Advanced Information and Knowledge Processing

Series Editors
Professor Lakhmi C. Jain
Lakhmi.jain@unisa.edu.au

Professor Xindong Wu
xwu@cs.uvm.edu

For other titles published in this series, go to
http://www.springer.com/series/4738

Elena Zudilova-Seinstra • Tony Adriaansen
Robert van Liere
Editors

Trends in Interactive Visualization

State-of-the-Art Survey

Springer

Editors
Elena Zudilova-Seinstra, PhD
University of Amsterdam
The Netherlands

Tony Adriaansen, BA
ICT Centre
Commonwealth Scientific and Discovery
Research Organisation (CSIRO)
Australia

Robert van Liere, PhD
Center for Mathematics and Computer Science (CWI)
The Netherlands

AI&KP ISSN 1610-3947
ISBN 978-1-4471-5939-1 ISBN 978-1-84800-269-2 (eBook)
DOI: 10.1007/978-1-84800-269-2

British Library Cataloguing in Publication Data

Printed on acid-free paper

Springer Science+Business Media
springer.com

Preface

Massive increases in data sizes and ongoing improvements in computational performance have created an urgent need for new systems that enable users to explore complex datasets and computations in an intuitive and flexible manner.

The field of Interactive Visualization studies how people interact with computers to create visual representation of information and how this process can be made more efficient. With this book, we have tried to compile a comprehensive overview of this young research field.

The book is a state-of-the-art survey of studies on Interactive Visualization. It examines research topics advancing the field, presents insightful findings and novel ideas, and describes applications across multiple disciplines. The book is intended for a broad audience and collects multidisciplinary articles that give readers insight into Interactive Visualization from various perspectives.

For instance, visualization experts can consult this book to find advanced methods for solving particular problems. Interaction designers will become familiar with the latest interaction techniques and input devices to perform visual exploration tasks. Scientists and engineers will realize new ways to examine complex datasets. Usability experts will be exposed to new and effective evaluation methodologies.

Furthermore, the book is appropriate for both undergraduate and graduate masters students and can be easily transformed into a handbook or a supplementary textbook for teaching courses such as scientific and information visualization, human–computer interaction, computer graphics, and interaction/interface design. To reflect a potential teaching taxonomy, we have organized the book into five parts.

I Introduction

Part I presents fundamentals of Interactive Visualization, surveys research in the field, examines existing challenges, and provides information about popular interactive frameworks for scientific and information visualizations.

II Challenges in Data Mapping

Part II deals with one of the most challenging tasks in Interactive Visualization, mapping and teasing out information from large complex datasets and generating visual representations. This section consists of four chapters.

Binh Pham, Alex Streit, and Ross Brown provide a comprehensive requirement analysis of information uncertainty visualizations. They examine the sources of uncertainty, review aspects of its complexity, introduce typical models of uncertainty, and analyze major issues in visualization of uncertainty, from various user and task perspectives.

Alfred Inselberg examines challenges in the multivariate data analysis. He explains how relations among multiple variables can be mapped uniquely into α-space subsets having geometrical properties and introduces Parallel Coordinates methodology for the unambiguous visualization and exploration of a multidimensional geometry and multivariate relations.

Christiaan Gribble describes two alternative approaches to interactive particle visualization: one targeting desktop systems equipped with programmable graphics hardware and the other targeting moderately sized multicore systems using packet-based ray tracing.

Finally, Christof Rezk Salama reviews state-of-the-art strategies for the assignment of visual parameters in scientific visualization systems. He explains the process of mapping abstract data values into visual based on transfer functions, clarifies the terms of pre- and postclassification, and introduces the state-of-the-art user interfaces for the design of transfer functions.

III Design and Evaluation

People's abilities and disabilities both tend to be underestimated in current visualization systems. Meanwhile, interactive visualisation systems should be easy to use and should not require sophisticated computer skills by users, as many are not computer experts. Part III addresses this research concern from two complementary perspectives: user-oriented and technology oriented. It includes three chapters.

To open this section, Roy Kalawsky explains why human perceptual and cognitive capabilities have to be taken into account when designing visualization techniques and tools. An example is discussed where the difficult technical challenges of creating an interactive three-dimensional visualization system on a PDA device have been overcome by applying knowledge of human perception and cognition.

Next, Martin Hicks reviews existing theories and principles for design of effective interactive visualization user interfaces, including Gestalt laws, data graphics, interaction design, and Human–Computer Interaction guidelines. To illustrate the principal benefits of applying these design principles, he discusses several case studies.

Then, Ingo Wassink et al. present a user-centred approach to the design of interactive visualization systems. They explain the importance of context-of-use in visualization design, evaluate different methodologies and techniques for user and task analysis, and discuss practical challenges in design and evaluation of collaborative visualization environments.

In the last chapter of this section, Ross Brown, Simon Joslin, and Penny Drennan describe the development life cycle of a collaborative virtual environment and introduce the automatic visualization framework to assist in evaluation and analysis of the usage data. To illustrate the framework benefits to the development team, a case study is presented and discussed in detail.

IV Novel User Interfaces

Effective user interfaces is one of the top research and development problems of Interactive Visualization. Part IV of the book is devoted to natural user interaction with the visualized data. This section contains three chapters.

Joseph LaViola Jr. et al. describe virtual environments for interactive visualization and data analysis for such domains as archaeology, biology, computational fluid dynamics, and geoscience. Results of experimental studies are presented that discuss benefits of Immersive Virtual Reality-based visualizations for end users.

Francis Marchese provides a comprehensive overview of novel interaction and visualization techniques applied to interactive exploration of molecular structures. He describes haptic displays and material molecular models along with mobile, multimodal, and collaborative visualization systems.

Finally, Jeffrey Heer et al. discuss systems that support collaborative visualization on the Web. They describe collaboration mechanisms for viewing, sharing, annotation, discussion, and publishing visualizations and review existing Web-based collaborative visualization systems.

V Integrating Visualization and Modeling

Part V of the book combines four chapters describing innovative visualization and data mining techniques, tools and systems capable of solving computational and imaging problems in various domains.

Judith Terrill et al. discuss how traditional data analysis and data mining tools can be enriched with multiple representations and interactions. They present a visual exploration environment that allows domain scientists to interactively measure and analyze experimental data. To demonstrate the use of quantitative visualizations, the description of three case studies is provided.

Yang Cai et al. present a new shape-based spatiotemporal reasoning method that combines computer vision, multiphysics simulation, and user interaction.

They describe case studies of tracking and predicting behavior of oceanographic phenomena and discuss results obtained from testing their algorithms using 2,384 satellite images.

Jean-Bernard Martens discusses how statistical models can be used for interactive analysis of experimental data. He introduces a special class of geometrical models that can be used to capture various data analysis scenarios and describes the interactive visualization program XGms that implements these models.

In the last chapter of this section, Kamran Sedig provides an overview of formal frameworks and tools for interactive mathematical visualizations. He explains what mathematical visualizations are and discusses general benefits of making them interactive.

Acknowledgments

To conclude the preface, we acknowledge the many people who made this book possible.

It has been a pleasure to work with the chapter authors, and we therefore thank all contributors. Without their support and commitment, it would have been impossible to bring this book to publication.

Also, we thank members of the International Review Board who participated in the refereeing process. We are grateful to: Charl Botha (Delft University of Technology, the Netherlands), Sabine Coquillart (National Institute of Research in Computer Science, France), Ellen Yi-Luen Do (Georgia Tech University, USA), Noureddine Elouazizi (University of Leiden, the Netherlands), Pilar Herrero (Universidad Politecnica de Madrid, Spain), Suguru Ishizaki (Carnegie Mellon University, USA), Roy Kalawsky (Loughborough University, UK), Gordon Kindlmann (Harvard Medical School, USA), Judith Klein-Seetharaman (Carnegie Mellon University, USA), Ulrich Lang (University of Stuttgart, Germany), David McGee (Adapx, USA), Frits Post (Delft University of Technology, the Netherlands), Bernhard Preim (University of Magdeburg, Germany), Jos Roerdink (University of Groningen, the Netherlands), Corina Sas (Lancaster University, UK), Margaret-Anne Storey (University of Victoria, Canada), Anna Vilanova Bartoli (Eindhoven University of Technology, the Netherlands), Frederic Vexo (Ecole Polytechnique Federale de Lausanne, Switzerland), Antony Unwin (Augsburg University, Germany), and Daniel Weiskopf (Simon Fraser University, Canada).

Finally, our special thanks go to Beverley Ford, Catherine Brett, and Helen Desmond from Springer, UK, for their assistance during the preparation of this book.

Contents

Preface v

Contributors xv

Part I Introduction

1 Overview of Interactive Visualization 3
Elena Zudilova-Seinstra, Tony Adriaansen, and Robert van Liere

Part II Challenges in Data Mapping

2 Visualization of Information Uncertainty: Progress and Challenges 19
Binh Pham, Alex Streit, and Ross Brown

3 Parallel Coordinates: Interactive Visualization for High Dimensions 49
Alfred Inselberg

4 Interactive Particle Visualization 79
Christiaan P. Gribble

5 Visual Parameters and Transfer Functions 99
Christof Rezk Salama

Part III Design and Evaluation

6 Gaining Greater Insight Through Interactive Visualization: A Human Factors Perspective 119
Roy S. Kalawsky

7 **Perceptual and Design Principles for Effective Interactive Visualizations** 155
Martin Hicks

8 **Applying a User-Centered Approach to Interactive Visualization Design** 175
Ingo Wassink, Olga Kulyk, Betsy van Dijk, Gerrit van der Veer, and Paul van der Vet

9 **A Visualization Framework for Collaborative Virtual Environment Usage Information** 201
Ross Brown, Simon Joslin, and Penny Drennan

Part IV Novel User Interfaces

10 **Virtual Reality-Based Interactive Scientific Visualization Environments** 225
Joseph J. LaViola Jr., Prabhat, Andrew S. Forsberg, David H. Laidlaw, and Andries van Dam

11 **Interactive Molecular Visualization at the Interface** 251
Francis T. Marchese

12 **Point, Talk, and Publish: Visualization and the Web** 269
Jeffrey Heer, Fernanda B.Viégas, Martin Wattenberg, and Maneesh Agrawala

Part V Integrating Visualization and Modeling

13 **Extending Measurement Science to Interactive Visualization Environments** 287
Judith Terrill, William George, Terence Griffin, John Hagedorn, John Kelso, Marc Olano, Adele Peskin, Steven Satterfield, James Sims, Jeffrey Bullard, Joy Dunkers, Nicos Martys, Agnes O'Gallagher, and Gillian Haemer

14 **Interactive Spatiotemporal Reasoning** 303
Yang Cai, Richard Stumpf, Michelle Tomlinson, Timothy Wynne, Sai Ho Chung, and Xavier Boutonnier

15 **Interactive Statistical Modeling with XGms** 321
Jean-Bernard Martens

16 Interactive Mathematical Visualizations: Frameworks, Tools, and Studies 343
Kamran Sedig

Index 365

Contributors

Tony Adriaansen
CSIRO ICT Centre, Epping, NSW 2121, Australia
tony.adriaansen@csiro.au

Maneesh Agrawala
University of California Berkeley, Berkeley, CA 94720, USA
maneesh@cs.berkeley.edu

Xavier Boutonnier
Carnegie Mellon University, Pittsburgh, PA 15213, USA
xab@cmu.edu

Ross Brown
Queensland University of Technology, Brisbane 4000, Australia
r.brown@qut.edu.au

Jeffrey Bullard
National Institute of Standards and Technology, Gaithersburg, MD 20899, USA
jeffrey.bullard@nist.gov

Yang Cai
Carnegie Mellon University, Pittsburgh, PA 15213, USA
ycai@cmu.edu

Sai Ho Chung
Carnegie Mellon University, Pittsburgh, PA 15213, USA
saic@andrew.cmu.edu

Andries van Dam
Brown University, Providence, RI 02912, USA
avd@cs.brown.edu

Betsy van Dijk
University of Twente, 7500 AE Enschede, the Netherlands
bvdijk@ewi.utwente.nl

Penny Drennan
Queensland University of Technology, Brisbane 4000, Australia
p.drennan@qut.edu.au

Joy Dunkers
National Institute of Standards and Technology, Gaithersburg, MD 20899, USA
joy.dunkers@nist.gov

Andrew Forsberg
Brown University, Providence, RI 02912, USA
asf@cs.brown.edu

William George
National Institute of Standards and Technology, Gaithersburg, MD 20899, USA
william.george@nist.gov

Christiaan P. Gribble
Grove City College, Grove City, PA 16127, USA
cpgribble@gcc.edu

Terence Griffin
National Institute of Standards and Technology, Gaithersburg, MD 20899, USA
terrence.griffin@nist.gov

Gillian Haemer
National Institute of Standards and Technology, Boulder, CO 80305, USA
gillian.haemer@nist.gov

John Hagedorn
National Institute of Standards and Technology, Gaithersburg, MD 20899, USA
john.hagedorn@nist.gov

Jeffrey Heer
University of California Berkeley, Berkeley, CA 94720, USA
jheer@cs.berkeley.edu

Martin Hicks
fhios Limited, The Media Centre, 3-8 Carburton Street, London W1W 5AJ, UK
mhicks@fhios.com

Alfred Inselberg
School of Mathematical Sciences, Tel Aviv University, Tel-Aviv 69978, Israel
aiisreal@post.tau.ac.il

Simon Joslin
Queensland University of Technology, Brisbane 4000, Australia
simonjoslin@gmail.com

Roy S. Kalawsky
Research School of Systems Engineering, Loughborough University,
Loughborough, Leicestershire LE11 3TU, UK
r.s.kalawsky@lboro.ac.uk

John Kelso
National Institute of Standards and Technology, Gaithersburg, MD 20899, USA
john.kelso@nist.gov

Olga Kulyk
University of Twente, 7500 AE Enschede, the Netherlands
o.kulyk@ewi.utwente.nl

David Laidlaw
Brown University, Providence, RI 02912
dhl@cs.brown.edu

Joseph J. LaViola, Jr.
University of Central Florida, Orlando, FL 32816, USA
jjl@cs.ucf.edu

Robert van Liere
Center for Mathematics and Computer Science, 1098 SJ Amsterdam, the Netherlands
robert.van.liere@cwi.nl

Jean-Bernard Martens
Eindhoven University of Technology, 5600 MB Eindhoven, the Netherlands
j.b.o.s.martens@tue.nl

Francis T. Marchese
Pace University, New York, NY 10038, USA
fmarchese@pace.edu

Nicos Martys
National Institute of Standards and Technology, Gaithersburg, MD 20899, USA
nicos.martys@nist.go

Agnes O'Gallagher
National Institute of Standards and Technology, Boulder, CO 80305, USA
abbie.ogallagher@nist.gov

Marc Olano
National Institute of Standards and Technology, Gaithersburg, MD 20899, USA
marc.olano@nist.gov

Adele Peskin
National Institute of Standards and Technology, Boulder, CO 80305, USA
adele.peskin@nist.gov

Binh Pham
Queensland University of Technology, Brisbane 4000, Australia
b.pham@qut.edu.au

Prabhat
The University of California, Berkeley, CA 94720, USA
prabhat@hpcrd.lbl.gov

Christof Rezk-Salama
University of Siegen, 57068 Siegen, Germany
rezk@fb12.uni-siegen.de

Steven G. Satterfield
National Institute of Standards and Technology, Gaithersburg, MD 20899, USA
steve.satterfield@nist.gov

Kamran Sedig
Middlesex College, The University of Western Ontario, London, Ontario, Canada
N6A 5B7, sedig@uwo.ca

James S. Sims
National Institute of Standards and Technology, Gaithersburg, MD 20899, USA
james.sims@nist.gov

Alexander Streit
Queensland University of Technology, Brisbane Q 4001, Australia
a.streit@qut.edu.au

Richard Stumpf
National Oceanic and Atmospheric Administration, Washington, DC 20230, USA
richard.stumpf@noaa.gov

Judith Terrill
National Institute of Standards and Technology, Gaithersburg, MD 20899, USA
judith.terrill@nist.gov

Michelle Tomlinson
National Oceanic and Atmospheric Administration, Washington, DC 20230, USA
michelle.tomlinson@noaa.gov

Gerrit van der Veer
Dutch Open University, 6419 AT Heerlen, the Netherlands
gerrit.vanderveer@ou.nl

Paul van der Vet
University of Twente, 7500 AE Enschede, the Netherlands
p.e.vandervet@ewi.utwente.nl

Fernanda B. Viégas
IBM T.J. Watson Research Center, Cambridge, MA 02142, USA
viegasf@us.ibm.com

Ingo Wassink
University of Twente, 7500 AE Enschede, the Netherlands
i.h.c.wassink@ewi.utwente.nl

Martin Wattenberg
IBM T.J. Watson Research Center, Cambridge, MA 02142, USA
mwatten@us.ibm.com

Timothy Wynne
National Oceanic and Atmospheric Administration, Washington, DC 20230, USA
timothy.wynne@noaa.gov

Elena Zudilova-Seinstra
University of Amsterdam, 1098 SJ Amsterdam, the Netherlands
E.V.Zudilova-Seinstra@uva.nl

Part I
Introduction

Chapter 1
Overview of Interactive Visualization

Elena Zudilova-Seinstra, Tony Adriaansen, and Robert van Liere

Abstract The book starts with the chapter presenting a comprehensive overview of Interactive Visualization. The chapter introduces fundamentals of Interactive Visualization, surveys research in the field, examines existing challenges and provides information about popular frameworks that can be used for the development of interactive data visualizations.

Keywords Interactive visualization model, User interaction, Virtual and Augmented reality, Multimodal and Collaborative visualizations, Interactive visualization frameworks.

1.1 Introduction

With the explosion of IT the amount of data at one's disposal is enormous. The data explosion has led to very large detailed datasets and the amount of details in these datasets continues growing at explosive rates. Nowadays the challenge is to extract and harness knowledge hidden in the collage of scientific data.

Visualization technologies empower users to perceive important patterns in a large amount of data, identify areas that need further scrutiny and make sophisticated decisions. However, without interactivity, visualization is often considered as an end point of the workflow or as a way of communicating observations.

Users need to manipulate and explore the data. The way people perceive and interact with visualizations can strongly influence their understanding of the data as well as the usefulness of a visualization system. Also, for many application domains it is unclear what the features of interest are and how to define them in such a way that they can be detected. As a result, the need for direct user interactions is becoming even more important.

In order to increase the users' ability to explore the data and better understand the results of experiments based on extensive calculations interaction and visualization capabilities need to be optimized so that access to the application data and associated features is apparent [35]. Effective integration of advanced visualization

E. Zudilova-Seinstra et al. (eds.) *Trends in Interactive Visualization*,
doi:10.1007/978-1-84800-269-2_1 © Springer-Verlag London Limited 2009

and interaction technologies has become a very important issue, especially in the field of scientific computing.

The relatively new concept of Interactive Visualization (IV) aims to address this research concern. Launched in the 1990s, the field of IV has become very successful due to the basic idea behind it: utilizing the broad bandwidth of the human sensory system in interpreting and steering complex datasets, processes and simulations from diverse scientific disciplines.

This chapter presents an overview of Interactive Visualization and is organized in the following way. In Sect. 1.2, we introduce a basic model of the IV process and discuss possibilities for user interaction with the visualized data. We report on the current state-of-the-art research in Sect. 1.3 and examine existing challenges and most pressing issues facing IV in Sect. 1.4. We then deal with a brief introduction and overview of some popular frameworks that can be used for the development of interactive visualizations in Sect. 1.5. We finalize with a summary in Sect. 1.6.

1.2 Interactive Visualization Process

The purpose of IV is to develop new scientific methods to increase person's abilities to explore and understand the data, so that an increased awareness of meaning in the data is possible [14]. IV allows a tighter connection between researchers, their models and the data being explored. The techniques of IV not only provide users with a vehicle to view the data but also permit them to use interaction capabilities to interrogate and navigate through datasets and communicate these insights with others.

IV is a complicated and iterative process implying two-way communication between the user and the visualization system [34]. Figure 1.1 shows a *basic model* of this process.

Data to be visualized is transformed into an image based on the visualization technique applied. An original dataset can vary for example from a single bit to a time-dependent 3D flow field. The image generated can be static or dynamic (e.g., time varying) and it can be combined e.g. with audio and/or haptic feedback. The

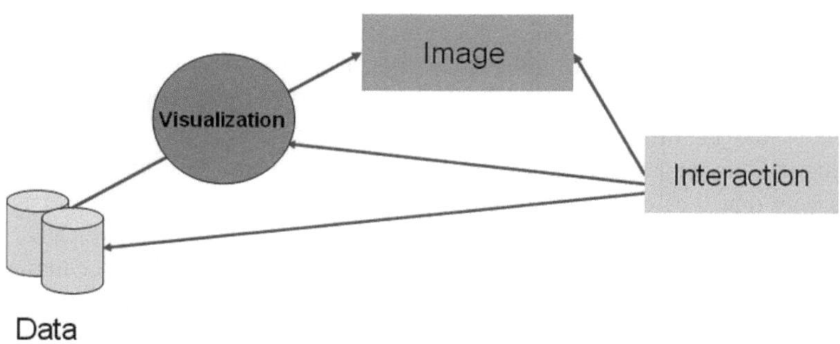

Fig 1.1 Interactive visualization process

user can interact with an IV system. Depending on user input, different visual representations will be generated.

(1) *The user may adjust visualization parameters/attributes* [11] such as shape, color, texture, brightness, blur, transparency, boundaries, sample rate, etc. Also, if an IV system supports several visualization techniques, the user may choose how he/she would like the final image to be rendered. In flow visualization, for instance, the following visualization techniques can be used: streamlines, vector glyphs, ribbons, streaklines, volume rendering, etc. [16]. Each technique allows the same data to be represented using different geometrical primitives and computer graphics methods. As can be seen in Fig. 1.2, for certain datasets some visualization techniques can be more suitable than others.
(2) *The user may interact with the visualized objects and scenes*. User interaction with the visualized data/space is based on accomplishing basic manipulation tasks such as selection, translation, rotation and scaling and often also locomotion and navigation [19]. The last two tasks are important for user orientation in a complex environment. The user may interact directly with visualizations via available interaction devices (e.g., 2D/3D mouse, tracked prop objects (Fig. 1.3, a), data-gloves, haptic devices, speech and gesture recognition, etc.)

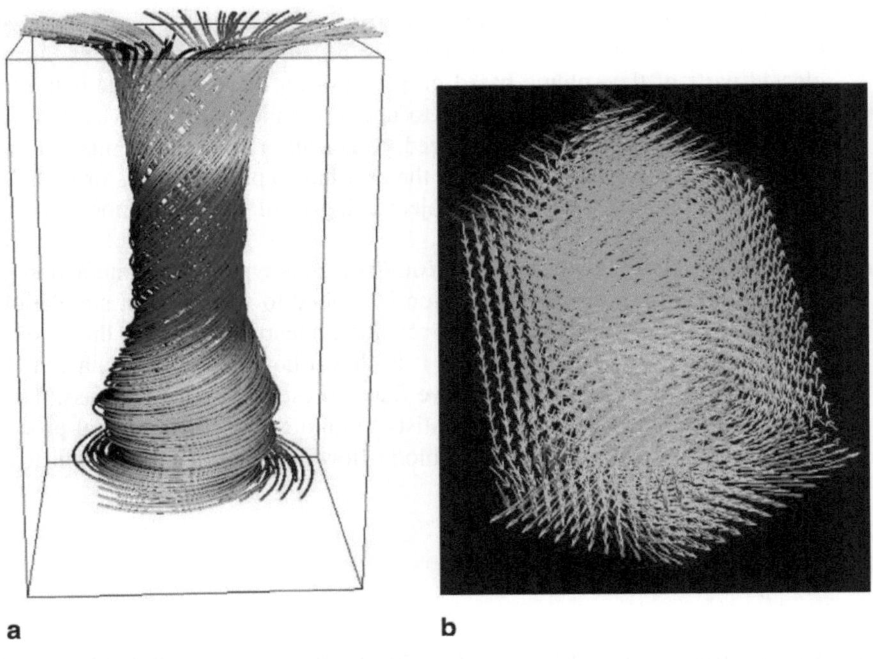

a **b**

Fig 1.2 Streamline (a) and glyph (b) based visualization techniques applied to validate the tornado CFD (Computational Fluid Dynamics) model (*See Color Plates*)

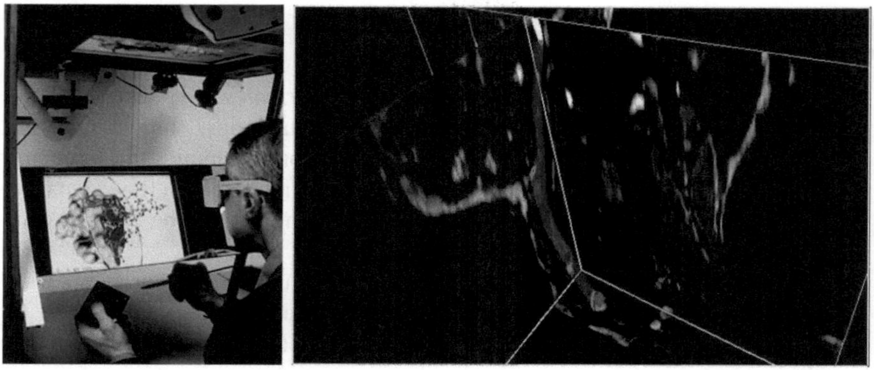

a b

Fig 1.3 Direct user interaction with the 3D visualization of a molecular structure (a); three orthogonal clipping planes within a 3D volumetric medical dataset (b) (Images courtesy of the Center for Mathematics and Computer Science (CWI) and the Division of Image Processing (LKEB), Leiden University Medical Center, the Netherlands) (*See Color Plates*)

or indirectly by altering active controls of the graphical user interface (GUI) of a visualization tool.

(3) *The user may extract features from the original dataset* for example by applying such methods as probing or clipping (Fig. 1.3, b). Clipping plays a decisive role in understanding volumetric datasets because it allows cutting away selected parts of the volume based on the position of voxels in the data set. Very often clipping is the only way to uncover important, otherwise hidden details of a data set. Probing is localized visualization and measurement of the data. For conducting a measurement, the user has to place markers or tools in specific positions on a visualized object using available interaction devices and/or GUI elements.

(4) *The user may modify the data to be visualized.* This type of user interaction is especially important when visualization is applied to verify/adjust simulation models used for the investigation of a scientific phenomenon or for the prediction of its behavior [36]. In Fig. 1.4, it is shown how the patient data can be modified by adding a spline primitive that represents a virtual bypass. This allows users like computational scientists to mimic a specific surgical procedure and to check the validity of a blood flow simulation model when it is applied to a particular case.

1.3 Major Research Themes

The extreme growth in data sizes has resulted in research on combining real-time computing and visualization. To allow real-time user interaction with big datasets, plenty of work has been done in the field of high-performance visualization [9, 18]

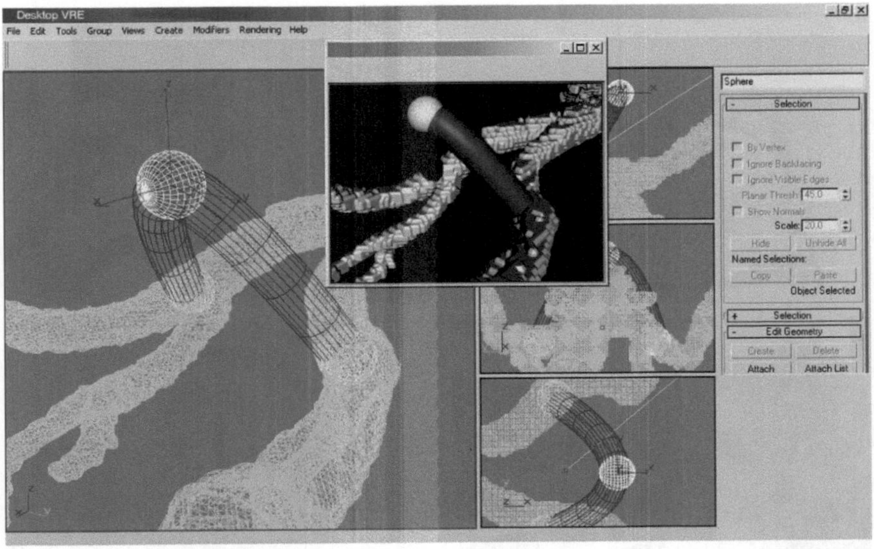

Fig 1.4 Interactive bypass placement using a spline primitive [37], © 2003 Springer Verlag, included here with kind permission of Springer Science and Business Media

and efficient feature extraction techniques [8, 24]. Often very large datasets present challenging visualization problems that are suitable for schemes in which multiple processors can work in parallel on the same image [3]. Another possibility is to provide users with direct control over the visualization pipeline [10] so that a user, for instance, can adjust mapping parameters and highlight certain aspects of the data.

Virtual visualization environments are becoming the established way of facilitating human interaction with large amounts of information. *Virtual reality* (VR) is a particular type of IV, where the visual representation of information is presented using an immersive display technology [7]. Immersion is measurable and depends on the rendering software and display devices. One system may have a higher level of immersion than others. Today's visualization workstations vary from non-immersive desktop systems to semi- and fully-immersive CAVE-like [5] virtual environments.

Multimodal visualization systems have become an important research area of IV as well. These are based on a combination of different interaction techniques e.g. direct manipulation, speech recognition, haptics, real time video and audio etc. These systems aim to provide efficient, convenient and natural interaction with the visualized data in a seamless way and will ultimately enable people to interact more fully using everyday skills [20].

Recent approaches to providing users with more natural methods of interacting with visualizations in VR have shown that more than one mode of input can be both beneficial and intuitive as a communication medium between humans and computer applications [15]. Although there are many different modes that could be used in

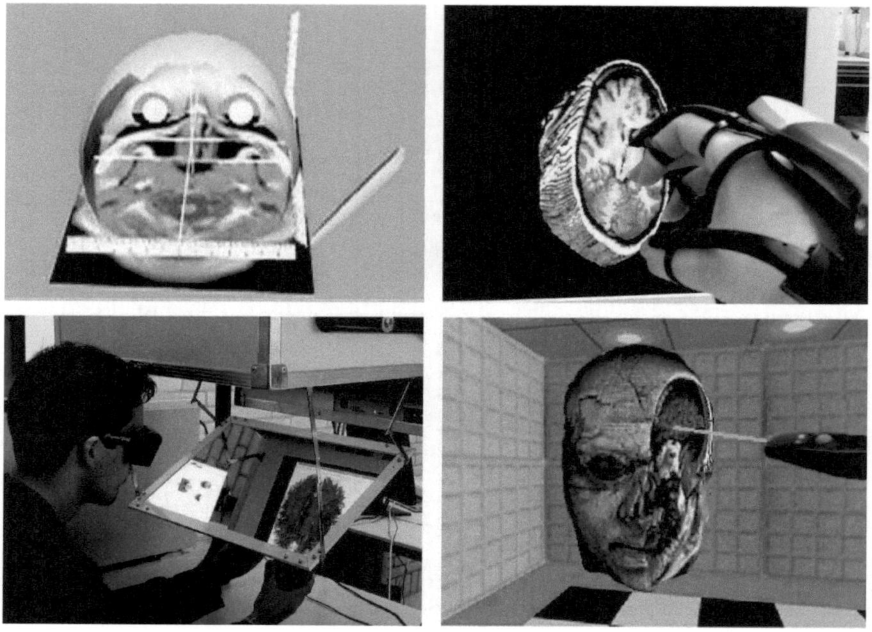

Fig 1.5 Interactive medical visualization in VR (Images courtesy of the CSIRO, Australia and the University of Amsterdam, the Netherlands [36], © 2004 Springer Verlag, included here with kind permission of Springer Science and Business Media) (*See Color Plates*)

VR-based applications, hand gestures and speech appear to be two of the most logical since users will typically be in environments that will have them immersed in a virtual world with limited access to traditional input devices like a keyboard or mouse.

The maturing VR techniques, together with the emerging haptic interfaces and multimedia networking technologies [1], provide ground for new enabling tools addressing computer-supported activities. They allow opinions to be shared, removing the data bottleneck of individual analysis and reducing the time to discovery. Interactive medical visualization (Fig. 1.5) is one of the most popular application domains for VR.

Augmented reality (AR) is also often used for purposes of IV, especially in the medical [17] and engineering contexts. AR is the process of overlaying computer-generated imagery to the real world, resulting in visualization of computer-generated data in the real world and interaction with these visualizations in a natural manner. AR-based visualizations are very well suited for the visualization of computer-aided design models in the field. For instance, AR can enable medical workers to instantaneously gain access to complex medical visualizations and make prognoses based on constantly updated data.

Devices used to display visualized images can vary from wall-sized to handheld. When existing IV techniques are adapted to handheld mobile devices, it becomes possible to harness the power of visualization anytime and anywhere [6]. A PDA-

Fig 1.6 Collaborative visualization on a large tiled panel display (Image courtesy of the SARA Computing and Networking Services, the Netherlands)

based application, for instance, can be used to control visualization parameters and make annotations for scientific visualizations running within an immersive virtual environment or an augmented reality system [13].

Large displays, on the other hand, allow people to gain insight into data in ways that are impossible with small displays. They are aimed at helping visualization by providing better performance, better accuracy and additional insight [2]. Thanks to large displays, people can use a greater amount of their field of vision to perceive a greater amount of data. Also, large displays enable users to engage in complex multi-tasking and allow multiple users (Fig. 1.6).

Collaborative visualization is one more well known type of IV, in which many people may interact with the same computer visualization to communicate their ideas to each other, or to explore information cooperatively. Frequently, collaborative visualization is used when people are physically separated. Networked visualization frameworks that support collaborative work have become increasingly important in many application areas in science and engineering [4], especially support for heterogeneous display environments, ranging from desktop systems or even PDAs to fully-immersive environments. Using several networked computers, the same visualization can be presented to each person simultaneously.

Special attention to IV has recently been gained in the HCI (Human-Computer Interaction) community. The aim is to employ HCI research in order to improve visualization tools available for science [27]. The development of design guidelines and metrics for the usability evaluation of IV systems is among the high priority tasks of HCI specialists today. Another open question is how to choose between modern display configurations and input devices in order to ensure good user experience while exploring complex data spaces and interacting with other people.

1.4 Challenges and Concerns

The major concern of IV today is the "big-data" problem. The greatest challenge is how to efficiently deal with a community of scientists who generate more data than they can possibly look at and understand [26]. For instance, when increasingly complex phenomena are being simulated, the resulting datasets are becoming too difficult to interpret without appropriate visualization tools. This requires novel high-performance visualization algorithms and feature extraction techniques [12].

Finding effective visual idioms for direct user interaction with visualizations is yet another challenge [21]. A major problem here is that user interfaces that seem natural from the developer's point of view often feel unnatural to users; and those that feel natural to users seem peculiar and full of special cases to visualization experts.

With the expanding volume of visual data, there is a need to develop novel interaction methods that maximize the user's understanding of the visual information. In this respect, the challenge is to leverage what is known about human perception so as to design user interfaces in a way that a typical viewer can intuitively extract the greatest amount of accurate and relevant information [25].

When visualization involves several sensory modalities, there are plenty of possibilities for errors. For instance, supporting multimodal interaction for a variety of users is a challenge with respect to the richness of interaction and display devices to be supported as well as effectively integrating these in a visualization environment. In addition, being able to optimize the user interface design space for the current context-of-use requires architectures that are able to modify interaction structures and inter-relationships at runtime [23]. Enabling such functionality in a distributed collaborative environment furthermore requires a certain amount of intelligence in the network to inform other sites about local changes at runtime and to learn from other participants' experiences.

Multimodal interaction adds to the uncertainty surrounding the choice between input modalities and the sequencing of input across modalities. Uncertainty leads to greater variability in user input, even for the same user, thus increasing the technical challenges. To provide a satisfying user experience, a multimodal interface has to conform to users' mental models and meet their expectations about the interaction and the domain.

Ideally, an IV system should be easy to use and not require sophisticated user skills, as many are not computer experts. Unfortunately, in reality the situation is far from ideal. Available usability metrics and guidelines have not been sufficiently applied yet to the field of IV.

There exists a major communication gap between HCI experts and those developing visualization algorithms and systems [35]. The former often consider visualization methods and techniques as tools oriented to computer scientists with very little relevance to HCI. Vice versa, to those working on scientific visualization, HCI concepts still often remain an after-thought rather than an essential component that affects the system's quality. In fact, new visualization techniques are rarely compared with previous results and their effectiveness is seldom quantified by user studies [9].

1.5 Interactive Visualization Frameworks

There are many frameworks available to assist in the development of interactive visualizations. Most of these are open source and freely downloadable. Six popular interactive visualization frameworks are listed below.

The Kitware Visualization Toolkit (VTK) [28] is a software system for 3D computer graphics, image processing and visualization. VTK supports a wide variety of visualization algorithms including scalar, vector, tensor, texture and volumetric methods along with advanced modeling techniques such as polygon reduction, mesh smoothing, cutting, contouring, etc. VTK provides algorithms to perform basic manipulation tasks using pointing devices (e.g., mouse or a trackball). Furthermore, VTK supports more advanced ways of interacting with visualizations based on the concept of so called "3D Widgets." The example of applying Plane and Spline Widgets to 3D medical visualization is shown in Fig. 1.7. A Plane

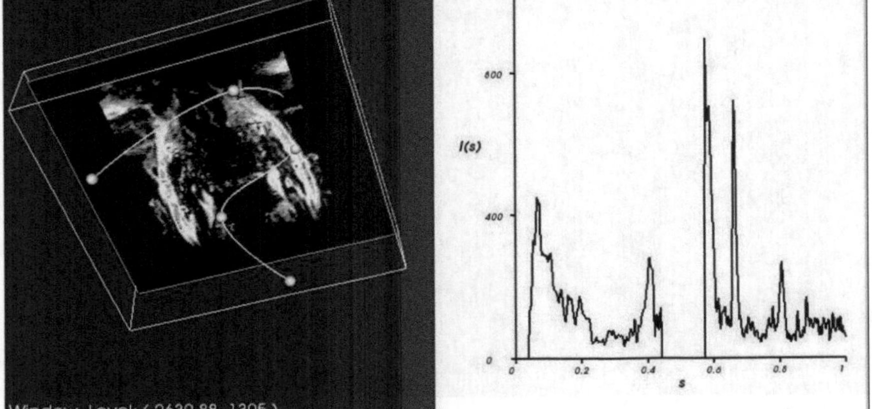

Fig 1.7 Applying 3D VTK Widgets to extract relevant features from the visualized MRA (Magnetic Resonance Angiogram) dataset

Widget is used to interactively construct a clipping/cutting plane through a 3D MRA dataset. A Spline Widget is used to extract profile information and to represent this data as a 2D graph.

Vis5D [33] is a framework for interactive visualization of large 5D datasets such as those produced by numerical weather models. It is possible to make isosurfaces, contour line slices, colored slices, volume renderings etc. of 3D data and then rotate and animate the images in real-time. Furthermore, VIs5D [33] permits the wind trajectory tracing and provides support for interactive data analysis.

The Medical Imaging Interaction Toolkit (MITK) [30] is an extension to the VTK visualization framework described above. It allows the construction of specifically tailored, interactive applications for medical image analysis. MITK performs coordination of multiple different visualizations of the same medical dataset with interactions that change the data either directly or indirectly by means of intermediate algorithms.

The Prefuse Information Visualization Toolkit (Prefuse) [32] supports a rich set of features for data modeling, visualization and interaction. It provides optimized data structures for tables, graphs and trees; a host of layout and visual encoding techniques; support for animation, dynamic queries, integrated search and database connectivity. The zipdecode shown in Fig. 1.8 can serve as an example of an IV application implemented in prefuse. The zipdecode is a web-based visualization of how US zip codes are mapped [22]. Every zip code is represented by a dot. As a user presses the number keys that correspond to a zip code, the dots from that area are highlighted.

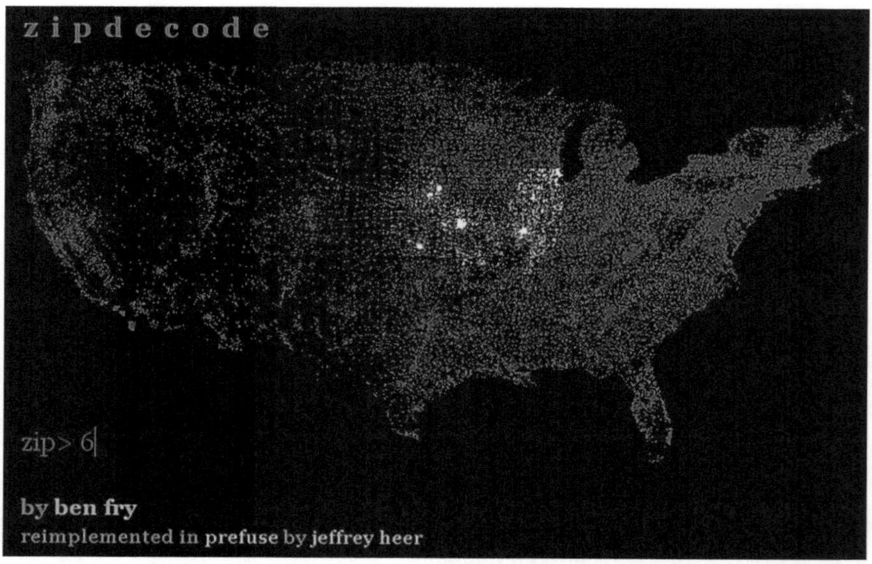

Fig 1.8 Zipdecode reimplemented using Prefuce Information Visualization Toolkit by Jeffrey Heer from the Computer Science Division, University of California, Berkley (Image generated by means of the demonstration software available at prefuse.org)

The Macrofocus InfoScope [29] is an interactive visualization tool to access, explore and communicate large or complex datasets. InfoScope is highly-interactive framework which aims to specifically assist in visualization of multi-dimensional datasets. It provides an overview of the global relationships between objects and embeds fine grain tasks. For instance, specific numeric values of attributes can be obtained by probing objects via multiple views and dynamic queries on a combination of attributes. All actions are supported by visual feedback embedded in a common frame of reference.

The Multimod Application Framework (MAF) [31] allows the development of multimodal visualization applications based on VTK and other specialized libraries. It provides high level components that can be easily combined to develop a visualization application in various scientific areas. Interaction inside MAF is accomplished by processing input events coming from both GUIs and interaction devices. MAF supports both 2D and 3D input and allows multiple device implementations.

1.6 Summary

The purpose of Interactive Visualization is to develop new scientific methods to increase a person's ability to explore the data and to better understand the results of experiments based on extensive calculations. The IV techniques not only provide users with the possibility of viewing the data but also permit them to use interaction capabilities to interrogate and navigate through datasets and communicate these insights with others [18].

Continuous improvements in computers' processing power and graphics capabilities have made it possible to incorporate a wide range of IV techniques in most computing application domains, including medicine, engineering, business and science. National laboratories have already embraced this technology and as IV penetrates the market, many institutions are using it to drive scientific discovery and competitive advantage [26].

This chapter provides an overview of Interactive Visualization. First, we introduce a basic model of the IV process and discuss four ways how the user may interact with the visualized data. In particular, the user may adjust visualization parameters/attributes, interact directly with visualized objects, interactively extract features from and apply changes to the data to be visualized.

We then consider a broad spectrum of research taking place in the field of IV, including high-performance algorithms and efficient feature extraction techniques, virtual and augmented reality, collaborative and mobile data visualization, multimodal user interaction and HCI design and evaluation principles applied to IV. We examine existing challenges and the most pressing issues facing IV. The complexity and size of data is considered, in addition to issues about user interface design. Special considerations concerning multimodal interaction are outlined and the importance of HCI from two points of view is given.

We finalize the chapter with an overview of available frameworks that can be used for the development of interactive visualizations. Both scientific and information visualizations are considered. We discuss the main functionality and features provided by the Kitware Visualization Toolkit [28], Vis5D [33], the Medical Imaging Interaction Toolkit [30], the Prefuse Information Visualization Toolkit [32], The Macrofocus InfoScope [29] and the Multimod Application Framework [31].

References

1. Adriaansen T and Gunn C (2003) An Experimental Implementation of a Networked Hapto-Acoustic Virtual Reality Environment Applied to Surgical Education Using the High Speed CeNTIE Research Network. In: Sun C et al. (eds.) Proceedings of the Seventh International Conference on Digital Image Computing: Techniques and Applications, DICTA Macquarie University, Sydney, Australia, CSIRO Publishing.
2. Ball R and North C (2005) An Analysis of User Behavior on High-Resolution Tiled Displays. In: Chittaro L et al. (eds.) Human Computer Interaction – INTERACT 2005, Springer LNCS 3585.
3. Bigler J, Stephens A and Parker SG (2006) Design for Parallel Interactive Ray Tracing Systems, SCI Institute Technical Report, UUSCI-2006–027, University of Utah, http://www.sci.utah.edu/publications/SCITechReports/UUSCI-2006-027.pdf, Accessed 11 February 2008.
4. Brodlie KW, Duce DA, Gallop JR, Walton JPRB and Wood JD (2004) Distributed and Collaborative Visualization. Computer Graphics Forum, 23(2): 223–251.
5. Cruz-Neira C, Sandin DJ and DeFanti TA (1993) Surround-screen Projection-based Virtual Reality: The Design and Implementation of the CAVE. In: Whitton MC (ed.) Proceedings of the 20th Annual Conference on Computer Graphics and Interactive Techniques – SIGGRAPH'93.
6. Chittaro L (2006) Visualizing Information on Mobile Devices. IEEE Computer, 39(3): 34–39.
7. van Dam A, Laidlaw DH and Simpson RM (2002) Experiments in Immersive Virtual Reality for Scientific Visualization. Computer and Graphics, 26(4): 535–555.
8. Doleisch H, Gasser M and Hauser H (2003) Interactive Feature Specification for Focus + Context Visualization of Complex Simulation Data. In: Proceedings of IEEE TCVG Symposium on Visualization, Grenoble, France, May 26–28, 2003.
9. Groner J, Lee M, Martin J, Moorhead R and Newman J (2005) A Concurrent Visualization System for High-Performance Computational Simulations. In: 16th IEEE Visualization 2005 (VIS 2005).
10. Jonhson C (2004) Top Scientific Visualization Research Problems. IEEE Computer Graphics and Applications, 4: 13–17.
11. Kaufman A (1994) Trends in Visualization and Volume Graphics, Scientific Visualization Advances and Challenges, IEEE Computer Society Press. Los Alamitos, CA, USA
12. Keim DA (2001) Visual Exploration of Large Data Sets. Communications of the ACM, 44(8): 38–44.
13. Kukimoto N, Nonako J, Koyamada K and Kanazawa M (2003) PDA-based Visualization Control and Interface for Virtual Environment. In: Villanueva JJ (ed.) Proceedings of the IASTED Conference on Visualization, Imaging and Image Processing.
14. LaViola JJ Jr (2000) MSVT: A Virtual Reality-based Multimodal Scientific Visualization Tool. In: Proceedings of the Third IASTED International Conference on Computer Graphics and Imaging, pp. 1–7.
15. de Leeuw W and van Liere R (2000) Multi Level Topology for Flow Visualization. Computers and Graphics, 24(3): 325–331.

16. Liao H et al (2005) Augmented Reality Visualisation for Navigation Surgery Using Integral Videography 3D Autostereoscopic Imaging. IFMBE News, 73, http://ifmbenewsiee.org/ifmbe-news, Accessed 10 February 2008.
17. van Liere R (1997) High Performance Visualization. ERCIM News, 31, http://www.ercim.org/publication/Ercim_News/enw31/van_liere.html, Accessed 11 February 2008.
18. Martens JB, Qi W, Aliakseyeu A, Kok AJF and van Liere R (2004) Experiencing 3D Interactions in Virtual Reality and Augmented Reality. In: Markopoulos P and Eggen B (eds.) Proceedings of the 2nd European Union Symposium on Ambient Intelligence (EUSAI 2004).
19. Nielson GM and Hamann B (1990) Techniques for the Interactive Visualization. In: IEEE Proceedings in Visualization, 90.
20. Oviatt S, Darrel T and Flickner M (2004) Introduction to Special Issue: Multimodal Interfaces that Fluex, Adapt, and Persist, Communication of the ACM, 47(1): 30–33.
21. Plaisant C (2004) The Challenge of Information Visualization Evaluation. In: Proceedings of Working Conference Advanced Visual Interfaces, ACM Press, pp. 109–116.
22. Post FH, Vrolijk B, Hauser H, Laramee SR and Doleisch H (2003) The State of the Art in Flow Visualization: Feature Extraction and Tracking. Computer Graphics Forum, 22(4): 775–792.
23. Reas C and Fry B (2007) Processing: A Programming Handbook for Visual Designers and Artists, MIT Press.
24. Rogers Y, Brignull H and Scaife M (2002) Designing Dynamic Interactive Visualisations to Support Collaboration and Cognition. In: Dill J et al. (eds.) Proceedings of IEEE International Conference on Information Visualization.
25. Shneiderman B (2003) Why Not Make Interface Better than 3D Reality? IEEE Computer Graphics and Applications, 23(6): 12–15.
26. Snel A and Willard CG (2005) Interactive Visualization: The End-User Experience. White Paper, IDC Analyze the Future, http://www.lite3d.com/uploads/idcwp_interactiveviz2.pdf, Accessed 11 February 2008.
27. Spence R (2000) Information Visualisation, ACM Press, New York, NY USA.
28. The Kitware Visualization Toolkit (VTK): (2008) www.vtk.org, Accessed 11 February 2008.
29. The Macrofocus InfoScope: (2008) http://www.macrofocus.com/public/products/infoscope/, Accessed 11 February 2008.
30. The Medical Imaging Interaction Toolkit (MITK): (2008) www.mitk.org, Accessed 11 February 2008.
31. The Multimod Application Framework (MAF): (2008) http://www.openmaf.org/maf, Accessed 11 February 2008.
32. The Prefuse Information Visualization Toolkit (Prefuse): (2008) prefuse.org, Accessed 11 February 2008.
33. Vis5D: (2008) http://www.ssec.wisc.edu/~billh/vis5d.html, Accessed 11 February 2008.
34. van Wijk JJ (2005) The Value of Visualization. In: Silva C, Groeller E and Rushmeier H (eds.), Proceedings IEEE Visualization 2005.
35. Zudilova-Seinstra EV and Adriaansen T (2006) Combining Visualisation and Interaction to Facilitate Scientific Exploration and Discovery. In: Fields T et al. (eds.) Proceedings of the International Conference "HCI 2006 Engage!", London, UK, 11–15 September.
36. Zudilova EV and Sloot PMA (2003) Virtual Reality and Desktop as a Combined Interaction-Visualisation Medium for a Problem-Solving Environment. In: Sloot PMA (eds.) Proceedings of the International Conference on Computational Science – ICCS 2003, Melbourne, Australia, June 2003.
37. Zudilova EV and Sloot PMA (2004) Multimodal Interaction in Biomedicine. In: Cai Y (ed.) Ambient Intelligence for Scientific Discovery: Foundations, Theories, and Systems, State-of-the-Art Survey, Springer LNAI, p. 3345.

Part II
Challenges in Data Mapping

Chapter 2
Visualization of Information Uncertainty: Progress and Challenges

Binh Pham, Alex Streit, and Ross Brown

Abstract Information uncertainty which is inherent in many real world applications brings more complexity to the visualisation problem. Despite the increasing number of research papers found in the literature, much more work is needed. The aims of this chapter are threefold: (1) to provide a comprehensive analysis of the requirements of visualisation of information uncertainty and their dimensions of complexity; (2) to review and assess current progress; and (3) to discuss remaining research challenges. We focus on four areas: information uncertainty modelling, visualisation techniques, management of information uncertainty modelling, propagation and visualisation, and the uptake of uncertainty visualisation in application domains.

Keywords Information uncertainty modeling, Management of information uncertainty propagation and visualisation, Application fields.

2.1 Introduction

Information uncertainty is a complex concept that needs to be addressed in many important real world applications. It refers to the impreciseness, vagueness, fuzziness, inconsistency, doubt or likelihood present in information. Information uncertainty comes from different sources and can be interpreted and modelled in various ways. Effective visualisation of information uncertainty provides deeper insights into the nature of data and its impacts on the working and decision making of practical systems. For example, to analyse the sustainability of a natural environment for planning purposes would involve the understanding of the characteristics of all species (animals, plants, etc.), their activities and the impacts of these activities upon the environment. However, data collected on species, their locations and activities are only accurate within a certain degree of precision. Furthermore, information derived from expert knowledge is mostly qualitative in nature. It requires effort for users to understand the structure, characteristics and interdependency of data, data transformations, propagation of uncertainty, trends and impacts due to changes to the systems and interactions between different components of the systems. The difficulty in embracing

E. Zudilova-Seinstra et al. (eds.) *Trends in Interactive Visualization*,
doi:10.1007/978-1-84800-269-2_2 © Springer-Verlag London Limited 2009

uncertainty while performing information analysis or decision making with visualisation support has often caused professionals either to ignore the uncertainty completely or to ignore situations where uncertainty is high. This practice would result in valuable knowledge being discarded and in outcomes with reduced quality, or in the worst case, incorrect outcomes as the uncertainty accumulates and propagates.

Some aspects of information uncertainly have been well researched, especially in the field of mathematics. There are currently various mathematical models for representing, measuring, understanding and minimising uncertainty. How to manage uncertainty and its propagation has also been well investigated. These models range from statistical, probability to fuzzy models (e.g. [1–6]). To a much lesser extent, research on visualisation of information uncertainty has only been carried out sporadically during the last decade. Earlier work has focused on a data-driven approach and visual data representations based on specific data types or triggered by the needs of specific applications. Later work attempted to address task-based and user objectives-based approaches and to investigate higher level issues such as software architecture frameworks of visualisation systems, and management of uncertainty modelling, propagation and adaptation. Although some significant progress has been made, the uptake of visualisation of information uncertainty is still slow due to a number of reasons. Firstly, different information uncertainty models might require different treatments, and judicious choices need to be made. Secondly, there is an artificial separation between modelling of the information itself and its uncertainty. Thus, non-standard techniques are required to map uncertainty parameters into visual elements. Thirdly, different visualisation approaches have their own drawbacks. While traditional data-driven approaches tend to neglect the needs of users, task-oriented approaches devise visualisation methods that suit a specific application but might not be applicable to another domain. User-objectives approaches require users to abstract the goals for each visualisation task being performed and to identify criteria for obtaining and ranking these goals (e.g. according to their priorities). Fourthly, there are no tools to integrate the modelling of uncertainty and its propagation with the visualisation process. Hence, it is very difficult to cater for adaptation during the analysis of "what-if" scenarios.

The overall aim of this chapter is to examine the problem of visualisation of information uncertainty in a more holistic manner. We identify important key issues and provide a review and assessment of current progress to address some issues that would help to identify areas where further investigation is needed. To this end, we adopt a top-down approach based on the needs of users for our analysis. Our goal is to identify remaining key research challenges in order to chart the way forward. It is hoped that this chapter will also provide a speedy starting point for new researchers to the field. One thing to note is that we do not attempt to review extensively on everything that has been done for specific applications because the literature is numerous. Instead, we bias this chapter towards work that has potential to be more generically applicable.

Section 2.2 provides a brief description of the sources of uncertainty and typical models for uncertainty. Section 2.3 analyses major issues in visualisation of uncertainty from different perspectives of users and tasks. How well some important issues have been addressed to date is examined in Sect. 2.4. Section 2.5 discusses remaining key research challenges while the summary of this chapter is given in Sect. 2.6.

2.2 Sources and Modelling of Information Uncertainty

Information uncertainty suffers from ambiguous terminology and meanings which are categorised in different ways by different researchers. For example, Klir [7] and Gershon [8] interpreted uncertainty as some deficiency or imperfection in information due to incomplete, inconsistent or too complicated information. Pang [9] used three categories: *statistical* – based on probabilistic and confidence; *error* – differences between estimates and actual values; and *range* – intervals of possible values. They also identified three sources of uncertainty: data acquisition stage through measurements, numerical models or data entry; data transformation stage through numerical calculations by computers with limited precision; and visualisation stage due to error and approximations of rendering algorithms and models. Thomson et al. [10] presented a general categorisation for uncertainty in geospatially referenced information, focusing on the tasks of information analysts in the field and using their descriptive terms.

We provide a more generic categorisation of uncertainty which is based on Zadeh's classification of information into three groups: factual, pseudo-measurement and pseudo-numerical, and perceptual-based. Factual information is numerical and measurement-based; while pseudo-measurement and pseudo-numerical information are approximately numeric (e.g. "this model is available in the 60's"). Perceptual-based information is mainly linguistic, but is also available in other forms such as image and sound-based (e.g. "this engine is nearly at the end of its useful life"). Uncertainty which may occur in all these information groups come from many sources. Table 2.1 shows typical sources of information uncertainty and their causes [11, 12]. Other categorisations mentioned above may be viewed as special cases of this categorisation.

Since the sources and causes of uncertainty are different, various mathematical models have been developed to faithfully represent different types of information. We summarise these models into four common types:

- *Probability* denotes the likelihood of an event to occur or a positive match. Probability theory provides the foundation for statistical inference (e.g. Bayesian methods) [1, 5].
- *Possibility* provides alternative matches, e.g. a range of errors in measurement [2].
- *Provability* is a measure of the ability to express a situation where the probability of a positive match is exactly one. Provability is the central theme of techniques such as Dempster-Shafer calculus.
- *Membership* denotes the degree of match and allows for *partially* positive matches, e.g. fuzzy sets [3, 6], rough sets [4].

For the rest of this chapter, we assume that all these four types of model can be used unless otherwise stated.

Table 2.1 Sources and causes of information uncertainty

Sources of information uncertainty	Causes
Limited accuracy	Limitation in measuring instruments, or computational processes, or standards.
Missing data	Physical limitation of experiments; limited sample size or non-representative sample.
Incomplete definition	Impossibility or difficulty in articulating exact functional relationships or rules.
Inconsistency	Conflicts arisen from multiple sources or models.
Imperfect realisation of a definition	Physical or conceptual limitation.
Inadequate knowledge about the effects of the change in environment	Model does not cover all influence factors; or is made under slightly different conditions; or is based on the views of different experts.
Personal bias	Differences in individual perception
Ambiguity in linguistic descriptions	A word may have many meanings; or a state may be described by many words.
Approximation or assumptions embedded in model design methods or procedures	Requirements or limitations of models or methods.

2.3 Major Issues in Visualisation of Information Uncertainty

There are a number of critical issues that need to be considered for visualisation systems of information uncertainty. They range from types of users and their specific needs, task requirements to visualisation approaches and computer – supported tools to provide an environment that enables users to effectively and efficiently manage, visualise, and interpret uncertainty information and their propagation.

2.3.1 User Types

Users of visualisation fall into three main types:

- *Users of systems with information uncertainty*: come from diverse application domains. They normally want to be able to interpret the data, especially how uncertainty and its propagation impact on the interpretation and the reliability of results. They may also wish to set up 'what-if' scenarios with varying parameters and different degree of uncertainty. These scenarios help to gain insight and facilitate future prediction and planning.
- *Designers of systems with information uncertainty*: require information on the internal structures of these systems for verification and analysis. These include the structures of rules, clustering effects, contributions of rules during operation and the effects of different operators on each task. Hence, accurate insight into

how uncertainty is modelled and propagated is of paramount importance. These designers might also wish to do comparative analysis or to seek for conditions under which an optimal outcome is obtained at each stage or at the final stage.

- *Designers of visualisation systems for information uncertainty*: usually wish to be able to evaluate the effectiveness of visualisation techniques in terms of understanding the impacts of uncertainty. They also wish to understand how users make use of visualisation, and to seek users' feedbacks on the systems' drawbacks in order to improve the systems by providing more suitable techniques and software tools.

2.3.2 Major Visualisation Tasks and Approaches

Most existing work concentrates on creating new visual representations and mappings for information uncertainty. However, there is a growing concern about the lack of formal theoretical frameworks which integrate uncertainty modelling with visualisation in order to provide deeper insight into the effects of information uncertainty for exploratory and predictive analysis. Methods for evaluating the effectiveness and usability of visualisation techniques are also limited. Furthermore, the issue of how to facilitate the task of managing uncertainty modelling, propagation together with interactive visualisation has virtually been neglected until recently. In this section, we discuss the main visualisation tasks and approaches, but leave the discussion on other tasks together with the needs for developing software tools to support these tasks to Sect. 2.3.4.

Although there is some variation in the requirements of different types of users, there exists some commonality that could be exploited in order to design an effective generic visualisation framework for information uncertainty. Visualisation tasks can be categorised into three main types:

- Interactive exploration and analysis of data uncertainty and its propagation. This is a sense making task which requires:
  - the depiction of the degree of uncertainty for each variable or rule together with the data;
  - the depiction of the effects on each operation by varying the degree of uncertainty or different uncertainty models; and
  - the understanding of the interactions of two or more variables or rules with their different degrees of uncertainty or different uncertainty models.
  - "what-if" scenario simulation with varying uncertainty conditions and constraints. This is not only useful for information analysis, but also for predictive planning and educational purposes.
- *Decision making and effects of uncertainty on decision making*. Decision making is a complex task which takes into account the interplay of many variables. Uncertainty and its propagation add significant complexity to the task. For each

application domain, methods for representing different aspects of uncertainty for variables may be required. In addition, to facilitate understanding and decision making, data should be depicted simultaneously with its uncertainty in ways that are useful and usable, while reducing information overloading effects.

- *Automated computer-supported exploration.* To facilitate information analysis and decision making, it is desirable to offer certain functionalities to enable useful and repetitive tasks to be performed automatically. Some typical ways to provide automated support include:

  - Highlighting unusual results, e.g. degree of uncertainty is too high.
  - Notification of special patterns given specified conditions.
  - Displaying alternatives, e.g. using different uncertainty models, or display techniques.
  - Comparing current results with previous ones.
  - Providing optimisation for certain tasks under specified constraints, e.g. to achieve the least degree of uncertainty.
  - Providing common statistical analysis in visual forms.
  - Providing a mechanism for users to write scripts (e.g. via a visual language) to perform a series of exploration tasks (e.g. simulating scenarios of different values of variables with different degree of uncertainty).

It is commonly recognised that there is a need to develop a formal approach towards visualisation to avoid the drawbacks of ad hoc solutions. Traditionally, visualisation follows a *data-driven* approach which focuses on the nature and structure of data sets. Hence, visualisation techniques were devised and categorised based on data formats (e.g. [13–15]). While this approach provides a coherent and structured framework, it does not take into account the needs of tasks or users.

Task-driven approaches have emerged from the specific requirements of application domains, with specific criteria to determine what insight should visualisation techniques provide (e.g. [16–18]). Hence, the outcomes are immediately useful within the context of the application. One thing to note is that uncertainty in different variables might exert different degrees of importance to different tasks and to different human information analysts. The main drawback of these approaches is the lack of a generic framework, hence the techniques work very well in one domain, but might not be transferable to other domains.

User-objective-driven approaches aim to reduce the limitations of focusing on specific tasks, while seeking to provide a coherent framework. An objective represents a goal that a user aims to achieve. For example, the task can be to identify the potential failures of power lines for different weather conditions, while the objective is to determine the degree of correlation between failures and weather conditions. Objectives are at a more abstract and generic level than tasks, hence it is possible to create a coherent visualisation framework that satisfies specific objectives.

A pertinent question is whether the selection of a specific approach would have significant impacts on the effectiveness of visualisation of information uncertainty?

2.3.3 Desirable Characteristics of Visualisation Systems for Information Uncertainty

To be effective, visualisation systems for information uncertainty should possess the following characteristics:

- *Intuitive, Interactive, Unambiguous, Real time*: Visualisation techniques need to be efficient, easy for users to understand and assess the effects of uncertainty on the fly.
- *Robust, Less error prone*: When the uncertainty information or its model changes, the visualisation system should continue to work correctly and reduce the introduction of errors by users.
- *Flexible:* Users should be able to easily map uncertainty information into alternative uncertainty models and visual features in order to explore the impacts of different visualisation and modelling techniques on their understanding and interpretation of data and tasks.
- *Seamless integration of information and its uncertainty:* There should not be an artificial separation of the information and its uncertainty.
- *Extensible*: The system should allow representations for multiple types of uncertainty modelling and visualisation techniques to be added as required.
- *Adaptive*: It should be easy to change, add, or remove information about the uncertainty space of a variable at any stage of the modelling and visualisation process.
- *Reducing data model-type lock-in*: If a data model is constructed using a particular information uncertainty modelling technique, the cost to change to another modelling technique should be minimised.
- *Consistent learning effects*: The system should provide consistent ways to identify relevant parameters to represent and map to visual elements, and to learn how uncertainty affects information analysis and decision making.

2.3.4 Computer-Supported Tools

To ease the burden of absorbing overloaded information while performing multiple processes, it is imperative that integrated software tools should be designed for the whole workflow cycle from data acquisition and data transform to the tasks of exploration, scenario simulation and decision making. Tools for managing uncertainty modelling together with the visualisation process are also required to pull all these tasks together to assist users with higher level tasks such as selection of modelling options, and organisation and comparison of visual mappings. More specifically, the systems should allow uncertainty propagation to be automated and its architecture should allow easy switching between different uncertainty models, and different ways of mapping to visual elements and display.

At a more advance level, it would be desirable to provide mechanisms to receive feedbacks from users, and to capture users' profiles in order to adapt the system to suit their needs. For example, if a user's patterns of tasks, data usage, uncertainty modelling methods and choice of visualisation techniques are recorded, the system can re-prioritise tasks and data organisation to make the work more efficient and reduce redundancy. Furthermore, the system can automatically provide or suggest tasks to be performed next according to detected patterns in order to improve efficiency.

2.4 Current Progress

To establish ground work in order to understand where future research is needed, we focus our discussion on four areas: (1) How have different types of uncertainty been modelled and visually represented?; (2) What visualisation techniques have been developed to extract more insights into information uncertainty, and how should they be effectively organised and used?; (3) How both uncertainty modelling and visualisation processes been managed?; and (4) How application domains have embraced information uncertainty visualisation and stimulated the development and improvement of visualisation techniques and computer-supported software tools?

2.4.1 Uncertainty Modelling

There are several well established methods for modelling information uncertainty. This section describes the main modelling techniques, their parameters, and how they are commonly visualised.

Information uncertainty is characterised by the potential for a unit of information to hold alternative values. Classical sets can be used to model this directly, where the members of a set represent competing alternatives [7]. For example, a medical professional may give a diagnosis as a set of possible diseases. The uncertainty about which outcome is correct is specified implicitly by the presence of multiple competing possibilities. The parameters of uncertainty are therefore described by the membership of the set. Classical set uncertainty models can be visualised using superimposition of alternatives, such as superimposed state spaces [19].

An anticipated potential error such as arises from imprecision in measurement is typically expressed by an *interval* of confidence. An interval is a specialised type of classical set that is defined over a continuous range. Therefore, the uncertainty can be specified more efficiently, where only the upper and lower boundaries and their inclusiveness need to be stored. All in-between values are implicitly included in the set of competing alternatives. Intervals are often visualised using *error bars*, which are markers that extend over the range of possible values to indicate the potential for variation. Volume rendering can be used to indicate the range of possibility in three dimensions [20]. For example, a magnetic resonance imaging device might have an error tolerance of 5 mm, which can be indicated by displaying a 5 mm thick transparent volume around the scanned result.

The practice of using a classical set to record information uncertainty helps to identify what the competing alternatives are. However, it does not discriminate between these alternatives. There is no statement made about whether one alternative is more or less certain than any other alternative. More sophisticated uncertainty modelling techniques associate a degree of certainty with each alternative, such as *likelihood* in probability theory or *degree of membership* in fuzzy set theory.

Probability theory describes uncertainty in terms of expectation that an outcome will eventuate. There are two schools in modern probability: frequentest and Bayesian. Frequentest probability theory defines the chance of a given result under random conditions. Thus, the ratio of the number of times an event occurs to the number of times an experiment is repeated will tend toward the probability of that event. Bayesian probability theory includes a method for revising probabilities, thus enabling them to represent belief. This revision is effected by Bayes' theorem, which relates conditional and marginal probabilities.

Variables that are modelled using probabilities are typically expressed using *probability distributions*, which encode a degree of likelihood for every possible value. There are several common distributions that can be represented succinctly, such as uniform and normal distributions. Uniform distributions define an even probability for every value within the set. The outcome from rolling a single die is an example of a uniform distribution. Normal distributions are defined by their mean and standard deviation. The sum of uniformly random variables results in a normal distribution.

Probabilistically described variables are often visualised using line and bar graphs of their probability density functions. These indicate the likelihood on one axis for a range of potential outcomes along the other axis. Typically, the likelihood is plotted on the vertical axis with the potential outcomes along the horizontal axis. Should such a graph have tall slender peaks then the outcomes in these peaks are likely to occur and predictions can be made with high confidence. Should the graph contain a broad even landscape then many values are similarly likely and predictions will be less accurate.

Visualising probability density functions provides a significant amount of information. However, common distributions can often be described intuitively in more succinct terms of specific statistical parameters. For example, the normal distribution is familiar to many viewers, who can interpret its meaning from mean and standard deviation alone. These statistical parameters can be exploited to provide visual support in graphs, scatter plots or volume visualisation.

While the classic set clearly separates member elements from non-members, rough- and fuzzy sets allow partial membership. These modelling techniques are often used to deal with uncertainty arising from missing information or linguistic vagueness.

Rough sets map members to one of three possible membership states: wholly outside the set, wholly inside the set, and partially inside. A common use for rough sets is in aggregation and sampling applications. An example is classifying the terrain types in sections of a satellite photograph. Regions that contain mixed terrain types can be partial members of multiple sets. Thus, a partially forested area is a partial member in the forest set. This information can be critical if forests must be avoided at all costs, for example.

Fuzzy sets allow a continuous range for the degree of membership. They are defined by a *membership function*, which maps possible members to their degree of membership. Similar to probability distributions, fuzzy membership functions are typically chosen for succinct representation using a small number of parameters. One such method is to use piecewise linear segments and store only the membership values at the discontinuities. Another common method is to use sinusoidal functions. Fuzzy data and rules can also be visualised using fuzzy parallel coordinates [21]. Fuzzy parallel coordinates use areas instead of lines to plot data on parallel coordinate. The size of the area indicates the support of the variable. Optionally, translucent or lighter shaded areas can be used to show regions of partial support. 3D parallel coordinates [22] use the third dimension to indicate the fuzziness. This has the advantage of making it easier to distinguish core and support for fuzzy sets. Fuzzy classifiers can intuitively be visualised as shapes [23], where the inputs are represented along each axis, while the color or opacity indicate the output level. For a two dimensional classifier, this representation results in a polygonal shape, while in three dimensions, this produces a volume.

In summary, uncertainty modelling methods are reasonably well understood when applied to a particular variable. However, one problem is the integration of information with its uncertainty so that the information interpretation remains accurate as uncertainty propagates. Another more difficult problem lies with the effects of uncertainty on multivariate variables, especially when they are of different types or different uncertainty models are used.

2.4.2 Visualisation Techniques

Data does not exist at an infinite precision, and as such, visualisation schemes should include approaches to highlight the amount of error attached to the data. This is a relatively new field within data visualisation, and work has been carried out into the appropriate representation of such error values (e.g. [20, 24, 25]) and the related area of fuzzy set representations (e.g. [26, 27]). Analysis of the present state of the art in visualisation shows that a number of visual features have been suggested and used for the visualisation of uncertainty. A précis of the possible features used is shown below [8, 20, 27]:

- Intrinsic Representations – position, size, brightness, texture, color, orientation and shape;
- Further Related Representations – boundary (thickness, texture, and colour), blur, transparency and extra dimensionality;
- Extrinsic Representations – dials, thermometers, arrows, bars, different shapes and complex objects – pie charts, graphs, bars, or complex error bars.

While these features are an effective metaphor of imprecision, there are two things to note. They may not have a direct perceptual connection to the concept of uncertainty and they do not include the temporal domain as a possible method for uncertainty representation. The general approach to mapping visual features to visualisation techniques is from an *objective-oriented* viewpoint, and is derived from a visualisation data ontology outlined in our previous work [28]. The mapping begins with the choice of *data attributes* to be represented: relationships, resemblances, order and proportion [8]. These attributes are then mapped to *visual features* depending on the *visualisation task* to be performed. The visualisation task is chosen to enhance the perception of the information required by the viewer for their specific objective in performing the data analysis. The knowledge required for such a task-oriented approach is encapsulated in an agent-based visualisation architecture [28].

Among the visual features listed, blurring has the most immediate and intuitive mapping to uncertainty, as it simulates the visual percept caused by an incorrectly focused visual system. Within the context of visualisation of uncertainty, this effectively smears the boundary between two values, inducing a sense of uncertainty as to what value occupies a particular spatial location. A number of visual features may be used in a similar manner, for example, *hue* and *luminance*. This blurring metaphor can be extended to the temporal domain via animation [24, 25, 29]. While animation has been previously used to represent error values, no one has analysed these animations in the light of the chart-junk described by Tufte and the overuse of visual vibrations in visualisations [30]. Furthermore, no one has fully investigated its applicability, especially within the context of perceptual constraints, when applied to the visualisation of uncertainty.

Successful visualisation of data is facilitated by the correct choice of visual features used to illustrate the magnitudes of data dimensions. The visual features are often chosen based upon their ability to act as a visual metaphor for the underlying data being represented [31]. With this in mind, we examine two major components of visualisation: the visual features used and their organisation into higher representations, with the aim to extract appropriate visual representations for the visualisation of fuzzy data. Two case studies are presented in the area of fuzzy rule visualisation for illustrative purposes, but the approach holds for other uncertainty visualisation applications.

2.4.2.1 Relevant Visual Features

Common visualisation techniques map various visual feature dimensions to data variables in order to highlight differences, to make comparisons, to show temporal effects, etc. We now delineate these features in turn and then show how they can be mapped to the level of imprecision within the data and be thus applied to the representation of fuzzy data. The features to be considered are: hue, luminance, size, transparency, depth, texture, glyphs, particles and blur.

Hue is heavily used to highlight data that is different, or to represent gradients in the data [30, 31]. Saturation of the hue can be used to highlight the precision or certainty of the data. The more saturated the hue, the more certain or crisp the value contained in that region is [32]. Pastel, or low saturation regions, have the appearance of washing into each other and can be used to indicate the fuzziness of spatial region boundaries [32]. The number of hue groups can also be used in the mapping of values (*cardinality*) and can indicate the level of precision in the values. The less precise solution has fewer variations in hue values, while a more precise solution has a smoother shaded appearance. Finally, bad hue choices can be used to indicate the location of uncertainty via a lack of background/foreground separation, e.g. red on purple. The lack of background/foreground separation can be a useful metaphor for uncertainty as the region may only just verge on being distinct, due to the proximity of the hue of the region to its background hue [33].

In a similar manner to hue, *luminance* may be used to signify categories and highlight differences within scalar data. Foreground and background effects could be used to show the appearance of entities within the data, i.e. the data could hover around JND (Just Noticeable Difference) values to indicate the ambiguity [33]. The cardinality of the luminance feature can be varied to show the precision of the data in a similar manner to the cardinality of the hue space.

Glyphs involving the size of the objects are often used to indicate the scalar component of vector information. An example of this is the variation of the size of error bars within to indicate the imprecision of the data point [30].

Opacity is similar to the concept of blending a colour with a background, except that the background can be any object behind the present object being rendered. In this context, it can be used to show the fuzziness of the data by mapping the possibility of the fuzzy variable to the opacity of the object in question.

Depth can be used to indicate an order or spatial positioning for the data. Data which is presented in stereo may have the algorithm modified to change the binocular fusion of the object to indicate fuzziness with the depth position of the data. Depth of field effects can be used, in a related manner to spatial blur caused by the removal of high frequency information.

Texture may be applied to objects to indicate the level of precision, ambiguity or fuzziness in the spatial location upon an object or upon a spatial location. Differences in colour and luminance and shape textures can be used to indicate the presence of ambiguous data. Certain shimmering effects, usually to be avoided in visualisation [30], can be used to indicate the presence of ambiguity within the region [34].

Both *glyphs* and *icons* present an unending list of possible shapes to use with regards to visualisation of fuzzy information. *Words* could also be used in this application, due to fuzzy terms being the currency of such rule-based systems. Words, along with other complex icon-like glyphs, have been used in visualisation applications.

Particles can be used to represent the fuzziness of a region or an object by varying the space between them, and the colour of the particles themselves. The particles can also be rendered with motion blur to again indicate the level of data imprecision. Cartography often uses a form of this by drawing dashed lines to represent imprecise lines and boundaries, or by using different dot densities to represent shading effects [26].

Blurring or *depth of field* effects from spatial frequency components being removed in the image plane can be used to show the indistinct nature of data points [35, 36].

2.4.2.2 Higher Spatial Representations of Data

The visual features listed previously are spatially arranged to form a coherent display in graphic forms which enable the perception of various patterns in the data.

2.4.2.2.1 2D Representations

2D graphs of various forms can be used to encode the colours and shapes into a display on a Cartesian system, in order to show the spatial relationships of values. These graphs may not necessarily related to a spatial locations. Some examples of graphs are: histograms, bar charts, tree diagrams, time histories of 1D slices, maps, iconic and glyph-based diagrams. The structure and inter-relationships of rules may be illustrated by graphs, trees and flowcharts. Variation in intensity or colour may be used to encode another dimension on a 2D graph which indicates the degree of impreciseness or fuzzy membership functions of the data displayed. Graphs may also be used to represent the fuzzy membership functions or alpha-cuts of a fuzzy set. Other techniques such as multi dimensional scaling [37] and parallel coordinates [21] provide ways to display multi-dimensional fuzzy data in 2D without losing any information.

For multi-dimensional scaling, the authors introduced an algorithm to generate 2D view of a set of fuzzy rules which minimises the inter-point distances. The rule set is then visualised as a 2D scatter plot, where different grey scales denote different classes and the size of each square denoting each class indicates the number of examples and hence the importance of the class. For the parallel coordinates approach, n Cartesian coordinates are mapped into n parallel coordinates and a n-dimensional point becomes a series of $(n - 1)$ lines connecting the values on n parallel axes. At the end of this section, as an example, we shall illustrate how the visualisation of fuzzy rules by parallel coordinates provided by these authors can be improved to make it more intuitive for users by judicious choice of visual features.

2.4.2.2.2 3D Representations

A 3D volume has spatial regions mapped to a location in n-dimensional space. The features of the volume partitions could be modified to indicate the precision of the data within the volume (e.g. varying intensity, colour saturation, texture, opacity). These techniques may be used to show classification boundaries in fuzzy classification methods. 3D height-field (expressed as surfaces) can also be used to represent fuzzy membership functions of data displayed in 2D graphs. To visualise hierarchical information, a cone tree method was introduced to represent a tree structure [38]. This technique is later used to produce a 3D flowchart to represent rule structure in a rule-based program to facilitate its understanding [39]. To extend these techniques to fuzzy rules, visual features described in the previous subsection can be integrated to the cone tree structure to express the degree of uncertainty in each rule (e.g. each node is displayed with different degree of opacity).

2.4.2.2.3 Dynamic Representations

Various visual features discussed in the previous subsection can be used to modify the animation to display object behaviour over time, e.g. using motion blur levels, flickering etc. to represent the precision of the measurements of the object motion in a plane simulation. The intention here is to cause the oscillations to be fast enough that the changes do not fuse, but shimmer between the two values to pre-attentively [40] indicate the location of uncertainty about values within a region. The reader is directed for further details to [29].

Each oscillation represents a change between lower and higher bounds of uncertainty values in the data set, represented by the visual feature change – the size of error in the data, or the membership value of a fuzzy set, for example. Various oscillation functions can be used. A step function produces a hard change between functions, a linear function is a linear interpolation between the two values, and a sin function is a smooth sinusoidal change between the two values. An example luminance oscillation visualisation is shown in Fig. 2.1.

Furthermore, these techniques can be extended to stereo displays, with the following figure showing vertex perturbations presented as a stereo pair (Fig. 2.2).

The centre region of the surface in Fig. 2.2, upon being viewed in stereo, is blurred by lack of binocular fusion and therefore represents uncertainty with a stereo form of blurring. Again, the parameters within this mode of delivery can be modified according to visual perceptual constraints.

2.4.2.3 Visualisation of Fuzzy Rules

In the last section, we mentioned how parallel coordinates and multiscaling can be used for representing fuzzy data and fuzzy rules. This section reviews other methods that explicitly cater for fuzzy rules. These methods fall into two categories: to model the causal flow between elements in a fuzzy system, and to represent fuzzy clustering

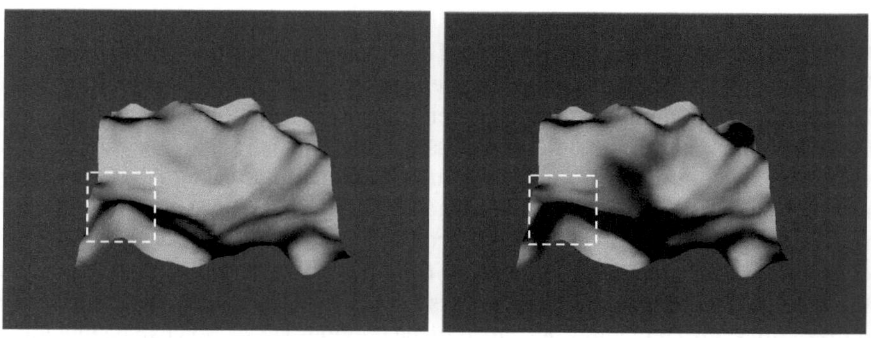

Fig. 2.1 Frames from a movie of the luminance oscillation technique, with the changes in values highlighted with the dashed rectangle (*See Color Plates*)

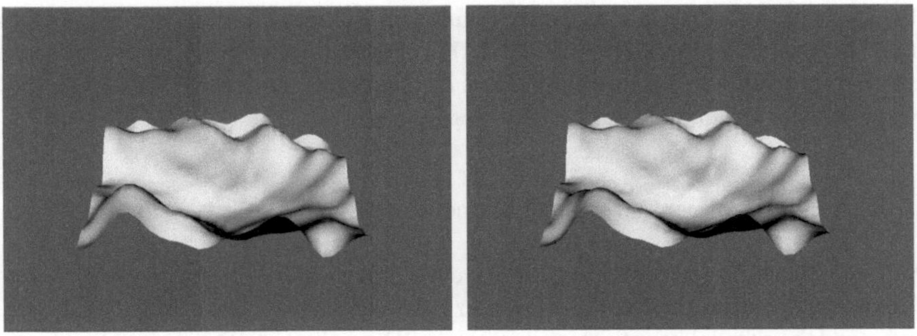

Fig. 2.2 Stereo pair with uncertainty at the peaks and in the centre rendered with vertex vibrations. This appears as a blurred uncertainty region due to an absence of binocular fusion (*See Color Plates*)

or classification of data. The first category aims to facilitate the understanding of the complex nature of a rule-based fuzzy control system, while the second category helps to analyse the effectiveness of fuzzy clustering algorithms.

2.4.2.3.1 Visualising Causal Fuzzy Relationships

Dickerson et al. [41] used fuzzy cognitive maps in the form of a graph to encode relationships in a complex interacting system (e.g. relationships between proteins in the expression of genetic information). This technique is useful for encoding expert information which is commonly present in fuzzy control systems. The 3D cone graph mentioned in Sect. 2.4.2.2 was later used by Gershon [25] to produce a 3D flowchart to represent the hierarchical rule structure in a rule-based program to facilitate its understanding. We shall show later how these techniques can be extended to visualising fuzzy rules, where appropriate visual features are integrated to the cone tree structure to express the degree of uncertainty in each rule (e.g. each node is displayed with different degree of opacity). The propagation of fuzzy rules can also be visualised by using a truncated double cone structure.

2.4.2.3.2 Visualising Fuzzy Data Clusters

Berthold and Holve [37] mapped an N-dimensional fuzzy rule to a point in 2D. The 2D function was constructed so that the error values between two rules are minimised. Rules are represented as squares with different grey intensities to distinguish the clusters. [42] used 2D and 3D plots with various thresholds to represent convex hulls of data point clusters. Glyphs with different shape and size are used for the data points. The authors also presented another method of using the colour hues from red (hot) to blue (cold) to represent the membership values of data points. Colour hues were also used by [43] to represent belief values in the form of a flame to facilitate decision making in an anaesthetic monitoring system. To show the classification boundaries resulted from fuzzy classification methods, Nürnberger et al. [23] used 3D illuminated surfaces. These surfaces can clearly demonstrate the effects of t-norm and t-conorm operators on the resultant surfaces. However, they do not show internal details for each class.

2.4.2.3.3 Improvement on Current Methods

We now present two cases where we have extended and improved the capabilities of existing visualisation methods for fuzzy data and fuzzy rules. In the first case, we extend the parallel coordinates approach to 3D graphs and 3D polygonal surfaces. In the second case, we integrate different visual techniques to cone trees to allow different types of information to be perceived.

2.4.2.3.4 3D Extension of Parallel Coordinates

Figure 2.3 shows an illustration of a method developed by Hall and Berthold [21], for representing multidimensional fuzzy rules using 2D parallel coordinates. Two rules are illustrated from their Iris data example, where four features are used for classification (sepal length, sepal width, petal length and petal width). They used the thickness or grey intensity of lines to indicate the fuzziness of points. One drawback is that it is difficult to visually distinguish fine grades of grey level on single lines. Another drawback is that it is not possible to perceive the core and support of a fuzzy set simultaneously. One way of addressing those limitations on visual perception is to use a 3D representation where the parallel coordinates are displayed on the x-y plane, and the fuzzy set membership functions are displayed as z-coordinates. Different alpha-cuts of fuzzy rules can be identified by applying horizontal cutting planes. The perception of different classes can be facilitated further by introducing surfaces with illumination and texture. Figure 2.3 demonstrates a visualisation of the same Iris data by lit and textured surfaces. Note how the alpha cutting of the membership function for Rule 2 on the Petal Length dimension is now easily perceived [16].

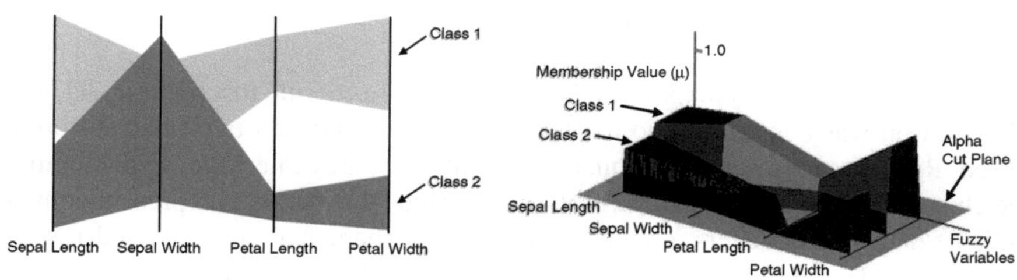

Fig. 2.3 A fuzzy parallel coordinate visualisation on the left showing membership values as levels of luminance. On the right is an improved 3D parallel coordinate visualisation of the Iris data with lit and textured surfaces, showing the same Iris data

2.4.2.3.5 Truncated Double Cone Structure for Visualising Fuzzy Rule Propagation

We introduce a truncated double cone structure to facilitate the visualisation and analysis of fuzzy rule propagation. The shape reflects the nature of the propagation starting from a small number of rules to a wider network of rules, then contracting its size during the de-fuzzification stage (Fig. 2.4). Each set of rules is displayed as a network on the surface of the double cone. The relationships between sets of rules are represented as connecting lines located within the double cone, which can be made visible by using transparency. Its structure is composed of concentric internal cones and parallel layers occupying the cone from top to bottom. The cone can be rotated around to examine the rules (shown by arrows in Fig. 2.4). Rules migrate through the concentric cones depending on criteria, e.g. the rules/variables that have the largest DOF (Degree of Fulfillment) are situated on the outer shell. Upright Trapezoids represent fuzzified input variables, inverted Trapezoids defuzzification output operators, Ellipses set operations and Crosses aggregation operators. These icons may have appropriate data superimposed onto the location. Lines use size, transparency or colour to indicate fulfilment values, and the output visual feature of the operator mimics the operator itself, e.g. the output of centroid defuzzification is the average thickness of the input lines.

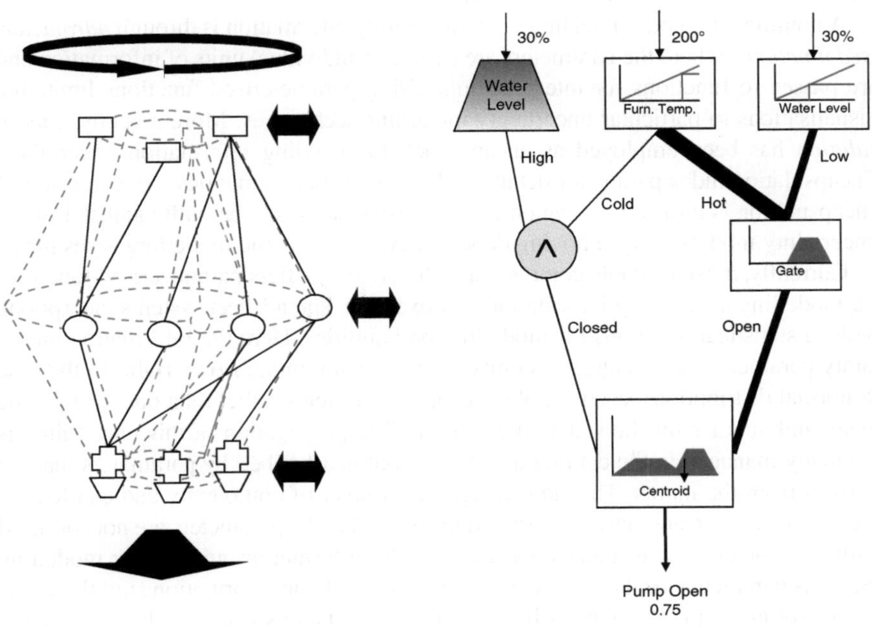

Fig. 2.4 Truncated double cone for visualising fuzzy rules and their propagation is shown in the diagram on the left. On the right is an example network diagram on the surface of the cones. The size and intensity of lines illustrate the fulfillment of rules. Fuzzy function diagrams have been overlaid to give further insight into the operation of the fuzzy rules

In summary, numerous visualisation techniques are currently available for information uncertainty. An important question to ask is which one is best to use for a particular task, and how uncertainty propagation can be tracked and interpreted properly? Another area of concern is the information overloading problem, that necessitates the development of *verity* visualisation approach which shows uncertainty together with the information itself, using the same graphical representation. For example, Wittenbrink et al. [44] used glyphs to represent fluid flows, where uncertainty is encoded in either the magnitude or orientation of the flow. Not all problems can be neatly resolved this way, but this highlights the need to reduce the cognitive stress exerted on users while embracing information uncertainty.

2.4.3 Management of Information Uncertainty Propagation and Visualisation

The addition of information uncertainty parameters adds complexity to the system for three reasons. Firstly, there is more information, which must be stored and managed. Secondly, new rules govern this new information, including the propagation of uncertainty information to other variables in the user's model. Thirdly, this new information poses unique visualisation challenges.

A common method for dealing with uncertainty information is through *parameterised functions*, where the parameters are treated as individual units of information and are passed to functions for interpretation. Using parameterised functions limits the visualisations to particular uncertainty modelling techniques. More recently, *encapsulation* has been employed as an approach to encoding information uncertainty. Encapsulation hides parameter details and enforces their semantics. An extension of encapsulation is *abstraction*, which enables visualisations to be built against abstract uncertainty models, thus removing dependency upon specific modelling types [45].

Currently, most available commercial software only offers parameterised functions for modelling uncertainty information. For example, spreadsheet systems incorporate built-in statistical functions for modelling probabilities. Here the information uncertainty parameters are managed as units of information in their own right. In the case of normal distributions, each variable occupies two fields rather than one, one for the mean and another for the standard deviation. The propagation of this uncertainty is manually managed in the data model. The output is described by parameters that are derived from the inputs. This adds a significant layer of complexity and can lead to accidental errors. Care must be exercised to ensure that the parameters are not confused with each other or with other data. Each of the information uncertainty modelling methods parameterises the uncertainty associated with the information slightly differently. Not all of the parameters have intuitive correlations between the information and the uncertainty. For example, breakpoints in a complicated piecewise linear fuzzy set may be difficult to comprehend, while the mean of a normal distribution is the most likely value, and therefore is easy to comprehend.

Encapsulation technique can encode not only information uncertainty parameters as mentioned above, but also the propagation of uncertainty [45]. This technique borrows from object oriented programming theory and enables uncertain variables to be treated with similar complexity to those without uncertainty information. The system is intrinsically aware of the parameters and can therefore enforce semantics. The parameters can be hidden, thus reducing perceived complexity and providing a multi-resolution view of the information model. Furthermore, rules for propagation of information uncertainty can by applied automatically.

There exist different mathematical models for the propagation of uncertainty (see e.g. [2, 46]). The appropriateness of a propagation model depends on the application. The user will therefore typically decide on particular models based on their own expertise and experience. However, a multiplicity of rules can be required in mixed representation cases. For example, the addition of a normally distributed variable to an interval-valued variable requires a different treatment to the addition of two normally distributed variables. This can result in an explosion of necessary uncertainty propagation rules to choose from.

To preserve uncertainty details through the operation requires that the modelling technique is sufficiently general to express the results. Klir [2, pp. 357] defines the *principle of uncertainty invariance*, which demands that the amount of uncertainty does not change when transforming between uncertainty theories. This will produce accurate results, but can have the effect of making the data unwieldy. Thus approximations are typically used.

One method that allows for approximation while reducing the number of rules required is *hierarchical propagation*. This method uses a hierarchy of the modelling techniques that is based on the level of detail that is encoded about the uncertainty [45]. Figure 2.5 shows the hierarchical structure for common categories of information uncertainty modelling techniques. The least amount of detail possible is uncertainty ignorance, where the potential for uncertainty is not known. At the next level of detail are two categories: known value, where the value of the variable is known to be truth and is therefore not subject to uncertainty; and estimate, where it is known that there exists uncertainty but nothing further is specified. The estimate is further

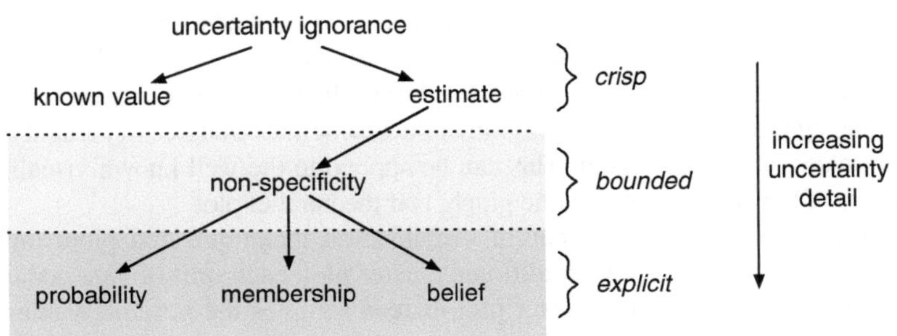

Fig. 2.5 The hierarchical framework orders categories of information uncertainty modeling techniques according to increasing levels of uncertainty detail

refined to the non-specificity class of techniques. These techniques specify the boundary between what is considered possible and what is not. This can be further refined to techniques that explicitly define the degree of uncertainty for candidate values: probability, in the frequentest sense; membership, such as fuzzy and rough sets; and belief, such as Bayesian probability or Dempster-Shafer methods.

The *hierarchical propagation* technique relies on making transitions between modelling techniques. The level of detail is *promoted* by extrapolating the required information and *demoted* by simplifying and reducing information. A tree search algorithm is used to establish a sequence of transitions to bring the operands into compatible uncertainty theories.

Visualisation of information uncertainty tends to be locked to the uncertainty modelling technique. This is largely due to the large number of methods for encoding information uncertainty, each of which is treated differently. A strong dependence eventuates between the uncertainty modelling technique and the visualisation. This creates a difficulty when the uncertainty modelling technique needs to be changed. According to Klir's *principle of requisite generalisation* [2, pp. 357], no a priori commitment should be made to any single technique. Changing the technique can be necessary in situations where the information changes. For example, a prediction might be modelled using an interval. Subsequently, when the event has come to pass and the outcome is known, it should be changed to a known value.

A method for overcoming the visualisation-uncertainty model lock-in problem is to use *abstraction*, where a single interface defines the contractual obligation for each uncertainty model. The visualisation can be built against the abstract interface, freeing it from the uncertainty modelling technique. The level of abstraction depends on the needs of the user. The *unified uncertainty model* (UUM) does not distinguish between different types of uncertainty and treats all methods as modelling a degree of uncertainty. This is useful for visualisation techniques that wish to highlight different levels of uncertainty within the same view. The *dual uncertainty model* (DUM) makes a distinction between the probabilistic views and the possibilistic views of uncertainty. This model is necessary for visualisations that need to distinguish between these approaches.

Both the UUM and DUM employ the concept of a *plural value*, where a plural value is an abstract construct for values that can simultaneously hold multiple states to different degrees. This can be expressed as a function that maps candidate states to their degree of certainty. Concrete analogues are the fuzzy membership function and the probability density function. For visualisation purposes, plural values are encoded as a set of ranges that define regions of interest. Each region of interest defines a degree of certainty function for values within the region. This can be applied to the well known visualisation techniques of the cluster plot, the line graph, and the parallel plot.

The cluster plot is an information visualisation technique that plots multiple values on the same axis. In the traditional cluster plot, each unit of data occupies a single point. The uncertainty cluster plot instead samples the possible values over the axis, usually using opacity to indicate the degree of certainty. In the case of an interval, the degree of certainty will be one over the range, resulting in a line for a 1-dimensional cluster plot.

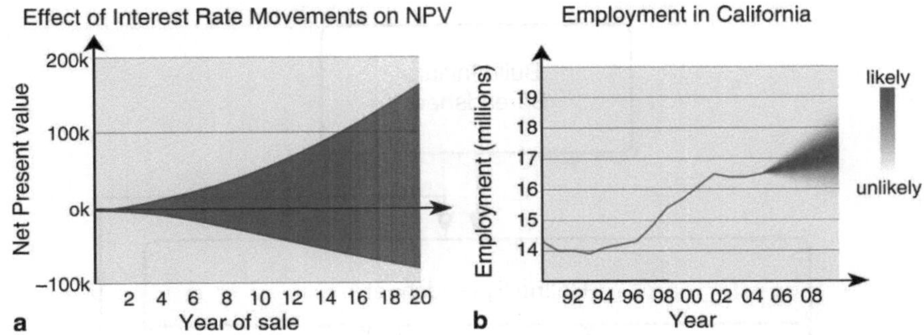

Fig. 2.6 Uncertainty line graphs (**a**) interval (**b**) normal probability distribution

A line graph is built from one or more series of values. It is a 2-dimensional graph: the value plotted against one axis, and the position within the series against the other axis. These points are then connected by a sequence of line segments. Extending the line graph to show uncertainty requires that every value be a plot of the uncertainty space, all of which is then connected to the next value plot in the series. The result is a polygon in the case of continuous plural values (e.g. Fig. 2.6a). The surface of the polygon can be textured with a sampling of the degrees of certainty over the range (e.g. Fig. 2.6b).

Parallel plots display multiple dimensions individually in sequence and use line segments to join points belonging to the same data unit together. There are two common approaches to uncertainty in parallel plots. The first uses blurring or opacity to indicate uncertainty and the second uses the third dimension. The first technique can be achieved in much the same way as the line graph given above. The second method needs to produce a geometric shape. The degree of certainty is mapped to a height value and a convex hull is formed between the height values at this parallel axis and the next.

Visualisation systems are commonly based on data-flow networks. However, the spreadsheet paradigm has been shown to offer some distinct advantages for visualisation [47, 48]. A spreadsheet visually lays out documentation, intermediate data, and model logic for inspection. The techniques for managing information uncertainty can extend the spreadsheet paradigm to provide a coherent managed system for information uncertainty visualisation.

An information uncertainty spreadsheet system requires three extensions to the spreadsheet paradigm. The first extension is to apply encapsulation at the cell level. Thus, each cell can contain a variable and its associated uncertainty details [45]. The second extension is to define the propagation models, which govern the propagation of uncertainty information from inputs to outputs in formulae. This means that the actual formulae within the user's spreadsheet do not need to be changed. The third extension is for the visualisation mapping system to adhere to an uncertainty abstraction model.

Figure 2.7 shows the process that a user will follow when building an information uncertainty spreadsheet. In the first step, an initial spreadsheet is built, typically

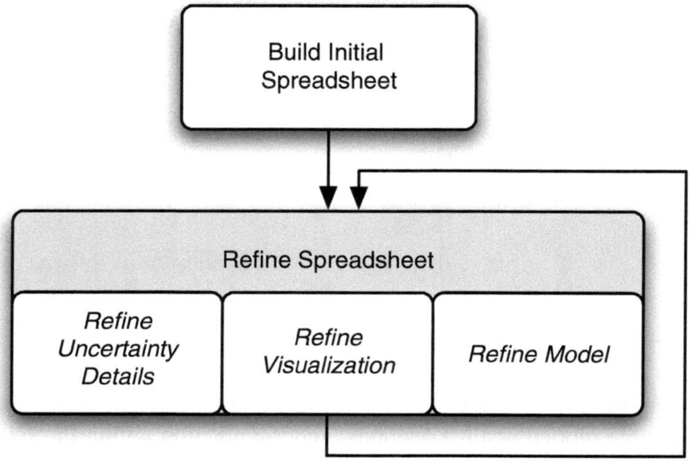

Fig. 2.7 Process for constructing an information uncertainty spreadsheet

using *uncertainty ignorance* data types. This step is similar to building a traditional spreadsheet and includes the spreadsheet structure, variables, and formulae. Next, the spreadsheet is iteratively refined in three ways: firstly, uncertainty detail is added to or removed from variables; secondly, visualisations are added, altered, or removed; and thirdly, the model can be refined in the traditional sense, such as changing formulae or adding variables.

Changes can be made to the uncertainty information in the model without these changes conflicting with the formulae. Furthermore, the use of abstraction allows these changes to propagate through to the visualisations. Therefore, the user can easily explore the impacts that different uncertainties can have on their system. The feedback is twofold. Firstly, changes are immediately reflected throughout the spreadsheet itself due to the propagation. Secondly, there is visual feedback from the visualisations.

Figure 2.8 shows an example of an information uncertainty spreadsheet and visualisation. The spreadsheet models the effect that changes in salary have over time and the resulting net income is plotted as a line graph. This is identical to a traditional spreadsheet-based model except that the salary growth variable is given as an interval. However, this small change has wide reaching effects. All calculated fields that are dependent on this field become themselves uncertain and the line graph expands to show the net income range.

In summary, it is critical to enable users to intuitively manage the propagation of information uncertainty together with its visualisation. To achieve a definite step in this direction, we have illustrated a spreadsheet paradigm as an effective method to manage data with or without uncertainty, and different uncertainty models in a unified fashion. Needless to say, this area still needs further investigation.

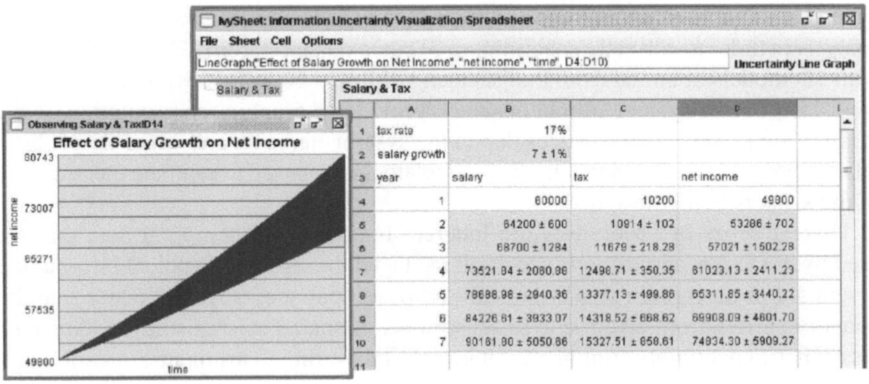

Fig. 2.8 Prototype information uncertainty spreadsheet system. The salary growth field (cell B2) is subject to uncertainty, which is propagated to other cells and from there to the visualisation (*See Color Plates*)

2.4.4 Applications of Information Uncertainty Visualisation

As information uncertainty is inherent in many real world problems, its visualisation is applicable for diverse domains. However, the level of sophistication of visualisation techniques deployed or developed vary substantially according to the ease of use and familiarity with technology of each domain. Early applications have arisen in engineering and scientific problems due to the need to deal with errors in measurements, approximations in numerical models, or statistical variations in experimental or simulation data. Prevalent use of remote sensing imagery, and spatial and temporal data has widely opened up the field to cover practically all application domains. In addition, recent focus on users' and customers' needs has brought forward different concepts of information uncertainty in social, humanity and business areas. As it is not possible to cover all application papers, we only select a few typical ones to highlight the usefulness and the degree of maturity of uncertainty visualisation in different application domains.

In engineering and scientific applications, uncertainty visualisation has facilitated error and range analysis, and decision making for the purposes of simulation, planning, surveying, maintenance and instrumentation. For example, Lodha et al. [24] investigated a number of different visualisation techniques for displaying uncertainty in streamlines of fluid flow: glyphs, envelopes, animation with motion blur, priority sequencing, trace viewpoints and rakes. Their system was designed to highlight the error differences when using different integration methods or a different step size for each method. Wittenbrink et al. [44] designed vector glyphs to show variation in uncertainty in the direction and magnitude of winds and ocean currents. The significance of their work lies in the verity approach which integrates the uncertainty information with the data in the visualisation, hence alleviates the information overloading problem. Khosrowshahi & Banissi [49] created 4D visualisation models using VRML to study the degradation of building floors for maintenance purposes. An important problem for surgical navigation systems is to perform error analysis in order to correctly superimpose 3D data obtained from 3D position sensors with 3D models obtained from images using different coordinate systems. Sakugari et al. [50] built a system simulator which provides a graphic representation of the registration graph, where vertices depict the system elements and edges depict their relative positions and orientations. This simulator is then used to estimate the accuracy of the sensors being designed.

Diverse types of uncertainty are inherent in spatial and temporal data that are used by numerous applications and often managed through geographical information systems. For example, maps are of limited positional accuracy, and raster satellite imagery suffers from errors due to sensor bias or spatial misregistration. Attribute data inherit uncertainty from the limitation of measuring instruments, or estimation methods, or simply their stochastic nature. Uncertainty is also introduced when maps are generalised to a finer scale from data available only in a coarser scale. Uncertainty in classification is another common problem, for example, classification of land based on vegetation cover, soil type and land use. Human subjective judgements provide another common source of vagueness and imprecision, especially for categorical data types.

Goodchild et al. [26] examined the problem of fuzzy spatial queries to retrieve fuzzy regions (ill-defined geographical footprints) from a spatial database, based on location or vernacular place names, instead of officially recognised place names. They also offered simple cartographical tools for displaying these fuzzy regions as well as tools for measuring the goodness of fit. Bastin et al. [51] used parallel coordinates to visualise the fuzzy memberships of multi-dimensional fuzzy clusters which result from the classification of landcover types in satellite imagery. Their visualisation toolkit also allows the tracking of classification process along each feature dimension. The uncertainty at each grid cell on a remotely sensed map can be described in terms of probability density functions. Dungan et al. [52] used surfaced graphs, contour colours and bar graphs to simultaneously visualise the four statistical variables that underlie these probability density functions (standard deviation, interquartile, mean and difference between mean and median). To simultaneously display information uncertainty together with the spatial data itself, Kardos et al. [53] explored the use of two hierarchical tree data structures: the region quadtree and the hexagonal or rhombus quadtree. A region with spatial or attribute data with a high level of uncertainty is displayed with less resolution than one with a low level of uncertainty. They also examined the effectiveness of using metaphors such as fog, blur, blinking pixels and colour mix for visualising uncertainty.

Hope [54] conducted an interesting study to test whether the inclusion of thematic uncertainty information would lead to better decision making. She used two case studies with different display methods: the selection of an airport location given the uncertain suitability of land parcels; and maritime navigation with positional uncertainty. The results showed that a significant percentage of the subjects did not respond rationally to uncertain information and disregard any option associated with high uncertainty, even though such an option might be the most optimal in terms of other factors. Subjects were also inclined to work with those uncertainty display methods which depict gradual transitions (e.g. graduate shading of a transition zone where positional uncertainty occurs; or probability of positional uncertainty), rather than a crisp-looking graphical entity (e.g. boundaries of 80% positional confidence interval) even though the meaning is the same.

Two strategic papers were offered in the field of geospatially reference information. The first paper was by Thomson et al. [10] who analysed the sources of uncertainty and how they are viewed and used by information analysts. They then offered a typological categorisation of these uncertainties and their quantitative representations. Their intention was to promote the use of such a framework for further development and evaluation of visualisation techniques. The second paper was by MacEachren et al. [55] who analysed the characteristics of geospatial uncertainty visualisation, and assessed the progress on available methods and tools, as well as their usefulness for information analysis and decision making. They also identified a number of key research challenges in this application domain.

Information uncertainty visualisation has also found its place in business, social and humanity areas. Typical applications in business include the estimation of price and cost, time completion, etc. For example, Kitchenham [17] developed a bidding model for software projects and methods for visualising the uncertainty in those factors that influence pricing decision and the decision on whether to bid or not. Monte Carlo simulation and animation were deployed to enable users to gauge the impacts of uncertainty in the model inputs and the extent of uncertainty in the model outputs. Biffl et al. [56] investigated how temporal uncertainty in task completion impacted on business success and planning. PERT charts and PlanningLines were used to visualise task relationships and temporal uncertainties for software engineering project planning. They concluded that the latter technique was far superior as users took less time to assess the implications of temporal task uncertainty and to complete tasks, while at the same time, making fewer mistakes.

Understanding users' or customers' needs and preferences is increasingly critical while developing new products, systems or technologies. Ohene-Djan et al. [18] explored simple visualisation methods to track how the opinions of customers are changed and gradually formed on media presentations such as television advertisement, video and music compositions, for commercial research market. They used colour spectra displayed on different shape configurations to express the diverse range of emotions and levels of certainty in the expressed opinions. Zenebe and Norcio [57] used fuzzy sets to model the subjectivity, vagueness and imprecision in customers' preferences, feedbacks, and their similarities with regard to movie genres. The display of degree of memberships and customer clusters with respect to movie genres, age and gender using cluster plots helped with the discovery of patterns in the preferences of customers, features of movie genres and understanding of their relationships.

In summary, the sophistication of visualisation techniques used or created depend largely on the level of expertise and familiarity of the technology and its uptake. The familiarity of existing tools currently being used in a specific domain also make them more likely to be adopted as potential candidates for uncertainty visualisation, or at least as initial starting points for development.

2.5 Key Research Challenges

The increasing uptake of information uncertainty visualisation by diverse real world application domains has stimulated a steady rate of research work in this area. However, many issues still need further research.

2.5.1 *Formal Methods for Assessing How Information Uncertainty Visualisation Techniques Benefit Information Analysis and Decision Making*

Although there have been some efforts to evaluate the effectiveness of specific techniques, currently there is no formal framework for evaluation that provide quantitative and qualitative assessment of how such visualisation help users understand, interpret and learn the impacts of uncertainty on their tasks. In other words, how much better is the performance of these tasks by embracing uncertainty? Does the complexity of introducing uncertainty into visualisation create more opportunities to make errors? Can different visualisation techniques and different uncertainty models be easily compared, and what are the criteria for comparison? Does the level of familiarity of uncertainty models and visualisation techniques significantly affect users' performance and discourage novices to adopt the technology? How important is the role of graphical user interfaces to enable users to intuitively explore, simulate and make decision with information uncertainty, especially when they have minimum knowledge of uncertainty modelling and analysis? Does a formal framework for visualisation based on a well-defined typological categorisation of uncertainty significantly improve the usability of visualisation techniques and comprehension of the implications of uncertainty on tasks? Do these impacts differ greatly for different types of tasks? All these questions require rigorous studies in order to not only assess the value of current uncertainty visualisation techniques and frameworks, but also to determine how they can be modified or improved in future.

2.5.2 *Intuitive Ways to Explore the Interactions of Multi Types of Uncertainty in Multivariate Data*

A common criticism of visualisation is that sophisticated and beautiful visual displays may not necessary add values to comprehension and interpretation. As information overloading is a major obstacle when embracing uncertainty, simplistic but intuitive methods would be more beneficial. How are multiple types of uncertainty represented and visualised? How do they interact? In particular, can data brushing techniques be developed further to enhance the capabilities of interactive exploration of uncertainty in multivariate data. To date, data brushing techniques have only been used in dynamic visualisation to select data subsets in order to perform operations in an intuitive and systematic way (e.g. [58, 59]). Another question is whether using other indicators besides visual elements to depict uncertainty would reduce the visual perception overload? For example, Lodha et al. [24] has used sound to augment visualisation of fluid flow. Can other senses such as vibration or touch be effectively used?

2.5.3 Integrated Tools for Management of High Level Tasks Together with Uncertainty Modelling and Visualisation

Visualisation systems tend to focus more on the development of low level tasks such as data representation, visual mapping and display, while leaving users to cope with high levels tasks such as simulation, decision making and information analysis themselves. As it is more difficult to gain insight into these tasks with added complexity due to uncertainty, it is imperative to pay attention to develop tools to manage the whole work flow. The tools should integrate the requirements of data visualisation with the requirements of different uncertainty models, as well as the requirements of these high level tasks. Users should be able to perform each task seamlessly, while switching between all options.

2.5.4 Visualisation Tools to Assist with Searching Fuzzy Databases and Vague Queries

Many databases associated with engineering, business and geographic information systems contain data with uncertainty, even though such data are often treated as crisp data. Uncertainty visualisation can certainly help to visualise the fuzzy outcomes of each query, but more importantly, it can assist users to see how search decisions are made given the interactions of uncertainty in variables, and how the results vary if the query is changed. In addition, users very often wish to make vague queries using approximate values or imprecise concepts. A visual method to depict such queries and how the search is refined would enhance the capacity of accessing appropriate and hopefully, more accurate information.

2.5.5 Integrating Human Behaviour to Tool Design and Task Performance Evaluation

As human behaviour, subjective judgements and preferences give rise to a major source of uncertainty, they have been subjected to various studies, notably for marketing research. An equally relevant question is how these factors affect the way uncertainty visualisation tools are used, and the way tasks are performed and interpreted? The answers to this question would assist with better tool design to provide deeper insights.

2.6 Summary

We have provided an analysis of major issues that need to be considered while developing and deploying visualisation systems or techniques for information uncertainty. We have also assessed progress in four important areas and discussed a number of key research challenges. In summary, the advance and uptake of uncertainty visualisation does not rely on how many more new visualisation techniques that can be devised, but on the development of a rigorous framework for evaluation on how useful and usable visualisation techniques are, with respect to the objectives of the users and the specific tasks they have to perform. To this end, it is imperative to develop good schemes for management of uncertainty modelling, uncertainty propagation and visualisation. Furthermore, the understanding of human behaviour and preferences has to play a crucial part in the design of these techniques and software tools.

References

1. Jacod, J. and P.E. Protter, *Probability Essentials 2 nd ed. 2003*, New York, New York: Springer.
2. Klir, G.J., *Uncertainty and Information: Foundations of Generalized Information Theory*. 2005, Wiley-Interscience Malden, USA.
3. Nguyen, H.T. and E. Walker, *A First Course in Fuzzy Logic*. 2000, Boca Raton, FL: Chapman & Hall.
4. Pawlak, Z., *Rough Sets: Theoretical Aspects of Reasoning about Data*. 1991, Dordrecht & Boston: Kluwer Academic Publishers.
5. Pearl, J., *Probabilistic Reasoning in Intelligent Systems*. 1988, Morgan Kaufmann.
6. Zadeh, L., Fuzzy Sets, *Information and Control*, 8: 338–353.
7. Klir, G.J., The many faces of uncertainty, in *Uncertainty Modelling and Analysis: Theory and Applications*, B.M. Ayyub and M.M. Gupta, Editors. 1994, Elsevier Science B.V. pp. 3–19.
8. Gershon, N., Visualization of an imperfect world. *Computer Graphics and Applications, IEEE*, 1998. 18(4): p. 43–45.
9. Pang, A.T., C.M. Wittenbrink, and S.K. Lodha, Approaches to uncertainty visualization, in *The Visual Computer*. 1997. pp. 370–390 vol. 13.
10. Thomson, J., et al., A typology for visualizing uncertainty, in *Proceedings of SPIE*. 2005. p. 146–157.
11. Pham, B. and R. Brown, Analysis of visualisation requirements for fuzzy systems, in *Proceedings of GRAPHITE 2003 (the 1st International Conference on Computer Graphics and Interactive Techniques in Australasia and South East Asia)*. pp. 181–187.
12. Reznik, L. and B. Pham, Fuzzy models in evaluation of information uncertainty in engineering and technology applications, in *Proceedings of the 10th IEEE International Conference on Fuzzy Systems*, Melbourne, Australia. 2001. pp. 972–975 vol. 3.
13. Card, S.K. and J. Mackinlay, The structure of the information visualization design space. 1997. IEEE Symposium on Information Visualization, IEEE Press, pp. 92–99, 125.

14. Chi, E., A taxonomy of visualization techniques using the data state reference model, in *IEEE Symposium on Information Visualization*. 2000, IEEE Press. pp. 69–75.
15. Tory, M. and T. Möller, Rethinking visualization: A high-level taxonomy, in *IEEE Symposium on Information Visualization*. 2004, IEEE Press. pp. 151–158.
16. Brown, R. and B. Pham, Visualisation of fuzzy decision support information: A case study, in *IEEE International Conference on Fuzzy Systems*. 2003, St Louis. pp. 601–606.
17. Kitchenham, B., Modeling software bidding risks. *IEEE Transactions on Software Engineering*, 2003. 29(6): pp. 542–554.
18. Ohene-Djan, J., A. Sammon, and R. Shipsey, Colour spectrum's of opinion: An information visualisation interface for representing degrees of emotion in real time, in *Information Visualization*. 2006. pp. 80–88.
19. Wittenbrink, C., A. Pang, and S. Lodha, *Verity Visualization: Visual Mappings*. 1995, Santa Cruz: Baskin Center for Computer Engineering & Information Sciences, University of California.
20. Johnson, C.R. and A.R. Sanderson, *A next step:* Visualizing errors and uncertainty. *Computer Graphics and Applications, IEEE*, 2003. 23(5): pp. 6–10.
21. Hall, L.O. and M.R. Berthold, *Fuzzy Parallel Coordinates*. Fuzzy Information Processing Society, 2000. NAFIPS. 19th International Conference of the North American 2000. pp. 74–78.
22. Pham, B. and R. Brown, Visualisation of fuzzy systems: Requirements, techniques and framework, in *Future Generation Computer Systems*. 2005. Vol. 21, (3) pp. 1199–1212.
23. Nürnberger, A., A. Klose, and R. Kruse, Discussing cluster shapes of fuzzy classifiers, in *18th International Conference of the North American Fuzzy Information Processing Society*. 1999. pp. 546–550.
24. Lodha, S.K., Pang, A., Sheehan, R.E. Wittenbrink, C.M. UFLOW: Visualizing uncertainty in fluid flow, in *Visualization '96. Proceedings*. 1996.
25. Gershon, N.D. Visualization of fuzzy data using generalized animation, in Visualization, *Visualization '92, Proceedings., IEEE Conference on*. 1992, Mitre Corp., McLean, VA, USA: Practical.
26. Goodchild, M.F., D.R. Montella, P. Fohl, and J. Gottsegen. Fuzzy spatial queries in digital spatial data libraries, in *IEEE World Congress on Computational Intelligence Fuzzy Systems Proceedings*. 1998. pp. 205–210.
27. Pham, B. and R. Brown. Analysis of visualisation requirements for fuzzy systems, in *Graphite Conference*. 2003, Melbourne, Australia, pp. 181–187.
28. Brown, R. and B. Pham. Visualisation of fuzzy decision support information: A case study, in *IEEE International Conference on Fuzzy Systems*. 2003, St Louis, USA: IEEE Press.
29. Brown, R., Animated visual vibrations as an uncertainty visualization technique, in *International Conference on Graphics and Interactive Techniques in Australasia and South East Asia*. 2004, ACM. pp. 84–89.
30. Tufte, E., *The Visual Display of Quantitative Information*. 1983, Cheshire, USA: Graphics Press.
31. Keller, P. and M. Keller, *Visual Cues*. 1992, IEEE Press Los Alamitos, USA.
32. Bin Jiang, Jian Liang Wang, Yeng Chai Soh, Robust fault diagnosis for a class of bilinear systems with uncertainty, in *IEEE Conference on Decision and Control*. 1999, IEEE. pp. 4499–4504.
33. Wandell, B., *Foundations of Human Vision*. 1st ed. 1995, Sunderland, USA: Sinauer.
34. Thomas, A., Contouring algorithms for visualisation and shape modelling systems, in *Visualisation and Modelling*, R. Earnshaw, J. Vince, and R. Jones, Editors. 1997, Academic Press: San Diego, USA. pp. 99–175.
35. Gershon, N.D., Proceedings., IEEE Conference on Visualization 1992, Mitre Corp., McLean, VA, USA Visualization of fuzzy data using generalized animation. 1992. pp. 268–273.
36. Kosara, R., S. Miksch, and H. Hauser, Focus + context taken literally, in *IEEE Computer Graphics and Applications*. 2002. pp. 22–29.
37. Berthold, M.R. and R. Holve, Visualizing high dimensional fuzzy rules, in *IEEE Fuzzy Information Processing Society*. 2000. pp. 64–68.
38. Robertson, G.G., J.D. Mackinlay, and S.K. Card, Cone Trees: Animated 3D visualizations of hierarchical information, in *Proceedings of the SIGCHI Conference on Human Factors in*

Computing Systems: Reaching through Technology. 1991, ACM Press: New Orleans, Louisiana, United States.
39. Fujiwara, Y., Visualization of the rule-based program by a 3D flowchart, in *6th International Conference on Fuzzy Theory and Technology (JCIS)*. 1998, NC, USA.
40. Treisman, A. and G. Gelade, A feature-integration theory of attention. *Cognitive Psychology*, 1980. 12: pp. 97–136.
41. Dickerson, J.A., et al. Creating metabolic and regulatory network models using fuzzy cognitive maps, in *IFSA World Congress and 20th NAFIPS International Conference, 2001. Joint 9th*. 2001, Dept.of Electr. Eng, Iowa State Univ., Ames, IA, USA: Practical.
42. Cox, Z., J.A. Dickerson, and D. Cook. Visualizing membership in multiple clusters after fuzzy C-means clustering, in *Visual Data Exploration and Analysis VIII*. 2001, SPIE Bellingham, Washington.
43. Lowe, A., R. Jones, and M. Harrison, The graphical presentation of decision support information in an intelligent anaesthesia monitor, *in Artificial Intelligence in Medicine*. 2001. 22: pp. 173–191.
44. Wittenbrink, C., A. Pang, and S. Lodha, Glyphs for visualizing uncertainty in vector fields, in *IEEE Transactions on Visualization and Computer Graphics*. 1996. Vol. 2, Issue 3 pp. 266–279.
45. Streit, A., B. Pham, and R. Brown, A spreadsheet approach to facilitate visualization of uncertainty in information, in *IEEE Transactions on Visualization and Computer Graphics*. 2007. p. Available as preprint Vol 14 Issue 1, pp. 61–72.
46. Halpern, J.Y., *Reasoning about Uncertainty*. 2003, The MIT Press Cambridge, USA.
47. Chi, E.H.-h., et al., A spreadsheet approach to information visualization, in *UIST '97: Proceedings of the 10th Annual ACM Symposium on User Interface Software and Technology*. 1997, ACM Press: New York, NY, USA. pp. 79–80.
48. Chi, E.H.-h., et al., Principles for information visualization spreadsheets, in *IEEE Computer Graphics and Applications*. 1998, IEEE Computer Society. pp. 30–38 Vol 18 Issue 4.
49. Khosrowshahi, F. and E. Banissi, Visualisation of the degradation of building flooring systems, in *Fifth International Conference on Information Visualisation*. 2001. pp. 507–514.
50. Sakuragi, F., et al., System simulator for structural description and error analysis of multimodal 3D data integration systems, in *Electronics and Communications in Japan (Part II: Electronics)*. 2007. Vol 90, Issue 8 pp. 45–59.
51. Bastin, L., J. Wood, and P.F. Fisher, Visualising and tracking uncertainty in thematic classifications of satellite imagery, in *IEEE International Geoscience and Remote Sensing Symposium, 1999. IGARSS '99 Proceedings*. 1999. pp. 2501–2503.
52. Dungan, J.L., D. Kao, and A. Pang, The uncertainty visualization problem in remote sensing analysis, *in IGARS'02 Proceedings* 2002. pp. 729–731 vol. 2.
53. Kardos, J., G. Benwell, and A. Moore, The visualisation of uncertainty for spatially referenced census data using hierarchical tessellations, in *Transactions in GIS*. 2005. Vol 9, Issue 1 pp. 19–34.
54. Hope, S., *Decision Making Under Spatial Uncertainty*. Masters Research thesis 2005, Geomatics, University of Melbourne.
55. MacEachren, A.M., et al., Visualizing geospatial information uncertainty: What we know and what we need to know, in *Cartography and Geographic Information Science*. 2005. Vol 32 pp. 139–160.
56. Biffl, S., et al., An empirical investigation on the visualization of temporal uncertainties in software engineering project planning, in *International Symposium on Empirical Software Engineering*. 2005. pp. 10.
57. Zenebe, A. and A.F. Norcio, Visualization of item features, customer preference and associated uncertainty using fuzzy sets, in *Annual Meeting of the North American Fuzzy Information Processing Society NAFIPS '07*. 2007. pp. 7–12.
58. Martin, A.R. and M.O. Ward, High dimensional brushing for interactive exploration of multivariate data, in *IEEE Conference on Visualization*. 1995. pp. 271.
59. Chen, H., Compound brushing [dynamic data visualization, in *IEEE Symposium on Information Visualization*. 2003. pp. 181.

Chapter 3
Parallel Coordinates: Interactive Visualization for High Dimensions

Alfred Inselberg

Abstract This story is about multidimensional visualization with **Parallel Coordinates** (abbr. ||-coords) which transform the search for relations in multivariate datasets into a 2-dimensional pattern recognition problem. The discovery process is illustrated by finding:

- ground features from remote sensing satellite data, and
- useful rules for gold, foreign currencies and stockmarket trading from a financial dataset.

A complex dataset with two categories is classified using a geometric classification algorithm based on ||-coords. The minimal set of variables required to state the rule is found and ordered by their predictive value. A visual model of a real country's economy is constructed showing how multivariate relations can be modeled by means of hypersurfaces. Interior points corresponding to feasible economic policies are constructed interactively finding that two sectors unknowingly compete for the same group of workers. An overview of modern ||-coords provides foundational understanding. The representation of an M-dimensional hypersurface is obtained from its $(M-1)$ subsets which are constructed recursively from its points. There are examples of surfaces where *convexity* can be seen in *any dimension* as well as non-orientability(as in the Möbius strip), and features like folds, crevices, bumps which are hidden or distorted in other types of displays. This is a prelude of what is on the way: **recursive multidimensional interactivity** for uncovering the secrets in massive datasets.

Keywords Parallel coordinates, Multidimensional visualization, Multidimensional geometry, Data mining, High dimensional datasets, Hypersurfaces, Nonlinear models.

3.1 Introduction

Visualization flourished in Geometry. Legend has it that Archimedes was absorbed in a diagram when he was killed by a Roman soldier. "Do not disturb my circles" he pleaded as he was being struck by the sword; the first recorded death in defense

E. Zudilova-Seinstra et al. (eds.) *Trends in Interactive Visualization*,
doi:10.1007/978-1-84800-269-2_3 © Springer-Verlag London Limited 2009

of visualization. Visual interaction with diagrams is interwoven with the testing of conjectures and construction of proofs. Our tremendous pattern recognition enables us to extract insight from images. This essence of visualization is abstracted and adapted in the more general problem-solving process to the extent that we form a mental image of a problem we are trying to solve and at times we say see when we mean understand.

My interest in visualization was sparked and nourished while learning geometry. Later, in the study of multi-dimensional geometry I became frustrated by the absence of visualization. How can we be doing Geometry without the fun and benefit of pictures? Is there a generic (i.e., widely applicable) way to make accurate pictures of multidimensional problems like Descartes epochmaking coordinate system for 2 and 3-D? What is sacred about orthogonal axes which use up the plane very fast? After all, in Geometry parallelism rather than orthogonality is the fundamental concept and they are not equivalent for orthogonality requires a prior concept of "angle." I played with the idea of a multidimensional coordinate system based on Parallel Coordinates. In the Euclidean plane $\mathbb{R}^2$ with *xy*-Cartesian coordinates, N copies of the real line R labeled $\overline{X}_1, \overline{X}_2, \ldots \overline{X}_N$ are placed equidistant and perpendicular to the x-axis as shown in Fig. 3.1. They are the axes of the Parallel Coordinates system, for the Euclidean N-dimensional space $\mathbb{R}^N$, all having the same positive orientation as the y-axis. A point C with coordinates $(c_1, c_2, \ldots, c_N)$ is represented by the complete polygonal line $\overline{C}$ (i.e., the lines containing the segments between the axes) whose N vertices are at the c_i value on the $\overline{X}_i$ -axis for $i = 1, \ldots, N$. In this way, a 1-1 correspondence between points in $\mathbb{R}^N$ and planar polygonal lines with vertices

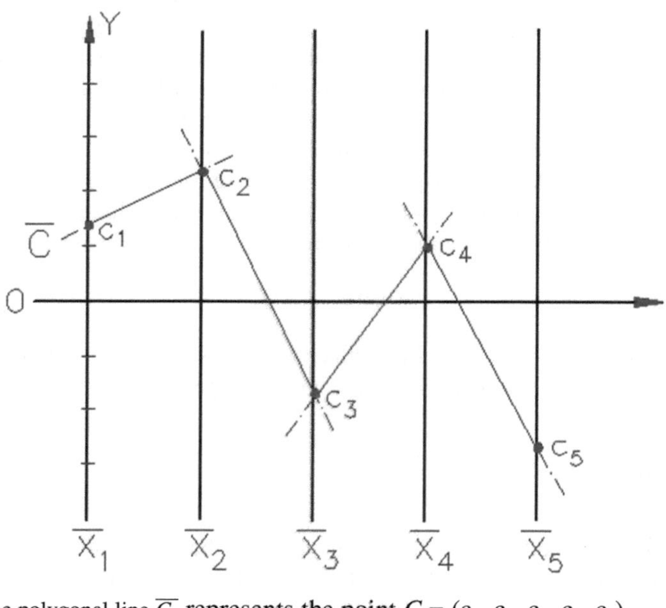

Fig. 3.1 The polygonal line $\overline{C}$ represents the point $C = (c_1, c_2, c_3, c_4, c_5)$

on the parallel axes is established. In principle, a large number of axes can be placed and be seen parallel to each other. The representation of points is deceptively simple and much development with additional ideas is needed to enable the visualization of multivariate relations or equivalently multidimensional objects.

Encouraged in 1959 by Professors S.S. Cairns and D. Bourgin, topologists at the University of Illinois where I was studying, I derived some of the basic properties like the *point* ↔ *line* duality. It was not until 1977 when, while teaching Linear Algebra I was challenged to "show" spaces of dimension higher than 3. I recalled Parallel Coordinates (abbreviated ||-coords). More questions about Parallel Coordinates were raised and the systematic development began. The comprehensive report [18] documented the initial results and followed by [21] became the foundations of the ||-coords methodology.

The collaboration with my colleagues the late B. Dimsdale(a long-time associate of John von Neuman), and A. Hurwitz lead to 5 USA patents (including Collision Avoidance Algorithms for Air-Traffic Control), J. Rivero [32], together with the students T. Chomut [5] (implemented the first ||-coords EDA (exploratory data analysis) software) and M. Boz [27] was fruitful as indicated by the partial list [19, 20, 22, 26] (applications to statistics) and [25]. The way was paved for new contributors and users: S. Cohan & Yang [6], H. Hinterberger [33], J. Helly [15], P. Fiorini [10], C. Gennings et al. (a sophisticated statistical application – response surfaces) [12], E. Wegman (promoted the EDA application using the *point* ↔ *line* duality in [21]) [38] and A. Desai & L. Walters [7]. The results of J. Eickemeyer [8], C.K. Hung [16], A. Chatterjee [2] and T. Mastkewich [29] were seminal. Progress continued A. Chatterjee et al. [3], M. Ward et al [37], C. Jones [28] to the most recent work of L. Yang [39] and H. Hauser [14], H. Choi and Heejo Lee [4] increased the versatility of ||-coords. This list is by no means exhaustive. As of this writing, a query for "parallel coordinates" on Google returned more than 70,000 "hits."

3.2 Visual and Automatic Data Mining

The first, and still more widespread, application of parallel coordinates is for exploratory data analysis (EDA). That is, the discovery of data subsets (relations) fulfilling given objectives. A dataset with *M* items has 2^M subsets anyone of which may be the one we really want. Our fantastic pattern-recognition ability and a good data display can penetrate this combinatorial explosion by recognizing patterns and the multivariate relations they represent. Extracting insight from images is the crux of data visualization.

For the visualization of multivariate problems numerous mappings encoding multidimensional information visually into 2-D or 3-D (see [11] and [34–36]) have been invented to augment our perception, which is limited by our 3-dimensional habitation. Wonderful successes like Minard's "Napoleon's March to Moscow," Snow's "dot map" and others are *ad hoc* (i.e. one-of-a-kind) and exceptional. Succinct multivariate relations are rarely apparent from **static** displays; **interactivity** is essential. Searching a dataset with M items for interesting, depending on the objectives, properties is inherently hard. The *visual cues*, our eyes can pick from a good data display, navigate the knowledge discovery process. Clearly, if the transformation: *data*→ *picture* clobbers information a great deal is lost right at the start. Good displays of datasets with N variables should preserve information and work for any number of variables N. Also they need to be computationally and space efficient. These considerations limit the use of the scatterplot matrix (abbr. SM) and other methods. The crucial value and role of visualization is not seeing "zillions of objects" but rather recognizing relations among them.

3.2.1 Exploratory Data Analysis with ||-coords

Parallel coordinates transform multivariate relations into 2-D patterns suitable for exploration and analysis. The exploration[1] paradigm is that of a *detective*, starting from the data, searching for clues leading to conjectures, testing, backtracking until *voila*... the "culprit" is discovered. The task is especially intricate when there are many variables (i.e., dimensions).

During the ensuing interaction think, dear reader, how similar queries can be done using other exploration methodologies including the ubiquitous spread-sheets. More important, what visual clues are available that would **prompt** the use of such queries. A few basics are recalled. In ||-coords due to the *point* ↔ *line* and other dualities, some but not all actions are best performed in the dual. The queries, which are the "cutting tools," operate on the display i.e. the *dual*. Their design should exploit the methodology's strengths and avoid its weaknesses; rather than mimic the action of queries operating on standard "non-dual" displays. As a surgeon's many specialized cutting tools, one of our early software versions had lots of specialized queries. Not only was it hard to classify and remember them but they still could not handle all situations encountered. After experimentation, I opted for a few (3) intuitive queries called **atomic** which can be combined via *boolean* operations to form complex intricate cuts. Even for relatively small datasets the ||-coords display can look uninformative and intimidating. Lack of understanding the basic underlying geometry and poor choice of queries limits the use of ||-coords to unrealistically small datasets. Summarizing, the requirements for successful exploratory data analysis are:

- an informative display without loss of information of the data,
- good choice of queries, and
- skillful interaction with the display.

Aside from starting the exploration without biases it is essential to understand the objectives. The task in the first example is the detection and location of various

[1] The venerable name "Exploratory Data Analysis" EDA is used interchangeably with the currently more fashionable "Visual Data Mining.".

ground features (i.e., built-up areas, vegetation, water etc.) on the map. There is a prominent lake, on the lower-left corner with an unusual shape like an upward pointing "finger.".

3.2.2 *An Easy Case Study: Satellite Data*

The first advice is not to let the picture intimidate you as can easily happen by taking an uninformed look at Fig. 3.4 (left) showing the dataset to be explored. It consists of over 9,000 measurements with 9 variables, the first two (X, Y) specify the location on the map in Fig. 3.2 (left), a portion of Slovenia, where 7 types of ground emissions are measured by satellite. The ground location, (X, Y), of one data item is shown in Fig. 3.2 (right), which corresponds to the map's region and remains open during the exploration. The query, shown in Fig. 3.3 (left), used to select the data item is called *Pinch*. It is activated by the button **P** on the tool bar. By means of this query, a bunch of polygonal lines (i.e., data items) can be chosen by being "pinched" *in-between* the axes. The cursor's movement changes the position of the s*elected* arrow-head which is the larger of the two shown. In due course various parts of the GUI are illustrated (*Parallax*[2]).

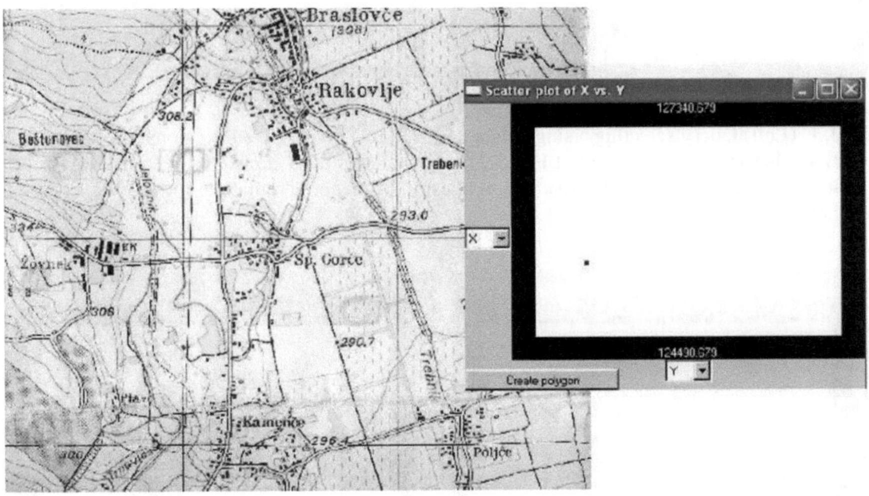

Fig. 3.2 Seven types of ground emissions were measured on this region of Slovenia. Measurements made by the Landsat Thematic Mapper. Thanks and acknowledgement to Dr. Ana Tretjak and Dr. Niko Schlamberger, Statistics Office of Slovenia, for providing the data. (Right) The display is the map's rectangular region. The dot marks the position where the 7-tuple shown in the next figure was measured

[2] MDG"s Ltd proprietary software — All Rights Reserved, is used by permission.

Follow up on anything that catches the eyes, gaps, regularities, holes, twists, peaks & valleys, density contrasts like the one at the lower values of B3 through B7. Using the *Interval* query, activated by the **I** button, starting at the minimum we grab the low range of B4 (between the arrowheads) stopping at the dense part as shown in Fig. 3.3 (right). The result, on the left of Fig. 3.4, is amazing. Voila we found the water[3] with the lake is clearly visible together with two other regions which in the map turn up to be small streams. Our scrutiny having been rewarded we recall the adage that a good thing may be worth repeating. Examining for density variations now *within the selected lower interval* of B4 we notice another. The lowest part is much denser. Experimenting a bit, appreciating the importance of interactivity, we select the sparse portion, Fig. 3.5, which defines the water's edge (right) 4 and in fact more. By dropping the lower arrow we see the lake filling up starting from the edge i.e. shallow water first. So the lower values of B4 reveal the water and the lowest "measure" the water's depth; not bad for few minutes of playing around.

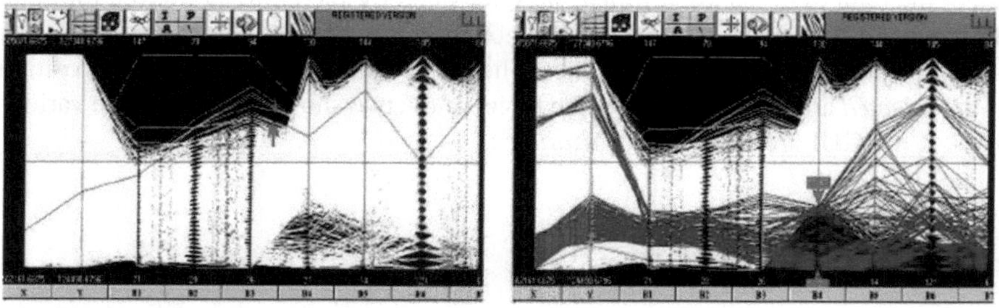

Fig. 3.3 (Left) Query selecting a single data item. (Right) Finding water regions. (Left)The X, Y (position, also shown on the right of Fig. 3.2), and values of the 7-tuple (B1, B2, B3, B4, B5, B6, B7) at that point. (Right)The contrast due to density differences around the lower values of B4 is the visual cue prompting this query

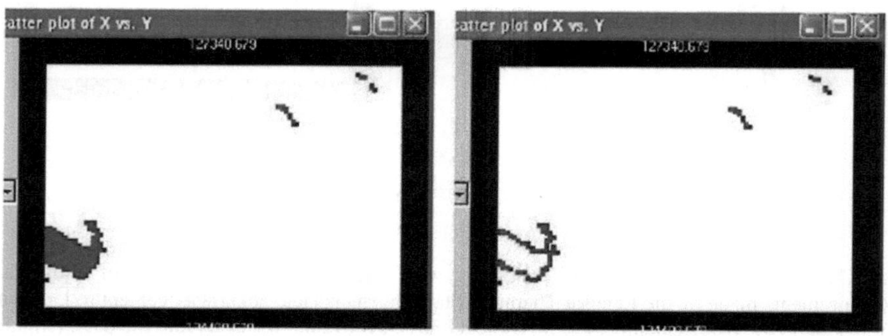

Fig 3.4 (Left) The lake – result of query shown in Fig. 3.4 (Right). On the right is just the lake's edge. It is the result of query shown in Fig. 3.5

[3] Suggesting that the Landsat Thematic mapper band 4 filters out water though unknown to me.

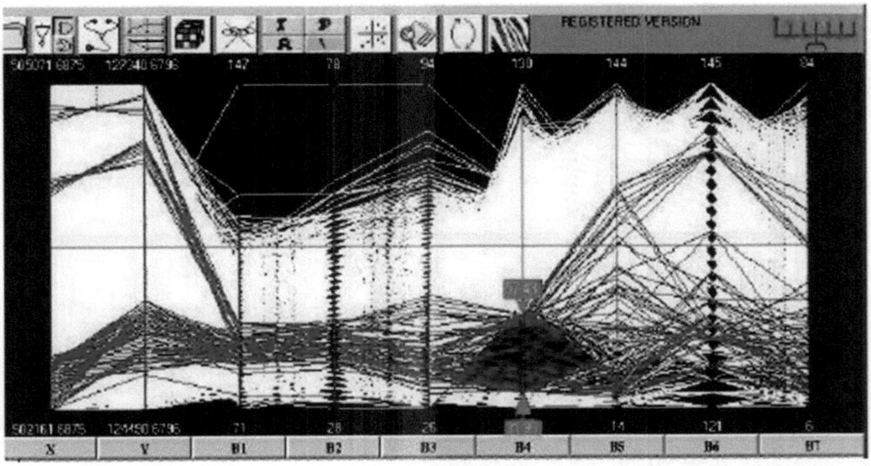

Fig. 3.5 Query finding the water's edge

But all this pertains to a single variable when we are supposed to be demonstrating multivariate exploration. This is a valid point but we did pick B4 among several variables. Further, this is a nice "warm-up" for the subsequent more involved examples enabling us to show two of the queries. The astute observer must have already noticed the regularity, the vertical bands, between the B1, B2 and B3 axes. This is where the *angle* query, activated by the **A** button, comes into play. As the name implies it selects groups of lines within a user-specified angle range. A data subset is selected between the B2, B3 axes as shown, with enlarged inter-axes distance better showing the vertical bands, in Fig. 3.6 (left) to select a data subset which corresponds on the map to regions with high vegetation. Clicking the **A** button and placing the cursor on the middle of one axis opens an angle, with vertex on the mid-range of the previous(left) axis, whose range is controlled by the arrow movements on the right axis. Actually this "rule" (i.e., relation among some parameters) for finding vegetation can be refined by twicking a couple of more parameters. This raises the topic of rule finding in general, *Classification*, which is taken up in Sect. 3.3.

The angle and pinch queries are motivated by the l line $\rightarrow$ point $\bar{l}$ duality

$$\ell : x_2 = mx_1 + b \leftrightarrow \bar{\ell} = \left(\frac{d}{1-m}, \frac{b}{1-m} \right) \tag{3.1}$$

in ||-coords illustrated in Fig. 3.7 where the inter-axes distance is d. As seen from its x-coordinate, the point $\bar{l}$ lies between the parallel axes when the line's slope $m < 0$, to the right of the $\bar{X}_2$ axis for $0 < m < 1$ and left of $\bar{X}_1$ for $m > 1$. Lines with $m = 1$ are mapped to the *direction* with slope *b*/*d* in the *xy*-plane; with d the inter-axes distance and b the constant (intercept) in the equation of *l*. This points out that dualities properly reside in the *Projective*, the *directions* being the *ideal points*, rather than the Euclidean plane. For sets of points having a "general" direction with negative slope,

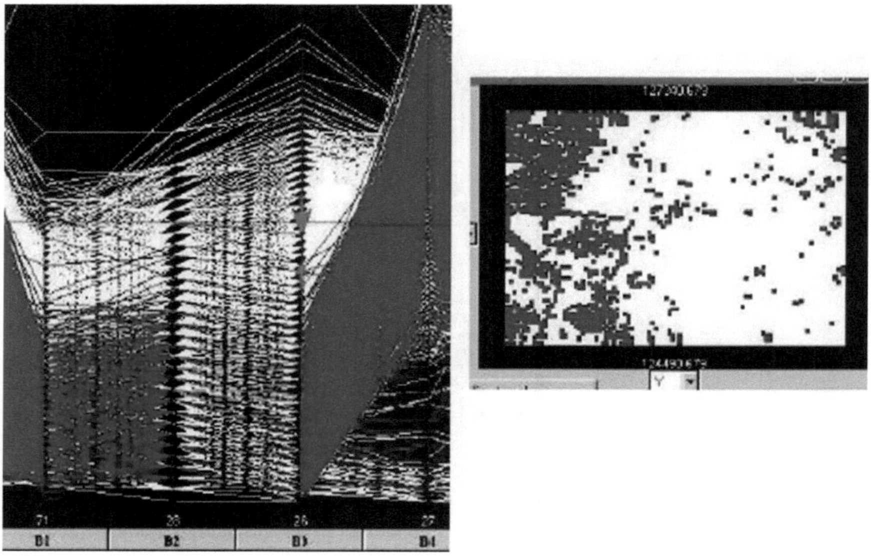

Fig. 3.6 Finding regions with vegetation

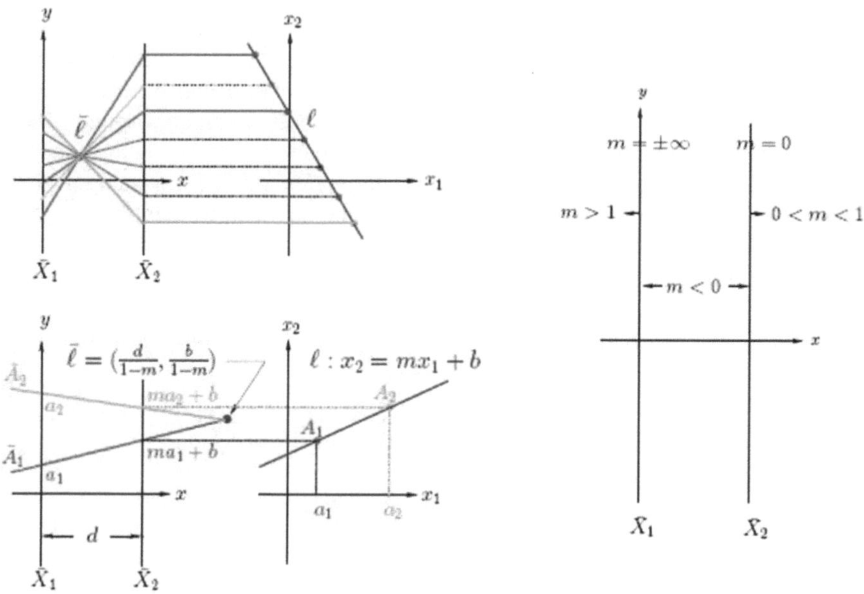

Fig. 3.7 Parallel coordinates induce a point $\bar{l} \leftrightarrow l$ line duality (left). (Right) The horizontal position of the point $\bar{l}$ representing the line l is determined only by the line's slope m. The vertical line l: $x_1 = a_1$ is represented by the point $\bar{l}$ at the value a1 on the $\bar{X}_1$ axis

i.e. are "negatively correlated," the lines representing them in || cross each other in between the axes and they can be *selected with the pinch query*. For positively correlated sets of points their corresponding lines cross outside the axes and can be *selected with the angle query*. All this exemplifies the need to understand some of the basic geometry so as to work effectively with the queries and of course, at first, design them well. The three atomic queries having been introduced there remains to learn how they can be combined to construct complex queries.

Prior to that, Fig. 3.6 (left) begs the question: "what if the B2 and B3 axes were not adjacent"? Then the pattern and hence their pairwise relation would be missed. Clearly the axes-permutation used for the exploration is important. In particular what is the minimum number of permutations among N-axes containing the adjacencies for all pairs of axes? It turns out [38]: M permutations are needed for even $N = 2M$ and $M + 1$ for odd $N = 2M + 1$. It is fun to see why. Label the N vertices of a graph with the index of the variables X_i; i = 1,…,N as shown in Fig. 3.8 for $N = 6$. An edge joining vertex i with j signifies that the axes indexed by *i, j* are adjacent. The graph on the left is a *Hamilton path* for it contains all the vertices. Such paths have been studied starting with Euler in the 18th century with modern applications to the "travelling salesman" problem and elsewhere ([13] pp. 66, [1] pp. 12). The graph corresponds to the axes index permutation 126354. On the right, the union with the additional two Hamiltonian paths, starting at vertices 2 and 3, forms the complete graph which contains all possible edges. Hence the 3 permutations 126354, 231465, 342516 contain all possible adjacent pairs; just try it. The remaining permutations are obtained from the first by successively adding 1 mod 6 to each digit and this works for general *N*.

Returning to EDA, the icon with the *Rubik's Cube on Parallax*'s toolbar activates a *permutation editor* which automatically generates the Hamiltonian permutations (abbr. HP). After scrutinizing the dataset display the recommended next step is to

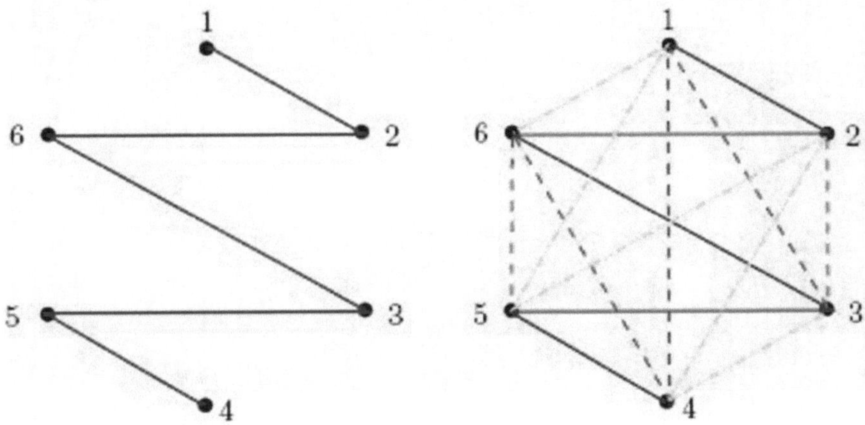

Fig. 3.8 (Left) First Hamiltonian path on vertices **1,…,6**. It corresponds to the (axes) index permutation **126354**. (Right) The complete graph as the union of the 3 distinct Hamiltonian paths starting successively at the vertices 1, 2, 3

run through the *O*(*N*/2) HP. This is how all nice adjacencies such as the one in Fig. 3.6 are discovered. Then using the editor, patch your own custom-made permutation containing all the parts you like in the *HP*. With this preprocessing cost the user sets her own best permutation to work with. Of course, there is nothing to prevent one from including axes several times in different positions and experimenting with different permutations in the course of the exploration.

3.2.3 Compound Queries: Financial Data

To be explored next is the financial dataset shown in Fig. 3.9, the goal being to discover relations useful for investments and trading. The data for the years 1986 (second tick on the 3rd axes) and 1992 are selected and compared. In 1986 the **Yen** had the greater volatility among the 3 currencies, interests varied in the mid-range, gold had a price gap while **SP**500 was uniformly low. By comparison in 1992, the Yen was stable while the Sterling was very volatile (possibly due to Soros' speculation that year), interests and gold price were low and the **SP**500 was uniformly high. Two Interval queries are combined with the *OR* boolean operator (i.e. Union) to obtain this picture.

We continue "looking for the gold" by checking out patterns that caught our attention. The data for 1986 is isolated in Fig. 3.10 and the lower range in the gold price gap is selected. Gold prices were low until the 2nd week in August when they jumped and stayed higher. The exploration was carried out in the presence of four

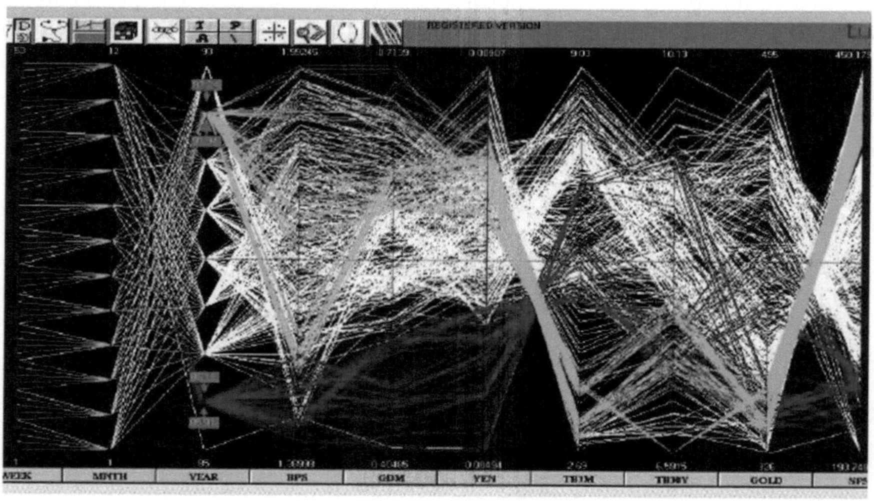

Fig. 3.9 Financial data. Quotes by Week-on Mondays, Month, Year – the first 3 axes fix the date; Sterling, **D**mark, **Yen** rates per $ 4th, 5th, 6th axes; **3M**TB, **30Y**TB interest rates in %,7th, 8th axes; Gold in $/ounce, 9th, **SP**500 index values on 10th axes (*See Color Plates*)

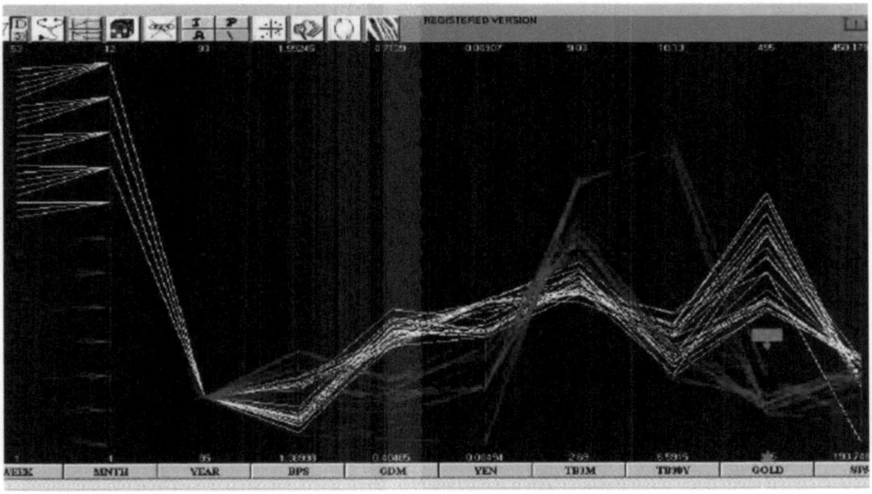

Fig. 3.10 Gold prices in 1986. Gold prices jumped in the 2nd week of August. Note the correlation between the low Dmark, high 3MTB rates and low Gold price range

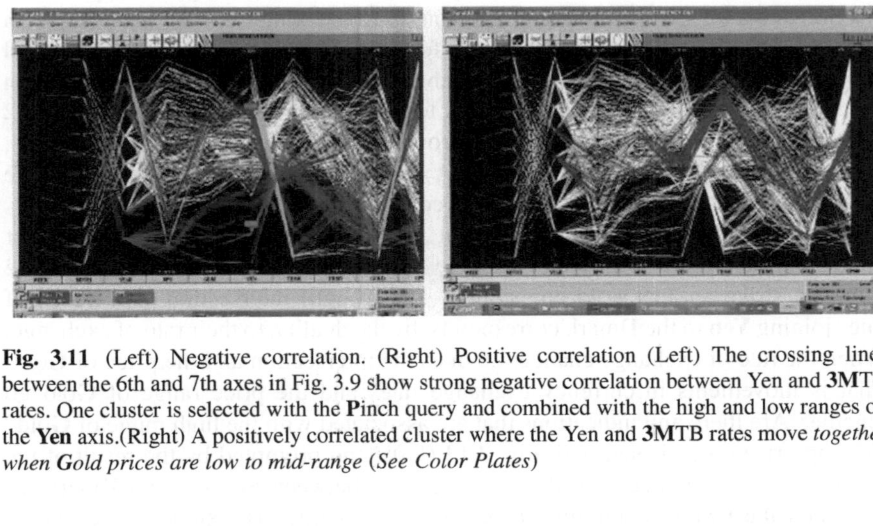

Fig. 3.11 (Left) Negative correlation. (Right) Positive correlation (Left) The crossing lines between the 6th and 7th axes in Fig. 3.9 show strong negative correlation between Yen and **3M**TB rates. One cluster is selected with the **P**inch query and combined with the high and low ranges on the **Yen** axis.(Right) A positively correlated cluster where the Yen and **3M**TB rates move *together when Gold prices are low to mid-range* (*See Color Plates*)

financial experts who carefully recorded the relation between low **Demark**, high **3M**TB rates and low **G**old prices. By the way, low Yen rate of exchange means the Yen has high value relative to the US $.

There are two bunches of crossing lines between 6th and 7th axes in Fig. 3.9 which together comprise more than 80% of the dataset. This and recalling the previous discussion on the line point mapping in Fig. 3.7 points out the strong negative correlation between **Yen** and **3M**TB rates. The smaller cluster in Fig. 3.11 (left) is selected. Moving from the top range of any of the two axes, with the **I** query, and

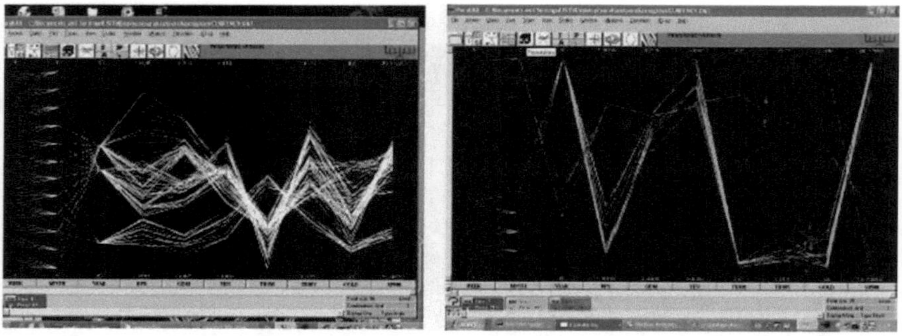

Fig. 3.12 (Left) Inverting the 3MTB axis. (Right) Variations in exchange rates. Now the lines between the **Y**en-**3M**TB and **3M**TB-**30M**TB axes in Fig. 3.11 (right) cross. Variations in the rate of exchange of the currencies correlate with movements in the price of **G**old

lowering the range causes the other variable's range to rise and is a nice way to show negative correlation interactively.

For the contrarians among us, we check also for positive correlation Fig. 3.11 (right). We find that it exists when **G**old prices are low to mid-range as happened for a period in the 90's. This is a free investment tip for bucking the main trend shown in Fig. 3.11 (left). It is also a nice opportunity for showing the *inversion* feature activated by the icon with 2 cyclical arrows. A variable is selected and the min/max values on that axes are inverted. Diverging lines (as for + correlation) now intersect Fig. 3.12 (left) making it easier visually to spot the crossing and hence the correlation. Actually, the recommendation is to work with the **A** query experimenting with various angle ranges using the inversion to check out or confirm special clusters.

When stuck don't just stand there but vary one of the variables watching for interesting variations in the other variables. Doing this on the **Yen** axis, Fig. 3.12 (left) we strike another gold connection. The (rough) intersection of a bunch of lines joining **Yen** to the **D**mark corresponds, by the duality, to their rate of exchange. When the rate of exchange changes so does the intersection and the price of **G**old! That is movements in currency exchange rates and the price range of **G**old go together. Are there any indications that are associated with the high range of **G**old? The top price range is selected, Fig. 3.13 (left), and prompted by the result of the previous query we check out the exchange rate between Sterling and **D**mark (or **Yen**) and the result is stunning: a perfect straight line. The slope is the rate of exchange which is constant when **G**old tops out. The relation between Sterling and Dmark is checked for different price ranges of **G**old, Fig. 3.13 (right), and the only regularity found is the one straight-line above. Aside from the trading guideline it establishes, it suggests "behind-the-scenes manipulation of the Gold market"… we could have said that but we won't. We perish this thought and proceed with the boolean complement, Fig. 3.14 (left) of an **I** (or any other) query. Not finding anything we select a narrow but dense range on the **Yen**, Fig. 3.14 (right) and notice an interesting relation between **D**mark, interest rates and **G**old.

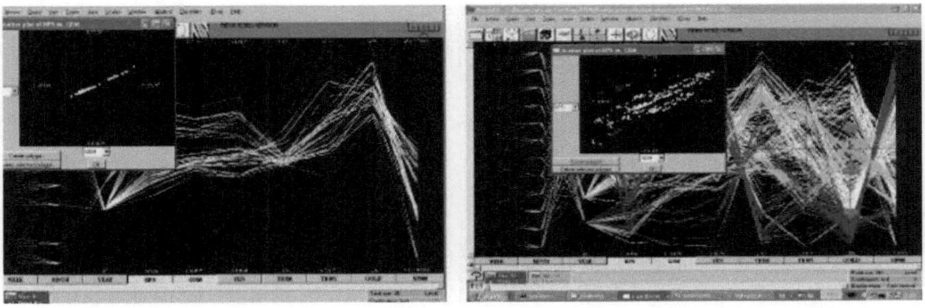

Fig. 3.13 (Left) High **G**old. (Right) Two price ranges of **G**old. (Left) Note the perfect straight line in the **S**terling vs. **D**mark plot. The slope is the rate of exchange between them and which remains constant when **G**old prices peak. (Right) The associated **S**terling versus **D**mark plots show no regularity

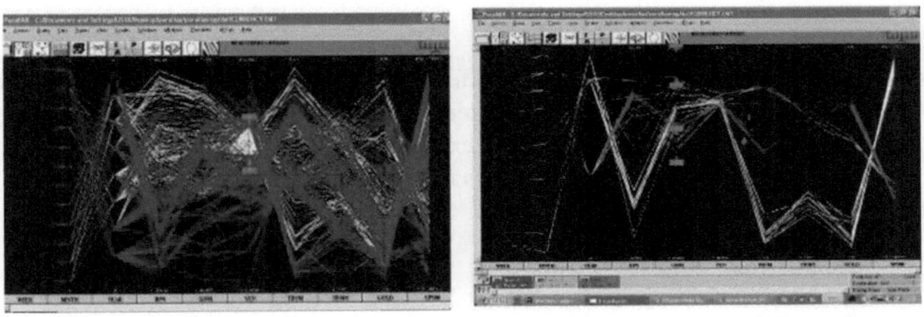

Fig. 3.14 (Left) The complement of an **I** query. (Right) **Y**en stable. (Right) For the **Y**en trading in a narrow range, high **D**mark goes with low **3M**TB rates, low **D**mark goes with high **3M**TB rates, while mid **3M**TB rates go with high **G**old

There is an exploratory step akin to "multidimensional contouring" which we fondly call **Zebra** activated by the last icon button on the right with the appropriate skin-color. A variable axis is selected, the **SP**500 axis in Fig. 3.15 (left), and divided into a number (user specified) intervals (here it is 4) and colored differently. This shows the connections (influence) of the intervals with the remaining variables which here is richly structured especially for the highest range. So what does it take for the **SP**500 to rise? This is a good question and helps introduce Parallax's classifier. The result, shown in Fig. 3.15 (right) confirms the investment community's experience that low **3M**TB and Gold correlate with high **SP**500. A comparison with the results obtained on this dataset with other visualization tools would be instructive though unfortunately not available. Still let us consider such an analysis done by the scatterplot matrix. There are 10 variables (axes) which requires 45 pairwise scatterplots. Let us assume that each is no larger than 5 × 5 cm square and a large screen monitor is available. Varying 1, 2 or more variables in tandem and observing the effects ***simultaneously*** over **all** the variables in the 45 squares may be possible

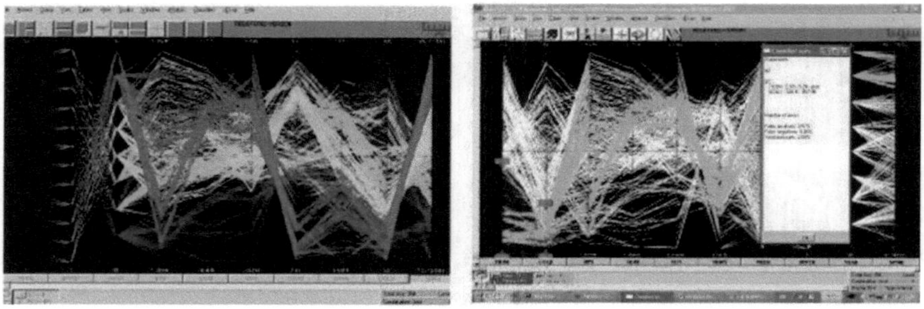

Fig. 3.15 (Left) The *zebra* query. (Right) The rule for high **SP**500. (Left) It partitions and colors the segments of values differently. A variable, here the **SP**500 axis, is divided it into equal (here 4) intervals. This quickly reveals interrelationships. Note especially those for the highest **SP**500 range. (Right) Both **3M**TB (the "short-bond" as it is called) and Gold are low and in this order of importance

but quite challenging. By contrast, the effects of varying **D**mark, *conditionally* for stable **Yen**, are easily seen on the two interest rates, **G**old as well as the remaining variables in one Fig. 3.14 (right). This example illustrates the difficulties due to high representational complexity which is $O(N^2)$ for the scatterplot matrix but $O(N)$ for ||-coords.

3.3 Classification

Though it is fun to undertake this kind of exploration, the level of skill and patience required tends to discourage some users. It is not surprising then that the most persistent requests and admonitions have been for tools which, at least partially, automate the knowledge discovery process [24]. Classification is a basic task in data analysis and pattern recognition and an algorithm accomplishing it is called a **Classifier** [9, 30, 31]. The input is a dataset P and a designated subset S. The output is a characterization, a set of conditions or rules, to distinguish elements of S from all other members of P the "global" dataset. The output may also be that there is insufficient information to provide the desired distinction.

With parallel coordinates a dataset P with N variables is transformed into a set of points in N-dimensional space. In this setting, the designated subset S can be described by means of a hypersurface which encloses just the points of S. In practical situations the strict enclosure requirement is dropped and some points of S may be omitted ("false negatives"), and some points of $P - S$ are allowed ("false positives") in the hypersurface. The description of such a hypersurface is equivalent to the rule for identifying, within some acceptable error, the elements of S. Casting the problem in a geometrical setting leads us to visualize how it may work. This entails:

1. use of an efficient "wrapping" (a convex-hull approximation) algorithm to enclose the points of S in a hypersurface S_1 containing S and in general also some points of $P - S$; so $S \subset S_1$,
2. the points in $(P - S) \cap S_1$ are isolated and the wrapping algorithm is applied to enclose them, usually also enclosing some points of S_1, producing a new hypersurface S_2 with $S \supset (S_1 - S_2)$,
3. the points in S not included in $S_1 - S_2$ are next marked for input to the wrapping algorithm, a new hypersurface $S3$ is produced containing these points as well as some other points in $P - (S_1 - S_2)$ resulting in $S \subset (S_1 - S_2) \cup S_3$,
4. the process is repeated alternatively producing upper and lower containment bounds for S; termination occurs when an error criterion (which can be user specified) is satisfied or when convergence is not achieved. After termination is obtained two error measures are available to estimate the rule's precision:

- *Train & Test.* A portion of the dataset (usually 2/3) selected at random is used to derive the classification rule, which is then tested on the remaining 1/3 of the data.
- *Cross-Correlation.*

It can and does happen that the process does not converge when P does not contain sufficient information to characterize S. It may also happen that S is so "porous" (i.e., sponge-like) that an inordinate number of iterations are required. On convergence, say at step $2n$, the description of S is provided as:

$$S \approx (S_1 - S_2) \cup (S_3 - S_4) \cup \ldots \cup (S_{2n-1} - S_{2n}) \tag{3.2}$$

this being the terminating expression resulting from the algorithm which we call **Nested Cavities** (abbr. **NC**).

The user can select a subset of the available variables and restrict the rule generation to these variables. In certain applications, as in process control, not all variables can be controlled and hence it is useful to have a rule involving only the accessible (i.e., controllable) variables. An important additional benefit, is that the minimal set of variables needed to state the rule is found and ordered according to their predictive value. These variables may be considered as the best *features* to identify the selected subset. The algorithm is display independent there being no inherent limitation as to the size and number of variables in the dataset. Summarizing for **NC**,

- an approximate convex-hull boundary for each cavity is obtained,
- utilizing properties of the representation of multidimensional objects in ||-coords, a very low polynomial worst case complexity of $O(N^2 |P|^2)$ in the number of variables N and dataset size $|P|$ is obtained; it is worth contrasting this with the often unknown, or unstated, or very high (even exponential) complexity of other classifiers,
- an intriguing prospect, due to the low complexity, is that the rule can be derived in near real-time making the classifier adaptive to changing conditions,
- the minimal subset of variables needed for classification is found,
- the rule is given explicitly in terms of conditions on these variables, i.e. included and excluded intervals, and provides "a picture" showing the complex distributions

with regions where there are data and "holes" with no data contributing important insights to the domain experts.

A *neural-pulse dataset* has interesting and unusual features. There are two classes of neurons whose outputs to stimuli are to be distinguished. They consist of 32 different pulses measured in a monkey's brain (poor thing!). There are 600 samples with 32 variables (the pulses).[4] Various classification methods were unable to obtain a rule. With **NC** convergence is obtained requiring only 9 of the 32 parameters for the classification rule for class # 1 with a 4% error. The resulting ordering shows a striking separation. In Fig. 3.16 the first pair of variables x_1, x_2 in the original order is plotted on the left. On the right the best pair x_{11}, x_{14}, as chosen by the classifier's selection speaks for itself. By the way, the discovery of this manually would require constructing a scatterplot matrix with 496 pairs, then carefully inspecting and comparing the individual plots. The implementation provides all the next best sections, some of which are shown in Fig. 3.17, to aid the visualization of the rule. The dataset consists of two "pretzel-like" clusters wrapping closely in 9-D one enclosing the other; showing that the classifier can actually "carve" highly

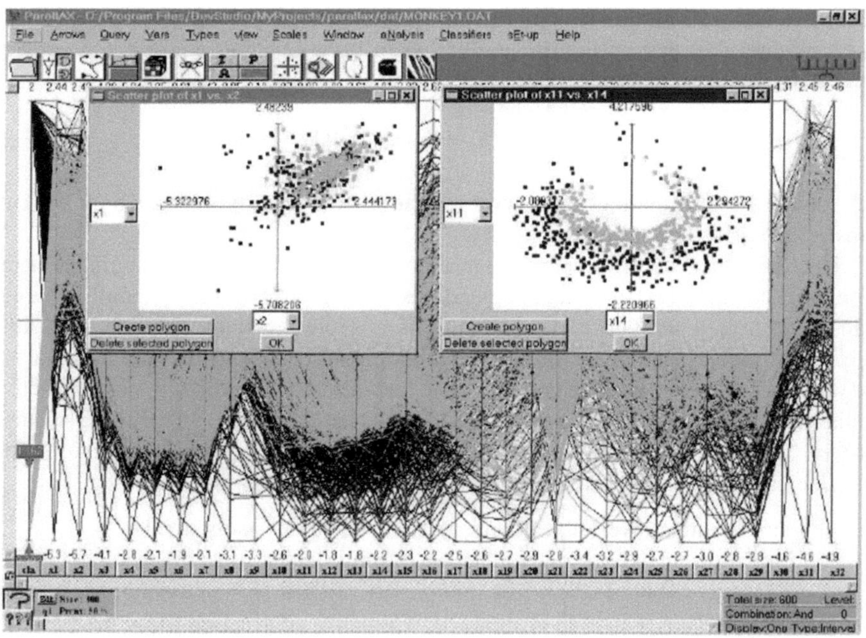

Fig. 3.16 The neural-pulses dataset with 32 parameters and two categories. Dataset is shown in the background. On the left plot are the first two parameters in the original order. The classifier found the 9 parameters needed to state the rule with 4% error and ordered them according to their predictive value. The best two parameters are plotted on the right showing the separation achieved

[4]I am grateful to Prof. R. Coiffman and group at the Math./CS Depts Yale University for this dataset.

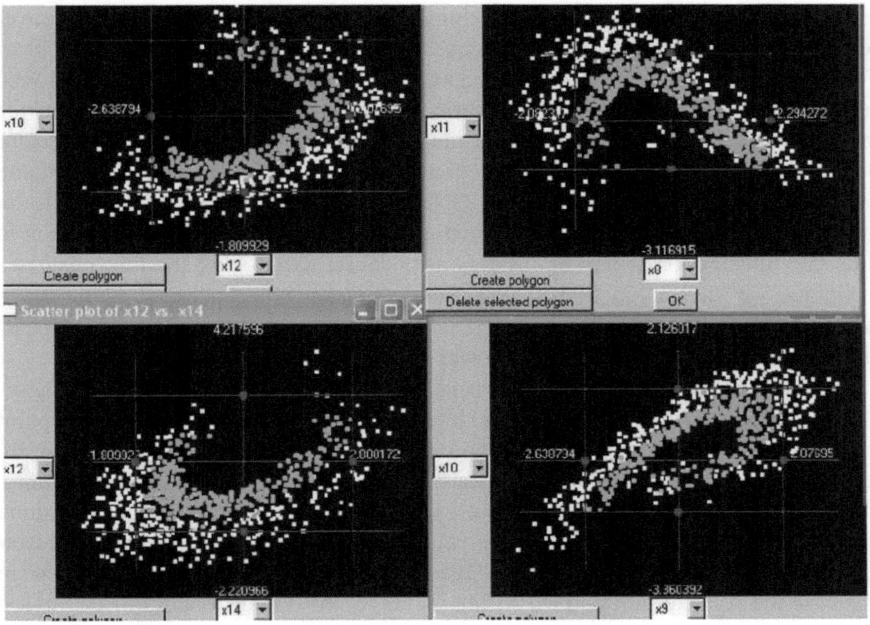

Fig. 3.17 Neural dataset classification. Further cross-sections of the hypersurface corresponding to the classification rule

complex regions. One can understand why separation of clusters by hyperplanes or nearest-neighbor techniques can fail badly for such datasets.

The rules are explicit, "visualizable," optimally ordering the minimal set of variables needed to state the rule without loss of information. There are variations which apply in some situations where the **NC classifier** fails, such as the presence of several large "holes" (see [24]). Further, keeping in mind that the classification rule is the result of several iterations suggests heuristics for dealing with the pesky problem of *over-fitting*. The iterations can be stopped just where the corrections in Eq. (3.2) become very small, i.e. the S_i consist of a small number of points. The number of iterations is user defined and the resulting rule yields an error in the test stage more stable under variations in the number of points of the test set. In addition, the user can exclude variables from being used in the description of the rule; those ordered last are the ones providing the smaller corrections and hence more liable to over-correct.

3.4 Visual & Computational Models

Finally we illustrate the methodology's ability to model multivariate relations in terms of hypersurfaces – just as we model a relation between two variables as a region in a 2-D plane. Then by using an interior point algorithm, as shown in

Fig. 3.24 of the next section, with the model we can do trade-off analyses, discover sensitivities, understand the impact of constraints, and in some cases do optimization. For this purpose we shall use a dataset consisting of the outputs of various economic sectors and other expenditures of a particular (and real) country. It consists of the monetary values over several years for the Agricultural, Fishing, and Mining sector outputs, Manufacturing and Construction industries, together with Government, Miscellaneous spending and resulting GNP; eight variables altogether. We will not take up the full ramifications of constructing a model from data. Rather, we want to illustrate how ||-coords may be used as a modeling tool. Using the Least Squares technique we "fit" a function to this dataset and are not concerned at this stage whether the choice is "good" or not. The function obtained bounds a region in R^8 and is represented by the upper and lower curves shown in Fig. 3.18.

The picture is in effect a simple visual model of the country's economy, incorporating its capabilities, limitations and interrelationships among the sectors. A point interior to the region, satisfies all the constraints simultaneously, and therefore represents (i.e., the 8-tuple of values) a feasible economic policy for that country. Using the interior point algorithm we can construct such points. It can be done interactively by sequentially choosing values of the variables and we see the result of one such choice in Fig. 3.18 (left). Once a value of the first variable is chosen (in this case the Agricultural output) within its range, the dimensionality of the region is reduced by one. In fact, the upper and lower curves between the 2nd and 3rd axes correspond to the resulting 7-dimensional hypersurface and show the available range of the second variable Fishing reduced by the constraint. This can be seen (but not shown here) for the rest of the variables. That is, due to the relationship between the 8 variables, a constraint on one of them impacts all the remaining ones and restricts their range. The display allows us to experiment and actually see the impact of such decisions downstream. By interactively varying the chosen value for the first variable we found, that it not possible to have a policy that favors Agriculture without also favoring Fishing and vice versa.

Proceeding, a very high value from the available range of Fishing is chosen and it corresponds to very low values of the Mining sector. By contrast in Fig. 3.18

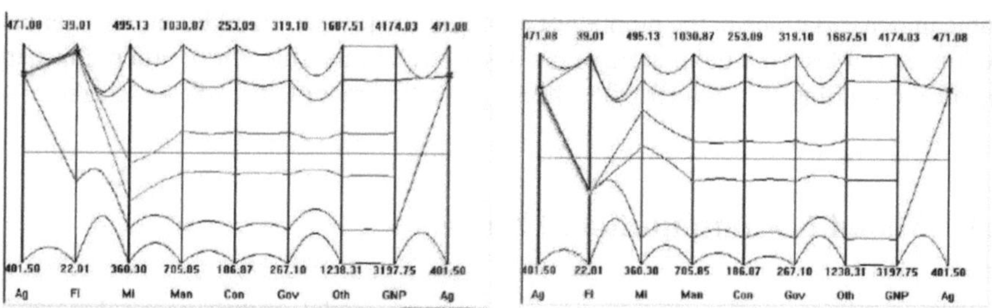

Fig. 3.18 (Left) Model of a country's economy. (Right) Competition for labor between the Fishing & Mining sectors. Choosing high Agricultural and high Fishing output forces low Mining output

(right) we see that a low value in Fishing yields high values for the Mining sector. This inverse correlation was examined and it was found that the country in question has a large number of migrating semi-skilled workers. When the fishing industry is doing well most of them are attracted to it leaving few available to work in the mines and vice versa. The comparison between the two figures shows the competition for the same resource between Mining and Fishing. It is especially instructive to discover this interactively. The construction of the interior point proceeds in the same way. In the next section in the discussion on surfaces this construction is shown for higher dimensional hypersurfaces.

3.5 Parallel Coordinates: The Bare Essentials

The overview covers the foundations of ||-coords up to the recent results and future prospects for innovative interactivity paradigms. For deeper excursions into ||-coords readers are referred to the textbook [23].

3.5.1 Lines

An N-dimensional line *l* can be described by the $N - 1$ linear equations:

$$\ell : \begin{cases} \ell_{1,2} : x_2 = m_2 x_1 + b_2 \\ \ell_{2,3} : x_3 = m_3 x_2 + b_3 \\ \dots \\ \ell_{i-1,i} : x_i = m_i x_{i-1} + b_i \\ \dots \\ \ell_{N-1,N} : x_N = m_N x_{N-1} + b_N, \end{cases} \tag{3.3}$$

each with a pair of adjacently indexed variables. In the $x_{i-1}x_i$-plane the relation labeled $l_{i-1,i}$, $N = 2,\dots,N$ is a line, and by the *line* ↔ *point* duality, Eq. (3.1), it can be represented by the point

$$\bar{\ell}_{1-1,i} = \left(\frac{1}{(1-m_i)} + (i-2), \frac{b_i}{(1-m_i)} \right) \tag{3.4}$$

Here the inter-axes distance is 1 so that $i - 2$ is the distance between the y (or $\bar{X}_1$) and $\bar{X}_{i-1}$ axes. Actually any $N - 1$ independent equations like

$$\ell_{i,j} : x = m_{i,j} x_j + b_{i,j}, \tag{3.5}$$

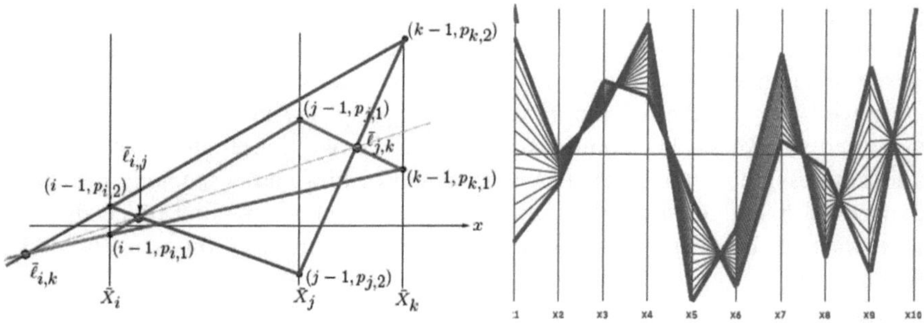

Fig. 3.19 Properties of multidimensional lines. (Left) The 3 points $\bar{l}_{i,j}$, $\bar{l}_{j,k}$, $\bar{l}_{i,k}$ are collinear for $i \neq j \neq k$. (Right) A line interval in 10-D

can equivalently specify the line l, for Eq. (3.5) is the projection of l on the $x_i x_j$ 2-D plane and $N - 1$ such independent projections completely describe l. There is a beautiful and very important relationship illustrated in (left) Fig. 3.19. For a line l in 3-D the three points $\bar{l}_{12}$, $\bar{l}_{13}$, $\bar{l}_{23}$ are collinear; the line so determined is denoted by $\bar{L}$. It is easy to see that a polygonal line on all the $N - 1$ points, given by Eq. (3.4) or their equivalent, represents a point on the line l. Two points in $\mathbb{R}^N$ determine a line l, so starting with the two polygonal lines the $N - 1$ intersections of their $\bar{X}_{i-1}, \bar{X}_i$ portions are the $\bar{l}_{i-1,i}$ representing points for l. A line interval in 10-D and several of its points is seen on the Fig. 3.19 (right). By the way, the indexing of the points $\bar{l}$, usually not shown to conserve display space, is essential and must be accessible when needed.

3.5.2 Planes & Hyperplanes

While a line can be determined from its projections, a plane even in 3-D can not. A new approach is called for [8]. Rather than discerning a p-dimensional object from its points, it is described in terms of its (p-1)-dimensional subsets constructed from the points. Let's see how this works. In Fig. 3.20 (left) polygonal lines representing a set of coplanar points in 3-D are seen. From this picture even the most persistent pattern-seeker can not detect any clues hinting at a relation among the three variables much less a linear one. The plane has dimension $p = 2$ so we look at lines (having dimension $p-1 = 1$) on the plane constructed by intersecting a pair of polygonal lines are obtained the $\bar{L}$ of the 3 point collinearity shown in Fig. 3.19 (left). The result shown on the right, is stunning. All the $\bar{L}$ lines intersect at a point which turns out to be characteristic of coplanarity but not enough to specify the plane. Translating the first axis $\bar{X}_1$ to the position X_1', one unit to the right of the X_3 axis and repeating the construction, based on the axes triple $\bar{X}_3\bar{X}_2\bar{X}_1'$, yields a second point shown in Fig. 3.21 (left). For a plane described by:

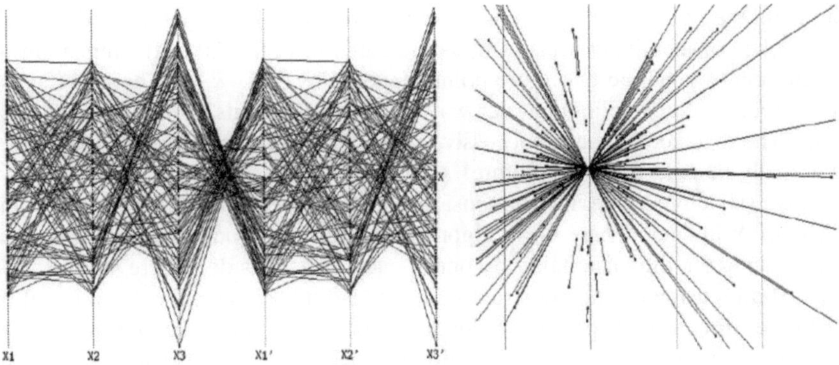

Fig. 3.20 (Left) skip Coplanarity! The polygonal lines on the first 3 axes represent a set of coplanar points in 3-D. (Right) Coplanarity! Forming lines on the plane, with the 3-point-collinearity property Fig. 19(left), the resulting lines intersect at point

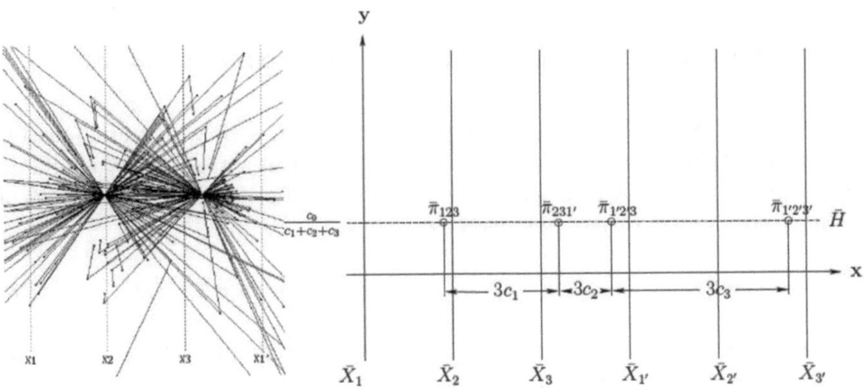

Fig. 3.21 Plane representation. (Left) The two points where the lines intersect uniquely determine a plane π in 3-D. (Right) From four points, constructed similarity by consecutive axes translation, the coefficients of π: $c_1x_1 + c_2x_2 + c_3x_3 = c_0$ can be read from the picture!

$$\pi : c_1x_1 + c_2x_2 + c_3x_3 = c_0 \tag{3.6}$$

The Cartesian coordinates of the two points, in the order they are constructed, are respectively

$$\bar{\pi}_{123} = \left(\frac{c_2 + 2c_3}{S}, \frac{c_0}{S}\right), \quad \pi_{1'23} = \left(\frac{3c_1 + c_2 + 2c_3}{S}, \frac{c_0}{S}\right) \tag{3.7}$$

for $S = c_1 + c_2 + c_3$. Three subscripts correspond to the 3 variables appearing in the plane's equation and the axes triple used for their construction, and distinguish them from the points with two subscripts representing lines. The 2nd and 3rd axes can also be consecutively translated, as indicated in Fig. 3.20 (left), repeating the construction to generate two more points denoted by $\bar{\pi}_{1'2'3}$, $\bar{\pi}_{1'2'3'}$. These points can also be found otherwise in an easier way. The gist of all this is shown in Fig. 3.21 (right). The distance between successive points is $3c_i$. The equation of the plane π can actually be read from the picture!

In general, a hyperlane in N-dimensions is represented uniquely by $N - 1$ points each with N indices. There is an algorithm which constructs these points recursively, raising the dimensionality by one at each step, as is done here starting from points (0-dimensional) and constructing lines (1-dimensional). By the way, all the nice higher dimensional projective dualities like *point* $\leftrightarrow$ *hyperplane*, *rotation* $\leftrightarrow$ *translation* etc. hold. Further, a multidimensional object, represented in ||-coords, can still be recognized after it has been acted on by projective transformation (i.e., translation, rotation, scaling and perspective). The recursive construction and its properties are at the heart of the ||-coords visualization.

3.5.3 Challenge: Visualizing Families of Proximate Planes

Returning to 3-D, it turns out that for points as in Fig. 3.20 which are "nearly" coplanar (i.e., have small errors) the construction produces a pattern very similar to that in Fig. 3.21 (left). A little experiment is in order. Let us consider a family of proximate (i.e., close) planes generated by

$$\Pi = \left\{\pi : c_1 x_1 + c_2 x_2 + c_3 x_3 = c_0, \quad c_i \in \left[c_i^-, c_i^+\right], \quad i = 0,1,2,3\right\}, \tag{3.8}$$

randomly choosing values of the c_i within the allowed intervals to determine several planes $\pi \in \Pi$, keeping at first $c_0 = 1$, and plotting the two points $\bar{\pi}_{1'2'3}$, $\bar{\pi}_{1'23}$ as shown in Fig. 3.22 (left). Not only is closeness apparent but more significantly the distribution of the points is not chaotic. The outline of two hexagonal patterns can be discerned. The family of "close" planes is visualizable and also the variations in several directions. These polygons can be easily constructed making it possible to see, estimate and compare errors or proximity *interactively*.

It can be proved that in 3-D the set of pairs of points representing the family of proximate planes form two convex hexagons when $c_0 = 1$ with an example shown in Fig. 3.22 (right), and are contained in octagons each with two vertical edges for varying c_0. In general, a family of proximate hyperplanes in N-D is represented by $N - 1$ convex $2N$-agons when $c_0 = 1$ or $2(N + 1)$-agons for c_0 varying. These polygonal regions can be constructed with $O(N)$ computational complexity. Choosing a point in one of the polygonal regions, an algorithm matches the possible $N - 2$ points, one each from the remaining convex polygons, which represent and identify hyperplanes in the family by $N - 1$ points.

We pose the thesis that visualization is not about seeing lots of things but rather discovering **relations** among them. While the display of randomly sampled points

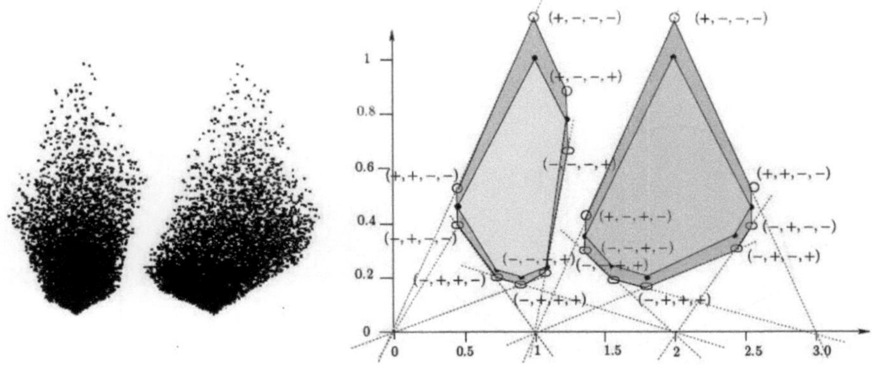

Fig. 3.22 A family of close planes. (Left) Pair of point clusters representing close planes. (Right) The hexagonal regions (interior) are the regions containing the points $\bar{\pi}_{123}$ (left) and $\bar{\pi}_{1'23}$ for the family of planes with $c_0 = 1$ and $c_1 \in [1/3, 1.5]$; $c_2 \in [1/3, 2.5]$; $c_3 \in [1/3, 1]$. For c_0 varying, here $c_0 \in [.85, 1.15]$, the regions (exterior) are octagonal with two vertical edges

from a family of proximate hyperplanes is utterly chaotic (the mess in Fig. 3.20 (right) from points in just one plane), their **proximate coplanarity relation** corresponds to a clear and compact pattern. With ||-coords we can focus and *concentrate* the relational information into patterns rather than wallow in the details, ergo the remark "without loss of information" when referring to ||-coords. This is the methodology's real strength and where the future lies. Here then is a visualization challenge: how else can proximate coplanarity be detected and seen?

3.5.4 Nonlinear Multivariate Relations: Hypersurfaces

A relation among 2 real variables is represented geometrically by a unique region in 2-D. Analogously, a relation between N variables corresponds to a hypersurface in N-D, hence the need to say something about the representation of hypersurfaces in ||-coords. A smooth surface in 3-D (and also N-D) can be described as the envelope of all its tangent planes. This is the basis for the representation shown in Fig. 3.23. Every point of the surface is mapped into the two points representing the *tangent plane at the point*. This generates 2 planar regions and for N-D there are $N-1$ such regions. These regions are *linked*, just as the polygons above, to provide the proper $N-1$ points representing each tangent hyperplane and from which the hypersurface can be reconstructed. Classes of surfaces can be immediately distinguished from their ||-coords display. For developable surfaces the regions consists of boundary curves only with no interior points, regions for ruled surfaces have grids consisting of straight lines, quadric surfaces have regions with conic boundaries these are some examples.

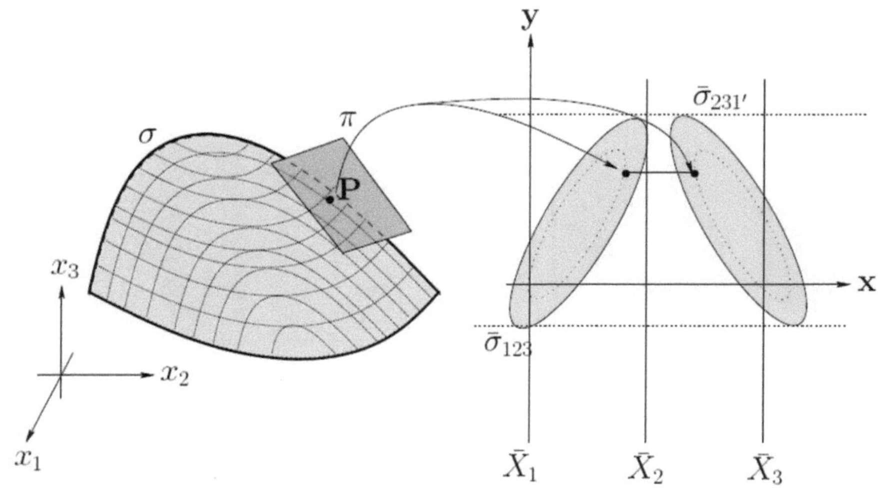

Fig. 3.23 Surface representation. A smooth surface is represented by two planar regions $\bar{\sigma}_{123}$, $\bar{\sigma}_{123'}$ consisting of pairs of points representing its tangent planes

There is a simpler but inexact surface representation which is useful when used judiciously as in the previous example Fig. 3.18. The polygonal lines representing points on the boundary are plotted and their envelope "represents" the surface; with the reminder that this is not a *unique* representation.

In Fig. 3.24 (left) are the upper and lower envelopes for a sphere in 5-D consisting of 4 overlapping hyperbolae which must be distinguished from those in Fig. 3.23 (right), which is exact and, interestingly enough are also hyperbolae, the curves determined by points representing the sphere's *tangent planes*. Retaining the exact surface description (i.e., its equation) internally, interior points can be constructed and displayed as shown for the 5-D sphere in Fig. 3.24 (left). On the right the same construction is shown but for a more complex 20-dimensional convex hypersurface ("model"). The intermediate curves (upper and lower) also provide valuable information and previews of coming attractions. They indicate a neighborhood of the point (represented by the polygonal line) and provide a feel for the local curvature. Note the narrow strips around *X*13, *X*14, *X*15 (as compared to the surrounding ones), indicating that at this state these are the critical variables where the point is bumping the boundary.

A theorem guarantees that a polygonal line which is in-between all the intermediate curves/envelopes represents an interior point of the hypersurface and all interior points can be found in this way. If the polygonal line is tangent at anyone of the intermediate curves then it represents a boundary point, while if it crosses anyone of the intermediate curves it represents an exterior point. The later enables us to see, in an application, the first variable for which the construction failed and what is needed to make corrections.

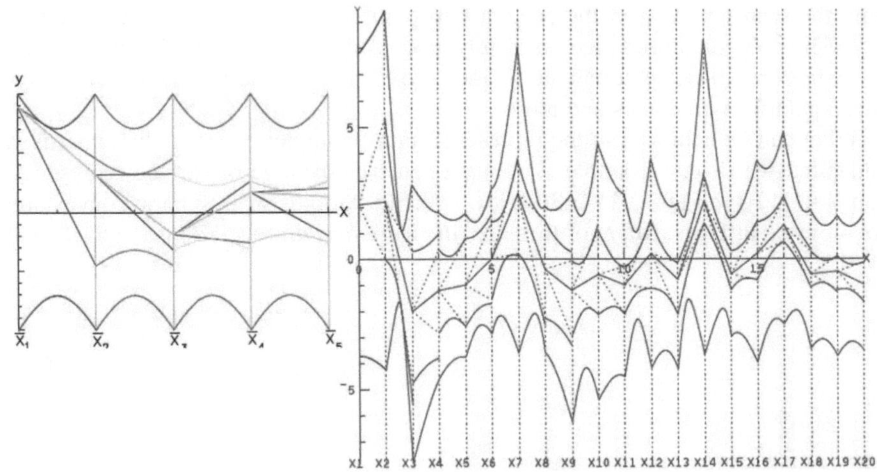

Fig. 3.24 Interior point construction. The interior point (polygonal line) construction on a sphere in 5-D (left) and for a convex hypersurface in 20-D (right)

By varying the choice of value over the available range of the variable interactively, sensitive regions (where small changes produce large changes downstream) and other properties of the model can be easily discovered. Once the construction of a point is completed it is possible to vary the values of each variable and see how this affects the remaining variables. So one can do trade-off analysis in this way and provide a powerful tool for, Decision Support, Process Control and other applications. As new data becomes available the model can be updated so that decisions are made based on the most recent information. This algorithm is used in the earlier example, shown in Fig. 3.18, to interact with a model of a country's economy.

3.6 Future

We are drowning in data and starving for knowledge.

Searching for *patterns* in the ||-coords data display is what skillful exploration is about. If there are multivariate relations in the display the patterns are there though they may be obscured by overlaps and that is not all. Our vision is not multidimensional. We do not perceive a room which is 3-dimensional from its points which are 0-dimensional, but from the 2-dimensional planes which enclose and define it. The recursive construction algorithm does exactly that for the visualization of p-dimensional objects from their p-1-dimensional subsets; one dimension less. We advocate including this algorithm within our armory of interactive analysis tools – **recursive interactivity**! Revisit Figs. 3.19 and 3.20 to note that relational information resides at the ***crossings***. Whatever p-dimensional relations exist are revealed by the pattern from the representation of the tangent hypeplanes of the corresponding hypersurface. The polygonal lines are completely discarded for the *relation is concentrated in the pattern*: linear relations into points, proximate coplanarity into convex polygons, quadrics into conics and more.

What can be achieved in the representation of complex relations by patterns is illustrated with some examples (a comprehensive coverage of surface representation is in [17]) in Figs. 3.25–3.30 folds, helicoid, Möbius strip, sphere, convex and non-convex surfaces. Many of these *results were first discovered interactively* and

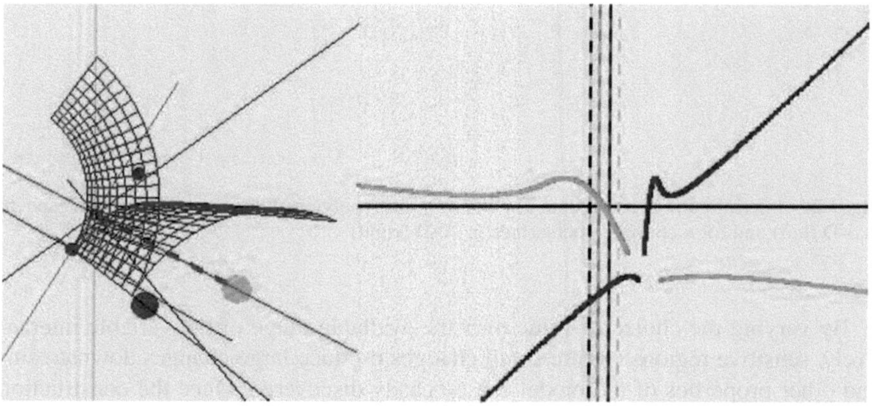

Fig. 3.25 A developable surface with a fold. The ||-coords representation illustrates the *developable* ↔ *curve* duality. The two *inflection points* represent the line of *cusps* in $\mathbf{R}^3$. The equivalent hypersurface in $\mathbf{R}^N$ is represented by $N - 1$ such curves all with inflection points at the same value of y

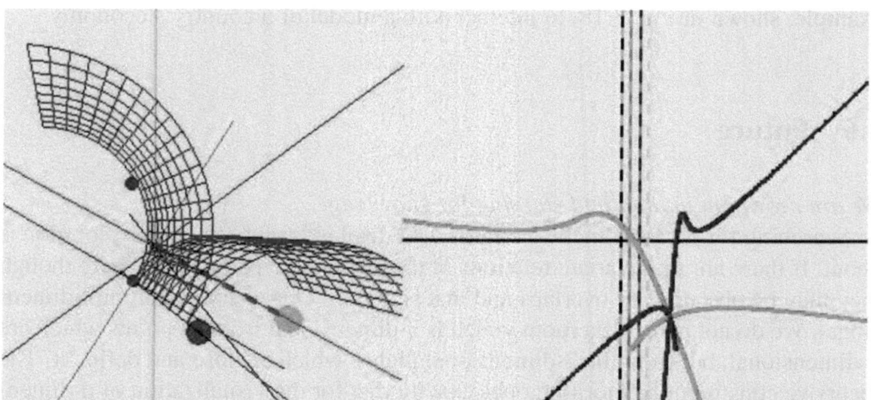

Fig. 3.26 Here there is a plane tangent, called *bitangent*, on the two extended leaves. It is represented by the coinciding *crossing points* for $\mathbf{R}^3$ and $N - 1$ for $\mathbf{R}^N$ occurring together with the inflection points in each of the representing curves

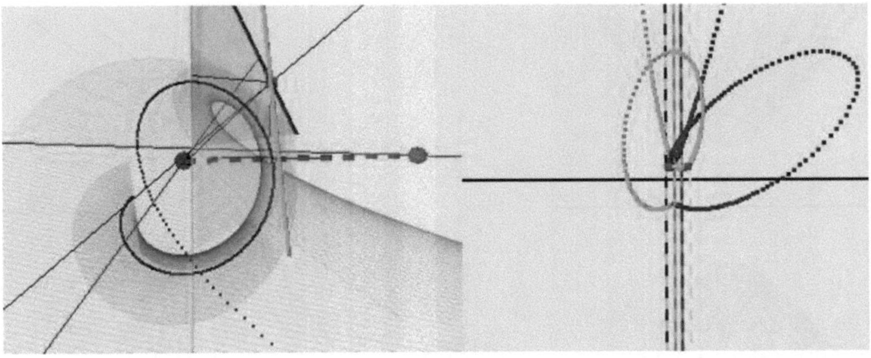

Fig. 3.27 A 3-D helicoid in Cartesian and ||-coords. The tangent plane determined by the two intersecting lines (left) is represented by a pair of points one on each of the curves at the same y (right). A helicoid in *N*-D is represented by $N-1$ such curves (*See Color Plates*)

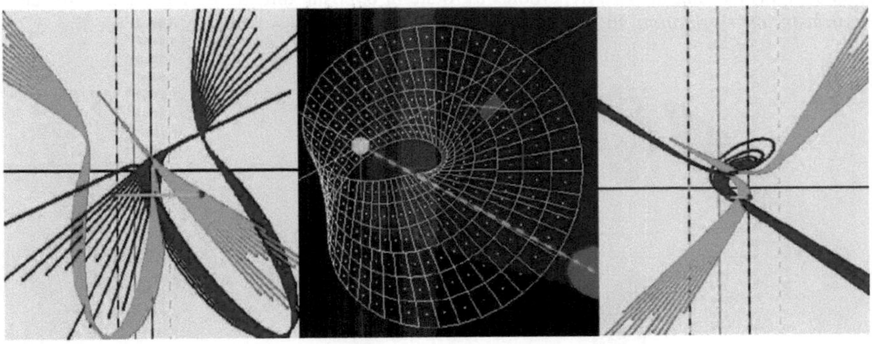

Fig. 3.28 Möbius strip and its representation for two orientations

then lead to mathematical proofs; in the true spirit of Geometry. These are state of the art results showing what is achievable and how easily it generalizes to N-D. Can one imagine a higher dimensional helicoid much less a non-orientable surface like the Möbius strip, non-convexities (bumps, crevices etc.) which unlike projections *are not hidden* in the representation. New vistas for interactive visualization emerge, transforming (rotating, translating) objects in N-space seeing the result in the representations, exploring for invariants which characterize surface properties (i.e., convexity, ruled etc.), developing intelligent agents to aid the exploration, classifying objects according to application-specific taxonomies and more. The challenge is speeding up the algorithms to reach real-time performance breaching the gridlock of multidimensional visualization. The secrets of massive datasets can then be unveiled interactively; the multidimensional relations *seen* as patterns – their *multidimensional graphs*.

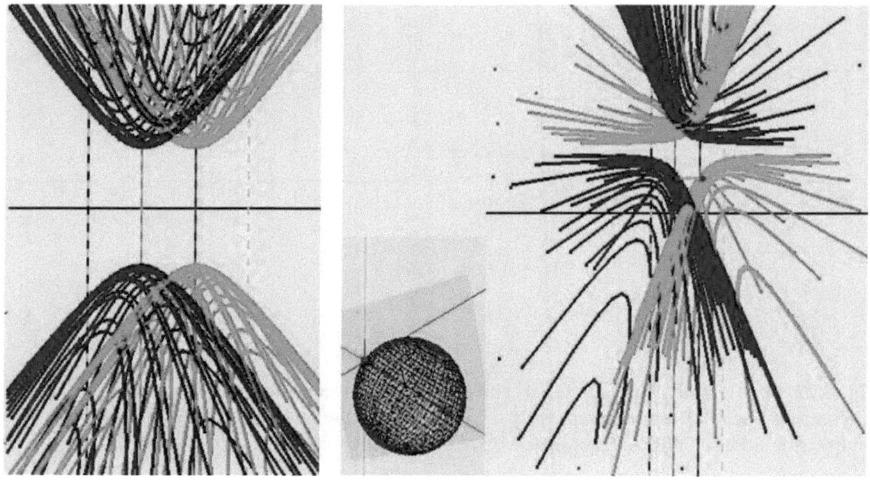

Fig. 3.29 Representation of a sphere centered at the origin (left) and after a translation along the x_1 axis (right) causing the two hyperbolas to rotate in opposite directions. This is an instance of the *translation* $\leftrightarrow$ *rotation*. In N–D a sphere is represented by $N-1$ hyperbolae – see Fig. 3.24

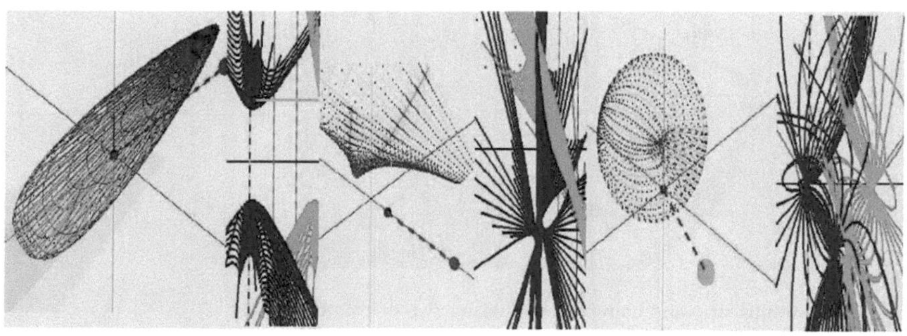

Fig. 3.30 Convex surfaces are represented by hyperbolic-like regions (left) Non-convexities: "bump" (center), three "dimples" represented by swirls (right)

3.7 Summary

This chapter is about the multidimensional system of Parallel Coordinates (abbr. ||-coords) how it came about and became popular in high dimensional data mining. Exploratory data analysis (EDA) is inherently complex. Our fantastic pattern-recognition ability can search and extract insights from the visual clues in a good data display. Data visualization is not just seeing "zillions of items but rather detecting relations among them as illustrated on" two real datasets discovering:

- ground features from remote sensing satellite data, and
- surprising rules for gold, foreign currencies and stockmarket trading.

The design of good queries and their operational environment is discussed during the knowledge discovery process. A complex dataset with two categories is classified using a geometric classification algorithm based on ||-coords. The algorithm has low computational complexity providing the classification rule explicitly and visually. The minimal set of variables required to state the rule is found and ordered by their predictive value. A visual model of a real country's economy is constructed from data on the output of economic sectors showing how multivariate relations can be modeled by means of hypersurfaces. Interior points corresponding to feasible economic policies are constructed interactively showing that two sectors unknowingly compete for the same group of workers. An overview of modern ||-coords provides foundational understanding. A relation between two variables is represented by a 2-dimensional region, and a relation between M variables is represented by an M-dimensional hypersurface. The representation of an M-dimensional hypersurface is obtained from its $(M-1)$ subsets which are constructed recursively from its points. There are examples of surfaces and their generalizations to higher dimensions. Properties like convexity can be seen in any dimension as well as nonorientability (as in the Möbius strip), and features like folds, crevices, bumps. This is a prelude of the future with recursive multidimensional interactivity uncovering the secrets in massive datasets.

Acknowledgements I am very grateful to David Adjiashvili who wrote the magnificent interactive software displaying the ||-coords representation of surfaces as seen in Figs. 3.25–3.30. Also I thank the two anonymous referees for their constructive and helpful suggestions.

References

1. B. Bollobas. Graph Theory. Springer-Verlag, New York, 1979.
2. A. Chatterjee. Visualizing Multidimensional Polytopes and Topologies for Tolerances. Ph.D. Thesis, Dept. Comp. Sci., Univ. of S. Calif., 1995.
3. A. Chatterjee, P. P. Das, and S. Bhattacharya. Visualization in Linear Programming Using Parallel Coordinates. Pattern Recognit, 26–11:1725–1736, 1993.
4. H. Choi and H. Lee. PCAV: Internet Attack Visualization in Parallel Coordinates, LNCS 3783, 454–466. Springer-Verlag, New York, 2005.
5. T. Chomut. Exploratory Data Analysis in Parallel Coordinates. M.Sc. Thesis, Dept. Comp. Sci. UCLA, 1987.
6. S. M. Cohan and D. C. H. Yang. Mobility Analysis in Parallel Coordinates. J. Mech. Mach., 21:63–71, 1986.
7. A. Desai and L.C. Walters. Graphical Representation of Data Envelopment Analyses: Management Implications from Parallel Axes Representations. Dec. Sci., 22(2):335–353, 1991.
8. J. Eickemeyer. Visualizing p-ats in N-Space Using Parallel Coordinates. Ph.D. Thesis, Dept. Comp. Sc., UCLA, 1992.
9. U. M. Fayad, G. P. Piatesky-Shapiro Smyth, and R. Uthurusamy. Advances in Knowledge Discovery and Data Mining. AAAI/MIT Press, Cambridge Mass, 1996.
10. P. Fiorini and A. Inselberg. Con_guration Space Representation in Parallel Coordinates. IEEE Conf. Rob. & Aut., 1215–1220, 1989.
11. M. Friendly and al. Milestones in Thematic Cartography. www.math.yorku.ca/scs/SCS/Gallery/milestones/, 2005.

12. C. Gennings, K. S. Dawson, W. H. Carter, and R. H. Myers. Interpreting plots of a Multidimensional dose-Response Surface in Parallel Coordinates. Biometrics, 46:719–735, 1990.
13. F. Harary. Graph Theory. Addison-Wesley, Reading, Mass., 1969.
14. H. Hauser. Parallel Sets: Visual Analysis of Categorical Data. Proc. IEEE Infovis, 2005.
15. J. Helly. Applications of Parallel Coordinates to Complex System Design and Operation. Proc. Nat. Comp. Grap. Assoc. vol. III, 541–546, 1987.
16. C. K. Hung and A. Inselberg. Parallel Coordinate Representation of Smooth Hypersurfaces. USC Tech. Report # CS – 92–531, Univ. of Southern California, Los Angeles, 1992.
17. C. K. Hung and A. Inselberg. Description of Surfaces in Parallel Coordinates by Linked Planar Regions, Mathematics of Surfaces XII, 177–208, LNCS 4647. Springer-Verlag, New York, 2007.
18. A. Inselberg. N-Dimensional Graphics. LASC Tech. Rep. G320-2711, 140. IBM, 1981.
19. A. Inselberg. Parallel Coordinates for Multidimensional Displays. Proc. IEEE Conf. on Spatial Infor., Sioux Falls, SD, 312–324. IEEE Comp. Soc., Los Alamitos, CA, 1984.
20. A. Inselberg. Intelligent Instrumentation and Process Control. Proc. 2nd IEEE Conf. on AI Appl., 302–307. IEEE Comp. Soc., Los Alamitos, CA, 1985.
21. A. Inselberg. The Plane with Parallel Coordinates. Visual Computer, 1:69–97, 1985.
22. A. Inselberg. Discovering Multi-Dimensional Structure with Parallel Coordinates (Invited Paper). In Proc. of ASA. Stat. Graphics 1–16. Amer. Stat. Assoc., 1989.
23. A. Inselberg. Parallel Coordinates: VISUAL Multidimensional Geometry and its Applications. Springer, New York, 2009.
24. A. Inselberg and T. Avidan. The Automated Multidimensional Detective. In Proc. of IEEE Information Visualization '99, 112–119. IEEE Comp. Soc., Los Alamitos, CA, 1999.
25. A. Inselberg and B. Dimsdale. Parallel Coordinates: A Tool for Visualizing Multi-Dimensional Geometry. Proc. of IEEE Conf. on Visualization, 361–378. IEEE Comp. Soc., Los Alamitos, CA, 1990.
26. A. Inselberg, M. Reif, and T. Chomut. Convexity Algorithms in Parallel Coordinates. J. ACM, 34:765–801, 1987.
27. A. Inselberg, M. Boz, and B. Dimsdale. Planar Conict Resolution Algorithm for Air-Traffic Control and the One-Shot Problem, in IBM PASC Tech. Rep. G320–3559. IBM Palo Alto Scientific Center, 1991.
28. C. Jones. Visualization and Optimization. Kluwer Academic Publishers, Boston, 1996.
29. T. Matskewich, A. Inselberg, and M. Bercovier. Approximated Planes in Parallel Coordinates. Proc. of Geom. Model. Conf., St. Malo, Vanderbilt Univ. Press, 257–266, 2000.
30. T. M. Mitchell. Machine Learning. McGraw-Hill, New York 1997.
31. J. R. Quinlan. C4.5: Programs for Machine Learning. Morgan Kaufman, San Francisco 1993.
32. J. Rivero and A. Inselberg. Extension al Analisis del Espacio De Fase de Systemas Dinamicos por las Coordinadas Parallelas. Proc. VII Systems EngrWorkshop, Santiago, Chile, 1984.
33. C. Schmid and H. Hinterberger. Comparative Multivariate Vis. Across Conceptually Different Graphic Displays. In Proc. of 7th SSDBM. IEEE Comp. Soc., Los Alamitos, CA, 1994.
34. E. R. Tufte. The Visual Display of Quantitative Information. Graphic Press, Connecticut, 1983.
35. E. R. Tufte. Envisioning Information. Graphic Press, Connecticut, 1990.
36. E. R. Tufte. Visual Explanation. Graphic Press, Connecticut, 1996.
37. M. O. Ward. XmdvTool: Integrating Multiple Methods for Visualizing Multivariate Data. Proc. IEEE Conf. on Vis., CA, 326–333. IEEE Comp. Soc., Los Alamitos, CA, 1994.
38. E. Wegman. Hyperdimensional Data Analysis Using Parallel Coordinates. J. Amer. Stat. Assoc., 85:664–675, 1990.
39. L. Yang. Prunning & Visualizing Generalized Association Rules in Parallel Coordinates. IEEE Knowledge Data Eng., 15(1):60–70, 2005.

Chapter 4
Interactive Particle Visualization

Christiaan P. Gribble

Abstract Particle-based simulation methods are used to model a wide range of complex phenomena and to solve time-dependent problems of various scales. Effective visualizations of the resulting state will communicate subtle changes in the three-dimensional structure, spatial organization, and qualitative trends within a simulation as it evolves. This chapter discusses two approaches to interactive particle visualization that satisfy these goals: one targeting desktop systems equipped with programmable graphics hardware, and the other targeting moderately sized multicore systems using packet-based ray tracing.

Keywords Interactive particle visualization, Particle-based simulation, Programmable graphics hardware, Packet-based ray tracing.

4.1 Introduction

Particle methods are commonly used to simulate complex phenomena in a wide variety of scientific domains. Using these techniques, computational scientists model such phenomena as a system of discrete particles that obey certain laws and possess certain properties. Particle-based simulation methods are particularly attractive because they can be used to solve time-dependent problems on scales from the atomic to the cosmological.

Frequently, millions of particles are required to capture the behavior of a system accurately. These massive simulations lead to very large, very complex datasets, such as the one depicted in Fig. 4.1, and make interactive visualization a difficult task. An effective particle visualization method will communicate subtle changes in the three-dimensional structure, spatial organization, and qualitative trends within the data as a simulation evolves, as well as enable easier navigation and exploration of the data through interactivity.

Many particle visualization methods project particle values to a three-dimensional grid, and the transformed data is then visualized using standard techniques such as direct volume rendering [22] or isosurface rendering [24]. Grid-based representations

E. Zudilova-Seinstra et al. (eds.) *Trends in Interactive Visualization*,
doi:10.1007/978-1-84800-269-2_4

Fig. 4.1 *Compaction of foam by a rigid plate*. Initial geometry is collected using micro-CT from a sample about 1 mm^3 in size. The CT data are converted to an equivalent distribution consisting of roughly seven million particles per time step [6]. Using interactive visualization tools, correlations between specific events in the simulation and the reaction force at the boundaries can be determined. Simulation data courtesy of Jerry Seidler and Erin Miller (University of Washington) and of Scott Bardenhagen (Los Alamos National Laboratory)

of the data are suitable for some, but not all, particle visualization tasks. For example, the need to simultaneously visualize both the large and small scale features within the data often make grid-based representations problematic. Additionally, interpolation may hide features or problems present in the original particle data [15], while isosurface extraction can be very time-consuming, particularly for large datasets. Alternatively, particle data can be represented directly by simple iconic shapes called glyphs. For many applications, a sphere or an ellipsoid is a natural representation of an individual particle.

As particle-based simulations continue to grow in size and complexity, effective visualization of the resulting state becomes increasingly problematic. First, these datasets are difficult to visualize interactively because of their size. An effective visualization algorithm must be capable of rendering such a large number of particles efficiently. Second, the intricacies of complex data are difficult to convey sensibly. Particle methods often simulate complex objects with subtle features that interact in complex ways, and detecting the salient features within the data is a critical step in correctly interpreting the simulation results.

Interactive visualization of particle-based simulation data typically serves one of three purposes: data analysis, code development, or generation of presentation and publication quality images. First, an interactive visualization process enables users to identify and explore the salient features of their data more effectively. For example, it is possible to correlate specific events in a given simulation with the behavior of each element in the simulation as it evolves (see Fig. 4.1). Second, the ability to debug ill-behaved solutions is an important consequence of highly accessible interactive visualization. Recognition of incorrect particle behavior has led to important advances in simulation algorithms, such as those described by Guilkey et al. [15]. Finally, interactive visualization makes generation of high quality animations and still images for presentation or publication fast and straightforward. An interactive environment allows a user to quickly identify optimal views in which each image or frame of an animation will convey the most pertinent information.

Interactivity in the context of particle visualization encompasses a wide range of activities. Interactive viewing and lighting enable investigators to identify and interrogate specific features within the data more easily. Interactivity also provides important visual cues from relative motion [33] and environmental frame of reference [37], whereas advanced features such as parameter range culling and color mapping provide opportunities for additional insights. Parameter range culling allows investigators to isolate particles with properties that lie within some range of values [12], and color mapping offers an effective way to communicate pertinent information beyond the spatial organization of objects within complex datasets [32]. Using interactive visualization tools, each of these features is under the full control of a user at run time and can be changed at interactive rates.

Applications in domains ranging from data mining [38] and computational fluid dynamics [5, 10] to diffusion tensor imaging [20] and structural mechanics [1, 15] employ particles to visualize scientific datasets. Glyph-based techniques render the data directly by representing each particle as a sphere, so many efforts have explored techniques to render large numbers of spheres efficiently, from rasterization on massively parallel processors [21],visualization clusters [23], custom hardware [17, 39, 40], and programmable graphics hardware [14] to interactive ray tracing on tightly coupled supercomputers [3, 25] and multicore systems [12].

Two recent approaches represent the current state-of-the-art in interactive particle visualization. On the one hand, programmable graphics processing units (GPUs) bring interactive particle visualization to the desktop [14]. On the other, interactive ray tracing on multicore systems enables advanced visualization features to be integrated in a straightforward manner. The remainder of this chapter discusses each of these methods in turn.

4.2 Programmable Graphics Hardware

Over the past several years, programmable GPUs have become an attractive option for visualizing a wide variety of scientific datasets. The GPU-based particle visualization algorithm discussed below combines point sprite rendering and software-based acceleration techniques to achieve interactive frame rates when rendering large, time-varying particle datasets. The algorithm also introduces an extension to the coherent hierarchical culling [4] algorithm that provides improved temporal coherence and better average performance for time-varying datasets.

4.2.1 Algorithm

In addition to interactive performance on desktop systems equipped with commodity graphics hardware, GPU-based approaches offer advanced data exploration capabilities that are consistent with those provided by interactive ray tracing systems running on tightly coupled supercomputing platforms. The critical components of the approach include: (1) rendering high quality particle glyphs efficiently, (2) achieving interactive performance with programmable GPUs, (3) handling time-varying data while maintaining interactivity, and (4) supporting enhanced data exploration and visualization techniques.

4.2.1.1 Rendering High Quality Particle Glyphs

The need to simultaneously visualize both large and small scale structures within particle datasets requires that each particle be rendered using a high quality representation. One approach would simply render a finely tessellated, view-aligned hemisphere for each particle. However, because each time step typically contains millions of particles, the required geometry would quickly overwhelm the system and result in poor performance.

View-aligned billboards can be used to alleviate this issue. Each billboard is rendered efficiently using the point sprite rendering capabilities of modern GPUs [16, 27]. Individual point sprites are specified by a vertex corresponding to the position of the particle, and per-vertex attributes control other aspects of its representation, including the radius and the scalar value used for color mapping. Vertex and fragment programs manipulate these data to render a high quality representation of each particle in an efficient manner (see Fig. 4.2).

4.2.1.2 Achieving Interactive Performance

The particle rendering process can be combined with software-based acceleration techniques to reduce the work load in each frame. For example, with view-frustum culling (VFC) [7], particles outside the current view volume are culled, saving the cost associated with rendering particles that are not visible. While each of the particles can be tested against the view volume individually, it is more efficient to cull large groups of particles by testing a bounding primitive encapsulating each

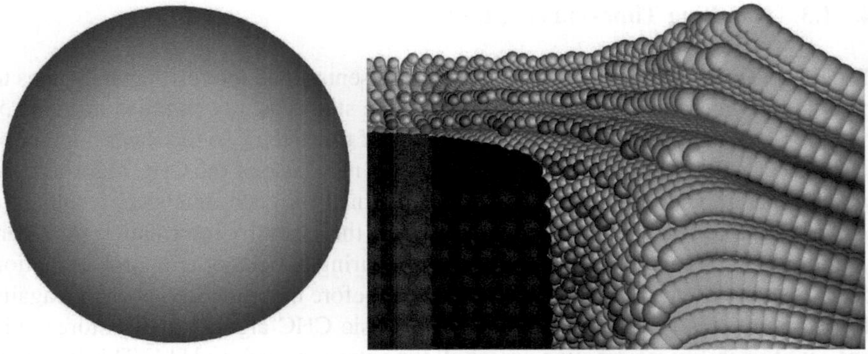

Fig. 4.2 *High quality particle rendering with point sprites*. View-aligned billboards serve as the base primitive. An individual particle is specified by a vertex position and other per-vertex attributes that control its representation (left). Efficiently rendering high quality particle glyphs enables simultaneous visualization of both large and small scale features within the data (right) (*See Color Plates*)

group. In this case, each bounding primitive corresponds to a node in a spatial subdivision structure such as an octree.

VFC provides a fast approximation to the potentially visible particles and typically improves performance over simply rendering all of the particles. Nevertheless, particles that are not visible may still be rendered, resulting in pixel overdraw and limiting the achievable performance.

To avoid this issue, VFC can be combined with other, more sophisticated culling techniques that utilize hardware-based occlusion queries [2]. Hierarchical stop-and-wait occlusion culling (HSW) is one such algorithm. In this method, the spatial subdivision structure is traversed depth-first, and an occlusion query is issued for nodes whose bounding boxes either intersect or are contained within the view frustum. The CPU waits for the result of the query before proceeding. If the node is not visible, its subtree is culled (interior node) or the associated particles are not rendered (leaf node) and traversal continues. Otherwise, the algorithm proceeds either by traversing the children of the node in a front-to-back order (interior node) or by rendering the associated particles (leaf node).

Hardware occlusion queries typically have a high latency, which leads to a load balancing problem between the CPU and the GPU. Coherent hierarchical culling (CHC) [4] is designed to address this issue. CHC exploits temporal coherence in the visibility classification of a node when rendering arbitrary occluders by reusing the results of occlusion queries issued in the previous frame. Visibility information is maintained with each node in the spatial subdivision structure. This simple solution also reduces query overhead: previously visible interior nodes are processed without issuing an occlusion query because the visibility status of such nodes can easily be determined from their children. Queries are issued only for previously visible leaf nodes and for the largest possible occluded nodes in the hierarchy.

4.2.1.3 Handling Time-Varying Data

The time-varying nature of particle datasets presents some interesting challenges to maintaining interactive performance. Each time step typically contains millions of particles, and there are often tens or hundreds of time steps, so the sheer number of particles can be problematic. Unfortunately, the naive use of the CHC algorithm, in which separate visibility information is maintained for each time step, results in a loss of frame-to-frame coherence. In particular, the visibility information for a particular time step quickly becomes out-of-date during periods of temporal animation because many frames may have been rendered before that time step is visible again. To overcome this issue, an extension to the basic CHC algorithm that stores only one set of visibility information across all time steps can be used [14].This information is always used to estimate the currently visible geometry, even if the estimate is based on the results of a different time step. This approach, which is called CHC-TV, often results in better coherence when the data are animated because the visibility classification of the geometry tends to change slowly between time steps.

4.2.1.4 Supporting Enhanced Data Exploration

Basic data exploration capabilities such as interactive viewing and lighting enable investigators to identify specific features within the data more easily. In addition, more advanced data analysis tools like color mapping and parameter range culling allow investigators to interrogate the data based on the state parameters from the simulation that are associated with each particle. Each of these features can be supported and controlled interactively at run time using the GPU-based approach.

Advanced particle visualization techniques can also be incorporated. For example, recent research results show that shading models such as ambient occlusion and physically based diffuse interreflection can enhance the perception of three-dimensional structure and spatial relationships within particle datasets [13]. Programmable GPUs support these shading models via multi-pass fragment processing (see Fig. 4.3). In particular, compressed precomputed luminance textures [11, 13] can be reconstructed on the GPU and mapped to the particles during interactive rendering. Similarly, the GPU can apply image-based silhouettes [3, 31] to the visualizations at interactive rates.

4.2.2 Results

The performance of the CHC-TV algorithm is compared to several other software-based acceleration techniques, including VFC, HSW, and the original CHC algorithm. To provide a bound on achievable performance, two additional algorithms are also investigated: (1) an "exact" algorithm that renders the exact visible set in each frame, as determined by a lengthy preprocessing phase; and (2) an "ideal"

Fig. 4.3 *Enhancing particle visualization.* Advanced visualization features can be implemented using multipass fragment processing. **a** Shading models such as physically based diffuse interreflection lead to enhanced perception of particle datasets.**b** Silhouette edges can be used to accentuate a set of view-dependent boundaries (*See Color Plates*)

algorithm that renders only the particles contained within the visible nodes of a spatial subdivision structure, also determined by a preprocessing phase. The exact algorithm provides a lower bound on frame time for a given interactive session (no rendering algorithm running on the same hardware can produce the correct results any faster), whereas the ideal algorithm provides a lower bound with respect to the given spatial subdivision structure (no occlusion culling algorithm using the same structure can be faster).

A dual processor system with 8 GB of physical memory and an NVIDIA GeForce 7800 GT graphics card serves as the test platform. Results were gathered for images rendered at 1024×768 pixels using prerecorded interactive sessions with two datasets, Container and Fireball. Table 4.1 presents the pertinent characteristics of each dataset. Table 4.2 shows the results for both datasets under each rendering algorithm, averaged over the interactive session, and Fig. 4.4 details the behavior of the Container dataset graphically.

Table 4.1 Particle datasets used in performance testing

	Container	Fireball
# Particles	386 M	20 M
# Time steps	138	21
Total data size	11 GB	315 MB

Occlusion culling algorithms typically provide the best performance for datasets exhibiting a high degree of self-occlusion (Container). In contrast, these algorithms simply add overhead to the rendering process and lead to lower performance for datasets that do not exhibit this property (Fireball)

Table 4.2 Comparing culling algorithms

Dataset	Method		# of particles rendered	Frame time [ms]	Speedup
Container	VFC	–	2108550	254.93	1.00
	HSW	1448	351060	120.83	2.11
	CHC	1939	469418	100.52	2.54
	CHC-TV	**1407**	**414098**	**88.37**	**2.88**
	Ideal	–	351060	47.11	5.41
	Exact	–	35425	7.45	34.22
Fireball	**VFC**	**–**	**711964**	**70.90**	**1.00**
	HSW	1623	363731	93.52	0.76
	CHC	1732	459410	77.03	0.92
	CHC-TV	1576	482659	81.82	0.87
	Ideal	–	363731	30.34	2.34
	Exact	–	25795	20.91	3.39

Several pertinent characteristics of each algorithm have been averaged over the given interactive session. CHC-TV provides the best performance for datasets exhibiting a high degree of self-occlusion, but VFC performs best for datasets that do not exhibit this property

When a dataset exhibits a high degree of self-occlusion, as in the case of the Container dataset, CHC-TV typically provides the best performance despite rendering more particles per frame than HSW. This result is a direct consequence of its ability to hide high latency hardware-based occlusion queries behind useful work. Moreover, CHC-TV maintains coherence during periods of temporal animation and thus provides better average performance for time-varying data when compared to the standard implementation of CHC.

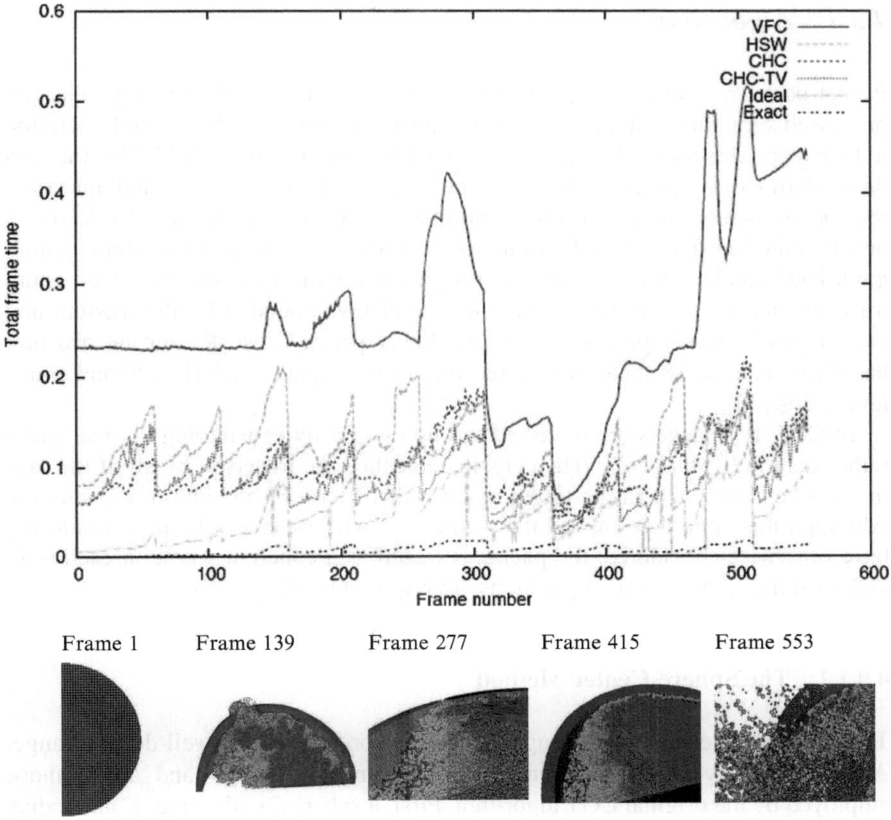

Fig. 4.4 *Characterizing interactive performance.* This graph shows the results of rendering the Container dataset over a prerecorded interactive session. Using the CHC-TV algorithm, average performance is roughly 10 frames per second on an NVIDIA GeForce 7800 GT graphics card, which provides a highly interactive environment for navigating and exploring large time-varying particle datasets

However, if a dataset does not exhibit a high degree of self-occlusion (as in the case of the Fireball dataset), the visibility tests simply add overhead, and VFC often provides better performance.

4.3 Interactive Ray Tracing

Packet-based ray tracing techniques and multilevel grids can also be used to achieve highly interactive performance [12]. In this approach, optimizations that exploit the properties of particle-based simulation data are used to tailor the coherent grid traversal (CGT) algorithm [36] for particle datasets, achieving both improved performance and reduced storage requirements.

4.3.1 Algorithm

Packet-based ray tracing [34] creates groups of spatially coherent rays that are processed simultaneously: each ray in the packet performs each traversal operation in lock-step. This packet-based approach enables effective use of SIMD instructions on modern CPUs, increases the computational density of the code, and amortizes the cost of memory accesses across multiple rays. Packet tracing has also lead to a new frustum based traversal algorithm for kd-trees [28] in which a bounding frustum guides and accelerates the traversal of ray packets. In this case, the cost of a frustum traversal step is independent of the number of rays bounded by the frustum and encourages large ray packets to achieve lower per-ray cost. Packet and frustum based ray traversal techniques have recently been adapted to BVHs [35] and multi-level grids [36].

In CGT, ray packets are traversed through a grid by considering vertical slices rather than individual cells. The cells in each slice are traversed by all of the rays in a packet, and each ray is tested against all of the objects within a given cell. Although this approach implies that some rays will traverse cells they would not have otherwise considered, the packet is traced as a coherent whole in each step, and no splitting or merging operations are required (see Fig. 4.5).

4.3.1.1 The Sphere-Center Method

Typically, particle radii are of roughly equal size or fall within a well-defined range. As a result, several observations permit optimizations over and above those employed by the original CGT algorithm. First, a sphere S with center C and radius

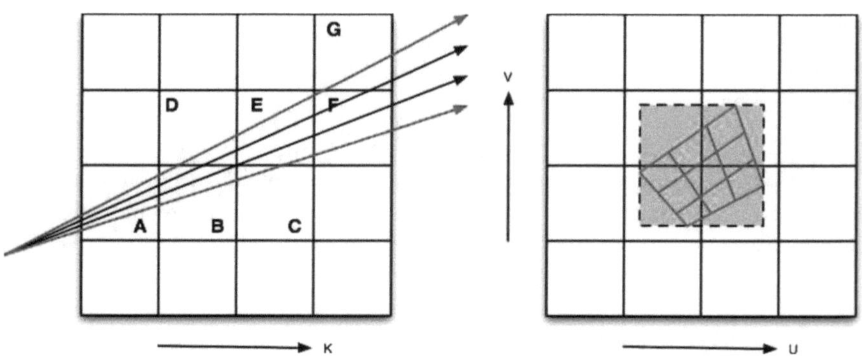

Fig. 4.5 *Packet traversal in a grid.* In CGT, rays step along vertical slices in the major traversal direction. Rays traverse the grid as a coherent whole, so no splitting or merging operations are required (left). The bounding frustum, which guides ray traversal, overlaps the same cells as the individual rays (right). (Images from Gribble et al., A Coherent Grid Traversal Approach to Visualizing Particle-Based Simulation Data, *IEEE Transactions on Visualization and Computer Graphics*, 13(4):758–768. Reprinted with permission)

r is symmetric, so determining whether S overlaps a frustum F is analogous to testing whether C is in the r-neighborhood of F. In particular, we can test whether the distance from C to any of the bounding planes of F is less than r. Second, testing whether the distance from C to the planes of F is less than r is the same as testing whether C is inside another frustum F_r that has been enlarged by the maximum radius r_{max}. Thus, by traversing the grid using an enlarged frustum, only those spheres whose centers lie inside that frustum must be intersected, and therefore each sphere must be stored in exactly one location: the cell in which its center is located. This approach is called the sphere-center method.

In a traditional grid, primitives often overlap multiple cells, which can be problematic. For example, data must be duplicated in each cell the primitive overlaps or, alternatively, references to the primitive data must be stored in these cells. The former approach can lead to a significant amount of redundant data, whereas the latter implies that spatially local primitives do not necessarily exhibit locality of reference; that is, primitives close to each other in the three-dimensional space of the scene may be separated by many bytes in address space. Although a preprocessing phase can be used to ensure that spatially local primitives reside together in address space as well [8], this approach is not well-suited to acceleration structures that are constructed on-the-fly during rendering.

Additionally, primitives that overlap many cells are problematic because rays will perform redundant intersections with these primitives as they traverse the grid. The original CGT algorithm uses a mailbox structure [19] to avoid these redundant intersections. However, mailboxes may not improve performance for grids when intersection tests are inexpensive, as in the case of spheres, and they may actually reduce performance if avoiding primitive intersections does not outweigh the cost of querying and updating the mailbox. The sphere-center method alleviates all of these problems. Data duplication is never required because the primitives are stored directly in the grid and the center of each sphere is guaranteed to lie in exactly one cell. As a consequence, locality of reference for spatially local primitives is improved without an explicit sorting or data reorganization process. The sphere-center method also obviates the need for mailboxes: spheres are stored in exactly one grid cell, and will be intersected no more than once during traversal.

4.3.1.2 Grid Organization and Construction

To improve performance, the grid can be organized hierarchically. Hierarchical grids typically divide densely populated regions of space more finely than empty regions. Although there are several ways to accomplish this task, the macrocell hierarchy described by Parker et al. [26] works well in practice [12, 36].

To support parameter range culling, the macrocell hierarchy differs from the one used in the original CGT algorithm and more closely resembles one used in interactive volume visualization applications [26]. In particular, a macrocell must store the minimum and maximum values of each data variable across all of the particles it contains, rather than a simple Boolean flag indicating an empty or nonempty condition.

For time-varying datasets, the sort-middle construction algorithm described by Ize et al. [18] is used to quickly rebuild the grid in each frame. In this approach, the construction-related tasks corresponding to disjoint sections of the grid are statically distributed among all of the threads in the system. The sort-middle insertion essentially performs a coarse parallel bucket sort of the particles by their cell locations, and each thread inserts the particles in its set of buckets into the appropriate grid cells. The regions corresponding to each bucket are disjoint, so each thread inserts its particles into different parts of the grid. Write conflicts are thus avoided, and mutexes or other synchronization primitives are not necessary.

4.3.1.3 Frustum Culling

The original CGT algorithm employs SIMD shaft culling [9] to prevent unnecessary intersection tests by quickly discarding triangles that lie outside the current bounding frustum. In this case, triangles are culled if all four corner rays of the current frustum miss the triangle on the same edge. Unfortunately, the SIMD shaft culling technique relies on primitives that posses planar edges, a property which spheres do not exhibit; as a result, this fast culling technique is not appropriate for particle visualization. However, a much simpler test can be used to quickly cull spheres and avoid unnecessary intersection tests: if the distance from the center of a given sphere to any of the planes of the bounding frustum is greater than the radius of the sphere, the rays bounded by the frustum cannot intersect the sphere. This test is used to quickly cull nonintersecting spheres.

4.3.1.4 Soft Shadows

Soft shadows from area light sources provide important visual cues about the relative position of objects in complex datasets. Soft shadows are preferable to hard shadows because the smooth transition from shadowed to unshadowed regions is less likely to be misinterpreted as a discontinuity in the underlying data. Although shadows and other global effects are difficult to implement in systems based on rasterization, these effects are easily integrated into an approach based on ray tracing.

In particular, packets of coherent shadow rays can be generated by connecting the hit point corresponding to a given primary ray with some number of samples on an area light source [34]. By constructing shadows rays in this manner, secondary ray packets share a common origin and can traverse a grid using the particle CGT algorithm in a manner identical to that used for primary ray packets. Using this approach, both the number of shadow rays and the size of the light source can be controlled interactively by the user and permits performance-for-quality trade-offs (see Fig. 4.6).

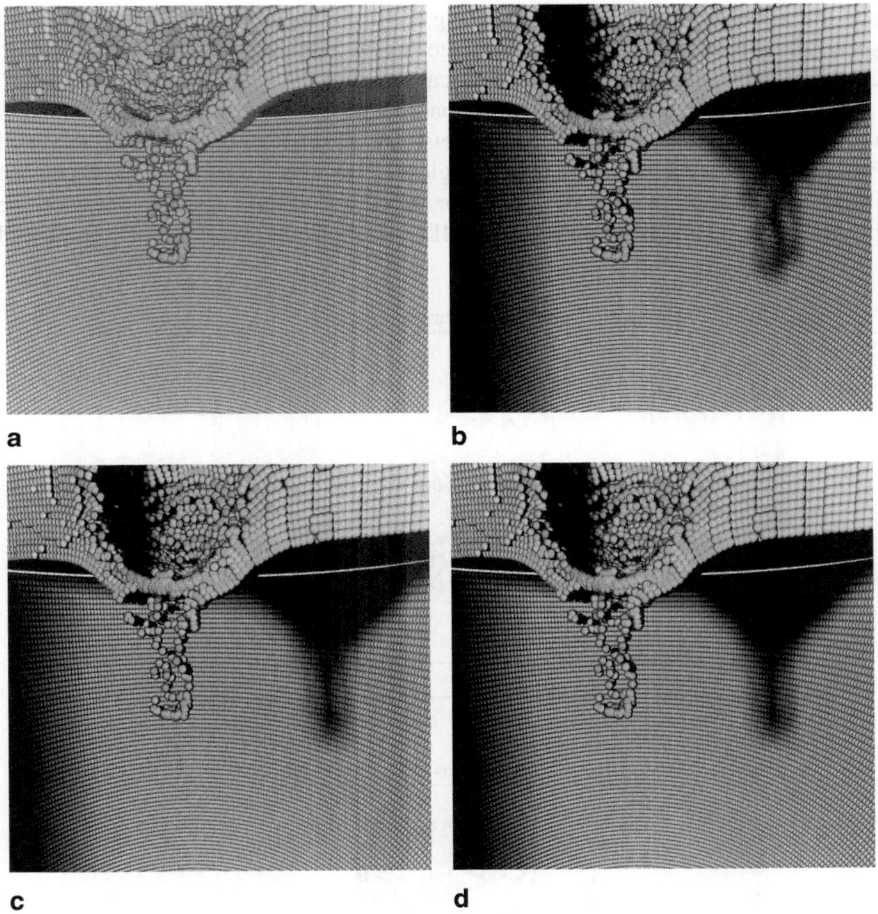

Fig. 4.6 *Rendering with soft shadows*. Soft shadows from area light sources provide important visual cues about the relative position of objects in complex datasets. Shadows and other global effects are easily integrated into an approach based on ray tracing such as the one described here. (Images from Gribble et al., A Coherent Grid Traversal Approach to Visualizing Particle-Based Simulation Data, *IEEE Transactions on Visualization and Computer Graphics*, 13(4):758–768. Reprinted with permission)

4.3.2 Results

The particle CGT algorithm is compared with two other particle visualization approaches. The first is based on an optimized single ray grid traversal algorithm in the Real-Time Ray Tracer (RTRT) [25], while the second leverages the GPU-based approach described above. The pertinent characteristics of the test datasets and the viewpoints used during rendering are given in Table 4.3. The results were gathered by rendering 1024 × 1024 images using a 16 core Opteron machine with 2.4 GHz processors and 64 GB of physical memory.

The results in Table 4.4 show that the particle CGT algorithm compares favorably with these approaches for the test datasets. The benefits of packet-based traversal become evident when compared to single ray traversal: interactive performance improves by a factor of 1.35–14.48 for the test datasets. Though some of the improvement results from the use of SIMD operations that are not easily employed

Table 4.3 Particle datasets used in performance testing

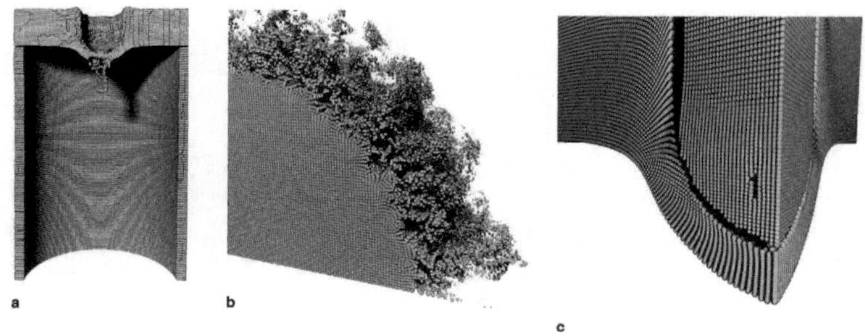

	Cylinder	JP8	Bullet
# of particles	212980	815345	2.1 M
Data size	6.50 MB	21.77 MB	47.75 MB
Frame rate	100.20 fps	99.88 fps	126.93 fps

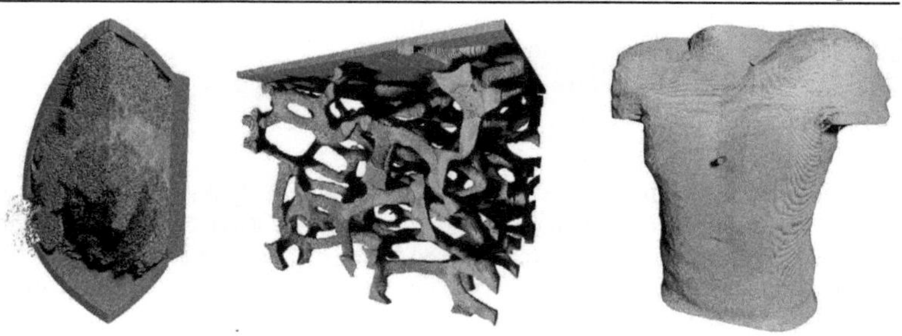

	Thunder	Foam	BulletTorso
# of particles	2.8 M	7.2 M	34.9 M
Data size	86.33 MB	136.52 MB	1.04 GB
Frame rate	40.86 fps	14.34 fps	18.31 fps

These datasets exhibit a wide variety of sizes and geometric complexity, and each represents a single time step of the full simulation. An implementation of the particle CGT algorithm is evaluated using the viewpoints and time steps shown above. (Images from Gribble et al., A Coherent Grid Traversal Approach to Visualizing Particle-Based Simulation Data, *IEEE Transactions on Visualization and Computer Graphics*, 13(4):758–768. Reprinted with permission)

Table 4.4 Comparison of particle visualization methods

Dataset	Particle CGT Gribble et al. [12]	RTRT Parker et al. [25]	GPU-based Gribble et al.[14]
Cylinder	100.20	12.60	5.78
JP8	99.88	6.90	17.40
Bullet	126.93	11.90	2.56
Thunder	40.86	14.90	8.10
Foam	14.33	6.40	2.04
BulletTorso	18.31	13.50	1.56

Frame rates achieved using the particle CGT algorithm and two state-of-the-art interactive particle visualization methods. The benefits of packet-based traversal become evident when compared to single ray traversal, and the algorithm also significantly outperforms an approach leveraging programmable graphics hardware. (Images from Gribble et al., A Coherent Grid Traversal Approach to Visualizing Particle-Based Simulation Data, *IEEE Transactions on Visualization and Computer Graphics*, 13(4):758–768. Reprinted with permission)

in single ray scheme, such an implementation usually provides an improvement of only a factor of 2–3; the remainder is a result of the cost amortization and algorithmic improvements inherent to a packet-based traversal method.

This algorithm also outperforms the approach based on programmable graphics hardware. Despite the fact that the test machine actually provides fewer raw FLOPS than the NVIDIA GeForce 7800 GT used for testing, the particle CGT approach outperforms this system by a factor of about 5 to almost 50 for the datasets tested.

4.4 Applications

Interactive visualization of particle-based simulation data assists investigators in the data analysis, feature detection, and code development tasks they often perform. The application of interactive particle visualization to simulations of foam compression (see Fig. 4.1) provides one example. In these simulations, a rigid plate compresses a foam material sample to roughly the level of full densification, or the point at which the total compressed volume is equal to the initial volume of the uncompressed material. Throughout the simulation, the various states of deformation of the foam, as well as the reaction force at the boundaries, are gathered. Using interactive visualization, it is possible to correlate specific events in the simulation with the reaction force at the boundaries, for example, the collision of one foam strut either with another strut or with the domain boundary. By determining visually exactly when these events occur, it is possible to recognize what relationship they have with the full computational domain, leading to specific insights like those described by Bardenhagen et al. [1].

Simulations of mechanical loading on angiogenesis, or the growth of micro blood vessels in a collagen matrix, provide another example. Initial geometry is constructed by transforming three-dimensional images of vessels grown in vitro into a particle representation. Images of samples that have been selectively stained with a fluorescent tag are collected using scanning-confocal microscopy and converted to an equivalent particle distribution. Mechanical loading is simulated by prescribing the displacement of a rigid plate at the top of the sample.

Early in the angiogenesis investigation, the computed reaction force holding the sample in place during loading was behaving in an unusual and unpredictable manner. Only upon viewing the particle data directly (13.2 million particles per time step in this case) was it evident that as particles moved through the computational grid, some were subject to very different levels of strain though these levels should have been nearly uniform. Recognition of this behavior led to an important modification of the simulation algorithm, as described by Guilkey et al. [15]. When these same data had been interpolated to the computational grid and visualized using volume rendering, these issues were not evident because interpolation had smoothed the nonuniformities.

4.5 Summary

Interaction scenarios involving very large, very complex datasets present many interesting and difficult challenges, both from an applications science and interactive visualization perspective. This chapter has discussed two approaches to interactive visualization for particle-based simulation datasets: one targeting desktop systems equipped with programmable graphics hardware, and the other targeting moderately sized multicore systems using packet-based ray tracing. Although the algorithms are motivated by the need to visualize data from a particle-based simulation technique called the material point method (MPM) [29, 30], both approaches are applicable to particle data from other simulation methods and other application domains as well.

The details of these algorithms are described, and implementations are evaluated using MPM data from simulations of structural mechanics problems. The GPU-based approach performs competitively with interactive ray tracing systems that require tightly coupled supercomputing platforms and offers the same capabilities that aid the data analysis, feature detection, and code development tasks investigators perform. Moreover, this system runs on hardware that is a fraction of the cost, which makes effective particle visualization more accessible.

Efficient ray tracing methods for multilevel grids, including ray packets, frustum based traversal, and frustum culling, provides a highly interactive approach for use with multicore desktop systems. The sphere-center method exploits the properties of particle-based simulation data to improve interactive performance and reduce storage requirements. As highly parallel multicore platforms become more prevalent, the price-performance ratio of interactive visualization systems leveraging such CPU-based methods will only improve.

The approaches to visualization of particle datasets presented in this chapter bring powerful data analysis and code development tools to the investigator's desktop, enabling interaction with millions of particles across the entire simulation. Moreover, because an investigator can interact with the whole dataset, a clear understanding of the state of each particle, as well as its relationship to the full computational domain, can be achieved. As particle-based simulation techniques continue to advance, the combination of interactive visualization and so-called "human-in-the-loop" problem solving environments may provide opportunities for additional insights through computational steering. The algorithms described above advance the current state-of-the-art by bringing interactive visualization of large, time-varying particle datasets to current and upcoming desktop computer systems.

References

1. S.G. Bardenhagen, J.U. Brackbill, and D. Sulsky. The material-point method for granular mechanics. Computer Methods in Applied Mechanical Engineering, 187:529–541, 2000.
2. D. Bartz, M. Meissner, and T. Huttner. Extending graphics hardware for occlusion queries in OpenGL. In Proceedings of the 1998 Workshop on Graphics Hardware, 97–104, 1998.
3. J. Bigler, J. Guilkey, C. Gribble, S. Parker, and C. Hansen. A case study: Visualizing material point method data. In Proceedings of the Eurographics/IEEE Symposium on Visualization, 299–306, May 2006.
4. J. Bittner, M. Wimmer, H. Piringer, and W. Purgathofer. Coherent hierarchical culling: Hardware occlusion queries made useful. Computer Graphics Forum (Proceedings of Eurographics 2004), 23(3):615–624, September 2004.
5. R. Bruckschen, F. Kuester, B. Hamann, and K. I.Joy. Real-time out-of-core visualization of particle traces. In Proceedings of 2001 IEEE Symposium on Parallel and Large-Data Visualization and Graphics, 45-50, 2001.
6. A. Brydon, S. Bardenhagen, E. Miller, and G. Seidler. Simulation of the densification of real open-celled foam microstructures. Journal of the Mechanics and Physics of Solids, 53:2638–2660, 2006.
7. H. Clark. Hierarchical geometric models for visible surface algorithms. Communications of the ACM, 19(10):547–554, 1976.
8. D.E. DeMarle, C.Gribble, and S.Parker. Memory-savvy distributed interactive ray tracing. In Eurographics Symposium on Parallel Graphics and Visualization, 93–100, 2004.
9. K. Dmitriev, V. Havran, and H.-P. Seidel. Faster ray tracing with SIMD shft culling. Technical Report MPI-I-2004-4-006, Max-Planck Institut für Informatik, 2004.
10. D. Ellsworth, B. Green, and P. Moran. Interactive terascale particle visualization. In IEEE Visualization 2004, 353-360, October 2004.
11. C.P. Gribble, C. Brownlee, and S.G. Parker. Practical global illumination for interactive particle visualization. Computers and Graphics, 2007. Submitted for publication.
12. C.P. Gribble, T. Ize, A. Kensler, I. Wald, and S.G. Parker. A coherent grid traversal approach to visualizing particle-based simulation data. IEEE Transactions on Visualization and Computer Graphics, 13(4):758–768, 2007.
13. C.P. Gribble and S.G. Parker. Enhancing interactive particle visualization with advanced shading models. In ACM Siggraph Third Symposium on Applied Perception in Graphics and Visualization, 111-118, July 2006.
14. C.P. Gribble, A.J. Stephens, J.E. Guilkey, and S.G. Parker. Visualizing particle based simulation data on the desktop. In British HCI 2006 Workshop on Combining Visualization and Interaction to Facilitate Scientific Exploration and Discovery, 1–8, September 2006.
15. J.E. Guilkey, J.A. Hoying, and J.A. Weiss. Computational modeling of multicellular constructs with the material point method. Journal of Biomechanics, 39(11):2074–2086, August 2006.

16. S. Gumhold. Splatting illuminated ellipsoids with depth correction. In Proceedings of 8th International Fall Workshop on Vi-sion, Modelling and Visualization 2003, 245–252, November 2003.
17. A. Herout and P. Zemcik. Animated particle rendering in DSP and FPGA. In 20th Spring Conference on Computer Graphics, 220–225, 2004.
18. T. Ize, I. Wald, C. Robertson, and S.G. Parker. An evaluation of parallel grid construction for ray tracing dynamic scenes. In Proceedings of the 2006 IEEE Symposium on Interactive Ray Tracing, 47–55, 2006.
19. D. Kirk and J. Arvo. Improved ray tagging for voxel-based ray tracing. In Graphics Gems II, 264–266. Academic Press, San Francisco, Calif., 1991. Interactive Particle Visualization 17
20. P. Kondratieva, J. Krüger, and R. Westerman. The application of GPU particle tracing to diffusion tensor field visualization. In IEEE Visualization 2005, 73–78, October 2005.
21. M. Krogh, J. Painter, and C. Hansen. Parallel sphere rendering. Parallel Computing, 23(7):961–974, 1997.
22. M. Levoy. Display of surfaces from volume data. IEEE Computer Graphics and Applications, 8(3):29–37, 1988.
23. K. Liang, P. Monger, and H. Couchman. Interactive parallel visulization of large particle datasets. In Eurographics Symposium on Parallel Graphics and Visualization, 111–118, 2004.
24. W. E. Lorensen and H. E. Cline. Marching cubes: A high reso-lution 3d surface construction algorithm. In International Con-ference on Computer Graphics and Interactive Techniques, 163–169, 1987.
25. S. Parker, W. Martin, P.-P. J. Sloan, P. Shirley, B. Smits, and C. Hansen. Interactive ray tracing. In Symposium on Interactive 3D Graphics, 119–126, 1999.
26. S. Parker, M. Parker, Y. Livnat, P.-P. Sloan, C. Hansen, and P. Shirley. Interactive ray tracing for volume visualization. IEEE Transactions on Visualization and Computer Graphics, 5(3):238–250, 1999.
27. G. Reina and T. Ertl. Hardware-accelerated glyphs for mono- and dipoles in molecular dynamics visualization. In Proceedings of the Joint Eurographics/IEEE TCVG Symposium on Visualization, 177–182, 2005.
28. A. Reshetov, A. Soupikov, and J. Hurley. Multi-level ray tracing algorithm. ACM Transactions on Graphics, 24(3):1176–1185, July 2005.
29. D. Sulsky, S. Zhou, and H. L. Schreyer. A particle method for history dependent materials. Computer Methods in Applied Mechanical Engineering, 118:179–196, 1994.
30. D. Sulsky, S. Zhou, and H. L. Schreyer. Application of a particle-in-cell method to solid mechanics. Computer Physics Communications, 87:236–252, 1995.
31. M. Tarini, P. Cignoni, and C. Montani. Ambient occlusion and edge cueing to enhance real time molecular visualization. IEEE Transactions on Visualization and Computer Graphics, 6(12):1237–1244, 2006.
32. E. R. Tufte. The Visual Display of Quantitative Information. Graphics Press, Cheshire, Connecticut, 2001.
33. S. Ullman. The Interpretation of Visual Motion. MIT Press, Cambridge, Mass., 1979.
34. I. Wald, C. Benthin, M. Wagner, and P. Slusallek. Interactive rendering with coherent ray tracing. Computer Graphics Forum, 20(3):153–164, September 2001.
35. I. Wald, S. Boulos, and P. Shirley. Ray tracing deformable scenes using dynamic bounding volume hierarchies. ACM Transactions on Graphics, 26(1):6,January 2007.
36. I. Wald, T. Ize, A. Kensler, A. Knoll, and S. G. Parker. Ray tracing animated scenes using coherent grid traversal. ACM Transactions on Graphics, 25(3):485–493, July 2006. (Proceedings of Siggraph'06).
37. L.R. Wanger, J.A. Ferwerda, and D.P. Greenberg. Perceiving spatial relationships in computer-generated images. IEEE Computer Graphics and Applications, 12(3):44–58, 1992.
38. K. Yin and I. Davidson. Further applications of a particle visualization framework. In Advanced in Knowledge Discover and Data Mining: 8th Pacific-Asia Conference, PAKDD 2004, 704–710, May 2004.

39. P. Zemcik, A. Herout, L. Crha, O. Fucik, and P. Tupec. Particle rendering engine in DSP and FPGA. In 11th International Conference and Workshop on the Engineering of Computer-based Systems (ECBS'04), 361, 2004.
40. P. Zemcik, P. Tisnovsky, and A. Herout. Particle rendering pipeline. In 19th Spring Conference on Computer Graphics, 165–170, 2003.

Chapter 5
Visual Parameters and Transfer Functions

Christof Rezk-Salama

Abstract Assignment of visual parameters is one of the most frequently applied operations in visualization systems. In practical applications, however, this assignment becomes a significant burden for the user due to its vast complexity. This chapter reviews state-of-the-art strategies for the assignment of visual parameters in scientific visualization systems. We introduce the transfer function as a mapping from abstract data values to visual properties. We clarify the terms pre- and post-classification and show the significance of multi-dimensional transfer functions. The chapter covers both image-driven and data-driven techniques for automatic transfer function design as well as general concepts for building intuitive user interfaces.

Keywords Scientific visualization, Visual parameters, Transfer function design, Usability.

5.1 Introduction

The purpose of scientific visualization is to generate meaningful images. Those images should depict certain properties of an underlying abstract data field in a way that is intuitively understandable for the user. As a consequence all visualization techniques require a type of mapping between abstract data values and a corresponding visual representation. One of the most frequently applied operations in this context is the direct assignment of visual attributes to data values. A simple example is the linear mapping of a scalar temperature or density sample to the hue value of a color in HSV space.

From the theoretical point of view, such a mapping is an arbitrary one in general, in the sense that there is no *correct* or *incorrect* mapping, as well as there is no correct or incorrect way a density or temperature value should *look like*. One might want to choose warm and cool colors to represent high and low temperatures, but this is simply a matter of choice for the domain scientist, probably based on existing conventions, and to a great extent on his own personal taste. The usefulness of the mapping, however, is determined by the way it helps the user finding the correct interpretation of the data.

E. Zudilova-Seinstra et al. (eds.) *Trends in Interactive Visualization*,
doi:10.1007/978-1-84800-269-2_5 © Springer-Verlag London Limited 2009

In complex visualization systems, finding appropriate settings that yield a desired visual appearance is often a tedious process of manual parameter tweaking. There are two different types of approaches to tackle such problems. Many researchers have developed algorithms to automate the assignment procedure. Other scientists work on concepts to facilitate the interactive process by making it more intuitive, controllable and goal-directed. Both the automatic approaches and the design of easy-to-use interfaces are still topics of active research. This chapter gives a survey on strategies for assignment of visual properties in scientific visualization.

5.2 Visual Parameters

We have already mentioned *color* as the most prominent visual attribute. Appropriate strategies for the generation of color maps for different purposes have been investigated by various researchers [4, 30, 42]. Color, however, is not the only visual attribute that is important.

A student who tries to visualize his first vector field will most likely start with a program which draws tiny arrows on the screen. This is a typical example for what is called a *vector glyph*. The length and direction of the arrow shows the magnitude and orientation of the vector field at a given point. We then draw differently colored arrows and use the color to encode another variable from the data set, say, local pressure. We can as well vary the thickness of the arrows to display additional variables.

As we see, *shape* is another important visual property. For more sophisticated vector and tensor glyphs, a variety of shapes can be generated using parametric functions such as the super-quadrics (Fig. 5.1, left) proposed by Kindlmann et al. [13].

Almost all rendering techniques in computer graphics separate the shape of an object from its appearance. The shape is specified by a geometric description, usually by a set of polygons. The appearance of an object is defined by textures, material properties and shading algorithms. Figure 5.1 (right) shows an isosurface extracted from the 3D computed tomography (CT) of the Veiled Chameleon [2]. The shape is defined by carefully selecting an appropriate iso-value. The appearance of the object is used to visualize data properties beyond the isosurface. The magnitude of the gradient vector at every point on the isosurface is encoded as the shininess of the Phong illumination term. Surface areas which have a high gradient due to the bone being close to the skin will appear more shiny. Likewise, surface areas with low gradient magnitude will reflect light more diffusely. This is an unusual example of data attributes being mapped to material properties.

Isosurface display is considered an *indirect* volume rendering technique. For *direct* volume rendering, a 3D scalar field is interpreted as a participating medium which simultaneously emits and absorbs light. The scalar variable is mapped to an *emission* and an *absorption* coefficient which is used to calculate light transport in

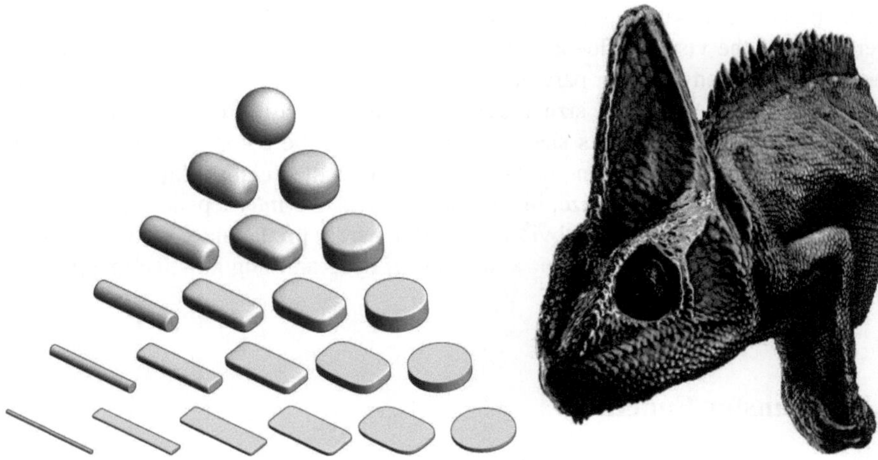

Fig. 5.1 Left: Superquadrics can be used to generate a variety of different shapes, such as spheres, discs and rods. Image courtesy of Gordon Kindlmann [13] © 2004 IEEE. Right: Isosurface rendering of the veiled chameleon computed tomography from the UTCT data archive [2]. The shininess of the surface encodes the gradient magnitude

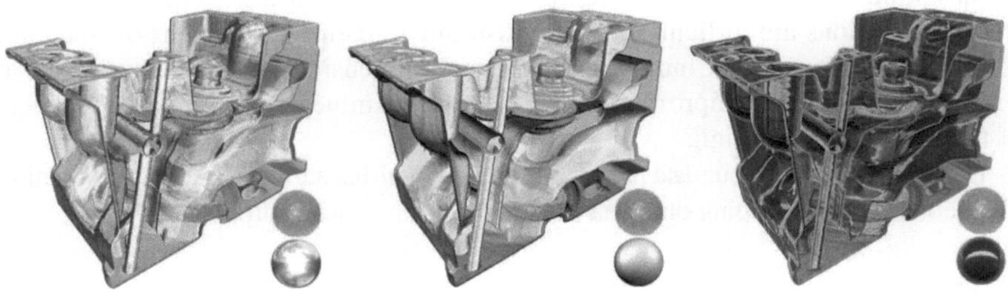

Fig. 5.2 Visualization of an engine block with different style transfer functions for illustrative rendering. Images courtesy of Stefan Bruckner [5] © 2007 Eurographics Association

a participating medium. While the emission coefficient is usually specified as an RGB color value representing the wavelength of the emitted light, the absorption coefficient is given as an achromatic opacity value. Bruckner and Gröller expand the transfer function to transfer more complex visual style for illustrative visualization, as illustrated in Fig.5.2.

As we see, there are numerous visual properties, including shape, color, transparency and material properties, which can be used to encode information from the underlying abstract data field. We have the freedom and flexibility to choose whatever visual attribute we believe is appropriate to depict a certain property of the underlying data set.

Nevertheless, in complex visualization systems, changing the mapping of one parameter may have considerably large influence on the final image. There may be other parameters which seem to have no effect on the visual result at all. Remarkably, the visual influence of a single parameter often strongly depends on the settings chosen for other parameters. Imagine a simple glyph, such as the arrow mentioned above, where the size and the color represent different data variables. If the glyph vanishes due to its size approaching zero, the color variable cannot be observed anymore. While in this simple example the relationship between the parameters is easy to recognize, in complex systems the interdependency of visual parameters is usually not that obvious and often hardly predictable. We will address this problem in Sect. 5.4.2. For now, let us start by examining how the mapping of visual parameters is achieved.

5.3 Transfer Function

A function which maps abstract data values to visual parameters is called a transfer function, regardless of whether it is specified explicitly as an analytic function or discretized as a lookup table. One of the most prominent examples of a transfer function in scientific visualization is the assignment of optical properties for direct volume rendering. However, we point out that the general principles are the same for any kind of mapping of abstract data to optical properties. In practice, useful transfer functions are difficult to accomplish due to their high degrees of freedom. This is especially true for multivariate and multidimensional data. Before we have a look at techniques to improve usability, we will examine the mathematical aspects of transfer function design.

Let D be the range of our data field and V be a set of visual attributes. A transfer function T is defined as the mapping of a data sample $d \in D$ to a visual attribute $v \in D$

$$\mathrm{T} : D \rightarrow V \tag{5.1}$$

In many scientific terminologies, this mapping step is called *classification*, because it categorizes data samples into different *classes*, represented by distinct visual attributes. While the above definition is fairly simple, things get more intricate if we look at the discretization of continuous data fields.

5.3.1 Mapping of Discrete Signals

To understand the sampling process, let us consider a 1D scalar field $s(x) \in \mathbf{IR}$ with $x \in \mathbf{IR}$. According to the Nyquist theorem, a continuous signal s can be fully reconstructed from a set of discrete sampling points s_i,

$$s_i = s(x_i) \text{ with } \quad x_i = i \cdot \Delta x; \qquad i \in \mathbf{IN} \tag{5.2}$$

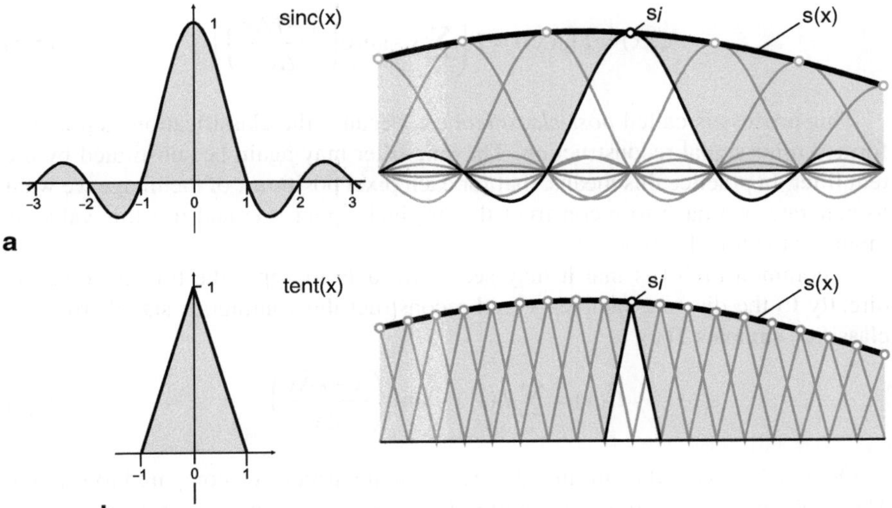

Fig. 5.3 Reconstruction filters for discrete 1D signals. The ideal sinc filter (top row) cannot be used in practice due to its infinite extent. The tent filter (bottom row) approximates the signal by piecewise linear segments, which linearly interpolate between adjacent sample positions

if the original signal s is band-limited with a limiting frequency F and the sampling step size Δx obeys

$$\Delta x < \frac{1}{2F} \tag{5.3}$$

In order to process continuous signals in our computer, we must discretize them according to this sampling theorem. In theory, we can then reconstruct the continuous signal $s(x)$ *without loss* by convolving the samples with a sinc filter (see Fig.5.3, top row):

$$s(x) = \sum_k s_k \cdot \mathrm{sinc}\left(\frac{x - \Delta x}{\Delta x}\right) \quad \text{with} \quad \mathrm{sinc}(x) = \frac{\sin(\pi x)}{\pi x} \tag{5.4}$$

Due to its infinite extent the sinc filter, however, is never used for reconstruction in practice. We usually set the step size x much smaller than required in Eq. 5.3 and replace the sinc by a tent filter for linear interpolation (Fig. 5.3, bottom row). It is important to note, that interpolation within a data grid means reconstructing the original *continuous* signal from its discrete samples. In most cases, however, this reconstruction is performed *lazily*, which means that signal values are reconstructed only on demand, e.g. values required to calculate the color of a pixel in the final image.

Now, in order to generate visual attributes C, the transfer function T must be applied to the scalar signal. For a given position x, we reconstruct the scalar signal $s(x)$ and apply the transfer function afterwards:

$$C(x) = T(s(x)) = T\left(\sum_k s_k \cdot \operatorname{sinc}\left(\frac{x - k\Delta x}{\Delta x}\right)\right) \tag{5.5}$$

This process is called *post-classification*, because the classification step is performed *after* signal reconstruction. The sinc filter may again be substituted by the tent filter. In practice this means, that for each pixel position x of the image we want to generate, we have to reconstruct the original signal $s(x)$ and use this value as input for the transfer function.

A common pitfall is that it may seem adequate to apply the transfer function directly to the discrete samples s_i and reconstruct the continuous signal from the classified samples $T(s_i)$:

$$\bar{C}(x) = \sum_k T(s_k) \cdot \operatorname{sinc}\left(\frac{x - k\Delta x}{\Delta x}\right) \tag{5.6}$$

Obviously, this will result in a different visual attribute $\bar{C}$ compared to Eq. 5.5. The application of the transfer function *before* signal reconstruction is called *pre-classification*. The question, whether pre- or post-classification is the correct way to apply a transfer function is easily answered by looking at resulting images. Figure 5.4 compares images obtained by pre- and post-classification. The left part of the figure shows an unstructured 2D grid with data values mapped to a HSV color scale. With pre-classification the image contains interpolation artifacts. The structure of the underlying grid is clearly visible, which should not be the case if reconstruction is done correctly. The right part shows a transparently rendered volume data set of the inner ear. The pre-classification image shows strong visual artifacts which appear rather disturbing to the observer.

How can these strong visual artifacts for pre-classification be explained? To find the answer we must take into account the frequency spectrum of the transfer function itself. While the original signal $s(x)$ might be band-limited with a Nyquist frequency of F, this does not hold true for the modified signal $T(s(x))$. Applying a transfer function changes the frequency spectrum of the signal. As a consequence, the step size Δx must be adapted to the new limit frequency. As can be seen in Eq. 5.6, the modified signal is reconstructed with the original step size, and this

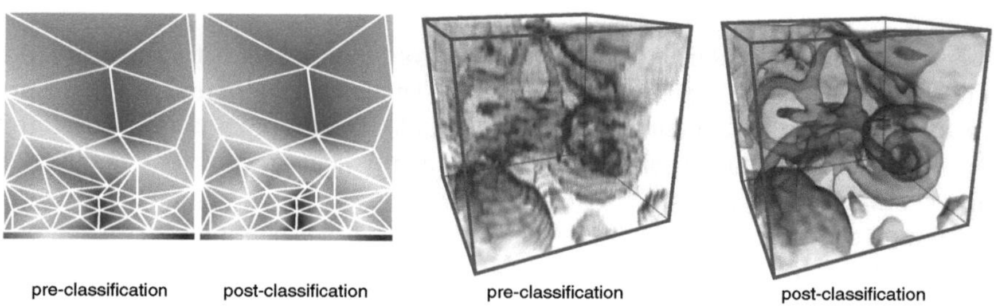

Fig. 5.4 Comparison of pre- and post-classification for the 2D heat distribution (left) and for a high-resolution CT of the inner ear (right) (*See Color Plates*)

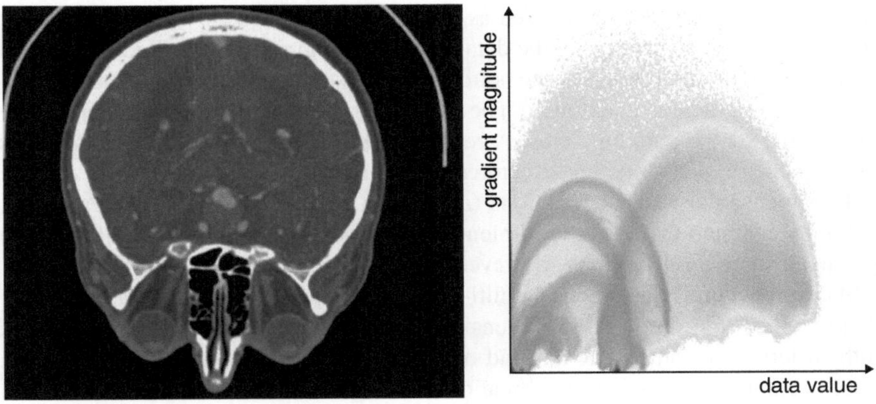

Fig. 5.5 Left: Slice image of a CT angiography of the human brain. Right: 2D histogram of data value and gradient magnitude for the same data set (*See Color Plates*)

finally leads to the visual artifacts observed in the result images. The higher the frequencies contained in the transfer function, the stronger these artifacts will become. With post-classification the original signal is reconstructed at the pixel resolution before transfer function assignment. It can be reconstructed even at sub-pixel accuracy if required for anti-aliasing purposes Fig.5.5.

As we see, a good piece of advice in general is to perform interpolation only in the data domain, not in the target domain of visual properties. This statement will become obvious, if we consider that both spaces may have different dimensions. For scientific data, the data domain is a spacial domain, with well-known spatial relationships between samples. In contrast, linear interpolation of color values depends, of course, on the color space. In other cases, such as the tensor glyphs shown in Fig.5.1, interpolation is hard or even impossible to perform in the target domain.

5.3.2 Multidimensional Transfer Functions

For multivariate data sets, a variety of different variables are given for each grid point. In weather simulation data sets, for example, those variables comprise velocities, temperature, pressure mixing ratios for cloud water, snow and ice and many others. To account for such data, n-dimensional transfer functions may be used, which take an input vector of data values $\mathrm{s} = (s_0, s_1, \ldots, s_n)^T$ to generate visual attributes:

$$C(x) = T(\mathrm{s}(x)) \tag{5.7}$$

Kniss et al. [16] show that even for scalar data, multi-dimensional transfer functions can be used if additional variables are computed from the scalar field, such as the gradient magnitude or the magnitude of the second-order derivative. Other variables, such as local curvature, can be used as well. The most frequently used 2D transfer function domain is spanned by the data value and its gradient magnitude, as shown in Fig.5.3B. The sharp peeks at the bottom of the histogram are homogenous materials with low gradient magnitude. The transitions between different materials are represented by the parabolic arcs. A respective bi-dimensional transfer function is thus capable of differentiating structures based on homogeneity.

Bi-dimensional transfer functions ($n = 1$) can be realized as 2D lookup tables. For transfer functions of higher dimensionality lookup tables will usually require too much memory. They can, however, be implemented as analytic functions or defined procedurally as a set of multi-dimensional primitives, such as Gaussians [17] or blobs [6]. While multi-dimensional transfer functions are more expensive both in terms of computational load and memory requirements, the benefit of a more accurate and flexible classification outweighs the drawbacks in most cases. For non-expert users, however, even one-dimensional transfer functions often are difficult to set up. In the following sections we are going to review strategies for automatic, or at least semi-automatic generation of transfer functions.

5.4 Usability

The purpose of a visualization system is to support the user in finding answers to very specific questions about the individual data set. A good visualization system should be intuitively useable by the domain scientist. Ideally, it should be easy to understand without detailed knowledge of the system internals, such as the rendering and mapping techniques. Transfer functions are integral parts at the core of each visualization system. Without sophisticated tools and techniques, however, transfer function design, is a tedious and time-consuming task. The reason for this is twofold:

The general representation of a transfer function has a lot of degrees of freedom. Managing the vast *complexity* of the transfer function, makes it difficult to handle in practice. Many design techniques thus aim at reducing the complexity of the transfer function by eliminating redundant low-level parameters. The first step in most approaches is some type of dimensionality reduction technique.

The second and more important problem with transfer function design is the lack of an appropriate mental model. According to the seminal work by Donald Norman [24], the process of human computer interaction can be coarsely divided into the user's *intension* to do something, the resulting *action* and the control over the *execution* of this action. The critical point for the user is to find an appropriate *action* to achieve his original *intension*. As an example, a physician who utilizes a volume rendering system to display his computed tomography data, would like to render the soft tissue transparently in order to examine the underlying structures. In most volume rendering systems, however, finding the appropriate action which leads to the desired result is a trial-and-error process. According to Norman's terminology the lack of an appropriate mental model of the user interfaces leads to a *gulf of execution.*

5.4.1 The Automation Problem

Many researchers have developed techniques to build an intelligent system, which determines an appropriate transfer function automatically, or at least comes up with an initial suggestion, which can be further edited and modified by the user. The usefulness of a transfer function, however, strongly depends on the underlying question the user wants to answer. Hence, the minority of automation techniques works fully autonomously and very few techniques automatically consider domain knowledge in the design process. Existing automatic and semi-automatic approaches can be divided into image-driven and data-driven techniques.

5.4.1.1 Image-Driven Techniques

The purpose of a transfer function is to create meaningful images. It thus seems obvious that we have to analyze images generated with different parameter settings in order to derive an optimal set of parameters. Such image-driven techniques mainly differ in the metric they use to evaluate the quality and significance of an image. State-of-the-art methods can be divided into interactive evolution algorithms and inverse design techniques.

Interactive evolution approaches are semi-automatic techniques which provide guidance for the user while he is exploring the parameter space interactively. Successful techniques are closely related to artificial intelligence systems. The most straight-forward technique is thumbnail selection [19]. The system proposes a set of rendered thumbnails images generated with a selection of different parameter settings.

The user selects one or more images that he finds most appropriate. Based on the user's selection, the system proposes a new set of thumbnails generated by a genetic algorithm. In fact, many techniques originally developed as artificial evolutionary art systems for design automation [18, 36, 38] can be adopted to the problem of transfer function design. One of the most general concepts for visual parameters in computer graphics and animation is the *Design Gallery* [22] which tries to build a distinctive set of visually distinguishable images.

Inverse Design techniques search for optimal parameter settings according to an objective quality measure. He et al. [9] have developed a technique for semiautomatic transfer function generation using stochastic search techniques. The search algorithm is controlled by evaluating an objective metric such as entropy, edge energy or histogram variance. Possible strategies for searching the huge parameter space most efficiently comprise genetic algorithms [8, 11], hill-climbing and simulated annealing [15]. Inverse design strategies can as well be based on concepts from artificial intelligence including sensor-actuator networks [25] and goal-based rendering [12].

While image-based techniques work quite well in practice, a general drawback is their unavoidable dependency on image-related parameters such as viewing position and pixel resolution. As a possible solution to the problem of view-dependence, image-driven techniques can be supplemented by approaches for automatic viewpoint selection. Many methods developed for image-based rendering [1, 10, 23, 32, 37] can be adopted for this purpose.

5.4.1.2 Data-Driven Techniques

Data-driven techniques analyze the volume data itself instead of the generated images. The process of transfer function design is thus decoupled from the influence of the image-related parameters mentioned in the previous section. Early approaches, such as the ones proposed by Fang et al. [7] and Sato et al. [34], derive optical properties by applying 3D image processing operations directly to the data. Bajaj et al. [3] propose a data-driven technique which generates a transfer function by evaluating statistical information about surface area and gradient magnitude of all the isosurfaces contained in the data.

The most prominent data-driven technique is a semi-automatic approach presented by Kindlmann and Durkin [14] in 1998. Their approach is capable of determining material boundaries within a given data set by evaluating statistical information about the first and second order directional derivatives. A material boundary is assumed if a maximum of the first-order derivative coincides with a zero-crossing of the second order derivative. The authors derive a *position function* $p(s)$, which describes the average distance of a data sample with scalar value s from an assumed boundary in the data set. Kindlmann and Durkin's approach turns out to be successful in determining material boundaries in unknown data sets.

Up to this point, all automatic or semi-automatic approaches to transfer function design tried to build a transfer function from scratch for every new data set. What was missing up until now are strategies for reusing existing transfer functions for similar data sets. The position function approach was utilized by Rezk-Salama et al. [28] to reliably adapt a pre-defined reference transfer function to individual data by non-linear distortion of the parameter axis. As displayed in Fig. 5.6, this work demonstrates that matching the position function of different data sets leads to more reliable results than matching the histograms only. Later, this adaptation approach was expanded to 2D transfer functions by Vega et al. [40].

Most existing applications provide a graphical user interface for the assignment of visual parameters. The histogram is one of the main means of orientation provided

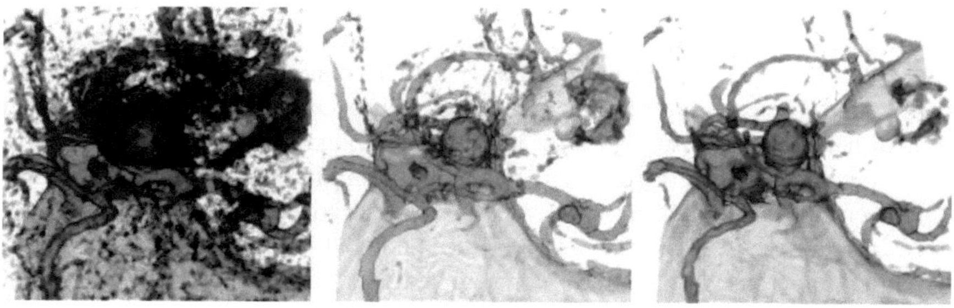

Fig. 5.6 Results of non-linear adaptation of predefined transfer function templates. Left: No adjustment. Middle: Adjustment based on histogram matching. Right: Adjustment based on matching the position functions

by the user interface for transfer function design. Among the very few approaches which incorporate domain knowledge into the classification process, is the work of Lundström et al. [20]. They introduce local histograms, which utilize a priori knowledge about spatial relationships to automatically differentiate between different tissue types. The classification is performed by a bi-dimensional transfer function, where the certainty of a voxel belonging to a specified tissue type is used as second parameter. The same group also introduced the α- histogram [21]. The basic idea is to split the data domain into disjoint subsets, then calculate separate histograms for these subsets. The values of the local histograms are raised to the power of $\alpha > 1$. The global histogram is finally calculated by summing the contribution from the modified local histograms. The authors show that the applied local exponentiation results in an amplification of homogenous regions of the data in the histogram.

5.4.2 *The Interface Problem*

The most actively followed path in transfer function design in recent years is the design of intelligent user interfaces. On the one hand, automatic approaches are often not flexible enough. They are difficult to adapt to a wide range of data sets. On the other hand, they are often not specific enough to account for the precise task the user wants to perform. In medical environments, fully automatic approaches are often not widely accepted due to the considerable amount of uncertainty. If automatic approaches fail to deliver satisfying results, non-expert users are often left alone. In this section we review general concepts developed in recent years to create goal-directed user interfaces.

5.4.2.1 Geometric Primitives

In order to reduce the effort of editing single entries in a color table, many user interfaces compose the color mapping from multiple independent geometric primitives. In practice, such component may comprise polylines, ramps and trapezoids [16], paraboloids [41] or other primitive shapes. Compared to simple color tables, where every entry can be edited separately, composition of primitives provide effective solutions for reducing the complexity of transfer functions. Most visualization algorithms, however, employ a given color table directly. Hence, primitive shapes must be converted to a tabular representation before usage. Few publications give details about the compositing of overlapping primitives. For opacity, the maximum is usually chosen and the color values are mixed according to their opacity ratio [29].

In practice, single functions are better suited for 1D classification of continuous simulation data from natural science and engineering. Such data often do not contain sharp structures which need to be separated from each other. For tomographic scans, a composition based on geometric primitives is advantageous, allowing the individual treatment of different spatial structure. Anatomical structures are often represented by geometric primitives in the transfer function domain. For multi-dimensional transfer function domains, single functions are rarely used, regardless of the scientific area, due to difficulties in providing appropriate user interfaces for editing. Roettger et al. [33] have developed a concept called spatialized transfer functions which generates primitives automatically by segmenting the 2D transfer function domain into disjoint regions. The user may then specify optical properties selectively for those regions.

5.4.2.2 Domains of Interaction

Kniss et al. have introduced the concept of dual domain interaction [16] for volume visualization. During their investigation on multi-dimensional transfer functions, the authors notice that finding appropriate settings is time-consuming if the user is not provided with some guidance. To this end they developed a dual user interface, which allows the user to probe the scalar field with a virtual pen in 3D (see Fig.5.7). The user can then decide to place a geometric primitive in the transfer function window to mark the data in 3D. With this approach it is easy for the user to point at interesting structures in the image domain, and to assign visual attributes in the parameter domain. The effect of changing visual parameters is immediately visible in the 3D image Fig.5.8.

The concept of interacting in different domains is not completely new. In the field of information visualization such an interaction is called *brushing*. Brushing represents an intuitive way for the user to visually select subsets of the data samples without the necessity to specify numerical ranges. Likewise, Pradhan et al. [26]

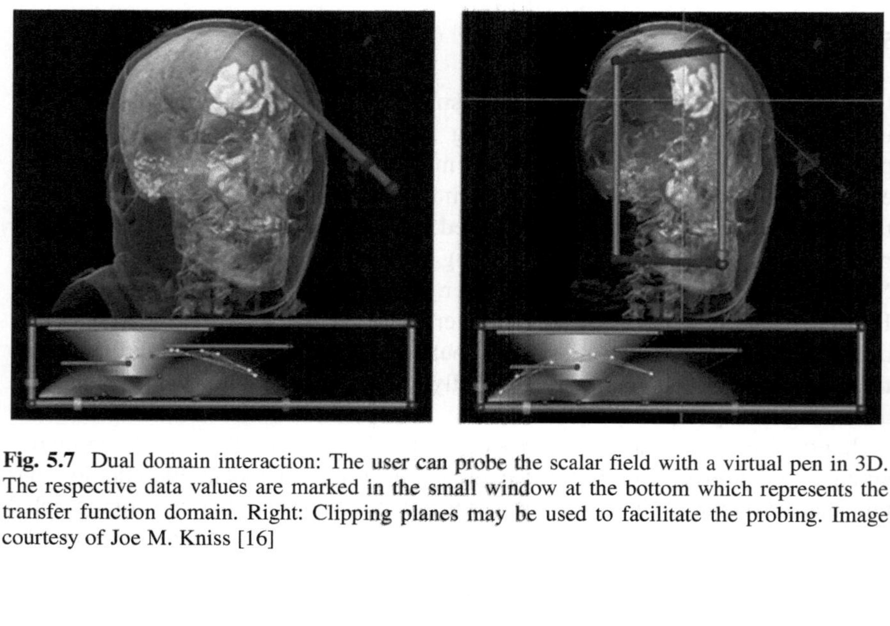

Fig. 5.7 Dual domain interaction: The user can probe the scalar field with a virtual pen in 3D. The respective data values are marked in the small window at the bottom which represents the transfer function domain. Right: Clipping planes may be used to facilitate the probing. Image courtesy of Joe M. Kniss [16]

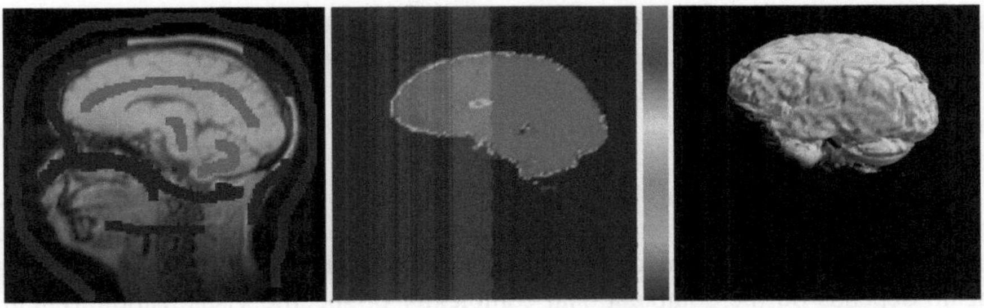

Fig. 5.8 Neural network approach to multi-dimensional transfer function design. The user marks regions of interest by roughly setting the boundaries. The system automatically derives a multidimensional classification using a neural network. Image courtesy of Fan-Yin Tzeng [39] © 2003 IEEE

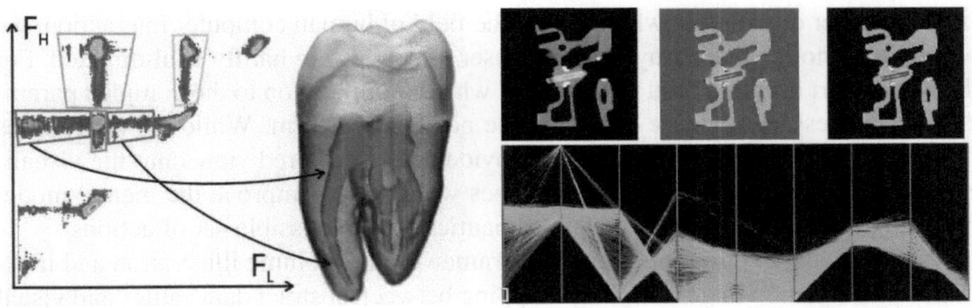

Fig. 5.9 Left: Example of an LH-histogram for the tooth data set. Image courtesy of Sereda et al. [35] © 2006 IEEE. Right: Parallel coordinates are used to select voxels with a given signature in a multi-dimensional parameter space. Image courtesy of Pradhan et al. [26] (*See Color Plates*)

demonstrate a visualization system which utilizes concepts borrowed from information visualization. They use parallel coordinates (see Fig. 5.9, left) to select regions in a multi-dimensional transfer function domain called the signature space including intensity, gradient magnitude and higher-order statistical moments.

Inspired by the work of Kindlmann and Durkin [14], Sereda et al. [35] introduce a new domain for interaction called the LH-histogram, or low-high-histogram (Fig.5.9, left). The LH-histogram can be viewed as a 2D map of the different spatial structures contained in the volume data set. Each spatial data sample with a gradient magnitude larger than a given threshold is considered a boundary sample. For each boundary sample a short pathline is traced along the gradient field in order to determine the low and the high intensity values used as 2D index into the map. While such an approach is highly efficient for expert users, it is not really intuitive to use for non-experts.

Tzeng et al. [39] suggest an intelligent visualization system with interaction in the spacial domain only, while hiding the transfer function domain completely. In their system the user marks regions of interest by roughly painting the boundaries on a few slice images. While he is painting, the marked regions are used to train an artificial neural network for multi-dimensional classification. Figure 5.8 shows an example slice image with the painted markings, the classified slice image and the final rendered 3D image from an MRI data set. Del Rio et al. have adapted this approach to specify transfer functions in an augmented reality environment for medical applications [31].

In practice, the applicability of such intelligent systems, which calculate the mapping during interaction strongly depends on the visual feedback provided to the user, the speed at which the effect of a user action is displayed in the image. This again depends on the computational complexity of specific visualization system, the size of the data set and the available memory bandwidth.

5.4.2.3 Semantic Models

If we consider domain knowledge from the field of human computer interaction, we will quickly notice that many graphical user interfaces are hardly goal-directed. For the non-expert user it is hard to figure out which modification to the complex parameters are necessary to cause the action he needs to perform. While the approaches described in the previous section still provide a data-centered view onto the visualization problem, there are novel approaches which try to improve the mental model of the application by providing clear semantics for the possible set of actions.

Rautek et al. [27] present a semantic framework for volume illustration and illustrative visualization in general. The mapping between abstract data values and visual properties is specified by rules based on fuzzy logic operations. The authors concept of semantic layers replaces the traditional transfer function setup and allows the user to specify the mapping from attributes to visual styles in natural language. Their system supports semantics like, "*if density is high and curvature is close to zero, then color coding is red.*" While fuzzy logic and the use of natural language represent a significant improvement, this approach does not immediately resolve the gulf of execution. If the non-expert user does not know, how to describe the structures of interest in terms of density or curvature values, the semantics will not help.

To this end Rezk-Salama et al. [29] suggest a general concept for tailoring the user interface to the visualization task. They target very specific visualization scenarios, such as routine examinations in medical practice. In their approach a visualization expert works together with a domain scientist to create a semantic model for the visualization task. With such a model, the user may directly select structures by name, such as *brain tissue* or *blood vessels* and directly adjust their visual parameters, such as color, contrast, or visibility. In order to create such a semantic model, a visualization task is performed several times on a collection of data sets which are considered representative for a specific examination scenario. Throughout this training phase the system collects the parameter vectors and analyzes them using principal component analysis.

Figure 5.10 shows a classified CT angiography data set with the separate anatomical structures brain, soft tissue and blood vessels. For this system, the authors have conducted a small user study. Physicians were presented with a semantic user

Fig. 5.10 Examples of a semantic model for CT angiography, with the anatomical structures, brain, soft tissue bone and vasculature (*See Color Plates*)

inter face without labels for the interaction elements (sliders and buttons). In most cases the physicians were capable of determining the semantics of actions triggered by the elements.

5.5 Conclusion

Transfer functions are at the heart of every visualization system. Transfer function design techniques are still an area of active research and will probably be for a very long time. The direction of research, however, has slightly changed in recent years. Transfer function design clearly shifts towards more user-centered applications, such as intelligent exploratory interfaces. Systems which hide most of the details of the underlying rendering algorithms are more intuitive to use by non-experts. Up until now only very few publications exist about including semantics into visualization systems. Especially for clinical systems, transfer function design must become faster and easier to achieve to become widely accepted. Semantic approaches have a high potential to achieve these goals.

We have only just begun to incorporate knowledge from other fields into our visualization systems to make them more flexible, more intuitive and more usable. In the near future we may expect important impulses from related fields such as computer animation and human computer interaction as well as influences from areas such as cognitive sciences.

Fully automatic transfer function design techniques are not widely accepted due to uncertainty in the data sets, which still needs to be resolved by the user. Scientific data sets contain much more information than can be displayed in a static image. The user must be provided with means of exploration, and this must include the transfer function as well. Fully automatic techniques are only applicable if structures contained in the underlying data are well-understood, which might be the case for simulation data, but usually not for measured data. For medical scans, and especially for pathologic cases, fully automatic techniques often fail. Nevertheless, they may be useful for generating good starting points for exploratory analysis.

Users of visualization systems increasingly ask for systems that are more usable and more efficient in practice. Companies which produce commercial systems have noticed that usability aspects are growing more important as a vital factor to secure market shares. In consequence, implementing general concepts to improve the usability and the acceptance of visualization systems is a research area of steadily growing importance.

At research facilities, multidimensional transfer functions have already become standard today. In commercial systems they are not yet widely used. The main reason for this might be that many commercial products are based on special-purpose hardware, which up until now only supports 1D lookup tables. The benefit of at least bi-dimensional classification, however, is incontrovertible, so we expect this will change in the near future.

5.6 Summary

There is a huge variety of different visual attributes that can be used to represent abstract data, including shape, color, transparency, and more complex optical properties such as emission and absorption coefficients, or specular reflectivity. Care must be taken to correctly reconstruct the original signal from discrete samples. We have seen that the sequence of reconstruction and classification operations makes a significant difference to the image quality and we have explained these differences with respect to sampling theory.

Transfer functions can be stored as lookup tables or applied procedurally as an explicit function. Multi-dimensional transfer functions are powerful and flexible, yet quite expensive with respect to computational cost and memory consumption. This chapter has given an overview of state-of-the-art techniques for automatic and semi-automatic techniques for parameter assignment. Image-driven techniques are based on interactive evolution or inverse design approaches. Data-driven algorithms analyze the data to generate meaningful parameter assignments. State-of-the art user interfaces for transfer function design are based on important strategies such as dual domain interaction and semantic models.

References

1. Arbel, T., Ferrie, F.: Viewpoint Selection by Navigation Through Entropy Maps. In: Proceedings of IEEE International Conference on Computer Vision (ICCV) (1999).
2. University of Texas at Austin, UTCT data archive, DIGIMORPH and CTLab. http://utct.tacc.utexas.edu. last visited July 2007.
3. Bajaj, C., Pascucci, V., Schikore, D.: The Contour Spectrum. In: Proceedings of IEEE Visualization (1997).
4. Bergmann, L., Rogowitz, B., Treinish, L.: A Rule-Based Tool for Assisting Colormap Selection. In: Proceedings of IEEE Visualization (1995).
5. Bruckner, M.E.: Gröller, (2007). Style Transfer Functions for Illustrative Volume Rendering. Computer Graphics Forum (accepted for publication) 26 (3)(2007).
6. Engel, K., Hadwiger, M., Kniss, J., Rezk-Salama, C., Weiskopf, D.: Real-Time Volume Graphics. AK Peters, Ltd. (2006).

7. Fang, S., Biddlecome, T., Tuceryan, M.: Image-Based Transfer Function Design for Data Exploration in Volume Visualization. In: Proceedings of IEEE Visualization (1998).
8. Goldberg, D.: Genetic Algorithms in Search, Optimization, and Machine Learning. Addison-Wesley (1989).
9. He, T., Hong, L., Kaufman, A., Pfister, H.: Generation of Transfer Functions with Stochastic Search Techniques. In: Proceedings of IEEE Visualization (1996).
10. Hlavac, V., Leonardis, A., Werner, T.: Automatic Selection of Reference Views for Image-Based Scene Reprentations. In: Proceedings of European Conference on Computer Vision (ECCV) (1996).
11. Holland, J.: Adaption in Natural and Artifical Systems. University of Michigan Press (1995).
12. Kawai, J., Painter, J., Cohen, M.: Rapidoptimization – Goal-Based Rendering. In: Proceedings in SIGGRAPH (1993).
13. Kindlmann, G.: Superquadric tensor glyphs. In: Proceedings of IEEE TVCG/EG Symposium on Visualization, pp. 147–154 (2004).
14. Kindlmann, G., Durkin, J.: Semi-Automatic Generation of Transfer Functions for Direct Volume Rendering. In: IEEE Symposium on Volume Visualization (1998).
15. Kirkpatrick, S., Gerlatt, C., Vecchi, M.: Optimization by Simulated Annealing. Science 220 (1993).
16. Kniss, J., Kindlmann, G., Hansen, C.: Interactive Volume Rendering using Multi-Dimensional Transfer Functions and Direct Manipulation Widgets. In: Proceedings of IEEE Visualization, pp. 255–262 (2001).
17. Kniss, J., Premoze, S., Ikits, M., Lefohn, A., Hansen, C., Praun, E.: Gaussian Transfer Functions for Multi-Field Volume Visualization. In: Proceedings of IEEE Visualization (2003).
18. Kochhar, S.: A Prototype System for Design Automation via the Browsing Paradigm. In: Proceedings of Graphics Interface (1990).
19. König, A., Gröller, E.: Mastering Transfer Function Specification by Using VolumePro Technology. In: Proceedings of Spring Conference on Computer Graphics (2001).
20. Lundström, C., Ljung, P., Ynnerman, A.: Extending and Simplifying Transfer Function Design in Medical Volume Rendering Using Local Histograms. In: Proceedings of IEEE/EuroGraphics Symposium on Visualization, p. 263270 (2005).
21. Lundström, C., Ynnerman, A., Ljung, P., Persson, A., Knutsson, H.: The a-Histogram: Using Spatial Coherence to Enhance Histograms and Transfer Function Design. In: Proceedings of Eurographics/IEEE-VGTC Symposium on Visualization (2006).
22. Marks, J., Andalman, B., Beardsley, P., Pfister, H.: Design Galleries: A General Approach for Setting Parameters for Computer Graphics and Animation. In: Proceedings in SIGGRAPH (1997).
23. Muehler, K., Neugebauer, M., Tietjen, C., Preim, B.: Viewport Selection for Intervention Planning. In: Proceedings of IEEE/Eurographics Symposium on Visualization (EuroVis), pp. 267–274 (2007).
24. Norman, D.: The Psychology of Everyday Things. Basic Books (2002).
25. van de Panne, M., Fiume, E.: Sensor-Actuator Networks. In: Proceedings in SIGGRAPH (1993).
26. Pradhan, K., Bartz, D., Mueller, K.: SignatureSpace: A Multidimensional, Exploratory Approach for the Analysis of Volume Data. Tech. rep., Department of Computer Science (WSI), University of Tuebingen, (2005).
27. Rautek, P., Bruckner, S., Grller, M.E.: Semantic Layers for Illustrative Volume Rendering. In: Proceedings of IEEE Visualization (2007).
28. Rezk-Salama, C., Hastreiter, P., Scherer, J., G.Greiner: Automatic Adjustment of Transfer Functions for 3D Volume Visualization. In: Proceedings of Vision, Modeling and Visualization (VMV) (2000).
29. Rezk-Salama, C., Keller, M., Kohlmann, P.: High-Level User Interfaces for Transfer Function Design with Semantics. In: Proceedings of IEEE Visualization (2006).

30. Rheingans, P.: Task-Based Color Scale Design. In: Proceedings of SPIE Applied Image and Pattern Recognition (1999).
31. del Rio, A., Fischer, J., Köbele, M., Bartz, D., Sträser, W.: Augmented Reality Interaction for Semiautomatic Volume Classification. In: Proceedings of Eurographics Workshop on Virtual Environments (EGVE) (2005).
32. Roberts, D., Marshall, A.: Viewpoint Selection for Complete Surface Coverage of Three-Dimensional Objects. In: Proceedings of British Machine Vision Conference (1998).
33. Roettger, S., Bauer, M., Stamminger, M.: Spatialized Transfer Functions. In: Proceedings of IEEE/EuroGraphics Symp. on Visualization, pp. 271–278 (2005).
34. Sato, Y., Westin, C.F., Bhalerao, A.: Tissue Classification Based On 3D Local Intensity Structures for Volume Rendering. IEEE Transactions on Visualization and Computer Graphics 6 (2000).
35. Sereda, P., Vilanova Bartoli, A., Serlie, I., Gerritsen, F.A.: Visualization of Boundaries in Volumetric Data Sets Using LH Histograms. Transactions on Visualization and Computer Graphics 12(2), 208–218 (2006).
36. Sims, K.: Artificial Evolution in Computer Graphics. In: Proceedings in SIGGRAPH (1991).
37. Takeushi, V., Ohnishi, N.: Active Vision Systems Based on Information Theory. Systems and Computers in Japan 29(11) (1998).
38. Todd, S., Latham, W.: Evolutionary Art and Computer Graphics. Academic Press (1992).
39. Tzeng, F.Y., Lum, E., Ma, K.L.: A Novel Interface for Higher-Dimensional Classification of Volume Data. In: Proceedings of IEEE Visualization, pp. 505–512 (2003).
40. Vega Higuera, F., Sauber, N., Tomandl, B., Nimsky, C., Greiner, G., Hastreiter, P.: Automatic Adjustment of Bidimensional Transfer Functions for Direct Volume Visualization of Intracranial Aneurysms. In: Medical Imaging 2004, vol. 5367, pp. 275–284. SPIE (2004).
41. Vega Higuera, F., Sauber, N., Tomandl, B., Nimsky, C., Greiner, G., Hastreiter, P.: Automatic Adjustment of Bidimensional Transfer Functions for Direct Volume Visualization of Intracranial Aneurysms. In: Proceedings of SPIE Medical Imaging (2004).
42. Ware, C.: Color Sequences for Univariate Maps: Theory, Experiments, and Principles. IEEE Computer Graphics and Applications 8 (1998).

Part III
Design and Evaluation

Chapter 6
Gaining Greater Insight Through Interactive Visualization: A Human Factors Perspective

Roy S. Kalawsky

Abstract This chapter is concerned with one of today's top scientific visualization research problems which relates to how humans respond to visualization. Visuali zation researchers rarely study or apply what is known about the visual system when designing visualization techniques. However, in order to produce an effective visualization, human perception must be understood otherwise the end result may not lead to a visualization that can be interpreted by the users. If this is to be avoided, the designer of a visualization system must make intelligent use of human perceptual and cognitive capability. Unfortunately, it is impossible to cover all the human perception issues of visualization in just one chapter. Therefore, in the main the use of interactive visualization has been focussed upon thus allowing the user to gain greater insight into their data. To help illustrate this, an example is given where the difficult technical challenges of creating an interactive 3D visualization system on a PDA device have been overcome by applying knowledge of human perception and cognition. This chapter hopes to 'demystify' this essential component of the visualization practitioner's toolbox by providing helpful insights and guidance on the human factors of interactive visualization. Finally, at the end of the chapter a series of useful tables of data showing the human factors that need to be considered in any interactive visualization system are given.

Keywords: Interactive visualization, Exploration, Distributed visualization, Remote visualization systems, Human Factors guidelines

6.1 Introduction

Visualization is becoming an increasingly important discipline because of its ability to facilitate the analysis and subsequent understanding of phenomena and emergent behaviour present in complex systems and higher dimensional data sets. Relatively recent developments in visualization hardware have made it possible to manipulate large and complex data sets in real-time to perform information retrieval, data mining and online analytical processing. These data sets arise from scientific experimentation, mathematical modelling, simulation, information analysis, geomet

E. Zudilova-Seinstra et al. (eds.) *Trends in Interactive Visualization*,
doi:10.1007/978-1-84800-269-2_6

rical modeling or through sensing of the real world (e.g. computer topography or magnetic resonance imaging for medical visualization).

Visualization also plays a key role in communicating information in wide and diverse fields. For example, it is feasible to create abstract or simplified visualizations that make communication of a complex phenomenon or situation much easier to understand by lay persons and non specialists. Examples include the daily weather map shown on television – the weather map is a very simplified view of the complex climatic and meteorological situation as predicted for that day or week. However, this visualization is a massive over simplification of the complex isotherms, isobars and general meteorological behaviour present over a given geographical region.

An important point to note is that visualizations are primarily designed for human interpretation. However, one of the top scientific visualization research problems of today has been stated as 'Research on the human visual system is vast, yet visualization researchers rarely study or apply what is known about the visual system when designing visualization techniques'. [27]. It is clearly important to understand how the human responds to visualization and this implies the designer of visualization systems must make intelligent use of human perceptual and cognitive capability. Therefore, in order to produce an effective visualization, human perception must be understood otherwise the end result may not lead to a visualization that can be interpreted by the user. Not surprisingly, it is common to come across examples where the visualization being produced actually masks important features of the visualization or makes the task of comprehending the information impossible.

A glance through any text book on human perception will highlight this as a complex field which should not be underestimated. Moreover, in order to produce a good visualization the designer has to balance a number of visualization parameters which are not equally weighted in terms of their impact on human performance and cognition.

The visualization system designer needs to be aware of standard conventions in visual representations. These should not be ignored. To illustrate this there are a number of standard conventions that employ specific colours (e.g. red, amber and green denotes danger, caution and safe respectively). If the use of these colours is reversed or jumbled up, then the user has to redefine their mental model of what a particular colour means. We have all probably seen examples of highly cluttered displays employing an ad-hoc selection of colours or unusual information coding representations where the meaning or any understanding of the visualization is virtually impossible. Shifts from normal visual convention should be avoided because of the confusion it can cause. Whilst many information coding conventions are written down in standards, the designer is more often than not free to choose his/her own definitions and conventions. However, unless proper care is taken the designer could easily code the visualization in a way that makes the user's task very difficult or impossible because there are conflicts in perceptual processing.

When visualizations involve other sensory modalities (auditory, tactile and proprioceptive) then there is an even greater room for error where the designer could make mistakes in information presentation – unless they understand the impact of certain combinations of sensory cues. Visualizations need not represent a static viewpoint. They can represent a moving observer within a scene (e.g.

a computer game or flight simulation). This kind of interactive visualization raises the question of sensory conflict if the observer remains stationary and the visualization represents a moving environment. In this situation, the observer's perceptual system has to deal with complex sensory conflicts. Whilst the observer's body is referenced to a stationary position in terms of vestibulo-ocular reflex [22] their visual system is being stimulated by a moving scene. In many cases the observer will feel as though he/she is moving through the visualization whilst in some instances they can feel nauseated because their body proprioceptive cues mismatch the visual cues. Such cues can be extremely powerful leading to illusions of self motion (vection) or a symptom known as simulator sickness [45, 49] rendering the system unusable. Interactive visualization raises important human factors issues in its own right. These need to be considered alongside the visual representation. However, where human perception and cognition is taken into account then highly usable visualizations can result, conveying exactly the level of understanding the user requires.

"He who loves practice without theory is like the sailor who boards ship without a rudder and compass and never knows where he may cast."

quote from Leonardo da Vinci

6.2 Visualization as a Tool for Gaining Insight

Visualization is the generic term used when creating images, illustrations or time based sequences (movies) to communicate information or provide greater insight and understanding of a complex phenomenon or process. Visualization is a general term used to cover scientific, financial, product, information, and medical fields to name but a few. More precise definitions exist. For example, 'information visualization is defined as the process of creating mental models of visually represented data' [51]. The information being communicated need not be real; it can also represent abstract information. Producing a visual representation to communicate a message is very common.

This chapter is concerned with a specific aspect of visualization and that is the use of interactive visualization thus allowing the user gain greater insight [53] into the inner nature of a particular system or behaviour. This insight comes from human powers of deduction and perception and from mapping observations against mental models of what is being seen. In this context insight has nothing to do with a computer's ability to process data. Instead it is associated with human cognition and the powers of reasoning within a logical framework.

Pictures are an excellent example of representational methods to communicate meaning. They exploit the human's ability to extract powerful understanding from a wide range of pictorial forms that would be largely invisible to a computer based system. The human mind is quite remarkable in extracting great understanding from apparently incomprehensible data if it is presented in a certain way. Alternatively, the human mind can be completely fooled by certain representations that are ambiguous. There are many examples of perceptual tricks or illusions [50] that can interfere with a true understanding of a particular information space.

An interesting collection of perceptual illusions can be found from (http://www.michaelbach.de/ot/). Arguably, the most disturbing illusions are those that occur when the sensory cues are in conflict due to technology constraints or induced by careless interface design.

Care should be taken with 'how real' the visualization should appear. When rendering abstract, non-realistic forms (such as iso-surfaces or stream tubes) photo-realism may not be an appropriate or helpful technique because this can impose extremely high processing overheads on the system or make image understanding more difficult. Nevertheless, image quality can be a major factor for some users. Although high quality photo-realistic images look good and help sell the concept to some people they do not necessarily add value to the scientific process. The key is to use an appropriate visualization technique with the right degree of image quality for the task in hand.

6.3 Achieving Insight and Understanding Through Exploration

An important requirement of a visualization system is to facilitate intelligent human perception and cognitive abilities in order to extract deeper knowledge and understanding from the resulting visualization. Instead of simply looking at visualization in a passive sense, it is essential in some situations to allow the user to interact with the data. This may mean manipulating one or more parameters at a time whilst observing the result, or simply moving the viewpoint around to reveal structure in the data that may be otherwise masked. One question often raised in interactive visualization systems is whether or not to use 2D, 3D or 4D representations (the fourth dimension being time). For complex scientific visualization, 3D and 4D is generally preferred because user tasks involve continuous variables (for example, temperature, current, voltage, angular velocity, rate of change, pressure) volumes and iso-surfaces. However, for information visualization, user tasks involve more categorical parameters and the discovery of data trends, correlations and clusters. Some information visualization users will try and analyse tens or even hundreds of variables in a particular investigation. The strategy they adopt is the exploration of a few relationships at a time through dynamic queries with 2D graphical representations (bar charts, line graphs, and scatter grams).

At a general level visualization users are following the steps defined by Johnson [27]:

- Observation and description of a phenomenon or group of phenomena.
- Formulation of a hypothesis to explain the phenomena.
- Use of the hypothesis to predict the existence of other phenomena or to predict quantitatively the results of new observations.
- Evaluation of the proposed methods and quantification of the effectiveness of their techniques.

6.4 Nature of Interactive Visualization

Visualisation has become a necessity for understanding the large data sets generated by scientific instruments such as telescopes, microscopes, particle accelerators and imaging machines. The complexity and sheer quantity of data generated by today's scientific instruments can make it virtually impossible to process information completely numerically. Whilst automated data analysis and reduction can play a role in this process, understanding is only currently achieved by human interpretation of the visualisation. A researcher's perception and understanding of a given visualisation can greatly increase by interactive exploration. The well known adage 'The purpose of computing is insight, not numbers' [20] supports this. Additionally, insight has been defined [23] as:

- The capacity to discern the true nature of a situation;
- The act or outcome of grasping the inward or hidden nature of things or of perceiving in an intuitive manner.

However, to what degree a visualization system achieves this purpose has been recently questioned [43]. North also attempts to list some important characteristics of insight as reproduced in Table 6.1

Scientific visualization techniques can translate large and/or multidimensional numerical data sets into images. Even though the human visual sensory channel is the widest information pipeline to the brain, (and our minds are particularly effective at abstraction, approximation and simplification) we can still find it difficult to analyse very large static images. To assist scientific interpretation, visualization data can be graphically rendered in terms of re-colouring, segmentation, sliced, or iso-surfaced, to name but a few. Unfortunately, these techniques can increase the complexity of the scientific visualization task if an inappropriate visualization technique is used. Properly prepared images enable the user to more readily correlate information, determine cause and effect relationships, and hopefully gain insight

Table 6.1 Important characteristics of insight (reproduced from text in [43])

Characteristic	Comment
Complex.	Insight is complex, involving all or large amounts of the given data in a synergistic way, not simply individual data values.
Deep	Insight builds up over time, accumulating and building on itself to create depth. Insight often generates further questions and, hence, further insight.
Qualitative	Insight is not exact, can be uncertain and subjective, and can have multiple levels of resolution.
Unexpected	Insight is often unpredictable, serendipitous, and creative.
Relevant	Insight is deeply embedded in the data domain, connecting the data to existing domain knowledge and giving it relevant meaning. It goes beyond dry data analysis, to relevant domain impact.

into the underlying principles embodied in the data. The scientific exploration processes can also be assisted by providing new insight through interaction with the visual representation. This interaction can be regarded as two categories:

1. Exploration of the 2D, 3D or 4D visualization
2. Exploration of the visualization parameters.

Interactively exploring a 3D visualization can greatly improve a researchers understanding of the 3D relationships in an environment through motion parallax [54] and improved spatial awareness. Also, parameter exploration allows the researcher to explore a 'what if ?' scenario and helps reveal otherwise occluded data and relationships. Visualization techniques readily transform complex data into 3D graphical representations that are easier for people to interpret than interpreting tables of raw data. Even though viewing a static image allows a certain amount of information to be extracted, it is also necessary for the user to either change the viewpoint or manipulate a given parameter and observe the effect. This level of interaction can allow the user to gain insight and understanding about behaviour of the underlying data sets.

Over the past decade human-computer interfaces have evolved considerably to the point where user interaction is predominantly a visuomanual activity as opposed to text input. Quite often with very complicated 3D renderings the information of interest is hidden until the scientist interacts with (r moves) their viewpoint with respect to the image. The value of user interaction with a scientific visualization should not be underestimated. In many visualization applications there is a focus on the structure of scientific visual representations. Whilst there is generally less concern with the visual properties of the visual image itself (i.e. brightness, contrast, choice of colours etc.) greater interest is targeted towards the spatial interpretation given to a vast range of visualization techniques. For example, iso-surfacing is a fairly standard technique used in scientific visualization which creates 3D surfaces or contours of constant scalar values. These contours provide discrimination between different threshold levels in the dataset and are intended to aid the scientists' perception. Even though this is a widely used technique the contour patterns of an image are well known to provide fairly incomplete evidence for the rich spatial environment that we perceive [18].

There are many other techniques that require a fair degree of understanding from the scientist in order to extract salient features and structures of interest. It should be noted that scale and structure cannot always be determined solely from the visual information alone. However, from a human perception perspective we are able to update our knowledge through observation of the consequences of interaction. It has been noted that the addition of motion in an image is important to help resolve some of the ambiguities of 3D surface segregation, which would otherwise present erroneous depth-order relations [26]. Stereo imagery has also been used to effect by some investigators but is not without problems. For example, certain scientific data, (such as medical imagery with moderate to high levels of transparency) cannot be viewed effectively by static stereo viewing alone. Interestingly, when stereo is used with user induced motion there is a noticeable enhancement and efficiency in the visual perception of the image [48].

Time-varying flow lines (streamlines) consist of particle traces that have been computed for a vector field. When a large number of streamlines are displayed simultaneously it is of great benefit to be able to rotate the image to resolve the perceptual ambiguities that exist in a static representation. These are a few of the many examples that highlight the importance of user interaction (and in particular user induced motion) as a means of aiding scientific visualization. Consequently, this means that user interaction should not be underestimated in terms of its contribution to perception of information and it should therefore be considered a key part of any visualization system. Accordingly, 'knowing-by-seeing' is an active, constructive process utilising considerable non-visual information, some of which is based on prior knowledge. Whilst one would not argue that visualization is unimportant [10] the author suggests that interactive visualization is very important when it comes to image interpretation. Absence of certain visual cues (when viewing a static image) could mask important results. In essence, factors which affect user interaction can also have an impact on the perceptual efficiency of image interpretation. Providing interactive visualization (as opposed to viewing a pre-rendered animation or sequence of images) has consi derable impact on the visualization system architecture.

6.5 Visualization System Architecture

The basic visualization pipeline is known as the Haber-McNabb visualization pipeline [19] and is shown in Fig. 6.1. It has been slightly modified by the author to aid explanation. Each stage performs a specific action as follows:

Data Analysis: Raw data is prepared for visualization by applying a range of techniques such as smoothing filters and interpolation.

Filtering: Appropriate sections of data are selected for visualization to create the data of interest or focus data.

Visualization Mapping: The data selected for visualization is mapped to geometric primitives (e.g., points, lines, surfaces and volumes) and their attributes (e.g., color, position and size).

Rendering: Geometric data is turned into a visual image by the computer graphics system.

The Haber-McNabb visualization pipeline is ideally suited to batch processing operations where the types of processing within the pipeline are known beforehand. However, this representation does not adequately describe the interactive visualization where real-time user interaction can occur at any of the stages. A modified (albeit

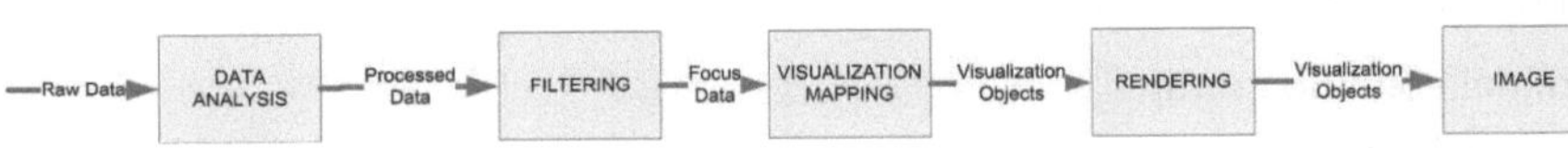

Fig. 6.1 Haber-McNabb visualization pipeline

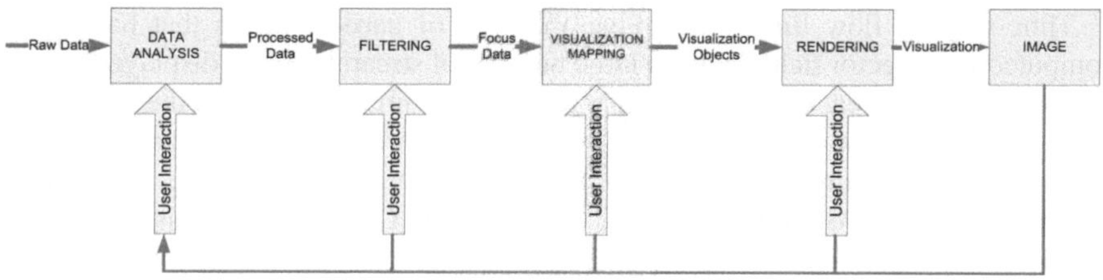

Fig. 6.2 Modified Haber-McNabb visualization pipeline showing interactive visualization

more complicated) visualization pipeline is shown in Fig. 6.2 as an interactive visualization system. It illustrates where user interaction can occur.

User interaction can occur at any of the stages shown – the nature of the user interface is dependant on the form of data being manipulated. Examples of user interaction can include the use of pull down menus, re-positioning sliders, selection of different pre-processing or filtering operations. Other more sophisticated user interactions involve manipulation of the rendering systems such as viewpoint selection and introduction of head position orientation data. These interactions do not normally operate on the incoming data and mainly affect the final stages of the pipeline.

6.6 Interactive Visualization: Giving Control to the User

Interactive visualization provides user control over the visualization pipeline during its execution such that the visualization workflow involves a sequence of steps – simulation parameter specification, computational simulation and results analysis [35]. This is an iterative process involving fine tuning the computational model or stages in the pipeline whilst it is running with the process being repeated until the desired results are obtained, or have reached the point where no further iteration is required. From a human computer interaction perspective, interactive visualization closes the loop between the user and his/her data analysis (or simulation) in a way that allows them to respond to results as they occur by interactively manipulating the input parameters. With sufficient computational resource, interactive visualization can lead to an enhancement in productivity through the reduction in time between optimization of visualization. However, one of the major benefits of interactive visualization is that it facilitates an exploration of 'what if analysis' and a greater understanding of the relationships in the original data.

Today, available computational graphics power has reached the stage where the user can control and interact with the visualization during its execution, or become part of the feedback loop involving:

- initial condition setup
- simulation execution
- results analysis

- change initial conditions
- re-run simulation etc.

It is interesting to note that when changes in parameters and their results become more instantaneous, cause-effect relationships become more evident.

There are several approaches to interactive visualization. One approach is shown in Fig. 6.3 and is based on a manual strategy where the user initiates a request, such as a change in one of the input parameters (for example temperature), and the visualization system responds directly by running the simulation with the parameter change in place. The simulation is a mathematical model of the phenomenon or system under investigation.

The user is an integral part of the feedback loop and has contact with simulation in the sense that he/she can affect the parameter space being searched. The downside is this system must be fully supervised and the display output from the simulations needs to be inspected to check for valid output. A further disadvantage is the detrimental effect of delayed visual feedback on operator behaviour especially if a long compute time is required. Long delays between job submission and results computation can lead to inefficient time spent waiting for the visualization to be computed.

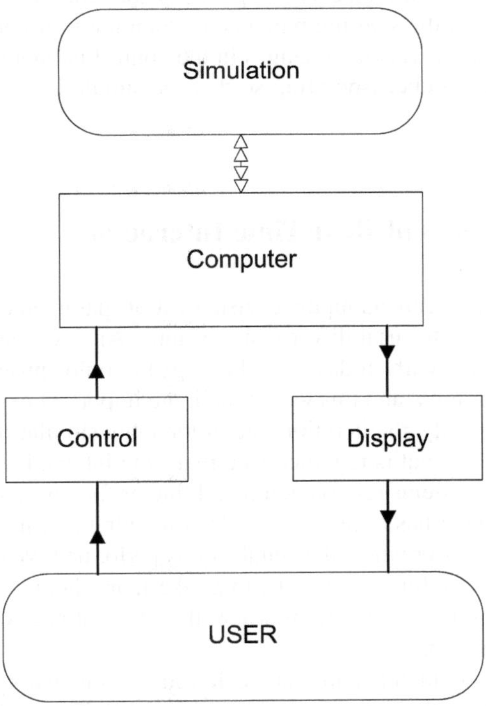

Fig. 6.3 Manual interactive visualization system

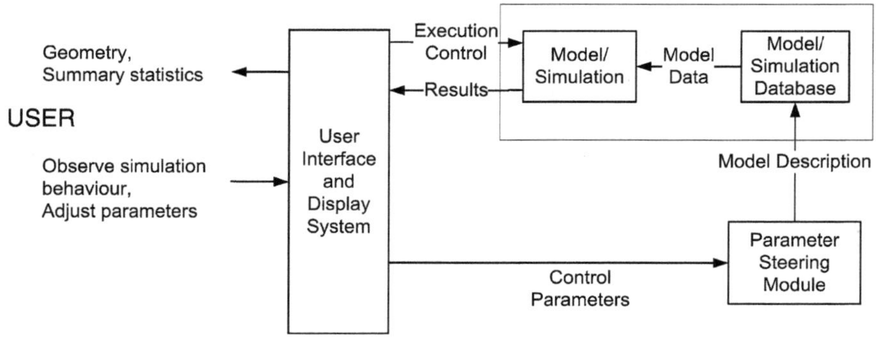

Fig. 6.4 Schematic showing data flow for a simple computational steering system

An alternative approach to interactive visualization is the use of computational steering [36]. Figure 6.4 gives a schematic showing data flow for a simple steering system. The resulting control system is based on running the mathematical model (computer simulation) against a set of predefined parameters set up by the user. The simulation can be initialised with the desired set of input conditions/data. Provided the parameter steering interface is designed so that the simulation periodically checks for changes in the steering parameters, then the user can inject changes as the simulation runs. By tracking changes in the control parameters it is possible to implement a degree of check-pointing so that the simulation can be re-run from a given point.

6.7 Requirements of Real-Time Interaction

The ability to control and manipulate visualization parameters interactively is a major contributor to the usability of the system. An ideal system (though not achievable currently with today's technology) would provide instantaneous response to any user input and this would facilitate important exploratory workflow processes. Unfortunately, the iteration rate of the main simulation loop is unable to get anywhere near to what is regarded as a real-time interactive rate. Most current generation steering systems rely on command line or file based parameter steering. Therefore, the scientist has to build up a file containing a sequence of instructions and parameter ranges over which the simulation is performed. Whilst this approach is reasonably satisfactory for applications that take many hours to execute, a single iteration is not so useful for situations where the scientist needs to manipulate data in an interactive fashion.

An in-depth human factors audit has reviewed the scientist's workflow involved in a number of large scale scientific investigations [30]. This audit captured the key user interaction requirements across a number of scientific applications and clearly indicated that the associated user interaction process is complex and involved. It necessitated a number of stages (or steps) from 'pre' job submission preparation through to the more highly interactive stages of interactive visualization. A key user interaction requirement emerging from the audit was the need to reduce the time delay between user input and the corresponding output from the simulation. Users tend to prefer the visual illusion of smooth motion for interactive rotation and animation.

6.8 Local Versus Distributed Visualization

Depending on the overall visualization system architecture and the type of pre-processing required the interaction time delay can be anything from fractions of a second to several minutes. In extreme cases the process required can take several hours. General advice regarding what constitutes an ideal response time in an interactive system has largely been the same for the past three decades [9, 39] and can be summarized as shown in Table 6.2. For a truly responsive steering system (in usability terms) it is necessary to be able to update visualisation viewpoints at a rate of at least 0.1 s (10 Hz). Unfortunately, it is impractical to expect all parts of the visualization system to be capable of updating at this rate. Indeed, in the case of extremely large scale simulations a single simulation loop may still take many hours to execute. However, this does not imply that all parts of the simulation needs to be tied to this long lead time computation. By separating the visualisation from the simulation loop it is possible to increase the responsiveness of the user's interaction. Depending on the nature of the task, close-coupled interaction with the intermediate data set can be very useful if not essential in understanding whether the simulation

Table 6.2 Effect of response time on user interaction

Response time	Comments
0.1 s	This is 'about' the limit for the user to feel that the system is responding instantaneously to his/her input. Normally no feedback would be necessary since the user is able to see the results of their interaction without any noticeable delay.
1.0 s	This is 'about' the limit for the user's flow of thought to stay uninterrupted. However, the user will often report a sense of loosing contact with his/her data. Typically, user feedback would need to be provided between 0.1–1.0 s.
10 s	This represents the limit for keeping the user's attention focused on the interface. For longer response times users will be easily distracted and will often try and perform other tasks while waiting for the task to finish. Ideally, feedback should be given in the form of a progress indicator. If the response time is unpredictable then the progress indicator becomes even more important. [41]

needs to continue. The exact system configuration has to take account of the capabilities of the resources available to the scientist.

By separating out elements of the visualization pipeline and distributing these across multiple resources it is possible to decrease the computational time of the earlier elements in the pipeline. A large scale visualization application has already been demonstrated [21] that can be distributed geographically over a high performance network. As an example, where the user has extremely limited local computation (and visualization) resources the whole simulation (including the visualization) could be remoted from the user. In addition, in very large scale simulations (up to tera-scale, which are employed to yield the necessary visualization data can be so demanding that a distributed system (harnessing the power of many computing resources) is the only viable solution. However, as soon as a distributed compute-visualization architecture is employed this raises a number of significant user interaction issues.

Whilst Figs. 6.2 and 6.3 depict data connectivity they do not show where critical time delays exist from a user interaction perspective.

In a distributed (remote) visualization system communication, delays or data transfer time can become significant depending on available network bandwidth. It is also important to note that actual network performance could vary according to network load demands at the time the simulation is run. It is important to design the overall system architecture so that the effect of these latencies has minimal impact on the user's interaction. Figure 6.6 shows typical interactive loops within a simple visualization system comprising separate compute and visualization resources. The author introduced an important parameter which refers to overall computational steering latency (CSL). CSL represents the time taken between the user inputting a steering demand and the resulting data display as a consequence of that input. By introducing this term one can clearly distinguish between the overall simulation time, and the considerably shorter time involved in interactively mani pulating the image for a viewpoint change.

One of the motivations for separating the visualization from the main simulation loop is to facilitate interactive exploration of the computed data. However, the iteration rate of the visualization machine then becomes an important factor in the usability of the system. As soon as the visualization is separated from the main simulation loop and the user is allowed to interactively manipulate parameters which affect the final visualization, a number of important user interface requirements need to be considered.

Three interaction loops have been identified where system delays will have an effect.

- Interaction loop 1 has the potential for dominating the CSL because this is concerned with the time it takes for an iteration of the simulation to occur. In certain cases the time delay could exceed several tens of hours.
- Interaction loop 2 assumes that the output from the main simulation loop is a set of data that requires some visualisation technique or filter applied to it in order to extract data of interest. Interaction at this level would involve the user running one or more visualisation techniques to identify features of interest.

- Interaction loop 3 is concerned with making small adjustments to the viewpoint of the rendered scene by the visualisation hardware so that different viewing positions may be displayed, or the data set may be 'flown' through. It is this interaction which demands extremely low latency due to close coupling between the user and the visualisation data.

Interactive flying through a data set ideally requires an update rate of 20 ms although 1 s can be tolerated. When update rates exceed a certain rate an effect known as pilot induced oscillation occurs [40] which makes control and interaction extremely difficult. The user tends to make over compensatory inputs into the system with the effect that the desired viewpoint overshoots the desired point. As soon as this sets in the user gets into a vicious circle and the image being displayed becomes very unstable. This has implications of where to perform the time critical user interactions such as interactive flythrough and exactly how much latency can be tolerated.

Apart from basic user interaction tasks such as resource discovery, job submission, resource management etc., the scientist is also interested in controlling (or steering) their applications by manipulating one or more simulation parameters. Current human-computer interaction theory highlights the need for direct manipulation interfaces rather than 'crude' command line or file based control methods. Ideally, steering would be done interactively whilst observing the result, pre-supposing that the response time of the overall simulation can meet the timing requirements – although this is unlikely for very large scale simulations.

An alternative way of looking at delays is to identify sources of system latency as illustrated in Fig. 6.5. This diagram shows the relative timings between simulation, visualization (comprising filtering, iso-surfacing, etc.) and the rendering of the image (display of a specific viewpoint). In an earlier section the author introduced the term computational steering latency (CSL) which makes it easier to distinguish between rendering time of an interactive image and the time it takes to perform a computational steering.

Figure 6.6 shows there are actually several interactive loops within typical computational steering systems. For example:

- The main simulation loop which generates the data set for visualisation.

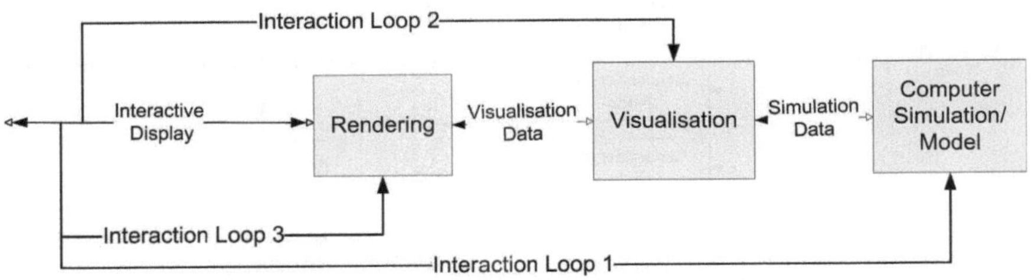

Fig. 6.5 Interactive loops within a simple visualization system

- The visualisation stage whereby the data is filtered to extract the data that needs to be rendered.
- The visualisation rendering stage where the actual visualisation is created.

There is a further source of latency in the system and this is due to communication delays between parts of the distributed system. Figure 6.7 illustrates the order of magnitude of response time between the different stages. It must be noted that the response time of the simulation loop of most large scale scientific applications is almost certainly not going to be real-time (with current technology) since the computation could take several hours. Consequently, if the user requires to manipulate some of the initial conditions then a full re-run of the simulation may be necessary. Filtering the resulting data set to create the dataset for visualization could be achieved in a much shorter timeframe but this obviously depends on the type of pre-processing required. Once a visualization data set has been produced the scientist often wants to explore interactively the resulting visualization to observe areas of interest. This exploration may involve operations such as image translation, rotation or navigation through the 3D data set. At the level of the visualization it is also possible that further pre-processing operations may be required such as 3D

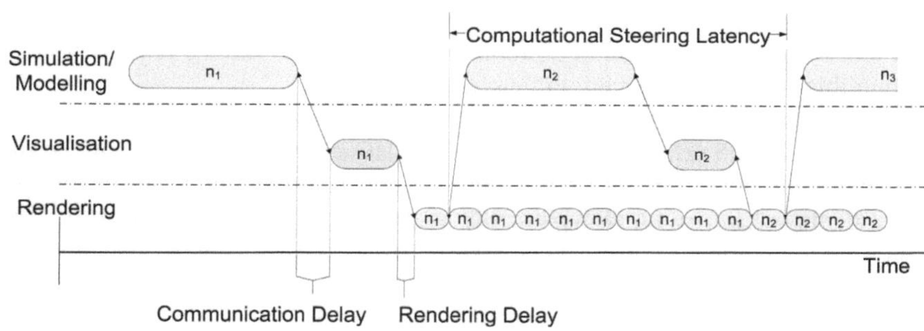

Fig. 6.6 System latencies in a distributed computing – visualisation system

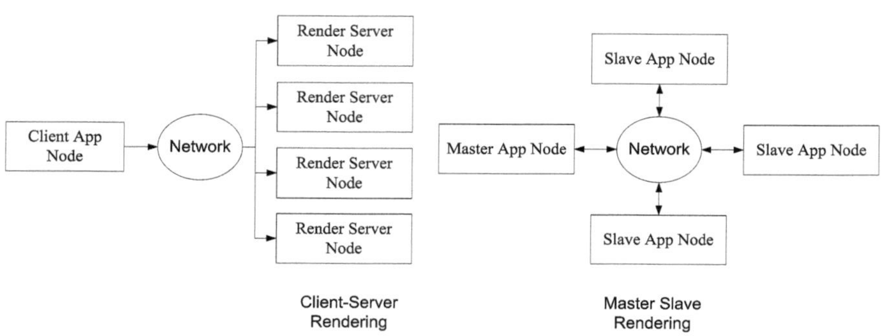

Fig. 6.7 Distributed visualisation rendering (from [52])

iso-surfacing or volumetric renderings. However, these tasks may not require a full re-run of the simulation in order to change the iso-surface thresholds. Consequently, the response time will be significantly less than the simulation time, even to the stage where near real-time interaction becomes possible.

6.9 Implications of System Architectures on Interactive Visualization

The importance of remote visualization was first recognised by [47] who noted the increasing reliance on the visualization of data by the scientific and engineering communities. Interactive scientific visualization requires a consistent, low-latency representation of the visualization and high band-width computation. Latency is a problem when analysing and interacting with large datasets and rendering 3-D structures, especially where the scientist is required to interactively manipulate the steering parameters of the computation. Early approaches to remote visualization relied on a client-server paradigm.

The distributed nature of grid resources and indeterminate network performance can introduce serious human computer interaction issues (As discussed earlier). Various techniques can be used to reduce these time delays by compressing data sent over the network, thus leading to a reduction in network bandwidth. However, this is not always commensurate with a guaranteed decrease in time delay or latency. Given the desirability to support interactive exploration it is considered good practice to separate the visualization rendering stage from the main compute/simulation loop because during an interactive session it will not tie down the visualization system response time to the long execution time of the simulation. If the user does not have local high-end visualization systems it is then feasible to employ a remote visualization or distributed system.

It is a reasonable assumption that any operation on a data stream has the potential to add a delay into the overall system pipeline, or possibly worse, to introduce a degree of distortion into the original dataset. The real question is how to trade off frame rate versus compression loss. Various techniques exist for supporting distributed visualization and specialised hardware has become available in terms of the processing that can be performed within dedicated hardware. This has led to a novel technique of remotely generating a compressed image and transmitting this to a user over a network. However, particular care has to be exercised in the use of data compression for images. There are both lossy and lossless compression techniques. The lossy compression techniques are ideal for low latency situations because of their low network bandwidth overhead requirements, but they should only be used where image compression can be tolerated.

As an alternative to presenting high quality rendered images whilst performing interactive tasks such as navigation and image rotation, it is feasible to render an image which is much simpler or has reduced quality. This means the image is purposely degraded to a point where sufficient visual cues remain and are adequate for the user to navigate around the dataset. As soon as the user interacts less with the visualization and finds the point of interest, the visualization is progressively rendered at a much higher level of fidelity, or with no compression. This technique has the advantage of minimising network bandwidth with increased frame rate during periods of high user interactivity. This visualization technique is known as 'adaptive rendering' and is based on a very similar approach that has already been successfully applied to virtual environments [17] and [55]. In grid based environments, different algorithms will be required to control the degree of adaptivity in order to maintain an adequate level of accuracy in the display during interaction and when viewing the image from a static viewpoint. These and other more sophisticated rendering techniques are able to make a significant contribution to reducing network bandwidth whilst providing an appropriate level of image fidelity during interaction.

6.10 Separation of Visualization from Main Compute Loop: Local Versus Remote Visualization

In a cluster rendering environment there are two general models for data distribution and management [11] – client-server and master-slave, refer to Fig. 6.7. Both client-server and master-slave models must support a form of frame synchronisation to prevent the scene becoming distorted. For example, the client must wait for all servers to finish rendering the scene before issuing the next frame. A master-slave approach may have additional order constraints to ensure correct composition of the rendered images.

The client-server model requires a single instance of the application, which runs on the client, through which all user interaction takes place. This approach can generally be accomplished with little or no alteration to the application, through replacing any graphics libraries used by the application [25]. In a master-slave approach there are multiple instances of the application controlled by a master, through which the user interacts. A master-slave approach generally requires less bandwidth than client-server approaches as only sporadic state changes, such as user interactions must be transmitted to all slaves. However this is generally not a transparent process to the application. The application must be aware of it's location in a cluster, in order to correctly manage a subset of the data domain and all state changes must be synchronised with all instances of the application. Many visualizations demand a cluster aware application from the outset, such as when the application must deal with data-sets larger than local memory. Client-server models face different challenges depending on the graphics mode implemented, retained or immediate. In immediate mode graphics such as OpenGL or DirectX all primitives are transmitted to the servers on every frame. As noted by [52], the distributions of all primitives on every frame in immediate mode graphics make software platforms such as Chromium bound by network bandwidth. A master-slave model is not affected by the graphics mode used as only application state-changes are transmitted between the master and slaves. Most software platforms for distributed rendering, such as Chromium [25], implement both a master-slave and client-server models.

6.11 Visualization Serving

A number of products such as Silicon Graphics VizServer [44] have emerged to meet the needs of remote visualisation. The basic concept is to produce rendered visualisations at geographically remote sites by compressing a rendered image in a remote visualisation system and transmitting the compressed data over a network. The local host runs a lightweight client which decompresses the image and makes this available to the user using fairly modest resources. VizServer currently supports five compression modules. Four of these modules use a lossy compression technique based around Block Truncation Coding (BTC) which compresses a 4 × 4 pixel block into two colours and a 4 × 4 pixel mask. Therefore, the time required to encode an image is governed only by the size of the image. Another compression technique known as 'compressed colour cell' is a basic implementation of BTC giving a compression ratio of 8:1 (16 bit pixel depth) where as an interpolated colour cell technique uses a 4 colour pixel mask and achieves a ratio of 4:1. A loss-less compression method (no details of the underlying compression method are given) but an upper bound of 4:1 ratio is stated.

Figure 6.8 illustrates the basic concept and shows the top level processes in the visualization pipeline (remote – local host). Depending on the compression technique the approach is not ideally suited to users who are connected through low bandwidth networks and require high quality images.

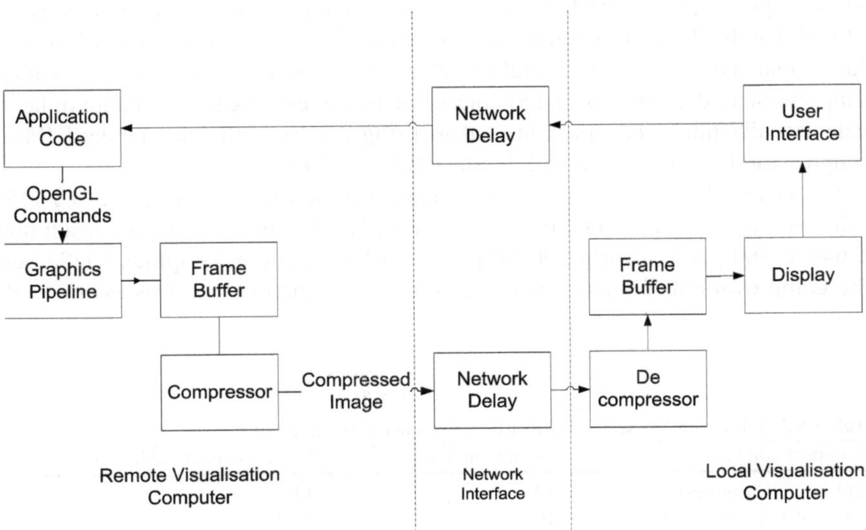

Fig. 6.8 Silicon graphics VizServer schematic

6.12 Performance trade-offs in Server-Client Remote Visualization Systems

There is no doubt that server-client visualisation systems offer scientists access to very powerful visualisation resources. However, despite various claims that the user will obtain relatively fast frame rates for reduced network bandwidth using server-client visualisation systems (compared to simply sending uncompressed visualisation data over the network), this only comes with a performance trade-off in other areas. The user needs to consider a range of inter-related performance issues such as resolution of the image and the compression method being employed.

To use server-client visualisation systems effectively it is important to recognize the inter-dependency of the key performance parameters. Parameters such as desired frame rate, required image size, network bandwidth and compression technique are all inter-related. Unfortunately, it is not possible to achieve high frame rates, low network bandwidth, high image resolution and lossless compression at the same time. The user must trade-off these parameters against the critical visualisation parameters of their application. Also, it is also worth noting that the requirements of a user, such as scene quality, network bandwidth, and frame rate may change with the context of the users activities. [2] developed a system which initial provided a coarse level-of-detail of the entire visualisation to allow the user to select a region of interest. This region was then progressively refined in idle client-cycles.

In order that the scientist's interaction is not impaired a consistent low-latency stream of images must be maintained. This places a high demand on networking resources. [37] noted that modern lossy compression algorithms such as MPEG and JPEG-2000 would provide better image compression, thus reducing demands on network bandwidth and therefore increasing client frame rates. However, Ma concluded that these algorithms would limit client frame rates to the rate at which compression or decompression took place due to the resource scarce nature of large scale visualizations and opted instead to using the less efficient standard JPEG compression in combination with lossless BZIP or LZO compression.

To get an idea of the sort of performance trade-off refer to Table 6.3 [15] which shows observed frame rate and network bandwidth for an image resolution of 640 × 480 pixels over a 100 Mbps network for Silicon Graphics VizServer. The compression techniques (with the exception of the one non lossless method)

Table 6.3 Observed VizServer frame rate versus network bandwidth

Compression technique	Frame rate (Hz)	Network bandwidth (Mbps)
Colour cell compression	12	11.1
Interpolated colour cell	10	18.4
No compression	8	59.0

used by VizServer are regarded as lossy techniques. This means a certain amount of data is lost in the compression/decompression process. The user needs to trade-off network bandwidth, frame rate of rendered images and image compression technique. However, the table does not show that during certain kinds of user interaction, such as roaming around the image, the performance can actually be significantly worse because the whole scene needs to be transmitted over the network rather than by small changes. An example of where this would occur is when the user panned a very wide field of view image from left to right. Consequently, the user needs to identify the parameters that are important to the application.

Some applications will not be able to tolerate any kind of image compression because data would be lost or interpolated. For example, in medical imaging applications the use of any form of compression is generally regarded as unacceptable, meaning that only lossless techniques are acceptable. This creates a serious problem for distributed visualization systems that depend on lossy compression techniques. A great deal of work still needs to be done in developing efficient lossless image compression techniques for grid applications.

For near or real-time response, the time taken for image compression and subsequent decompression can become an important factor. The user should be aware these techniques may have an impact on their data – especially when any technique employs compression technology. Dynamic stereo imagery also represents an interesting challenge for image compression systems since it is important to maintain the correct timing relationship between left and right eye images. Some compression techniques are unable to present truly consistent images between the left and right eye and lead to the introduction of strange visual artifacts in the stereo image. An extreme case would when the right eye image contained significantly more information than the left eye. (This mainly applies to partially overlap stereo viewing systems.) As soon as movement is introduced by the user this can lead to visually perceptible differences between the images, caused by the compression technique.

6.13 Future Enhancements to Improve user Interaction

A more advanced approach to computational steering is one where the user has partial or advanced supervisory control as shown in Fig. 6.9. An additional control feedback loop is placed between the control and display which allows the system to continue to operate without user intervention. A supervisory steering control system allows the scientist to operate at a much higher level of interaction. Instead of changing specific system parameters he/she can set steering objectives or targets for the simulation. In this case the user submits a job and establishes a set of steering objectives or targets. The resulting simulation then proceeds autonomously and is under the control of a special solver which aims to converge on the goals defined by the scientist. Obviously checks and balances need to be put in place to halt a

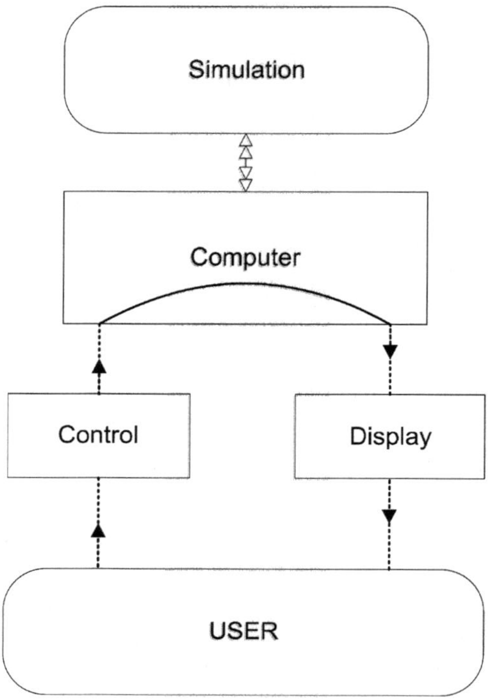

Fig. 6.9 Supervisory steering control

simulation if the desired results are not achievable. With careful design it would be possible to allow conventional steering parameter input as well as high level monitoring and interaction with steering targets. Such a system would still provide intermediate results of the computation to the user who is then free to manipulate the steering parameters as desired.

The design of the steering objective function broker is complex since it has to incorporate a model of the inter-relationships between the individual steering parameters. These relationships will be dependent on the nature of the scientist's application. At a simple level it would be possible to implement a system which iteratively searches between the dynamic ranges of each parameter as specified by the scientist. A more advanced system would embody agent technology to more intelligently control the simulation.

The supervisory steering control system has the potential to save the scientist a great of time by taking over the time consuming aspects of their task. This concept has been used in other disciplines. Other supervisory control systems have been employed in complex human in the loop systems (vehicle navigation, auto pilots etc.) to great effect. It is only a question of time before computational steering benefits from the same technology (Fig. 6.10).

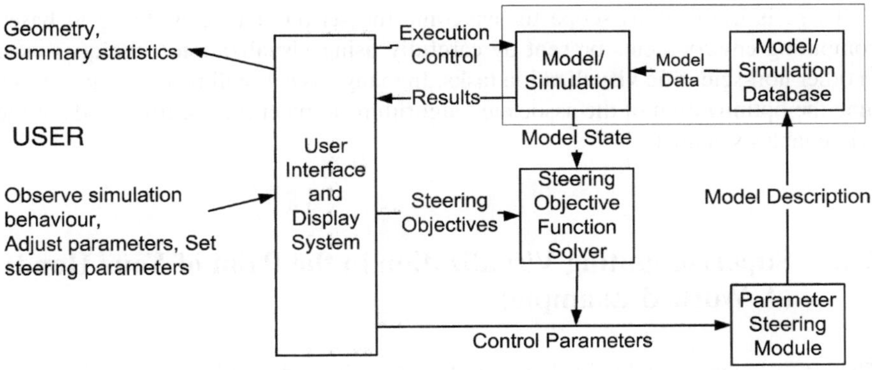

Fig. 6.10 Supervisory steering control system

6.14 Adaptive Rendering (Progressive) Refinement of Image Quality)

It is worth mentioning briefly another development that has the potential to improve user interaction in a visualization system where large data sets are manipulated. Instead of presenting a consistent rendered image during periods of interactivity it is possible to present a much simpler or degraded image which is adequate for the navigation stages of interactivity. However, as soon as the user finds the point of interest and interacts less with the image, the visualisation is then rendered at a much higher level of fidelity or even with no compression. This type of visualisation system is known as an adaptive rendering system and is used in the virtual reality and gaming fields. The author has been investigating this kind of visualisation technique but researchers have also applied similar techniques in virtual environments [17, 55].

In grid based environments different algorithms will be required to control the degree of adaptivity in order to maintain an adequate level of accuracy in the display during interaction, and whilst viewing the image from a static viewpoint. These and other more sophisticated rendering techniques should be able to make a significant contribution by reducing network bandwidth whilst providing an appropriate level of image fidelity during interaction. Adaptive rendering becomes very useful when extremely large datasets need user interaction in order to understand the complex visualisation structures. However, particular care must be taken to ensure that the adaptive rendering solution does not actually increase the cognitive workload of the user. Further research is required to develop adaptive rendering algorithms that take account the variability of the latencies in a grid based architecture. This work will need to examine the context of use of the interactive visualisation to ensure that the scientist's workflow and cognitive processing is not affected by a particular adaptive visualisation solution.

There is tremendous scope to overcome the serious latencies that grid based computing environments present by carefully using visualization techniques used in other non-scientific visualization tasks. In many cases it will be necessary to fine tune the optimization of the associated algorithms to meet the specific needs of the grid enables scientist.

6.15 Supercomputing Visualization in the Palm of Your Hand: (A Worked Example)

The UK e-Science RealityGrid project (http://realitygrid.org) has been undertaking computational chemistry studies at atomistic and mesoscale levels with the goal of improving simulation productivity by enhancing the scientist's interaction with the underlying computational model. Prior to the introduction of the grid [13, 14] large computing jobs would typically take days or weeks to complete. In a typical example, the scientist's workflow involved launching an initial application then monitoring its progress before spawning ten or more concurrent simulations. As the simulations proceeded the scientist was required to monitor the convergence or otherwise of the group average. Decisions would be taken at various intervals to terminate, extend or launch new jobs. Second or further chained simulations could be launched at the same time as the first, or a short time later.

Even though RealityGrid has achieved a dramatic speed increase from 26 days of continuous computing to less than 48 h [16] the scientist still has to frequently monitor their simulation – this means being able to connect to the simulation and check the parameters of interest during the 48 h period. Unfortunately, being tied to a desktop computer for this length of time is unacceptable so a solution was required that could allow the scientist to work away from their desk was highly desirable. To address this challenge a user centered approach was adopted [5, 6, 12, 32] to identify required system and performance requirements. A human factors audit was performed to capture current working practices and provide a detailed context sensitive description of how RealityGrid scientists undertook their research. The following inter-related usability factors [42] were considered:

- Understanding of how the users utilise their tool sets
- Consideration of what people are good and bad at
- Identifying what might improve the way people do things currently
- Listening to what users want
- Involving the end users in the design process
- Employing tried and tested user-based techniques during the design process
- Understanding of the limitations of the human physical and cognitive system

The human factors audit identified the following requirements for a lightweight user interface for computational steering:

- Remote access to grid based resources at any time and from any location
- Wireless connectivity

- Intuitive interaction – with minimal learning
- Consistent user interface between standard desktop scientific applications
- Connectivity with standard (proprietary) and bespoke computation grid enabled applications
- High resolution, highly interactive 3D visualization
- Ability to graph data as it is computed
- Ability to interactively steer a computation through a set of user selectable input parameters
- Collaborative visualization – shared visualization with other users
- Minimum latency during interaction
- Mobile device (PDA or mobile phone) desirable interface provided it could be made to work.

The requirement for interactive exploration of the resulting visualization was extremely high on the list of priorities because this greatly increases the scientists understanding of the data space [32]. A system engineering framework [29] was employed to define system architecture requirements. In this application, the set of steering libraries [6] that were developed to allow the user's simulation to be distributed over a grid architecture as shown in Fig. 6.11 were adopted.

A lightweight visualization system was created to provide a set of grid-enabled software components and middleware. The basis of lightweight visualization was to facilitate efficient and collaborative remote user access to high-end visualization on the grid.

6.15.1 Implementation of the RealityGrid PDA Client

The lightweight visualization system can be hosted on a PDA, mobile phone, laptop or desktop computer and comprises four Grid-enabled components (Refer to Fig. 6.5).

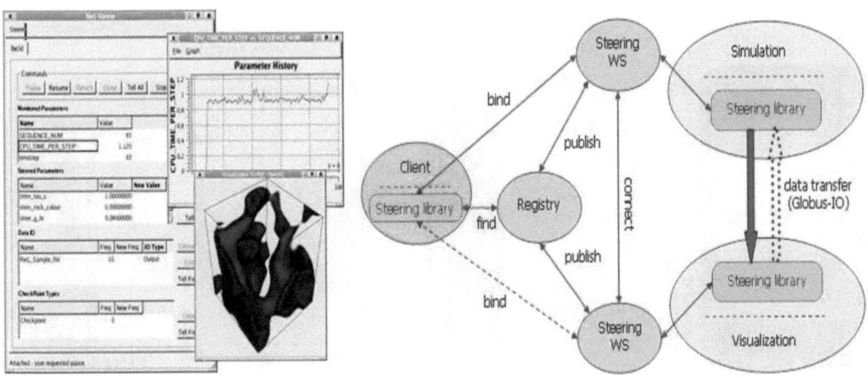

Fig. 6.11 Simple RealityGrid steering (Right) [6]). The RealityGrid steerer provides a visual front-end to all of the Grid-based computational steering (Left)

The RealityGrid PDA Client was designed as an intuitive visual front-end, enabling the user to discover their applications on the RealityGrid, steer their simulations in real-time and interact with high-end visualizations as if the supercomputing applications were running locally. The PDA Client provides convenient, remote, handheld access to the primary aspects of supercomputing functionality:

Resource discovery enables the scientist to find experiment software components on the grid and associate the remote user interface to the grid applications to support real-time interaction. The PDA Client's first task at start-up is to retrieve its contained list of all the user's currently deployed and active jobs on the grid. The PDA interface enables the user to select an individual job to interact with. The PDA Client will then establish a remote connection or 'attach' to the job over the grid and display the appropriate computational steering or visualization interface, depending on the type of job selected.

Real-time computational steering The computational steering interface of the PDA Client has been developed to specifically provide the same level of usability plus all the facilities that the user can access on their desktop or laptop computer (Refer to Fig. 6.3). Whilst attached to a running simulation the PDA Client updates its user interface with fresh simulation parameter data (Refer to Fig. 6.12) once every second. This received data can also be plotted in a 2D line graph (Refer to Fig. 6.12).

The user remotely steers a simulation by entering new parameter values into an input dialog, which is displayed by the user interface. The inputted new parameter values are then dispatched to the grid to update the relevant parameters within the simulation. Once the required steering activity has been instigated it is reflected back to the PDA interface, through a client-requested parameter update, almost instantaneously.

Visualization The PDA Client can provide user access to the high-end 3D visualization capabilities (Refer to Fig. 6.13). for a wide range of existing or established scientific visualization codes. The PDA Client has initially been developed to provide a remote handheld interface to the RealityGrid-instrumented application (Refer to Figs. 6.12 and 6.13). The configurable visualization interface has been designed to

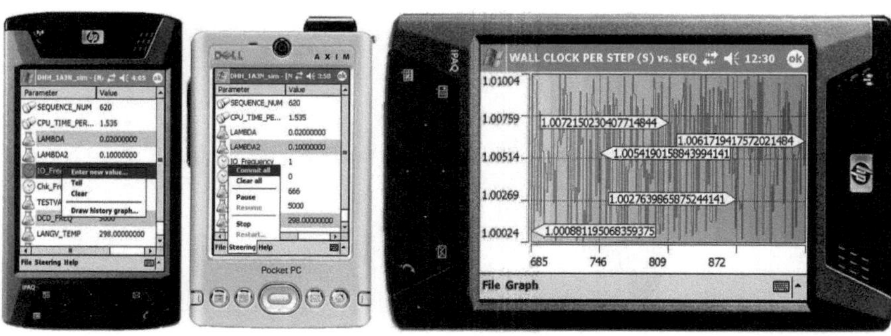

Fig. 6.12 The computational steering interface of the RealityGrid PDA Client (*See Color Plates*)

provide the same user services and level of user interaction as that of the desktop computer front-end (Refer to Fig. 6.14) ensuring a familiar user interface on the PDA.

The user can remotely configure the image encoder settings to enable varying levels of image compression, in order to adapt the client for use on low or medium bandwidth wireless networks with higher levels of image compression yielding increased image serving throughput on slower networks. This method also allows the system to produce images with lossless compression when required.

When designing the visualization interface for the PDA Client, it was essential to provide the user with a real sense of engagement with their visualization application and not leave them feeling remote or disconnected from it. The user interface provided interactive feedback as the user interacts remotely with the visualization

Fig. 6.13 The RealityGrid PDA Client is able to configure itself to provide remote user access and interaction for visualization applications on the grid (*See Color Plates*)

Fig. 6.14 The RealityGrid PDA Client visualization interface has been specifically designed to provide the same user services as the integrated VMD front-end (*See Color Plates*)

dragging the PDA stylus across the display screen results in almost immediate changes in image rotation, translation and zoom as required. Also, incorporating different modes of input and image encoding has enabled the user to adapt the performance of the PDA Client to remain responsive to variable network performance.

The PDA Client has been extremely well received by the many users who tried it out. Feedback has been very positive and the ease of use has been particularly welcomed. An understanding of what is important from a human perception perspective with respect to interactive visualization has helped ensure that parts of the system architecture which improve interactive performance, and the scientific exploration process have been appropriately optimized.

6.16 A Selection of Best HF Guidelines for User Interaction

During the course of the e-Science human factors audit and other investigations it has been possible to put together a series of best practice and highly recommended criteria for interactive visualization systems. These recommendations are listed in the following tables and are backed by scientific references.

6.16.1 Guidelines for Display Technologies: 1

Functional Requirements	Guidelines
Fully Immersive Displays Head-Coupled System Head-Mounted Displays (HMD) Augmented Reality Display (AR)	Ensure display resolution is adequate for the task Take extra care that the optical system does not cause accommodation/vergence problems Ensure that see through transmission is suitable for task – most systems tend to attenuate real world information too much.
Semi-Immersive Displays Spatially Immersive Display Screen projection Curved screens (Reality Centres, etc.)	Determine field of view versus resolution requirements for task. Rear projection may be better in some applications because contrast may be better in higher ambient lighting conditions. It is difficult to avoid a hot spot (i.e. a conspicuously higher luminance in the image centre) Rear projected CAVE displays tend to have reduced contrast caused by veiling glare from surrounding display screens. Front projection is generally adequate for most applications [46]. Curved projection screens require special distortion correction to be applied. This is usually accomplished by the deflection/scanning circuitry of CRT projectors. LCD/DLP projectors can be used but it is not possible to correct the distortion effects.
Field of regard (FOR)	The field of regard refers to the total field of view, viewable by a user with the full range of head movements. For a head mounted display this is 360° but for a projected or desktop display this is much less. FOR should be carefully matched to the task since increasing the FOR could incur abnormal head movements and lead to neck strain.

(continued)

(continued)

Functional Requirements	Guidelines
Field of view (FOV)	Amount of virtual environment observed without any head movement, measured in units of visual angle. Angle is a function of the width of the display and the viewer's distance from the display [31]. Wider fields of view promote greater situation awareness. Wide fields of view (without increase in viewing angle) distort the perceived distance from objects [38]. Projection based display systems can achieve FOV angles up to 270°. Wide fields of view provide a very compelling sense of motion in the virtual environment [56].
Spatial resolution	Ability of the system to resolve small details. Limiting resolution is defined as the number of lines per degree of a high-contrast grating Input at which the observer can no longer distinguish the separate lines in the resulting display image. The limiting resolution should at least be equivalent to the observer's visual acuity. A limiting resolution of 15 lines is acceptable for many applications [46]. As a guide a limiting resolution of 60 lines would be ideally required. (Clapp, 1985) Spatial resolution is critical for reading tasks.

6.16.2 Guidelines Display Technologies: 2

Functional Requirements	Operational Guidelines
Depth perception	
Binocular cue (stereopsis)	Not everyone has the capability for stereo vision. Users in experiments or tasks where stereo depth perception is important should be screened for good stereo acuity. Objects less than 1 m away, depth differences of less than 1 mm may be perceived Depth perception starts to degrade at object distance 10 m and not effective beyond 135 m.
Monocular cues	Monocular cues for objects 10–20 m away give more accurate depth perception than stereopsis.
Inter-Pupillary distance (IPD)	Extremely important parameter for stereo viewing systems. Typical range of IPD adjustment 50–76 mm [3]. Designers rarely take IPD into account, which is serious. System designers should provision for this adjustment since unadjusted IPD produces eyestrain and distorts space perception.
Viewing region and distance	Maximum parallax distortion of 8°, the minimum viewing distance is equal to the required width or height (whichever is greater) of the viewing region, multiplied by 57/ 8. Refer to [46].
Display Frame rate/ Update frequency	Frequency of complete display refresh. Frame rate depends on: Scene complexity expressed as:- No. of polygons processed, and Pixel fill rate (no. per second) Maximum frame movement that gives an impression of continuous movement is 15 arcmin

(continued)

(continued)

Functional Requirements	Operational Guidelines
	Min. required update frequency ($frames^{-1}$) = object angular speed ($arcmins^{-1}$)/15. [46]. For most applications, an update rate of 33 ms (30 Hz) will be sufficient. [46]. For stereo applications (Frame sequential – a frame rate in excess of (100 Hz) required) Fast moving objects in the scene require a higher frame rate to avoid image blurring. [28] and [46] Low update rates cause blurring, double imaging and user interaction problems. [28]. Low refresh rate causes luminance flicker. Note: User's sensitivity to flicker is higher for wide fields of view at high luminance.
Image lag	Delay incurred by the graphics system and head tracking system (if used). The effect is a lag between corresponding input and resulting image. Comprises: Tracker latency + Display generator lag + Frame update rate Delays can be problematical if lags are in excess of 40 to 80 ms where real time interaction required.[28] Image lags are known to cause motion sickness symptoms [24, 33].
Feedback	It is good engineering practice to incorporate adequate feedback in a direct manipulation interface. The control order determines the optimum kind of feedback for the user, whether isometric (rigid and force sensitive) or isotonic (free moving and position sensitive). [8].
Visual feedback	The user should be given an indication of when they have chosen an object for selection (e.g. highlighting the object or its bounding box).
Object recognition	Light and shadowing [1] and motion parallax play a more important role than motion cues, stereo and texture gradients.
Visual fidelity requirements	Level of visual realism must be based upon a task analysis and what has to be recognised. If texture is important, for discriminating between geological features then it must take precedence over say, image update rate.
Motion cues	Motion cues must be accompanied by appropriate vestibular inputs. Perceptual mismatch between vestibular and visual perception can result in motion sickness. Regularly spaced texture and level surfaces can help support accurate perception of gradients, slant and optic flow (cues that humans use to judge motion and orientation in the natural world) [34].
Auditory feedback	An audible tone can be used to indicate when the user has successfully selected a virtual object has led to a doubling of improvement in user performance over purely visual displays. [7].

6.16.3 Guidelines for Selecting Input Devices for Virtual Design Environments

Functional Requirements	Guidelines
Modes of movement direction	
Hand directed	Hand (orientation and position) determines the direction of motion through the virtual environment.
Pointing mode	Direction of motion through the virtual environment depends on the current orientation of the user's hand or hand held input device. **Advantages**: Very flexible mechanism allowing arbitrary flying through the virtual environment.
Crosshairs mode	User positions the cursor (usually attached to the user's hand) **Advantages**: intended for novice users who are used to interacting with desktop workstations and personal computers using mice Disadvantages: requires the user to keep the cursor in line with the desired destination and can lead to arm fatigue
Dynamic scaling	**Advantage**: provides a virtual map of the entire environment making it possible to locate your final destination
Head line of sight directed and orbital mode	Flying directed to wherever the user points their head. Easy to understand and good for novice users Disadvantage: User cannot turn their head to look around while flying through the virtual environment. Head referenced mode – the object of interest always appears directly in front of the user, irrespective of where they turn their head. Objects rotate around the user, with their positions relative to the user's head line of sight.
Object driven	Direction is controlled by objects in the environment such as moving cameras. **Disadvantage**: requires a means of controlling the position of the camera unless autonomous.
Goal driven	The user is presented a list of destinations, which are displayed either as text or as a set of icons (virtual menu) or graphically in the form of virtual maps. The user can point to a destination and be transported under program control.

6.16.4 Direct User Interaction

Functional Requirements	Guidelines
Modes of speed control	
Constant speed	Typically based on the size of the virtual environment the user must traverse (calibrated so that the user can traverse the environment in a reasonable amount of time) Disadvantages: leads to a jerky, start/stop kind of motion and a tendency to overshoot destination.

(continued)

(continued)

Functional Requirements	Guidelines
Constant acceleration	Movement starts at a slow speed that is reasonable for short flights through the virtual environment. Velocity increases exponentially. **Advantages**: OK if size of the environment is very large and contains lots of detail that needs to be navigated around. **Disadvantages**: The correct rate of acceleration is tricky to maintain.
Hand controlled	Speed through the environment is based on how far the user's hand is extended in front of their body. Linear or exponential mappings are used. **Disadvantages**: a) User quickly develops fatigue from having to hold their arm outstretched b) Restriction in the dynamic range that can be mapped onto the possible range of arm motions and still be controllable. c) Confusing, especially for novice users
	Ensure movement in virtual environment maps onto real world actions. More intuitive.
	Provide a fast mode so that movement between two points can be achieved very quickly.
	Employ a fully automatic navigation mode with a constant speed mode or logarithmically diminishing speed mode to desired destination.
	Many VR systems only have a limited usable working volume of 1 – 2 m radius. This is limited by the tracking system.
	Physical space is typically much smaller than virtual space. This requires use of navigational techniques.
Devices	
Physical controls	Devices such as joysticks, trackballs, buttons and sliders, steering wheels, handle bars, treadmill, keyboard input, voice control, speed controls such as accelerator pedal, dial or slider mounted on the hand held input device. **Advantages:** Readily available and easy to incorporate into an application. Joysticks and dials are useful if more precise control of the orthogonal components of motion is required. Commonly called a dials and button box in CAD. **Disadvantages:** lack a natural mapping between movement of the device and motion in the virtual world.
Virtual controls	3D joysticks, glove based interfaces **Advantages:** tremendous flexibility **Disadvantages:** no haptic feedback; lack of haptic feedback present a general difficulty of interacting with a virtual object
Direct user interaction	Includes hand tracking, gesture recognition, pointing, gaze direction, etc.
Physical devices	Includes buttons, sliders, dials, joysticks and steering wheels These are well suited for the fine positioning of an object Often lack the natural mappings that facilitate an interaction task
Object Selection Mechanism	Mechanism required to select (e.g. a button press, gesture or voice command)

(continued)

(continued)

Functional Requirements	Guidelines
Local	The desired object is within reach and the user can interact with it directly. Objects are selected by moving a cursor (typically attached to the user's hand) until it is within the object's selection region (e.g. a bounding box)
Action-at-a-distance	Fall outside the immediate reach of the user Accomplished using 'virtual laser beams or spotlights' that project out of the user's hand and intersect with the object in the virtual world. Also some form of virtual cursor can be moved within the selection zone.
Gaze directed	Based upon the user's current gaze direction. The user looks at an object to be selected and then indicates a selection via a selection signal (e.g. the user turning his/her head to line up a target object and a cursor floating in the middle of his/her field of view.
Voice Input	**Disadvantages**: Increased mental workload due to remembering the names of all objects. Increased in clutter in the virtual world due to the need to label all objects. Issue of poor of reliability of current voice systems. Need to train recogniser for each person.
List Selection	Virtual selection list Advantage: The user does not have to see the object to select it
Object selection	Object selection is made easier if user works at different scales.
Precision selection	Zero-order control – optimal if user requires to reach a short distance at a precisely fixed position or location [56]. Isometric control – optimal for first-order dynamics and isotonic control (typically a sensor that responds to the position and orientation of the hand) [57].
Object manipulation	Joysticks reduce problems of fatigue but do not allow direct manipulation of virtual objects. Object position is controlled by a 3D cursor. [4]. Manipulation of objects is greatly facilitated with the use of constraints. Lack of constraints is one of the biggest problems in the manipulation of virtual objects – users are restricted to gross interactions and are unable to perform precise manipulation.
User fatigue	User fatigue is problem because an arm is raised for long periods of time. [4]. Isotonic position control (glove based systems) is the most 'direct' interface. The major problem is fatigue. Limited output range (therefore clutch needed) is also a disadvantage. Good for novice VR users because they can use the system without much learning. Isometric rate control devices (e.g. space ball) are less fatiguing. Lack of feedback (proprioception) is a problem. Users need to develop skill.

6.16.5 Object Manipulation

Function Requirements	Guidelines
Object Displacement	Three parameters that must be specified when manipulating an object: Change in position Change in orientation Centre of rotation

(continued)

(continued)

Function Requirements	Guidelines
Hand-specified	A very intuitive means to change position and orientation of a virtual object is to allow the user to grab it (typically initiated by a button press or a grab gesture and move it like an object in the real-world. Move in a 1:1 correspondence with the user's hand or a gain factor can be applied to the motion of the object. Magnitude of the gain factor will result in fine or gross positioning of the object. Gain factor can be based upon some ratio such as the speed of the user's hand motion (analogous to the control-to-display ratio used in mouse interaction.
Physical controls	Joystick, slider or dials are excellent for precise positioning of objects because each degree of freedom can be controlled separately. The absence of natural mappings can make it difficult to place an object at some arbitrary position and orientation.
Virtual controls	Virtual menu or toolbox can be used to position objects.
Centre of rotation	Hand-centred rotation is directly related to the manipulation of objects in the real world. Alternatives include rotation about the centre of an object or rotation about some user specified centre of rotation.
Scaling	Allows a used view small detail by scaling up the selected object or; to get a better global understanding of the environment by scaling it down and viewing it as a miniature model. Two parameters: centre of scaling and the scaling factor. Non-uniform scaling allows the user to control the scale of a selected object along each dimension separately
Centre of Scaling	The point to which all objects move when scaling down and where all points move from when scaling up.

6.16.6 Virtual Menus

Function	Guidelines
Virtual Menus	1D menus are perfect for the selection of a single item from a limited set of options. Avoid 3D interaction with conventional menus (such as pull down menus and dialogue boxes. The user finds it quite difficult to select specific options. Virtual menu design relates directly to principles of 2D user interface design: consistency, feedback, natural mappings, good visibility.
Positioning of virtual menu in the virtual environment	Options include: floating in space. Whenever the user wishes to move the menu he/she must pick it or grab it and move it to a new location. **Disadvantage**: Easy to lose track of the menu location in space Poor image quality of HMDs makes it impossible to select between options. Noise and errors in tracking make it difficult to interact with virtual items.
Way-finding	Use of a compass rose, depicted in a perspective view and in a 2D map can help users navigate and remain spatially orientated.

6.17 Summary

This chapter has tackled one of today's top scientific visualization research problems which relates to how humans respond to visualization. Visualization researchers rarely study or apply what is known about the visual system when designing visualization techniques. However, in order to produce an effective visualization, human perception must be understood otherwise the end result may not lead to a visualization that can be interpreted by the users. This chapter has provided guidance to help the designer of a visualization system to make intelligent use of human perceptual and cognitive capability. Unfortunately, it has been impossible to cover all the human perception issues of visualization in just one chapter. Therefore, in the main the use of interactive visualization has been focussed upon thus allowing the designer to focus on what helps the user gain greater insight into their data. To help illustrate this, an example was given where the difficult technical challenges of creating an interactive 3D visualization system on a PDA device were overcome by applying knowledge of human perception and cognition. This chapter has tried to 'demystify' this essential component of the visualization practitioner's toolbox by providing helpful insights and guidance on the human factors of interactive visualization. Finally, at the end of the chapter a series of useful tables of data showing the human factors that need to be considered in any interactive visualization system have been provided. Whilst a full appreciation of the complexities and interactions of the human perceptual system is not easy to comprehend the effort is well worthwhile since it can make the difference between a system that really works and one that looks ok but actually hinders the user.

Acknowledgements The author would like to acknowledge the support of the application and computer scientists within the RealityGrid project (www.RealityGrid.org) (University College London, University of Manchester, University of Oxford, Loughborough University, Edinburgh Parallel Computing Centre and Imperial College). In particular, the author would like to thank Dr Simon Nee and Ian Holmes who were his research assistants in the RealityGrid project. Ian Holmes also helped write Sect. 6 15 of this chapter. Also, I would like to thank Prof Peter Coveney (University College London) and Stephen Pickles (University of Manchester) for their encouragement in taking the output of the in-depth human factors audit to a fully working solution. The Reality-Grid work was carried out under grant GR/R67699 from the EPSRC. This chapter also draws on a report entitled 'Human Factors Audit of Selected e-Science Projects', and on the work of the vizNET project, both of which were funded by the Joint Information Systems Committee (JISC). JISC provides expertise and guidance on information and communications technology for the UK academic community. Their support is gratefully acknowledged.

References

1. Barfield, W. et al. (1988) The mental rotation and perceived realism of computer-generated three-dimensional images. International Journal of Man-Machine Studies 29: 669–684.
2. Boada, I. and Navazo, I. (2003) Optimal Exploitation of Client Texture Hardware Capabilities on a ClientServer Remote Visuali-zation Framework. ICCSA, LNCS series, 468-477.

3. Boff, K. R. and Lincoln, J. E. (1988) Engineering Data Compendium – Human Perception and Performance, Vol. I, Sensory Process and Perception. New York, John Wiley.
4. Boman, D. K. (1995) International survey: virtual environment research. Computer: 57-65.
5. Bradley, D. (2004). RealityGrid – Real Science on Computational Grids. e-Science 2004: The Working Grid.
6. Brooke, J. M. et al. (2003) Computational Steering in RealityGrid. Proceedings of the UK e-Science All Hands Meeting, Nottingham.
7. Frederick P. Brooks, Jr., Ming Ouh-Young, James J. Batter, P. Jerome Kilpatrick, Project GROPEHaptic displays for scientific visualization, Proceedings of the 17th annual conference on Computer graphics and interactive techniques, p. 177–185, September 1990, Dallas, TX, USA.
8. Buxton, W. (1993) HCI and the inadequacies of direct manipulation systems. SIGCHI Bulletin 25(1): 21–22.
9. Card, S. K., Robertson, G. G., Mackinlay, J. D. (1991). The information visualizer: An information workspace. Proceedings in ACM CHI'91 Conf, New Orleans, LA.
10. Card, S. K., Mackinlay, J. D., Shneiderman, B. (1999) Readings in Information Visualization: Using Vision to Think. San Francisco, California, Morgan Kaufmann Publishers, Inc.
11. Chen, Y., Chen, H., Clark, D. W., Liu, Z., Wallace, G., Li, K. (2001) Software environments for cluster-based display systems. IEEE Symposium on Cluster Computing and the Grid: 202-210.
12. Coveney, P. V. (2003) Computational Steering on Grids – A Survey of RealityGrid. Proceedings of the Second Annual RealityGrid Workshop, University College London, UK.
13. Foster, I. and Kessleman, C. (1999) The Grid: Blueprint for a New Computing Infrastructure. Morgan Kaufmann Publishers.
14. Foster, I. et al. (2003) The physiology of the grid: An open grid services architecture for distributed systems integration. Grid Computing: Making the Global Infrastructure a Reality. F. Berman, G. Fox and A. J. G. Hey: 217-246.
15. Fowler, J. E. (2000) Evaluation of SGI Vizsever. NSF Engineering Research Center, Mississippi State University: 12.
16. Fowler, P. W. et al. (2004) Exact calculation of peptide-protein binding energies by steered thermodynamic integration using high performance computing grids. EPSRC e-Science All Hands Meeting, Nottingham.
17. Funkhouser, T. A. and Sequin, C. H. (1993) Adaptive display al-gorithms for interactive frame rates during visualization of complex virtual environments. Computer Graphics (SIGGRAPH '93), Los Angeles, CA.
18. Gregory, R. L. (1993) Seeing by exploring. Pictorial Communication in Virtual and Real Environments. S. R. Ellis, M. K. Kaiser, and A. J. Grunwald, Taylor and Francis. Inc. Bristol, PA, USA
19. Haber, R. B. and McNabb, D. A. (1990) Visualization Idioms: A Conceptual Model for Scientific Visualization Systems. IEEE Computer Society Press.
20. Hamming, R. W. (1962) Numerical Methods for Scientists and Engineers. McGraw-Hill.
21. Harting, J., Venturoli, M., Coveney, P. V. (2004) Large-scale grid-enabled lattice Boltzmann simulations of complex fluid flow in porous media and under shear. Philosophical transactions: Mathematical. Physical and Engineering Sciences 362(1821): 1471–2962.
22. Highstein, S. M. et al. (2004) The Vestibular System. Berlin, Springer.
23. Houghton, M., Company (2003) The American Heritage Dictionary of the English Language. Boston, Houghton Mifflin Company.
24. Howarth, P. A. and Costello, P. J. (1997) The Development of a Test Battery for Virtual Reality Users. Taylor & Francis.
25. Humphreys, G., Houston, M., Ng, R., Frank, R., Ahern, S., Kirchner, P. D. (2002) Chromium: A Stream Processing Frame-work for Interactive Rendering on Clusters. Proceedings of SIGGRAPH '02.
26. Ittelson, W. H. (1968). The Ames Demonstrations in Perception. New York, Hafner.
27. Johnson, C. (2004) Top Scientific Visualization Research Problems. IEEE Computer Graphics and Applications 24(4): 13–17.

28. Kalawsky, R. S. (1993). The Science of Virtual Reality and Virtual Environments. Wokingham, Berks, Addison-Wesley-Longman.
29. Kalawsky, R. S. and Holmes, I. R. (2007) Overcoming Engineering Challenges of Providing an Effective User Interface to a Large Scale Distributed Synthetic Environment on the US Teragrid: A Systems Engineering Success Story. San Diego, California, USA, Systems Engineering: Key to Intelligent Enterprises.
30. Kalawsky, R. S. and Nee, S. P. (2004) e-Science RealityGrid – Human Factors Audit Requirements and Context Analysis. Loughborough University.
31. Kalawsky, R. S. et al. (1999) Human factors evaluation techniques to Aid understanding of virtual interfaces. BT Technology Journal 17(1): 128–141.
32. Kalawsky, R. S. et al. (2005) Improving scientists interaction with complex computational-visualisation environments based on a distributed grid infrastructure. Philosophical Transactions of the Royal Society of London. Series A 363(1833): 1867–1884.
33. Kennedy, R. S. A. L. and Michael, G. (1995) Implications of balance disturbances following exposure to virtual reality systems. 1995 Virtual Reality Annual International Symposium, Proceedings of the IEEE.
34. Lee, J. D. and Moray, N. (1992) Trust, control strategies and allocation of function in human-machine systems. Ergonomics 35: 1243–1270.
35. Leech, J., Prins, J. F., Hermans, J. (1996) SMD: Visual steering of molecular dynamics for protein design. IEEE Computational Science & Engineering 3(4): 38–45.
36. Liere, R. V. et al. (1997) Computational steering. Future Generation Computer Systems 12(5): 441–450.
37. Ma, K. and Camp, D. M. (2000) High Performance Visualization of Time-Varying Volume Data Over a Wide Area Network. The 2000 ACM/IEEE Conference on Supercomputing, Dallas, Texas, United States.
38. McGreevy, M. W. and Ellis, S. R. (1986) The effect of perspective geometry on judged direction in spatial information instruments. Human factors 28: 439–456.
39. Miller, R. B. (1968) Response time in man-computer conversational transactions. Proceedings in AFIPS Fall Joint Computer Conference.
40. Mitchell, D. G., Hoh, H., Roger, A. L., Bimal, K., David, H. (1994) The Measurement and Prediction of Pilot-In-The Loop Oscillations. AIAA Guidance, Navigation, and Control Conference, Scottsdale, AZ.
41. Myers, B. A. (1985). The importance of percent-done progress indicators for computer-human interfaces. Proceedings in ACM CHI'85 Conference, San Francisco, CA.
42. Newman, W. M. and Taylor, A. S. (1999) Towards a Methodology Employing Critical Parameters to Deliver Performance Improvements in Interactive Systems. Interact '99 Conf.
43. North, C. (2006) Visualization Insights: Toward Measuring Visualization Insight. IEEE Computer Graphics and Applications 26(3): 6–9.
44. Ohazama, C. (1999) OpenGL Vizserver White Paper. Silicon Graphics Inc.
45. Oman, C. M. (1991) Sensory conflict in motion sickness: an observer theory approach. Pictorial communication in virtual and real environments. S. R. Ellis, M. K. Kaiser and A. J. Grunwald, Taylor & Francis, Inc.: 362-376.
46. Padmos, P. and Milders, M. (1992) Quality criteria for simulator images: A literature review. Human Factors (6).
47. Parulkar, G. M., Bowie, J., Braun, H., Guerin, R., Stevenson, D. (1991) Remote visualization: challenges and opportunities. Proceedings of the 2nd conference on Visualization '91, San Diego, California, IEEE Computer Society Press.
48. Russell, G. and Miles, R. (1987) Display and perception of 3D space-filling data. Applied Optics 26(6): 973.
49. Seay, A. F. et al. (2002) Simulator sickness and presence in a high field-of-view virtual environment. Conference on Human Factors in Computing Systems – CHI '02 Extended Abstracts on Human Factors in Computing Systems, Minneapolis, Minnesota, USA, ACM Press.
50. Seckel, A. (2003) Incredible Visual Illusions: You Won't Believe Your Eyes. Arcturus Publishing.

51. Spence, R. (2001) Information Visualization. Edinburgh Gate. Harlow, Essex, England, ACM Press Books.
52. Staadt, O. G., Walker, J., Nuber, C., Hamann, B. (2003) A survey and performance analysis of software platforms for interactive cluster-based multi-screen rendering. Eurographics Workshop on Virtual Environments – International Immersive Projection Technologies Workshop.
53. Sternberg, R. J. and Davidson, J. E. (1996) The Nature of Insight. Cambridge MA, MIT Press.
54. Ware, C. and Franck, G. (1996) Evaluating stereo and motion cues for visualizing information nets in three dimensions. ACM Transactions on Graphics 15(2): 121–140.
55. Watson, B., Walker, N., Ribarsky, W. R., Spaulding, V. (1998) The effects of variation in system responsiveness on user performance in virtual environments. Human Factors 40(3): 403–414.
56. Wickens, C. D. (1986) The Effects of Control Dynamics on Performance. Handbook of Perception and Performance. K. B. A. Kaufman 39.1-39.60.
57. Zhai, S. and Milgram, P. (1993). Human performance evaluation of manipulation schemes in virtual environments. Proceedings in IEEE Virtual Reality Annual International Symposium (VRAIS), Seattle, WA.

Chapter 7
Perceptual and Design Principles for Effective Interactive Visualisations

Martin Hicks

Abstract This chapter reviews some influential theories and design principles for informing the design of effective interactive visualisation user interfaces (UIs). Several theories and principles are reviewed encompassing perceptual organisation, data graphics, and design principles (e.g. Gestalt laws, data graphics, interaction design and Human-Computer Interaction guidelines). Some example case studies are included in order to illustrate the principal benefits of applying these design principles within the UI. The objective of this review of the principles and approaches to graphical presentation is to highlight how they can be used to emphasise and reveal the most salient properties of a data visualisation, whether it is intended for scientific or for business use. Certain principles are further proposed as a generic set of guidelines for the design of interactive visualisations, which are summarised at the end of the chapter.

Keywords Interactive visualisations, Perceptual organisation, Design principles, Interaction design, HCI.

7.1 Introduction

With the advent of informational systems and databases of increasing size and complexity, advanced techniques are required to visualise them. The processes of information and scientific data visualisation seek to address the problem of representing various data types for the user, so that the data can be readily interpreted and communicated. Claims pertaining to the benefits of visualisations are well documented [4, 31, 34, 38]. A much cited study by cognitive theorists Larkin and Simon [16] illustrates why visualisations can be effective. Larkin and Simon compared physics problem solving tasks comparing diagrams and sentential representations. They claimed that one principal benefit of diagrammatic representations is that 'diagrams can group together information that is used together thus avoiding large amounts of search for the elements needed to make a problem solving inference' [16]. Similarly, Reinhard et al. [25] claim that graphics serve as external representations that

E. Zudilova-Seinstra et al. (eds.) *Trends in Interactive Visualization*,
doi:10.1007/978-1-84800-269-2_7

are very effective for making inferences, finding salient characteristics, and structuring the course of problem solving dependent on the content. Besides facilitating problem solving, graphics can display the prominent features of a problem space and support the visualisation of goal structures.

One of the most important issues in information and scientific visualisation is mapping data attributes into graphical properties, so that the informational content is effectively conveyed. However, there are typically several possible mappings which may lead to different visualisation techniques and designs. Selecting and creating the most effective design among all the alternatives for a given situation usually requires considerable knowledge and creativity on the part of the designer. While an understanding of the data characteristics as well as the relevant graphical properties is important in constructing visualisation techniques, being aware of the comprehensibility of any image or graphic is essential for the effective presentation of the information inherent in the data [26].

With the development of graphical user interfaces (GUIs) there are several influential theories of perceptual organisation and approaches to data graphics that are particularly relevant to interactive visualisation design, including Gestalt theory and perceptual principles surrounding pre-attentive processing. In addition, there are several design principles within the scope of data graphics, interaction design and HCI that can further inform the designer when developing visualisations as manipulable UIs. The following sections review the relevant principles and approaches to graphical presentation, using case study examples to emphasise how they can be incorporated to reveal the most salient properties of a data visualisation.

7.2 Gestalt Theory in User Interface Design

Gestalt theory, expressed as a series of laws, explains how individual elements from the environment may be visually organised into fields or structures [15]. Traditionally, within UI design the Gestalt laws are used to suggest how static visual elements should be presented in order to achieve effective visual results. Ware [38] proposes that the Gestalt laws easily translate into a set of design principles for information displays. Nine Gestalt laws and related design principles are presented in Table 7.1.

Card et al. [4] and Ware [38] illustrate how the principles in Table 7.1 can be applied to the design of an informational display. Ware [38] suggests that spatial proximity is one of the most powerful perceptual organising principles and one of the most useful in design. Objects that are located close together are perceptually grouped together. However, proximity is not the only factor involved in predicting perceived groups. For example, in Fig. 7.1, the dot labelled *x* is perceived to be part of cluster *a* rather than cluster *b*, even though it is as close to the other points in cluster *b* as they are to each other. Slocum [32] termed this effect the spatial concentration principle, whereby we perceptually group regions of similar element

Table 7.1 Gestalt principles of organisation (Tovée [36]; Ware [38])

Rule	Boundaries
Pragnanz (Good Form)	Every stimulus pattern is seen in such a way that the resulting structure is as simple as possible
Proximity	The tendency of objects near each other to be grouped together into a perceptual unit
Similarity	If several stimuli are presented together, there is a tendency to see the form in such a way that the similar items are grouped together
Symmetry	A stimuli will appear incomplete if it is not balanced or symmetrical
Closure	The tendency to unite contours that are very close to each other
Continuity	Neighbouring elements are grouped together when they are potentially connected by straight or smooth curving lines
Common fate	Elements that are moving in the same direction tend to be grouped together
Familiarity	Elements are more likely to form groups if the groups appear familiar or meaningful
Figure & ground	Foreground and background elements are distinguished in a visual field

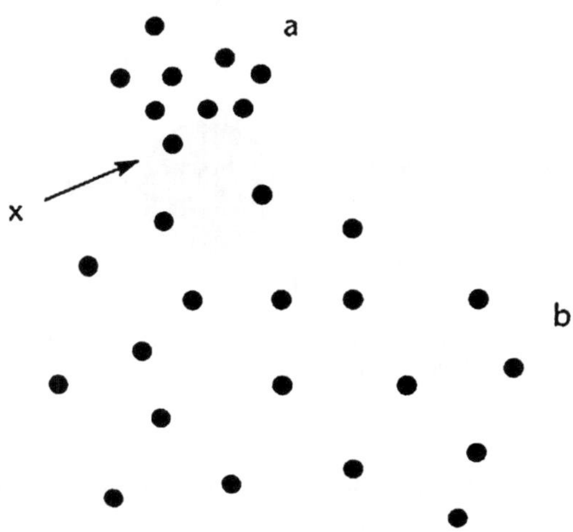

Fig. 7.1 The dot labelled *x* is perceived as part of cluster *a* rather than cluster *b* (Ware [38])

density. Ware [38] considers that the application of the proximity law in display design is relatively straightforward. The simplest and most powerful way of emphasising relationships between data entities in a display is to place them in proximity.

The principle of continuity can be applied to the construction of diagrams consisting of networks of nodes and the links between them. Continuity implies connectedness, and Palmer and Rock [24] argue that connectedness is a more fundamental organising principle than proximity, colour, size or shape, as illustrated at Fig. 7.2 below.

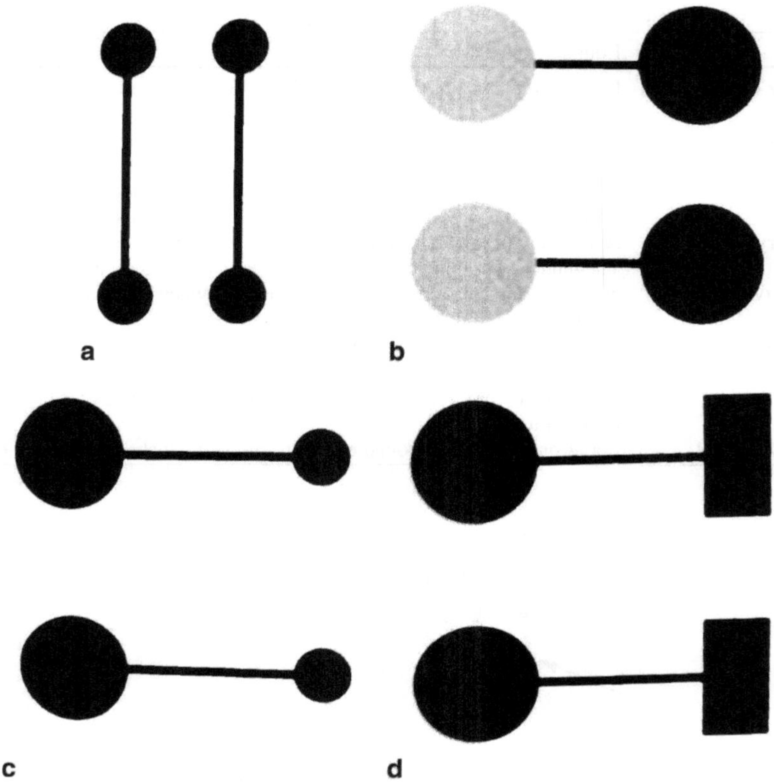

Fig. 7.2 Connectedness is a powerful grouping principle and stronger than (**a**) proximity, (**b**) colour, (**c**) size, and (**d**) shape (Ware [38])

Another powerful organising principle is symmetry. A visual object will appear as incomplete if the visual object is not balanced or symmetrical [10]. The symmetrically arranged pairs of lines in Fig. 7.3 are more strongly perceived as forming a visual whole than the lines merely positioned in parallel. A possible application of symmetry in tasks is where analysts are searching for similarities between disparate sets of time-series data. It may be easier to perceive similarities if these time series are arranged using vertical symmetry as shown in Fig. 7.4, rather than incorporating more conventional parallel plots.

Regarding the principle of closure, a closed contour tends to be viewed as an object. Fisher and Smith-Gratto [10] argue that 'open shapes make the individual perceive that the visual pattern is incomplete' and the 'sense of incompletion serves as a distraction to the learner'. Gestalt theorists also argue that there is a perceptual tendency to close contours that include gaps, which illustrates why we perceive Fig. 7.5a as a complete circle occluded by a rectangle rather than a circle with a gap in it (Fig. 7.5b).

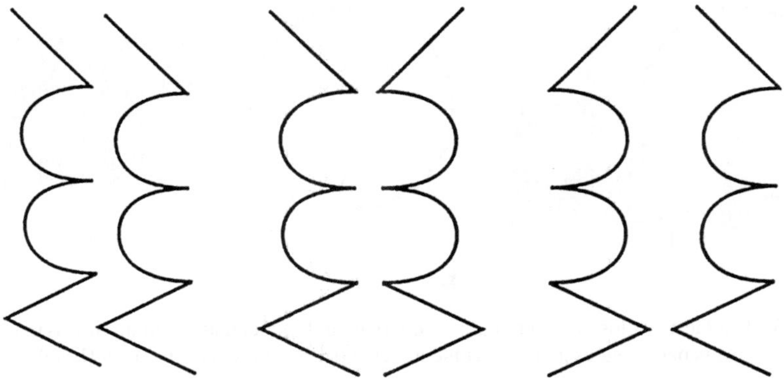

Fig. 7.3 The patterns in the centre and on the right are reflected about a vertical axis, producing bilateral symmetry and a stronger sense of a whole figure than the pattern on the left (Ware [38])

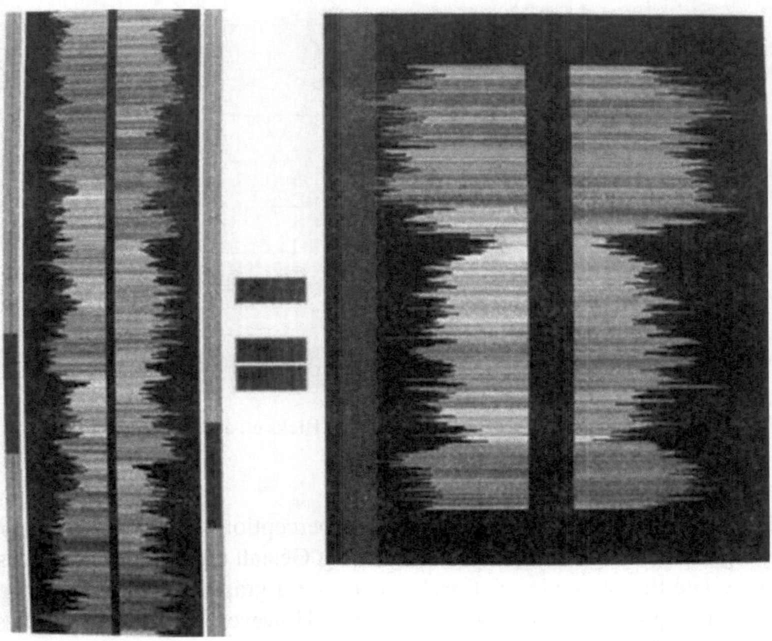

Fig. 7.4 An application designed to support recognition of similar patterns in time-series plots. Two subsets of the extended sequences are shown on the right (Ware [38])

7.2.1 Application of Gestalt Principles

Some limitations of Gestalt theory have been exposed. Moore and Fitz [19] analysed the visual dimensions of diagrammatic instructions using Gestalt principles. They argue that although Gestalt theory broadly concerns grouping and distinguishing

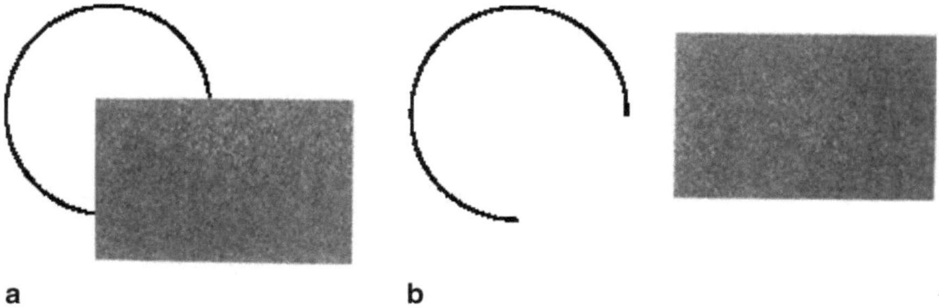

Fig. 7.5 The Gestalt closure principle predicts that find perceptual solutions involving closed contours – (**a**) is perceived as a circle behind a rectangle, not a broken ring as in (**b**) (Ware [38])

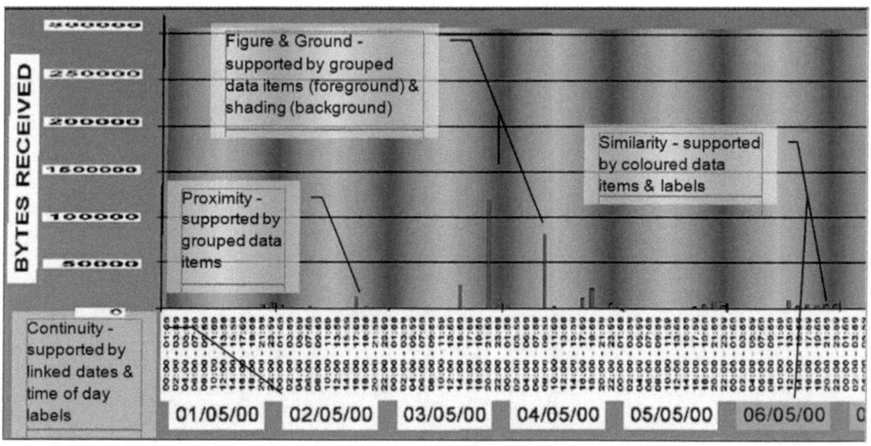

Fig. 7.6 2D graph supporting four Gestalt principles (Hicks et. al [11])

entities, it does not involve organising those perceptions into object categories or assigning them a name. They further argue that Gestalt theory does not necessarily accommodate the semantic relationship between a graphic and the explanation in the surrounding text in instructional diagrams. However, more recent studies have identified benefits associated with incorporating Gestalt principles in graphical displays. Findings from studies incorporating graphs and charts [17, 27, 28, 40] indicate that graphical representations incorporating Gestalt principles such as connectness similarity and proximity can reduce cognitive demands for information interpretation tasks. Based on their evaluation of an instructional multimedia application, Chang et al. [5] indicated that all the identified Gestalt principles were beneficial for informing UI design and promoting learning, although they concluded that the relative benefits of these principles should be investigated more thoroughly in subsequent research, to arrive at better guidance for visual designers.

Figures 7.6 and 7.7 (below) show a 2D graph (Fig. 7.6) and 3D time-series plot (Fig. 7.7), based on previous work by the author [11]. Both representations depict equivalent information (showing emails received during a one month period) for presentation on a desktop Virtual Reality (VR) environment. Both Figs. 7.6 and 7.7 further indicate whether four Gestalt principles (continuity, figure and ground, proximity and similarity) have been wholly or partially supported.

The proximity and similarity principles are universally supported by both representations. Both displays organise data items according to date (including coloured weekend dates) and time of day. The 3D time-series plot has additional null markers (coloured yellow), while the grid itself is divided into weekly intervals, thus supporting perceptual grouping when the x- and z-axis are not fully visible. The Gestalt principle of continuity states that we are more likely to construct visual entities out of visual elements that are smooth and continuous, rather than ones that contain abrupt changes in direction [38]. The principle of good continuity is evident in Fig. 7.6, where date and time of day labels are linked together along the x-axis of the 2D graph. Although only part of the display is visible, this grouping implies continuity or connectedness along the remainder of the x-axis that is out of view. The principle is only partially supported by the 3D time-series plot, as connectedness is reduced where the date and time of day labelling is separated along the x- and z-axis in 3D space, as evident in Fig. 7.7. An important distinction between the 2D and 3D displays is how effectively they support the figure-ground principle. Whereas the 2D graph supports four Gestalt principles (see Fig. 7.6), the figure-ground principle is only partially supported by the 3D time-series plot, as the contrast between the y-axis label and data items can vary according to the viewpoint adopted within 3D space.

Clearly, the application of Gestalt principles has important implications for the design of interactive visualisations. Ware [38] suggests that while the Gestalt laws

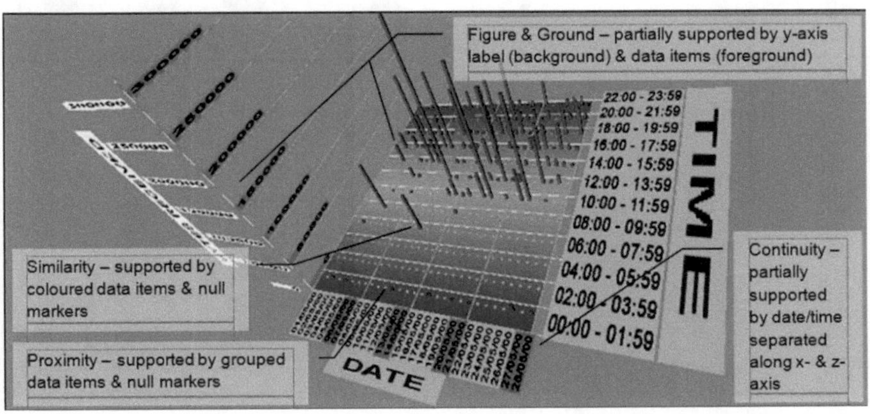

Fig. 7.7 3D time-series plot supports proximity, similarity, and partially supports continuity and figure-ground Gestalt principles (Hicks et. al [11])

of perception leads to principles that may seem obvious to the visual designer they are often overlooked or violated. Objects that should be grouped together are commonly placed far apart in displays. This does not necessarily support the perceptual organisation of items of interest.

7.2.2 Pre-attentive Processing

The perceptual organisation supported by Gestalt principles highlights the underlying mechanism of pre-attentive processing, which logically occurs before conscious attention. According to Ware [38], 'an understanding of what is processed pre-attentively is probably the most important contribution that visual science can make to a data visualisation'. In view of the advantage of deriving insight without the need for conscious attention, an obvious question for the interaction designer is – 'How do we make information pop out?' – Ware [38] provides an in-depth discussion of pre-attentive processing in the context of the human visual system. However, as an overview it is useful to illustrate how we can do certain things to symbols to make them more likely to be visually identified – even after a very brief exposure [38]. Certain simple shapes or colours can 'pop out' from their surroundings, as highlighted by the examples (a – d) shown in Fig. 7.8 below. Spence [34] suggests

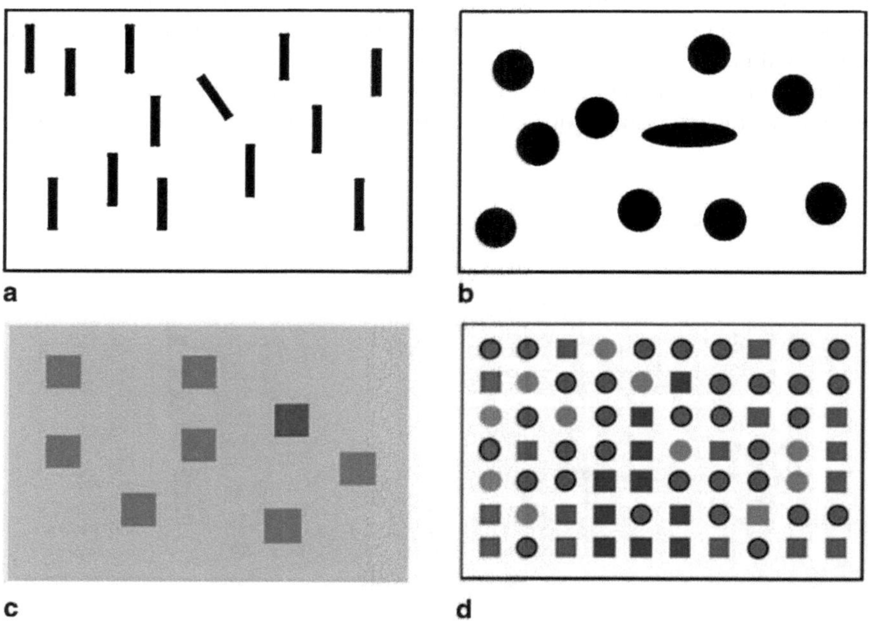

Fig. 7.8 (**a**) Orientation – the 'odd one out' can be quickly identified, (**b**) Different shapes can often pop out, (**c**) A different colour can be identified pre-attentively, (**d**) Pre-attentive processing does not occur – careful scrutiny is required to locate the orange square (Spence [34]) (*See Color Plates*)

that the first two examples shown in Fig. 7.8a) and b) – allow the viewer to quickly identify the 'odd one out'. Similarly, in c), pre-attentive processing allows us to quickly perceive where the blue square is located. However, in d), pre-attentive processing does not occur as more careful scrutiny is required to locate the orange square target. This is because the viewer is required to discriminate between both colour (orange and blue) and shape (square and circle) in order to identify the orange square target in the collection of items.

Figures 7.9 and 7.10 below provide examples of how Gestalt principles and pre-attentive mechanisms can be effectively used within two different visualisations. Firstly, Fig. 7.9 below shows the Filmfinder interface [1], an interactive representation to allow a user to select a film to watch on video. On the main (scatterplot) display each coloured square identifies a film. Colour encodes genre (horror, musical, etc.) – horizontal position along the x-axis indicates the year of production and vertical position along the y-axis indicates duration. The Filmfinder interactive representation exploits the Gestalt principles of spatial proximity and similarity, allowing the viewer to pre-attentively perceive outlier items as well as to perceptually group similar items together (i.e., by colour and/or proximity).

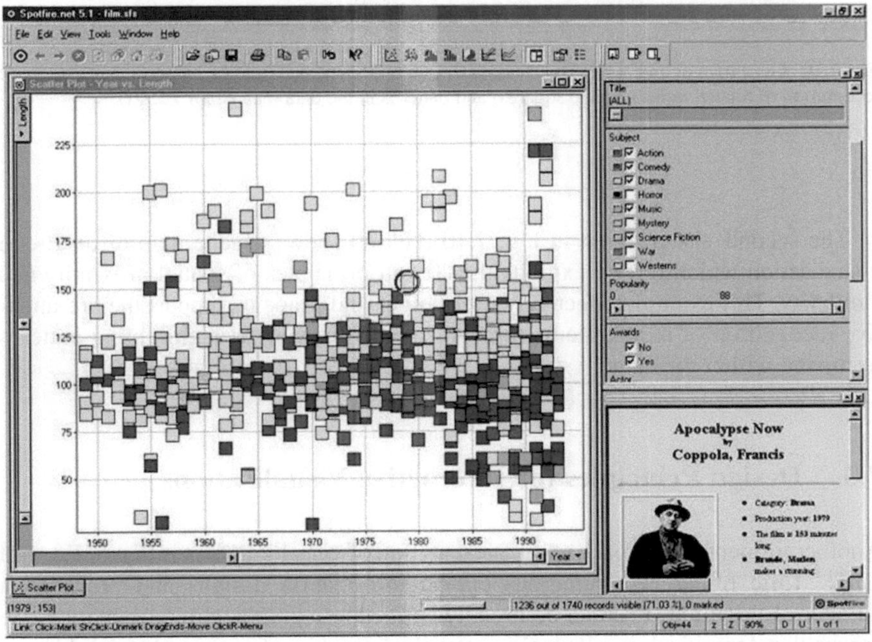

Fig. 7.9 The Filmfinder interface [1] exploits Gestalt principles (spatial proximity, similarity) allowing the viewer to quickly perceive dissimilar items (outliers) as well as similar items (grouped by colour and proximity)

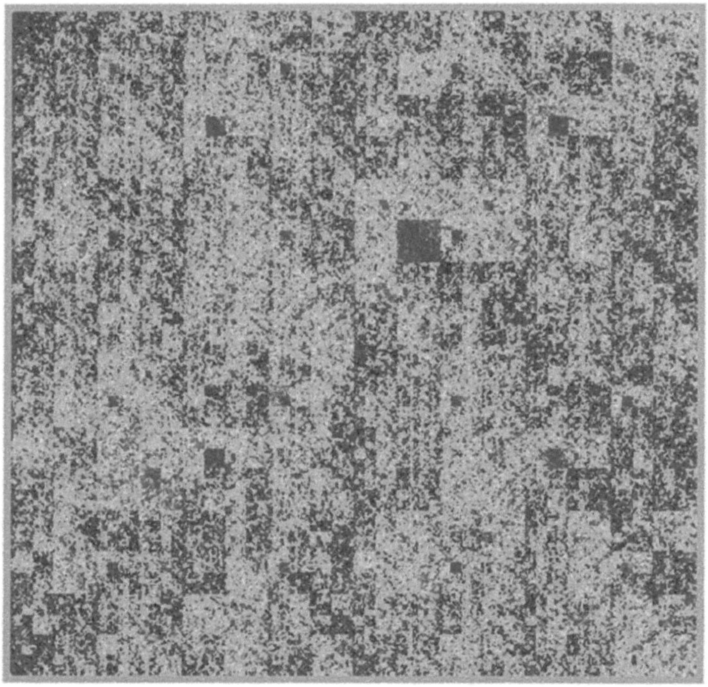

Fig. 7.10 Gene map of an E-coli visualisation. Colour and shape and used to support the pre-attentive recognition of related items (orange squares) and patterns in the data (*See Color Plates*)

The second visualisation in Fig. 7.10 (below) shows a gene map of an E-coli visualisation which further exploits the Gestalt principles of spatial proximity and similarity. This example effectively uses colour and shape to support the pre-attentive recognition of related items (orange squares) as well as highlighting patterns occurring within the data.

7.3 Design Principles for Interactive Visualisations

Another influential approach to the presentation of visual graphics is that of Edward Tufte. Tufte researched numerous classic information designs and proposed a number of principles that can be broadly applied to a graphical representation. He argues that 'graphical excellence' in statistical graphics, for example, should consist of complex ideas communicated with clarity, precision and efficiency. Essentially, Tufte [37] maintains that graphical displays should:

1. Show the data
2. Induce the viewer to consider the substance (data) of the graphic rather than its methodology, design, or production
3. Avoid distorting the information conveyed
4. Present large numerical sets in a small space
5. Make larger data sets coherent
6. Encourage the eye to compare different parts of the data
7. Reveal the data at several layers of detail
8. Serve a clear purpose: description, exploration, tabulation, or decoration
9. Be closely integrated with statistical and verbal descriptions of a data set

Tufte [37] further considers that when viewing a visualisation consisting of incomprehensible, cluttered graphics, or 'chartjunk', there is a temptation to remove data. In this sense, clutter is considered to be attributable to poor design and not the data presented within the graphic. Thus, if a visualisation is too cluttered, the design should be simplified without compromising the data. The principle of avoiding cluttered graphics, or 'chartjunk', in graphic design has been translated by other authors in terms of guidelines and heuristics. Nielsen [20] refers to the avoidance of clutter and the elimination of extraneous graphics as a usability heuristic to maintain simplicity and aesthetic integrity in graphical design. Similarly, Card et al. [4] argue that, in some instances, certain representations, for example, bar charts, pie charts, histograms may include 'chartjunk 3D' – eye-catching and appealing graphics that serve little purpose and distract the user's attention away from the data.

Another related principle is the data-ink ratio, a means for measuring the value of a graphic by comparing the ink used to the data represented. More specifically, Tufte [37] measures the amount of ink used to represent data against the total amount of ink used in the drawing. If the data-ink ratio is high, the author has effectively used 'their ink to convey measured quantities'. With a low ratio, the graphic has less of what Tufte calls 'non-erasable' ink. An example of non-data ink erasure is range frames. The frame of an x-y plot is essentially non-data ink. Most of the frame can be erased, for example, leaving only the minimum and maximum values without loss of information or meaning.

As Tufte's main focus is producing paper graphical forms, and on information representation and not necessarily information structure, information architects question the value of his accounts for their own work. According to Brown [3], information architects, particularly those involved with interface design, might consider a digital equivalent of the data-ink ratio: the data-pixel ratio, comparing the pixels used for representing the interactive parts of the interface with the total number of pixels used. However, Brown suggests that Tufte's approach does not take into account the subtleties of interaction and usability, concluding that 'Tufte's principles do not take the user's motivation into account, concentrating instead on the data alone. Indeed, for information architects, the deliverable's audience must guide its design as much as the data does' [3].

While Brown's statements may hold some validity, Tufte's work has clear implications for informing the design of graphical displays. Tufte's nine basic principles for graphical excellence can broadly be applied to any graphic, be it paper or computer-based. In addition, Tufte's [37] treatment of multidimensional data has informed more recent techniques (parallel coordinates, iconic displays, dimensional stacking, hierarchical plotting, dynamic methods, and worlds within worlds – see Card et al. [4]; Keim and Kriegel [14] for a detailed review).

7.3.1 Design Principles Based on Dialogue Styles

A further set of principles for interactive visualisations can be based on design principles associated with dialogue styles. Dix et al. [9] proposes that a major concern for general design guidelines of interactive software is the subject of dialogue styles. Generally, these styles pertain to the means by which the user communicates input to the system, including how the system presents the communication device. Several basic dialogue styles can be incorporated in the design of UIs including, menus, fill-in-forms, question/answer, command languages, function keys, direct manipulation, and restricted natural language. Guidelines for these different dialogue styles are well documented in the literature [18, 31, 33].

A dialogue style relevant to the development of interactive visualisations is exemplified by the model describing the activity of manipulating objects and navigating through virtual spaces by exploiting the user's knowledge of their interactions in the physical world. The term 'direct manipulation', originally coined by Shneiderman [30], refers to a continuous presentation of objects which have physical (rather than symbolic) actions. The design properties of a graphical representation incorporating direct manipulation objects have been suggested by Card et al. [4], who state that such designs should reflect the way people manipulate objects in the real world, and should include the following aspects:

- Continuous representations of objects and actions (maintains visual momentum)
- Objects should be manipulated by physical actions or directional keys
- Operations should be visible, rapid and reversible
- Direct manipulation objects should be designed as recognisable objects and reflect real world actions

Norman's [21, 22] set of design principles are invaluable in characterising direct manipulation interfaces in terms of the behaviour of objects and their relation to each other. The primary design principles are *affordances*, *constraints*, *mappings*, *consistency*, and *feedback*. Norman [22] defines affordance as 'a term that refers to the properties of objects – what sorts of operations and manipulations can be done to an object'. In other words, the affordances of a visual element are the cues that it provides to communicate what actions can be performed with it.

When designing interface objects, such as buttons or sliders, it is important that the actions to be performed are obvious. Perceptual affordances, such as the representation of a pointing hand pushing a slider, simulate the action of a real object.

Similarly, sequential affordances occur when acting on a perceptual affordance, lead to feedback indicating a new affordance. For example, by selecting and clicking on the box of a scroll bar, the feedback provided indicates the box in an animated state. Figure 7.11 below shows four different examples of affordance.

The Filmfinder interface shown in Fig. 7.9 incorporates affordances such as sliders and scroll bars. Sliders can be used to specify other attributes of a film such as director or actor. Scroll bars can be used to confine attention to a particular span of years and film length, where more detail can be displayed. Such affordance techniques support the exploration of a space of parameter values to enhance user operations.

Whereas affordances suggest the scope of an object in terms of what it can do and how users can interact with it, constraints limit the possibilities that can be performed [29]. Physical constraints restrict the possible operations of an object. For example, the visual appearance of the shaft in the scroll bar box defines the physical limits of movement of the scroll bar. Logical constraints, however, work by constraining the order, position or location of objects. 'Context persistence' is an example of logical constraints in the Selective, Dynamic, Manipulation (SDM) paradigm [7]. The rationale for this constraint is that many data analysis tasks require users to focus on or manipulate a set of objects in the visualisation, while maintaining some relationship between the focus objects and the environment. Thus, SDM operations are logically constrained to maintain various degrees of context between the focus object set and its environment.

An important advantage associated with SDM is that it allows users to maintain scene context, or visual momentum within the interface. For example, when objects are displaced, users need to get feedback on the original object positions in order to maintain context with the rest of the environment. One way that SDM achieves this is by having multiple representations of an object. Each data object is represented by two graphical representations: the 'body' and the 'shell'. Object shells are left behind in the home position (in white) when the object bodies are drawn out and displaced. Object shells always appear in the original object width and height.

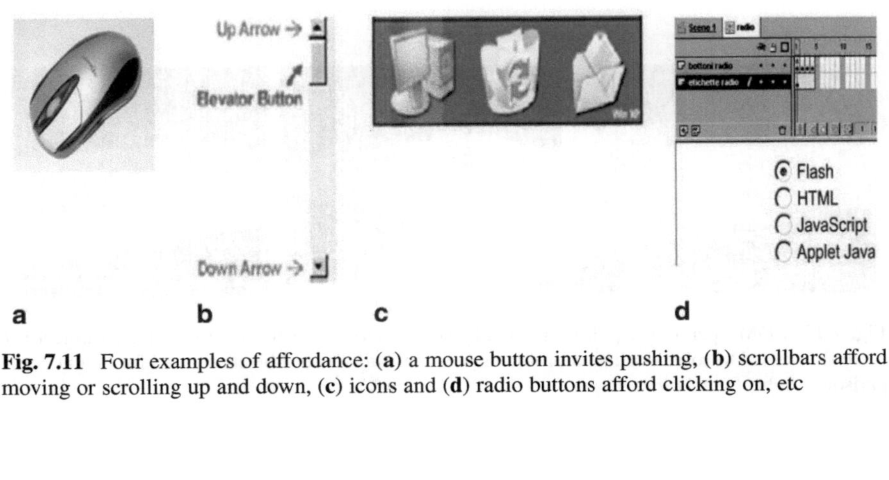

a b c d

Fig. 7.11 Four examples of affordance: (**a**) a mouse button invites pushing, (**b**) scrollbars afford moving or scrolling up and down, (**c**) icons and (**d**) radio buttons afford clicking on, etc

Figure 7.12 (below) shows examples of object sets (left and centre) which have been displaced and their shells, left behind at the original positions, widths and heights (in white).

Allowing users to maintain context while navigating an informational space can potentially enhance the usability and perceived satisfaction of interactive visualisations. In their study comparing zoomable map-based interfaces, Hornbaek et al. [12] found that users preferred a map-based interface with an overview, as it helped them to keep track of their position on the map. However, maps providing rich semantic navigational cues without an overview allowed users to navigate faster. Hornbaek et al. [12] suggest that depending on task demands, zoomable interfaces featuring integrated overview and detail views can increase complexity, requiring additional cognitive and motor effort.

Visualisations can further support the mapping of different data attributes to a variety of visual variables, including position, colour, texture, motion, etc. [38]. Each different mapping allows some relationships to become more distinct, while others become less distinct. Allowing the user to interactively adjust mappings can be advantageous, although such mapping changes are in direct conflict with the important principle of consistency. Designing for consistency by ensuring consistent logical operations (e.g. order or position of selectable objects and choice of colour hues) can ensure that interfaces are easier to learn and less error-prone. Finally, the key principle of feedback to provide visual (and if appropriate, auditory and tactile) information is an inherent property in interface design.

Wiss and Carr [39] consider that while most visualisations provide indirect manipulation via a control panel or a set of tools, the direct manipulation of the graphical elements themselves is often more efficient for improving the usability of the visualisation. Providing affordances for interaction is therefore a challenge in designing interactive visualisations. North et al. [23] propose that guiding principles for designing the Visible Human Library interface (see Fig. 7.13 below), were derived from techniques which include direct manipulation. They suggest that these principles have been successfully incorporated in many exploration interfaces. Filtering processes by issuing dynamic queries enables users to drag sliders, click on options, and receive rapid visual feedback to identify desired data for retrieval.

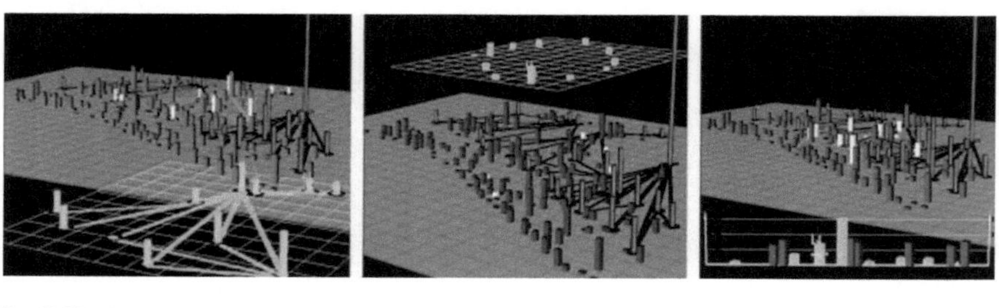

Fig. 7.12 SDM operations: pulling focus objects (green) to the front (left), selected object set (green) is raised to solve occlusion problems (centre), two sets of objects created for height comparisons (right) (*See Color Plates*)

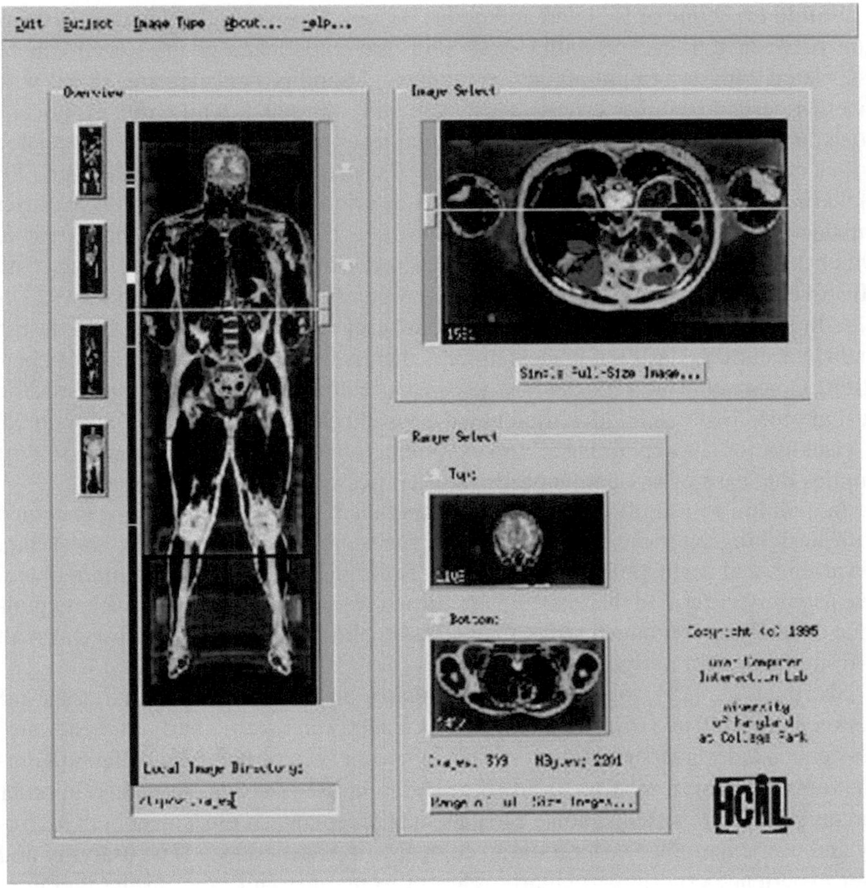

Fig. 7.13 The Visible Human Explorer [23] – dragging sliders animates the cross-sections through the body (*See Color Plates*)

7.4 Usability and User Experience Goals

The design principles associated with direct manipulation provide useful guidance for the development of interactive visualisations. As with other interdisciplinary approaches, such as Human-Computer Interaction (HCI), cognitive engineering, human factors, and Computer-Supported Cooperative Work (CSCW), the development of interactive visualisations as information systems needs to be concerned with designing systems that match user's goals, expectations, and motivations. With the development of visualisation prototypes incorporating manipulable UIs, it is possible to form generalisations from existing HCI and interaction design principles.

Within the scope of HCI and interaction design, Sharp et al. [29] make a distinction between top-level usability goals and user experience goals, which can be associated with designing interactive products. Usability goals are concerned with meeting certain usability criteria associated with a product, while user experience goals are concerned with enhancing the quality of the user experience associated with a product. Several core characteristics of usability are defined by Nielsen [20] including: learnability, memorability, efficiency in use, reliability in use and user satisfaction. A main reference for usability can be considered as 'the extent to which a product can be used by specified users to achieve specified goals with effectiveness, efficiency and satisfaction in a specified context of use' (ISO 9241–11). In addition, other usability criteria relating to aspects of interface design include accuracy, clarity of presentation, comprehensibility, and flexibility of operation. Constantine and Lockwood [8] propose that more focused and specific design objectives can be identified based on user role characteristics. For example, a visualisation incorporating complex interactions with large amounts of data implies that ease of navigation needs to be addressed in interface design.

In addition to usability criteria, user experience goals are primarily concerned with designing interactive products to be fun, enjoyable, pleasurable, satisfying, rewarding, and aesthetically pleasing [29]. Such goals differ from the more objective usability criteria in that they are concerned with how users subjectively experience an interactive product, rather than assessing how useful or productive a system is from the system perspective.

Sharp et al. [29] suggest that recognising and understanding the trade-off between usability and user experience goals is important, particularly as this awareness enables designers to understand the consequences of pursuing different combinations of them in relation to fulfilling different user's needs. Arguably, in order for any interactive visualisation UI to gain user acceptance it must meet both usability and user experience criteria for an enjoyable user experience. The usability and user experience criteria particularly relevant to interaction design in the literature [18, 20, 31, 35] were reviewed by the author. These criteria, together with the relevant design principles associated with direct manipulation are proposed as a generic set of guidelines for interactive visualisation UIs in Table 7.2 below.

Table 7.2 Design principles for an interactive visualisation UI

Design principle	Description	Reference
Consistency	Consistent sequences of actions should be required in similar situations; identical terminology should be used in the interface (e.g. commands, prompts, menus, and help screens)	[18, 20, 31, 35]
Cater to universal usability	Recognise the needs of diverse users. Add features for novices (explanations) and for experts (shortcuts) to enrich interface design and improve perceived system quality.	[20, 31]
Provide feedback & visibility of system status	Provide users with system feedback and status information: make them aware of their progress.	[18, 20, 31, 35]

(continued)

(continued)

Design principle	Description	Reference
	Provide adequate visual feedback in manipulation of direct manipulation objects.	[21, 22]
Permit reversible actions	Reversible actions can reduce user anxiety and encourages exploration of unfamiliar options. Allow actions to be visible, rapid and reversible.	[4, 31, 35]
Support error handling, prevention & recognition	Prevent serious errors from occurring and provide mechanisms to assist users to recognise, diagnose and recover from errors. Use clear, explicit error messages.	[18, 20, 31]
Support internal locus of control	Provide status information and feedback within easy view to keep users aware and informed. Indicate progress in task performance.	[20, 31, 35]
Reduce memory load	Keep displays simple, consolidate multiple pages. Incorporate 'see & point' techniques rather than 'remember & type'. Make all available actions/commands salient.	[20, 31]
User control	Clearly mark exits. Allow user to initiate and control actions. Provide obvious means to redo/undo commands and actions.	[18, 20, 35]
Simple and aesthetic integrity	Graphical elements should incorporate simple design (use natural dialogue, eliminate extraneous words or graphics). Avoid clutter. Information should appear in a natural and logical order.	[18, 20]
Incorporate logical constraints wherever possible	Provide logical constraints in the position or order of direct manipulation objects or graphical elements.	[21, 22]
Incorporate perceptual affordances	Ensure that operations and manipulations to be performed on a direct manipulation object or graphical element are made obvious.	[21, 22]
Incorporate mapping of data attributes	Ensure appropriate support for the mapping of different data attributes to visual variables, including position, colour, texture, motion, etc.	[21, 22, 38]
Strive to attain a pleasurable user experience	Ensure that interactions with a visualisation UI creates a fun, enjoyable, pleasurable, satisfying, rewarding, and aesthetically pleasing user experience.	[13, 29]

7.5 Summary

Designing effective interactive visualisations as graphical representations or UIs is a multifaceted problem and some of the relevant design principles for supporting this process have been reviewed in this chapter. The influential theories relating to perceptual organisation and data graphics previously described are highly relevant for informing the design of both informational and scientific interactive visualisations. As aforementioned, being aware of the comprehensibility of any image or graphic is essential for the effective presentation of the information inherent in the data [26]. From a design perspective, a number of authors concur that the user-centred design of visualisations or a comprehensive set of design guidelines is rare in the visualisation literature [2, 6]. Arguably, the development of visualisations as scientific and business data applications and manipulable UIs necessitates the application of usability and user experience criteria in the design and evaluation process. Moreover, this usability and user criteria common to HCI and interaction design were summarised as several generic, high-level design principles for this purpose, together with principles related to the concept of direct manipulation (see Talbe 7.2). Finally, certain principles derived from theoretical accounts discussed in this chapter [16, 21, 37] are further referenced by Card et al. [4] as the ways or principal means by which visualisations can amplify cognition, notably by:

1. Increasing the memory and processing resources available to users
2. Reducing the search for information
3. Using visual representations to enhance the detection of patterns
4. Enabling perceptual inference operations
5. Using perceptual attention mechanisms for monitoring
6. Encoding information in a manipulable medium.

Card et al. [4] elaborate further on these principal means by which visualisations aid cognition, which can be adapted as cognitive properties of interactive data visualisations based on scientific and business applications. As Card et al. [4] suggest, interactive visualisations can enhance cognitive effort by several separate mechanisms, but the efficiency of these different mechanisms further depends on the appropriate mappings of data into a visual form fit for the human perceiver.

References

1. Ahlberg, C., and Shneiderman, B. (1994) Visual information seeking using the filmfinder Conference Companion of CHI'94, ACM Conference on Human Factors in Computing Systems, 433.
2. Brath, R.(1997). 3D Interactive Information Visualization: Guidelines from experience and analysis of applications. http://www3.sympatico.ca/blevis/thesis49guide.html
3. Brown, D. (2002). Three Lessons From Tufte: Special Deliverable #6. http://www.boxesandarrows.com/archives/three_lessons_from_tufte_special_deliverable_6.php
4. Card, S. K., Card, J. D., and MacKinlay, B. Shneiderman, (1999). Readings in Information Visualisation – Using Vision to Think. Morgan Kaufmann Publishers.
5. Chang, D., Dooley, L., and Tuovinen, J. E. (2002). Gestalt theory in visual screen design – A new look at an old subject. In Proceedings of WCCE2001 Australian Topics: Selected Papers from the Seventh World Conference on Computers in Education, Copenhagen, Denmark. Conferences in Research and Practice in Information Technology, 8. McDougall, A., Murnane, J., and Chambers, D., Eds., ACS. 5 x2013;12. http://crpit.com/confpapers/CRPITV8Chang.pdf
6. Chen, C., and Czerwinski, M. (2000). Empirical evaluations of information visualisations: An introduction. In *International Journal of Human-Computer Studies*, 53(5), 631–635.
7. Chuah, M. C., Roth, S. F., Mattis, J., and Kolojejchick, J. A. (1995). SDM: Selective dynamic manipulation of visualizations. In *Proceedings of UIST '95, ACM Symposium on User Interface Software and Technology* Pittsburgh. 61–70.
8. Constantine, L. L., and Lockwood, L. A. D. (1999). *Software For Use. A Practical Guide to the Models and Methods of Usage-Centered Design.* New York: Addison-Wesley, ACM Press.
9. Dix, A., Finlay, J., Abowd, G. and Beale, R. (1997). *Human-Computer Interaction.* Cambridge: Prentice Hall.

10. Fisher, R. M., and Smith-Gratto, K. (1998–99). Gestalt theory: A foundation for instructional screen design. *Journal of Educational Technology Systems*, 27(4): 361–371.
11. Hicks, M., O'Malley, C., Nichols, S., and Anderson, B. (2003). Comparison of 2D and 3D representations for visualising telecommunications usage. *Behaviour & Information Technology*, 22(3): 185–201, Taylor & Francis Ltd.
12. Hornbæk, K., Bederson, B., Plaisant, C. (2002). Navigation patterns and usability of overview + detail and Zoomable user interfaces for maps. *ACM Transactions on Human-Computer Interaction*, 9(4): 362–389.
13. Jordan, P. W. (2000). *Designing Pleasurable Products*. London: Taylor and Francis.
14. Kein, D. A., and Keim, H. -P. Kriegel, (1994). VisDB: Database exploration using multidimensional visualization. IEEE Computer Graphics and Applications, Sept. 1994, 4049.
15. Koffa, K. (1935). *Principles of Gestalt Psychology*. London: Routledge and Kegan Paul.
16. Larkin, J. H. and Simon, H. A. (1987). Why a diagram is (sometimes) worth ten thousand words. *Cognitive Science*, 11, 65–99.
17. Lewandowsky, S., and Behrens, J. T. (1999). Statistical graphs and maps, Handbook of Applied Cognition, eds F.T. Durso, R.S. Nickerson, R.W. Schvaneveldt, S.T. Dumais, D.S. Lindsay, M.T.H. Chi, Chichester, UK, WILEY, pp. 513–549.
18. Mayhew, D. J. (1992). *Principles and Guidelines in Software User Interface Design*. Englewood Cliffs, NJ: Prentice Hall.
19. Moore, P. and Fitz, C. (1993). Gestalt theory and instructional design. *Journal of Technical Writing and Communication*, 23(2): 137–157.
20. Nielsen, J. (1993). *Usability Engineering*. San Francisco: Morgan Kaufman. Nielsen, J. (1994). Heuristic evaluation. In Nielsen, J., and Mack, R. L. (eds.) *Usability Inspection Methods*. New York: John Wiley & Sons.
21. Norman, D. (1988). *The Psychology of Everyday Things*. NY: Basic Books.
22. Norman, D. A. (1992). *Turn Signals are the Facial Expressions of Automobiles*. Reading, MA: Addison-Wesley.
23. Ahlberg, C., and Shneiderman, B. (1994) Visual information seeking using the filmfinder Conference Companion of CHI'94, ACM Conference on Human Factors in Computing Systems, 433.
24. Palmer, S. E., and Rock, I. (1994). Rethinking perceptual organization: The role of uniform connectedness. *Psychonomic Bulletin and Review*, 1(1): 29–55.
25. Reinhard, P., Hesse, F. W., Hron, A., and Picard, E. (1997). Manipulable graphics for computer-supported problem solving. *Journal of Computer Assisted Learning*, 13: 148–162.
26. Senay, H., and Ignatius, E. (1999). Rules and Principles of Scientific Data Visualization. http://www.siggraph.org/education/materials/HyperVis/percept/visrules.htm.
27. Shah, P., and Carpenter, P. A. (1995). Conceptual limitations in understanding line graphs. *Journal of Experimental Psychology General*, 124(1): 43–61.
28. Shah, P., Mayer, R. E., and Hegarty, M. (1999). Graphs as aids to knowledge construction: Signalling techniques for guiding the process of graph comprehension. *Journal of Educational Psychology*, 91(4): 690–702.
29. Sharp, H., Rogers, Y., and Preece, J. (2007). Interaction Design: Beyond Human-Computer Interaction. John Wiley & Sons, Inc.
30. Shneiderman, B. (1983). Direct manipulation: A step beyond programming languages. *IEEE Computer*, 16(8): 57–69.
31. Shneiderman, B. and Plaisant, C. (2005). Designing the User Interface – Strategies for Effective Human-Computer Interaction (Fourth Edition). Addison-Wesley Longman Inc.
32. Slocum, T. S. (1983). Predicting visual clusters on graduated circle maps. *American Cartographer*, 10(1): 59–72.
33. Smith, S. L., and J. N. Mosier, (1986). Guidelines for Designing User Interface Software. Mitre Corporation Report MTR-9420, Mitre Corporation.
34. Spence, R. (2007). *Information Visualization*. Longman: Higher Education.
35. Tognazzini, B. (1992). *Tog on Interface*. Reading, MA: Addison-Wesley.
36. Tovée, M. J. (1996). *An Introduction to the Visual System*. Cambridge, UK: Cambridge University Press.

37. Tufte, E. R. (1983). The Visual Display of Quantitative Information. Graphics Press.
38. Ware, C. (2004). Information Visualisation – Perception for Design. Academic Press, Morgan Kaufmann.
39. Wiss, U., and Carr, D. (1998). A Cognitive Classification Framework for 3-Dimensional Information Visualization. Research report LTU-TR--1998/4--SE, Luleå University of Technology.
40. Zacks, J., and Tversky, B. (1999). Bars and lines: A study of graph communication. *Memory & Cognition*, 27(6): 1073–1079.

Chapter 8
Applying a User-Centered Approach to Interactive Visualisation Design

Ingo Wassink, Olga Kulyk, Betsy van Dijk, Gerrit van der Veer, and Paul van der Vet

Abstract Analysing users in their context of work and finding out how and why they use different information resources is essential to provide interactive visualisation systems that match their goals and needs. Designers should actively involve the intended users throughout the whole process. This chapter presents a user-centered approach for the design of interactive visualisation systems. We describe three phases of the iterative visualisation design process: the early envisioning phase, the global specification phase, and the detailed specification phase. The whole design cycle is repeated until some criterion of success is reached. We discuss different techniques for the analysis of users, their tasks and domain. Subsequently, the design of prototypes and evaluation methods in visualisation practice are presented. Finally, we discuss the practical challenges in design and evaluation of collaborative visualisation environments. Our own case studies and those of others are used throughout the whole chapter to illustrate various approaches.

Keywords Design process, User analysis, Task analysis, Domain analysis, User profile, Task model, Visualisation design, Evaluation.

8.1 Introduction

Humans have remarkable perceptual capabilities that tend to be underestimated in current visualisation designs [68]. Often, this is due to the fact that designers do not analyse who the users are, what tasks they want to perform using the visualisations, and what their working environments are [39].

One of the key questions, of course, is: what is successful visualisation? Usability factors, such as efficiency, satisfaction and ease of use, are used in user interface design to express the quality of interactive systems [45, 70]. Besides these generally applicable usability factors, the quality of visualisations will depend on whether they meet their goals. For instance, scientific visualisations aim to support the data exploration and decision making process [8, 72]. In this case, text books

E. Zudilova-Seinstra et al. (eds.) *Trends in Interactive Visualization*,
doi:10.1007/978-1-84800-269-2

and lecture material can form a valuable source to gain more insight into goals of visualisation techniques these scientists frequently use.

Last but not least, the success of visualisations depends on the user: a good visualisation for one user may be a poor visualisation for another, because of the variance in user group characteristics and the differences in tasks to be performed [92]. Amar and Stasko [2] refer to this as the Worldview Gap: what is being visualised and what needs to be visualised. People give preference to the visual representations that strongly match their putative mental model, not so much the structure of the information [27].

Caroll [9] stated that "When we design systems and applications, we are, most essentially, designing scenarios of interaction". This is also true for interactive visualisation design. It is a process of system design used for creating and manipulating visualisations. We define an interactive visualisation system as a system that not only provides different views on data (objects, structures, processes), but also enables dialogues to explore and to modify the data. Such systems should be designed for specific tasks and specific user groups. Therefore it is essential to analyse what kind of visualisation techniques should be used to support the tasks at hand and what types of interaction techniques best fit the particular user groups [25, 39, 91]. Analysing users in their context of work and finding out how and why they use different information resources is essential to provide interactive visualisation systems [39, 90]. Designers should actively involve the intended users throughout the whole visualisation design process, from the analysis to the evaluation stage [33, 74].

In this chapter, we present a user-centered design approach for interactive visualisation systems. We explain the iterative visualisation design process. Subsequently, we will discuss different techniques for the analysis of the users, their tasks and environments, the design of prototypes and evaluation methods in visualisation practice. Finally, we discuss the practical challenges in design and evaluation of collaborative visualisation environments. Our own case studies and those of others are used to illustrate and discuss differences in approaches.

8.2 User-Centered Visualisation Design

Visualisation design employs an iterative, user-centered approach that globally can be split into three phases: the early envisioning phase, the global specification phase, and the detailed specification phase. In the early envisioning phase, the current situation (the users, their environments and their tasks) is analysed, resulting in user profiles and requirements. In the global specification phase and the detailed specification phase, solutions are proposed and presented to the users and other stakeholders. Each of these phases can contain more than one iteration, while each iteration consists of three activities [67] (see Fig. 8.1).

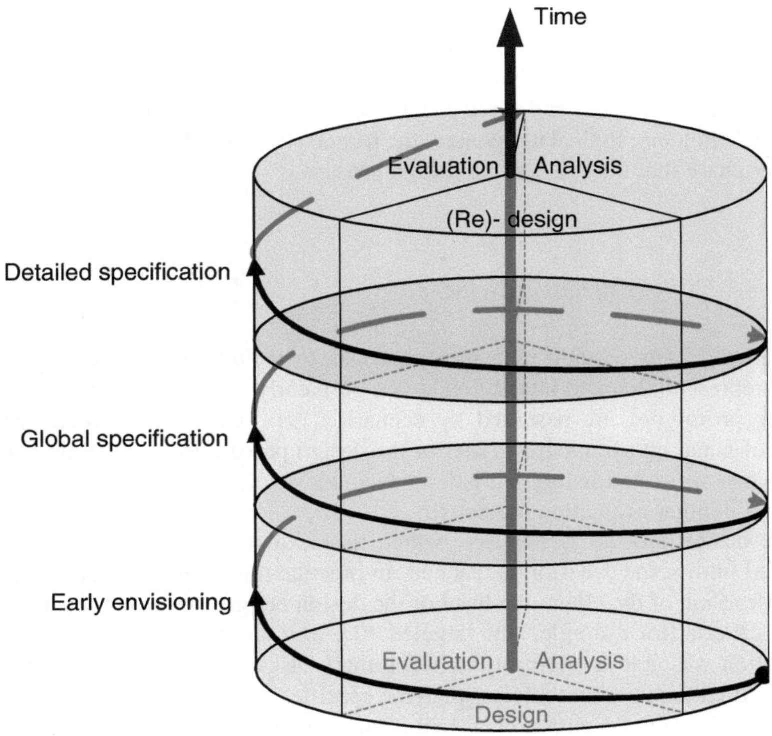

Fig. 8.1 User-centered visualisation design process

8.2.1 Analysis

Analysis of the users, their environments and their tasks. The first cycles, that are part of the early envisioning phase, concern the current tasks and context. Later cycles, that are part of the specification phases, concern proposed changes in the current situation and concern the systems to be built [82].

8.2.2 Design

The creative activity in which proposals for solutions are developed using the results from the analysis. In the first cycles the results are scenarios of the tasks and situations where the solutions will be applied. Later solutions will concern the use of future technology, resulting in low-fidelity (Lo-Fi) prototypes [45, 64]. In still later cycles, that are part of the detailed specification phase, one can include interactive high-fidelity (Hi-Fi) prototypes and finally beta-versions of the new system. In all cycles, the product is both an explicit (and often formal) record of the proposed design decisions, and a representation intended to present to the users and other stakeholders. In the later phases, the formal records will be aimed at the engineering phase that may follow the design process.

8.2.3 Evaluation

Evaluation of any visualisation technique has to include an assessment of both visual representation and interaction styles. At a early stages of development, low-fidelity prototypes are assessed by scenarios [9], observations, focus groups, interviews and questionnaires. Later in the design process interactive high-fidelity prototypes are tested using heuristic evaluation, cognitive walkthrough, usability testing and other evaluation methods.

The design process is iterative, which means that the whole design cycle is repeated until some criterion is reached. In practice this criterion could be the targeted deadline of the client, the level of the design budget, or having reached ergonomic criteria (for example, "the targeted 90% of a sample from the intended user population was able to perform the bench mark tasks with the new system within the specified time period with less than the specified maximum number of errors"). The key point of the design cycle is that from the very beginning of the design process, stakeholders are involved to provide design ideas and feedback.

The design cycle does not guarantee successful visualisation design, however it helps to discover problems in the early stage of design. When a proposed solution is designed, usability problems will be found in the evaluation that follows design. The analysis of the next iteration will help understand why these problems exist [39].

8.3 Analysing the Users, Their Tasks and Their Domain

Users differ in perceptual abilities and therefore have different needs in visualisation use [86]. Besides differences in perceptual abilities, other factors, such as gender, age, culture, education, cognitive and physical abilities, and economic status, are reported to play an important role [54, 69]. Additionally, different users have different tasks to perform and therefore have different needs visualisation systems have to meet [2].

Due to these differences, it is essential to perform a detailed analysis of the users, their environments and their tasks, before starting with the design of visualisation systems [20]. Several questions have to be answered [6, 45, 61, 67, 70]:

- Who will be the users and what are their characteristics?
- What are their tasks?

- What are the objects and processes that need to be visualised?
- What kind of insight should the visualisation support?

User, domain and task analysis are performed in order to gain insight into the needs and working practices of the intended users. Kujala and Kauppinen [39] argue to do these analyses to identify the core set of common needs and the conflicting needs. The output of the user, domain and task analysis consists of user profiles and requirements.

In our user study [42], we performed a user and domain analysis in the bioinformatics domain. We explored the working practices and experiences of scientists with bioinformatics tools and visualisations. In this domain, scientists from different disciplines, such as bioinformatics, biology, chemistry and statistics, have to collaborate to solve life science questions which cannot be solved by scientists from a single discipline. They work with huge amounts of data stored in on-line databases and use tools to access these databases and to analyse and modify the data stored in them. These scientists have different expertises in computer science, programming, and using console applications. The tools currently available are often complex and unsuitable for non-bioinformaticians [70]. Additionally, scientists from different disciplines use their own type of visualisation to gain insight into the problem and to provide "their piece of the puzzle".

One of the problems in this domain is how to combine different types of visualisation and link the information available in the different visualisations [42]. Current bioinformatics tools do not meet the needs of the scientists. To help them perform their tasks, a new generation of tools and interactive visualisations has to be developed [37].

8.3.1 Selecting the User Group

Different types of users often have distinct goals, perform different tasks and use different tools. It is important to distinguish these different types of user, because of their different goals in relation to the interactive visualisation system [16, 38]. For example in life science, biologists need to be able to detect differences between DNA sequences, whereas statisticians need to combine sample results in order to calculate the reliability of detected differences [42].

Ideally, the results of a user study should cover all user groups [15]. However, in practice, it is only possible to involve a limited number of users. Therefore, a careful selection of the participants is required to gain insight in characteristics of the typical (or prototypical) users and who could be relevant special types of users.

Wilson et al. [88] noticed that one of the main problems in user-centered design is to convince stakeholders of the need to involve users. And when users are involved, they are often selected by the stakeholders, for example managers. This results in an unrepresentative user selection, mostly consisting of expert users and early adopters who are willing to use the product.

In the bioinformatics domain, two groups of users can be distinguished based on their expertise with bioinformatics applications [34, 42]. The first group consists of bioinformaticians, who are expert users. Because of their education and job traditions, they are regular users of bioinformatics applications. They often have a lot of programming experience and use specialised bioinformatics tools, which are mostly console applications.

The second user group consists of biologists, who are the novice users of bioinformatics applications. They are not familiar with console applications and often have no programming experience at all. Because they need to use bioinformatics tools to perform and to interpret their experiments, they use web front-ends to access these tools. These front-ends are often direct translations of the console applications and contain a lot of parameters for configuration. Additionally, a large number of tools is available, which often confuses the biologists as to which one to use [65].

For example, ClustalW [12] is a frequently used tool in the bioinformatics domain. It is a sequence alignment tool, used for comparing DNA or protein sequences. The tool uses as input a set of DNA or protein sequences, often provided by the users by copy-paste actions of sequences found at other websites. The result is a static visualisation showing the alignments of the sequences. The tool provides a lot of parameters to optimise the alignments. However, most biologists do not understand the algorithm behind the tool [55] and therefore often only use the default settings [42].

Another problem is that most sequence alignment tools only achieve at maximum a 50% accuracy [77]. Therefore, scientists have to manually correct these alignments using their expert knowledge, such as knowledge about structures of protein families. Interactive sequence alignment tools exist to help scientists perform these post-edits. For example, Jalview [13] is an interactive visualisation tool for editing sequence alignments. Additionally, Jalview provides different types of visualisations of the alignment, such as a phylogenetic tree (see Fig. 8.2).

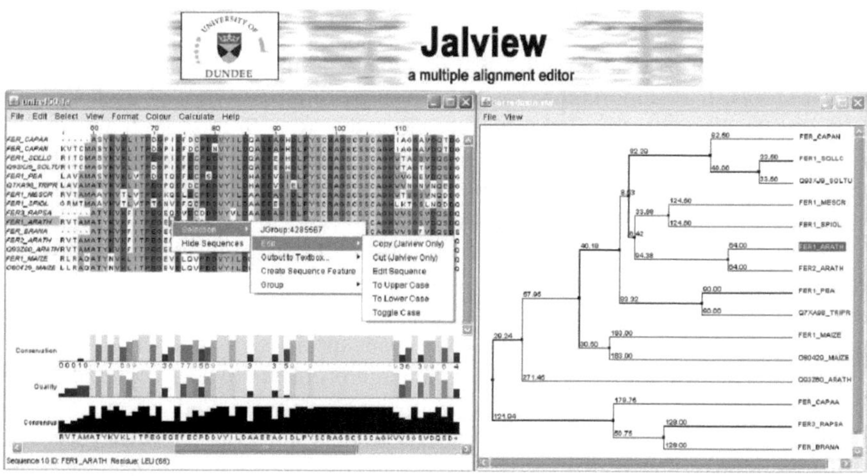

Fig. 8.2 Jalview, a sequence alignment editor for improving automatic sequence alignments. Right: an interactive visualisation of a sequence alignment. Left: a phylogenetic tree, based on the alignment (*See Color Plates*)

If both novice and expert users have to use the same visualisation system, it is important to design help for the novice users and short-cuts for the experts. All of them could be using the same visualisation system if they are all taking the same role. A good but classic example of differentiating user interfaces for novice and expert users is the Training Wheels approach of Carroll and Carrithers [10]. In this approach, novice users only can perform an essential but safe set of actions to use the applications. When users become more skillful, more advanced functionality becomes available to them. Another approach to help novice users is the use of wizards for helping these users to achieve a particular goal [34].

8.3.2 Collecting Data

There are two main types of user analysis techniques: quantitative and qualitative techniques [67]. In quantitative techniques, also known as studies in breadth, users' input is used to discover the different types of users and the differences in their needs. One has to be careful that measuring quantitative data does not lead to design decisions based on democracy, but on the distribution of requirements among the users. Quantitative data are often easier to compare, but a large sample is needed to measure both general and exceptional requirements.

Qualitative techniques are studies in depth, which means that more detailed information is gathered on how tasks are done. Since they require much time per participant, the number of participants is often limited.

We will describe three user study techniques frequently used in the practise of interactive visualisation, one quantitative technique (questionnaire) and two qualitative techniques (interview and observation).

8.3.2.1 Applying A Questionnaire

Questionnaires are often used to get quantitative data from large user groups and may under certain conditions be suitable for translation into statistical information [45]. The response rate is often a problem, especially when no direct contact with the participants exists [5, 67]. A questionnaire is represented as a list of closed or open questions or a combination of both. It is important to design a questionnaire carefully, because questions can easily be misunderstood and it is not always possible to explain them during the session. To prevent such problems, it is suggested to perform a pilot study on a small group in advance [67].

Sutcliffe et al. [76] performed a user study to discover the user specific needs of the representation of information retrieval systems. They used a questionnaire in a pilot study among seventeen users, mostly researchers and students. The results of the questionnaire were used to split the group into novice users and expert users and to discover interesting aspects to focus on during the observations. The number of participants is too low to generalise results, but it can be useful as a quick method when a clear hypothesis is not known yet. However, Benyon et al. [5] argue that if the time required to construct a questionnaire is taken into account, with a small number of participants an interview will provide the same information or more with little or no extra effort. The advantage of interviews is, that the interviewer is available to explain questions and ambiguities [67].

We [42] used a questionnaire to gain insight into the experiences of novice users with bioinformatics tools. The participants were forty-seven life science students who were learning to use bioinformatics tools and resources during a course. The students did not have much expertise using these tools and therefore were not able to give extensive feedback. A questionnaire was a suitable method for getting quantitative response. We provided space at the end for comments and motivations. However such space is not often used and if used, the comments and motivations are mostly very diverse and therefore difficult to interpret. By distributing the questionnaire during the weekly classroom lectures, we got a high response rate (90%).

8.3.2.2 Interviewing the Users

Due to the opportunity to ask more detailed explanations, interviews form a main source of knowledge of working practices. Interviews can vary from structured to unstructured [67]. A structured interview is based on prepared questions in a fixed order and has much in common with a questionnaire. In an unstructured interview, the questions are not specified in advance, but develop spontaneously during the interview. The analysis is often difficult and the danger exists that the interviewer gets "carried away" in subsequent interviews, triggered by topics discussed in former interviews [90]. In practice, most interviews are semi-structured, which combines features of both structured and unstructured interviews [5, 67].

Nardi and Miller [49] used interviews to investigate how spreadsheet users with different programming skills and interests collaborate to develop spreadsheet applications. The focus of the study was to find out how these spreadsheets stimulated collaborative work and structured the problem solving process. Their study contains eleven interviews with spreadsheet users, followed by an analysis of some of their spreadsheets. They distinguished three types of spreadsheet users based on their skills in programming: the non-programmers, local developers and programmers. These three classes of users make it easier to understand the roles of different users and how these users collaborate. For example, local developers serve as consultants for non-programmers and in their turn seek programmers for assistance. The study shows that spreadsheets form a communicable means for sharing programming skills and knowledge about advanced spreadsheet features from experienced users to less experienced users.

Both novice users and expert users need to be investigated, because the first group is required for establishing a user profile, the latter for collecting information about expert procedures [45]. Interviews are time consuming, and therefore only a limited group of participants can be chosen. Therefore, we [42] have chosen to only interview expert users in the bioinformatics domain, because these expert users could give extensive feedback about their working practices and the bioinformatics resources they use. As mentioned, the novice users were analysed by distributing a questionnaire. The interviews with the expert users took place in the interviewees' working environment to make the participants feel more comfortable, which is also known as contextual inquiry [7]. These expert users mentioned that visualisation is very important in interdisciplinary research for discussing experiment design and results, however, it is often underused.

Closely related to interviews are focus groups: not just one person is interviewed but a group of persons [48, 67]. An advantage of focus groups is that they enable discussion among participants. One participant's opinion or knowledge will trigger additional comments and ideas from the others. However, a trained facilitator is required to lead the discussion in order to prevent some participants from dominating the process.

Kulyk et al. [41] arranged a focus group to get participants' opinions about a real-time feedback system on social dynamics in meetings. Such a system visualises different aspects of meetings, such as speaking time and visual attention of participants, in order to improve group cohesion. The focus group addressed five questions to discuss the idea of such a feedback system and showed that participants thought such a system will improve the efficiency of meetings.

8.3.2.3 Observing the Users

Interviews and questionnaires are both useful analysis techniques for getting information on users. However, participants often fail to mention relevant aspects of their working practices and working environments, because they are either not aware of them (tacit knowledge [58]), or do not see the importance for the analyst [14, 67]. Observation is a useful technique for gathering this more implicit type of information. The observer watches the participants perform a set of normal working tasks in their natural environment to get to know the working practices of the participants.

Ethnographic observation is a frequently applied observation method that aims to observe people in their natural setting ("community of practice") without intending to influence their behaviour. The method originates from the study of (unknown) cultures. It is used in social sciences to understand group behaviour or organisational activities [67]. A classical example is the study of Latour and Woolgar [44], who observed a group of life scientists in their work environment to gain insight into both their group behaviour and their working context.

We [42] performed an ethnographic observation in the bioinformatics domain to gain insight into the way scientists from different disciplines collaborate during meetings. In such a context, it is not allowed to disturb the collaboration process for asking questions. Therefore, ethnographic observation is essential. If explanation is needed, this can still be asked after the meetings.

A drawback of ethnographic observation is that participants are aware of being observed. Consequently, there is the risk they do tasks in a prescribed or expected way instead of the way they normally do them. Participants can also get nervous by being observed, which can result in mistakes. One should be aware that the mere presence of an observer in the community of practice does make a difference. People have to get used to this “intruder”, trust the person, and accept the presence and the habit of the ethnographer to be “nosy”.

8.3.2.4 Combining Techniques

Most analyses are not based on a single technique, but consist of a combination of quantitative and qualitative methods [38]. Benyon et al. [5] argue for complementing interviews and questionnaires with observations. Combining different techniques in order to pursue a single goal is also known as triangulation [67]. After their pilot study by means of a questionnaire, Sutcliffe et al. [76] continued their user analysis of information retrieval systems by doing observations of novice and expert users. Both novice users and expert users were given the same set of tasks to perform. The participants were asked to think aloud and both their verbal and physical actions were recorded. The think-aloud technique is a valuable add-on to standard observation to understand what goes on in a person’s mind [67], however, people feel sometimes strange or scared doing this.

Consolvo et al. [14] refer to Labscape [3], a ubiquitous computing environment that helps biologists to do their experiments. The Labscape environment is a workflow-based environment which enables scientists to model and to visualise their procedures. During experiment execution, it structures and provides the information needed and enables the scientist to capture and structure generated data. Consolvo et al. combined interviews and contextual field research to discover the needs of the intended users of the Labscape environment. Contextual field research (CFR) has much in common with observation but in contrast to observation, interaction with users is allowed. CFR is a good technique for gathering qualitative data [14]. It is conducted in the users’ “natural” environment and the users perform their normal daily activities. Like in normal observation, a disadvantage of CFR is that users are aware of being observed.

Chen and Yu [11] compared and combined the results of existing user studies in information visualisation techniques into a meta-analysis. The advantage of such an approach is that qualitative and quantitative user studies can be combined. If existing user studies are compared, it is important to decide on the criteria for considering studies to be comparable. Examples of criteria Chen and Yu used are the topic of the study, the amount of data used and the variables measured.

8.3.3 Structuring the Data

The analysis activity delivers complex data sets that need to be translated into user profiles, task models and descriptions of the working environments [39]. User profiles cover information about the abilities and disabilities of the users, their working environment and cultural diversity [70, 92]. Task models contain information about what tasks users currently perform and how different people are involved in performing them [84]. Task models can also be used to indicate directions to improve the current situation [2]. The description of the working environment contains information about the layout of the environment as well as information on the objects and the tools to modify these objects [82].

In our case study [42], we described profiles for three types of users in the life science domain. The first user group covers the domain experts. This group consists of the bioinformaticians who both create and use the bioinformatics tools and are familiar with console applications and programming. The second user group consists of novice users, mostly biologists. The user profiles describing the novice users show that these users often have problems using the bioinformatics tools provided by domain experts. The third group describes multidisciplinary life science teams. This profile describes that visualisation is an important means during discussion, however it is often underused in life science.

Vyas et al. [85] collected data using various methods, such as contextual interviews, diary keeping and job-shadowing, to investigate the working environment in academic research. They translated the collected data into personas, which could be used as requirements for the system to be designed. A persona is a fictitious person usually described in 1–2 pages [15]. Like user profiles, a persona is based on data collected from user studies and represents the most relevant user characteristics. However, personas represent extreme characters or characters in extreme conditions. Vyas et al. defined their personas based on demography and behaviour differences. Each persona forms a base on which to build realistic scenarios [28]. Additionally, personas form a communicable representation of what is known about the users [85].

The models of the users, their tasks and their environment together provide both constraints the future design has to meet and directions of how to improve the current situation. These models are used as input for the design and evaluation activities to reason about what valid design solutions are for the intended users.

8.4 Designing Prototypes

Although the whole process is called "visualisation design process", we use the label "design" to indicate the activity in which designers create things. Designing means generating solutions based on the results of analysis activities. As Fallman [21] said:

"Design is a matter of making; it is an attitude to research that involves the researcher in creating and giving form to something not previously there."

Design is a creative activity; brainstorming and generating alternatives play an important role [67]. The results of design are proposed solutions. These solutions are in the first place proposed or intended changes in the users' task world, by changing, or creating new procedures, tools and/or objects. In order to analyse the intended solutions and to communicate them to the users and other stakeholders at an early stage, one needs to represent these solutions in the form of scenarios, mock-ups, simulations, interactive prototypes or beta-versions of products. The representations are used for two purposes. Firstly, they can function as proof of concept to test whether things are acceptable and whether they can be expected to meet the needs they aim to fulfill. Secondly, they act as communication media between the designer, users and other stakeholders.

Two types of prototypes can be distinguished [67]: Low Fidelity (Lo-Fi) prototypes and High Fidelity (Hi-Fi) prototypes. The first type of prototypes does not aim to look like, or behave like, the intended end-product, but is used to test early design ideas or partial solutions among the users and stakeholders. The latter type simulates the end-product and is used to demonstrate its working without the necessity of a full implementation.

8.4.1 Low Fidelity Prototypes

Low fidelity prototypes such as sketches support creativity during design [29, 43, 71]. Proposed design decisions can still be rather vague, as well as somewhat playful. Stakeholders feel free to react and to propose alternatives, and will readily elaborate and expand, since it is clear to them that details are not fixed, nothing final has been decided yet [43]. Fuchs [26], for example, used sketches to demonstrate the setup of a future office environment (Fig. 8.3).

This approach is closely related to storyboarding. Storyboarding is a technique taken from movie making in which a series of sketches illustrate user interaction with visualisations in a cartoon like structure [5, 81]. Van der Lelie [81] mentioned that different styles of storyboarding (from sketchy to detailed) can be used to reach different goals, such as exploration, discussion or presentation. Storyboards can show different states of the interaction design, however real interaction is not possible. Sutcliffe et al. [75] used storyboarding for demonstrating their initial ideas about user interface design for information retrieval systems. The critiques about these storyboards by stakeholders helped them to gain more insight into the tacit knowledge of the users.

Paper-based prototyping is a fast approach in which sheets of paper are used to suggest different system states during interaction. Stakeholders and users are willing to interpret them as early suggestions of how the intended interface should react to their behaviour. This approach was used to illustrate the initial ideas about the interaction with a user interface [64]. Each window was drawn on a separate sheet and one of the designers "plays" the computer by simulating the interactions by moving the different sheets. Rettig [64] argues that paper-based prototyping allows one to demonstrate a systems at an early stage of development and to try out far more ideas than is possible with high-fidelity prototypes.

Fig. 8.3 Office of the future, a single user is collaborating with multiple participants at remote sites. Picture taken with permission from [26], © 1999 Springer Verlag

Sketches, storyboards and paper based prototypes are all cheap approaches for creating low fidelity prototypes. Designers are not restricted to technological limitations, do not have to spend time on programming and can still identify and solve usability problems at an early stage of design [71].

8.4.2 High Fidelity Prototypes

When design ideas have matured and early solutions have been assessed and decided, representations of an intended system become less exploratory. High-fidelity prototypes will look and behave like the expected end-product and can be mock-ups or even fully working products.

However, problems arise when implementation depends on technology that is not fully available yet. One way to deal with this problem is to create video prototypes to demonstrate ideas to the users in the form of acted scenarios in which the future technology is suggested to be available [78].

Bardram et al. [4] created virtual video prototypes to show the use of context aware, advanced communication techniques in hospitals. They use the label "virtual" video prototyping to indicate a mixture of conventional videos with computer animation to imitate future technologies. The video prototype shows how PDA's and interactive walls support nurses and doctors doing their daily working practices. These devices are used for video conferencing, visualising patient data and showing the activities to be performed by the particular employee.

Bardram et al. [4] claim that a video prototype will force designers to make their ideas concrete, since they have to instruct the actors what to do. The main limitation of video prototyping is that there is no possibility for real users to interact with the intended system and to experience real use. Still, a video prototype can be a good starting point for discussion with stakeholders, since they get a clear impression of the future product and may get inspired how to improve it.

A similar solution is faking future technology by using existing technology. For example, Holman et al. [30] designed Paper windows, a system that illustrated the use of digital paper. The technology of digital paper was not mature enough to demonstrate it. Holman et al. solved this by faking the technology using video projection on normal white paper. Users can interact with the prototype using pen, fingers, hand and gesture based input. The digital paper supports advanced actions, such as copying the paper's content to another piece of paper or grabbing the laptop's screen content.

A Wizard of Oz experiment is another way of demonstrating new ideas to the stakeholders without using actual technology. The intended users work with a system that is only a mock-up of the real system. The experimenter acts as a wizard and secretly intercepts the communication between the user and the system and executes the actions the user wants to perform [67].

Kelley [35] used this type of experiment in the early eighties to demonstrate the CAL programme, which is a calendar programme for computer-naïve professionals. It uses natural language speech input (English) to interact with the system. Kelley performed a Wizard of Oz experiment to simulate and evaluate the ideas of the CAL programme input. By performing this type of experiment, he only had to partially implement the system and could ignore the limitations of natural language processing techniques.

Kulyk et al. [41] used this type of experiment to evaluate their real-time feedback system for small group meetings. As we mentioned before, the system visualises non-verbal properties of peoples' behaviour during team meetings in order to improve the productivity of the meetings. Real implementation requires reliable computer vision and speaker recognition techniques. By performing a Wizard of Oz experiment, the use of the system could be evaluated without the need of implementing the whole system.

8.4.3 From Prototypes to End-Products

Evaluation at an early stage of development allows the solution of usability problems with less effort than after implementation [64]. On the other hand, once a design is implemented, it can and should be evaluated in the community of practice (intended context of use with the intended users) in order to check commitment to the requirements [67]. Whatever the status of the prototype, whether it is a simulation or real interactive version of the intended system, its goal is still to assess design decisions and possibly to reconsider them. Evaluation of the end-product is different as the goal is to test the implementation, which may include machine performance, platform independence, maintainability and portability. Still, even in the case of an end-product, in most cases new (and unexpected) usability problems will emerge, triggering a redesign for next releases of the product.

8.5 Evaluation in Visualisation Design Practice

New generations of interactive visualisations not only have to meet user requirements but also have to enhance exploration of large heterogeneous data sets and provide domain-relevant insight into the data [37, 65]. This raises challenges in evaluation of visualisations. Innovative and complex designs need to be tested in order to check whether they meet user requirements. Existing evaluation methods are not fully applicable to new visualisation spaces and related advanced user interfaces [37]. Evaluation of any visualisation technique has to include an assessment of both visual representation and interaction styles [89]. House et al. [31] underline the low quality of published evaluations, in the sense that the findings are not appealing for visualisation practitioners since such results do not lead to design principles and guidelines to guide them. There are only few successful attempts to transform the results from different evaluation studies into general design guidelines or heuristics [11, 31, 79]. General guidelines would be useful for the visualisation community in general, including designers, developers and marketing specialists of interactive visualisation techniques.

8.5.1 Case Studies of Evaluations

Kobsa [36] compares three different commercial information visualisation systems. In this experiment, each of the participants performed a set of predefined tasks. Mean task completion time was measured in combination with observations to measure ease of use. He found that users achieved only 68–75% accuracy on simple tasks. In this study, the success of visualisation systems was found to depend on the following factors: flexibility of visualisation properties, freedom of operating the visualisation, visualisation paradigm and visualisation-independent usability problems. Kobsa concludes that there is room for improvement in effectiveness of visualisations.

The lack of a generic framework is also a common problem in evaluation of visualisations. Very few studies are devoted to frameworks for design and evaluation of information visualisation techniques [2, 24, 37, 89]. Such models can help to perform evaluations in a structured way. For example, Figueroa et al. [24] introduce a methodology for the design and exploration of interactive virtual reality

(VR) visualisations. They evaluated performance and user preference with several design alternatives during the early stage of development of a VR application. Alternative interaction techniques were presented to users in order to choose a technique they prefer most [23].

Koua and Kraak [37] developed a framework for the design and evaluation of exploratory geovisualisations for knowledge discovery. This study addresses the lack of evaluation methodologies and task specifications for user evaluations of geovisualisations. In contrast, Amar and Stasko [2] presented a knowledge task-based framework to support decision making and learning. Their study classifies limitations in current visualisation systems into two analytic gaps. First, the worldview gap between what is shown to a user and what actually needs to be shown to make a decision. Second, the rationale gap between perceiving a relationship and expressing confidence in the correctness and utility of that relationship. In order to diminish these gaps, new task forms are presented for systematic design and heuristic evaluation. For example, an interactive visualisation system can bridge the rationale gap by clearly presenting what comprises the representation of a relationship, and present concrete outcomes where appropriate. A similar study by Winckler and Freitas [89] proposes a task-based model to construct abstract visual tasks and generate test scenarios for more effective and structured evaluations.

A number of studies also demonstrate the practical use of various methods for evaluation of visualisations. For example, Tory and Möller [79] report on heuristic evaluation [51] of two visualisation applications by experts in human-computer interaction. They conclude that expert reviews provide valuable feedback on visualisation tools. They recommend to include both experts and users in the evaluation process and stress the need for development of visualisation heuristics based on design guidelines.

Allendörfer et al. [1] use the cognitive walkthrough [52] method to assess the usability of CiteSpace, a knowledge domain visualisation tool to create visualisations of scientific literature. The cognitive walkthrough method is typically suitable for evaluation of systems with structured tasks for which action sequences can be scripted. In CiteSpace tasks are exploratory and open-ended. Allendörfer et al. adapted the cognitive walkthrough method to be fit for evaluation of knowledge domain visualisation systems. This study confirms that each evaluation method has to be adjusted for the specific domain, the intended users and the evaluation purpose.

As explained earlier in Sect. 8.3, focus groups can be used during the analysis phase to generate ideas for the visualisation designs. Focus groups, combined with interviews and questionnaires, are also common techniques in evaluation practice. Figueroa et al. [24] demonstrate the evaluation of interactive visualisations using the focus group method. The main purpose of using focus groups in this study [24] was to establish users' attitudes, feelings, beliefs, experiences, and reactions in a better way than with interviews or questionnaires. For more information on focus groups, interviews and questionnaires, see Sect. 8.3.

Usability testing is the most widely used method later in the design process [60]. In usability testing, performance is measured of typical users interacting with a high-fidelity prototype or an actual implementation of a system. Usability testing is typically done in artificial, controlled settings with tasks defined by the evaluator. Users are observed and their interactions with the system are recorded and logged. These data can be used to calculate performance times and to identify errors. In addition to these performance measures, user opinions are elicited by query techniques (interviews, questionnaires) [60]. In addition to traditional performance measurements, several studies illustrate that visual and spacial perception, for example the users' ability to see important patterns, should be also included in the evaluation measures of the interactive visualisations [31]. North and Shneiderman [53] evaluate users' capability to coordinate and operate multiple visualisations in spatial information representations. The study of Westerman and Cribbin [87] reports evaluation results of the effect of spatial and associative memory abilities of users in virtual information spaces. Other important evaluation aspects are, among others, influence of shared visualisations on multidisciplinary collaboration, cognitive abilities and cognitive load, peripheral attention, awareness, and engagement.

8.5.2 Controlled Laboratory Tests Versus Field Studies

In addition to the controlled usability tests that are usually performed in the laboratory, it is necessary to evaluate an interactive system in the real context of use [19]. Unfortunately, there are very few studies in which the evaluation of visualisations is done in the real context of use. One example is a field study of Trafton et al. [80] on how complex visualisations are comprehended and used by experts in the weather forecasting domain.

Another example is a longitudinal field study performed by Seo and Shneiderman [66], including participatory observations and interviews. This study focused on evaluation of an interactive knowledge discovery tool for multiple multi-dimensional genomics data. This contextual evaluation aimed to understand the exploratory strategies of molecular biologists. While exploring the interactive visualisation, biologists were excited to discover genes with certain functions without, however, knowing how the correlations between a gene and its function are established.

In another study [27], it was found that traditional evaluation methods are not suited for multi-dimensional interactive visualisations. Therefore, the authors focused on initial testing by observing users trying out the prototypes using representative tasks. A combination of techniques was used in this study for data capturing, namely logging software, video recordings, note taking, and verbal protocol, which helped to disambiguate detailed interactions.

The field studies described here aimed to understand the actual use of visualisation tools by real users in the real use context. Though constraints like time and budget often tend to limit evaluation to the controlled laboratory settings, field studies are needed to find out what people do in their daily environment.

8.5.3 *Evaluation Setup*

Several practical issues, such as stage in the design, particular questions to be answered and availability of user groups, affect the selection of suitable evaluation techniques. When setting up the user test, it is important to define the goals and the main questions to be addressed. Depending on what type of design ideas or decisions are to be tested, there may be a need to develop or adjust a visualisation prototype created in the design phase (see Sect. 8.4) to engage users in evaluation scenarios. Planning the evaluation includes time for preparation, finding participants, choosing an optimal location, and performing a pilot test to measure how much time each part and the whole test session will take. All these aspects are important for the success of the evaluation study.

Simple tasks are often used in current evaluations of visualisations. However, new exploratory visualisations require more realistic, motivating, and engaging tasks [56]. Such tasks can be derived from the task analysis performed in the early envisioning phase (see Sect. 8.3). Another possibility is to study related literature for relevant tasks or adopt a task from the Information Visualisation Benchmark Repository [22], based on the collection of the results from the InfoVis context [23]. This repository contains low-level tasks for evaluation of the interactive systems for visualising multiple datasets. Amar and Stasko [2] propose a taxonomy of higher-level analytic tasks that can provide support for designers and evaluators of interactive visualisation systems. In addition, it is important to let users explore the visualisation interface freely (if possible using their own data) and ask them to explain what they are able to understand [56].

Some evaluation experts suggest to invite an outside evaluation facilitator in order to avoid being biased [48]. A related solution is to split roles (e.g. evaluator, technical support person, observer, video/audio monitoring person, etc.) and use a separate evaluation protocol for each role. This helps to organise the evaluation and effectively distribute tasks [18].

It is important to ensure privacy of participants during and after the experiment [18]. It is sensible to use a special consent form which, among other things, asks permission for audio/video recordings [47]. For further information on the practical steps in conducting an evaluation study see [18].

8.6 Challenges in Design of Collaborative Visualisation Environments

Most published evaluation studies focus on "single user – single visualisation system" interaction. Another challenge for the visualisation designer is collaborative exploration of information. This requires new and advanced visualisation environments. Special evaluation methods are needed in order to adequately address the aspects of collaborative work in such environments [62]. Refined methodologies and reliable measures are required to assess aspects such as, for example, knowledge discovery and decision making quality. A framework should be constructed in order to adopt evaluation practices from fields like computer supported cooperative work and ubiquitous services [32, 50, 59].

New systems for collaborative use of visualisation are emerging. I-Space [73] is an example of a visualisation environment for multidisciplinary exploration of the human genome. MacEachren et al. [46] present a collaborative geovisualisation environment for knowledge construction and decision support. The e-BioLab is a collaborative environment that aims to facilitate multidisciplinary teams during project meetings on molecular biology experiments [40, 63]. The large high-resolution display in this environment allows scientists to gain new insights into the results of their experiments and to explore genomics data (see Fig. 8.4). We are currently conducting a series of field studies in this laboratory to develop novel concepts to support group awareness during project meetings [40, 83].

One more demonstration of multiple visualisations design is the persuasive multi-displays environment designed by Mitsubishi Research Lab [17]. Such environments may include peripheral awareness displays – systems in the environment that stay in the periphery of user's attention [57]. Ubiquitous computing services allow feedback to the users in the periphery of their attention. The awareness supporting signs can be generated from multi-modal cues sensed by the perceptive services embedded in the environment [32]. The evaluation of awareness displays focuses on effectiveness and unobtrusiveness and the ability of visual representation to communicate information at a glance without overloading the user [32, 57].

We sketch a user-centered approach for designing visualisation environments to enhance multidisciplinary group collaboration in life sciences [83]. We are currently

Fig. 8.4 Scientists interacting with multiple visualisations using large displays in e-BioLab, MAD/IBU, University of Amsterdam (*See Color Plates*)

performing case studies to find out how to support collaboration in daily work practice between biologists, bioinformaticians, and biomedical researchers. Scenarios are used for empirical studies in micro-array experiments [63].

8.7 Summary

Visualisation systems are often designed for specific user groups which have specific goals and work in specific environments. Analysing users in their context of work and finding out how and why they use different information resources is essential to provide interactive visualisation systems that match their goals and needs. This chapter presents a user-centered approach for design of interactive visualisation systems. Based on our own case studies and other visualisation practices, we have described three phases of the iterative visualisation design process: the analysis, design, and evaluation phase. The whole design process is iterative and the actual users need to be actively involved throughout the whole process. They give input about requirements and provide information that helps to assess whether designs match their needs.

We have discussed different techniques and methods for the analysis of users, their tasks and domain. Subsequently, the design of prototypes and evaluation methods in visualisation practice have been presented. An overview of evaluation studies has illustrated that there is a need for design guidelines specifically for interactive visualisations. These guidelines should differentiate between multiple types of users performing different tasks in different contexts to achieve different goals. Both controlled laboratory studies and field studies are needed to provide the necessary knowledge of how users interact with visualisations and of how visualisation tools affect their working practices.

Finally, we have discussed the practical challenges in design and evaluation of visualisations for multiple users. Enhancing collaboration and exploration of information through natural interaction is a new challenge for the visualisation designers. We have demonstrated that collaborative and multi-display environments demand new frameworks for design and evaluation of interactive visualisations for collaborative use. Fundamental comparative research is needed to assess the reliability and validity of different techniques for user-centered design of such environments. Essential insights in a wider range of disciplines such as human visual perception, cognitive science, and social psychology in combination with traditional user-centered design methods can guide us towards the most promising venues of investigation. Eventually, as we understand more of our target users in their actual work environments, visualisations will become not only efficient and effective, but also more pleasurable and fun to interact with.

Acknowledgements This work was part of the BioRange Programme of the Netherlands Bioinformatics Centre (NBIC), which is supported by a BSIK grant through the Netherlands Genomics Initiative (NGI).

References

1. K. Allendörfer, S. Aluker, G. Panjwani, J. Proctor, D. Sturtz, M. Vukovic, and C. Chen. Adapting the cognitive walkthrough method to assess the usability of a knowledge domain visualisation. In IEEE Symposium on Information Visualisation (InfoVis'05), 2005. IEEE Computer Society Press.
2. R. Amar, and J. Stasko. A knowledge task-based framework for design and evaluation of information visualisations. In M. Ward and T. Munzer, editors, IEEE Symposium on Information Visualisation (InfoVis'04), volume 04, 143–149, Austin, TX, USA, 2004.
3. L. Arnstein, C.-Y. Hung, R. Franza, Q. H. Zhou, G. Borriello, S. Consolvo, and J. Su. Labscape: A smart environment for the cell biology laboratory. *IEEE Pervasive Computing*, 1(3):13–21, 2002.
4. J. Bardram, C. Bossen, A. Lykke-Olesen, R. Nielsen, and K. H. Madsen. Virtual video prototyping of pervasive healthcare systems. In W. Mackay and J. A. W. Gaver, editors, Proceedings of the Conference on Designing Interactive Systems (DIS'02), 167–177, New York, NY, USA, 2002. ACM Press.
5. D. Benyon, P. Turner, and S. Turner. Designing Interactive Systems: People, Edinburgh, 2005. Addison Wesley, Harlow.
6. B. Berry, J. Smith, and S. Wahid. Visualizing case studies. Computer Science TR-04- 12, Virginia Tech, Blacksburg VA, 2004. Technical Report.
7. H. Beyer. Contextual Design: Defining Customer-Centered Systems, San Francisco, USA, 1997. Morgan Kaufmann.
8. S. Card and J. Mackinlay. The structure of the information visualisation design space. In J. Dill and N. Gershon, editors, IEEE Symposium on Information Visualisation (InfoVis'97), 92–100, Phoenix, Arizona, USA, 1997. IEEE Computer Society Press.
9. J. Carroll, editor. Scenario-Based Design: Envisioning Work and Technology in System Development, 1995. John Wiley and Sons, New York, NY.
10. J. M. Carroll and C. Carrithers. Training wheels in a user interface. *Communication of the ACM*, 27(8):800–806, 1984.
11. C. Chen and Y. Yu. Empirical studies of information visualisation: A meta-analysis. *International Journal of Human-Computer Studies*, 53(5):851–866, 2000.
12. R. Chenna, H. Sugawara, T. Koike, R. Lopez, T. Gibson, D. Higgins, and J. Thompson. Multiple sequence alignment with the clustal series of programs. *Nucleic Acids Research*, 31(13):3497–3500, 2003.
13. M. Clamp, J. Cuff, S. M. Searle, and G. J. Barton. The jalview java alignment editor. *Bioinformatics*, 20(3):426–427, 2004.
14. S. Consolvo, L. Arnstein, and B. Franza. User study techniques in the design and evaluation of a ubicomp environment. In G. Borriello and L. E. Holmquist, editors, Proceedings of the 4th International Conference on Ubiquitous Computing, 73–90, Göteborg, Sweden, 2002. Springer-Verlag, Berlin.
15. A. Cooper. The Inmates are Running the Asylum: Why High Tech Products Drive Us Crazy and How To Restore The Sanity, volume 1, Sams, Indianapolis, IN, USA, 1999.
16. G. C. der Veer, M. van Welie, and C. Chisalita. Introduction to groupware task analysis. In C. Pribeanu and J. Vanderdonckt, editors, Proceedings of the First International Workshop on Task Models and Diagrams for User Interface Design (TAMODIA'02), 32–39, Bucharest, Romania, 2002. INFOREC Publishing House Bucharest.
17. P. Dietz, R. Raskar, S. Booth, J. V. Baar, K. Wittenburg, and B. Knep. Multiprojectors and implicit interaction in persuasive public displays. In Working Conference on Advanced Visual Interfaces (AVI'04), 209–217, 2004. ACM Press, New York, NY.
18. J. F. Dumas and J. C. Redish. A Practical Guide to Usability Testing, 1993. Greenwood Publishing Group Inc, Westport CT.
19. K. Dunbar. The Nature of Insight, chapter How Scientists Really Reason: Scientific Reasoning in Real-World Laboratories, 365–395, Cambridge, MA, 1995. The MIT Press.

20. O. Espinosa, C. Hendrickson, and J. Garrett. Domain analysis: A technique to design a user-centered visualisation framework. In D. Keim and G. Wills, editors, INFOVIS'99: Proceedings of the 1999 IEEE Symposium on Information Visualisation, 44–52, Washington, DC, USA, 1999.
21. D. Fallman. Design-oriented human-computer interaction. In G. Cockton and P. Korhonen, editors, Proceedings of the SIGCHI Conference on Human Factors in Computing Systems, 225–232, Ft. Lauderdale, Florida, USA, 2003. ACM Press, New York, NY.
22. J. Fekete, G. Greinstein, and C. Plaisant. Infovis contest, 2004. http://www.cs.umd. edu/hcil/iv04contest Retrieved 14–12–2007.
23. J. Fekete and C. Plaisant. Information visualisation benchmark repository, 2004.http://www. cs.umd.edu/hcil/InfovisRepository/ Retrieved 14–12–2007.
24. P. Figueroa, W. F. Bischof, P. Boulanger, and H. James Hoover. Efficient comparison of platform alternatives in interactive virtual reality applications. *International Journal of Human-Computer Studies*, 62:73–103, 2005.
25. F. Fikkert, M. D'Ambros, T. Bierz, and T. Jankun-Kelly. Interacting with visualisations. In A. Kerren, A. Ebert, and J. Meyer, editors, Human-Centered Visualisation Environments, volume 4417 of Lecture Notes in Computer Science, chapter 3, 77–162. London, 2007. Springer Verlag, Berlin.
26. Fuchs. Beyond the desktop metaphor: Toward more effective display, interaction, and telecollaboration in the office of the future via a multitude of sensors and displays. In S. Nishio and F. Kishino, editors, AMCP'98: Proceedings of the First International Conference on Advanced Multimedia Content Processing, 30–43, London, UK, 1999. Springer-Verlag, Berlin.
27. M. Graham, J. Kennedy, and D. Benyon. Towards a methodology for developing visualisations. *International Journal of Human-Computer Studies*, 53:789–807, 2000.
28. J. Grudin and J. Pruitt. Personas, participatory design, and product development: An infrastructure for engagement. In T. Binder, J. Gregory, and I. Wagner, editors, Participatory Design Conference 2002, 144–161, Malmo, Sweden, 2002.
29. D. G. Hendry. Sketching with conceptual metaphors to explain computational processes. In J. Grundy and J. Howse, editors, Proceedings of the Visual Languages and Human-Centric Computing (VL/HCC'06), 95–102, Washington, DC, USA, 2006. IEEE Computer Society Press.
30. D. Holman, R. Vertegaal, M. Altosaar, N. Troje, and D. Johns. Paper windows: Interaction techniques for digital paper. In W. Kellogg and S. Zhai, editors, Proceedings of the SIGCHI Conference on Human Factors in Computing Systems (CHI'05), 591–599, Portland, Oregon, USA, 2005. ACM Press, New York, NY.
31. D. House, V. Interrante, D. Laidlaw, R. Taylor, and C. Ware. Panel: Design and evaluation in visualisation research. In IEEE Visualisation Conference, 705–708, Minneapolis, United States, 2005.
32. R. Iqbal, J. Sturm, O. Kulyk, J. Wang, and J. Terken. User-centred design and evaluation of ubiquitous services. In International Conference on Design of Communication: Documenting and Designing for Pervasive Information, 138–145, Coventry, United Kingdom, 2005. ACM Press, New York, NY.
33. ISO-13407. Human-Centered Design Processes for Interactive Systems. Technical report, ISO, 1998.
34. H. Javahery, A. Seffah, and T. Radhakrishnan. Beyond power: Making bioinformatics tools user-centered. *Communications of the ACM*, 47(11):58–63, 2004.
35. J. Kelley. An empirical methodology for writing user-friendly natural language computer applications. In A. Janda, editor, Pro-ceedings of the SIGCHI Conference on Human Factors in Computing Systems (CHI'83), 193–196, New York, NY, USA, 1983. ACM Press.
36. A. Kobsa. An empirical comparison of three commercial information visualisation systems. In A. Jacobs, editor, Proceedings of the IEEE Symposium on Information Visualisation 2001 (INFOVIS'01), 123–130, Washington, DC, USA, 2001. IEEE Computer Society Press.
37. E. Koua and M. Kraak. A usability framework for the design and evaluation of an exploratory geovisualisation environment. In E. Banissi, K. Borner, C. Chen, M. Dastbaz, G. Clapworthy,

A. Failoa, E. Izquierdo, C. Maple, J. Roberts, C. Moore, A. Ursyn, and J. Zhang, editors, Eighth International Conference on Information Visualisation (IV'04), volume 00, 153–158, Parma, Italy, 2004. IEEE Computer Society Press.
38. S. Kujala and M. Kauppinen. Identifying and selecting users for user-centered design. In R. Raisamo, editor, NordiCHI: Nordic Conference on Human-Computer Interaction, volume 82, 297–303, Tampere, Finland, 2004. ACM Press, New York, NY.
39. O. Kulyk, R. Kosara, J. Urquiza-Fuentes, and I. Wassink. Human-Centered Visualisation Environments, volume 4417 of Lecture Notes in Computer Science, chapter Human-Centered Aspects, 13–75, Human-centered aspects, 2007. Springer, Berlin.
40. O. Kulyk, E. van Dijk, P. van der Vet, and A. Nijholt. Do you know what I know? Situational awareness and scientific team-work in collaborative environments. In A. Nijholt, O. Stock, and T. Nishida, editors, Social Intelligence Design 2007. Proceedings Sixth Workshop on Social Intelligence Design, volume WP07–02 of CTIT Workshop Proceedings Series, 207–215, London, UK, 2007. Centre for Telematics and Information Technology, University of Twente, Enschede, the Netherlands. ISSN=1574–0846.
41. O. Kulyk, C. Wang, and J. Terken. Real-time feedback based on nonverbal behaviour to enhance social dynamics in small group meetings. In S. Renals and S. Bengio, editors, Machine Learning for Multimodal Interaction, volume 3869 of Lecture Notes in Computer Science, 150–161, Edinburgh, UK, 2006. Springer, Berlin.
42. O. Kulyk and I. Wassink. 2006. Getting to know bioinformaticians: Results of an exploratory user study. In E. Zudilova-Seinstra and T. Adriaansen, editors, HCI 2006 Engage, Combining Visualisation and Interaction to Facilitate Scientific Exploration and Discovery, London, UK, 30–37,
43. J. A. Landay and B. A. Myers. Sketching interfaces: Toward more human interface design. *IEEE Computer*, 34(3):56–64, 2001.
44. B. Latour and S. Woolgar. Laboratory Life, Beverly Hills, CA, 1979. Sage publications.
45. S. Lauesen. User Interface Design, 2005. Addison Wesley, Harlow.
46. A. MacEachren, M. Gahegan, W. Pike, I. Brewer, G. Cai, E. Lengerich, and F. Hardisty. Geovisualisation for knowledge construction and decision support. *IEEE Computer Graphics and Applications*, 24:13–17, 2004.
47. W. E. Mackay. Ethics, lies and videotape. In SIGCHI Conference on Human factors in Computing Systems, 138–145, Denver, Colorado, United States, 1995. ACM Press/Addison-Wesley Publishing Co, Harlow.
48. D. Morgan. Focus Groups as Qualitative Research, London, 1997. Sage.
49. B. A. Nardi and J. R. Miller. An ethnographic study of distributed problem solving in spreadsheet development. In F. Halasz, editor, Proceedings of the 1990 ACM Conference on Computer-Supported cooperative work (CSCW'90), 197–208, New York, NY, USA, 1990. ACM Press.
50. D. Neale, J. Carroll, and M. Rosson. Evaluating computer-supported cooperative work: Models and frameworks. In ACM Conference on Computer Supported Cooperative Work (CSCW'04), 112–121, Chicago, Illinois, USA, 2004. ACM Press, New York, NY.
51. J. Nielsen. Usability Engineering, San Francisco, 1994. Morgan Kaufmann.
52. J. Nielsen and R. L. Mack. 1994. Usability Inspection Methods, John Wiley & Sons, New York, NY.
53. C. North and B. Shneiderman. Snap-together visualisation: Can users construct and operate coordinated visualisations? *International Journal of Human-Computer Studies*, 53:715–741, 2000.
54. D. G. Novick and J. C. Scholtz. Universal usability. *Interacting with Computers*, 14(4):269–270, 2002.
55. P. A. Pevzner. Educating biologists in the 21st century: Bioinformatics scientists vs bioinformatics technicians. *Bioinformatics*, 20(14):2159–2161, 2004.
56. C. Plaisant. The challenge of information visualisation evaluation. In Working Conference on Advanced Visual Interfaces, 109'116, Gallipoli, Italy, 2004. ACM Press, New York, NY.

57. C. Plaue, T. Miller, and J. Stasko. Is a picture worth a thousand words?: An evaluation of information awareness displays. In Conference on Graphics Interface, 117'126, Ontario, Canada, 2004. Canadian Human-Computer Communications Society.
58. M. Polanyi. 1983. The Tacit Dimension, Paul Smith Publishing, Gloucester MA.
59. R. Poppe, R. Rienks, and E. van Dijk. Evaluating the future of hci: Challenges for the evaluation of emerging applications. In T. Huang, A. Nijholt, M. Pantic, and A. Pentland, editors, Artificial Intelligence for Human Computing, 234–250, Berlin, 2007. Springer Verlag, ISBN=3–540–72346–2.
60. J. Preece, Y. Rogers, and H. Sharp. Interaction Design: Beyond Human-Computer Interaction, New York, 2002. John Wiley and Sons Ltd.
61. R. Pressman and D. Ince. 2000. Software Engineering, volume 5, McGraw-Hill, London.
62. M. Ramage. 1999. The Learning Way: Evaluation of Cooperative Systems. PhD thesis, Lancaster University.
63. H. Rauwerda, M. Roos, B. Hertzberger, and T. Breit. The promise of a virtual lab in drug discovery. *Drug Discovery Today*, 11(5–6):228–236, 2006.
64. M. Rettig. Prototyping for tiny fingers. *Communications of the ACM*, 37(4):21–27, 1994.
65. P. Saraiya, C. North, and K. Duca. An evaluation of microarray visualisation tools for biological insight. In M. Ward and T. Munzer, editors, Proceedings of the IEEE Symposium on Information Visualisation (INFOVIS'04), 1–8,Washington, DC, USA, 2004. IEEE Computer Society Press.
66. J. Seo and B. Shneiderman. Interactively exploring hierarchical clustering results. *Computer*, 35(7):80–86, 2002.
67. H. Sharp, Y. Rogers, and J. Preece. 2007. Interaction Design, volume 2, John Wiley & Sons, Ltd, New York, NY.
68. B. Shneiderman. The eyes have it: A task by data type taxonomy for information visualisations. In R. S. Sipple, editor, Proceedings of the 1996 IEEE Symposium on Visual Languages, 336–343, Los Alamitos, CA, 1996. IEEE Computer Society Press.
69. B. Shneiderman. Universal usability. *Communications of ACM*, 43(5):84–91, 2000.
70. B. Shneiderman and C. Plaisant. 2005. Designing the User Interface, Addison-Wesley, Reading MA.
71. C. Snyder. 2003. Paper Prototyping: The Fast and Easy Way to Design and Refine User Interfaces, Morgan Kaufman, San Francisco.
72. R. Spence. Information Visualisation, Edinburgh Gate, 2001. Addison-Wesley, Reading MA.
73. B. Stolk, F. Abdoelrahman, A. Koning, P. Wielinga, J. Neefs, A. Stubbs, A. de Bondt, P. Leemans, and P. van der Spek. Mining the human genome using virtual reality. In Eurographics Workshop on Parallel Graphics and Visualisation, 17–21, 2002. Germany Eurographics Digital Library.
74. D. Stone, C. Jarrett, M. Woodroffe, and S. Minocha. 2005. User Interface Design and Evaluation: Series in Interactive Technologies, Morgan Kaufmann, San Francisco.
75. A. Sutcliffe. Advises project: Scenario-based requirements analysis for e-science applications. In S. J. Cox, editor, UK e-Science All Hands Meeting 2007, 142–149, Nottingham, UK, 2007.
76. A. Sutcliffe, M. Ennis, and S. Watkinson. Empirical studies of end-user information searching. *Journal of the American Society for Information Science*, 51(13):1211–1231, 2000.
77. J. D. Thompson, F. Plewniak, and O. Poch. A comprehensive comparison of multiple sequence alignment programs. *Nucleic Acids Research*, 27(13):2682–2690, 1999.
78. B. Tognazzini. The starfire video prototype project: A case history. In B. Adelson, S. Dumais, and J. Olson, editors, Conference on Human Factors in Computing Systems, 99–105, Boston, Massachusetts, United States, 1994.
79. M. Tory and T. Möller. Evaluating visualisations: Do expert reviews work? *IEEE Computer Graphics and Applications*, 25:8–11, 2005.
80. G. J. Trafton, S. S. Kirschenbaum, T. L. Tsui, R. T. Miyamoto, J. A. Ballas, and P. D. Raymond. Turning pictures into numbers: Extracting and generating information from complex visualisations. *International Journal of Human-Computer Studies*, 53:827–850, 2000.

81. C. van der Lelie. The value of storyboards in the product design process. *Personal and Ubiquitous Computing*, 10(2–3):159–162, 2006.
82. G. van der Veer and M. van Welie. Task based groupware design: Putting theory into practice. In D. Boyarski and W. A. Kellogg, editors, Proceedings of the Conference on Designing Interactive Systems (DIS'00), 326–337, New York, NY, USA, 2000. ACM Press.
83. P. van der Vet, O. Kulyk, I. Wassink, F. Fikkert, H. Rauwerda, E. van Dijk, G. van der Veer, T. Breit, and A. Nijholt. Smart environments for collaborative design, implementation, and interpretation of scientific experiments. In T. Huang, A. Nijholt, M. Pantic, and A. Pentland, editors, Workshop on AI for Human Computing (AI4HC), 79–86, Hyderabad, India, 2007.
84. M. van Welie, G. van der Veer, and A. Koster. Integrated representations for task modeling. In P. Wright, E. Hollnagel, and S. Dekker, editors, Tenth European Conference on Cognitive Ergonomics, 129–138, Link¨oping, Sweden, 2000.
85. D. Vyas, S. Groot, and G. der Veer. Understanding the academic environments: From field study to design. In G. Grote, editor, 13th European Conference on Cognitive Ergonomics, Switzerland, 119–120, New York, September 2006. ACM Press, New York, NY.
86. C. Ware, D. Christopher, and J. Hollands. Information Visualisation: Perception for Design, volume 2, San Fransisco, CA, USA, 2004. Morgan Kaufmann.
87. S. Westerman and T. Cribbin. Mapping semantic information in virtual space: Dimensions, variance and individual differences. *International Journal of Human-Computer Studies*, 53:765–787, 2000.
88. S. Wilson, M. Bekker, P. Johnson, and H. Johnson. Helping and hindering user involvement – a tale of everyday design. In S. Pemberton, editor, CHI'97: Proceedings of the SIGCHI Conference on Human Factors in Computing Systems, 178–185, New York, NY, USA, 1997. ACM Press.
89. M. A. Winckler, P. Palanque, and C. M. Freitas. Tasks and scenario-based evaluation of information visualisation techniques. In 3rd annual conference on Task models and diagrams, 165–172, Prague, Czech Republic, 2004. ACM Press, New York, NY.
90. L. E. Wood. Semi-structured interviewing for user-centered design. *Interactions*, 4(2):48–61, 1997.
91. J. Zhang. A representational analysis of relational information displays. *International Journal of Human-Computer Studies*, 45(1):159–74, 1996.
92. J. Zhang, K. Johnson, J. Malin, and J. Smith. Human-centered information visualisation. In R. Ploetzner, editor, International Workshop on Dynamic Visualisations and Learning, Tübingen, 2002. Digital Enterprise Research Institute, University of Innsbruck.

Chapter 9
A Visualization Framework for Collaborative Virtual Environment Usage Information

Ross Brown, Simon Joslin, and Penny Drennan

Abstract Due to the popularity of modern Collaborative Virtual Environments, there has been a related increase in their size and complexity. Developers therefore need visualisations that expose usage patterns from logged data, to understand the structures and dynamics of these complex environments. This chapter presents a new framework for the process of visualising virtual environment usage data. Major components, such as an event model, designer task model and data acquisition infrastructure are described. Interface and implementation factors are also developed, along with example visualisation techniques that make use of the new task and event model. A case study is performed to illustrate a typical scenario for the framework, and its benefits to the environment development team.

Keywords Collaborative virtual environments, Massively multiplayer online role-playing games, Game design, Content usage visualisation.

9.1 Introduction

Quality Assurance (QA), and related phases of Collaborative Virtual Environment (CVE) testing, such as focus groups and beta testing, are time consuming processes for modern companies. Firstly, there is the problem of how to generate and test the sheer magnitude of content that is required for the millions of users of games such as *World of Warcraft* (WoW) [1] and *Second Life* [2]. Magnitude problems like these are also further exacerbated by the introduction of next generation hardware content requirements, giving further opportunities for realism, at the expense of testing this higher quality content for usage problems[1].

A large segment of every game development budget and timetable is invested in QA for an environment [3]. Thus, any approach that will help game development companies and other creators of digital content to increase the efficiency of their verification

[1] The framework in this chapter is part of our proposed solution to problems facing CVE developers, we have coined the term *Digital Asset Manufacturing* (DAM) - the adoption of large scale industrial manufacturing techniques in the creation of digital content.

E. Zudilova-Seinstra et al. (eds.) *Trends in Interactive Visualization*,
doi:10.1007/978-1-84800-269-2_9 © Springer-Verlag London Limited 2009

process should reap major cost savings, and provide a related increase in the quality of the environment. Secondly, there are the considerable maintenance requirements of persistent content that is required for this genre of software, due to ongoing usage. This includes monitoring present content in persistent worlds, which may highlight people engaging in anti-social behaviour, or the presence of bugs and problems with mechanics and content usage. The expense of online environments greatly increases with the addition of more and more complex content, requiring large open beta testing communities (in the order of thousands of people) to verify the content of a game [4]. We believe there is a need for software to aid this process, both in automated data mining and via improvements in the effective management of user groups.

One approach to alleviating these problems is to use collaborative visualisation of usage data from the environment, as it is a powerful tool for enhancing insight into patterns within information [5]. Related work has been carried out in the area of data capture and visualisation for real-time monitoring purposes in other domains which have similarities to the CVE domain. Some that have been developed include applications for network monitoring and complex system control [6]. In particular, visualisation has been useful in the telecommunications, electrical generation and industrial control domains [7]. There have also been some relevant game industry implementations [8] and work has been developed on the visualisation of gameplay [9], but it is ad hoc in nature, as there has been no development of a complete collaborative framework for the logging, management and visualisation of gameplay data.

In this chapter, we outline a complete data logging framework for a CVE usage visualisation system. We analyse the process of CVE development, and provide a developer-oriented, collaborative approach to the visualisation of usage data. For the purposes of this work, the focus has been on online games of the Massively Multiplayer Online Roleplaying Game (MMORPG) genre. We show with examples that the results from work with game systems have application across all forms of CVEs.

The chapter is divided into the following sections. Sect. 9.2 reviews the existing research in the area of environment usage data visualisation. Sect. 9.3 outlines our approach which is grounded in a task-based analysis of the design and testing of computer games. Sect. 9.4 analyses the CVE development life cycle to place the framework correctly in development team processes. Sect. 9.5 describes a generalised environment event model derived from the analysis of development tasks. In Sect. 9.6, a framework is described for event data acquisition, management and visualisation. Interfaces to the visualisation framework are discussed in Sect. 9.7. Finally, examples of gameplay visualisations designed for CVE developers illustrating the final output of the framework are included in Sect. 9.8. Sect. 9.9 is a case study of the framework used in a typical game development scenario.

9.2 Related Work

Virtual environment data mining and player usage analysis techniques have been a related area of research since at least 1999 [9–12]. Simple data models and visualisations have been developed to analyse user interaction with generic virtual environments.

Early efforts to visualise user actions in CVEs began with 2-dimensional map overlays created for the geographical level designers of the world. Beginning at a user-centric starting point, the visualisations specifically demonstrated to the designer the areas of maximum (or minimum) user flow and the areas of environment more seen (or less seen) by users [13].

The concept of Virtual Prints, a mapping of Virtual Footprints, Virtual Fingerprints and Virtual Fossils was proposed to aid navigation, provide useful feedback, work as a history mechanism and support social navigation [14]. For users in the world, the prints are effectively an in situ visualisation of the actions of other users, as they continue the legacy of the actions of users in the VE.

Digital games introduce competition to CVEs, an element otherwise not often seen. The only development of competitive behaviour visualisations so far considers the spectator, but not the designer [9]. The visualisations capture high level data such as: player distribution over time, areas of intense combat activity, fire coverage, occupancy coverage, support fire coverage and medic efficacy and could be useful to a level designer when ascertaining the equality between two halves of the map. However, the designer was not the focus of the work and no analysis has been performed on mappings between designer tasks and appropriate visualisations.

The Zereal simulation platform defines a methodology and data model to record and simulate the events of MMORGs [12]. The extensible model favours simplicity over details. It does not deal with quests, inventories, item collection etc. For many designer questions, it would be necessary to utilise a secondary model such as a relational database to query the records. Thawonmas et al. [11] then analyse the raw MMORPG log data from Zereal to identify player types. From a raw log file, character types have been identified from the actions that a player performed.

From these readings, it can be seen that there is a lack of general collaborative frameworks to CVE data visualisation, especially with respect to developing a system to integrate into various aspects of the development life cycle and workflow issues within a large development organisation. Using the newly developed framework as a basis, we have developed an event model that captures specific information tailored to a particular member of the game development team [15]. The event model considers modularity like other work, but the implementation shown ultimately collects information to answer specific questions about the CVE that would be asked by designers.

9.3 Approach

Visualisations can help a designer analyse a CVE to find and highlight the difference between expected and actual use. We believe that it would be helpful to the designer to see when, where and what their users are doing, with the hope of understanding how and why. Therefore the approach we have used in developing our model is to gather and present information relevant to the task of the designer. We aim to provide an approach and software architecture that enables analysis from this perspective.

Firstly, we analyse the development life cycle and derive key processes that are carried out which would require the services of a visualisation system. Within these processes we identify the major tasks carried out by the designers and other process stake holders. Using the designer tasks we extract a set of events that need to be monitored for each designer task, and then apply an appropriate visualisation to see that event data, and identify patterns that are congruent with the task. Conceptually, this is represented as a diagram in Fig. 9.1.

In general, there are two types of CVEs which cater to large numbers of people. The first game type, is the Massively Multi-player Online Roleplaying Game, or MMORPG. MMORPGs are large, persistent environments, structured around game objectives, which require collaboration or competition between players. They usually contain an element of fantasy, and player activities are focused on combat and the acquisition of experience points to 'level up', as well as armor, weapons and other in-game items. The second type of CVEs don't incorporate combat to the extent of MMORPGs and are instead social environments supporting large scale social networking and player interactions. An example of the first type of CVE would be World of Warcraft, with its focus on fantasy, combat and acquisition of armor and items. An example of the second type of CVE would be Second Life, with its extensive supporting structures for social interaction between players. MMORPGs are therefore a subset of CVEs in general, with their focus on combat and competition. It is difficult to classify Second Life as a game, as any goals that players have are created by the player, instead of the game, which is counter-intuitive to the notion of a game [16].

We therefore take the approach of integrating the requirements for these domains together, in order to show the general approaches required for the development of such CVEs. For this chapter, the acronym CVE will apply to both the gaming and non-gaming domains. However, the emphasis is from a gameplay approach, due to the richness of user interactions within a goal oriented environment. We take the approach that a game is essentially a CVE with strong goal oriented tasks that have to be completed. We also emphasise the online persistent forms of CVEs that are

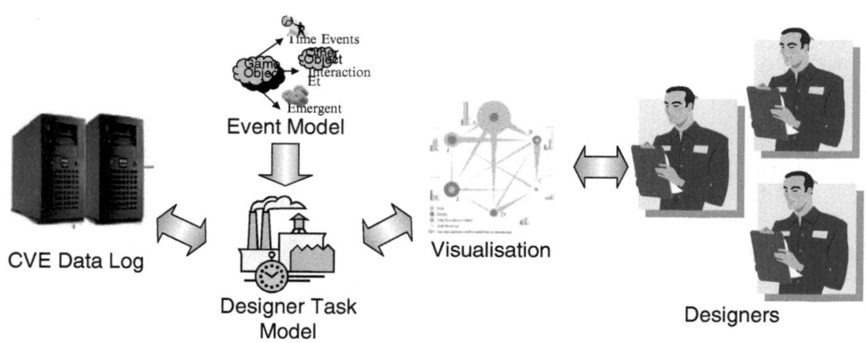

Fig. 9.1 Conceptual diagram of the visualisation approach taken. Each visualisation being a view of the environment event model, modulated by factors aligned with designer tasks

growing in popularity and application, as the content is often modified and analysed during the life of the game, and requires a detailed understanding of the usage of the environment for administration purposes. An example of a more generic task for a CVE is the management of the Second Life economy, monitoring the exchange of goods, and how this affects the social fabric of the virtual environment.

9.4 CVE Development Life Cycle Analysis

The visualisation framework needs to fit into a model of development company processes, in order to maximise its effectiveness within the workflow of an organisation. To do this, there must be analysis of the stages in the development of a game, to ascertain how such a framework may be integrated into the relevant stages, to enhance the efficiency of the workers involved. Referring to the list of development phases as outlined in [3] indicates a game log visualisation system would fit into the Prototype Development, Quality Assurance and Maintenance stages of the game development life cycle. At each of these stages, there is CVE usage log data that can be acquired and analysed for usability purposes. Concentrating these life cycle stages, there are five potential uses of visualisation software that could enhance game development: *Focus Testing, Balancing, Beta Testing, Live Console* and *Ad Hoc Queries.*

Focus Testing is a stage which involves the gathering of a small number of users early in the development cycle, to test early prototypes. During Focus Testing, the desired information is concentrated on the gross usage characteristics. The visualisations are focused on estimating ease of play and enjoyment at this stage, as the prototype is a feasibility analysis in this phase of development. Designers would be particularly interested in the correlations between reported user enjoyment, and the user log information. That is, they would be interested in discovering what aspects of the CVE are affecting the user experience.

Balancing, as it suggests, is the balancing of character capabilities in order to provide fairness, yet enough challenge to create engaging interactions. Data is required here from preliminary focus testing to assist the balancer in the process of understanding the dynamics between users within the environment. Balancers would be interested in the correlations between user capabilities, and the reported enjoyment of the environment.

Quality Assurance/Beta Testing are related processes of bug fixing and usage analysis for the process of finalising the build for release. Visualisations at this stage will target finding bugs in interfaces and mechanics, content, and usability factors. Visualisations will be about correlating reported bugs with logged data, to discern the exact component that has been uncovered as being faulty.

The Live Console phase will allow for all stake holders to modify persistent world servers to increase usability. At this stage the aim is to modify CVE parameters, and to specify problems that will need to be addressed in future world add-ons and game versions. In particular, they require an exception reporting approach to the data logging, in order to investigate aberrant behaviour on the part of players, from antisocial user interactions, to malevolent scripted bots, to problems experienced by users with content.

Finally, Ad-Hoc Queries refers to the expectation that during any stage of the game development process, and into the game maintenance phase, any usage data will be queried to ascertain patterns of behavior, even from older versions or other CVEs for comparison purposes. This means that an extensible and easy to use framework should be developed that would allow any game development stakeholders to design and execute their own queries, in much the same manner as is performed in other large dataset application domains [17].

9.5 Event Model

The event model is derived from the factors highlighted in a focus group held with games company designers, and in effect encapsulates the information that is desired by future users of such a visualisation framework. Eight members of the Brisbane game development community met with the researchers to ascertain the user requirements for a proposed data logging and visualisation system, and assisted with event model development. The focus groups included a questionnaire session which enabled them to highlight user behaviours that they prioritised from a presented list, with the opportunity to add their own behaviours. User behaviours and events that were identified as highly prioritised by focus group participants were related to user *immersion experience*, *mission uptake* and *social factors*.

From these three areas a general event model has been developed to support the logging of desired game elements. This event model is similar in structure to those used for remote network monitoring [18], with unique CVE oriented additions. For each event component the following event types have been defined that emanate from objects in the game.

1. Time Events (TE) – logging at specified time intervals, such as location of player at particular time.
2. Interaction Events (IE) – battles, interactions with other objects in the environment, for example, usage of CVE content like weapons or virtual houses.
3. Emergent Events (EE) – events that emerge from internal state changes, for example, death events from internal loss of health.

The animation/rendering thread associated with each object in the environment generates these events if the object has been selected to be part of a log data stream. A detailed list of designer task relevant events that should be logged were derived from further discussion with focus group attendants, and are listed in [15, 19]. We now described the software framework which will be used to generate events and manage the data created for visualisation by game development stake holders.

9.6 CVE Data Logging and Visualisation Framework

The visualisation framework is a set of software tools that accesses a special build of the environment (called a *CVE logging build*) to expose the event model. This logging build has a thread attached to the environment objects, which generates the events during interactions by users. Data within the environment engine model is thus selected for logging according to the event model previously defined. Furthermore, discussions with the focus group showed a strong desire for a simple turn key solution with a low barrier to entry, while still allowing extensions for specialist visualisations.

In this framework, game source code classes have a logging method added via a preprocessing pass on the source code during the build. The logging approach has the single function of exposing class internals through the event model. Some variables may be tagged as time events, and so will be written to a logging file via a timer attached to the class. Interaction events will require the identification of object interaction methods in the code. The preprocessing pass can then insert appropriate functions into the class interaction methods. Emergent events use a watch approach on key class parameters, and so if these parameters pass a certain threshold, then the logging method writes an entry to the game log system. In effect, this is an extended form of typical Integrated Development Environment (IDE) debugging systems.

The event model is the basic structure around which the framework is developed. An interface approach to the event model is therefore required to allow users to select the event information they require from the game. The framework exposes five interfaces to the event model:

- In Situ – the event log is specified within the actual game logging build itself.
- Aggregate – a summary aggregated interface to regions and environment content is presented to obtain environment wide large scale visualisations of usage data.
- Programmer – the event model is exposed via the programming IDE to enable tagging and marking up of environment engine object data.
- Player – players also feed information into this framework by providing a game logging build to allow players to report their experience of gameplay passages.
- Live Console – designers and controllers of a virtual environment will wish to have a running view of the CVE, with the ability to exposing event information in a collaborative manner.

Each of these interfaces are designed to facilitate the generation of data logging streams within the testing phases of the game development life cycle previously described. The interface requirements for these components are analysed in more detail in Sect. 9.7.

The system is conceptually a Service Oriented Architecture (SOA) [20] to allow external applications to communicate with the system, and the encapsulation of services within the major components of the visualisation and data logging architecture.

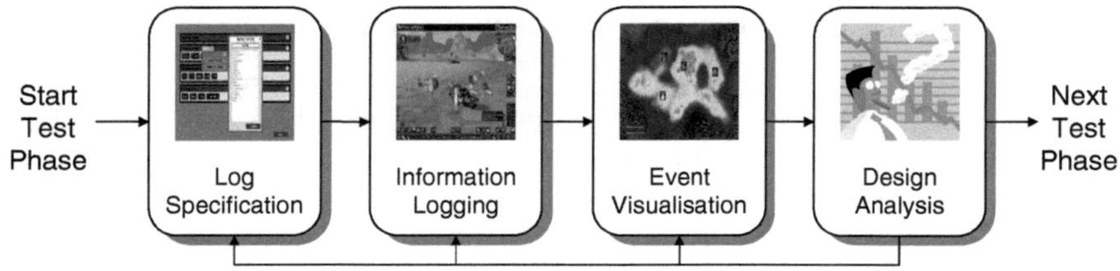

Fig. 9.2 The four main stages in the visualisation framework workflow: Log specification, information logging, event visualisation and finally design analysis

This design will assist with the development of a collaborative approach to using the visualisation system, especially during remote beta testing sessions, where the log specification, processing and display options can be run with other users and designers. In each case the user is selecting gameplay event log data streams to store and analyse, these stream specifications are stored in a file and used by the preprocessing pass to insert the code necessary into the classes to expose the event model data streams.

The process typically follows the workflow shown in Fig. 9.2. Firstly, logging of information is made that is congruent with analysis tasks performed by designers, usually by aggregate and in situ interfaces. For such environments, the reports of good and bad experiences in regions of the environment need to be correlated with other data and displayed to indicate what is happening with the users. A course of action is then taken to remove the problem within the virtual environment. While the details of each stage may be different and use different interfaces and components, the main stages of log specification, user response gathering, visualisation and decision making are executed many times in CVE testing. An example workflow case study is described in detail in Sect. 9.9.

9.7 Interface Design

This visualisation system is integrated into the games development toolset via the test engine build, and a separate visualisation tool for aggregated and console views of the CVE event model. The event model is also exposed via a programmer interface that will be integrated within the IDE environment. This allows specification of the game play log via a compilation of the game engine, using a language preprocessor to expose event model streams to disk logs.

The environment engine will also allow for a special build component exposing an in situ environment that enables the designer to mark up objects within the game in an intuitive manner. The designer(s) can select objects in the environment while playing or traversing the game in a collaborative manner with colleagues, and specify log information for that object or its object class. For example, the designer may select a region within the CVE, and specify a log of purchases by a selected user in the environment.

During testing phases, a player interface to the data logging system is presented for reporting enjoyment levels of particular sections of the game via a simple interface. This allows time stamps of player enjoyment levels to be recorded, and then correlated with other data available, such as usage logs and videos of the faces of people using the environment.

A separate tool provides an aggregated view to the event model, allowing the specification of higher level logs and visualisations, for example, they may wish to log the spell weapon usage for an entire class of wizards in a particular region. This would be separate to the engine build, allowing a more aggregated view of the event model that does not require traversal of the game environment for usage.

The framework also interfaces with the other tools in the pipeline, via the IDE the programmers use, and integrates into the compile tool chain for engine and content. The event model exposure via data streams from the game logging build becomes a part of the environment nightly build procedure. In effect, this log becomes useful archival information about the game design, and can be potentially used for future software by comparison of usage across different versions of the same CVE.

We now illustrate interfaces to the framework for the log specification, and related testing phases for an online game. Each visualisation and interface component is related to tasks performed by game development stakeholders in each section of the game development life cycle. Each of the interfaces uses Shockwave mockups, based on World of Warcraft screen dumps as a case study for the designs. It is a straightforward task to refactor the interfaces to work within more general environments such as Second Life, due to similar requirements.

9.7.1 *In Situ Log Specification*

Figure 9.3 illustrates a shock wave mockup of a designer using the In Situ interface. Following our WoW case study, a priest character has been selected, with the menu

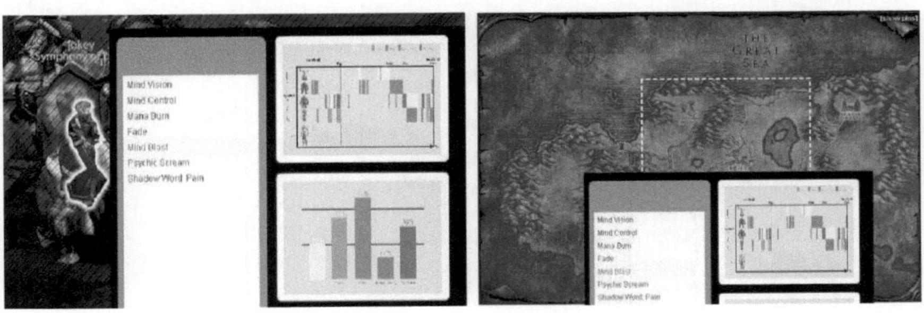

Fig. 9.3 Illustration of the in situ interfaces, with the designer highlighting a priest game character in the left image (white halo to left of menu), and requesting a data log and visualisation of the "Mind Blast" weapon. On the right a map region (white dotted rectangle) is being selected for the same weapon monitoring within the game (*See Color Plates*)

options being presented to log the mind-blast weapon usage (content usage event) and visualisation specification of the data.

This query may also be specified by highlighting a region within a map. The menus expose the internal event model for the objects in the game, as stored in the log specification file.

The main advantage of this interface is that a designer may be playing the game, discovers a problem, and is inspired to log some game play data while actually being in the game itself. It also allows colleagues to collaborate with each other in selecting content that should be watched for usability problems in a very ad-hoc and spontaneous manner, thus capturing subtle problems with the environment being tested. Finally, it also allows a highly intuitive mode of interaction with the game event model.

9.7.2 Aggregate Log Specification

The aggregate interface shown in Fig. 9.4 allows developers to specify large scale data logging streams, or to use standard streams for game wide factors, such as content usage across the entire server. This interface is stand alone from the game build and produces a data logging specification to be later processed. Game objects and regions are exposed and selected at an aggregate level, thus the main advantage of this interface is the ability to easily create large scale, game wide, data logs.

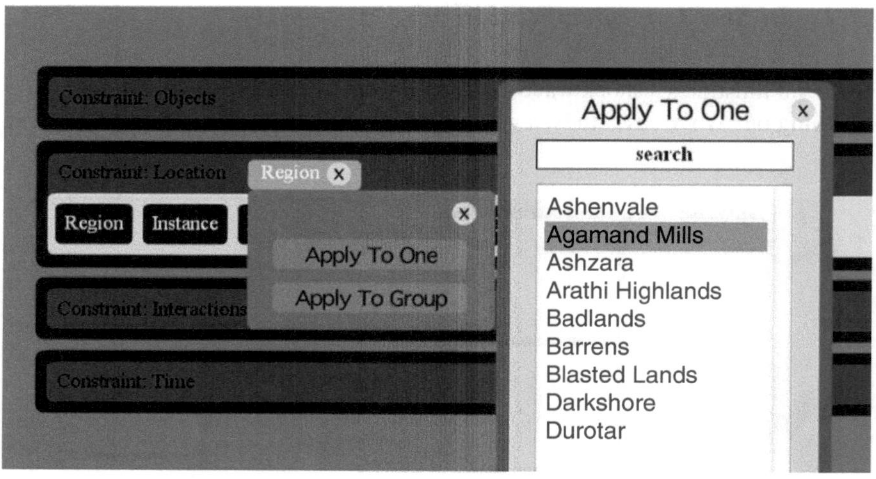

Fig. 9.4 Illustration of the aggregate interface, facilitating the tracking of large scale data streams applied to whole regions of a CVE. In this example, as per the case study in Sect. 9.2, the Agamand Mills are selected from the new content being tested and analysed, as it is the area of interest for the new environmental area

The interaction modes for such an aggregate interface will tend to be a menu driven system. Here, previously specified CVE usability log specifications will be loaded, ready for selection by designers. But, as with the in situ interface, it will allow the users to access the event model as exposed in the log specification file, to select log data streams of their own choice.

9.7.3 Collaborative Console Views

Figure 9.5 illustrates a live console interface to the logging framework while the game is playing. Selected game event data streams are visualised as rows of temporal visualisations for the game console, and are configurable by the designers. Games maintenance staff can thus monitor the state of various game event streams for problems.

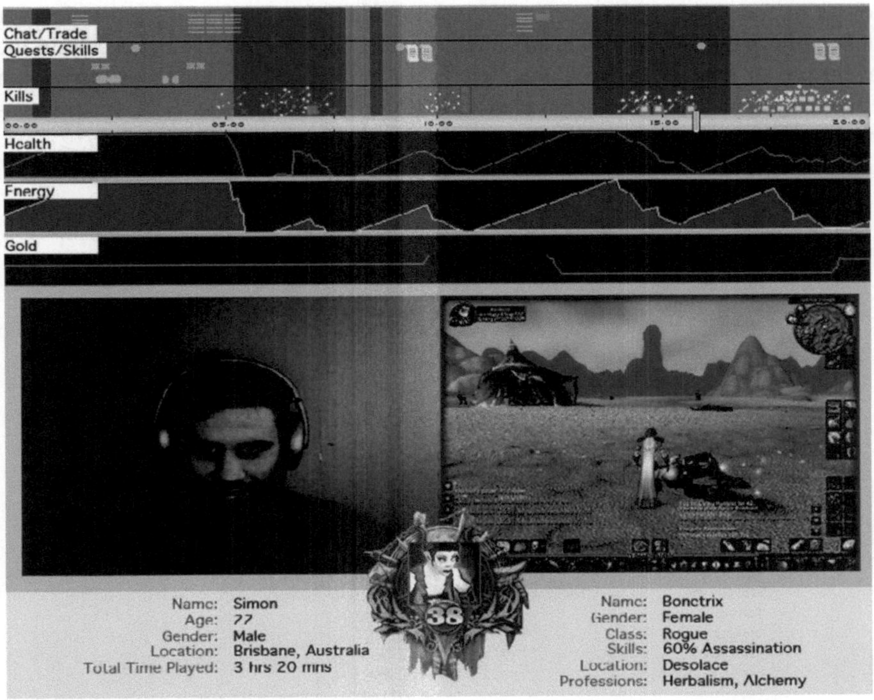

Fig. 9.5 Mock up of an example live console interface to a WoW. The console view also allows for collaboration with beta testers of a game, in order to view video footage of emotional responses, logged play in situ in the game environment and a matching of these with timeline based event indicators

Such a console view enables scalable management of a testing session. Designers can test with as many as several thousand focus testers at once and still be able to talk with them on a one to one basis as needed. For example, a designer can link up to any user over video chat and discuss relevant game events. The designer can review visualisations of data or videos of user faces via this interface. The live console shows the designers the current status of environment testers. A designer can initiate conversation with any player, and can, via testing interfaces shown in Fig. 9.5, watch the player via video hook up to analyse facial expressions during usage, and correlate it with usage events generated by the event model. This approach facilitates a collaborative and distributed mode to environment testing, allowing designers to scale up from focus group and user testing to support the size of modern online environments, in order to give a thorough testing environment.

9.7.4 Programmer Log Specification

The programmer IDE interface to the event model allows the specification of a data log from code itself, refer to Fig. 9.6. Programmers may wish to log game data for debugging purposes, and so need an interface that allows them direct access to the event model from the source code itself. For example, the logging of Interaction Events by a programmer may reveal collision detection problems in the environment engine logic.

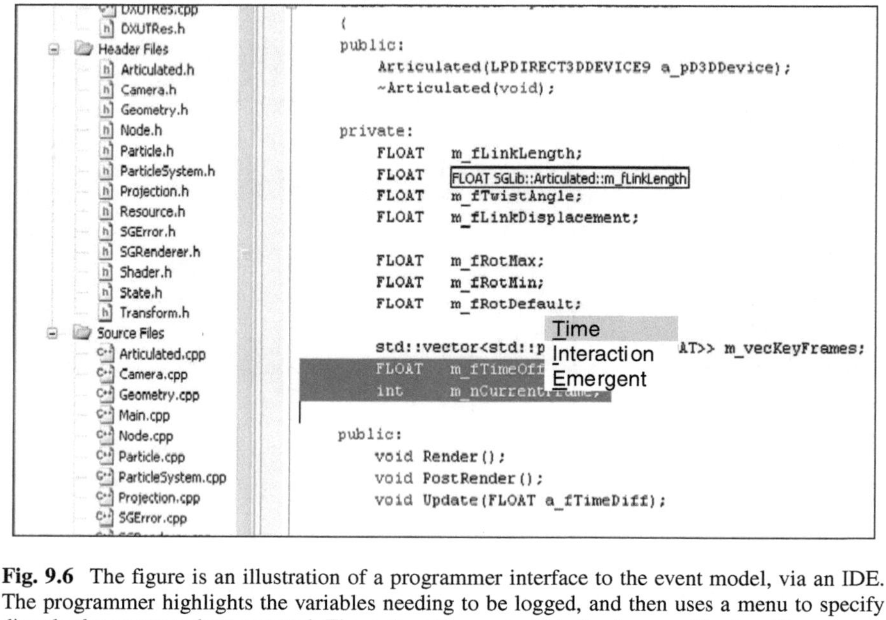

Fig. 9.6 The figure is an illustration of a programmer interface to the event model, via an IDE. The programmer highlights the variables needing to be logged, and then uses a menu to specify directly the events to be generated. These streams are stored in the log specification file

9.7.5 Player Test Phase Interfaces

In this section we illustrate the interfaces for testing phases for users. By this stage a log specification has been made, so the event model is being logged for the designers, in the background. However, during testing, users will be required to provide feedback on various aspects of the game. Therefore, a mechanism must be created for capturing such information, for large scale testing. Interviewing users, while invaluable, is not practical for large scale testing, which may involve tens of thousands of people. Part of the log specification will therefore provide an interface for the users to record subjective impressions of enjoyment during the usage of the CVE.

From our analysis of the testing phases performed in Sect. 9.4, we show the interfaces required for incorporating subjective impressions into the usage data logging framework. Focus testers generate subjective information, with regards to their impressions of level design, mechanics, balancing, missions, crafting, amongst other factors. Figure 9.7 illustrates such an interface for a focus group session. The interface allows the subjective impressions of immersion experienced by the user to be included into the logging build streams for future analysis. Subjective impressions from users provide much insight into environment usability, and need to be included into any data logging scheme.

For example, if a large number of people tag a particular environment component as being not enjoyable, then the designers can easily visualise other data

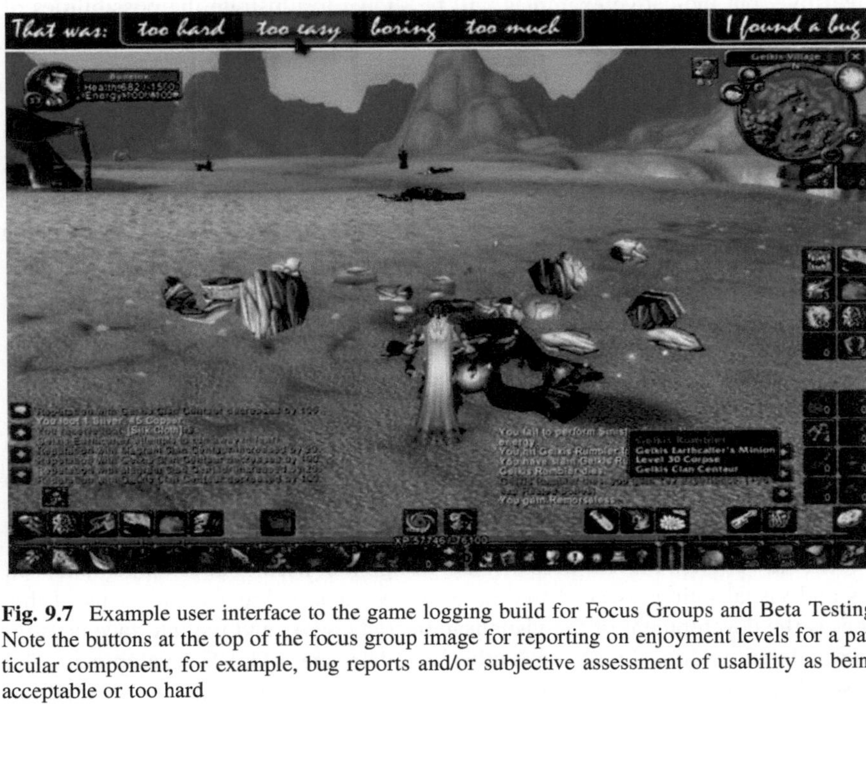

Fig. 9.7 Example user interface to the game logging build for Focus Groups and Beta Testing. Note the buttons at the top of the focus group image for reporting on enjoyment levels for a particular component, for example, bug reports and/or subjective assessment of usability as being acceptable or too hard

around that time stamp to find out why it was sub-optimal under focus testing. In addition, the simple interface is less intrusive than interviews by designers, which will provide more honest answers. This information can supplement the already used approaches of video and audio capture in small groups. The designer can upload the last 30 seconds of player video footage when problems occur or subjective inputs indicate usability issues.

The use of an integrated questionnaire interface for QA and Beta testing also helps organise and manage beta testing sessions, thus assisting beta tester reporting. The data used can also be used for environment balancing visualisations. As with focus testing, the principle is to expose players to a simple interface extension within the game logging build, allowing subjective information to be easily correlated with other usage data, and integrated into the runtime log data model.

9.8 Visualisation Techniques for Collaborative Virtual Environment Data

We have analysed the design and implementation stages for CVE development, to derive the general tasks that designers need to perform. We now proceed to provide event model data for each of these major tasks, and provide an example visualisation to enable the analysis of appropriate environment events. This will not be exhaustive, but indicative examples will be shown to illustrate the possibilities of this framework. We also model the following examples around the concept of missions within a game. These mission examples can map effectively to general CVE tasks, as the creation of more general visualisations for CVE environment is very similar to those generated for government and social organisations [21], and so these mission designs can be re-factored for more general interactions within CVE environments for administrative purposes.

The environment event model is exposed to the developer via the visualisations presented. The event model is processed by a designer task model to produce the base level visualisations. In this section we generate a number of visualisations for the following designer tasks: environment traversal, social networks and economics, that were identified during a focus group meeting as priorities [22]. These categories may blur, and a fully configured system will allow a game development team to configure their own specialized visualisations. However, it was found during the industry focus groups that preconfigured visualisations would be preferred, due to ease of use by a design team. In the end, these visualisations do not differ in nature, except that some are created and stored for reuse as turn-key visualiszation solutions for the team.

It should be noted that the actual visual design tool used to develop personalised logs and visualisations is not listed here for the sack of brevity, the focus of this paper is the development of the visualisation framework, and the interface components and their relationships to each other, and the stages of CVE development. The log specification file will be human readable and thus can be edited by a text editor, or a visual front end (in addition to those interfaces listed) to specify complete details for the game log variables to be sampled. But if required, the visualisation development tool for this framework can follow the nature of other visualisation toolkits allowing visual and programming interfaces to be personalised from previous usage information [23].

9.8.1 Environment Traversal Visualisation

A major insight into virtual environment usage is derived from analysis of the environment traversal performed by users. The designer task here is to understand content usage, in the form of map locations, to examine where people are moving and to identify regions that are not being used, or conversely, are being too heavily used. This designer task requires the use of a number of timed events to be monitored, thus the location events will be sampled at an appropriate interval for client server loading. An alpha blended line, from point to point in the sample space, is then rendered over the map surface. An example is shown in Fig. 9.8, with the trails overlaid onto the map surface in the 3D world. The alpha blending value is normalised for the total number of events, so the heavy concentrations of movements are easily discerned as opaque regions on the ground surface.

9.8.2 Social Network Visualisation

Another designer task is the monitoring of social networks that form within the environments. For this example, the visualisation incorporates an analysis of how a social network is performing internally, for the benefit of the team members, and

Fig. 9.8 Example of visualisation to support the content usage task, via capturing of location time events from the event model. These location time events are represented via an alpha blended line joining them together in the game model itself. A World of Warcraft example is shown on the left, and a similar example utilising a Second Life map is shown on the right

for designers to understand team dynamics within the environment. For the game example, the analysis requires the analysis of Combat Events and Death events from the event model, bringing out the statistics of the environment partakers involved. The help given to each member can be gained from character to character interactions in team battles with the same opponent.

The Interaction Event data is then visualised as a graph, with deaths as a blue circle, kills as a green circle and the amount of help given in battle as a weighted edge, with thickness indicating the amount of help. This visualisation can then be analysed for the relative contributions of the team members. In the example shown in Fig. 9.9, it can be seen that team member A is a strong contributor to the gaming group, while team member C is effectively an absent member. This type of visualisation can be used in other environments for similar teamwork analysis, for example, economic interactions between producers of content, and consumers of content in an environment such as Second Life.

9.8.3 *Economic Visualisation*

One of the major areas highlighted in focus groups was the need for economic visualisations which indicate trading and gathering of items as Content Interaction events between players and items in the map. In Fig. 9.10 an economic visualisation example is shown for both a game (WoW) and non-game (Second-Life), as similar

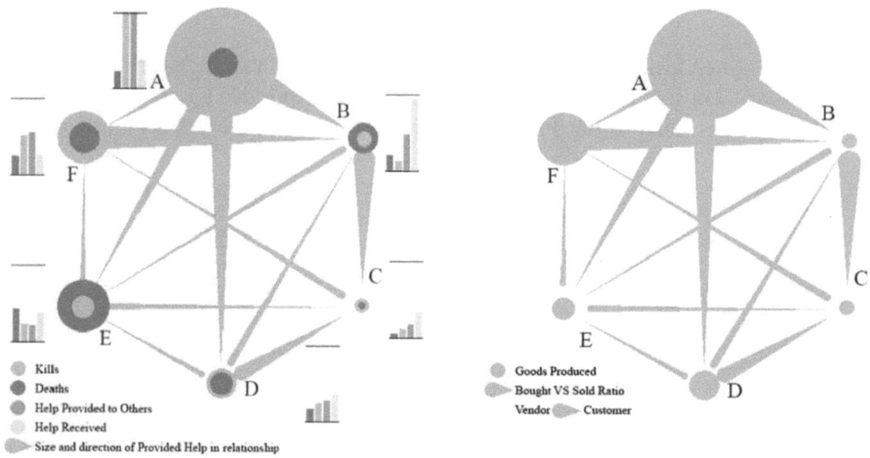

Fig. 9.9 Example of social networking visualisation of a team showing their kills (light part of node circle – green) and deaths (dark part of node circle – blue) with the graph edges representing help contributed to each member by other members in the group (left). On the right hand side, a similar graph is used to show the production of goods within Second Life by each person in a selected group, and the amount of produce they purchase from other people, giving insight into the economic networks occurring in the environment

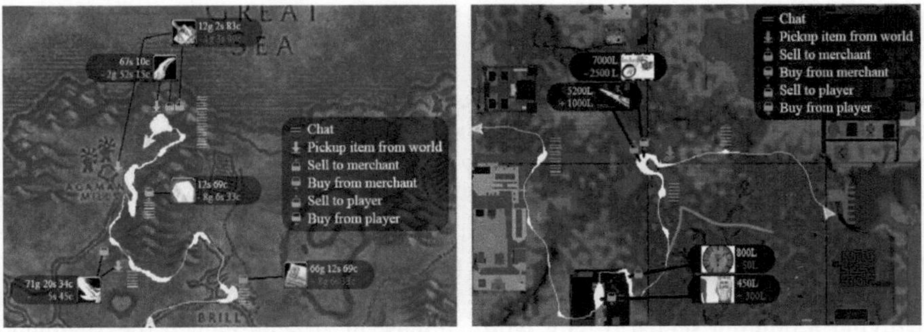

Fig. 9.10 Map indicating locations of a player chatting, trading, and using environmental content, for both World of Warcraft (left) and Second Life (right). The difference in transaction price to the average world price is shown. Both visualisations give designers insight into the usage of the environment from an economic perspective (*See Color Plates*)

design issues need to be addressed around the area of content creation, exchange, economic effects and how they correlate with the actual spatial arrangement of the environment. The example annotations indicate the amount of gold or other content collected or traded, and will help designers with analysis of interactions between players at this level, to find economic patterns of usage, or non-usage of items in areas of the online game.

9.9 Visualisation Framework Case Study

To show an example of how the described framework may be used, a simulated MMORPG case study is described with a typical game design scenario derived from WOW game screen captures[2]

This case study will not illustrate all possible components, but it will highlight how designers can use the visualisation system to explore problems highlighted by users of the environment, and how they can then investigate problems with the game using the components. It will highlight the usage of the visualisation and data logging components that facilitate collaborative and critical examination of CVE design issues, and embeds these into the visualisation workflow approach we described previously in Sect. 9.4. While the example is for a game environment, the content design and usage issues are similar for any 3D virtual environment, such as Second Life.

[2] The scenario was developed from an example given by developers during the game focus group discussions, and in no way is representative or endorsed by Blizzard Entertainment creators of World of Warcraft. World of Warcraft® ©2004-–2008 Blizzard Entertainment, Inc. All rights reserved. World of Warcraft and Blizzard Entertainment are trademarks or registered trademarks of Blizzard Entertainment, Inc. in the U.S. and/or other countries.

9.9.1 Background

A new MMORPG game add-on has been released for public beta testing. This release includes an update pack with many new and complex puzzle-like environments with non-linear relationships between actions taken by the player and the resultant consequences. The game is thus at the final quality assurance beta testing phase, and as is typical for an MMORPG, is being released to a group of beta testers who have signed up for the chance to play a prerelease version of the game.

An important new component of the game has a new environmental section involving a hunting scenario with wild animals, in an area named the Agamand Mills. In a valley section of the environment, there is a mini-ecosystem consisting of wild deer and wolves where the populations are held in balance, modeling a real population of predator and prey. However, if the wild deer are killed, then a number of wolves starve making it easier to traverse a section of the map near this valley.

9.9.2 Log Specification and Execution

The registered beta users are given a debug build of the game engine containing the user interface for registering problems with the game. The game build also contains software which allows live linkups to the console management system, for conversations with the designers, facilitating a remote focus group approach. While playing the game, users are able to report quickly to the game server log that they are not happy with a particular level section via the interface overlay shown in Fig. 9.7. The designers have enabled a default configuration for this debug build that allows the aggregate logging of the location of the players, usage of content, kills by players and player deaths in the area around Agamand Mills, as per the interface shown in Fig. 9.4. A test server running the game with the beta testers is implemented, logging the information as required.

9.9.3 Data Visualisation

After the registered beta testers were playing the game for a time, it was noticed by the designers of the level that a large number of the users were dying before completion. A number of players noted, via the game interface, that the region near the mountains was no fun to play.

The designers then referred to spatial locations of deaths on the level and found that most of the players were being killed in a particular region on the map, this location was correlated highly to the place where critical comments were made by the users (refer to Fig. 9.11, left diagram). The designers then queried the nature of the deaths for that region via a map visualisation interface, as shown in Fig. 9.3.

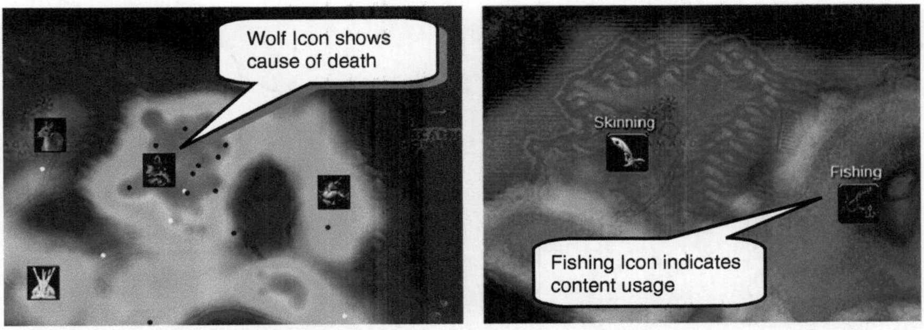

Fig. 9.11 On the left is a spatial map of the deaths in the level, and their correlation with locations of negative comments by players (shown by black dots), with an overlay of content interactions for that region (deaths and kills). On the right is a spatial map showing traversal in the area around the wolf deaths, including overlays of interaction with content by players (*See Color Plates*)

The majority of deaths came up as being by wolves in the area, too numerous to attack properly and survive (refer to Fig. 9.11, left diagram). These deaths puzzled the designers, as the players it seemed were not killing enough deer to enable safe passage through the area.

Visualisations of the content interaction events showed a lot of fishing being performed by people in the area near the lake, as there was a mini-game involving fishing in that area of the valley (refer to Fig. 9.11, right diagram). But the players were not then going to hunt the deer nearby. The designers then entered the game, just near the fishing area, and noted that the nature of the outlay of the land is too hilly to see the deer in the other section of the level (refer to Fig. 9.12). It was concluded that even if the players did see the deer, it had also not been made obvious to kill the deer, thus almost all players faced the full onslaught of fit wolves later in the level.

9.9.4 Results Analysis and Action Plan

After using the visualisation system to focus in on the problem parameters, the development team had a meeting. Upon reflection, the fishing game was much more obvious to play, and its engaging quality had distracted players from the correct path through the level. The problem was resolved with the following derived from previous replays and analysis of the results of the visualisation: the fishing sub-game was removed due to its distracting nature; the terrain model was modified to allow visual line of sight to the deer grazing in the other section of the game; an animated scenario was shown to the players of wolves eating the deer, as a hint as to how to beat the wolves; the power balance of the wolves was modified to allow more of a chance for the players.

Fig. 9.12 Scene from case study game, indicating a lack of ability to see the deer and wolf environment over mountain ridge on traversal of the level

Further logs indicated less users were dying at this location of the level. Interaction event visualisations also showed more people were deciding to kill the deer in order to weaken the wolves in the environment. The play results thus showed that it had become an appropriately challenging puzzle for players to solve for the game environment.

9.10 Summary

This chapter described a complete collaborative framework for gameplay data logging and visualisation for online games. We have analysed the game development process to produce mappings from a general event model to the design and use of a data logging framework. Data acquisition, data management, user interface and hardware scalability factors have also been analysed. Furthermore, we have used the event and designer task model to design task relevant visualisations for some typical design assessment scenarios. A case study was then used to show the utility of the framework, in particular, the workflow process involved in using the framework in a typical scenario. As an end result, we have proposed a modular framework that can be applied with minor additions to numerous designer tasks within the many forms of CVEs now appearing in both the entertainment and business sectors of the community.

Acknowledgements The authors acknowledge the financial assistance of Microsoft Research Asia (Beijing).

References

1. Blizzard (2007) World of Warcraft Home Page, www.worldofwarcraft.com/index.xml Accessed July 2007.
2. Linden (2007) Second Life Home Page, www.secondlife.com Accessed July 2007.
3. Irish D (2005) The Game Producer's Handbook. Premier Press, Boston, USA.
4. Blizzard (2004) Blizzard Beta Testing FAQ., www.blizzard.com/wow/faq/faq_beta.shtml Accessed March 2007.
5. Keller P, Keller M (1993) Visual Cues. IEEE Press, Piscataway, USA.
6. Alberto Gonzalez P, Rolf S (2006) Adaptive Distributed Monitoring with Accuracy Objectives. SIGCOMM Workshop on Internet Network Management. ACM Press, Pisa, Italy.
7. Handschin E, Leder C (2001) Automatic Decision Ssupport with a New Visualization Concept for Power Systems. Power Tech Proceedings, Porto, Portugal 2:5.
8. Emergent (2007) Emergent Game Technologies: Metrics, www.emergent.net/index.php/homepage/products-and-services/metrics/metrics Accessed March 2007.
9. Hoobler N, Humphreys G, Agrawala M (2004) Visualising Competitive Behaviours in Multi-User Virtual Environments IEEE Visualization Austin, USA:163–170.
10. Robert PB-A, Simeon JS (2001) An Integrative Framework for Knowledge Extraction in Collaborative Virtual Environments. International ACM SIGGROUP Conference on Supporting Group Work, Boulder, Colorado, USA:61–70.
11. Thawonmas R, Ho J-Y, Matsumoto Y (2003) Identification of Player Types in Massively Multiplayer Online Games. 34th Annual Conference of the International Simulation and Gaming Association (ISAGA), Chiba, Japan:893–900.
12. Tveit A, Rein O, Iversen JV, Matskin M (2003) Scalable Agent-Based Simulation of Players in Massively Multiplayer Online Games. 8th Scandinavian Conference on Artificial Intelligence (SCAI'03), Bergen, Norway:80–89.
13. Chittaro L, Ieronutti L (2004) A Visual Tool for Tracing Users' Behavior in Virtual Environments. Working Conference on Advanced Visual Interfaces, Improving Interaction:40–47.
14. Grammenos D, Filou M, Papadakos P, Stephanidis C (2002) Virtual Prints: Leaving Trails in Virtual Environments. Workshop on Virtual Environments 2002, Navigation and Interaction, Barcelona, Spain:23 131-ff.
15. Brown R, Joslin S, Drennan P (2007) The Gameplay Visualisation Manifesto: A Framework for Logging and Visualisation of Online Gameplay Data. ACM CIE, Vol. 5.
16. Salen K, Zimmerman E (2004) Rules of Play: Game Design Fundamentals. The MIT Press, Cambridge, MA.
17. Jake Yue C, John VC, Ning G (2005) A Complex Biological Database Querying Method. ACM Symposium on Applied Computing, Santa Fe, USA:110–114.
18. Mansouri-Samani M, Sloman M (1993) Monitoring Distributed Systems. *Network* 7:20–30.
19. Joslin S, Brown R, Drennan P (2006) Modelling Quest Data for Game Designers. The 2006 International Conference on Game Research and Development, Perth, Australia 1234371:184–190.
20. Erl T (2005) Service-Oriented Architecture: Concepts, Technology, and Design. Prentice Hall Professional Technical Reference, Upper Saddle River, USA.
21. Tufte E (1983) The Visual Display of Quantitative Information. Graphics Press, Cheshire, USA.
22. Brown R, Joslin S, Drennan P (2007) MMOG Visualisation Project Wiki, wiki.qut.edu.au/display/gameplayvis/Home Accessed March 2007.
23. Brown R, Pham B (2003) Visualisation of Fuzzy Decision Support Information: A Case Study. 12th IEEE International Conference on Fuzzy Systems, St Louis, Missouri, USA:601–606.

References

Part IV
Novel User Interfaces

Chapter 10
Virtual Reality-Based Interactive Scientific Visualization Environments

Joseph J. LaViola Jr., Prabhat, Andrew S. Forsberg, David H. Laidlaw, and Andries van Dam

Abstract Immersive Virtual Reality (IVR) has some production applications (e.g., in vehicle design and psychiatric treatment), but it is often viewed as an expensive, over-hyped technology with insufficient and/or unproven benefit over conventional desktop systems. With steady research progress at many institutions and advances in hardware and software technologies, immersive scientific visualization is another application area in which IVR is having a positive impact and is beginning to attract more attention from the scientific community. At Brown University, we have been researching immersive scientific visualization systems by developing interactive systems with domain scientists in a variety of fields, including archaeology, biology, computational fluid dynamics (CFD), and geoscience. Anecdotal and formal evaluations show the benefits range from mild to very significant – benefits include speeding up and providing broader analysis, greater spatial understanding, enabling new types of exploration, helping in undergraduate as well as graduate courses, and debugging data acquisition methods. In this chapter, we present a number of these systems developed at Brown University and discuss the results of our experimental findings on the efficacy of IVR-based interactive visualization.

Keywords Immersive virtual reality, Scientific visualization, Interactive visualization, 3D interfaces, Surround screen display, Virtual environments.

10.1 Introduction

Scientists studying the physical world frequently need to analyze complex data sets (multidimensional, multivariate, time-varying) and models. Our group of interactive visualization researchers subscribes to the theory that in order to best understand such data we must "impedance match" display and interaction devices as best we can with human motor and sensory capabilities, in a task-dependent way. We feel

E. Zudilova-Seinstra et al. (eds.) *Trends in Interactive Visualization*,
doi:10.1007/978-1-84800-269-2_10

that for 3- or higher-dimensional data this is best done by immersive virtual reality (IVR) systems, with their ability to provide greatly enhanced 3D depth-perception via head-tracked stereo. There is also mounting evidence that IVR's ability to let users be "inside" their data or model and to interact directly with the data by moving their heads, bodies and hands (body-centric interaction) speeds up the processes of perception and interpretation. Scientific visualization and IVR are both technologies that have a history of invention and development spanning over multiple decades. Indeed, the use of IVR for scientific and information visualization dates back to the early uses of virtual reality [7]. In multiple articles [14, 15, 28, 29, 34, 40, 48], examples have been presented of applications combining these two technologies, as well as evidence for their effectiveness ranging from anecdotal or observational to controlled quantitative user studies. There have also been important studies [8, 26, 34, 35] trying to document how one measures the degree and effectiveness of the dominant psychophysical experiences of presence and immersion provided by IVR; roughly these two experiences relate respectively to the feeling "of being there" and the feeling of being surrounded by a model or data set.

Among the reasons for the potential effectiveness of immersive environments for scientific visualization are (1) the ability to use body-centric interaction, e.g., moving one's head and/or body to gain a different point of view, and using one's hands, potentially aided by voice, to interact with the data or model. Such interactions can be more fluid and more efficient, i.e., with reduced cognitive load, than those controlled by the standard desktop display's keyboard and mouse-driven graphical user interface. (2) the ability to move quickly between large-context views and more detailed views and to have 3D depth-perception significantly enhanced by stereo and low-latency head movement (motion parallax). Being able to hold a model or data set in a fixed position and moving one's point of view, whether on the outside or inside, is far more natural and efficient than holding one's viewpoint fixed and moving the data set. However, head/body movement is not sufficient by itself and a variety of techniques exist [3] for examining new locales within one data set or model using physical interaction devices such as a 3D mouse or tracked glove. (3) the ability to have not only fully immersive environments such as those produced by a head mounted display (HMDs) or CAVE™ [10] but also semi-immersive environments (e.g., Fishtank VR [43] on the desktop or tiled-display walls [41] that still allow head-tracking and use of one's peripheral vision.

At Brown University, we have been developing IVR-based interactive visualization systems and studying their effectiveness for the last 15 years using our Cave, a variant of the CAVE™ and Fishtank VR. In this chapter, we highlight a number of these systems and discuss some of our experimental findings on the efficacy of IVR-based interactive scientific visualization. Readers should note that many other academic institutions and organizations have worked on multiple aspects of Virtual Reality for a number of years. We cannot possibly do justice to all of our colleagues within the space constraints of a single chapter. Indeed that would be an entire book in its own right! If readers are interested, they may refer to the following sampling of literature as a good starting point: [2, 5, 9, 10, 12, 16, 17, 24, 30, 31, 36, 38, 39, 44].

10.2 IVR-Based Interactive Visualization Systems

Brown University has had a long history in developing interactive scientific visualization systems with carefully designed and evaluated user interfaces from both a visualization and interaction point of view. We believe immersive virtual reality has the potential to provide substantial benefit for these complex visualization problems. In this section, we discuss some of the IVR-based interactive visualization systems we have developed.

10.2.1 Widget Library

In the early 1990s, we began work on 3D user interfaces for desktop and immersive scientific visualization applications working with NASA Ames Research Center over a five year period. The work was inspired by Bryson's Virtual Windtunnel project [6, 7], one of the first systems to explore how scientific visualization could be conducted in IVR. The final user-interface project with NASA led to the development of a stand-alone library for creating and interacting with 3D widgets. The core of the library was a set of building blocks for constructing custom 3D widgets and functions that handle direct manipulation of the widgets (see Fig. 10.1).

In addition to the basic widget building blocks, the library supported interactive shadows and gestural navigation controls (i.e., translation forward and backward, virtual trackball rotation, and film-plane translation) using a single mouse button. These camera controls were derived from the camera controls used in the SKETCH system [46].

In particular, we developed interaction techniques for positioning probes in three-dimensions, controlling both spatial and non-spatial parameters of several visualization techniques, utilizing six-degrees-of-freedom input devices, navigating a 3D virtual world, managing voice annotations, in addition to developing an approach for rapid-prototyping custom input devices.

As an extension to the work done with NASA, we explored how multimodal interfaces could be used in an IVR-based visualization system with the Multimodal Scientific Visualization Tool (MSVT) [22]. MSVT used a rear-projected display device and combined speech input with pinching postures and gestures. The main objective of MSVT (see Fig. 10.2) was not only to build a natural and intuitive interface for a scientific visualization application, but also to explore different multimodal input combination styles [25] such as when two modalities complement each other (e.g., a user asking for a visualization tool with speech while simultaneously pointing to where it should be placed).

10.2.2 Virtual Cardiovascular Laboratory

Towards the late 1990s, we began to focus more on multi-disciplinary collaborations with doctors and scientists to see how IVRs could help them with their visualization

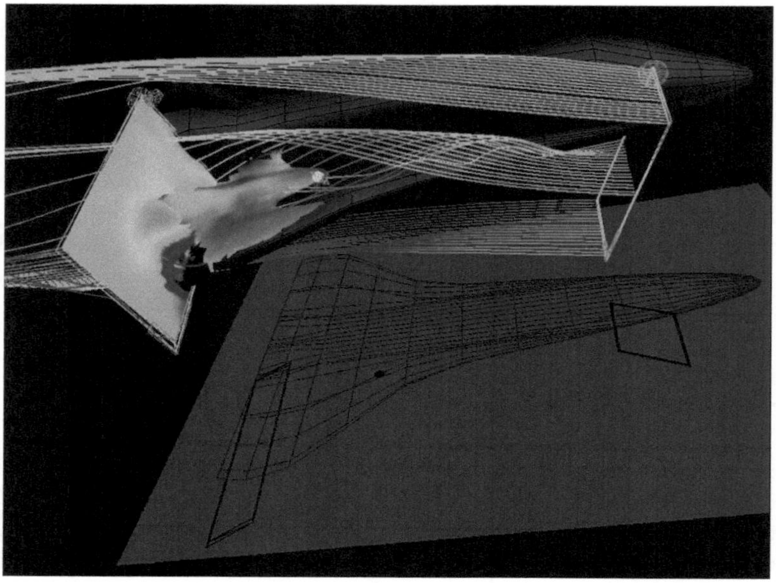

Fig. 10.1 Three example widgets developed as part of the Brown Widget Library developed in the mid-90s under NASA sponsorship to help scientists interactively visualize flow data past a space shuttle model. A color plane of flow speed (far left), an isosurface of flow speed widget (around the bluish-gray surface geometry), and a streamline source widget are shown. Each may have visualization parameters adjusted via direct manipulation of geometry "handles" making up the widget, as well as be transformed (resized, translated, or dragged via interactive shadows) (*See Color Plates*)

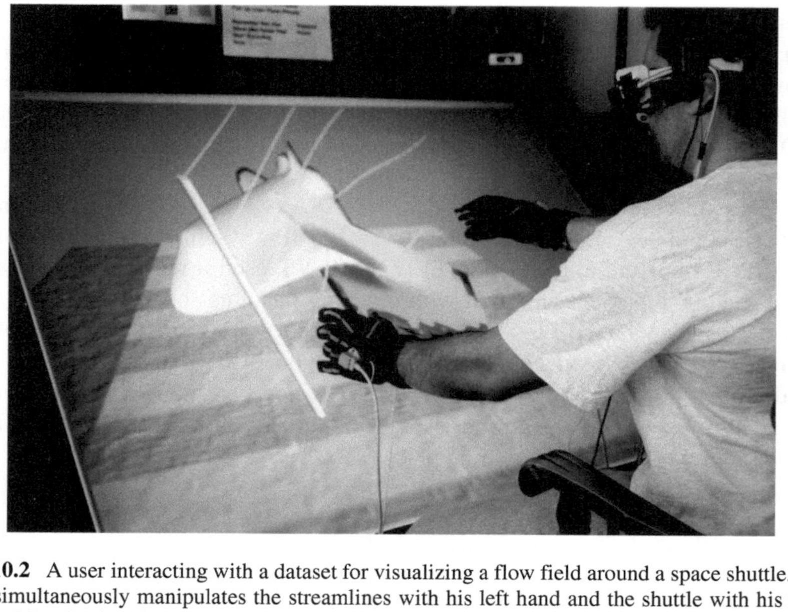

Fig. 10.2 A user interacting with a dataset for visualizing a flow field around a space shuttle. The user simultaneously manipulates the streamlines with his left hand and the shuttle with his right hand while viewing the data in stereo. The user asked for these tools using speech input

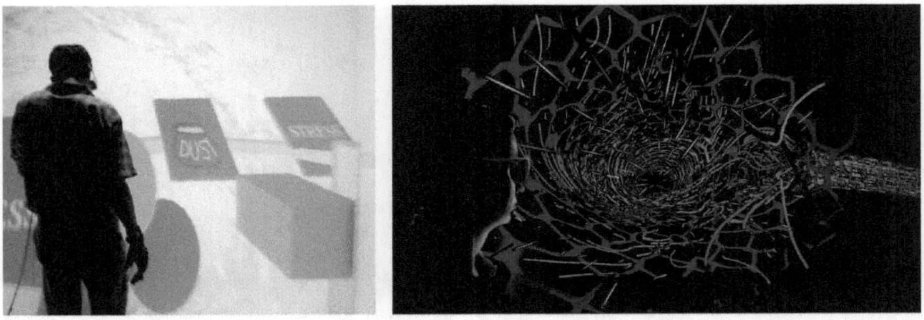

a b

Fig. 10.3 **a** A user looking at the virtual toolbelt in the Virtual Cardiovascular Laboratory. **b** A visualization of an artery using particle flurries

problems. One of the first systems we built along this path was for visualizing coronary artery grafts. These grafts regularly fail for unknown reasons, possibly related to the characteristics of fluid flow around these new arterial bifurcations. When they fail, they require repeated heart surgeries and often cause heart failure. Thus, doctors need tools to better understand cardiovascular hemodynamics.

We built a *Virtual Cardiovascular Laboratory* [14, 37] that coupled numerical simulation of graft geometry with an immersive surround-screen virtual environment for studying the resulting flow data (see Fig. 10.3). To support 3D interaction, we used trackers and pinching postures so users could pull themselves through space to examine artery structure. When users looked down, a virtual toolbelt appeared so they could grab dust for advecting particles through the flow, an "Alka-Seltzer" widget for creating a persistent source of advecting particles, and widgets for choosing wall coloring, streamlines, and rakes.

This system has not yet resulted in novel scientific results partly because we are still learning how to simulate the models of interest. Nevertheless, domain scientists believe the virtual cardiovascular laboratory quickly verified previously discovered results due to the human-sized visualizations (vessel walls and the data within were scaled-up such that they were about eight feet in diameter) that researchers could move inside of and carefully study intricate flow features throughout the volume. Researchers previously studied these kinds of flows in a laboratory setting with life-sized models (vessels on the order of millimeters in diameter with fluids flowing through them) and photographs of dyes injected into the vessel were carefully analyzed to piece together the overall 3D flow behavior.

10.2.3 ARCHAVE

Archaeologists base the analysis of data from an excavation site on the physical descriptions recorded in trench reports, site plans, drawings, and photographs. One of

Fig. 10.4 Users exploring the Great Temple Petra with the ARCHAVE system

the main challenges they must face is in understanding the complex spatial relationships existing between the artifacts and the site's architecture. Furthermore, site excavations are a destructive process so accurately capturing and later integrating data reliably is also important. To assist archeologists with their research, we developed the ARCHAVE system, a surround screen IVR application that puts users in a three-dimensional model of *in situ* architectural ruins [1]. Specifically, ARCHAVE was used to visualize the great temple site in Petra, Jordan and the associated trenches and artifacts that have been excavated over the years (see Fig. 10.4).

With ARCHAVE, users navigate in the environment, using a 3D mouse and wear a tracked glove to query the database site information. A standard database of artifact finds has been consistently updated since excavations began in 1993, and it can be queried in real time from the application. Users can also use a miniature version [23] of the full-scale model as a reference to quickly travel anywhere in the virtual environment.

10.2.4 Fluid Mechanics of Bat Locomotion

Building on the work done for ARCHAVE and the Virtual Cardiovascular Laboratory, we began collaborating with researchers from computational fluid dynamics and evolutionary biology to study bat flight fluid dynamics using visualization (see Fig. 10.5). Bats are energy efficient and highly maneuverable, making the study of bat flight likely to yield insights of use in future technological application, such as the development of unmanned flying machines. The mechanisms of their flight are currently not well understood and are challenging to study.

The data field describing airflow around the bat's wings can be described by a combination of many quantities including velocity, vorticity, pressure, and rate of strain. Each of these is a function of both space and time. Additional data describe the intricate motion of the score of bones in each wing, the deformation of the flexible surface of the wing, and interactions between the flow and the surface of

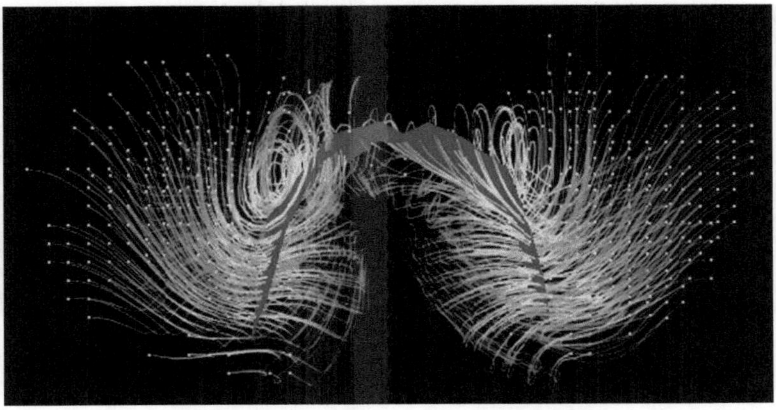

Fig. 10.5 Snapshot from an immersive visualization of bat flight highlighting vortical structure, a signature of lift, near the bat wing surface (*See Color Plates*)

the bat. To address the challenge of creating effective tools to visually portray the complex kinematics of the anatomy together with the fluid dynamics, we formed strong collaborations with visual designers at the Rhode Island School of Design (RISD). Visual designers, particularly illustrators, are trained specifically to solve constrained visual problems, and this training can effectively carry over into virtual environment (VE) applications.

With the designers' input, we developed a surround-screen IVR system for visualizing bat flight using several different visualization techniques including particle "eels" that followed pathlines, vorticity-seeded time-varying streamlines for visualizing vortices, and advecting vortex-seeded "snow" to capture wake structures. The user has control over the density of visual elements, how they are distributed in space, and the mapping of color and opacity to flow quantities. These controls allow users to explore a continuum between localized visualization of detected vortices and the contextual flow around them [28].

10.2.5 Diffusion MRI Visualization

In addition to visualizing bat flight and coronary artery grafts, we also developed techniques to visualize diffusion MRI data in IVR, primarily gathered from brain tissues. Diffusion tensor MRI, often abbreviated DTI, is an imaging modality that measures fiber-tract trajectories in fibrous soft tissues such as nerves and muscles. The datasets produced are volumetric, with six interrelated values at each spatial location, and hence are a significant challenge to visualize and understand.

We developed stream tube and stream surface geometric models [48] that relate to the interesting structures in the tissue while representing the DTI data with a

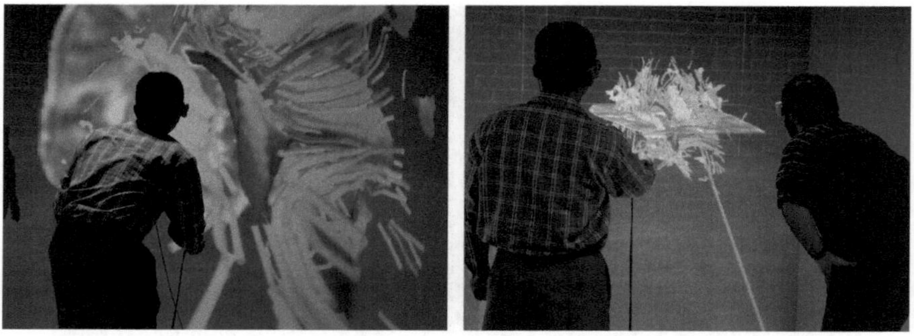

Fig. 10.6 Users interacting with the brain dataset in the Brown University Cave (*See Color Plates*)

focus on studying white-matter structures to understand changes due to a number of pathologies and for pre-operative planning for tumor surgery. In the VE, geometric models representing the white matter structures and planes showing sections of anatomical scan data generally are kept stationary above a virtual table. The user walks around and adjusts his head position to observe the data from different perspectives (see Fig. 10.6). We generated a yellow line akin to a laser pointer from a 3D mouse in the direction the mouse is pointing. The line stops where it hits an object. The user can use this virtual laser pointer to indicate a region of interest to others, which is particularly useful in the case because different users see different views. The user can also change the position of the slice or cycle through axial, coronal, and sagittal sections with the buttons on the 3D mouse [49].

10.2.6 ADVISER

Collaborations with the geological sciences department at Brown has led to the development of the Advanced Visualization in Solar System Exploration and Research system (ADVISER), that lets researchers go "into the field" using our surround screen VE (see Fig. 10.7). Places like Mars and Antarctica are mimicked in ADVISER using satellite data and other computed data like climate models. ADVISER's implementation is a set of tools that provides planetary geoscientists with the capability to operate and analyze data as if they were on or near the surface of a planet. These tools let these scientists go virtually into the field, perform traverse planning for rover missions, take measurements, and conduct global climate model simulations [15].

Users navigate across planetary surfaces using a 3D mouse to point in a particular direction, moving along that vector at a speed proportional to how hard they push on an analog joystick mounted on the device. In addition, they can also bring a Tablet PC into an ADVISER session. The tablet provides them with a 2D view of a planetary surface where they can sketch out paths they want to explore.

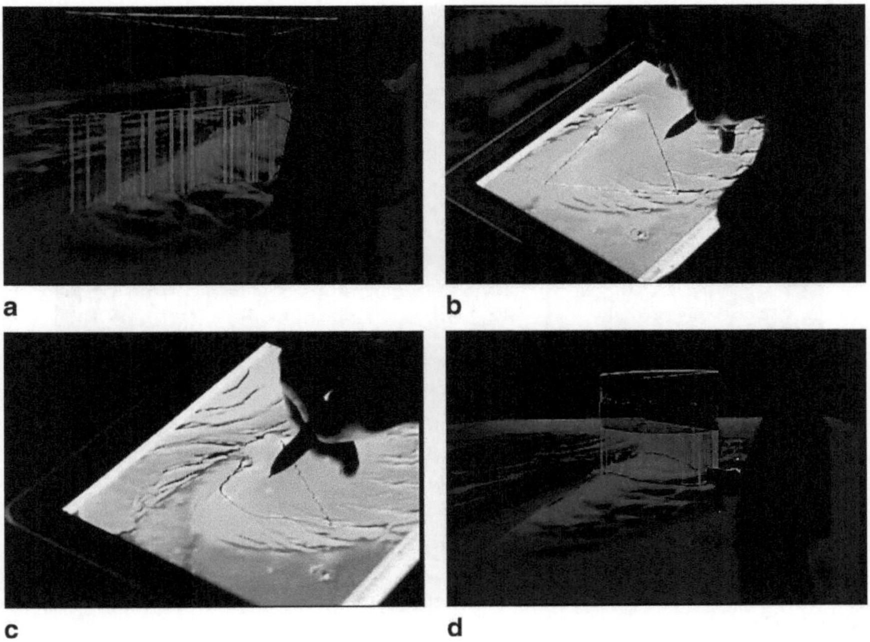

Fig. 10.7 A traverse planning operation in ADVISER. **a** Initial traversal is visualized in the IVR by a line that snaps to the terrain and vertical bars that connect it to a graph of slope (opaque bars indicate slopes too steep for rovers traversal, transparent bars indicate safe slopes), **b** The TabletPC's view of the initial traverse. **c** The user sketches out a new traverse and **d** the system updates the traverse and slope visualization (*See Color Plates*)

10.2.7 VOlume eXplorer

Laser scanning confocal microscopy has revolutionized biological science research during the past 10–15 years by providing biologists with the ability to collect high resolution images while eliminating out-of-focus information which is associated with image degradation. Despite the dramatic technological improvements that confocal microscopy and the development of new synthetic fluorescent molecules have brought to the biological sciences, the reconstruction and analysis of a series of optical sections still poses a profound challenge to most researchers. As part of a collaboration with developmental biologists, we designed and implemented Cave VOX, (VOlume eXplorer) a system for studying digitized volumes of multi-channel data from confocal microscopy (see Fig. 10.8).

VOX's user interface uses a set of rectangular widgets on the left wall of our Cave. These widgets are permanently displayed at fixed positions. We chose to display them in the plane of the screen so they are always projected at the same position, independent from where the head-tracked user is looking. Due to the unavoidable

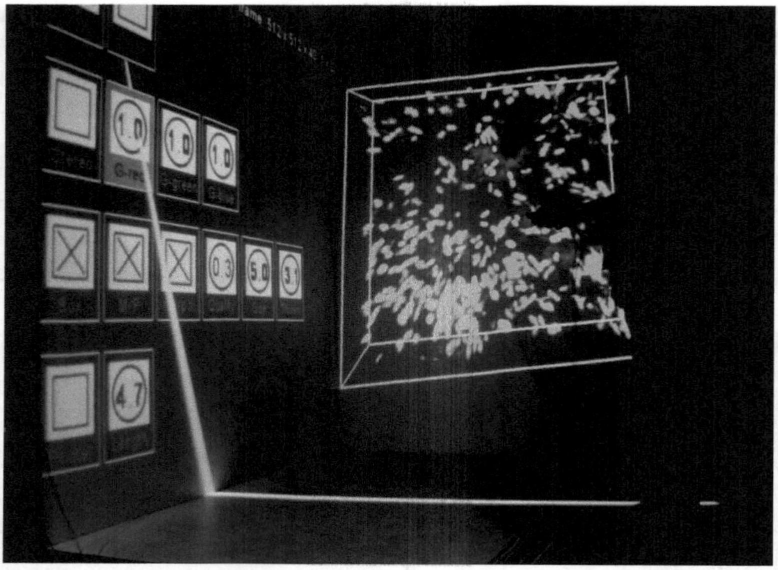

Fig. 10.8 A scientist can adjust visualization settings to tune the 3D visualization on the front wall of the Cave

tracking lag, this gives them a much more stable feel than free-floating widgets, and even for non-tracked users, they are always in the same place and therefore easily accessible [33].

10.3 Analysis of IVR-Based Interactive Visualization

We aim to be toolsmiths [4], adopting the problems that scientists in other disciplines have and using them to drive our research to create effective visualization and interaction tools. To measure progress we gathered data from anecdotal and formal evaluations. Results from several of our studies are reported below. More thorough discussions of our evaluations can be found in the papers cited in this section.

10.3.1 Anecdotal Findings

Below we report anecdotal feedback on several systems described above. This feedback is from domain scientists and we believe indicative of relevant properties of the systems, but due to its informal nature none of the results should be considered statistically significant in the sense of traditional formal evaluative experiments.

10.3.1.1 ARCHAVE

Over the course of several years four different versions of ARCHAVE were used by archaeologists to analyze data collected at the great temple site in Petra, Jordan. The prototyping and development process is described in [40]. The evaluation process is further described in [1]. Relevant results from those works are summarized here.

The evaluation process helped confirm the value of an immersive spatial visualization of the excavation record and also suggested a number of directions for improvement. One experiment involved two researchers who were interested in studying lamp and coin finds. We found that users performed three categories of tasks: queries of site information to generate and explore hypotheses, site exploration and pattern finding, and visual confirmation of hypotheses generated on-site.

Feedback suggested that their use of the system changed their mental model of the site as compared to participating in the excavation and searching the excavation data via a desktop database interface. They were also able to identify patterns in the finds that had not been identified during the excavation or found using the earlier online tools. They were enthusiastic about having IVR available, especially if it were extended from the prototype stage to cover more types of artifacts.

10.3.1.2 Diffusion MRI Visualization

We performed two experiments motivated by our brain visualization research. The results summarized here are also reported in [11]. The first experiment was an anecdotal comparison of Fishtank VR with our Cave. Overall, participants reported several advantages for the Cave, including its size, the larger field of view, the ability to interact more expressively with gestures, and the ability to walk around. They also noted several advantages of Fishtank VR, including sharper, crisper imagery, a more compact display, less noticeable claustrophobia, and a better ability to support collaboration. Four of the five participants subjectively preferred Fishtank VR.

Our second experiment evaluated the accuracy and speed of participants in performing a visual search task. In addition to comparing Fishtank VR and the Cave, it included in the comparison a reduced-resolution fish tank configuration that better matched the resolution of the Cave. Our findings were that users were more accurate and faster using the Fishtank VR configurations than using the Cave.

While both of these experiments seem to favor Fishtank VR, we believe that this is not only application-specific, task-specific, and also unduly influenced by the visual attributes of the configurations. With a significantly brighter and higher resolution Cave configuration that came much closer to matching those two key attributes of the Fishtank VR system, many of the differences would likely disappear. The particular visual search task that we used was a spatially localized one. With tasks that benefit from more contextual information, such as architectural walk-throughs, the surround-screen configurations are very suitable. Some of the other scientific applications that we report on share the need for spatial context that the Cave configuration can provide.

10.3.1.3 VOlume eXplorer

Over a period of three years, the VOX system was used extensively by the research community at Brown and our collaborators at peer institutions. We have collaborated closest with Brown Professor Kristi Wharton who researches developmental biology. A stereo-capable desktop version of VOX has been setup in her lab and now almost every dataset acquired is viewed with it to verify the scan is high enough resolution and quality to give a clear answer to the experimental question of interest, as well as for the analysis itself. Biologists walk the 10 min to the Cave building to view virtually all spatially complex datasets with "CaveVOX." Professor Wharton reports it is extremely useful to explore datasets in more detail and her group uses the Cave to draw conclusions from the data. To help make the immersive 3D data analysis experience more readily available to a greater number of biologists we will in early 2008 deploy with University support a head-tracked, stereo display (specifically, a stereo-capable Samsung 50″ DLP HD TV) in the University's biology imaging department. This scaled down version of the "Cave experience" will run the same VOX software on the Samsung display and sit side-by-side with conventional desktop analysis tools, easily accessible to dozens of research groups gathering 3D volume data, and is a direct result of the impact CaveVOX has made on researchers studying volume datasets. In this section we highlight specific instances where VOX was used for scientific investigations.

Our collaborators utilize VOX's advanced rendering capabilities to effectively visualize large datasets from laser scanning confocal microscopy. Visualization in IVR additionally helps them in fully appreciating the complexity (spatial and multi-channel) of the datasets. Over the past three years, our scientific collaborators have examined hundreds of datasets in the Cave. On several occasions, important observations have been made which had gone un-noticed on the desktop platform. Some instances of such observations have been accurate estimation of number of co-localizations in specimens. Co-localization is a phenomenon wherein multiple dyes fluoresce in the same voxel (the same voxel contains red and green expression, hence resulting in a yellow colored voxel). Conventional 2D image-based techniques tend to flatten the stack of images; hence even if there are disparate red and green pixels, but then happen to be along the same line-of-sight, one observes a yellow pixel. A 3D interactive visualization easily and efficiently eliminates this false count.

Similarly, discovery of experimental acquisition problems was facilitated by IVR. Problems with intensity falloff (as the laser signal optically penetrates a thick sample) are not apparent in comparison of subsequent 2D images, but a 3D stereoscopic visualization greatly assists in perceiving the falloff. In one instance, a problem was discovered with the way in which experimental samples were being placed on the slides – the slides were flattening the samples; hence the aspect ratios of various organs were inaccurate. Again, this flattening was not obvious from a 2D representation, it was only when the data was viewed in a 3D environment that the problem became obvious and the experimental setup was corrected.

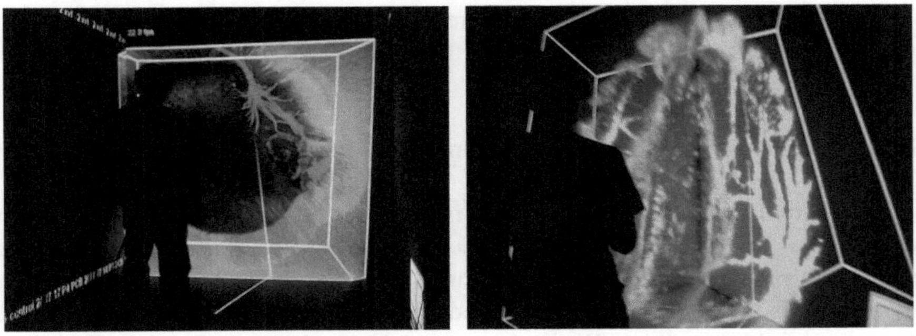

Fig. 10.9 Biologists examine neuronal branching structures in two different zebrafish embryo datasets. The task is to count the number of primary, secondary and tertiary neuronal branches for a population of zebrafish embryos

A series of detailed quantitative analyses were performed in the Cave on zebrafish embryo datasets. We now discuss two such analyses which were impossible to do on a 2D desktop system but were made possible because of IVR. Bilateral symmetry in zebrafish is broken during early embryonic development. Key players in this process are cells with tiny hair-like structures, called cilia, which line the inside of a fluid-filled vesicle. The cilia are motile and generate a counter-clockwise flow of fluid in the vesicle. In turn, this counter-clockwise flow of fluid is important for left-sided development of the heart and left-sided gene expression in the developing brain. Visualizing the vesicle structure in a Cave allowed the researchers to "step inside" a magnified vesicle and study the structures within. In their words, "We were puzzled how a sphere could generate a directional flow. The data sets in the Cave revealed a local patch of cilia and suddenly the generation of a counter-clockwise flow of fluid started to make sense." Researchers then proceeded to make quantitative measurements on the distribution of cilia. This task was nearly impossible to do on a conventional desktop system; the Cave version helped the researchers to quickly process over 50 datasets. The result was an important discovery of an asymmetry in the cilia distribution which explained the asymmetric fluid flow [19].

Another set of investigations with zebrafish embryos was directed towards quantifying the branching structures of neurons (see Fig. 10.9). In order to propose a reasonable model it was important to make the measurements on a large population. Again, the Cave was used to process over 50 datasets effectively in a short period of time. Researchers said they used the Cave system because doing the same analysis of branching structures at the desktop was very hard. The results of the investigation are currently being processed [20].

10.3.1.4 ADVISER

ADVISER is impacting geoscience at Brown University. Over 20 geoscience publications have used it in data analysis. While no formal evaluations have been published on the system yet, we report here a general and specific application of the system with feedback from geoscientists. For further reading, please see [15, 18].

General Application: Going Virtually into the Field

A fundamental capability of ADVISER is allowing the free exploration of a 3D environment. Professor Jim Head has decades of geoscience research experience and reports moving through a 3D environment makes it easier to understand an environment's intricacies than simply studying a 2D map. In this way, ADVISER has been used to explore 3D environments for both research and education. Researchers have explored Mars with ADVISER to:

- stand inside craters and consider illumination and solar insulation leading to formation and preservation of ice deposits,
- assess polar layered deposits caused by the planet's recent climate change,
- plan and review candidate rover traverses for a proposed NASA mission to Mars's North Polar cap, and
- analyze a simulation of the Martian atmosphere.

Geoscientists doing field work in Antarctica's Dry Valley region (which has geological characteristics similar to some areas of Mars) previewed geographic, geological, and safety aspects of their trip using ADVISER. After the field trip, ADVISER was used to review at once data collected over multiple trips to the Antarctic Dry Valley and helped resolve problems that emerged in the field.

Instructors have used ADVISER to teach introductory-level courses as well as graduate seminars. In "Geological Sciences 5: Earth, Moon, and Mars" over 100 students per year study Mars, choose an area of it to pursue a specific scientific question, and then use ADVISER to visit Mars and work to answer their question. All students report the ADVISER assignment gives them new insights into the geology and topography of Mars and a greater appreciation for its spatial relationships. One student commented about ADVISER, "It's like going to a foreign country rather than reading about it in a book!"

Specific Application: Strike and Dip

The North Pole of Mars has layered terrain composed of water ice and dust. The individual thickness and brightness of layers are clues to the planet's recent climate record. Furthermore, layer spacing and 3D relationship to other layers are important for understanding their emplacement and evolution. ADVISER can overlay high resolution Mars Orbiter Camera data (which reveals alternating dust and ice layers) over Mars Orbiter Laser Altimeter topographic data in order to calculate each layer's thickness and geometry. A recent hypothesis states ice and dust layers encode a distinctive climate signal related to orbital parameter variations – similar to periodic changes in obliquity and eccentricity that cause ice ages on Earth. Strike and Dip measurements performed in ADVISER with a "virtual field toolkit" describe subsurface layer orientation and structure. The geologist uses tools to identify multiple exposed points along a particular layer and compute best-fit planes from the points. A standard calculation produces the strike-and-dip measurements and can reveal whether the layers are flat or distorted beneath the surface. The value of IVR for strike and dip calculations lies in the significantly higher confidence geoscientists have when identifying a series of points belonging to the same layer. With conventional monoscopic displays of satellite data (a popular approach to visualizing and then labeling layers) there are frequent ambiguities due to interactions between the reflectance of surface material and shading from topographic features. These situations can be easily resolved using ADVISER to drape high-resolution satellite imagery over high-resolution topological data and interactively view the area quickly from several vantage points.

10.3.2 Formal Evaluations

In this section we report results from formal studies designed to measure some aspect of the systems and carefully control for other variables. Subjects were recruited and paid to participate in the studies. Standard statistical methods were applied when analyzing the collected data. The experiments we summarize in this section have all been published elsewhere and their details can be found in citations below.

10.3.2.1 VOlume eXplorer

Following our positive anecdotal experience with developmental biologists in their use of VOX in the Cave and the positive scientific return, we wanted to see if the Cave statistically differed from other technologies and conducted a formal evaluation which would mimic the relatively free-form scientific exploration of datasets by these scientists. This is in contrast to most participant studies which focus on interaction techniques, presence and usability. In such studies, participants are typically asked to perform relatively simple "benchmark" tasks. In this study, we focused on free-form exploration of scientific data without emphasis on speed/accuracy performance tradeoff. We use an open-ended "think aloud" protocol which encourages participants to explore and talk about their exploration without any constraints.

Twelve users, all familiar with confocal datasets; participated in the study. All users explored the Desktop, Fishtank VR and Cave environments in random orders; and underwent a brief training phase on each platform. Once users indicated that they were comfortable with the interaction; they proceeded onto the testing phase. During the testing phase participants explored confocal datasets; talked about their observations and responded to questions about each dataset. After the testing phase, users were asked to choose a single platform (out of the three) and examine two

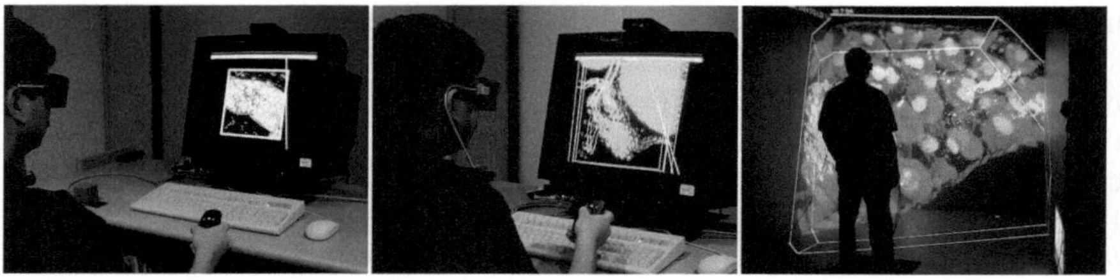

Fig. 10.10 Experimental setup for the exploring scientific datasets. Scientists examine a range of datasets on a conventional desktop (left), Fishtank (middle), and Cave (right) environment. (Note: different datasets are shown on each display in these images.)

more datasets. Following this, users filled out a post-questionnaire which noted their quantitative responses on a Lickert scale. A debriefing at the end helped us collate their subjective responses.

The selected tasks involved looking at real confocal datasets from the egg-chamber, brain, and gut regions of a fruit-fly (see Fig. 10.10). An expert biologist assisted us in preparing the datasets and a list of exhaustive features that were present in the data. A table with questions related to features and a weight associated with each question was also determined in advance by the expert. The questions and tasks were inspired by real-life analogues; the tasks emphasized understanding spatial relationships including characterizing the general features in a volume, identifying co-located features, and reporting geometric relationships in the datasets. Performance of participants was assessed based on a review of the videotape of each session. Participants were awarded points based on their observations in accordance with the table prepared by the expert.

Prabhat et al. [29] presents detailed results from the study; we only highlight the major results in this section. All significance results presented in this chapter were conducted with ANOVA at 5% level of significance. Briefly, we found that users performed significantly better in platforms with higher levels of immersion (Cave > Fishtank VR > Desktop, $p < 0.0001$). All twelve participants chose the Cave (over the Fishtank VR or Desktop) when presented with a choice to continue exploration on new datasets. In the post-questionnaire, participants generally rated the Cave higher than Fishtank VR and Desktop for a range of metrics (learning about datasets, answering specific questions about datasets, confidence in finding features, etc.). While the Cave was rated slightly higher than the Fishtank VR configuration, it should be noted that the Desktop was very poorly rated across all metrics. When asked to list major advantages and disadvantages of the various platforms, participants subjectively rated the Cave highly for its large display area, wide field of view and its immersive capabilities. They subjectively liked the clarity and crispness of the Fishtank VR display, but complained of the small size and FOV. All users disliked the desktop and complained of the lack of stereo. Everyone acknowledged the inferior brightness of our current Cave (as compared to Fishtank VR and Desktop), and yet they preferred the Cave for its immersive capabilities.

Fig. 10.11 Experimental setup for performing specific scientific tasks. Users examine a neuron dataset on a desktop (left), Fishtank (middle), and Cave (right)

Building on the results from the study reported in earlier section, we decided to restrict the range of tasks and come up with focused tasks. We did not want to lose the relevance to domain science analysis conducted by scientists; hence we chose three tasks motivated by real problems that neuroscientists need to tackle. An expert neuroscientist prepared datasets for this study. We chose to examine neuronal datasets; the tasks were to:

- count the number of spines along a dendrite
- count the number of contact points between multiple axons and dendrites
- count the number of pyramidal neurons (see Fig. 10.11).

An identical protocol (as reported in the last experiment) was used. Twelve subjects, this time with varying background in neurosciences, were recruited for the tasks. Users went through a training phase where they were exposed to a sample neuron dataset; they then performed the three tasks on unique datasets. All platforms were presented in random order. After the testing phase; subjects were asked to move to a neutral location and choose a platform for performing the three tasks on new datasets. Subjects then chose a platform, conducted the tasks and finished up the experiment with responses to a post-questionnaire followed by debriefing.

Sanchez et al. [32] reports on the detailed results from the study. In brief, we found similar trends to the results for the developmental biology study. Users rated the Cave higher than Fishtank VR, and Fishtank VR higher than the Desktop system. There were a few differences in the choice phase though. For spatially complex tasks (such as finding contact points between axons and dendrites) most subjects chose the Cave over Fishtank VR and the Desktop. For counting the number of spines, the same held true (most subjects preferred the Cave). But for counting the number of pyramidal neurons, subject responses were mixed. There was no clear preference between either the Cave or Fishtank VR.

10.3.2.2 ADVISER

The ADVISER system (described in the previous section) was applied in an educational outreach setting. We incorporated the system into an undergraduate laboratory exercise and evaluated the usefulness of the system. In the exercise,

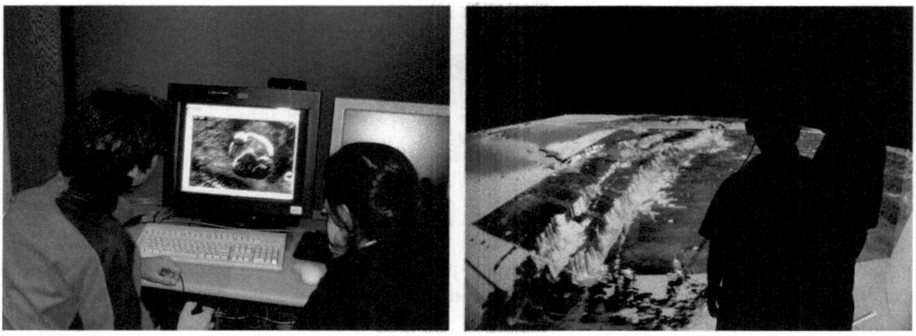

Fig. 10.12 Student using the ADVISER system to explore the surface of Mars

undergraduate students gather information and insights while exploring the Martian surface in a computer-rendered immersive virtual reality system (see Fig. 10.12). Students choose an area on Mars for virtual exploration, formulated geological questions, and pursue their investigation using a real-time 3D terrain exploration tool. Ninety students completed a follow-up survey and reported that using a conventional desktop and our Cave contributed significantly to the learning experience, and that they would choose the immersive environments over standard 2D maps in the future exercises.

In general we observed that students highly prefer a Cave-like system to a conventional desktop display for learning about topography datasets (ANOVA $F = 11.594$, $p < 0.0001$). This preference is indicated by their ratings and choice of Cave as the preferred medium for future exploration. Both Cave and desktop media are preferred, however, to a standard 2D image based investigation ($F = 29.91$, $p < 0.0001$). Students' subjective responses are positive about the insights gained from the Lab exercise; we consequently believe that 3D visualization is a valuable tool in teaching students about topographical and geological datasets.

10.4 Summary

In this chapter, we have presented a variety of different IVR-based interactive visualizations systems developed at Brown University. These systems provide support for scientists in archaeology, computational fluid dynamics (CFD), biology, and the geosciences. By working directly with these scientists, we have been able to show, both anecdotally and formally, that IVR-based visualization systems have important benefits that enable scientists to do their jobs better. The systems we have developed in the Cave have provided insights, in some cases, that would not have otherwise been discovered or would have taken a significantly longer time.

We are observing that IVR is making a positive impact on visualizing scientific data with complex 3D spatial relationships and also provides significant benefit to some tasks where magnifying the projection of the data helps find features faster or otherwise not seen. Body-centric interaction appears to be another important component of IVR's benefit. However, understanding when and why IVR applies generally remains an area of active research, and there is no clear-cut formula for when IVR is the right tool. It is generally necessary to try visualizing your data in IVR, and potentially tailor an interactive visualization to your particular needs.

The reader should bear in mind that our old Cave system was built in 1998 and is much dimmer than a conventional desktop display; the spatial resolution is also much lower (10 dpi, whereas we estimate 25–30 dpi would make it comparable to a typical 72 dpi desktop monitor because the Cave wall surfaces are viewed at a greater distance than a desktop screen). Still, the Cave outperformed Fishtank VR and conventional monitors in many situations. We think the greatest advantage will come from a brighter display that reveals a comparable dynamic range of visual data, and that, as the spatial complexity of data increases, higher resolution would result in greater benefit. Modern projectors already provide very high brightness display, and tiling them is a standard approach now for achieving higher resolutions.

Biologists and geoscientists at Brown, as a result of our initial collaborations, are installing head-tracked, stereo-capable displays in their buildings. While single walls are not fully immersive environments, these conveniently located systems coupled with other research tools are a significant step towards production use of immersive virtual reality for these scientific domains. We intend to continue partnering with scientists at Brown and elsewhere who are struggling to understand their data both in the early stages, like many of the projects reported here, and later with systems deployed in their laboratories where their daily work takes place.

Appendix: IVR Hardware Configurations

One of the key characteristics of IVR is that special hardware is needed beyond the traditional desktop computer (i.e., monitor, keyboard, and mouse) to support the high level of immersion and more fluid interaction that benefits IVR-based interactive visualization. There are a variety of different input and output hardware configurations that can be employed in these applications, and, in this appendix, we will briefly discuss ones we have worked with over the years. A thorough discussion on IVR input and output devices can be found in [3].

A.1 Display Configurations

In many cases with interactive visualization virtual environments (VEs), we want to present users with a head-tracked stereoscopic display so they can see visualizations in immersive 3D with appropriate motion parallax. A tracking system is required to create motion parallax when users move in the VE, and these devices are discussed in the next section. For the stereoscopic display, there are several different types that can be used.

A.1.1 Monitors

Conventional monitors coupled with a pair of stereo glasses makes for a simple yet effective visual display for interactive visualization applications. When a user is head tracked this configuration is commonly referred to as "Fishtank VR" [43]. These configurations are relatively inexpensive compared to other visual display devices, such as workbenches and surround screen devices, and provide excellent spatial resolution. However, monitors are not very immersive and the user has a very limited range of movement due to its small field of regard (FOR), the amount of physical space surrounding the user in which visual images are displayed.

A.1.2 Surround-Screen Displays

A surround-screen display is a visual output device that has three or more large (anywhere between 8 to 12 feet in width and height) projection-based display screens that surround the human participant (often referred to as a CAVE™ [10]). They provide high spatial resolution, a large FOR and a large field of view (FOV), the maximum number of degrees of visual angle that can be seen instantaneously on a display. This high FOV lets users leverage their peripheral vision. As with a monitor, surround screen devices provide stereopsis with stereo glasses. Additionally, real and virtual objects can be mixed in the environment.

One of the biggest disadvantages of surround screen display devices, as well as any projection-based display system, is that user can have difficulties seeing objects in stereo under certain conditions. When the user gets close to the display or when objects appear to be right in front of the user, it becomes more and more difficult for a user to fuse the two images together. Eye strain is a common problem in these situations. Another issue is the physical/virtual object occlusion problem. The problem arises when the user tries to move a physical object behind virtual objects. Although a user can physically move an input device behind a graphical object, visually, the device will appear in front of the graphical object, since it is actually being projected on the screen. This is a common problem with any projection-based display device (or Fishtank VR configuration) and can hinder the immersive experience and break the 3D illusion produced by stereo.

A.1.3 High-Resolution Display Walls

High-resolution display walls (e.g., tiled display surfaces) are becoming increasingly popular for interactive visualization applications. Display walls can be constructed by combining several LCD screens or projectors. These displays offer greater image fidelity than other immersive and desktop displays because the increased number of pixels displayed over a large area can fill most of a user's FOV. For example, Princeton University developed the Scalable Display Wall (18 feet long and 8 feet high) with a resolution of 6,000 by 3,000 pixels using 24 projectors [41]. Other examples can be found in [27]. High-resolution display walls have many of the same benefits and problems associated with surround screen displays in terms stereo image fusion, FOV, and the physical/virtual object occlusion problem. Since high-resolution display walls do not surround the user with visual imagery, they have a much smaller FOR compared to a surround screen device.

A.1.4 Workbenches

Another type of projection-based display is the Responsive Workbench™, originally developed by [21]. In general, workbenches make for an intuitive display for certain types of applications. Relative to surround screen displays, workbench screen sizes are smaller, which improves visual quality. In many device designs, the display can be rotated so the screen's orientation relative to the user is anywhere from completely horizontal to almost vertical, making the device quite flexible.

In general, users have limited mobility when interacting with a workbench because the display is not head coupled like a head-mounted display (see below) and does not surround them in a room-sized display. Therefore, as with monitors, the range of viewpoints from which a user can see 3D imagery is restricted since, for some viewpoints, all or part of the screen would not be visible. For example, it would not be possible for a user to see the bottom of a stationary, graphical object by physically looking underneath it, since the display surface would no longer be in the user's FOV thus breaking the 3D illusion.

A.1.5 Head Mounted Displays

Thus far we have focused on stationary displays (i.e., visual devices that do not move with the user). Here, we will discuss visual displays where the user is attached (i.e., head-coupled) to the display device. Head-coupled display devices used for IVR-based interactive visualization is the head mounted display (HMD). A head mounted display's main goal is to place images directly in front of the user's eyes using one (for monoscopic viewing) or two (for stereoscopic viewing) small screens. Since, the screens may or may not be placed directly in front of the user's eyes, a combination of refractive lenses and/or mirrors (depending on the optical technique used) are used to present and sometimes magnify the images shown to the user.

One of the biggest advantages of HMDs is that the user can have complete physical visual immersion (i.e., a 100% FOR) since the user always sees the virtual world regardless of head position and orientation. Even though HMDs have a 100%

FOR, many of them have small FOVs (i.e, between 30 and 50 degrees in horizontal or vertical) which can cause performance problems. Even high-end HMDs have limited FOVs when compared to surround screen displays. Since the real world is completely blocked out of the user's view, interaction while wearing an HMD usually requires some type of graphical representation of either one or both hands or the input device used. These graphical representations can be as simple as a cube or as sophisticated as a hand model containing thousands of polygons. HMDs also put a strain on the types of input devices that can be used since the user cannot physically see the device in order to use it. HMDs are more claustrophobic than the other types of displays because they do eliminate all real world cues, and unless trackers are wireless, also have entangling cords that add to the cumbersomeness, weight and discomfort of HMDs for prolonged work sessions.

A.2 Input Device Configurations

In IVR-based interactive visualization systems, users can use stereoscopic displays to see and interact with their data spatially in 3D. Thus, VEs afford a much greater variety of interaction capabilities than a traditional desktop computing environment. There are many different types of input devices that can be used in an IVR-based interactive visualization application, and, in this section, we briefly discuss the most common devices.

A.2.1 Motion Trackers

Motion tracking devices are one of the most common and fundamental interaction devices used in VEs. Since they can track different parts of a user's body, they provide a critical piece of functionality in terms of head, hand, and device tracking. Head tracking is important for motion parallax and providing the correct stereoscopic viewpoint as users move around the VE, while hand and device tracking is important for users to interact with data spatially in six dimensions (three translation and three rotation degrees of freedom).

There are a variety of different tracking systems and technologies used in VEs today and they all have advantages and disadvantages [45]. For example, *magnetic trackers* have good range, and are generally accurate to within 0.1 inches in position and 0.1 degrees in orientation, but any ferromagnetic or conductive objects present in the room with the transmitter will distort the magnetic field, thus reducing the accuracy. *Acoustic trackers* are relatively inexpensive and lightweight, but often have a short range, low sampling rates (compared with optical and inertial trackers which can have sampling rates above 1 KHz), and their accuracy suffers if acoustically reflective surfaces are present in the room.

Inertial trackers use a variety of inertial measurement devices such as angular rate gyroscopes and linear accelerometers. These devices can produce measurements at high sampling rates but suffer error accumulation from sensor biases, noise, and drift. *Optical trackers* use computer vision techniques and optical sensors such as cameras and infrared emitters. They often suffer from the occlusion problem because they sometimes cannot pick up information about parts of the user's body that are occluded by other parts. Finally, *hybrid tracking* attempts to put more than one tracking technology together to help increase accuracy, reduce latency, and, in general, provide a better virtual environment experience. For example, combining inertial and acoustic tracking or inertial and optical tracking technologies have been successful in providing robust tracking solutions. The major difficulty with hybrid trackers is that the more components added to the system, the more complex the device becomes.

A.2.2 3D Mice

In many cases, tracking devices are combined with other physical widgets such as buttons, sliders, knobs, and dials to create more functionally powerful input devices. These *3D mice* are hand held or worn input devices which combine motion tracking with a set of physical interface widgets placed in various configurations.

The distinguishing characteristic of 3D mice opposed to regular 2D mice is that a user physically moves them in 3D space to obtain position and/or orientation information instead of just moving the device along a flat surface. Therefore, users can hold the device or, in some cases, wear them. Additionally, with orientation information present, it is trivial to determine where the device is pointing (i.e., the device's direction vector) which is used in many fundamental 3D interaction techniques for working with visualization data where it is useful to be able to point at specific locations in three-space. These devices can also be considered 6D mice in many cases because they often provide both 3D orientation and 3D position information. Because of their general applicability, they can be mapped to many different interaction techniques, and, in one form or another, they are often the primary means of communicating user intention in 3D interfaces. A variety of these devices have been developed over the years including the "bat" [42], Ascension Technology Corporation's Wanda, and the FingerSleeve [47].

A.2.3 Other Input Devices

A variety of other input devices can be utilized in IVR-based interactive visualization applications. For example, data gloves that sense a user's finger motion can be used to grab virtual objects and manipulate data. Joysticks and gamepads such as the Xbox 360 or Nintendo Wii controllers can be used in these environments as well.

Finally, pen-based tablets such as Tablet PCs and PDAs can be used in IVR-based visualization applications. These types of devices are becoming increasingly popular in both desktop 3D and in VE applications because they give the user the ability to interact with a "pen and paper" interface and bring 2D interaction techniques such as handwriting and menu-based techniques into 3D immersive environments [13, 15].

References

1. Acevedo, D., E. Vote, D. H. Laidlaw, and M. Joukowsky (2001) Archaeological Data Visualization in VR: Analysis of Lamp Finds at the Great Temple of Petra, a Case Study. In *Proceedings IEEE Visualization 2001,*IEEE Press, 493–496.
2. Bowman, D. (1999) Interactive Techniques for Common Tasks in Immersive Virtual Environments: Design, Evaluation and Application. PhD Thesis. Georgia Institute of Technology.
3. Bowman, D., E. Kruijff, J. LaViola, and I. Poupyrev (2004) *3D User Interfaces: Theory and Practice*, Addison Wesley.
4. Brooks, F. P., Jr. (1996) The Computer Scientist as Toolsmith II. *Communications of the ACM*, 39(3):61–68.
5. Brooks, F. P., Jr. (1999) What's Real About Virtual Reality? *IEEE Computer Graphics and Applications*, 19(6):16–27.
6. Bryson, S. (1996) Virtual Reality in Scientific Visualization. *Communications of the ACM*, 39(5):62–71.
7. Bryson, S., and C. Levit (1991) The Virtual Windtunnel: An Environment for the Exploration of Three-Dimensional Unsteady Flows. *IEEE Visualization 1991*, IEEE Press 17–24.
8. Burns, E., S. Razzaque, A. T. Panter, M. C. Whitton, M. R. McCallus, and F. P. Brooks (2006) The Hand is Slower than the Eye: A Quantitative Exploration of Visual Dominance Over Proprioception. *Presence: Teleoperators and Virtual Environments*, 15(1):1–15.
9. Chung, J, M. Harris, F. Brooks, Jr., H. Fuchs et-al. (1989) Exploring Virtual Worlds with Head-Mounted Displays. In *SPIE Proceedings Vol 1083 Non-Holographic True 3- Dimensional Display Technologies*.
10. Cruz-Niera, C., D. Sandin, and T. Defanti (1993) Surround Screen Projection-Based Virtual Reality. In *Proceedings of SIGGRAPH'93*, ACM Press, 135–142.
11. Demiralp, C., C. Jackson, D. Karelitz, S. Zhang, and D. H. Laidlaw (2006) CAVE and Fishtank Virtual-Reality Displays: A Qualitative and Quantitative Comparison. *IEEE Transactions on Visualization and Computer Graphics*, 12(3):323–330.
12. Feiner, S., and C. Beshers (1990) Worlds within Worlds: Metaphors for Exploring N-Dimensional Virtual Worlds. In *Proceedings of UIST '90 (ACM Symposium on User Interface Software and Technology)*, 76–83.
13. Forsberg, A., J. J. LaViola Jr., and R. C. Zeleznik (1998) ErgoDesk: A Framework for Two and Three Dimensional Interaction at the ActiveDesk. In *Proceedings of the Second International Immersive Projection Technology Workshop*, Ames, Iowa.
14. Forsberg, A., M. Kirby, D. H. Laidlaw, G. Karniadakis, A. van Dam, and J. L. Elion (2000) Immersive Virtual Reality for Visualizing Flow Through an Artery. In *Proceedings of IEEE Visualization 2000*, IEEE Press, 457–460.
15. Forsberg, A., Prabhat, G. Haley, A. Bragdon, J. Levy, C. I. Fassett, D. Shean, J. W. Head III, S. Milkovich, and M. Duchaineau (2006) Adviser: Immersive Field Work for Planetary Geoscientists. *IEEE Computer Graphics and Applications*, 26(4):46–54.
16. Fuchs, H. (1998) Beyond the Desktop Metaphor: Toward More Effective Display, Interaction, and Tele-collaboration in the Office of the Future via a Multitude of Sensors and Displays.

In *1st International Conference on Advanced Multimedia Content Processing* (AMCP), Osaka, Japan.

17. Grant, B., A. Helser, and R. M. Taylor II (1998) Adding Force Display to a Stereoscopic Head-Tracked Projection Display. In *Proceedings of the Virtual Reality Annual international Symposium*, 81–88.
18. Head, J. W., A. van Dam, S. G. Fulcomer, A. Forsberg, Prabhat, G. Rosser, and S. Milkovich (2005) ADVISER: Immersive Scientific Visualization Applied to Mars Research and Exploration. *Photogrammetric Engineering & Remote Sensing*, 71(10):1219–1225.
19. Kreiling, J., Prabhat, and R. Creton (2007a) Analysis of the Kupffer's Vesicle in Zebrafish Embryos using a Cave Automated Virtual Environment, Developmental Dynamics, 2007 July; 236(7):1963–1969.
20. Kreiling, J., A. Crawford, and R. Creton (2007b) Quantitative Analysis of Neuronal Branching Patterns in Zebrafish Embryos, Paper is still in preparation.
21. Kruger, W., and B. Froelich (1994) The Responsive Workbench. *IEEE Computer Graphics and Applications*, 14(3):12–14.
22. LaViola, J. (2000) MSVT: A Virtual Reality-Based Multimodal Scientific Visualization Tool. In *Proceedings of the Third IASTED International Conference on Computer Graphics and Imaging*, 1–7.
23. LaViola, J., R. Zeleznik, D. Acevedo, and D. Keefe (2001) Hands-Free Multi-Scale Navigation in Virtual Environments. In *Proceedings of the 2001 Symposium on Interactive 3D Graphics*, 9–15.
24. Macedonia, M. R, D. P. Brutzman, M. J. Zyda, D. R. Pratt, P. T. Barham, J. Falby, J. Locke (1995) NPSNET: A Multi-Player 3D Virtual Environment over the Internet. In *Proceedings of the 1995 Symposium on Interactive 3D Graphics*, ACM Press, 93-94.
25. Martin, J. C. (1998) TYCOON: Theoretical Framework and Software Tools for Multimodal Interfaces. *Intelligence and Multimodality in Multimedia Interfaces*, (Ed.) J. Lee, AAAI Press.
26. Meehan, M., S. Razzaque, B. Insko, M. Whitton, F. Brooks (2005) Review of Four Studies on the Use of Physiological Reaction as a Measure of Presence in Stressful Virtual Environments. *Applied Psychophysiology and Biofeedback*, 30(3):239–258.
27. Ni, T., G. Schmidt, O. Staadt, M. Livingston, R. Ball, and R. May (2006) A Survey of Large High-Resolution Display Technologies, Techniques, and Applications. *IEEE Virtual Reality 2006*, IEEE Press, 223–234.
28. Pivkin, I., E. Hueso, R. Weinstein, D. H. Laidlaw, S. Swartz, and G. Karniadakis (2005) Simulation and Visualization of Air Flow Around Bat Wings During Flight. In *Proceedings of International Conference on Computational Science*, 689–694.
29. Prabhat, A. Forsberg, M. Katzourin, K. Wharton, and M. Slater (2008) Evaluation of Desktop, Fishtank and Cave Environments for Exploring Confocal Microscopy Datasets. To Appear in *IEEE Transactions on Visualization and Computer Graphics*.
30. Rosenberg, L. B. (1993) Virtual Fixtures: Perceptual Tools for Telerobotic Manipulation. In *Proceedings of the IEEE Annual International Symposium on Virtual Reality*, IEEE Press, 76–82.
31. Sanchez, M. V., and M. Slater (2005) From Presence to Consciousness Through Virtual Reality. *Nature Reviews Neuroscience* 6(4):332–339.
32. Sanchez, M. V., M. Slater, A. Forsberg, and Prabhat (2008) Using Virtual Reality for Neuronal Visualization, Paper is still in preparation.
33. Schulze, J. P., and A. S. Forsberg (2005a) A Comparison of a Cave and a Fish Tank VR System for Counting Biological Features in a Volume, Technical Report CS-05–02, Brown University, Department of Computer Science.
34. Schulze, J. P., A. S. Forsberg, and M. Slater (2005) Analysis of Subject Behavior in a Virtual Reality User Study. In M. Slater (Ed.), *Presence 2005: The 8th Annual International Workshop on Presence*, 255– 260.
35. Slater, M. (1999) Measuring Presence: A Response to the Witmer and Singer Questionnaire. *Presence: Teleoperators and Virtual Environments*, 8(5):560–566.

36. Slater, M., M. Usoh, and A. Steed (1994) Depth of Presence in Virtual Environments. *Presence*, 3:130–144.
37. Sobel, J., A. Forsberg, D. H. Laidlaw, R. Zeleznik, D. Keefe, I. Pivkin, G. Karniadakis, P. Richardson, and S. Swartz (2004) Particle Flurries: Synoptic 3D Pulsatile Flow Visualization. *IEEE Computer Graphics and Applications*, 24(2):76–85.
38. Sutherland, I (1968). A Head-Mounted Three Dimensional Display. In *Fall Joint Computer Conference, AFIPS Conference Proceedings*, 757–764.
39. Taylor II, R. M., W. Robinett, V. L. Chi, F. P. Brooks, Jr., W. V. Wright, R. S. Williams, and E. J. Snyder (1993) The Nanomanipulator: A Virtual-Reality Interface for a Scanning Tunneling Microscope. *Computer Graphics (Proceedings of SIGGRAPH 93)*, ACM Press, 127–134.
40. Vote, E., D. Acevedo, D. H. Laidlaw, and M. Joukowsky (2002) Discovering Petra: Archaeological Analysis in VR. *IEEE Computer Graphics and Applications*, 22(5):38–50.
41. Wallace, F., O. J. Anshus, P. Bi, H. Chen, Y. Chen, D. Clark, P. Cook, A. Finkelstein, T. Funkhouser, A. Gupta, M. Hibbs, K. L. Zhiyan Liu, R. Samanta, R. Sukthankar, and O. Troyanskaya (2005) Tools and Applications for Large-Scale Display Walls. *IEEE Computer Graphics and Applications*, 25(4):24–33.
42. Ware, C., and D. R. Jessome (1988) Using the Bat: A Six-Dimensional Mouse for Object Placement. In *Proceedings of Graphics Inteface'88*, 119– 124.
43. Ware, C., K. Arthur, and K. S. Booth (1993) Fishtank Virtual Reality. In *Proceedings of INTERCHI'93*, 37–42.
44. Wartell, Z., W. Ribarsky, and L. Hodges (1999) Third-Person Navigation of Whole-Planet Terrain in a Head-Tracked Stereoscopic Environment. In *Proceedings of the IEEE Virtual Reality*, IEEE Press, 141–148.
45. Welch, G., and E. Foxlin (2002) Motion Tracking: No Silver Bullet, but a Respectable Arsenal. *IEEE Computer Graphics and Applications, Special Issue on "Tracking"*, 22(6):24–38.
46. Zeleznik, R. C., K. P. Herndon, and J. F. Hughes (1996) SKETCH: An Interface for Sketching 3D scenes. In *Proceedings of SIGGRAPH'96*, ACM Press, 163–170.
47. Zeleznik, R. C., J. LaViola, D. Acevedo, and D. Keefe (2002) Pop-Through Buttons for Virtual Environment Navigation and Interaction. In *Proceedings of Virtual Reality 2002*, IEEE Press, 127–134.
48. Zhang, S., C. Demiralp, D. Keefe, M. DaSilva, B. D. Greenberg, P. J. Basser, C. Pierpaoli, E. A. Chiocca, T. S. Deisboeck, and D. H. Laidlaw (2001) An Immersive Virtual Environment for DT-MRI Volume Visualization Applications: A Case Study. In *Proceedings of IEEE Visualization*, IEEE Press, 437–440.
49. Zhang, S, C. Demiralp, and D. H. Laidlaw (2003) Visualizing Diffusion Tensor MR Images Using Streamtubes and Streamsurfaces. *IEEE Transactions on Visualization and Computer Graphics*, 9(4):454–462.

Chapter 11
Interactive Molecular Visualization at the Interface

Francis T. Marchese

Abstract: Physical and computer models of molecules are designed to embody chemical knowledge of the molecular world. Over the past forty years interactive molecular visualization software has transformed the way chemical scientists build and use molecular models. This chapter surveys interactive molecular visualization from the point of view of the molecular model, showing the convergence of its visual, haptic, and tangible instantiations, and their use to represent chemical structure and dynamics.

Keywords: Molecular visualization, Molecular model, Haptic interface, Steered molecular dynamics, Tangible display

11.1 Introduction

This chapter discusses interactive molecular visualization (IMV). The first interactive molecular visualization system (IMVS) was built in early 1965 by Cyrus Levinthal at MIT's project MAC. Levinthal's program allowed a user to orient a line drawing of a three-dimensional molecular model with a plastic "globe" (the predecessor to the torque ball) that could be twisted or pushed in any desired direction to change the speed and orientation of a rotating molecular model [35]. By placing a light pen on the computer display, it was possible to select from a menu, choose an object, or zoom into important parts of the molecule. In the forty-plus years since this system appeared, chemical scientists have written interactive molecular visualization software employing mobile [16], immersive [9, 11, 26, 37, 38, 41], and collaborative technologies [6, 24, 39, 40, 55], capitalizing on nearly every innovation in computing that has appeared since that time.

Today's innovations in interactive molecular visualization are taking place at the interface – the interface between the scientist and the molecular model, and the interface between the software and data. In the former case, the haptic perceptual channel is used to make a stronger bond between chemist and molecular model; in the latter, a better interface between interactive visualization software and molecular data is created.

E. Zudilova-Seinstra et al. (eds.) *Trends in Interactive Visualization*,
doi:10.1007/978-1-84800-269-2_11

We begin here with a discussion of the molecular model, the focal point of chemical representation, and hence, the core of any visualization system. In Sect. 11.3 mainstream IMVSs are categorized and discussed. Section 11.4 covers how haptics are used in IMVSs. Finally, Sect. 11.5 returns to the physical model as an interface to IMVSs. Those interested in mobile, immersive, and collaborative molecular visualization should explore the references cited above. For a wealth of general information about molecular visualization with links to software, models, systems, tutorials, etc. see Eric Martz's website *World Index of Molecular Visualization Resources* or visit MolviZ.Org.

11.2 Molecular Models and Modeling

Material [8, 12] and computer molecular models [13] are scientific instruments that have a well-documented history as integral components of the chemical research and education process. They transcend representational medium (e.g., paper sketch, three-dimensional computer rendering, material model) [23], and are derivable from, validated and verified through experiment and theory. Material molecular models such as those assembled from the ubiquitous wooden ball-and-stick and space-filling model kits have been used for over 125 years to represent, reason about, and communicate the underlying physical laws that govern chemical structure and process. Indeed, the awarding of Nobel Prizes in chemistry to Linus Pauling for his work on the structure of the chemical bond [42], and Watson and Crick for the double helix structure of DNA [60], was recognition of the power of material molecular model building.

Today, computer models and simulations have for the most part replaced material models as the essential tools in the refinement and analysis of experimental data, and as a means for building plausible molecular structures that are predictive aids in the design of new experiments. By expressing the chemical rules and theories that guided material model builders within molecular modeling software, chemists have been able to investigate the structure, properties, and dynamics of extremely complex molecular systems that may include millions [15, 49, 59] or billions of atoms [28, 46].

There are two general approaches to molecular modeling. The first is the application of quantum theory, which reduces the problem of molecular structure and property determination to solving the Schrödinger equation. Quantum mechanical theories are rigorous, computationally intensive, first principles methods that are employed when an understanding of the origins of electronic structure, spectra, and reactivity is required [20]. The second approach, called molecular mechanics [22, 32], applies Newtonian mechanics and classical electrostatics to describe the physical basis behind molecular models in which atoms are defined as point charges with associated masses. Potential functions compute the molecular potential energy as a sum of energy terms that describes the deviation of bond lengths, bond angles, and torsion angles away from equilibrium values, augmented by terms for non-bonded pairs of atoms describing van der Waals and electrostatic interactions. Molecular mechanics methods may be applied to the computation of static stable molecular structures that represent local energy minima on the hypersurface defined by atomic distances, angles, and torsion angles, or to the computation of the dynamical behavior of a molecular system. The former method allows for comparison of the structural states of similar systems, while the latter techniques, known as molecular dynamics simulations, founded on Newton's laws of motion, provide information about the dynamical processes that underlie the evolution of molecular structure over time (e.g., the folding of an amino acid chain into a protein's native structure).

The molecular modeling process itself is defined by the complexity of the problem to be solved and the availability of computer resources required to solve the problem. Historically, the most interesting chemical systems have been either too large or too complex to model in real time, typically taking days, weeks, or months to model. As a result, IMVSs have been used as part of the data generation and analysis process, either for creating input files for modeling and simulation programs, or as viewers of intermediate or final results. Now, many molecular mechanics and simulation programs run efficiently on parallel computers, and can scale well to hundreds-of-thousands of processors, making it possible to solve structure optimization problems and perform dynamic simulations at interactive rates. These innovations in computation have permitted the creation of computational steering environments in which IMVSs are front-ends to molecular mechanics and dynamics programs. In computational steering, a scientist has interactive control over a computational process during its execution. In so doing, the scientist can respond to results as they occur by interactively manipulating parameters to visually explore a what-if analysis, or immediately observe cause-effect relationships among variables.

11.3 Mainstream IMVSs

Mainstream IMVSs are WIMP-based (Windows, Icons, Menus, and Pointing) and are used for *viewing*, *building/editing*, and *searching/steering*. Molecular viewers are programs that read molecular structure and property files created by experiment and theory, displaying them as three-dimensional models. These viewer programs enable the user to render molecular structures in different graphical styles (e.g., ball-and-stick and space filling spheres). One can interactively rotate, pan, and zoom; compute bond distances, angles, and dihedral angles; adjust rendering parameters, such as the number, color, and position of light sources, background color, and the material properties of graphical objects (e.g., metal, plastic). More extensive capabilities include: stereographic display; superposition of multiple graphical representations; calculation and display of molecular properties such as charges, electrostatic interactions, atomic volumes, and molecular orbitals; and the simultaneous display and alignment of multiple molecules.

A variety of freely available molecular *viewers* has been developed, including VMD [25], Jmol [21], KineMage [47], SwissPDBViewer/DeepView [19], PyMol [10], Chimera [43], and PMV [50], to name but a few. Each of these systems exhibits a basic set of viewing attributes, and supports high quality molecular rendering. In addition, they may be characterized as being OS agnostic, open source, and open architecture systems, designed for extensibility. For example, VMD has been adapted for virtual environments, speech/gesture input [52], and is the IMV front-end for a molecular dynamics program called NAMD [44]. Jmol is written in Java. It works as either an applet or application, allowing the embedding of IMVs within web pages. Kinemage (Kinetic Image) reads an ASCII input file that contains source data, annotated display lists for visualization scenarios, and accompanying descriptive comments that can be shared, edited, appended to, and evolve over time. PMV (Python Molecular Viewer) is dynamically extensible, allowing new commands to be developed independently, placed in libraries, and imported as needed.

An example of a molecular *viewer* is shown in Fig. 11.1. Here VMD displays the structure of DNA bound to the Cro repressor protein. Each molecule has been selected and drawn in a different style. The DNA double helix is represented by a solvent accessible surface (SAS), which defines at each position on DNA's surface the closest point of contact made by a water molecule. The color of this surface has been selected to enhance DNA's phosphate backbone (green) and the major and

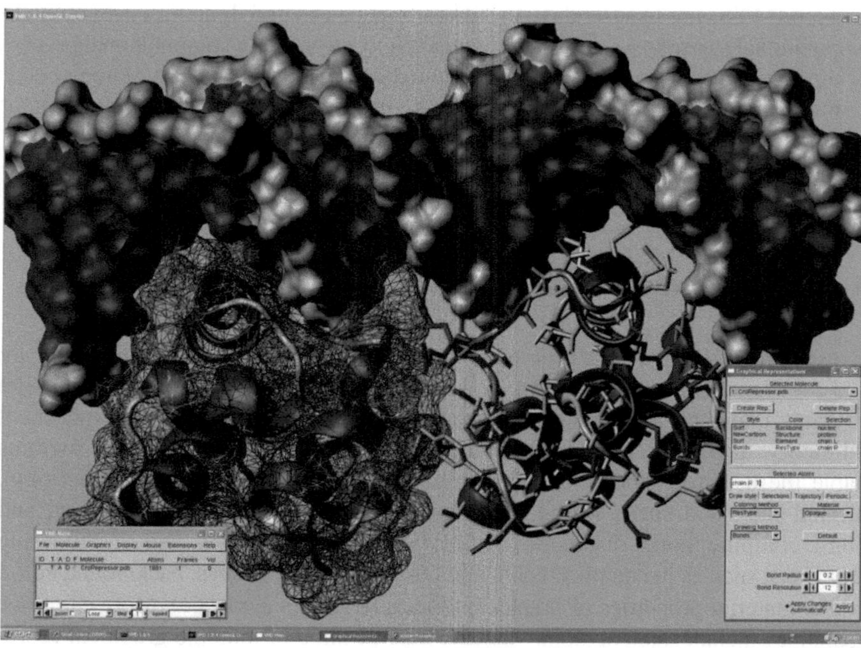

Fig. 11.1 A snapshot of the VMD molecular viewer with its main menu displayed on the lower left hand corner and rendering style on the lower right [25]. The molecular complex shown is the Cro protein bound to the DNA double helix

minor grooves (blue). The two parts of the Cro protein are displayed with molecular representations superimposed. Stick figures present the bonding network, while solid ribbons illustrate the general three-dimensional path the protein's amino acid chain traces through space. Ribbon color has been selected to indicate the kinds of structure the peptide backbone can assume (e.g., helix, sheet, coil, turn). In addition, the left hand protein's SAS is displayed in wireframe to show how the protein fits into DNA's major groove while still revealing its internal structure.

Molecular *builders/editors* include all the capabilities of molecular viewers. Additionally, they provide resources for interactively constructing molecules from scratch or for editing pre-existing structures. Typically, users select from a menu of atom, functional group, or larger collection of molecular fragments (e.g., amino or nucleic acids), and interactively connect them. Geometric parameters such as bond distances, angles, and dihedral angles may be set by the user or assigned by the software utilizing built-in standard atomic geometric parameters. The molecular models constructed by *builders/editors* are approximations to optimal molecular representations because they only use the best chemical guesses at structure. As a result, *builders/editors* save these models as files for subsequent input to a wide variety of molecular modeling programs that either optimize molecular structure (that is, find the most energetically favorable structure by varying a select set or all geometric parameters) or simulate its dynamics.

Unlike *viewers,* most interactive molecular *builders/editors* are part of commercial products distributed by companies such as Wavefunction, Gaussian, Accelrys, Openeye, Chemaxon, MDL, and CambridgeSoft. There are a number of non-commercial programs that include ECCE [5] and ArgusLab [57]. ECCE is designed to support structure building, job submission, and data analysis of large-scale quantum mechanical calculations on computer clusters and supercomputers. ArgusLab builds molecules for submission to mainstream quantum and molecular mechanics code, as well as providing its own computations. In the latter case data generation and analysis are tightly coupled.

IMVSs used for *searching/steering* are real-time interfaces to molecular mechanics and simulation programs that allow a scientist to intervene in the execution of a running simulation. By using the capabilities of molecular viewers and editors it is possible for a scientist to change interatomic distances and angles on-the-fly. The goal of these systems is to capitalize on the scientist's knowledge to facilitate the *search* for the best structural and energetic solutions for a molecular system, or to visually explore new or existing dynamical pathways by *steering* a simulation's direction.

An example of the use of an IMVS as part of the *search* process is in the area of molecular docking in which the general problem to be solved is how to determine the best interaction between two molecules [56]. This is an important problem in the design of drugs, because the better the drug interacts with a biological molecule (e.g., protein), the more effective it is. For example, a drug's (ligand's) shape often determines its activity, because it possesses a structure that can fit, or dock, into a complementary part of a protein (receptor) in such a way as to maximize its cohesion or binding, and hence its efficacy.

Molecular docking is a numerical optimization problem in which the goal is to find the lowest energy of a molecular system by minimizing the intermolecular interaction energy between the two molecules. Docking systems are implemented by employing three different strategies. First, a ligand may be positioned manually. The molecular system is then modeled using molecular mechanics with interatomic distances and angles adjusted to find the minimum energy structure. Second, the ligand is positioned in an approximate location, and molecular dynamics is used to optimize the ligand-receptor relationship. In both strategies, available experimental data is used to help select a site on the receptor at which the ligand is expected to bind. Third, in situations where little is known about the geometry of the ligand-receptor interaction, molecular modeling is used to select and evaluate potential molecular complexes. Here, the automated determination of docking sites can significantly retard the docking process because of the sheer number of possible ligand-receptor combinations that must be searched and evaluated. This search space may be reduced through a scientist's visual inspection, selection, and evaluation of likely binding sites, thus accelerating the process. And once ligand orientations have been generated by the automated docking algorithm, IMV can facilitate the identification of the correct ligand binding structure.

A typical docking scenario is as follows. First, the ligand-receptor molecules are displayed in an appropriate graphical representation (e.g., SAS). These molecules are rotated to study their shape and charge patterns. Second, concave regions on the receptor molecule are identified that are likely to be binding sites. Third, the ligand is hand docked to each of the identified receptor regions based on shape and charge complementarity. After each hand docking, the ligand-receptor structure is optimized. Finally, the energetically best ligand orientations are compared.

The second use of an IMVS as a front-end to simulations is in the *steering* of molecular dynamics calculations [27]. Here, the scientist applies external forces to a single atom or groups of atoms by grabbing and tugging them toward a target position. These applied forces reduce energy barriers, thereby increasing the probability of occurrence of unlikely molecular dynamic events. In so doing, it is possible to force a protein to unfold in order to study its trajectories, coerce the binding and dissociation of substrates during enzyme reactions, and increase recognition of ligands by their receptors.

There are three stages to steering. First, the scientist develops a hypothesis for the mechanism of the chemical process to be simulated based on his or her *a priori* understanding. This leads to a specification of external forces to apply to the system. Second, the simulation is conducted with the weakest force possible to complete the process within an affordable amount of computer time (e.g., days or weeks). Third, analysis of the simulation relates the applied force to the progress of the system along the chosen reaction path.

Steering a dynamics simulation amounts to adding restraints or forces to the computation. Typically this can be done in an IMVS by grabbing an atom with a pointing device, and attaching to it a vector which points in the direction of the restraint. An image of such an operation using VMD as the IMVS is shown in Fig. 11.2. Here, a spherical ion is to be steered through a cylindrical channel

Fig. 11.2 Visualization of restraint attachment (solid arrow) and guidance (cone) using VMD. A potassium ion (sphere) is guided through the helical channel embedded within a cell wall (zigzag molecular structures). Water molecules occupy both ends of the channel [54]. © 2001 ACM, Inc. Included here by permission

(helix). A vector restraint is attached to the sphere and guided by a conical probe that is attached to a pointing device (e.g., mouse). The size of the vector corresponds to the magnitude of the force. Large forces effect a rapid change in the system, and are used in real-time where a trajectory is explored. By directly connecting this restraint to a pointing device, interactive steering is performed. Small forces are used for incremental steering of long-running batch simulations. These simulations are checked intermittently to visualize the simulation's progress and to make incremental adjustments to the restraints.

Searching/steering systems can run in either monitor or interaction mode. In monitor mode, the scientist may track the system as it evolves over time, using tools available in the IMVSs. For example, the system may be rotated, translated, or zoomed; and each molecule's graphical style may be changed. In interaction mode, the scientist can intervene in a docking optimization by moving or twisting the ligand - the docking algorithm then resumes in the new configuration; in steered molecular dynamics, forces are adjusted and the simulation continues.

Searching/steering systems have been enormously successful at solving complex biomolecular problems [53]. A number of programs exist, including: Stalk [34], VRDD [1], and DockingShop [36] for docking; SMD [33], IMD [54], and MolDRIVE [29] for steering. Besides possessing a different simulation backend, each uses a different graphical interface. For example, Stalk, VRDD, SMD, IMD, and MolDRIVE work in immersive environments, while DockingShop does not. DockingShop supports a rich widget-based user interface, the others do not. At a

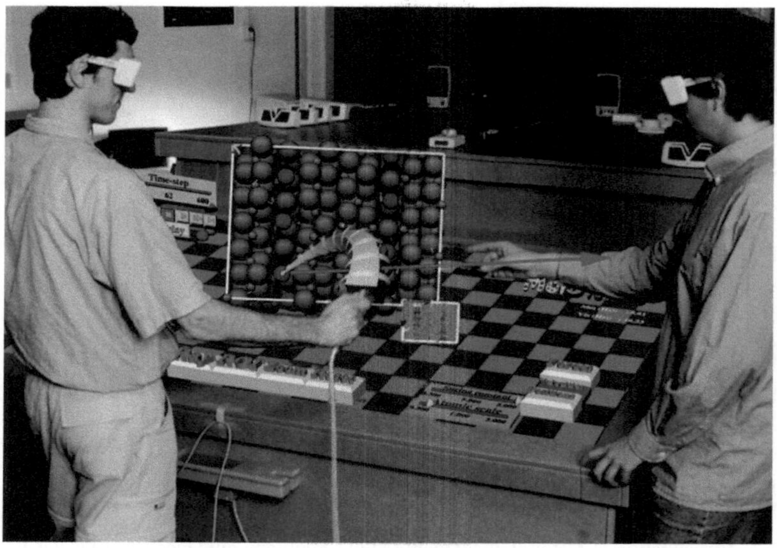

Fig. 11.3 MolDRIVE system running on a Responsive Workbench. A virtual spring manipulator (bent cone-shaped polyhedron) is employed to produce visual feedback of user-applied forces to atoms in a real-time simulation [29]. Reprinted with permission of M. Koutek (*See Color Plates*)

minimum, each system displays molecular structure and a text message containing the energy value of the current state of the system. Beyond this, VRDD produces both visual and auditory feedback of forces. Color is used to show how tight a fit exists between ligand and receptor. If the ligand is steered to an orientation that clashes with the receptor, the user is alerted with a metal-hitting sound. These additional cues provide a simple way of amplifying and communicating essential structural and energetic information resident in these simulations. Finally, MolDRIVE provides real-time visual force feedback by displaying a deformable spring stylus whose shape communicates a sense of the magnitude of force applied to a particle by a user. Figure 11.3 shows a composite image of MolDRIVE running on a Responsive Workbench [30], an immersive stereographic table, in which two scientists are performing real-time steering of atomic dynamics within the β-alumina crystal. The scientist on the left holds a six degree-of-freedom tracker upon which the virtual spring manipulator (bent cone-shaped polyhedron) is superimposed. The arrow at the manipulator's tip displays the magnitude and direction of the force to an atom that has been computed from the spring's stretching and bending deformations.

What is interesting about these systems from an information communication perspective is their limited sensory feedback. Their heavy reliance on molecular representation implies the scientist must shoulder the majority of the cognitive load for visualization. However, since most systems of this kind are built by chemical scientists, who are trained to use molecular models, there is a greater reliance on a scientist's cognitive skills. The challenges confronting scientists is that the visual channel may be perceptually incomplete, and its further augmentation should impart a greater richness of information.

11.4 Touch

Direct manipulation is an important concept in user interface design. Within a direct manipulation interface [14] a user manipulates computer-generated objects by using physical actions that correspond to real-world activities. In response, the software rapidly updates representations providing interactive feedback. All IMVSs possess direct manipulation interfaces. By dragging a mouse across the image of a molecule, a chemist makes the molecule rotate, translate, or scale in real-time. This translation of a user's real-world hand motion into a molecular object's action engenders a strong connection between real and virtual worlds, supporting a telepresence transcending two spatial domains. This is particularly true in systems that support stereographic rendering in which the molecule appears to leap out of the computer screen into the chemist's space.

Direct manipulation may be taken one step further by providing haptic control of molecular objects. By using haptic computer technology it is possible to communicate additional information about a molecule's physicality [45]. Computer haptics is a field analogous to computer graphics concerned with the algorithms needed to generate and display the touch and feel of virtual objects to a human [51]. A haptic display [48] is composed of three parts: a force-feedback device that generates computer-controlled forces to convey to the user a sense of the natural feel of virtual objects; a physical model of the object that the user is attempting to perceive; and a haptic renderer that computes the forces required to comprehend the model. A haptic renderer detects collisions between a probe and a virtual object to create a response. As a user manipulates a probe over a molecular model's surface, collisions are detected and translated by the modeling or simulation software into reaction forces. The strength of these forces depends upon the depth of the probe's penetration into the molecule's surface. These forces are then returned to the user through the haptic device.

The first haptic display system used for molecular visualization was GROPE-III, developed by Fred Brooks and coworkers [7]. GROPE-III combined a six degree-of-freedom plus grip Argonne Remote Manipulator (ARM), normally used for sample manipulation within a sealed laboratory glove box, with a workstation and large screen display. It ran a program called Docker that allowed a chemist to interactively dock a drug molecule within a protein's active site (Fig. 11.4). It computed the forces and torques between the drug and protein molecules arising from electrostatic charges and interatomic collisions, and displayed them visually and through haptic feedback so the chemist could feel their strength. Experiments showed that chemists could position the drug molecule in the protein's active site in such as way as to create the most energetically stable drug-protein complex up to twice as quickly with haptic feedback augmentation as opposed to using only

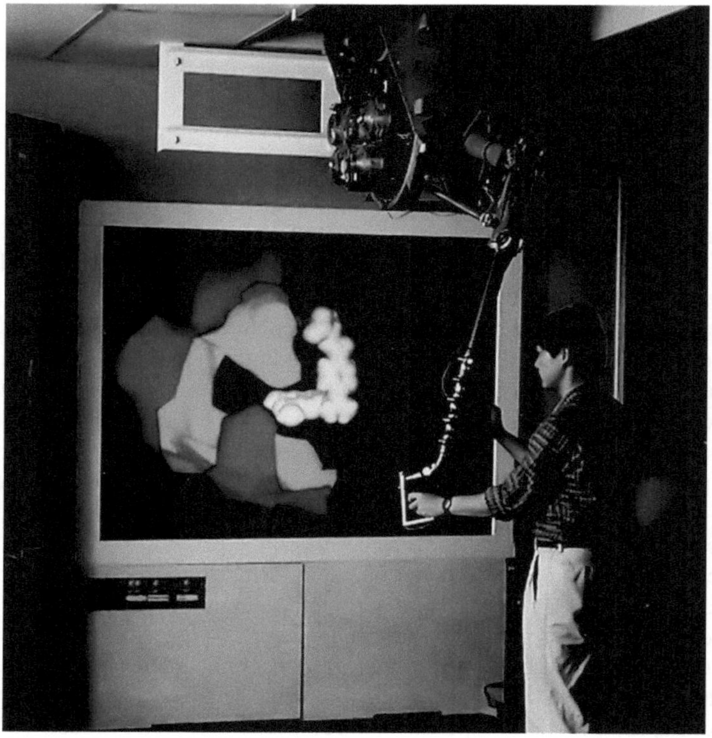

Fig. 11.4 The GROPE-III force feedback system is used to guide a ligand into a protein's active site [7]. © 1990 ACM, Inc. Included here by permission

visual representations. Scientists also had a better sense of how the drug fit into the receptor site when they were able to feel the intermolecular forces.

The availability of relatively inexpensive and more compact haptic feedback tools, such as Sensable's PHANToM, has made it possible to build or adapt IMVSs to include haptic interactions. The prototypical system is IMD (interactive molecular dynamics) created by combining the molecular viewer VMD with the NAMD molecular dynamics code [25]. When combined with force-feedback hardware, VMD supports real-time feedback and steering of NAMDs molecular dynamics simulations. IMD consists of three modules: a haptic device controlled by a server which generates forces, a molecular dynamics simulation for determining the effects of applied forces, and the VMD display system [54].

IMD was first demonstrated on a dual processor graphics workstation. The system studied was a gramicidin A channel composed of 4,385 atoms. Gramicidin A channels are found in cell walls, allowing the transport of ions and water through the cell wall in and out of the cell (c.f. Fig. 11.2). In their analysis of the IMD simulations, these researchers found a number of challenges must be overcome for true interactive molecular dynamics. First, because simulation, rendering, and haptic feedback necessarily occur at greatly differing time scales, synchronization of these processes creates significant latency. Second, molecular rendering is geometry intensive - hence time consuming. They solved the first problem by decoupling the system components so the system runs as three independent communicating threads. The second problem was solved by drawing more simplified molecular representations. The first application of IMD to a research problem was in the study of the selectivity and regulation of the membrane channel protein GlpF and the enzyme glycerol kinase [18]. In this research, NAMD was run on a 32 CPU cluster, a computational resource sufficient to allow IMD to execute at interactive rates.

A number of haptic enabled IMVSs have appeared since IMD. Bayazit, Song, and Amato [3] built a system for binding rigid ligands. A PHANToM device is used to move the ligand about the protein and investigate the potential energy field associated with its automated binding path generator. Lai-Yuen and Lee [31] have developed a custom haptic force-torque feedback tool and software system for docking flexible ligands that can be used to screen docking candidates and give the user a real-time sense of a ligand's flexibility. Bidmon and coworkers [4] built an interactive haptic visualization system for analysis of protein dynamics. By attaching the PHANToM stylus to an atom, the user's hand is dragged around in space following the motion of the selected atom over time when a protein trajectory is played back. This motion tracking allows the analysis of anisotropic protein dynamics. The user can directly feel motion in all three dimensions without perceptual issues as there would be for stereoscopic vision. Wollacott and Merz [62] built a system called HAMStER for docking small molecules that offers both visual and haptic feedback of intermolecular forces.

In all these projects the rate determining step in the IMV process is the computation of the physical model. As such, the effort in the development of *searching/steering* systems has focused on creating intermediate, computationally tractable representations that either involves a static, pre-computed database of energies or the segmentation of a complex molecular model so that the IMVS only registers the segment that is actively being visualized. The goal of these systems is to capture enough of the model's attributes to simultaneously maintain its realism and support interactive visualization. However, IMD's research success suggests that by decoupling *searching/steering* system components, it is possible to improve the system as a whole by improving each component individually.

11.5 Return of the Material Model

When compared with material models even haptically augmented stereographic rendering can convey only a limited sense of a molecule's physicality. Material models by their very nature are physical entities. They can be oriented and reoriented, measured, assembled, disassembled, and rearranged by hand. A scientist who guides his or her hands over the hills and valleys of a molecular surface model can feel its contours, hardness, and texture because the hand's tactile and kinesthetic sensory systems respond to the spatial (and possibly temporal) distribution of the model's physical forces. This haptic contact becomes the interface between a human's physical actions and the molecular world.

The power of a material molecular model as a visualization medium has been demonstrated by Bailey and coworkers [2] in their study of virus capsid structure. Virus capsids are highly symmetrical (icosahedral or helical) structures that envelope a virus's genetic material. They are built from highly irregular shaped proteins that fit together like pieces of a puzzle. In their study of the black beetle virus structure, neither computer graphics nor numerical analysis had been able to reveal how these three-dimensional parts interlocked. These researchers resorted to rapid prototyping technology in order to automatically fabricate three-dimensional material models of the proteins that comprise the capsid. Rapid prototyping utilizes three-dimensional printing technology to transform computer created models into material objects made from substances such as polymers, paper, or powdered gypsum (e.g., see Fig. 11.5a). Once the material models of the virus components had been manufactured it became immediately obvious to the scientist holding these components in his hand that they fit together in a peg-in-hole mechanism.

This contact between human and material model may be used to control an IMVS by employing the physical model as a tangible interface to a software system. Tangible interfaces are systems that use physical artifacts to represent and control digital information [58]. A core characteristic of a tangible interface is its seamless integration of representation and control, with a physical object being both the representation of information and physical control for directly manipulating its underlying associations. In the system built by Gillet and coworkers [17], an auto-fabricated molecular model (Fig. 11.5a) is used as part of an augmented reality system that combines the physical model with its virtual counterpart, giving the illusion of a real interaction. Computer-based spatial tracking and rendering methods

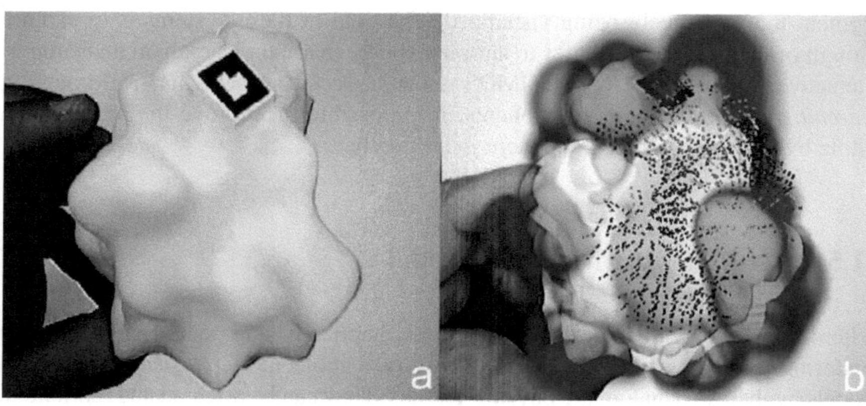

Fig. 11.5 Auto-fabricated molecular model of a protein with attached registration marker (**a**), and with superimposed computed properties (**b**) [17]. © 2004 IEEE. Included here by permission (*See Color Plates*)

are used to capture the position and orientation of the model and superimpose it with computed molecular properties. As the user manipulates the physical model, it is tracked by a video camera and displayed on a computer screen with a virtual representation (e.g., another 3D rendering of the same molecule, textual labels, or a 3D animation) superimposed over the video display, and spatially registered with the model (Fig. 11.5b). The result is a tight binding between physical and virtual molecular models, blending the best attributes of both.

Finally, physical molecular models need neither be static nor unintelligent. By embedding microcontrollers within physical molecular models it is possible to distribute molecular computation. For example, the Posey computationally-enhanced hub-and-strut construction kit employs a ball and socket connection that allows users to move parts of an assembled model [61]. Hubs and struts are opto-coupled in the ball and socket joints using infrared LEDs and phototransistors. As a user builds and configures a model, wireless transmitters in Posey's hubs send connection and geometry information to a host computer. It, in turn, assembles a representation of the physical model that can then be used by programs in any application domain.

One of the first applications of Posey is Molecule Explorer, a demonstration of Posey's use in chemical modeling in which its hubs and struts correspond to atoms and bonds, respectively. The number of sockets on a hub represents the atom's valence, which is the number of atoms that can bond to it. As the user snaps together Posey parts, the Molecule Explorer displays a picture of the molecule. The program has a small database of compounds that it searches as the user makes the Posey model. It uses this database to identify the molecule that the user has made so far, as well as suggests possible molecule completions. Figure 11.6 shows the $HOCH_2$- fragment of an ethanol molecule (CH_3CH_2OH). One four-socket hub represents a carbon

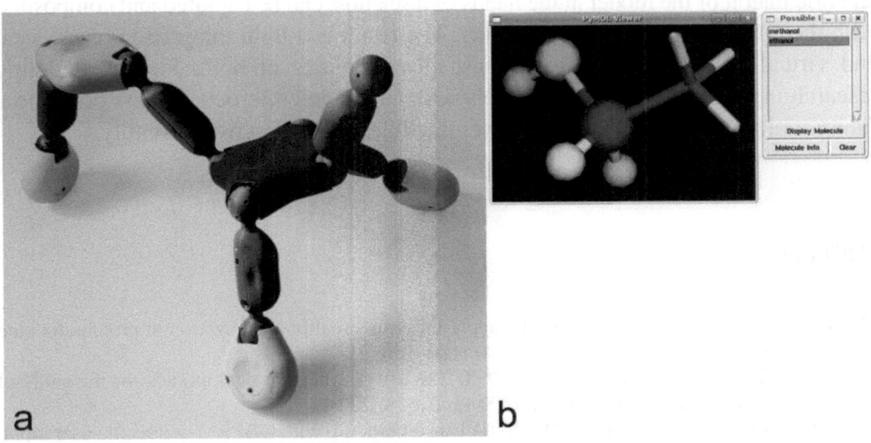

Fig. 11.6 Posey model of ethanol fragment (**a**) and computer image constructed in Molecular Explorer (**b**) [61]. Printed with permission of M. Gross (*See Color Plates*)

atom; one two-socket hub represents an oxygen atom; and three single-socket hubs represent hydrogen atoms. All struts connecting all hubs represent single bonds. The remaining unattached strut awaits the connection of the second carbon hub to complete the molecular backbone.

The power of Posey is its feedback in response to physical manipulations that are part of the model building process. Although work on systems like Posey is just beginning, computationally enhanced construction kits show promise for making physical molecular models less static, a better representation of molecular reality, and improving their integration into the IMV process. This research holds promise for the construction of future physical molecular models that are not just molecular avatars but realistically embody molecular reality.

11.6 Summary

In the mid-1960s Cyrus Levinthal built the first interactive molecular visualization system (IMVS). Until then, chemists had constructed and used physical models as the standard mode of molecular representation. In the forty years since his IMVS appeared, IVMSs have infiltrated all of chemical education and research, running on computer systems from PDAs to CAVEs, and replacing physical molecular models as the standard mode of representation. Today's mainstream IMVSs are employed routinely for building molecular models, and viewing complex molecular structure and dynamics. By augmenting graphics systems with touch, chemical scientists can not only feel molecular forces, but also push and pull on atoms to change the course of real-time simulations. Ironically, recent studies in IMV have come full circle - returning to the physical model as the center of interest. Researchers have utilized the molecular model as a tangible display and interface to an IMVS. The position and orientation of the model in the hands of a scientist can be captured and composited with the contents of an IMVS's display. The result is a tight integration of physical and virtual models exploiting the best characteristics of both. Finally, fledgling research in articulated physical models with embedded microcontrollers points to a future molecular model that is reactive, intelligent, and a mirror of reality.

References

1. Anderson A, Weng Z (1999) VRDD: applying virtual reality visualization to protein docking and design. J Mol Graph Model 17(3–4): 180–186, 217.
2. Bailey M, Schulten K, Johnson JE (1998) The use of solid physical models for the study of macromolecular assembly. Curr Opin Struc Biol 8: 202–208.
3. Bayazit OB, Song G, Amato NM (2001) Ligand binding with OBPRM and haptic user input. In: Proceedings of the 2001 IEEE international conference on robotics and automation (ICRA'01), pp. 954-959.

4. Bidmon K, Reina G, Bos F, Pleiss J, Ertl T (2007) Time-based haptic analysis of protein dynamics. In: Proceedings of the second joint eurohaptics conference and symposium on haptic interfaces for virtual environment and teleoperator systems. IEEE Computer Society, Washington, DC, pp. 537–542.
5. Black G, Daily J, Didier B, Elsethagen T, Feller D, Gracio D, Hackler M, Havre S, Jones D, Jurrus E, Keller T, Lansing C, Matsumoto S, Palmer B, Peterson M, Schuchardt K, Stephan E, Sun L, Swanson K, Taylor H, Thomas G, Vorpagel E, Windus T, Winters C (2006) ECCE, a problem solving environment for computational chemistry. Pacific Northwest National Laboratory, Richland, Washington, DC.
6. Bourne PE, Gribskov M, Johnson G, Moreland J, Weissig H (1998) A prototype molecular interactive collaborative environment (MICE). In: Altman R, Dunker K, Hunter L, Klein T (eds) Pac symp biocomput, pp. 118-129.
7. Brooks FP, Ouh-Young M, Batter JJ, Kilpatrick PJ (1990) Project GROPE: Haptic displays for scientific visualization. In: Proceedings of the 17th annual conference on computer graphics and interactive techniques, Dallas, TX. SIGGRAPH'90. ACM Press, New York, pp. 177–185.
8. de Chadarevian S (2004) Models and the making of molecular biology. In: de Chadarevian S, Hopwood N (eds) Models: the third dimension of science. Stanford University Press, California, pp. 339–368.
9. Chastine JW, Zhu Y, Brooks JC, Owen GS, Harrison RW, Weber IT (2005) A collaborative multi-view virtual environment for molecular visualization and modeling. In: Proceedings of the coordinated and multiple views in exploratory visualization (Cmv'05). IEEE Computer Society, Washington, DC, pp. 77–84.
10. DeLano WL (2002) The PyMOL molecular graphics system. DeLano Scientific, San Carlos, CA. http://www.pymol.org.
11. Drees RC, Pleiss J, Schmid RD, Roller D (1998) Integrating molecular modeling tools and virtual reality engines: an architecture for a highly immersive molecular modeling (HIMM) environment. In: Proceedings of the computer graphics international 1998. IEEE Computer Society, Washington, DC, pp. 391–392.
12. Francoeur E (1997) The forgotten tool: the design and use of molecular models. Soc Stud Sci 27: 7–40.
13. Francoeur E, Segal J (2004) From model kits to interactive computer graphics. In: de Chadarevian S, Hopwood N (eds) Models: the third dimension of science. Stanford University Press, California, pp. 409–429.
14. Frohlich DM (1993) The history and future of direct manipulation. Behav Inform Technol 12(6): 315–329.
15. Geshi M, Hoshi T, Fujiwara T (2003) Million-atom molecular dynamics simulation by order-N electronic structure theory and parallel computation. J Phys Soc Jpn 72(11): 2880–2885.
16. Gilder JR, Raymer M, Doom T (2001) PocketMol – a molecular visualization tool for the Pocket PC. In: 2nd IEEE international symposium on bioinformatics and bioengineering (BIBE'01). IEEE Press, pp. 11–14.
17. Gillet A, Sanner M, Stoffler D, Goodsell D, Olson A (2004) Augmented reality with tangible auto-fabricated models for molecular biology applications. In: 15th IEEE visualization 2004 (VIS'04), pp. 235–242.
18. Grayson P, Tajkhorshid E, Schulten K (2003) Mechanisms of selectivity in channels and enzymes studied with interactive molecular dynamics. Biophys J 85: 36–48.
19. Guex N, Peitsch MC (1997) SWISS-MODEL and the Swiss-PdbViewer: an environment for comparative protein modeling. Electrophoresis 18: 2714–2723.
20. Jensen F (2007) Introduction to computational chemistry, 2nd edn. John Wiley and Sons, Ltd., Chichester, England.
21. Herráez A (2006) Biomolecules in the computer: Jmol to the rescue. Biochem Mol Biol Edu 34(4): 255–261.
22. Hinchliffe A (2003) Molecular modelling for beginners. John Wiley and Sons, Ltd, Chichester, England.

23. Hoffmann R, Laszlo P (1991) Representation in chemistry. *Angew Chem Int Ed (Eng)* 30: 1–16.
24. Huang CC, Couch GS, Pettersen EF, Ferrin TE (1996) Chimera: an extensible molecular modeling application constructed using standard components. Pacific symposium biocomputing, p. 724.
25. Humphrey W, Dalke A, Schulten K (1996) VMD – visual molecular dynamics. J Mol Graphics 14: 33–38.
26. Ihlenfeldt W-D (1997) Virtual reality in chemistry. *J Mol Model* 3: 386–402.
27. Izrailev S, Stepaniants S, Isralewitz B, Kosztin D, Lu H, Molnar F, Wriggers W, Schulten K (1998) Steered molecular dynamics. In: Deuflhard P, Hermans J, Leimkuhler B, Mark AE, Reich S, Skeel RD (eds) Computational molecular dynamics: challenges, methods, ideas, vol. 4 of Lecture notes in computational science and engineering. Springer-Verlag, Berlin, pp. 39–65.
28. Kadau K, Germann TC, Lomdahl PS (2006) Molecular-Dynamics comes of age: 320 billion atom simulation on BlueGene/L. Int J Mod Phys C 17: 1755–1761.
29. Koutek M, van Hees J, Post FH, Bakker AF (2002) Virtual spring manipulators for particle steering in molecular dynamics on the responsive workbench. In: Stürzlinger W, Müller S (eds) Proceedings of the workshop on virtual environments 2002 (Barcelona, Spain, May 30–31, 2002). ACM International Conference Proceeding Series, vol. 23. Eurographics Association, Aire-la-Ville, Switzerland, 53ff.
30. Krueger W, Froehlich B (1994) The responsive workbench. *IEEE Comput Graph* 14(3): 12–15.
31. Lai-Yuen SK, Lee Y (2006) Interactive computer-aided design for molecular docking and assembly. Comput-Aided Des App 3(6): 701–709.
32. Leach A (2001) Molecular modeling: Principles and applications, 2nd edn. Prentice-Hall, New Jersey.
33. Leech J, Prins JF, Hermans J (1996) SMD: visual steering of molecular dynamics for protein design. IEEE Comput Sci Eng 3(4): 38–45.
34. Levine D, Facello M, Hallstrom P, Reeder G, Walenz B, Stevens F (1997) Stalk: an interactive system for virtual molecular docking. IEEE Comput Sci Eng 4(2): 55–65.
35. Levinthal C (1966) Molecular model-building by computer. Sci Am 214(6): 42–52.
36. Lu T, Ding JH, Crivelli SN (2005) DockingShop: a tool for inter-active protein docking. In: IEEE computational systems bioinformatics conference – workshops (CSBW'05), pp. 271–272.
37. Luo Y, Guo P, Hasegawa S, Sato M (2004) An interactive molecular visualization system for education in immersive multi-projection virtual environment. In: Third international conference on image and graphics (ICIG'04). IEEE Computer Society, Washington, DC, pp. 485–488.
38. Marchese FT (2002) A stereographic table for biomolecular visualization. In: Proceedings of the sixth international conference on information visualization: IV'02. IEEE Computer Society, Washington, DC, pp. 603–607.
39. Marchese FT, Mercado J, Pan Y (2003) Adapting single user visualization software for collaborative use. In: Proceedings of the seventh international conference on information visualization: IV'03. IEEE Computer Society, Washington, DC, pp. 252–257.
40. Marchese FT, Brajkovska N (2007) Fostering asynchronous collaborative visualization. In: Proceedings of the 11th international conference information visualization: IV'07. IEEE Computer Society, Washington, DC, pp. 185–190.
41. Moritz E, Meyer J (2004) Interactive 3d protein structure visualization using virtual reality. In: Fourth IEEE symposium on bioinformatics and bioengineering (BIBE'04), p. 503.
42. Pauling L (1960) The nature of the chemical bond, 3rd edn. Cornell University Press, Ithaca, New York.
43. Pettersen EF, Goddard TD, Huang CC, Couch GS, Greenblatt DM, Meng EC, Ferrin TE (2004) UCSF Chimera – A visualization system for exploratory research and analysis. J Comp Chem 25(13): 1605–1612.
44. Phillips JC, Braun R, Wang W, Gumbart J, Tajkhorshid E, Villa E, Chipot C, Skeel RD, Kale L, Schulten K (2005) Scalable molecular dynamics with NAMD. J Comp Chem 26: 1781–1802.

45. Prytherch D, McLundie M (2002) So what is haptics anyway? Research Issues in Art Design and Media, Spring (2): 1-16.
46. Rapaport DC (2006) Multibillion-atom molecular dynamics simulation: design considerations for vector-parallel processing. Comput Phys Comm 174: 521–529.
47. Richardson DC, Richardson JS (1992) The kinemage: a tool for scientific communication. Protein Sci. 1(1): 3–9.
48. Salisbury K, Conti F, Barbagli F (2004) Haptic rendering: introductory concepts. IEEE Comput Graph 24 (2): 24–32.
49. Sanbonmatsu KY, Tung CS (2006) Large-scale simulations of the ribosome: a new landmark in computational biology. J Phys Conf Ser 46: 334–342.
50. Sanner MF (1999) Python: a programming language for software integration and development. J Mol Graph Model 17: 57–61.
51. Sharma G, Mavroidis C, Ferreira A (2005) Virtual reality and haptics in nano- and bionanotechnology. In: Rieth M, Schommers W (eds) Handbook of theoretical and computational nanotechnology, vol. X. American Scientific Publishers, Stevenson Ranch, CA pp. 1–33.
52. Sharma R, Huang TS, Pavovic VI, Zhao Y, Lo Z, Chu S, Schulten K, Dalke A, Phillips J, Zeller M, Humphrey W (1996) Speech/Gesture interface to a visual computing environment for molecular biologists. In: 13th International conference on pattern recognition (ICPR'96), p. 964.
53. Sotomayor M, Schulten K (2007) Single-molecule experiments in vitro and in silico. *Science* 316(5828): 1144–1148.
54. Stone J, Gullingsrud J, Grayson P, Schulten K (2001) A system for interactive molecular dynamics simulation. In: Hughes JF, Séquin CH (eds) ACM symposium on interactive 3d graphics. ACM SIGGRAPH, New York, pp. 191–194.
55. Su S, Loftin R, Chen D, Fang Y, Lin CH (2000) Distributed collaborative virtual environment: PaulingWorld. In: Proceedings of 10th international conference on artificial reality and telexistence, pp. 112–117.
56. Teodoro M, Phillips GN, Jr, Kavraki LE (2001) Molecular docking: a problem with thousands of degrees of freedom. In: Proceedings of the 2001 IEEE international conference on robotics and automation (ICRA 2001). IEEE press, Seoul, Korea, pp. 960–966.
57. Thompson MA (2006) ArgusLab 4.0. Planaria Software LLC, Seattle, http://www.ArgusLab.com.
58. Ullmer B, Ishii H (2000) Emerging frameworks for tangible user interfaces. *IBM Syst* 39 (3&4): 915–931.
59. Vashishta P, Rajiv KK, Nakano A (2006) Multimillion atom simulations of dynamics of oxidation of an aluminum nanoparticle and nanoindentation on ceramics. *J Phys Chem B* 110: 3727–3733.
60. Watson JD, Crick FHC (1953) Molecular structure of nucleic acids. *Nature* 171: 737–738.
61. Weller MP, Do EY, Gross MD (2008) Posey: Instrumenting a poseable hub and strut toy. In: TEI 2008 – second international conference on tangible and embedded interaction, Bonn, Germany Feb 18–21, ACM Press, to appear.
62. Wollacott AM, Merz KM, Jr (2007) Haptic applications for molecular structure manipulation. J Mol Graph Mod 25: 801–805.

Chapter 12
Point, Talk, Publish: Visualization and the Web

Jeffrey Heer, Fernanda B. Viégas, Martin Wattenberg, and Maneesh Agrawala

Abstract: The power of data visualization comes from social as well as visual processes. Visual analysis is often a group effort, as people share findings, confer with colleagues, and present results. Furthermore, thanks to the Web, collaborative data analysis tools are becoming more broadly available, taking new forms and reaching audiences of unprecedented scale. This chapter discusses the design of systems that support collaborative visualization on the Web, where users can interact across both time and space. We use a simple mantra---point, talk, publish---to guide discussion of the design decisions required by asynchronous collaborative visualization. We describe a number of collaboration mechanisms for view sharing, annotation, discussion, and publishing in interactive visualization, and present case studies of current systems. We also discuss theoretical frameworks that help guide future research in this emerging area.

Keywords: Visualization, Asynchronous collaboration, Social data analysis, Web

12.1 Introduction

Visual analysis is rarely a solitary activity. A lone accountant may spot an irregularity in a graph of retail sales – but then she's likely to confer with a colleague, who may show the graph to a lawyer, who later might present it to a jury. Such scenarios of collaboration and presentation are common in business and scientific visualization. One implication is that designers should pay attention not just to the graphical features of visualization tools, but to the collaborative aspects as well. Just as a good visualization takes advantage of the power of the human visual system, it can also exploit our natural social abilities. At minimum, it should enable people to communicate about what they see so they can point out discoveries, share knowledge, and discuss hypotheses.

The social aspects of visualization have taken on new importance with the rise of the Web. The existence of a globally available network has vastly expanded the feasible scale of collaboration and has enabled new forms of collective analysis.

E. Zudilova-Seinstra et al. (eds.) *Trends in Interactive Visualization*,
doi:10.1007/978-1-84800-269-2_12 © Springer-Verlag London Limited 2009

While collaboration in small groups remains ubiquitous, it is now also possible for thousands of people to work with a visualization tool together. Users may be members of an extended team (employees of a large company on an intranet) or strangers (visitors to a public web site). These scenarios are driven by the fact that users can interact remotely from anywhere on the globe and asynchronously log into the system at different times.

Because of its growing importance, this chapter focuses on remote asynchronous collaboration around visualization. This area sits at the intersection of several disciplines, including visualization, computer-supported cooperative work (CSCW), and sensemaking. The amount of related work can be dizzying, so we've organized it around a motto that sums up our experience designing visualizations: *"Point, talk, publish."* Pointing refers to the need for users to establish common ground by sharing specific views of data. Talking includes discussions that take place as people ask questions and propose hypotheses. Publishing encompasses activity aimed at broad audiences, on the web or an intranet. We use the point-talk-publish mantra as a guide for summarizing prior research and discussing design features that enable collaborative interaction around visualization.

12.2 Situating Web-Based Collaborative Visualization

Collaboration has been well studied in contexts that are not directly related to information visualization. The study of how computer systems can enable collaboration is referred to as *computer-supported cooperative work*, or CSCW. Because collaboration occurs in a variety of situations, CSCW scholars often use a "time-space" matrix [21] to outline the conceptual landscape (Fig. 12.1). The time axis represents whether participants interact at the same time or not (synchronously or asynchronously) – for example, instant messaging is a largely synchronous communication

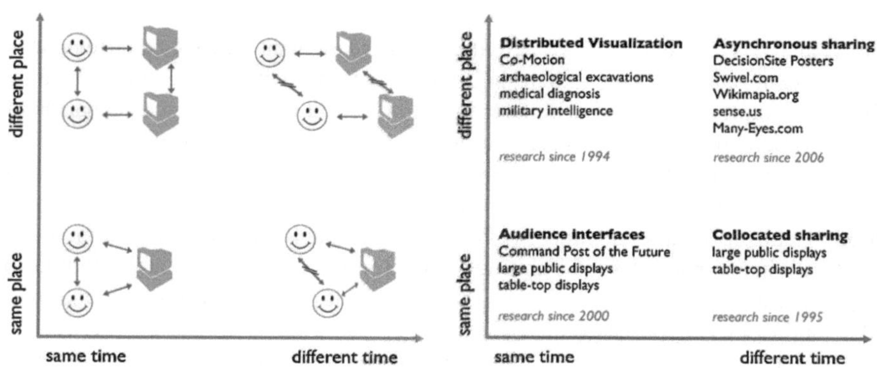

Fig. 12.1 Space/Time matrix characterizing different forms of group work. The image on the right situates prior work in collaborative visualization

medium, while email is asynchronous. The space axis describes whether users are collocated or geographically distributed.

Most work on collaborative visualization has been done in the context of synchronous scenarios (Fig. 12.1, left): users interacting at the same time to analyze scientific results or discuss the state of a battlefield. Before moving on, it is worth quickly revisiting some of this research. Collocated collaboration usually involves shared displays, including large wall-sized screens and table-top devices (e.g., [12, 15]). Systems supporting remote collaboration have primarily focused on synchronous interaction [1, 4], such as shared virtual workspaces (e.g., [7]) and augmented reality systems that enable multiple users to interact concurrently with visualized data (e.g., [3, 8]). In addition, the increasing availability of table-top and large public displays has prompted researchers to experiment with asynchronous, collocated visualization (same place, different time), often in the form of ambient information displays (e.g., [6]).

In this chapter, however, we focus on the kind of collaboration that is most common over the Web: remote asynchronous collaboration (the top right quadrant of the time-space matrix). One reason for our interest is that partitioning work across both time and space holds the potential of greater scalability in group-oriented analysis. For example, one decision making study found that asynchronous collaboration resulted in higher-quality outcomes – broader discussions, more complete reports, and longer solutions – than face-to-face collaboration [2]. This focus on collaboration across both time and space carries direct implications for our point-talk-publish mantra that we review below.

Some researchers, particularly in scientific visualization, have used the web as a platform for visualization. For example, Lefer and Pierson [22] developed a web architecture that leverages a network of workstations to provide visualization images on demand. Jankun-Kelly et al. [20] additionally enable interaction over the web, using the web browser as an exploratory interface to server-side visualization technology. Rhyne [25] describes a design concept for providing web-based visualizations of data from the United States Environmental Protection Agency, presaging a number of recent developments. However, though these systems provide access to visualizations through the web, they remain grounded in a single-user model of usage. To support asynchronous collaboration around visualizations, a deeper connection must be forged between visualization and collaborative technologies.

Although research on remote, asynchronous collaboration around visualizations is still in its infancy, a number of recent projects provide insights into this type of collaborative interaction. One of the common themes is the value of the conversations that occur in the context of visualization. The term *communication-minded visualization* [26] has been used to describe tools that are designed to foster these conversations. In the next sections, we first discuss design decisions and trade-offs faced by system designers when building visualization systems that enable users to point, talk, and publish at an Internet scale. We then present case studies of existing systems that exemplify different approaches for supporting asynchronous collaboration. We end with a discussion of theoretical perspectives and likely future directions for this field. Overall this chapter has two primary goals. The first goal is to introduce the design space of asynchronous collaborative visualization and the trade-offs between different design approaches. The second goal is to highlight open questions in need of further research, with the hope of spurring work in an area that has the potential to change the way everyday people relate to information.

12.3 Point

"Look at this cluster..."

Before people can have a substantive discussion, they have to agree on what they're talking about. Establishing common ground – in which a group of people determines that they are all referring to the same thing – is a well-studied process in psychology [10]. For example, in face-to-face communication people constantly monitor their mutual understanding. Facial expressions, body language, and simple utterances such as "uh-huh" and "hmm?" provide grounding cues of a person's current level of understanding.

In visualization, the challenge is to establish graphical as well as verbal common ground. Because collaborators need to relate actions and comments to a common visual environment, they require easy ways to share views of interest as well as point to specific items and patterns in those views. In face-to-face interaction, physical gestures and speech help meet this goal. For remote collaboration, however, new forms of pointing are necessary.

12.3.1 View Sharing

One way to establish grounding when looking at a visualization remotely is to share screenshots. Unfortunately, as static pixel reproductions of the original application, screenshots cannot support interaction or drilling down for details. Thus, collaboration begins and ends with the screenshot itself since it is impossible to refine the view or investigate alternate hypotheses. More extended collaboration requires users to share data as well as pixels, content as well as form.

To provide such "deep" view sharing, interactive visualization systems must represent and export their internal state. To reproduce a specific view, the state must include both the data (or a pointer to the data) and the parameter settings that control the view: zoom levels, color choice, and so forth. The resulting state representations can then serve as *application bookmarks* into specific views. Such bookmarks can take multiple forms. For example, saving internal state to an external file format is common for many desktop applications, including a number of visualization tools. However, the file must then be transferred to collaborators who must in turn have the same application and access to the same data. While such a system allows view sharing, the overhead is prohibitively high.

In contrast, web-based systems can exploit URLs (Universal Remote Locators) to represent specific views. URLs enable simple and flexible sharing since users can cut and paste a URL into an e-mail, instant message, or blog. The URL may include a string that encodes the parameters of the visualization directly, or it may be more efficient for the web server to store the state internally, much like a saved file, and provide a URL with an identifier for the state record.

12.3.2 Highlighting and Annotation

Once they have shared a view and are looking at the same thing, collaborators often need to highlight particular features, such as interesting trends and outliers. People working in the same room typically point, wave, or use other physical gestures. These gestures can be quite nuanced, often communicating much more than "look here." For example, the space between the thumb and index finger can communicate an interval within the data, while a swooping, accelerating movement of the hand may reinforce corresponding increases in value [9, 19].

Systems for remote collaboration face two challenges: first, to support flexible pointing behaviors (or *deictic* reference) in the absence of literal hand gestures. Second, to balance the tension between the fluidity of visualizations that rely on interaction and animation and the fact that pointing is easiest when a visualization is set in a single static state.

A standard way to point in a visualization is *brushing*: selecting and highlighting a subset of the data. Naturally, these selections should be sharable as part of the state of the visualization [18]. In addition, a palette of visual effects richer than simple highlighting can let users communicate different intents. For example, following time-varying values of selected items in a scatter plot is easier when the selected items leave trails as they move over time. The selected items and their trails are even more salient if non-selected items are simultaneously de-emphasized. Brushing-based forms of pointing have the advantage that the pointing action is tied directly to the data, allowing the same gesture to affect different views of the same data.

A more expressive method of pointing in visualizations is the use of freeform *graphical annotations*. Drawing a circle around a cluster of items or pointing an arrow at a peak in a graph can direct the attention of remote viewers; at the same time, the angle of the arrow or shape of the hand-drawn circle may communicate emotional cues or add emphasis. However, while such drawing and vector graphic annotations allow a high degree of expression, they only apply to a single view in the visualization, without any explicit tie to the underlying data. Freeform annotations can persist over purely visual transformations such as panning and zooming, but they are not "data-aware" and may become meaningless in the face of data-oriented operations such as filtering or drill-down. A promising research direction is hybrid approaches that combine aspects of both brushing and graphical annotation. The resulting techniques could create graphical annotations that are tied to data points so that they can be "recycled" in other views of the data.

12.4 Talk

"Look at this cluster... It seems to relate to GDP."

After establishing common ground – the subject of conversation – the next step is to start talking. Not only is communication essential for sharing hypotheses and insights, it is also crucial for group task coordination. The main challenge for designers is choosing how to link a verbal conversation to its graphical subject. Indeed, the linking of verbal and nonverbal content is one of the differences between collaborative visualization and other forms of groupware.

The simplest form of linking is to embed application bookmarks within a standard discussion forum, interspersing links to desired views within the text. This form of *independent* discussion is unidirectional, linking from text to the visualization. The reverse approach is *embedded discussion*, placing conversational markers directly within the visualization, such as "sticky note" comments attached to annotated geographic regions or brushing selections. This approach provides unidirectional links that point from the visualization to text.

A hybrid technique is *doubly-linked* discussion, which allows comments to link to specific views as in independent discussion, while also enabling comments to be retrieved in situ as visualization views are visited. For example, as users explore a visualization, they can dynamically retrieve the comments related to the current view. Conversely, searchable comments listings can likewise provide pointers back into the visualization. Directly associating commentary with a specific visualization state disambiguates its context while supporting serendipitous discovery of relevant discussion during exploration. Such doubly-linked discussion allows users to more quickly and easily understand their collaborators' remarks about a specific view.

12.5 Publish

"Look at this cluster... It seems to relate to GDP. Does anyone have more data on this?" – Posted by Mary, on her blog

Traditionally, collaboration around data analysis has been bounded, involving a fixed set of team members working with a fixed set of tools. The Internet opens new opportunities for participation at a massive scale by erasing both of these limits. Not only can you collaborate in your class or in your work environment, you are able to work with users across the globe whom you will never meet in person. An analytic debate may begin on one web application only to continue on another completely separate platform, such as a personal blog, which further increases the scale of participation. The "publish" portion of our mantra is shorthand for any action that makes this leap from a bounded context to an unbounded one.

The removal of traditional team and application boundaries, and the concomitant change in scale, carries implications for the design of collaborative visualization systems. Web applications exist within an ecosystem of collaboration and discussion. It behooves the system designer to integrate collaborative sites with external discussion mechanisms. The Spotfire system, for example, provides a way to export a visualization as a web "poster" that may be emailed or placed on an intranet. On the Many Eyes site (described in detail later) there is a one-click "blog this" button that allows users to place a fully interactive version of a visualization into any HTML page. Furthermore, comments, visualizations, and data sets on Many Eyes are available as RSS feeds, making alerts readily available through standard feed readers.

While there are obvious benefits to drawing in bloggers who are used to carrying out discussions on their sites, there is also the potential for "discussion drain," where on-site conversations do not achieve critical mass. Similarly, publishing fully interactive visualizations may lead to reduced traffic to the central visualization service, where richer collaboration features might be available. An initial set of interviews with Many Eyes users indicates this is a complex trade-off [11]. Managing the tension between integration with the outside world and keeping a site inhabited is a crucial area for future work.

12.6 Collaborative Visualization Systems Today

In this section, we discuss contemporary visualization systems that support asynchronous collaborative analysis (shown in Fig. 12.2). In particular, we contrast the individual design decisions made and how they affect the ability of collaborators to point, talk, and publish.

12.6.1 DecisionSite Posters: Adding Collaboration to a Single-User Tool

DecisionSite Posters is a feature of the Spotfire product sold by TIBCO, Inc. Users of Spotfire's desktop-based visualization system can capture snapshots of their analyses and publish them on an intranet as "posters." View sharing and pointing is supported, as each poster has a unique URL that can be easily distributed. Each poster supports talking, in the form of unthreaded text comments on a side panel. However, posters do not allow graphical annotations, limiting the ability of collaborators to point at specific trends or outliers.

As described by Viégas and Wattenberg [26], the communication capabilities in DecisionSite Posters have been used in an unexpected way. Instead of engaging in complex conversations by using the comment panel, as envisioned by the system's designers, users have largely used the tool for presenting their findings to colleagues – to publish more than talk. The ability to create comments with pointers into the visualization provides an easy way to choreograph a step-by-step presentation

12.6.2 Swivel: Sharing Data on the Web

Swivel.com is a web site that supports sharing and discussion around data. The service appears to be modeled on media-sharing sites such as YouTube. In keeping with this model, Swivel allows users to upload data sets and talk about them in attached discussion forums. In addition, the site automatically generates graphs by combining columns from uploaded data sets into bar charts, pie charts, and scatter plots. Pointing behavior on the site appears limited.

Although the graphs on Swivel are not interactive, the site provides an example of social data analysis in action, in particular the importance of the "publish" stage of collaborative visualization. While there do not seem to be many extensive conversations in Swivel's discussion area – that is, little on-site pointing and talking – there has been significant use of Swivel's graphs among bloggers who wish to discuss statistics. In other words, it is the ability to publish graphs for use in other contexts that is most valuable to Swivel's users.

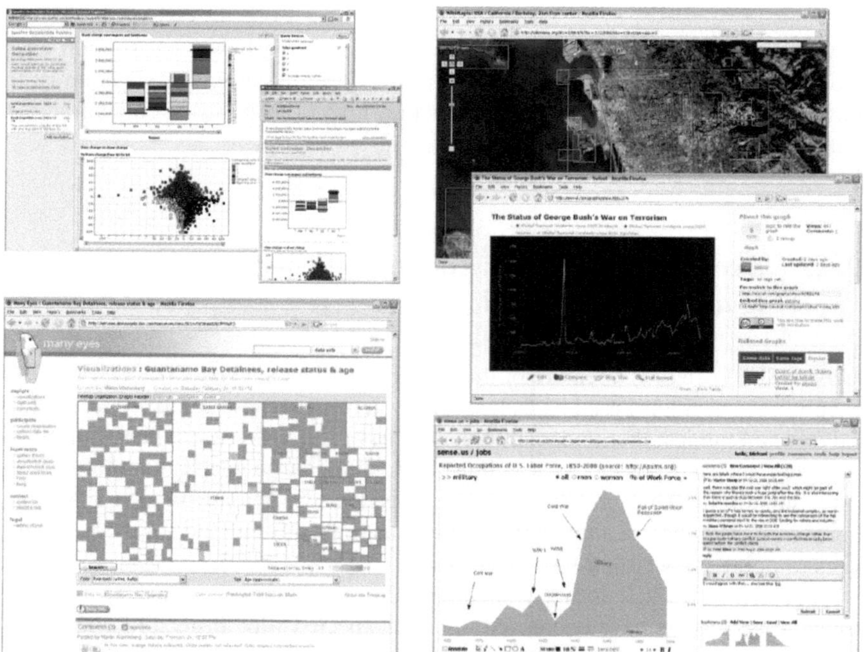

Fig. 12.2 Asynchronous collaborative visualization systems. Clockwise from top-left: Spotfire decisionSite posters, Wikimapia, Swivel, sense.us, and Many Eyes (*See Color Plates*)

12.6.3 Wikimapia: Collaborative Geographic Annotation

Wikimapia.org is a web site enabling collective annotation of satellite imagery. The site provides a zoomable browser of satellite photos across the globe, along with the ability to select geographic regions for annotation with names and additional data (Fig. 12.2). View sharing is supported through automatically updating URLs. As the view is panned or zoomed, the current URL updates dynamically to reflect the current zoom level and latitude and longitude values. Pointing is supported through annotations. Users can draw rectangular and polygonal annotations, which scale appropriately as the map is zoomed. To avoid clutter, annotations are filtered as the view is zoomed; the viewer does not see annotations that are too small to be legible or so large they engulf the entire display, improving the scalability of the system.

Wikimapia supports talking using an embedded discussion technique. Each annotation serves as a link to editable text. Descriptive text about a geographic region can be edited by anyone, similar to articles on Wikipedia. Individual comments are avoided, with contributions instead being aggregated through group editing. Discussion also occurs through voting. When annotations are new, users can vote on whether they agree or disagree with the annotation. Annotations that are voted down are removed from the system. For instance, the small town of Yelapa, Mexico is located on an inlet in a bay near Puerto Vallarta. However, the bay has a number of inlets very close together. As a result, contributors posted multiple conflicting annotations for Yelapa. Through voting, users discarded the incorrect regions and preserved the correct annotation.

12.6.4 Sense.us: Social Data Analysis of U.S. Census Data

Sense.us is a prototype web application for social visual data analysis [17]. The site provides interactive visualizations of 150 years of United States census data, including stacked timelines, choropleth maps, and population pyramids. With a URL-based bookmarking mechanism, it supports collaboration through doubly-linked discussion, graphical annotations, bookmark trails, and searchable comment listings.

Talking occurs via a doubly-linked conversation model. Pointing occurs through free-hand annotations; view sharing is facilitated by URLs that automatically update as users navigate the visualizations. Searchable comment listings provide links back into the visualization, while navigating in a visualization automatically causes related comments to be retrieved for the current view. By tying commentary directly to specific view states, comments become less ambiguous, enabling deictic remarks such as "that spike" or "on the left" to be more easily understood. Sense.us also allows users to collect view links in a "bookmark trail" of view thumbnails. Users can then drag-and-drop view thumbnails from the trail into a comment text field, thereby adding a hyperlink to the saved view within the comment. In this way, users can provide pointers to related views and create tours through the data.

The sense.us prototype was initially available on a corporate intranet which provided employees with blogs and a social bookmarking service. Users of sense. us found ways to publish their findings, typically by taking screenshots and then placing them on blogs or the bookmarking service with application bookmarks. These "published" visualizations drew additional traffic to the site.

Studies of the sense.us system found interesting patterns of social data analysis. Users would make observations about the data, often coupled with questions and hypotheses about the data. These comments often attracted further discussion. For example, within a visualization of the U.S. labor force over time, a spike and then decline in the number of dentists prompted discussion ranging from the fluoridation of water to the specialization of dental work, with a rise in the number of hygienists corresponding to the decline of dentists. There was also an interesting interaction between data analysis and social activity. Users who tired of exploring visualizations turned their focus to the comment listings. Reading others' comments sparked new questions that led users back into the visualization, stimulating further analysis.

12.6.5 Many Eyes: Web-Based Visualization and Publishing

Many-Eyes.com [27] is a web-based service that combines public data sharing with interactive visualizations. Like social data analysis sites such as Swivel, site members can upload data sets and comment on them. Unlike Swivel, however, Many Eyes offers a palette of 15 interactive visualization techniques – ranging from bar charts to treemaps to tag clouds – that visitors may apply to any data set. Other users may leave comments on the visualizations, including bookmarks that are tied to particular states. A basic form of data-centric deixis is possible through highlighting mechanisms within each visualization; for example, in a treemap a user can click on individual rectangles to leave highlights that persist when the view is bookmarked.

The pointing and talking capabilities of Many Eyes are used in a variety of ways. The site contains some lengthy conversations around visualizations, although the great majority of visualizations have no comments. One class of visualizations, how ever, did lead to lengthy onsite discussions: visualizations that sidestepped sober analysis and were instead playful, joyful, or just plain funny. One person, for example, initiated a game based on a visualization of Shakespearean poetry in which he used the highlighting mechanisms to pick out alphabetically ordered words to make pseudo-Elizabethan epithets. These games frequently attracted many "players."

The Many Eyes site also can be viewed as a publishing platform, since the visualizations that users create are publicly visible and may be linked to from other web pages. Many bloggers have taken advantage of this, and perhaps as a result the longest discussions around Many Eyes visualizations seem to take place offsite. Indeed, the deepest analyses we have seen of Many Eyes visualizations have occurred as part of blog entries that reference the site. In one example, a blog at the

Sunlight Foundation (a political reform organization) published a Many Eyes tag cloud to analyze messages between the U.S. Congress and the U.S. Department of Defense. The blog entry framed the results as a funny-but-sad surprise: the most common phrases had nothing to do with current pressing issues, but rather requests for congressional travel. In another case, a user created a visualization of the "social network" of the New Testament. Not only was this visualization linked to from more than 100 blog entries, but another user went to the trouble of recording a YouTube video of himself interacting with the visualization and narrating what he learned. These phenomena again underscore the importance of publishing mechanisms for collaborative visualization.

12.7 Future Directions

The systems above highlight varied forms of collaborative analysis around interactive visualizations, but also reveal areas in need of further investigation. Here we consider theoretical perspectives on information access and collaboration to inform future efforts. For additional discussion of theoretical perspectives on collaborative visualization, we refer interested readers to [16].

12.7.1 Information Foraging

One source of insight for improving collaborative visualization systems is an examination of the ways that humans search for information. Information foraging theory [23, 24] describes how people navigate when searching for information, based on an analogy with the strategies used by animals foraging for food. Recently, several researchers have begun to extend the theory to collective tasks [23, 26]. *Information patches* – small, easily explored subsets of a large collection of data – and *information scent* – hints that a subset of data might be a valuable or relevant information patch – can be co-opted for collaboration around visualizations. Imagine, for example, that many people are analyzing a data set that contains an important undiscovered pattern. The best strategy might be to avoid redundant searching, that is, follow an approach in which individuals explore distinct parts of the data set in parallel, with some overlap to account for human error. Social information foraging theory may be applied to determine how to parameterize such a search, helping direct users to the patches where pointing and talking are most needed.

How are regions of high information scent communicated to the group? In social foraging, fruitful patches are often signaled by the activity of others. For example, users can point to promising areas on overview displays. Collaborative analysis systems can also automatically provide *social navigation* mechanisms by providing indicators of others' activity and visitation patterns [14]. This enables collaborators to see both highly visited areas of interest and underexplored data regions. One approach is to provide activity indicators within the visualization itself. For example, Wattenberg and Kriss [28] describe a prototype that grays out previously visited data elements, making unvisited regions more visually salient. To provide foraging cues without disrupting the visualized data, Willett et al. [29] visualize visitation and comment counts within the dynamic query widgets used to navigate the visualizations. They find that these "scented" widgets particularly aid unique discoveries when users are unfamiliar with the data. Other forms of enhanced navigation cues might further improve the efficiency of collaborative analysis.

12.7.2 Coordination and Communication

Another important aspect of collaborative action is awareness of others' activities, allowing collaborators to coordinate their work by gauging what others have done and where to allocate effort next [5, 13].Within asynchronous contexts, participants require awareness of the timing and content of past actions. This suggests that designs should include both history and notification mechanisms for following actions performed on a given artifact or by specific individuals or groups. Browseable histories of past action are one mechanism, as are subscription and notification technologies such as RSS (Really Simple Syndication). An open question for future designs is what forms of awareness information might better facilitate collaborative analysis in interactive visualizations.

The rubrics of coordination and communication are also helpful for organizing open questions related to explicit pointing and talking. For example, Sect. 12.4 introduced various ways that discussions can be associated to visualizations: embedding, linking, and double linking. The comparative efficacy of these approaches is currently unclear. In one recent investigation [17], users found doubly-linked discussion easy to understand and comments exhibited deictic remarks such as "here" and "that spike" that were dependent on the linked view. Still, more research is needed and many questions remain unexplored. Should threaded discussions be preferred to flat comment listings? How should doubly-linked discussion be applied across multiple views?

These questions become thornier at the scale of a web-based audience. If a large number of people want to contribute to an analysis, the sheer scale may be overwhelming. Effective coordination mechanisms are needed to integrate the contributions of multiple users. How can conversations be structured so that individual contributions are more effectively integrated? What filtering or aggregation methods are the most useful? For example, Wikipedia uses collaborative revision of individual documents to integrate the efforts of editors, while online voting systems use statistical aggregation. For visual analysis, contributions may include observations of interest (indicated through pointing), insightful questions, explanatory hypotheses, and supporting evidence. Other viewers may then want to voice their support or disdain for hypotheses or evidence, perhaps through voting. A usable, structured conversation system that can aggregate these contributions and support summarization of discussions may increase the scale of the feasible audience for web-based visualization.

12.8 Summary

In this chapter, we introduce an emerging use of interactive visualization: collaborative visual analysis across space and time. The Web has opened up new possibilities for large-scale collaboration around visualizations and holds the potential for improved analysis and dissemination of complex data sets. We use a simple mantra – *point, talk, publish* – to guide discussion of the design space of asynchronous collaborative visualization and identify promising avenues for future research.

Pointing actions call attention to interesting visualization views and patterns. Designers can enable successful pointing through view sharing techniques that allow remote collaborators to see the same image, and through highlighting and annotation techniques that clearly identify interesting patterns.

Talking involves discussion around views, including observations, questions, and hypotheses about the data. A primary design challenge is linking text and visuals in a way that supports comprehension; approaches include linking to visuals from independent text, embedding conversational markers directly within the visualization, and doubly-linking text and visuals, such that text that references particular views can also be dynamically retrieved during exploration and interaction.

Publishing consists of disseminating insights gained through pointing and talking and extending conversations to the web at large. Publishing is achieved through view sharing and embedding both static and interactive visualizations into external web sites, extending the reach of web-based visualization services.

Each of these points in the design space have been explored in an emerging class of collaborative analysis applications, including the commercial product Spotfire DecisionSite Posters, the research prototype sense.us, and public websites such as Swivel.com, Wikimapia.org, and Many-Eyes.com. Each application provides usage examples of successful collaboration, involving cycles of observation, questioning, and hypothesis around interactive visualizations.

Looking forward, frameworks such as information foraging theory [23, 24] provide guidance for future iterations of collaborative visualization systems. Information Foraging theory suggests that both individual user contributions and automatic presentation of activity metrics can help users direct their interests to the regions of data where their contributions will make the greatest impact. In this way, collective intelligence can be more effectively leveraged by the many eyes now looking at an increasing array of public data sets.

Acknowledgments Image of TIBCO Spotfire DecisionSite Enterprise Analytics Software provided by TIBCO Software Inc. TIBCO, TIBCO Software, Spotfire and Spotfire DecisionSite are trademarks or registered trademarks of TIBCO Software Inc. in the United States and/or other countries. The graph from Swivel.com was created by user Seema, and is available at http://www.swivel.com/graphs/show/8052276 under a Creative Commons Attribution license.

References

1. Anupam, V., Bajaj, C.L., Schikore, D., Shikore, M.: Representations in distributed cognitive tasks. IEEE Computer 27(7), 37–43 (1994).
2. Benbunan-Fich, R., Hiltz, S.R., Turoff, M.: A comparative content analysis of face-to-face vs asynchronous group decision making. Decision Support Systems 34(4), 457–469 (2003).
3. Benko, H., Ishak, E.W., Feiner, S.: Collaborative mixed reality visualization of an archaeological excavation. In: Proceedings in IEEE International Symposium on Mixed and Augmented Reality (ISMAR 2004), pp. 132–140. Arlington, VA (2004).
4. Brodlie, K.W., Duce, D.A., Gallop, J.R.,Walton, J.P.R.B.,Wood, J.D.: Distributed and collaborative visualization. Computer Graphics Forum 23(2), 223–251 (2004).
5. Caroll, J., Rosson, M.B., Convertino, G., Ganoe, C.H.: Awareness and teamwork in computer-supported collaborations. Interacting with Computers 18(1), 21–46 (2005).
6. Carter, S., Mankoff, J., Goddi, P.: Building connections among loosely coupled groups: Hebb's rule at work. Journal of Computer-Supported Cooperative Work 13(3), 305–327 (2004).
7. Chuah, M.C., Roth, S.F.: Visualizing Common Ground. In: Proceedings of International Conference on Information Visualization (IV), pp. 365–372 (2003).
8. Chui, Y.P., Heng, P.A.: Enhancing view consistency in collaborative medical visualization systems using predictive-based attitude estimation. In: Proceedings of IEEE International Workshop on Medical Imaging and Augmented Reality (MIAR'01). Hong Kong, China (2001).
9. Clark, H.H.: Pointing and placing. In: S. Kita (ed.) Pointing. Where Language, Culture, and Cognition Meet, pp. 243–268. Erlbaum (2003).
10. Clark, H.H., Brennan, S.E.: Grounding in communication. In: L.B. Resnick, R.M. Levine, S.D. Teasley (eds.) Perspectives on Socially Shared Cognition, pp. 127–268. American Psychological Association (1991).
11. Danis, C., Viégas, F.B., Wattenberg, M., Kriss, J.: Your place or mine? visualization as a community component. In: Proceedings of ACM Conference on Human Factors in Computing Systems (CHI) (2008).
12. Dietz, P.H., Leigh, D.L.: DiamondTouch: A multi-user touch technology. In: Proceedings of ACM Symposium on User Interface Software and Technology (UIST), pp. 219–226 (2001).
13. Dourish, P., Belotti, V.: Awareness and coordination in shared workspaces. In: Proceedings of ACM Conference on Computer-Supported CooperativeWork, pp. 107–114. Toronto, Ontario (1992).
14. Dourish, P., Chalmers, M.: Running out of space: Models of information navigation. In: Proceedings of Human Computer Interaction (HCI'94) (1994).
15. General Dynamics: Command post of the future. Accessed: November, 2007. URL http://www.gdc4s.com/content/detail.cfm?item=2a58f8e2-ef2b-4bb1-9251-42ee4961dd7f.
16. Heer, J., Agrawala, M.: Design considerations for collaborative visual analytics. In: Proceedings of IEEE Symposium on Visual Analytics Science and Technology (VAST), pp. 171–178 (2007).
17. Heer, J., Viégas, F.B.,Wattenberg, M.: Voyagers and voyeurs: Supporting asynchronous collaborative information visualization. In: Proceedings of ACM Conference on Human Factors in Computing Systems (CHI), pp. 1029–1038 (2007).
18. Heer, J., Agrawala, M., Willett, W.: Generalized selection via interactive query relaxation. In: Proceedings of ACM Conference on Human Factors in Computing Systems (CHI) (2008).
19. Hill, W.C., Hollan, J.D.: Deixis and the future of visualization excellence. In: Proceedings of of IEEE Visualization, pp. 314–319 (1991).
20. Jankun-Kelly, T., Kreylos, O., Ma, K.L., Hamann, B., Joy, K.I., Shalf, J., Bethel, E.W.: Deploying web-based visual exploration tools on the grid. IEEE Computer Graphics and Applications 23(2), 40–50 (2003).
21. Johansen, R.: Groupware: Computer Support for Business Teams. The Free Press, New York (1988).

22. Lefer, W., Pierson, J.M.: Using network of workstations to support a web-based visualization service. In: Proceedings of Euro-Par'99, pp. 624–633 (1999).
23. Pirolli, P.: Information Foraging Theory: Adaptive Interaction with Information. Oxford University Press (2007).
24. Pirolli, P., Card, S.K.: Information forgaging. Psychological Review 106(4), 643–675 (1999).
25. Rhyne, T.: Scientific visualization and technology transfer. IEEE Computer 28(7), 94–95 (1995).
26. Viégas, F.B., Wattenberg, M.: Communication-minded visualization: A call to action. IBM Systems Journal 45(4), 801–812 (2006).
27. Viégas, F.B., Wattenberg, M., van Ham, F., Kriss, J., McKeon, M.: Many Eyes: A site for visualization at internet scale. IEEE Transactions on Visualization and Computer Graphics 12(5), 1121–1128 (2007).
28. Wattenberg, M., Kriss, J.: Designing for social data analysis. IEEE Transactions on Visualization and Computer Graphics 12(4), 549–557 (2006).
29. Willett, W., Heer, J., Agrawala, M.: Scented widgets: Improving navigation cues with embedded visualizations. IEEE Transactions on Visualization and Computer Graphics 13(6), 1129–1136 (2007).

Part V
Integrating Visualization and Modeling

Chapter 13
Extending Measurement Science to Interactive Visualization Environments

Judith Terrill, William George, Terence Griffin, John Hagedorn, John Kelso, Marc Olano, Adele Peskin, Steven Satterfield, James Sims, Jeffrey Bullard, Joy Dunkers, Nicos Martys, Agnes O'Gallagher, and Gillian Haemer

Abstract We describe three classes of tools to turn visualizations into a visual laboratory to interactively measure and analyze scientific data. We move the normal activities that scientists perform to understand their data into the visualization environment, which becomes our virtual laboratory, combining the qualitative with the quantitative. We use representation, interactive selection, quantification, and display to add quantitative measurement methods, input tools, and output tools. These allow us to obtain numerical information from each visualization. The exact form that the tools take within each of our three categories depends on features present in the data, hence each is manifested differently in different situations. We illustrate the three approaches with a variety of case studies from immersive to desktop environments that demonstrate the methods used to obtain quantitative knowledge interactively from visual objects.

Keywords Measurement, Metrology, Visualization, Immersive visualization.

13.1 Introduction

The National Institute of Standards and Technology (NIST) was established in 1901 as the National Bureau of Standards. Although NIST's mission has expanded over the years, metrology, or measurement science, has remained a central theme. Measurement science has traditionally meant measurements on laboratory data that are made during the course of an experiment. However it is not always possible to perform desired measurements on laboratory data while the physical experiment is taking place. For example, a reconstruction phase may be needed to get the data into a form where it can be measured. An example is tomographic reconstruction, for which a great deal of information in the form of image data has to be carefully filtered, transformed, etc. to yield useful quantitative information. In addition laboratory experiments today are increasingly being replaced by computational experiments. Here, it may be too time consuming, expensive or impossible to do the laboratory experiment, and while quantitative data is typically gathered during

E. Zudilova-Seinstra et al. (eds.) *Trends in Interactive Visualization*,
doi:10.1007/978-1-84800-269-2_13

numerical simulations, there are also many reasons why additional measurements may need to be taken during a post-processing stage. Measurements and analyses from within interactive visualization environments provide unique capabilities in this regard.

There are a variety of other motivations beyond pure measurement for adding interactive analysis to visualizations. Computational and laboratory experiments are generating increasing amounts of scientific data, and often, the complexity of the data makes it difficult to devise a priori methods for its analysis. Also, data currently is derived from new landscapes, such as the nanoworld, where we have little experience. There may be ancillary data, from databases for example, that may be required for understanding. Finally, just having the capability at hand to quantify the visualization speeds understanding.

Most visualization techniques excel at providing a **qualitative** view of the visualized data. We are developing interactive measurement and analysis capabilities in desktop, three dimensional (3D) desktop, and immersive visualization environments, that bring **quantitative** data measurement into traditional qualitative visualization. We classify quantitative tools for visualization into three categories as follows:

Quantitative Measurement: These are of two types: (1) interactive measurement tools analogous to physical measurement tools such as tape measures, and generalizations thereof; and (2) interactive tools to measure more abstract properties of data

Quantitative Output: These are tools to perform interactive analyses and represent their output as quantitative data alongside raw data as it is visualized, and

Quantitative Input: These are tools using values or graphs as part of an interactive interface to help drive the direction of a visualization (visualization steering)

With real time qualitative and quantitative visual exploration and interaction, scientists can easily perceive complex relationships in their data, quickly ascertaining whether the results match expectations, and often obtain unexpected answers from visual observation. To support our classification for quantitative visualization tools, this chapter presents three case studies of visualizations at NIST incorporating quantitative tools for use by the domain scientist. In each of these three, the domain scientists played central roles, collaborating with computer scientists to develop visualizations and methods of interaction that produced valuable scientific measurements and insight.

13.2 Related Work

This work is not the first attempt to perform measurements in visualization environments [4, 3, 13, 15, 22, 23]. The most relevant work within immersive visualization environments is described by Reitinger et al. who present a set of virtual reality tools for making measurements (distance, angle, and volume) for surgical planning [25]. They point out that the virtual environment affords more natural interactions, so the user is able to make measurements more effectively than could be done on a non-interactive system, and this has certainly been our experience. Our work involves the implementation of some similar measurement tools, as well as some novel measurement tools, and incorporates interactive tools for statistical analyses and investigation of the measurement data derived from the 3D scene. Moreover, our toolbox is not specific to any one application; the tools are general and can be moved from application to application.

On the commercial side, simple measurement capability has begun to appear in a variety of software e.g. Acrobat 3D [1], and Amira [19]. On the desktop, measurement of 3D objects requires the ability to directly access any point in 3D space. This 3D desktop capability has existed for years in CAD software, but CAD systems are design tools – the scales of interest are an integral part of the design. In scientific visualization, the investigative scales generally come out of the data, and are not usually designed. This chapter will not address how to build a 3D desktop but rather assumes it exists and describes analytical techniques to gather and understand data in the 3D world. Immersive environments by their nature allow access to any part of space. So measurement in these environments is straightforward. We design our applications to work both on the desktop and immersively.

13.3 Case Studies

A few widely varying examples of the use of a 3D visualization environment to gather new information from data are described below. Each uses one or more of our three types of quantitative techniques that add to the productivity of understanding and quantifying that particular application.

13.3.1 Tissue Engineering

Tissue engineering has been identified by NIST as a biotechnology area in which metrological analyses are required to lower the cost barrier for product commercialization. To this end, NIST is developing methods to measure tissue engineered scaffold structures and analyzing scaffolds interactively. Scaffold structure is known to have a large influence on cell response, and this in turn affects the success of the final tissue engineered product. These structures are manufactured and then scanned using X-ray microcomputed tomography. The 3D structure is then reconstructed mathematically. Thresholding enables extraction of the scaffold which is visualized using a polygon approximation. We study the visualization with quantitative methods.

For tissue engineering, we use all three classes of quantitative visualization tools within an immersive visualization environment to determine the fidelity of a manufactured tissue engineered scaffold to a design specification [12]. Each of the quantitative measurement tools places measurement objects into the virtual world that are, in some sense, surrogates for the features being measured. The user interacts with these objects in the immersive environment with a 3D cursor that is controlled by the position of the hand-held motion-tracked wand. The researcher can position and stretch those surrogate objects to fit the features of the data representations under study. The measurement of those features can then be taken from the known dimensions of the surrogates, and the user is able to analyze and interact with those measurements. So far, we have developed three such measurement tools: linear, cylindrical, and ellipsoidal. We envision these tools as the first of a set that will form a general purpose tool-box for the measurement of dimensional quantities in a virtual laboratory.

The linear measurement tool lets the user stretch line segments to measure the linear distance between any two points. This is a virtual tape measure that provides a continuous numeric display of the length while the user is stretching each line segment. The cylinder measurement tool places wire-frame cylinders into the scene which the researcher can move, orient, and stretch in any dimension in order to match tubular features in the scene. The resulting dimensions of the wireframe cylinders can then be recorded to measure these features of the scene. Similarly, the ellipsoidal measurement tool enables the researcher to place wire-frame spheres into the scene. These spheres can then be interactively stretched into any ellipsoidal form and moved and oriented to match features of the scene. The various quantitative features of each ellipsoid can be recorded to measure these features.

All these positioning and stretching interactions are direct manipulations of the objects. For example, the user manipulates a linear measurement by grabbing one end of the line segment (point and click) and moving it to a new location (drag and drop). During the interaction, the system shows a continuous display of the rubber band line segment, with a continually updated numeric display of its length.

As these linear, cylindrical, or ellipsoidal measurements are taking place, a second set of quantitative output tools allows the scientist to analyze the compiled measurements graphically, while they are being gathered. At any time, the user can display a histogram of the current set of measurements together with their mean and standard deviation. Finally, the histogram can be used as a quantitative input tool, allowing the user to sweep out a portion of the histogram and have the system highlight the corresponding line segment measurements whose lengths lie in that portion of the histogram.

This closes the loop between measurement, analysis, and visualization. Here it lets the researcher see the relationship between the spatial location of measurements and their positions in the distribution of measurements. For example, we are able to highlight and examine all fibers whose diameters are less than 30% of the design size to see whether they are spatially clustered within the scaffold. Note also that the highlighting based on interaction with the histogram could be regarded as a form of *brushing* [2]. In the immersive system, this interaction takes place through a panel that is an element in the 3D virtual scene. Figure 13.1 shows the cylindrical measurement tool with its accompanying analysis panel as it might appear in the immersive visualization environment.

We performed linear measurements both on the "as-designed" scaffold model (generated synthetically from the design) and on the image of the actual manufactured scaffold material in the visualization environment. The former are intended to validate the measurement method, while the latter are used to understand the scaffold structural characteristics and fabrication method. We derived descriptors such as gap width, spacing of fibers, angles between intersecting struts, etc., and compared the results to those from the as-designed scaffold. We found that the inter-junction strut diameter was about 19% smaller than the as-designed model and the at-junction strut diameter (or layer thickness) was about 33% smaller than the as-designed model. However the angular measurements correspond very closely to the design [10].

The manual nature of these measurement tools presents some ease-of-use issues for the user. For example, when making large numbers of measurements in the immersive environment, user fatigue becomes a substantial issue. We also found that it was often difficult to align the surrogate objects with the surfaces that represent the objects being measured. The steadiness of the hand became a factor and many small adjustments were often required to get the desired result. This alignment problem was ameliorated in the immersive environment by interactively

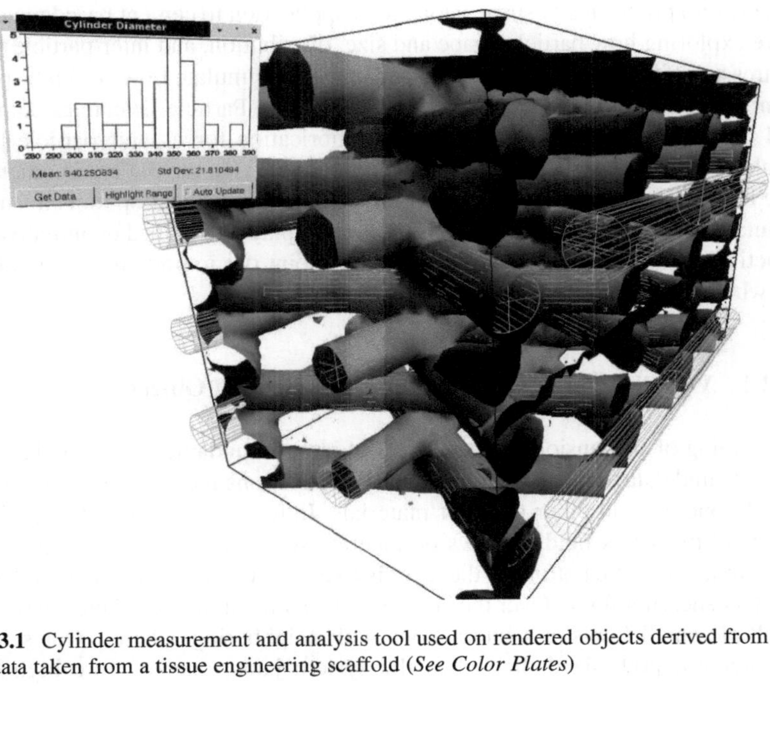

Fig. 13.1 Cylinder measurement and analysis tool used on rendered objects derived from measured data taken from a tissue engineering scaffold (*See Color Plates*)

enlarging the virtual scene so that small mis-positionings would have less impact. However, it is also important to keep in mind that the (typically polygonal) representations that are displayed in the virtual environment are themselves only approximations of the real objects being measured. The researcher may choose not to place a surrogate object exactly aligned with the data representation based on his or her scientific judgment about how the virtual object approximates the real object.

Researchers reported that interactive measurement of the data provides valuable quantitative information for the scaffold manufacturers and scientists. They were able to look at multiple attributes at the same time, enabling the identification of manufacturing defects. The ability to interactively make physical measurements of objects in the virtual world and to display and interact with statistics derived from these measurements has let researchers efficiently collect and understand the data that they need. These domain scientists identified several areas in which this work could be extended: the integration of a fluid flow simulation to quantitatively understand nutrient transport issues in the scaffold; the imaging of cells growing on the scaffold structure; and inclusion of automated measurement techniques used side-by-side with the manual measurement methods described above.

13.3.2 Flow of Suspensions

This research is focused on advancing our fundamental understanding of the rheological (flow) properties of suspensions with application to cement based materials. We are exploring how particle shape and size, distribution, and inter-particle forces and stresses affect the properties of suspensions. We simulate flows of both spheres and more realistic particle shapes using a Dissipative Particle Dynamics computational model that includes hydrodynamics, lubrication forces, interparticle forces and takes into account the local surface curvature [18]. In the 3D environment, we create both *quantitative input* and *quantitative output* visualization tools to analyze computational output. We use analysis tools to display and embed quantitative data interactively as it is investigated. Visual clues point out important aspects of data from which quantitative information can be derived.

13.3.2.1 Visualization of Stress in Flows of Spherical Objects

The jamming of suspensions is the subject of intense fundamental research. In particular, its understanding is useful for many applications including flow and placement of concrete and other granular materials. In this visualization, the goal is to understand the stress field in flows of spheres. We simulate a layer of spheres in suspension, where the bottom of the layer is fixed and the top of the layer undergoes a constant shearing force. Over the course of the simulation, the spheres participate in multiple small low-stress interactions with neighboring spheres. Our scientist collaborator hypothesized that when the system jams, one or more high-stress chains would form from sphere to sphere to sphere through the system, possibly dissipating quickly as the system breaks free.

In order to see the stress field, we create a visual representation of the stress value between each pair of spheres (an output of the simulation). As shown in Fig. 13.2, the stress between each pair of interacting spheres is represented as a line. The sphere positions are implied from the line end points. We do not visualize the actual spheres because with their simple, known shape, they would just obscure the important data in the visualization. 3D time sequence animation allows a qualitative understanding of the system stress. As can be seen from the representation of stress in the figure, patterns of the stress can be ascertained visually, illuminating the directions along which the stress is being transferred through the system. The stress chains of the system are of significant importance to the researchers. This quantitative information embedded in our data makes these chains explicit to the scientist during the visualization.

A slider selecting the upper and lower stress values to display gives real time quantitative interaction with the data. This provides the researchers with an interactive

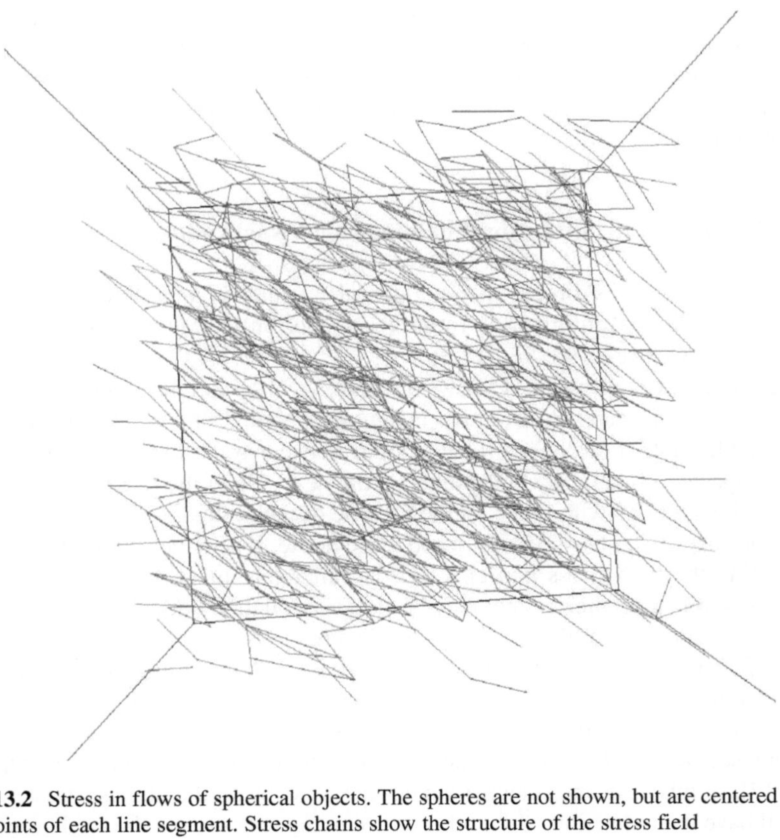

Fig. 13.2 Stress in flows of spherical objects. The spheres are not shown, but are centered at the endpoints of each line segment. Stress chains show the structure of the stress field

tool to visually explore the data by dynamically viewing the stress data through a data window defined by the slider controlled stress range, and allows the user to visually remove the data of low interest and focus on the areas where stress chains and potential jamming/locking occurs.

An example of an identified stress line propagating from top to middle to bottom of the system is shown in Fig. 13.2. Another slider provides control of the animation speed. When a stress chain in the system occurs, it typically exists for a short period of time. A higher animation speed allows for a quick overview of the system. Reducing the animation to very slow or to a full stop allows an identified area and time step to be studied in more careful detail. The capability to focus on particular lines of stress and study them in frame-by-frame detail provides information to the scientist not otherwise available without these visible clues.

13.3.2.2 Visualization of Stress in Flows of Realistic Shapes

Flows of realistic random particulate shapes require new methods to obtain the qualitative and quantitative information needed by the scientists for a full understanding of the stress. The shape of the rocks, not just the distance between the rocks, influences stress chains and jamming. The physics of these flows requires different analytical tools than would be needed to study the flow of spheres. We therefore create a combination of our measurement techniques within the visualization environment.

13.3.2.3 Hybrid Realistic/Non-Photorealistic Visualization

We visualize the rocks directly, but augment the visualization with embedded data to provide additional information to the researcher on interactions between rocks and the per-rock stress (see Fig. 13.3).

The addition of these values allows quantitative observations and measurement, as opposed to the purely qualitative insight provided by most visualizations. In addition, blue dots show the interaction points between rocks in the simulation. The system repeats toroidally, so blue points on the near side of the closest rocks correspond to interactions with rocks on the far side of the system.

As the suspension becomes more and more dense, it becomes increasingly difficult to find the high-stress particles in a visualization, much less chains of such particles. While a smaller system may be simple enough to understand without further visualization tools, the larger system in Fig. 13.3 and our biggest system to date, 2025 rocks, require extra visualization tools, such as culling the less interesting rocks, in order to allow the scientist to find potential jamming.

We gain inspiration from prior work in Focus + Context, primarily seen in information visualization [9, 14, 16, 21], and from non-photorealistic rendering in graphics [7, 8, 17]. In this case, the scientist would like to focus on the highest stress rocks, but still have the indication of the other surrounding rocks to put the total system in

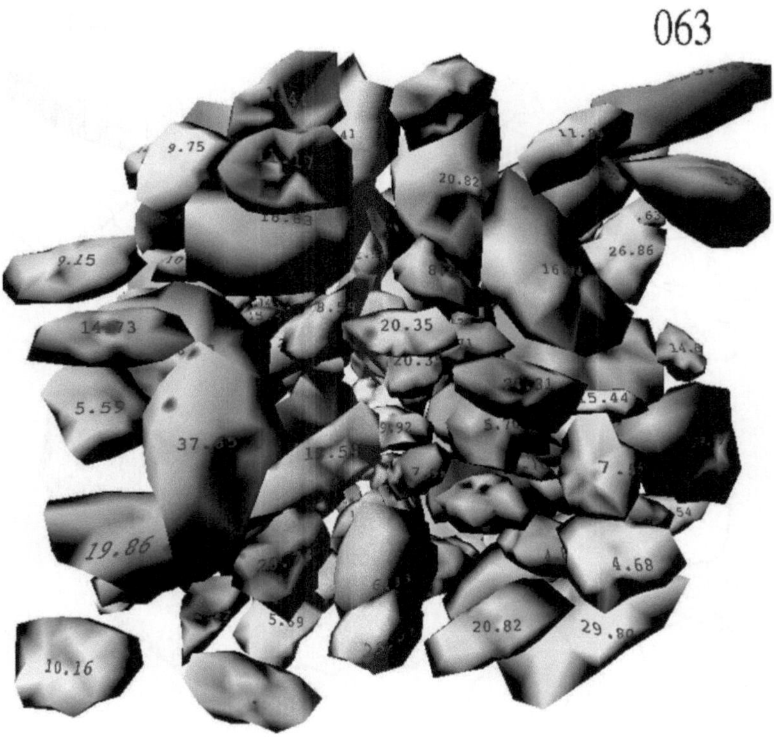

Fig. 13.3 Frame 63 in a simulation of the flow of rocks in a suspension. The per-rock stress is shown with a gray-yellow color scale, and also with a numeric value printed on the face for each rock (*See Color Plates*)

context. To achieve this, we turn to non-photorealistic rendering techniques to show these rocks in a sketchy style. The result, shown in Fig. 13.4, is quite effective, especially when seen in motion. The coherent motion of each low-stress rock's silhouette enhances the ability to recognize and distinguish individual rocks. In this visualization, we can clearly see a diagonal chain of rocks from the upper right, wrapping briefly to the opposite side of the simulation (recalling that the simulation wraps toroidally).

In addition, it is useful to track the high-stress rocks from a single frame of the simulation through the entire simulation. That allows the scientist to see how those specific rocks move into gridlock, and how they escape it and continue on afterwards. For example, in some simulation runs, a small rock can be seen to move and twist to a new location while larger rocks remain locked in place, almost like working a 3D jigsaw puzzle. Then the larger rocks release, the stress goes down, and the aggregate motion continues.

To assist the scientist in choosing a frame to display, we create a quantitative input visualization tool using a graph of the total system stress per frame as a form

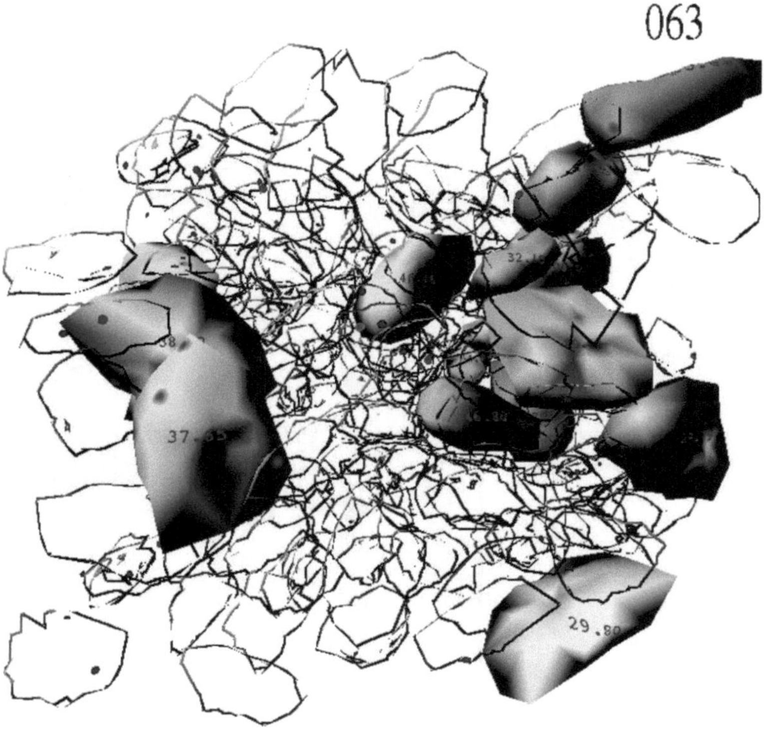

Fig. 13.4 Frame 63 in a simulation of the flow of rocks in a suspension. Lower stress rocks are shown in sketch mode

of slider (Fig. 13.5). The graph is generated in a preprocess using the statistical package [24], and a selection bar is overlaid on top of it. The scientist can drag this selection bar to choose a frame. For example, frames just before a steep drop-off in stress are of particular interest, since they may indicate a time step when the rocks in the aggregate were binding, then one moved to release the pressure. Other interactions with the GUI in Fig. 13.5 enable toggling features of the visualization: closest point spots, stress colors, stress values, and solid/sketchy style transition value.

The sparse visualization of Fig. 13.4 makes it much easier to see and understand the per rock digital stress measurements. The measurement value of total rock stress is centered on the face of the rock closest to the viewer, so as the system is rotated and manipulated, whether on the desktop or in the immersive visualization environment, the text always remains at the correct orientation. Some interactive rotation is generally necessary to see the values on hidden rocks, but with many fewer rocks displayed as solid photo-realistic entities, it is straightforward to find a suitable view to read the data from each rock.

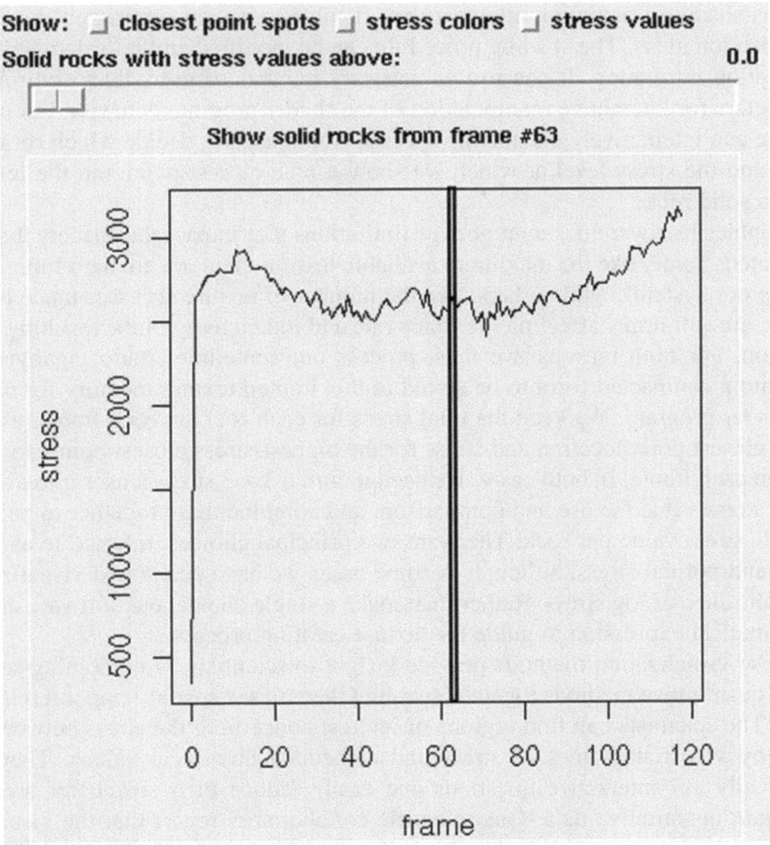

Fig. 13.5 GUI for interactive exploration of the visualization

13.3.2.4 Shading-Based Visualization Environment

This set of visualizations is created with a procedural-shading based add-on to our visualization environment [5, 12, 20]. A shader is a short procedure which determines the color (i.e. shading) and opacity of each point on a surface. Our shaders are written in the OpenGL Shading Language [26] and run in the graphics hardware at each pixel on each rock. This procedure determines the color and opacity of that pixel, referring to the current rock and frame number, position of the pixel on the rock, and data packed into a couple of floating point texture values. This procedure is responsible for creating the sketchy appearance for less important rocks, the stress color scale for solid rocks, placing the spots on the rock surface, and writing the numeric values on each rock.

This shading framework allows a very flexible means to experiment with new visualization ideas. The shading procedure can be modified and reloaded while the application is running. It can use an arbitrary number of user-slider controllable parameters for interactive manipulation of the shader program behavior. For example, we can interactively change the specific frame used to decide which rocks are solid, and the stress level at which we show a blue closest point and the level to show a solid rock.

Graphics hardware has a number of limitations that impact the shaders that can be created. Some, like the maximum available texture memory, are hard limits (512 MB on our system), while others, like the number of texture accesses made by the shader, are soft limits affecting the frame rate and interactivity of the resulting visualization. For both reasons, we must process our sometimes multi-gigabyte raw data into a compacted form to be stored in this limited texture memory for use by the shader program. We keep the total stress for each rock on each frame, as well as the closest point location and stress for the highest-stress closest points for each rock on each frame. In both cases, we need to turn a 3×3 stress tensor into a single scalar stress value for use and comparison, and combine these together to produce a single stress value per rock. There are two principal choices, referred to as shear stress and normal stress, although in some cases we have performed visualization using distance or log stress. Rather than make a single choice, our software takes a mathematical expression to guide the texture creation process.

These visualization methods provide insight to scientists by combining several of our quantitative methods together enabling them to see spatial-temporal relationships. The scientists can find regions of interest concerning the stress between the rocks by visualizing lines of stress and embedded numerical values. They can graphically ask interactive questions and easily reduce their search for areas of important quantitative data. Our scientific collaborators report that the visualizations enable them to validate the physical correctness of the simulation, to detect problems, and to tune parameters of the model. The quantitative displays and interactions also enable the researchers to find and to focus on locations and periods of rapid change in stress.

13.3.3 Cement Hydration

Scientists can also use the 3D visualization environment to test the accuracy of their experimental methods, whether they are using computational or laboratory bench methods. This is an example of an application in which visualization was useful for debugging a complex numerical model. Both physical and graphical measurement tools can be used to understand the model and collect valuable numerical results.

As a basic construction material, it is important to understand the complex properties of cement. Providing strength and structure to a large part of the man-made world, concrete has a complex mechanism for phase changes and development over time once it is poured. Models that can successfully predict the flow, hardening, and strength of concrete are currently being created. The Inorganic Materials Group within BFRL/NIST has new computational models for cement hydration that track both solvent and solute components whose concentrations vary over many orders of magnitude. Because the new software models equations of change that are extremely complex, it is important to have detailed visual output, both to test the accuracy of the models and to be able to understand the relative magnitudes of the various components across the volume of the system being studied. Precise quantitative visual information is required.

To provide this kind of quantitative visualization, we can create a variety of different visual modes of output within a given visualization environment. A high concentration species within a given volume can be visualized by tracking a surface created from points at which the concentration of that component is at a designated isovalue. Components whose volume fractions change with time can be tracked by watching the decay or growth of a particular isosurface. Gradients of concentrations can be viewed by watching a series of semi-transparent isosurfaces, each representing a different isovalue of the component of interest. Time sequences of these isosurfaces provide clear visible information about the accuracy of the equations in the computations that produce the surfaces. We have developed an adaptive isosurface approach that reveals more features by changing the isosurface values over time based on characteristics of the data set. Low concentration ionic species can be tracked by looking at individual slices across the volume and watching the changes in isolines of the concentration of that ion. The scientist can zoom into a particular region of interest, for example, a seed point for the growth of a new species in the system, and carefully step through and watch the generation of that species.

To provide more quantitative information, we provide a quantitative measurement tool, with which the scientist can interactively select particular regions of interest and query the precise concentrations of components in that region. 2D plots can be brought up in the visualization environment to show the volume fractions of each species at a particular point in space and time during the time analysis. In Fig. 13.6, we see a 3D display of isosurfaces of the various components in the modeled system together with graphs depicting the volume fraction of each component and the values used for the adaptive isosurface display.

The system allows for flexibility in choosing exactly which components and in which sub-volume the scientist would like to generate quantitative information. Testing the accuracy of the models and outputting this type of quantitative information are essential to the understanding of cement hydration. Because of the complexity of the system, quantitative visualization provides a creative way to obtain more information from the output of this model than purely qualitative methods. The ability of scientist to visually query locations of interest within the data and graphically examine those regions helps to narrow the search for important information.

Researchers have reported that these methods provide insight into cement paste microstructure, particularly the 3D spatial relationships among the cementitious compounds. This enables the scientists to: validate the computational algorithms; to gain insight into the chemical relationships among phases (common reactants,

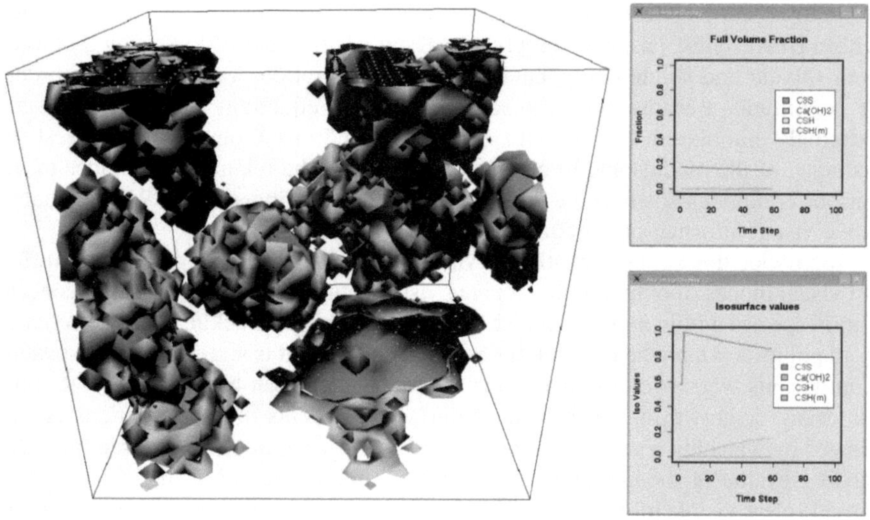

Fig. 13.6 Visualization of the cement hydration model with quantitative displays (*See Color Plates*)

nucleating agents, etc.) based on the spatial proximity that these phases have with each other; and to interpret macroscopic properties of cement in terms of changes in the three-dimensional microstructure. Future work could include the integration of interactive quantitative local chemical analysis, virtual microcalorimetry, the measurement of the thickness of cementitious compounds, and other numeric methods in the virtual environment.

13.4 Summary

Most visualizations excel at presenting a qualitative view of complex data, allowing scientists to quickly make overall judgments and locate interesting features in their data. The focus at NIST on measurement science has led us to introduce quantitative measurement tools into our visualizations. In this chapter, we present a classification of these tools into *Quantitative Measurement*, *Quantitative Output*, and *Quantitative Input*. Quantitative measurement tools allow direct in-visualization measurement of derived quantities such as lengths, volumes, etc. Quantitative output tools analyze the visualized data and present concrete values or graphs alongside the visualization or embedded in it. Quantitative input tools use direct, physically meaningful values or graphs as input to the visualization. These quantitative visualization tools can be used alone or together to enhance traditional qualitative visualizations. Through measurement, visualization can become a more effective instrument for quantitative science.

This chapter also presents three case studies demonstrating the use of quantitative visualizations in collaboration with domain scientists. We present quantitative input and several forms of quantitative measurement for analyzing X-ray microcomputed tomography data of a tissue engineering scaffold. We show quantitative output and several types of quantitative input for flow of particles in suspension. Finally, we present quantitative output and quantitative measurement within a cement hydration simulation. These case studies have shown how the integration of these quantitative methods can direct scientist(s) to otherwise unknown features of interest and then provide tools to single out and analyze those features. These tools allow scientists to view large amounts of numerical data from computational simulations and see subtle problems with the numerical calculations when resulting output has inconsistent features. They also provide data mining information on large data sets, assessing statistically important features in the data.

Future work includes the implementation of additional quantitative interactive measurement and display tools, the application of these methods to non-spatial data [6], and development of methods for analysis and display of uncertainties in the input data and in our interactive measurements. We note that laboratory measurements on physical objects always have an uncertainty associated with them. We will be applying this same standard to measurements and analyses of virtual objects.

Disclaimer Certain commercial equipment, instruments, or materials are identified in this paper to foster understanding. Such identification does not imply recommendation or endorsement by the National Institute of Standards and Technology, nor does it imply that the materials or equipment identified are necessarily the best available for the purpose.

Acknowledgment The Flow of Suspensions computations were performed under Award SMD-05-A-0129, "Modeling the Rheological Properties of Suspensions: Application to Cement Based Materials," for NASA's National Leadership Computing System initiative on the "Columbia" supercomputer at the NASA Ames Research Center.

References

1. Adobe Software (2007) : http://www.adobe.com.
2. Becker, R. A. and Cleveland, W. S. (1987) Brushing scatterplots. Technometrics, 29(2):127–142.
3. Bethel, E. W., Bastacky, S. J., and Schwartz, K. S. (2002) Interactive stereo electron microscopy enhanced with virtual reality. In: A. J. Woods, J. O. Merritt, S. A. Benton, M. T. Bolas, L. Spector, I. Parmee, and H. G. Beyer (Eds.), *Stereoscopic Displays and Virtual Reality Systems IX*. SPIE, San Jose, CA, pp. 391–400.
4. Brady, R., Pixton, J., Baxter, G., Moran, P., Potter, C. S., Carragher, B., and Belmont, A. (1995) Crumbs: A virtual environment tracking tool for biological imaging. In: *Proceedings of IEEE Symposium on Frontiers in Biomedical Visualization*.
5. Corrie, B. and Mackerras, P. (1993) Data shaders. In: *Proceedings of the 4th Conference on Visualization*. pp. 275-282.

6. Devaney, J., Satterfield, S., Hagedorn, J., Kelso, J., Peskin, A., George, W., Griffin, T., Hung, H., and Kriz, R. (2005) Science at the speed of thought. In: *Ambient Intelligence for Scientific Discovery: Lecture Notes in Artificial Intelligence*, vol. 3345, pp. 1–24.
7. Diepstraten, J., Weiskopf, D. and Ertl, T. (2002) Transparency in interactive technical illustrations. Computer Graphics Forum 21(3):317–325.
8. Feiner, S. K. and Seligmann, D. D. (1992) Cutaways and ghosting: Satisfying visibility constraints in dynamic 3D illustrations. The Visual Computer, 8(5–6):292–302.
9. Flider, M. J. and Bailey, B. P. (2004) An evaluation of techniques for controlling focus + context ccreens. In: *Proceedings of Graphics Interface 2004*. pp. 135-144.
10. Hagedorn, J., Dunkers, J., Peskin, A., Kelso, J., Henderson, L., and Terrill, J. (2006) Quantitative, interactive measurement of tissue engineering scaffold structure in an immersive visualization environment. Biomaterials Forum, 28(4):6–9.
11. Hagedorn, J., Dunkers, J., Satterfield, S., Peskin, A., Kelso, J., and Terrill, J. (2007) Measurement tools for the immersive visualization environment. Journal of Research of the National Institute of Standards and Technology, 112(5):257–270.
12. Hanrahan, P. and Lawson, J. (1990) A language for shading and lighting calculations. In: *SIGGRAPH '90: Proceedings of the 17th Annual Conference on Computer Graphics and Interactive Techniques*. ACM Press, New York, pp. 289–298.
13. Hastreiter, P., Rezk-Salama, Ch., Tomandl, B., Eberhardt, K. E. W., and Ertl, T. (1998) Fast analysis of intracranial aneurysms based on interactive direct volume rendering and CTA. In: W. M. Wells, A. Colchester, and S. Delp (Eds.), *Medical Image Computing and Computer-Assisted Interventation – MICCAI'98*. Springer, Berlin, pp. 660–668.
14. Jayaraman, S. and North, C. (2002) A radial focus + context visualization for multi-dimensional functions. In: *Proceedings of the Conference on Visualization '02 IEEE*, Washington, DC, pp. 443–450.
15. Kim, M., Milgram, P., and Drake, J. (1997) Virtual tape measure for 3D measurements in micro-surgery. In: *Engineering in Medicine and Biology Society, Proceedings of the 19th Annual International Conference of the IEEE*, pp. 967–969.
16. Leung, Y. K. and Apperley, M. D. (1994) A review and taxonomy of distortion-oriented presentation techniques. ACM Transactions on Computer-Human Interaction (TOCHI), 1(2):126–160.
17. Markosian, L., Kowalski, M. A., Goldstein, D., Trychin, S. J., Hughes, J. F. and Bourdev, L. D. (1997) In: *Proceedings of the 24th Annual Conference on Computer Graphics and Interactive Techniques*. ACM Press, New York, pp. 415–420.
18. Martys, N., George, W. and Lootens, D. (2007) Spatial-temporal correlations in startup-up flows of colloidal suspensions. *In preparation.*
19. Mercury Computer Systems (2007): http://www.tgs.com.
20. Perlin, K. (1985) An image synthesizer. In: *Proceedings of the 12th Annual Conference on Computer Graphics and Interactive Techniques*. ACM Press, New York, pp. 287–296.
21. Pfitzner, D., Hobbs, V. and Powers, D. (2003) A unified taxonomic framework for information visualization. In: *Proceedings of the Asia-Pacific Symposium on Information Visualisation*. Australian Computer Society, Adelaide, Australia, pp. 57–66.
22. Preim, B. and Bartz, D. (2007) *Visualization in Medicine*. Morgan Kaufmann, Burlington, MA.
23. Preim, B., Tietjen, C., Spindler, W., and Peitgen, H.-O. (2002) Integration of measurement tools in medical 3D visualizations. In: *IEEE Visualization*, pp. 21–28.
24. R Package for Statistical Computing (2007): http://www.r-project.org.
25. Reitinger, B., Schmalstieg, D., Bornik, A., and Beichel, R. (2006) Spatial analysis tools for virtual reality-based surgical planning. In: *Proceedings of the 2006 IEEE Symposium on 3D User Interfaces*. pp. 37–44.
26. Rost, R. J. (2005) *OpenGL(R) Shading Language, 2nd Edition*. Addison-Wesley Professional, Boston, MA.

Chapter 14
Interactive Spatiotemporal Reasoning

Yang Cai, Richard Stumpf, Michelle Tomlinson, Timothy Wynne, Sai Ho Chung, and Xavier Boutonnier

Abstract Spatiotemporal reasoning involves pattern recognition in space and time. It is a complex process that has been dominated by manual analytics. In this chapter, we explore the new method that combines computer vision, multi-physics simulation and human-computer interaction. The objective is to bridge the gap among the three with visual transformation algorithms for mapping the data from an abstract space to an intuitive one, which includes shape correlation, periodicity, cellular shape dynamics, and spatial Bayesian machine learning. We tested this approach with the case studies of tracking and predicting oceanographic objects. In testing with 2,384 satellite image samples from SeaWiFS, we found that the interactive visualization increases robustness in object tracking and positive detection accuracy in object prediction. We also found that the interactive method enables the user to process the image data at less than 1 min per image versus 30 min per image manually. As a result, our test system can handle at least ten times more data sets than traditional manual analysis. The results also suggest that minimal human interactions with appropriate computational transformations or cues may significantly increase the overall productivity.

Keywords Pattern recognition, Image processing, Data mining.

14.1 Introduction

For centuries, scientists have been using shape-based spatiotemporal reasoning to study natural phenomena. There is ample evidence that the interactive visual reasoning methods play a central role in the formation of major theories. For example, in 1596, the Dutch mapmaker Abraham Ortelius discovered the remarkable fit of the contours of South American and African continents. Making an analogy with the motion of floating ice, he suggested that the Americas were torn away from Europe and Africa. In parallel, engineers and technologists have also widely used spatiotemporal reasoning in creating technological artifacts. For example, Nicola Tesla claimed that the first alternating current motor he built ran perfectly because he had visualized and *run* models in his mind before building the prototype [7, 8].

E. Zudilova-Seinstra et al. (eds.) *Trends in Interactive Visualization*,
doi:10.1007/978-1-84800-269-2_14

Spatiotemporal reasoning involves pattern recognition in terms of space and time. It is a complex process that has been dominated by manual analytics, in which the analyst *conceives* and *interacts* with objects in the non-verbal thoughts, so-called "*the mind's eye.*" We not only see things, but also construct them and interact with them. To build an interactive visualization system, we have to understand how humans and computers perform visual reasoning in space and time, and combine them in a coherent way.

Human vision system is well-developed to detect, track and predict the motions of animals. Our nerve system is fine-tuned to observe patterns, anomalies and differences. For example, scientists use sea color images to monitor harmful algal blooms and river plumes. Criminologists use geological profiles to catch serial killers [17]. Coastguards monitor vessels at sea and alert any anomalous routes. Oncologists classify cancer tumors based on the motion patterns of in vitro cells. Unfortunately, this visual processing is tedious, time-consuming and not reliable. For example, visually detecting and tracking chlorophyll anomaly objects from satellite images takes 30 min per frame. As a result, only a fraction of available collected images can be analyzed. The bottleneck becomes significant as the information flow increases. On the other hand, automated feature extraction and tracking algorithms [3, 4] can speed up the process. However, they are not always robust, especially in complex or unseen situations.

Interaction is necessary to narrow the gap (see Fig. 14.1). Many ill-structured discovery problems can be solved by human-computer interaction, for example, the interactive data mining system that helps users gain insight from the dynamically created virtual data space [16], the interactive visualization environment for data discovery within continuous, time-varying data streams [5, 23], and the game-based interactive scientific visualization system for biological education.

Interaction is not just simple communication. It involves abstraction. One compelling example of the interactive visual system is the ability to recover object information from the interactive sparse input. For example, we humans are well-trained to recognize biological motion. Human infants as young as 3 months of age can perceive biological motion [9]. In Johansson's experiment, the activity and

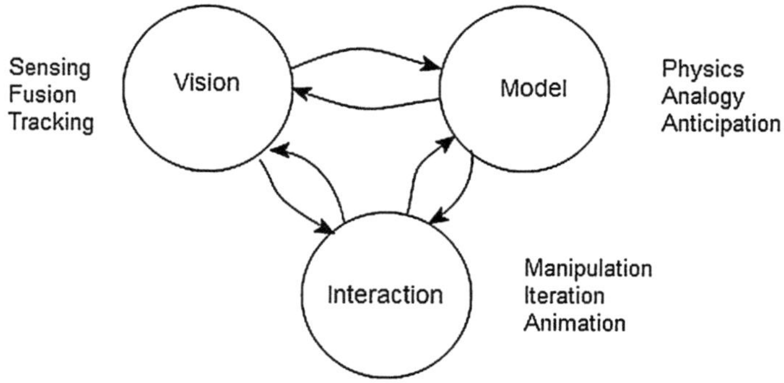

Fig. 4.1 Shape-based spatiotemporal reasoning, where computer vision and physical models enable a human-computer problem solving environment

identity of an animate creature are created using just a dozen light points placed on the individual's body [12]. When viewing point-light displays, observers can identify the emotional state of the subject [2]. Understanding how people interact with three-dimensional objects in everyday work and life can eventually help us design more effective discovery. Hubona and Shirah investigated how various spatial depth cues, such as motion, stereoscopic vision, shadows, and scene background, are utilized to promote the perceptual discovery and interpretation of the presented imagery in three-dimensional scientific visualization [11].

The mind's eye is guided by mental models that are mainly commonsense. In early days, the modeling was done by *Gedanken* Experiments (http://en.wikipedia.org/wiki/Thought_experiment, captured on January 3, 2008) or analogy. Today, the qualitative physical knowledge can be simulated on a computer. For example, deformable finite meshed templates are used to model faces [20]. Particle filters [27] are used to describe the spatiotemporal feature distributions as particle dynamics. Field theories have been developed to represent cognition dynamics with physical analogy. For example, Leyton's shape process theory [15] reveals the rules for recovering original shapes based on symmetry and other properties. Lewin [14] uses metaphors from well-known systems (e.g. physics), in order to understand and explain a rather unknown system (e.g. psychology). In explaining phenomena around the concept of behavior, Lewin uses the metaphor of a "force field," such as psychological tension, psychological force, and fluidity.

Studies of Cellular Automata (CA) suggest the possibility of modeling artificial life forms [10, 22], biological motion [24–26], and urban dynamics [6]. Furthermore, CA has been employed in simulating and verifying various types of physical interactions, such as the expansion patterns of different lattice gases, surface tension of liquids, and diffusion-limited aggregation [1]. Although CA's rules are simple and local, they can simulate complex spatiotemporal interactions that are challenging to other computational methods.

14.2 Spatiotemporal Tracking and Prediction Problems

The goal of this study is to develop a computational framework that incorporates computer vision, multi-physics simulation, and human-computer interaction for the shape-based spatiotemporal reasoning.

Combining vision with modeling and interaction enables us to automate the data pre-preprocessing and increase accuracy in the overall spatiotemporal reasoning process. In contrast to the conventional data mining algorithm that is normally context-free and independent from the physical constraints, this study introduces a visual multi-physics model to simulate the physical, biological, and chemical phenomena. This provides a mechanism to explore the "deep knowledge" about spatiotemporal patterns while the accurate computational models are unavailable or impractical. For example, the current data assimilation for weather models takes

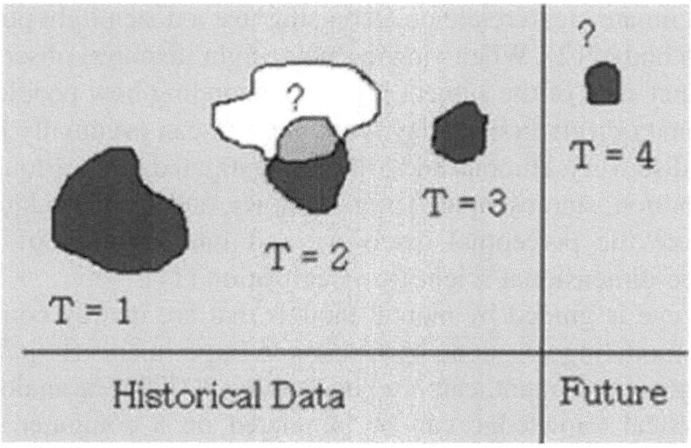

Fig. 14.2 The spatiotemporal object tracking and prediction problems

several hours, preventing real-time weather forecasting. Machine learning has been a key feature in many data mining algorithms.

In this study, we extend learning algorithms to spatial and temporal space and integrate the two with vision and simulation models. As learning models can be data mining tools alone, they also support vision and simulation models for calibration or optimization of parameters. Moreover, human-computer interaction and scientific visualization methods are introduced as comprehensive interface that increases the robustness of the process.

Assume a deformable object that can move and split into pieces, we aim to develop computational algorithms for tracking and predicting the movement of the object from images and sensory data. For the tracking problems, given an object in an image sequence ($t = 1, \ldots, n$), we try to find the object at $t = n + 1$ and beyond. For the prediction problems, given databases of historical data and current physical and biochemical conditions, we try to predict the occurrence of the object of interest at a particular time and location. Figure 14.2 illustrates a generalized spatiotemporal data mining problem.

To validate the methods developed in this study, we conducted case studies with the real world databases: tracking and prediction of harmful algal blooms in the Gulf of Mexico, based on the satellite images from SeaWiFS and NOAA and the in-situ data from NOAA.

14.3 Shape Correlation

Given a selected object in a very large imagery database, tracking the movement of the object over time with multiple sensors is a challenging task for both humans and computers. For example, it takes about 30 min for scientists to analyze one frame of the multi-spectrum satellite image. On the other hand, computer vision-based tracking is faster, though not very reliable in many cases.

The goal of interactive tracking is to combine machine vision with human-computer interaction so that the computer takes care of most of the time-consuming iterative tasks and humans contribute minimal initiation and evaluation processes.

The interaction protocol is developed for human-computer interaction during the tracking task. In the protocol, the user identifies the tracking target. The computer takes over the tracking frame by frame and superimposes the tracking results on top of the original images. At a certain point, the computer stops the tracking and sends the signal to the user for more information. After the re-initiation, the computer moves on until the next break point. The key element in this protocol is the context-awareness algorithm. In this study, we use the Correlation Filter [13] to measure the similarity of the object in the current frame and the object in the previous frame. The correlation filter is built by using Fast Fourier Transform and Correlation Theorem:

$$C = IFFT(FFT(a) * conj(FFT(b))) \tag{14.1}$$

where a is the test image while b is the reference object in the previous image to be tracked. $X = FFT(x)$ and $x = IFFT(X)$ represent Discrete Fast Fourier Transform and Inverse Discrete Fast Fourier Transform respectively.

$$X(k) = \sum_{j=1}^{N} x(j)\omega_N^{(j-1)(k-1)} \tag{14.2}$$

$$x(j) = \sum_{j=1}^{N} X(k)\omega_N^{-(j-1)(k-1)} \tag{14.3}$$

where $\omega_N = e^{(-2\pi i)fN}$, N denotes the length of the vector and symbol. The symbol * denotes array multiplication and *conj* returns the complex conjugate of the argument. The pixel that gives the highest correlation value has the highest confidence that the reference object is at that pixel location. The correlation filter alone cannot reliably track the object over a long period of time because it faces a dilemma when the object breaks into pieces. The computer would select one of the pieces and track it. The scenario, therefore, is not what we want for object tracking due to lack of control of the process. Figure 14.3 shows the scenario in which the object breaks into two pieces and the computer is attracted to the small piece at the fourth frame.

With the interaction protocol, the user initiates the object tracking by clicking on the target shape. The Correlation Filter is used to indicate the change of the similarity of the objects between images. If there is a large difference in the values given by the Correlation Filter between two consecutive images, we can conclude that the objects have changed significantly during this time period. The computer would stop and wait for user's input.

In our object tracking experiment for a series of 79 images from SeaWiFS chlorophyll anomaly channel, when the object breaks into more than one piece, the user can select more than one object and multiple targets to be tracking targets. See the results in Table 14.1, Figs. 14.4 and 14.5. In frame 48, the correlation dropped by more than 50% from the previous frame. Originally, the algorithm would stop at this point because it would not be able to identify the object being tracked. However, instead of terminating the tracking, the computer prompts the user to select a particular object in the new image so that the tracking can continue.

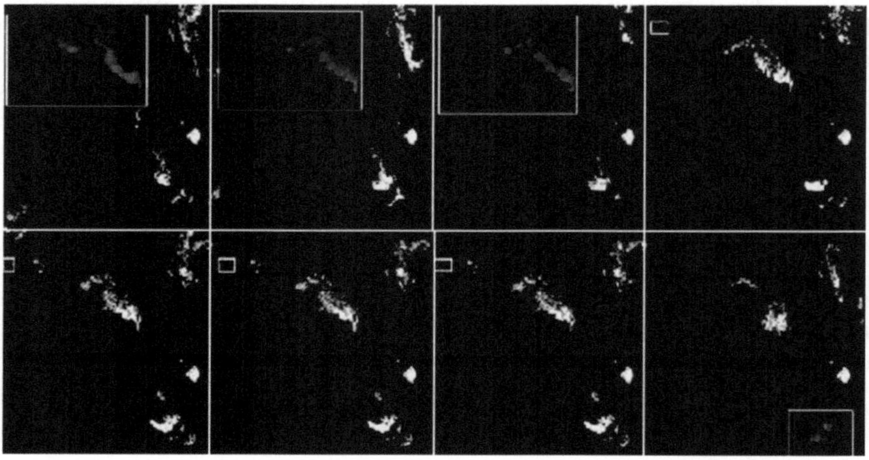

Fig. 14.3 Automatic tracking of a target which has split into two pieces (*See Color Plates*)

Table 14.1 Automated versus interaction (79 image samples from SeaWiFS and NOAA)

Case	Automatic	Interactive
Acceptance % for the coherent target	73/79 = 92%	73/79 = 92%
Acceptance % for the target split into two pieces	48/79 = 60%	71/79 = 90%

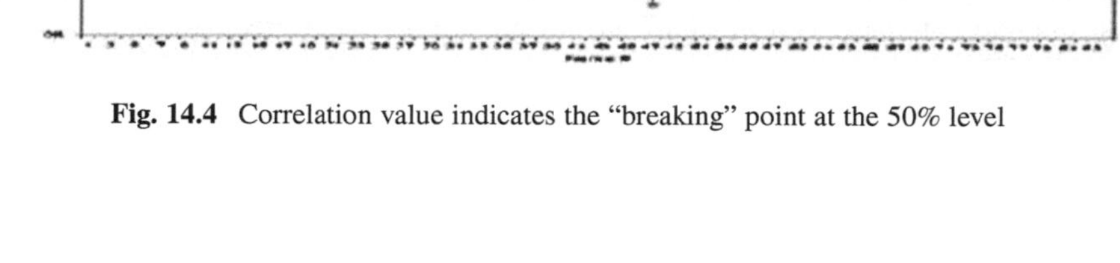

Fig. 14.4 Correlation value indicates the "breaking" point at the 50% level

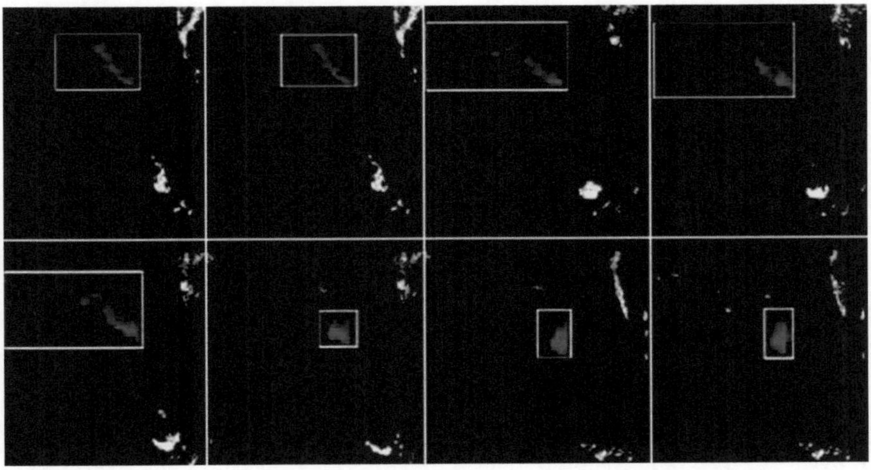

Fig. 14.5 Interactive tracking results: the computer tracks the object and the user makes decision at the "breaking point," notified by the computer (*See Color Plates*)

14.4 Spatial Periodicity

Although humans are capable of identifying spatial temporal and patterns, such as the repetitions in textures and the rhythms in music, human perceptions often miss the hidden patterns if the data set is complex. Computational transforms are needed for semi-automatically identifying underlying patterns. Perhaps the best known is the Fourier Transform, which attempts to explain a data set as a weighted sum of sinusoidal basis elements. However, none of the available methods directly search for periodicities, repetitions, or regularities in the data. Sethares builds on a classical technique, called the Buys-Ballot table, for the determination of hidden periodicities, the Periodicity Transform [18,19]. In his method, the algorithm searches for the best periodic characterization of the length N signal x. The underlying technique is to project x onto a periodic subspace.

In this study, we expand the one-dimensional Periodicity Transform into the two-dimensional space of the cellular automata. We construct spatial and temporal windows to allow the user to select the region of interest (in the red box of longitude and latitude coordinates) on a particular time frame. The algorithm starts by cropping the data within the ROI (Region of Interest) box and sorting the data by time. Then it takes the Fast Fourier Transform (FFT) and extracts the highest value. For each point, we take the average value of the corresponding time. We then simply reprocess the remaining signals.

The outputs include the detected periods and their energy. This method enables the user to interact with spatial periodicity transform in an interactive mode, which is very important to many applications such as oceanographic studies. From the Fourier Transform, we select the frequency of the component with the highest energy. Then we turn this frequency (f) into a period (p) with the formula:

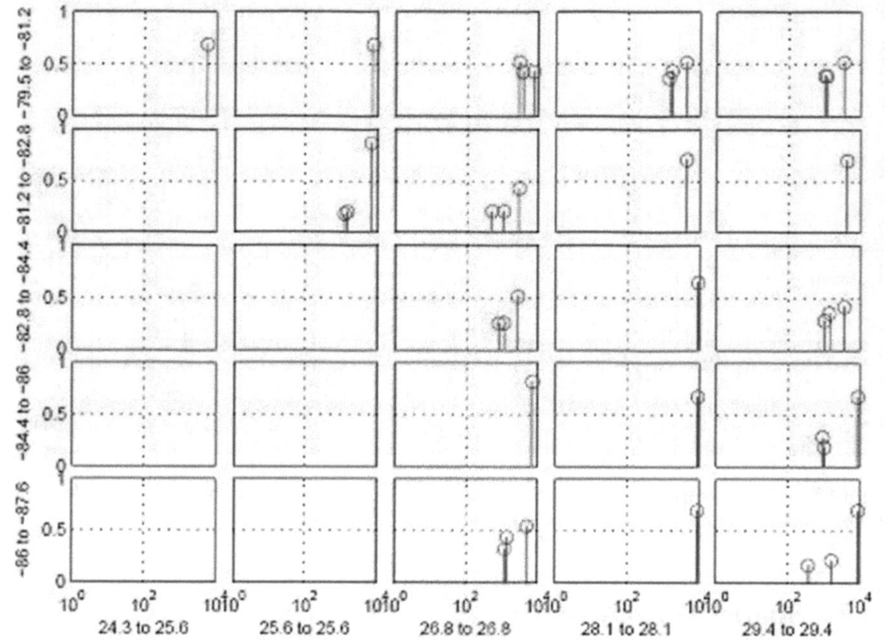

Fig. 14.6 Spatial based Frequency Analysis

$$p = \frac{1}{f} \quad \text{for all points } x_i \tag{14.4}$$

The equation of the power (energy) is the following:

$$Power = \| x \|^2 = \frac{1}{p^2} \sum_{i=0}^{p^2-1} x(i)^2 \tag{14.5}$$

There are many ways to render the spatial periodicities. First, we use the two-dimensional rendering to tile the individual period spectrum diagram into a two-dimensional matrix. Each cell has its periodicities along with their powers. This matrix is called cellular periodigram and is represented in Fig. 14.6. The advantage of this method is its all-in-one solution. However, its scalability is limited by the number of cells per screen.

Second, we use two-dimensional colored cells to represent the power (energy) for a particular period component, e.g., 365.25 days. In this case, a user needs to select the period component as an input. Figure 14.7 illustrates an example of the two-dimensional power ratios in a database of *Karenia Brevis* cell counts in the Gulf of Mexico for 40 years. The brighter the cell, the higher the power ratio, which means that the probability of finding the target every year at the same time is higher. Due to the heterogeneity of the data set, pre-processing is necessary. Pre-processing consists of computing a space mean of the number of cells and the estimation of

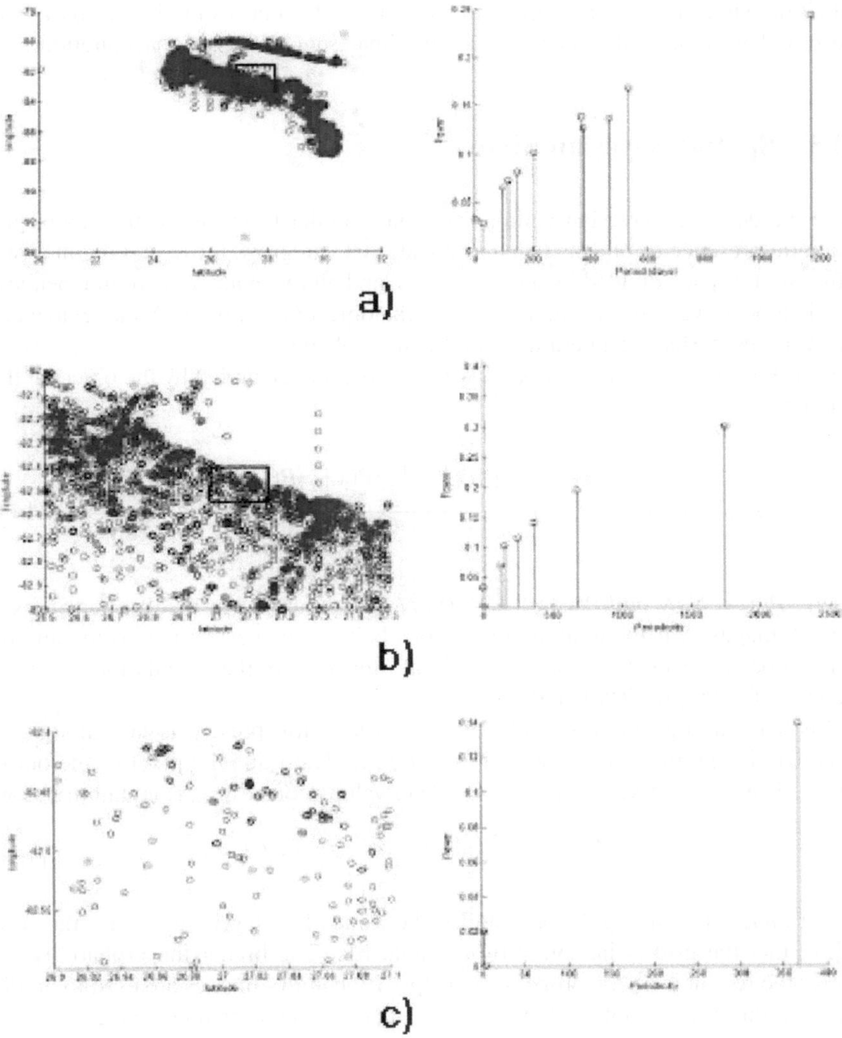

Fig. 14.7 Zooming windows for the interactive visualization of the periodicity: all samples with narrow time window and the periodicity detection (a), median window (ROI) selection and the periodicity detection (b), and small window (ROI) selection and the periodicity detection (c)

missing data spots where we do not have measurements. Based on the periodicity transform and human-computer interaction, we can see on Fig. 14.7c that for each set of data, we have a one-year period component.

We assign an interactive window for two-dimensional data points. In the right window, we display the associated results of the periodicity transform, where the x-coordinate is the period and the y-coordinate is the power ratio of the component. Figures 14.7a through 14.7c are examples of the interactive visualization results. The data is drawn from 40 years of the *Karena Brevis* cell counts from Florida coast. Each piece of data contains the geographical coordinates and levels of concentration.

14.5 Spatial Bayesian Model

Here we define a Bayesian cellular automata model to represent the spatial and temporal presence of objects (such as algae) that can grow, move and die in a two-dimensional space divided by a grid of cells, and all the evidences are independent. In this model, we consider the location of the object $(x; y)$, time (t), and evidence e (such as the surface temperature), and historical images, in which c denotes the presence of the object. The probability of the location occupied by the object at that time is:

$$P(c|x,y,t,e_1,e_2\ldots,e_k)=\frac{P(c)P(x|c)P(y|c)P(t|c)\prod_{i=1}^{k}P(e_i|c)}{P(x,y,t,e_1,e_2,\ldots e_k)} \tag{14.6}$$

where, $P(c) = N_c/N$ and $P(x \mid c) = N_{xc}/N$. N_c is the number of pixel occurrences of c in all images, N is the total number of pixels in all images, and N_{xc} is the number of pixel occurrences of c at location x in all images. Similar calculations to $P(x|c)$ are made for $P(y|c)$, $P(t|c)$, and $P(e|c)$.

Just calculating the probability of the artificial life present is not enough. To visualize this prediction, we need a threshold to determine the pixel of the output image. The output pixel $O(x|y)$ is a Boolean value decided by the equation below:

$$O(x,y)=P(c|x,t,e_1,e_2,\ldots e_k)\geq\alpha \tag{14.7}$$

For images outputting the probability, the value of each grid represents the probability that the grid is inhabited by artificial life. The higher the probability, the darker the region is on the probability image. Probability images are used to predict the location of life given the location, time, and any additional evidence.

We now investigate the interactive spatiotemporal reasoning methods in the context of our real-world scientific research projects in oceanographic studies. The team tested the system with the field data of cell counts from the Gulf of Mexico area and SeaWiFS satellite images from NASA. To evaluate the results quantitatively, a few measurements are defined, e.g. positive accuracy, which describes the percentage of predictions which were correct when Harmful Algal Bloom cell count, is greater than or equal to 5,000 (cell/liter). The measurements in Tables 14.2 and 14.3 are defined as following:

- Positive accuracy is the percent of the cases in which target is present and the model predicted correctly.
- Positive accuracy = confirmed positive/(confirmed positive + false negative).

Table 14.2 Interactive prediction results (2,384 satellite image samples)

Method	False positive	Combined positive	False negative	Combined negative	Sum	Positive detection (%)	Positive accuracy (%)	Negative accuracy (%)
Image only	44	17	6	306	373	86.60	73.91	87.43
SB[a] w/o SDT[b]	161	423	142	1658	2384	87.29	74.87	91.15
SB w/SDT	176	445	120	1643	2384	87.74	78.76	90.32
SBw/SDT&Int[c]	166	441	124	1653	2384	87.84	78.05	90.87
SBw/SDT&Or[d]	173	445	120	1646	2384	87.71	78.76	90.49

[a] Spatial Bayesian model
[b] Sparse data treatment
[c] Interpolated images
[d] Original images

Table 14.3 Manual-only results (188 satellite image samples)

Method	False positive	Combined positive	False negative	Combined negative	Sum	Positive detection	Positive accuracy	Negative accuracy
Results	5	36	23	124	188	85.1%	61.2%	96.12%

- Positive detection is the percent of all predictions that are correct.
- Positive detection = (confirmed positive + confirmed negative)/(sum).

We have 5,000 SeaWiFS satellite images, in which 2,616 images are used for training data and 2,384 images are used for testing. From Tables 14.1 and 14.2, we can see that the interactive method's positive detection rate and positive accuracy are higher than manual method. However, the negative accuracy is lower than manual one. Comparing the number of samples in each method, the interactive method is capable to process ten times more samples than the manual method but in shorter time.

14.6 Cellular Shape Models

Conventional data mining models do not involve physical parameters. On the other hand, traditional physical models only deal with particular phenomena with required calibration processes. In this study, we try to merge the two with a simple multi-physics model and an interaction process that overlays the results from the simulated model on top of the collected data.

We build the simulation model for predicting the spatiotemporal dynamics of shape. Given the results obtained from the previous sections, we can create scenarios of object movements by modeling the shape dynamics with diffusion, growth, shrink, transport and collision. The growth diffusion function changes the object shape by a predefined structuring element. The dilation or erosion morphology is based on the assumption of a glass-like surface where no friction exists. They can only deform the outline of a shape *uniformly* based on the population. It does not reflect the intrinsic, external non-linear, or random factors that contribute to the shape process. In order to simulate the non-uniform shape growth, we use the percolation clustering.

The CA simulation model can then use the predicted output and simulate future shape deformations, collisions, and wind translations using surface current conditions, such as temperature, which would reflect how the shape deforms, grows, and shrinks. The dynamics are detailed by simulating predictions and comparing them to the actual movement of artificial life. The error of simulation compared to actual movements will allow humans to better understand the dynamics of the internal and external factors of artificial life. With better understanding, the CA model can be improved to incorporate more rules regarding artificial life. This cycle can be repeated for the computer and human to learn together. Figure 14.8 shows the concept of the interaction.

Figure 14.9 shows an example of the percolation process started from a given shape [21]. In the real world, it is rarely the case that cells are allowed to grow or

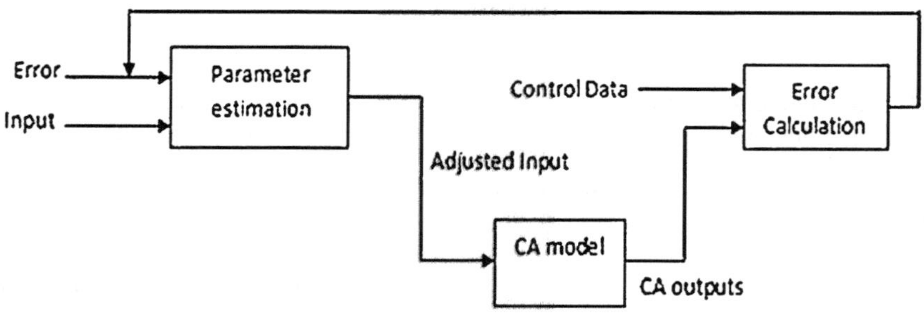

Fig. 14.8 Interactive parameter estimation with CA visualization and manual adjustment

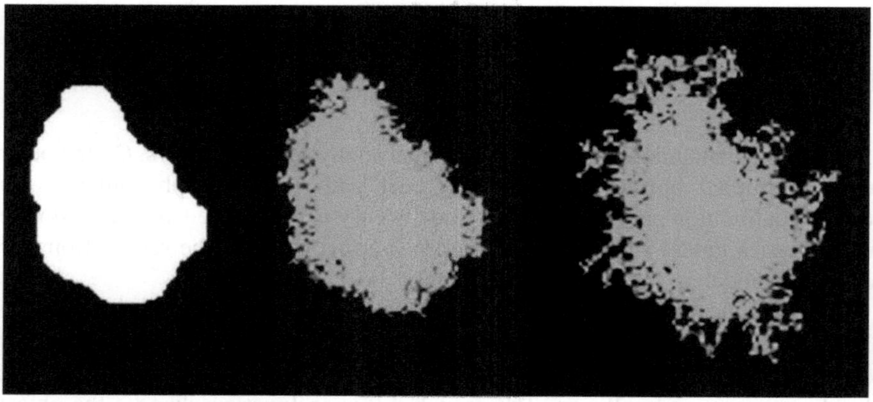

Fig. 14.9 Diffusion with resistance (*See Color Plates*)

move uninhibitedly in an infinite amount of space; rather, their growths and movements are often affected by environmental factors such as winds and currents, and the presence of obstacles. A collision causes deformation. The extent of a deformation depends on the elasticity of an object. A rigid object will stop at the collision contact point and keep the same shape.

We classify objects as rigid, elastic, and flexible. The two extreme cases are straightforward. Rigid objects do not deform after the impact. Flexible objects completely deform along the outline of the collided hard objects. For the case of an elastic object and a rigid object, we use the following rules to model the deformation:

1. *Detect the collision points.*
2. *Move a portion of the collided cells sideways; the ratio is proportional to the elasticity of the object. The bigger the elasticity, the more the cells are moved sideways.*
3. *Continue to deform until the motion stops.*

Figure 14.10 shows simple dynamics of growth and collision of the artificial life, which starts at the left frame with a very small region. Through some internal factors, the life becomes larger. But once the growth hits the wall, the growth spreads

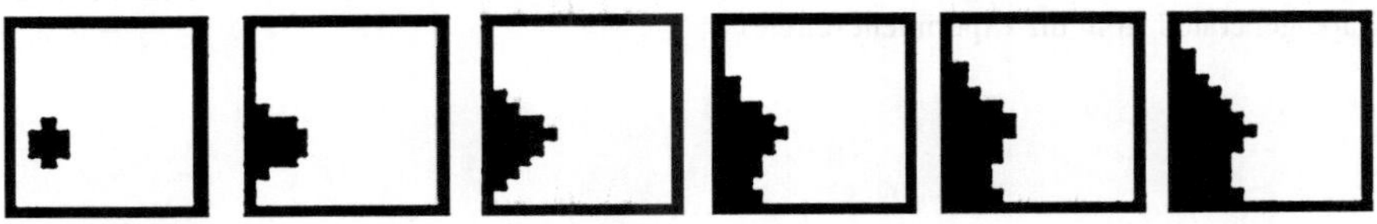

Fig. 14.10 A simulated result of the cellular growth and collision. From left to right, the cells grow and deform at the left border

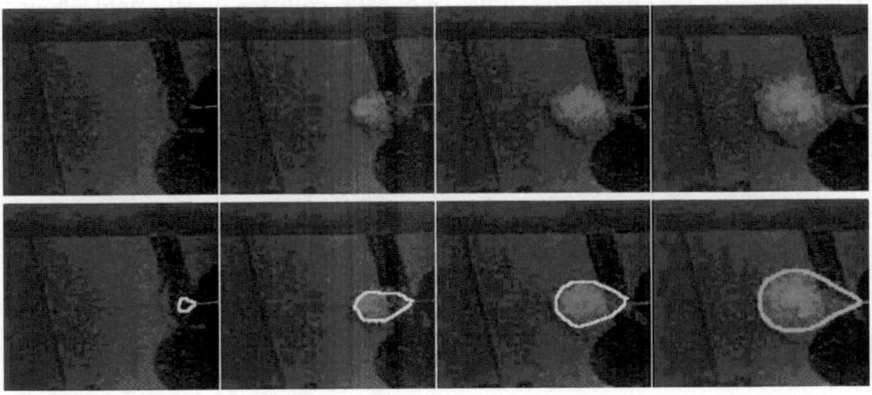

Fig. 14.11 Example of the output and interaction: the first row video is the physical river plume simulation with ink. The second row video is the superimposed results, where the yellow color in the first three images outlines tracked plumes and the green color in the last image indicates the envelop of the predicted shape (*See Color Plates*)

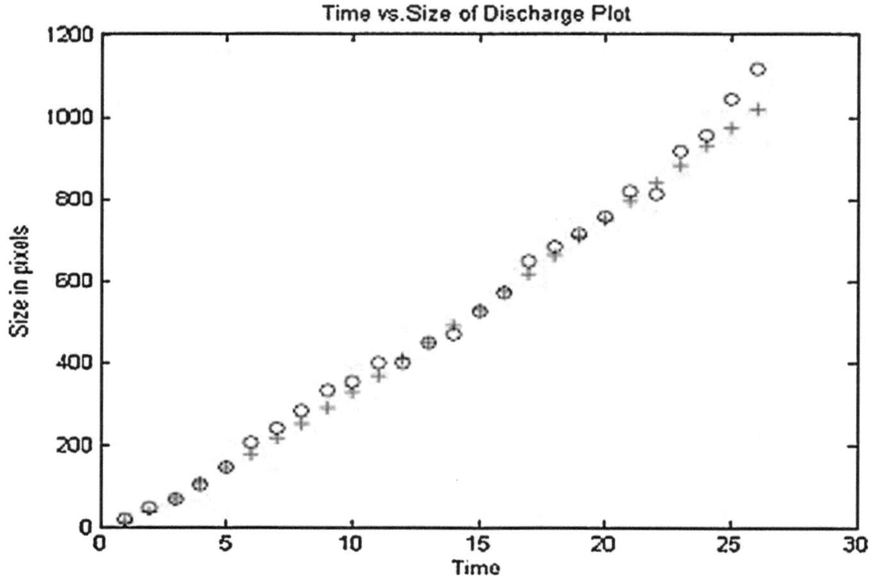

Fig. 14.12 A comparison between the spatiotemporal prediction results (cross) and the actual shape generated from the experiment (circle)

to the side starting from the third frame. The frames above were generated using a Cellular Automata simulation with a relatively low elasticity.

To simulate the dynamics of artificial life, diffusion using Cellular Automata is implemented for the growth and shrinking of cells, collision of cells onto a boundary, and wind translations. The simulation rules are listed in the Appendix.

Figure 14.11 shows an example of the visualization of the river plume tracking and prediction process with the interactive cellular automata. For comparison between the spatiotemporal prediction results and the actual generated shape we refer to Fig. 14.12.

14.7 Summary

The shape-based spatiotemporal reasoning algorithms in this chapter incorporate computer vision, multi-physics simulation, and interaction for solving the spatiotemporal tracking and prediction problems. Embedding computer vision into the conventional data mining algorithms enables us to automate the data pre-processing and increase accuracy in the overall process. In contrast to the conventional data mining or machine learning algorithms, which are normally context-free and independent from the physical constraints, we introduce a visual multiple physics model Cellular Automata to simulate the physical, biological and chemical phenomena. This provides a mechanism to explore the deep knowledge of spatiotemporal reasoning while the accurate computational models are not available or impractical.

In this study, the human-computer interactions are embedded into the shape-based spatiotemporal reasoning process with multi-modal interfaces such as desktop computers and stereo projectors. The interactive visualization is not only a display but also a learning and problem solving process.

We test this approach with the oceanographic data mining from NASA's 8-year SeaWiFS satellite database along with NOAA's 50-year in-situ cell count databases. We find that the interactive visualization increases robustness in object tracking and positive detection accuracy in object prediction.

We find that the interactive method enables the user to process the image data at less than 1 min per image versus 30 min per image manually. As a result, our test system is able to handle significantly more data sets (e.g., 2,384 satellite image samples) than traditional manual analysis (e.g., 188 satellite image samples).

The empirical benchmarks suggest that the visual interactions can improve the data mining quality. However, where, when, and how to engage the visual interaction are key factors in the process. The results also suggest that minimal human interactions with appropriate computational transformations or cues may significantly increase the overall productivity.

Appendix: Cellular Shape Dynamics Simulation Rules

The growth rule is as followed given the growth amount N:

1. Pick an arbitrary cell neighboring the region of life
2. If the sum of neighboring cells 2 and the arbitrary cell is "0" then make the cell "1"
3. Repeat steps 1 and 2 until the desired N has been reached

The shrink rule is as followed given the shrink amount M:

1. Pick an arbitrary cell on the edges of the region of life
2. If the sum of neighboring cells 2 and the arbitrary cell is "1" then make the cell "0"
3. Repeat steps 1 and 2 until the desired N has been reached, or a maximum iteration threshold has been reached.
4. If the threshold is reached, it means the region of life has shrunk to a very condensed region and will not easily reduce in size.

The collision rule is as followed given elasticity E:

1. If any cells cross the boundary, proceed to the next step.
2. Treat the rows and columns outside of the boundary as "1"

3. If the sum of neighboring cells around any cell is "4" then make the cell "1." This phase will add the cells onto the boundary row, or in the case that the region of life has already collided with a boundary, add cells close to the previously collided cells.
4. Repeat this step *E* times since the more elastic the collision, the more the cells will spread.

The wind translation rules are as followed given wind speed *W* and direction:

1. Using a constant for speed of translation with relationship to wind speed.
2. Move the shape at the speed of one iteration at a time in the x and y direction.
3. If there is a collision with a boundary, spread along the boundary, but continue moving.

Acknowledgments This study is supported by NASA ESTO grant AIST-QRS-04-3031 and National Science Foundation grant CT-ER 0716657. The authors appreciate the comments and suggestions from Karen Meo, Kai-Dee Chu, Steven Smith, Gene Carl Feldman and James Acker from NASA. Also, many thanks to Professors Christos Faloulus and William Eddy of Carnegie Mellon University for their input. The authors also thank Brenda Battad for her text editing.

References

1. Bandini, S. and Pavesi, G. (2002) Controlled generation of two-dimensional patterns based on stochastic cellular automata, Future Generation Computer Systems, 18: 973–981
2. Blake, R. (1993) Cats perceive biological motion, Psychol. Sci. 4: 54–57
3. Chen, J., Silver, D. and Liang, J. (2003) The Feature Tree: Visualizing Feature Tracking in Distributed AMR Datasets. In: IEEE Parallel Visualization and Graphics Symposium
4. Correa, C., Silver, D. and Chen, M. (2006) Feature Aligned Volume Manipulation for Illustration and Visualization, IEEE Transactions on Visualization and Computer Graphics (Proceedings Visualization/Information Visualization 2006), 12(5)
5. Cowell, A. J., Havre, S., May, R. and Sanfilippo, A. (2005) Scientific Discovery Within Data Streams, Ambient Intelligence for Scientific Discovery, Vol. 3345, Springer
6. Essam, J. W. (1980) Percolation theory, Rep. Prog. Phys. 43: 833
7. Ferguson, E. S. (1977) The minds eye: Non-verbal thought in technology, Science 197(4306): 827–836
8. Ferguson, E. S. (1992) Engineering and the mind's eye. Cambridge, MA: MIT Press
9. Fox, R. and McDaniel, C. (1982) The perception of biological motion by human infants, Science 218: 486–487
10. Hardy, J. (1976) Molecular dynamics of a classical lattice gas: Transport properties and time correlation functions, Phys. Rev. A 13(5): 1949–1961
11. Hubona, G. S. and Shirah, G. W. (2005) Spatial Cues in 3D Visualization, Ambient Intelligence for Scientific Discovery, Vol. 3345, Springer
12. Johansson, G. (1973) Visual perception of biological motion and a model for its analysis, Percept. Psychophys. 14: 201–211
13. Kumar, B. V. K. V., Mahalanobis, A. and Juday, R. D. (2005) Correlation Pattern Recognition, Cambridge University Press
14. Lewin, K. (1975) Spatial Cues in 3D Visualization, Ambient Intelligence for Scientific Discovery, Greenwood Press, Westport
15. Leyton, M. (1992) Symmetry, Causality, Mind, MIT Press.

16. Pryke, A. and Beale, R. (2005) Interactive Comprehensible Data Mining, Ambient Intelligence for Scientific Discovery, Vol. 3345, Springer
17. Rossmo, D. K. (1999) Geographical Profiling, CRC Press
18. Sethares, W. A. and Staley, T. W. (1999) Periodicity transforms, IEEE Transact. Signal Process. 47(11): 2953–2962
19. Sethares, W. A. and Staley, T. W. (2001) Meter and periodicity in musical performance, *J. New Music Res.* 22(5): 1–11
20. Sonka M., Boye, R., and Hlavac, V. (1998) Image Processing Analysis, and Machine Vision (2nd edition). PWS Pub Co.
21. Stauffer, D. (1994) Introduction to Percolation Theory, Taylor and Francis
22. Toffoli, T. and Margolus, N. (1987) Cellular automata machines: a new environment for modeling, MIT Press
23. Vrolijk, B. (2007) Interactive visualisation techniques for large time-dependent data sets. PhD thesis, Delft University of Technology, The Netherlands, June 2007, ISBN 978-90-8559-293-8
24. Wolfram, S. (1983) Statistical mechanics of cellular automata, *Rev. Mod. Phys.* 55: 601–644
25. Wolfram, S. (1984a) Cellular automata as models of complexity, *Nature* 311: 419–424
26. Wolfram, S. (1984b) Universality and complexity in cellular automata, *Physica D* 10: 1–35
27. Zhou, S., Chellappa, R. and Moghaddam, B. (2005) Tracking and recognition using apprearance-adaptive models in particle filters, *IEEE Trans. Image Process.* 13(11): 1491–1506

Chapter 15
Interactive Statistical Modeling with XGms

Jean-Bernard Martens

Abstract This chapter intends to clarify how statistical models can be used in the interactive analysis of experimental data. It is discussed how maximum likelihood estimation can map experimental data into model parameters, and how confidence intervals on these parameters play a key role in drawing inferences. One frequent inference is whether or not similar data collected in two different experimental conditions require a significant change in model parameters, hence indicating that the conditions are not equivalent. Another frequent inference is whether a simple or a more complex model needs to be adopted for describing observed data. It is argued that the user, who has insight into the problem underlying the data, should be allowed to play an active part in selecting models and specifying the inferences of interest. Hence, the need for interactive visualization is identified and the program XGms that has been developed for this purpose is discussed. The fact that the statistical models implemented within XGms are geometrical in nature simplifies their visualization and interpretation.

Keywords: Statistical modeling, Interactive modeling, Model visualization, Data analysis

15.1 Introduction

There is a widespread interest in establishing and understanding relationships between variables, where a variable is defined as any measurable aspect that can take on different values. Sometimes this interest is motivated by sheer curiosity, in which case it can suffice to establish whether or not there is a relationship between the variables of interest. In industrial or scientific settings, however, the interest is often triggered by practical or theoretical necessity, and more quantitative descriptions of relationships are usually required.

An established way of testing and describing relationships between variables is by means of statistical analysis. Statistics can aim at drawing inferences about whether or not variables are related, such as in the case of a T-test or chi-squared

E. Zudilova-Seinstra et al. (eds.) *Trends in Interactive Visualization*,
doi:10.1007/978-1-84800-269-2_15

test [13], or can aim at estimating quantitative relationships between observed data, such as in the case of regression. In order to argue the need for more intuitive interactions in statistical data analyses, we highlight a number of characteristics of current practice.

First, a statistic is a single number derived from the data, and detailed characteristics of the data, such as individual data points that do not satisfy a global relationship, can be obscured by such statistics. Statistics should therefore be used primarily to verify effects that can also be visualized through other means, such as with scatter or parallel plots [20] or confidence intervals [12, 19]. Therefore, most popular statistical packages, such as SPSS, Statgraphics, DataDesk, etc., offer interactive visualizations for both exploratory data analysis (i.e., the stage in which hypotheses are construed and statistical methods are selected) and for illustrating the results of statistical analyses. The required analyses themselves however most often need to be specified using command-line entry or menu selection, which requires a substantial familiarity with the available methods, their properties and their limitations.

Second, in order to compress a large set of data into a single number (or a few numbers), assumptions need to be made about the data being interpreted. For example, the widely used analysis of variance (ANOVA) assumes that the observed data is normally distributed across conditions, with varying average, but constant variance. Being able to rapidly switch between alternative assumptions, such as changing to non-constant variance, and to adequately visualize the impact of such changes, is essential for gaining insight into the validity of such assumptions. Currently, such an exploration of alternatives cannot be performed in an intuitive way. Selecting alternative statistical methods and finding the relevant information in the wealth of textual and graphical output provided by these methods is what is now most often required. This is a slow and non-intuitive way of working.

Third, a plethora of statistical methods have been developed in order to cope with alternative data characteristics (such as whether the data is discrete or continuous, interval or ordinal) and with different hypotheses (such as, testing for equal averages or variances). Because of this complexity, a statistical expert may be needed to help select the most adequate method. Since this is seldom feasible, most users tend to restrict themselves to the most simple and best-known methods, even in cases where such methods are clearly not the best choice (or even simply inappropriate). Although the underlying mathematical models for many of the existing methods are more closely related than most people seem to be aware of, end users are not able to perceive these communalities. A better visualization of the models being available for approximating the data can potentially lead to choosing more appropriate methods, which in turn is likely to result in better abstractions from the data.

In this chapter, we propose that interactive visualization can help to make statistical data modeling more intuitive and appropriate. More specifically, we propose to enable the user to interactively control different aspects of a general statistical model in order to explore a range of alternative model descriptions, rather then having to select from a list of available statistical methods. Moreover, we propose an output visualization that is closely related to this general model so that the consequences of alternative model choices can be easily appreciated. We also propose that the user, who has insight in the problem underlying the observed data, should be allowed to play an active role in the model estimation process by providing reasonable guesses, hence avoiding local optimizations. Such interactive feedback and feed-forward is deemed crucial when developing an understanding of observed data.

In Sect. 15.2 of this chapter, we introduce some fundamentals of statistical modeling, including maximum likelihood estimation and (asymptotic) confidence intervals. In Sect. 15.3, we discuss a class of geometrical models that are both intuitive and flexible, i.e., able to model data with very different characteristics. The majority of this section is dedicated to illustrating how the model can be used to address a diversity of statistical problems, such as ordinal and linear regression, factor analysis and multidimensional scaling. In Sect. 15.4, we describe the interface of XGms, the interactive visualization program that implements these geometrical models. We end up by identifying important contributions and aspects for future development.

15.2 Statistical Modeling

15.2.1 Single Data, Single Model

A statistical model describes the *probability* of any possible outcome of an experiment. More precisely, $\boldsymbol{x}$ let be the vector of observations and let $P(\boldsymbol{x};\, \theta)$ be the probability of this observation vector in case the vector of model parameters is equal to θ. Once the actual observation $\boldsymbol{x}$ is known, $P(\boldsymbol{x};\, \theta)$ can be viewed as a function of the parameter vector θ. This function is called the *likelihood function* (LF) for the model, given the observation vector $\boldsymbol{x}$. Let us illustrate this concept by means of a simple example. Suppose that the experiment consists of N independent observations of a binary output, and that the number of positive (1) and negative (0) outcomes is n and $N - n$, respectively. The outcome of such an experiment could be modeled by a binomial distribution with probability p for a positive outcome, i.e.,

$$P(n, N-n; p) = \frac{N!}{n!(N-n)!} p^n (1-p)^{N-n} \tag{15.1}$$

This corresponds to assuming that all observations are performed independently and that p is constant across observations. Since n and N are known from the observation, the LF only depends on the model parameter p.

From all possible models, we want to select the one that best describes our actual data vector $\boldsymbol{x}$. According to the *maximum likelihood* (ML) principle, the optimum choice θ for the parameter vector θ is such that the likelihood function $P(\boldsymbol{x};\, \theta)$ is maximized. Since probabilities are often exponential functions, it is customary to maximize the (natural) logarithm of the LF, i.e., $L(\theta) = \log P(\boldsymbol{x};\, \theta)$, as a function of θ. Once the ML parameter estimate $\hat{\theta}$ is known, then we can construct the log likelihood profile (LLP) $\Lambda(\theta) = 2[L(\theta) - L(\hat{\theta})]$. In case of our simple binomial model, the log likelihood function (LLF) is equal to

$$L(p) = \log \frac{N!}{n!(N-n)} + n \log p + (N-n)\log(1-p) \tag{15.2}$$

Maximizing this function with respect to the parameter p, i.e.,

$$\frac{dL(p)}{dp} = \frac{n}{p} - \frac{N-n}{1-p} = 0, \tag{15.3}$$

results in the optimal ML estimate $\hat{p} = n / N$, and a LLP equal to

$$\Lambda(p) = 2N(\hat{p} \log \frac{\hat{p}}{p} + (1-\hat{p}) \log \frac{1-\hat{p}}{1-p}) \tag{15.4}$$

This LLP is plotted in Fig. 15.1a for two possible experimental observations with the same optimal ML estimate $\hat{p} = n / N$, but different total number N of observations. Note that the minimum becomes more pronounced as the number of observations N increases, and that the parabolic approximation to the LLP (to be defined below) also improves.

Intuitively, we expect that more extensive data sets, with a higher number of observations, lead to more accurate predictions for the model parameters than smaller data sets. Within statistical modeling, this is formalized through the concept of

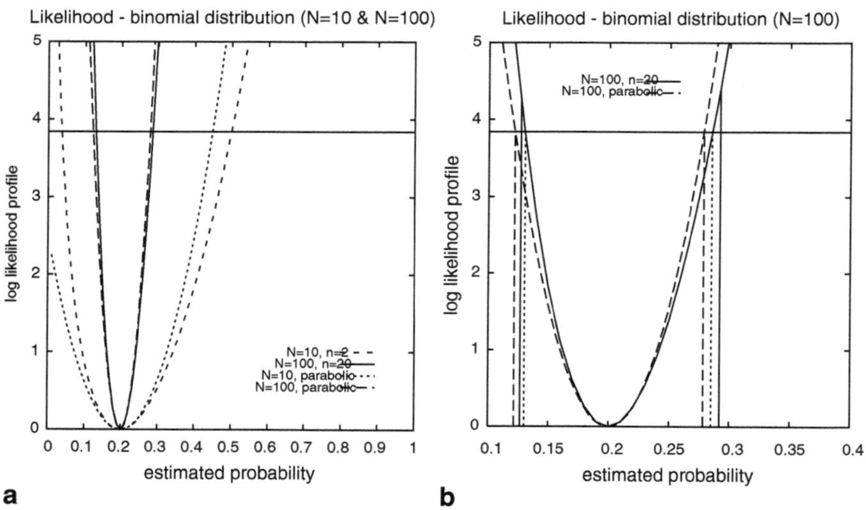

Fig. 15.1 Log likelihood profiles and their parabolic approximations for a binomial model with one (probability) parameter p. Figure (**a**) shows the model for two different observation vectors with identical ML estimate, $\hat{p} = 0.2$ i.e., (2, 8) (N = 10) and (20, 80) (N = 100). An enlarged view for observation (20, 80) is shown in Fig. (**b**). The vertically drawn lines in this figure indicate the exact 95% confidence interval for the model parameter p. The dashed and dotted vertical lines show two different, asymptotically correct, approximations. The horizontal line is the $\chi^2_{0.05}(1) = 3.84$ boundary

confidence intervals (CIs). More precisely, we expect the ML parameter estimate $\hat{\theta}$ to vary slightly in case of repeated experiments. This is captured by the statistical nature of the model, since a model with constant parameter vector θ will give rise to different observations $\boldsymbol{x}$ on successive (simulated) trials. Without going into detail (see [14, 17] for more in-depth treatments), a $100(1 - \alpha)\%$ CI is a region in parameter space, surrounding the ML estimate $\hat{\theta}$, such that the "true" model parameter vector θ is expected to fall within this region with an estimated probability of $100(1 - \alpha)\%$ (the most frequently adopted choice is 95%, or $\alpha = 0.05$). The hypothesis that a model with assumed parameter vector θ_o describes the data can then be rejected with $100(1 - \alpha)\%$ confidence if this vector falls outside the $100(1 - \alpha)\%$ CI. Exact determination of these CIs is only possible in relatively simple special cases, such as the binomial model discussed above [6]. The exact 95% CI for the parameter p in case of an (20, 80) observation is indicated by the drawn vertical lines in Fig. 15.1b. Since $p_o = 0.3$ falls outside of the 95% CI, we can reject the hypothesis that the probability p underlying our observation is $p = 0.3$ (we can for instance not reject the hypothesis that $p = 0.25$).

The popularity of ML estimates can be largely attributed to the fact that there exist approximations to the CIs that can be derived in very general cases and that are asymptotically correct, i.e., in case the number of observations is (infinitely) large. Provided the number of parameters in the model is k (this is the number of elements in the parameter vector θ), then the "likelihood ratio" approximation [14] to the CI is obtained by

$$\Lambda(\theta) < \chi^2_\alpha(k) \tag{15.5}$$

where $\chi^2_\alpha(k)$ is such that the area from $\chi^2_\alpha(k)$ to infinity under the chi-squared distribution curve with k degrees of freedom is equal to α (which means that the area under the curve between 0 and $\chi^2_\alpha(k)$ is equal to $1 - \alpha$). These chi-squared values are tabulated in almost all textbooks on statistics, e.g., [4, 13]. The "likelihood ratio" approximation to the 95% CI for the parameter p in the binomial model of Fig. 15.1b is indicated by the dotted vertical lines. The boundary values for the interval are obtained by intersecting the LLP $\Lambda(p)$ with the horizontal line at height $\chi^2_{0.05}(1) = 3.84$. Note that the asymptotic CI (ACI) is (slightly) smaller than the true CI.

In case the LLP around the optimum ML estimate $\hat{\theta}$ can be approximated by a parabolic function, which is guaranteed to be the case when the number of observations is large (due to the central limit theorem), then the CI can be shown to be approximately equal to an ellipsoid with expression

$$(\theta - \hat{\theta})^t \cdot I(\hat{\theta}) \cdot (\theta - \hat{\theta}) = \chi^2_\alpha(k), \tag{15.6}$$

where the k x k matrix of the negated second derivatives to the log likelihood function, i.e.,

$$I(\hat{\theta}) = \left[-\frac{\partial^2}{\partial\theta_i \partial\theta_j} L(\hat{\theta}); i, j = 1, \ldots k \right] \tag{15.7}$$

is called the observed *Fisher information matrix* [14]. For the binomial model with one parameter p, this matrix reduces to a single number

$$I(\hat{p}) = -\left.\frac{d^2L(p)}{dp^2}\right|_{p=\hat{p}} = \frac{N}{\hat{p}\,(1-\hat{p})} \tag{15.8}$$

which corresponds to a parabolic or "Wald" approximation to the LLP, i.e.,

$$\hat{\Lambda}(p) = \frac{N}{\hat{p}(1-\hat{p})}(p-\hat{p})^2 \tag{15.9}$$

The "Wald" approximation to the 95% CI for the parameter p in the binomial model is indicated by the dashed vertical lines in Fig. 15.1b. The boundary values for the interval are obtained by intersecting the parabolic approximation $\hat{\Lambda}(p)$ to the LLP with the horizontal line at height $\chi^2_{0.05}(1) = 3.84$.

15.2.2 Multiple Data and/or Models

In the above discussion we have assumed that there is only one observation vector $\boldsymbol{x}$ and one model of interest, with model parameter vector $\boldsymbol{\theta}$. In practice, the situation is usually more complex in at least two respects.

First, we often have different observation vectors $\boldsymbol{x}_1,\ldots,\boldsymbol{x}_K$ that correspond to different experimental conditions, and the question of interest is whether or not the experimental conditions have a significant effect on the observations. In order to compare such observations, we can model them using an identical model with varying parameters. More specifically, if the observation vectors $\boldsymbol{x}_1,\ldots,\boldsymbol{x}_K$ are modeled by different ML estimated parameter vectors $\hat{\theta}_1,\ldots,\hat{\theta}_K$ within a common model, then the statistical question (or hypothesis) of interest is whether or not the model parameters $\hat{\theta}_i$ and $\hat{\theta}_j$, or a selected subset of them, are significantly different. Since many different comparisons are possible, interactive visualization can be used to select only the interesting ones, and to adequately visualize the comparison results.

Second, we might be interested in testing different models, of increasing complexity, on the same observation vector $\boldsymbol{x}$. If the first model has k_θ parameters, and the second model is an extension of the first one with $k_\varphi > k_\theta$ parameters, then the latter model is expected to have a higher log likelihood (LL). The statistical question of interest is knowing whether or not this increase in LL is sufficiently substantial to warrant the increase in number of parameters, in which case the more complex model should be preferred. If this increase in LL is not substantial enough, then the simpler model should be preferred. Exploring such alternative models in an efficient way will be another objective of using interactive visualization.

In order to address the first aspect, we will need a slightly more general formulation of ML estimation than the one provided before. More specifically, we will need to know how to determine CIs for subsets of parameters. Let us divide the parameter vector $\theta = (\theta_1, \theta_2)$ into two subsets of parameters (with k_1 and k_2 components, respectively, so that $k_1 + k_2 = k$) and rewrite the LLP as $\Lambda(\theta) = \Lambda(\theta_1, \theta_2)$. It has been demonstrated [14] that the LLP for the "wanted" parameter vector θ_1 equals

$$\Lambda(\theta_1) = \Lambda(\theta_1, \hat{\hat{\theta}}_2(\theta_1)), \tag{15.10}$$

where $\hat{\hat{\theta}}_2(\theta_1)$ is the "unwanted" parameter vector that maximizes $\Lambda(\theta_1, \theta_2)$ for a fixed value of θ_1. This log likelihood profile tends to a χ^2-distribution with k_1 degrees of freedom for large data sets, so that an $100(1 - \alpha)\%$ ACI for the subset θ_1 of "wanted" parameters can be obtained by setting

$$\Lambda(\theta_1) < \chi^2_\alpha(k_1) \tag{15.11}$$

Alternatively, a parabolic approximation [14]

$$\tilde{\Lambda}(\theta_1) = (\theta_1 - \hat{\theta}_1)^t \cdot (I_{11} - I_{12} I_{22}^{-1} I_{21}) \cdot (\theta_1 - \hat{\theta}_1) \tag{15.12}$$

to the log likelihood profile can be obtained, where the matrices I_{ij}, of size $k_i \times k_j$, for $i,j = 1,2$, are derived by subdividing the original observed Fisher matrix of size $k \times k$, see equation (15.7), in sub-matrices, i.e.,

$$I = \begin{bmatrix} I_{11} & I_{12} \\ I_{21} & I_{22} \end{bmatrix} \tag{15.13}$$

We now demonstrate how this result can be used to derive an ACI for the difference between model parameters. Assume that the same model, with different model parameters θ_i and θ_j, is used to model the observation vectors $\boldsymbol{x}_i$ and $\boldsymbol{x}_j$, respectively. If both experiments are performed independently, then the probability for the combined observation vector $(\boldsymbol{x}_i, \boldsymbol{x}_j)$ is the product $P(\boldsymbol{x}_i, \theta_i)$. $P(\boldsymbol{x}_j, \theta_j)$, so that the LLF is simply

$$L(\theta_i, \theta_j) = \log P(\boldsymbol{x}_i; \theta_i) + \log P(\boldsymbol{x}_j; \theta_j); \tag{15.14}$$

where the probability function $P(\boldsymbol{x}; \theta)$ is identical for both observation vectors. The following coordinate transformation

$$\delta_{ij} = \frac{\theta_i - \theta_j}{2}, \theta_i = \rho_{ij} + \delta_{ij} \tag{15.15}$$

$$\rho_{ij} = \frac{\theta_i + \theta_j}{2}, \theta_j = \rho_{ij} - \delta_{ij}$$

can be used to express this LLF $L(\theta_i, \theta_j) = L(\delta_{ij}, \rho_{ij})$ in terms of two new parameter vectors (δ_{ij}, ρ_{ij}). The procedure in the previous paragraph tells us how to derive an ACI for the difference vector δ_{ij}. We can reject the hypothesis that both model vectors θ_i and θ_j are equal if the zero vector lies outside of this ACI. The procedure is easily adapted in case we only want to compare a subset of the model parameters. More precisely, by further subdividing the difference vector $\delta_{ij} = (\delta_{ij}(1), \delta_{ij}(2))$ into two subsets, we can apply the above procedure to create an ACI for the difference vector $\delta_{ij}(1)$ with the parameters of interest (removing both $\delta_{ij}(2)$ and θ_{ij} as unwanted parameters).

We now address the second aspect mentioned above, i.e, that of selecting between increasingly complex models for the same observation vector $\boldsymbol{x}$. More specifically, assume that the LLFs are $L_\theta(\mu) = \log P_\theta(\boldsymbol{x};\ \theta)$ for the simpler model with k_θ parameters, and $L_\phi(\phi) = \log P_\phi\ (\boldsymbol{x};\ \phi)$ for the more complex model with k_ϕ parameters. The probability functions are now different, since the two models are different. It has been demonstrated [17] that the log likelihood difference (LLD)

$$\Delta\Lambda = 2 \cdot [L_\phi(\hat{\phi}) - L_\theta(\hat{\theta})] \tag{15.16}$$

where $\hat{\theta}$ and $\hat{\phi}$ are the optimal ML estimates for the model parameters, is asymptotically χ^2-distributed with $k_\phi - k_\theta$ degrees of freedom. Hence, only in case this LLD exceeds the threshold $\chi^2_\alpha(k_\phi - k_\theta)$ do we consider adopting the more complex model description over the simpler one. Note that, in practice, there frequently arise situations where we prefer to stick to a simpler model that is easier to interpret, despite the statistical argument to the contrary.

15.3 Geometrical Models for Statistical Data Analysis

Now that we have established how parameters of statistical models can be estimated from observations and know how ACIs can be used to draw inferences between alternative models, or model parameters, we can direct our attention to a specific class of statistical models.

According to the principle of *homogeneity of perception* [7], different variables associated with a set of objects are often related, and the relationships may be visualized by linking them to geometrical properties of a stimulus configuration. More specifically, distances between points representing objects can be related to observed (dis)similarities between these objects, while coordinates of object points along different axes can be associated with measurements on different attributes. Such models provide a geometrical interpretation for popular statistical methods such as multiple regression (MR) and multidimensional scaling (MDS) [1, 3, 7, 11]. In case of MR, part of the model (i.e., the object positions) is a priori provided, based on some theoretical or physical understanding of the objects of interest. In case of MDS, these object positions are estimated from the experimental data.

In order to clarify the above concepts, we illustrate part of the geometrical model that is implemented within our program XGms in Fig. 15.2. We assume that N different objects, represented by object positions $\boldsymbol{x}_i$, for $i = 1,\ldots,N$, have been assessed on K_a different attributes, and that measurements have been repeated R_a times, so that A_{kij} is the j-th measurement, for $j = 1,\ldots,R_a$, of object i on attribute k, for $k = 1,\ldots,K_a$. According to the model, the object configuration $\{\boldsymbol{x}_i;\ i = 1,\ldots,N\}$ is shared by all attribute measurements. The mapping of an object position $\boldsymbol{x}_i$ to a response A_{kij} for attribute k depends on the prediction vector $\boldsymbol{a}_k$, the proportionality factor f_k, the offset factor c_k, the noise standard deviation σ_{ak} and the possibly nonlinear but monotonically increasing response function $R_{ak}(\cdot)$, for $k = 1,\ldots,K_a$. How

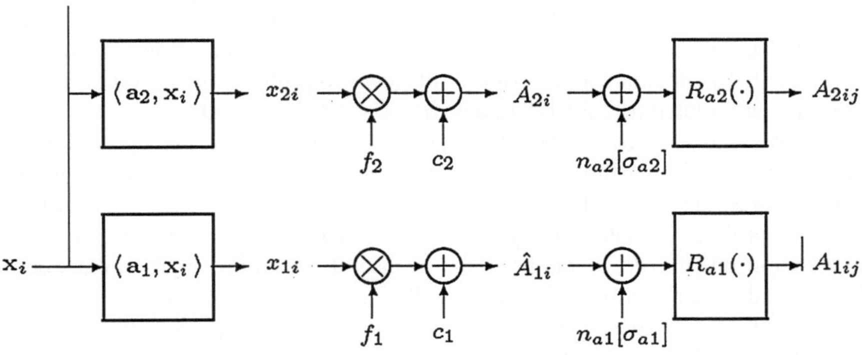

Fig. 15.2 Geometrical model relating object positions $\boldsymbol{x}_i$ to measurements A_{kij} for variable k on object i, during repetition j. The objects within an experiment are described by positions $\boldsymbol{x}_i$, while the attribute vector $\boldsymbol{a}_k$, regression coefficients c_k and f_k, and response mechanism $R_{\alpha k}$ describe the mapping to the variable measurements on these objects. The response variability in successive trials j around the predicted mean value $\hat{A}_{ki}$ for variable k on object i is modeled by a noise source n_{ak} with (constant) standard deviation $\sigma_{\alpha k}$

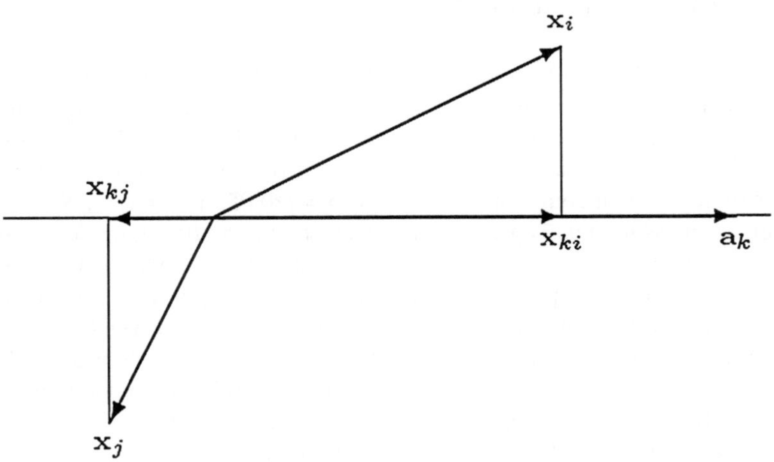

Fig. 15.3 Geometrical interpretation of attribute predictions. If $\boldsymbol{x}_{ki}$ is the orthogonal projection of the vector $\boldsymbol{x}_i$ onto the axis with direction $\boldsymbol{a}_k$, then the inner product definition implies that $<\boldsymbol{a}_k, \boldsymbol{x}_i> = <\boldsymbol{a}_k, \boldsymbol{x}_{ki}>$. The projected vector can be expressed as $\boldsymbol{x}_{ki} = x_{ki} \cdot \boldsymbol{a}_k / ||a_k||_2$ since it is aligned with the vector a_k. The numbers $\boldsymbol{x}_{ki}$ and $\boldsymbol{x}_{kj}$ can be interpreted as coordinates on the axis with direction $\boldsymbol{a}_k$ for two different objects i and j

object position $\boldsymbol{x}_i$ is mapped into an (average) score x_{ki} for object i on variable k is illustrated in Fig. 15.3. When the same objects are scored very differently on different attributes, then this is reflected within the model as attribute vectors $\boldsymbol{a}_k$ with different orientations. Such distinct orientations are obviously only possible in case the dimension n of the space exceeds one. Note that the model in Fig. 15.2 is statistical in nature because of the inclusion of the (Gaussian) noise sources n_{ak}. For a detailed mathematical description of how the probabilities of observed data values A_{kij} are related to the model parameters, we refer to [10, 11].

The proposed geometrical model is especially flexible in how object positions are mapped into attribute measurements. In this way, observed data with very different characteristics can be handled within a common model, and different alternative assumptions about the data characteristics can be easily compared. More specifically, the response function $R_{ak}(\cdot)$ can be linear in case of *interval* (or metric) data, but is also allowed to be a non-linear, monotonically increasing function, in case of *ordinal* (or non-metric) data. Both power-like functions [15] and monotonically increasing spline functions [16] are supported. The response function can optionally be quantized, i.e., limited to a discrete set of output values, in case of *discrete* data, such as in case of a measurement variable with integer instead of real values [10]. Variables with different ranges and accuracies can be handled by adapting the linear regression coefficients c_k and f_k and the noise standard deviations σ_{ak}.

15.3.1 Example 1. Binary Data

We start with a simple illustrative example where the stimulus configuration is one-dimensional, i.e., each condition under test is represented by a single number x_i, for $i = 1,\ldots,N$. We assume that a constant number of $R_a = 100$ binary (positive/negative) measurements are performed in each of $N = 19$ conditions, and that the fraction of negative outcomes in condition i is $p_i = i*0.05$, for $i = 1,\ldots,19$. Since the same binary measurement is performed in each condition, the number of measured attributes is $K_a = 1$. Such data can be analyzed using the model of Fig. 15.2 by adopting a nonlinear mapping $R_{a1}(\cdot)$ that quantizes the output to two levels, representing the positive and negative outcomes. A small fraction of negative outcomes in case i should map to an average prediction $\hat{A}_{1i}$ well above the quantization threshold of the nonlinearity (corresponding to a small probability of generating a value below the threshold), while an equal fraction of negative and positive outcomes should map to a position close to the quantization threshold.

The estimated positions for the different conditions are plotted in Fig. 15.4. For reasons explained in [10], the stimulus configuration is always centered around the origin and its variance is normalized. The estimation program determines that the offset c_1 in the model is equal to the threshold value of the quantizing nonlinearity $R_{a1}(\cdot)$, which defaults to 0, and that the scale factor f_1 is equal to 0.864 times the noise standard deviation $\sigma_{\alpha 1}$, which defaults to 1. This implies that the standard deviation of the noise on the stimulus configuration in Fig. 15.4 equals $\sigma_{a1}/f_1 = 1.157$.

During the ML estimation, only the stimulus configuration is visualized, because calculating ACIs at each iteration step would significantly slow down the estimation process. The ACIs are moreover only required when inferences need to be drawn from the data. Therefore, Fig. 15.4 is only generated in response to an

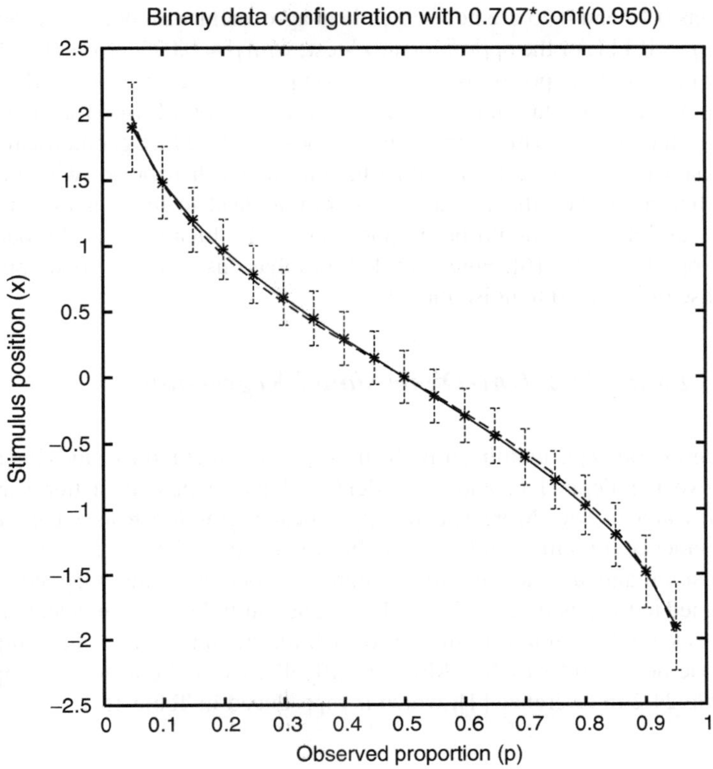

Fig. 15.4 Estimated stimulus positions for binary data with a constant decrease in observed fraction p of positive responses. The intervals equal $1/\sqrt{2}$ times the 95% CIs on the estimated positions. The dashed curve is proportional to the logarithm of the odds ratio $\log((1-p)/p)$

explicit user request. Although extensive statistical tests (following the ML principles discussed in the previous section) can be reported textually, the figure being presented is a deliberate approximation that is much easier to interpret. Indeed, if all $N(N-1)/2 = 171$ stimulus distances $x_i - x_j$ would need to be reported and checked for statistical significance, a long list that is difficult to inspect would be the result. Of course, we could prune this list by only reporting the results for neighboring stimulus positions. Instead, we have adopted an approximate graphical rendering that has recently been promoted by several authors [12, 19]. It has been shown that, provided the standard errors on the estimated positions are approximately constant (an assumption that is reasonably satisfied in our case), we can perform a simple visual inspection in order to identify statistically significant differences. More precisely, if we render $1/\sqrt{2}$ times the estimated 95% CI around each position, then non-overlapping intervals are equivalent to statistically significant differences. Note for instance that observed proportions 0.05 and 0.15 are significantly different according to this criterion (which is in agreement with both the exact Fisher test [5], with $p = 0.0317$, or the approximate χ^2-test [13], with $p = 0.018$), while observed proportions 0.15 and 0.25 are not (which is in agreement with both the exact Fisher test, with $p = 0.111$, or the approximate χ^2-test, with $p = 0.077$). Note that the intervals between stimulus positions x_i can be compared on a linear scale (because of the assumption of constant noise variance), which is not allowed for the observed fractions p_i themselves. This is one of the purposes of building geometrical models. If the noise would be logistically rather than normally distributed (which is only a minor difference), then theoretical considerations lead to the conclusion that the stimulus configuration should be proportional to the logarithm of the odds ratio, i.e., $x_i \propto \log((1 - p_i)/p_i)$ [6]. Figure 15.4 shows that this is also a good approximation in case of a Gaussian noise model.

15.3.2 Example 2. One-Dimensional Regression

Linear regression [4] is undoubtedly the most popular method for studying associations between independent and dependent variables when the latter variable is continuous and metric. More specifically, linear regression tests whether or not there is evidence for a linear relationship between both variables. The model in Fig. 15.2 can simultaneously test the linear regression between one independent variable, assigned to the positions x_i, for $i = 1,..,N$, and multiple (K_a) dependent variables. In order to keep the discussion simple we will restrict ourselves to the simple case of only one dependent variable. More specifically, we will consider example data from Table 24.2 in reference [4], which is reproduced in Table 15.1.

Table 15.1 Measured concentration of chlorine in a product as a function of the number of weeks after production (Reproduced from [4], Table 24.2)

Weeks	Chlorine concentration
8	0.49, 0.49
10	0.48, 0.47, 0.48, 0.47
12	0.46, 0.46, 0.45, 0.43
14	0.45, 0.43, 0.43
16	0.44, 0.43, 0.43
18	0.46, 0.45
20	0.42, 0.42, 0.43
22	0.41, 0.41, 0.40
24	0.42, 0.40, 0.40
26	0.41, 0.40, 0.41
28	0.41, 0.40
30	0.40, 0.40, 0.38
32	0.41, 0.40
34	0.40
36	0.41, 0.38
38	0.40, 0.40
40	0.39
42	0.39

The model of Fig. 15.2 describes linear regression between the dependent variable A_{1ij} (observed chlorine concentration within a medicine) and the independent variable x_i (number of weeks since production) in case the response function is linear, i.e., $R_{a1}(A) = A$ (with inverse $T_{al}(A) = R_{al}^{-1}(A) = A$). Within the program XGms, the result of the regression is presented in a scatter plot, where the regressed values $\hat{A}_{1i} = c_1 + f_1 \cdot x_i$ are used as coordinates along the horizontal axis, and the transformed measured values $T_{a1}(A_{1ij})$ are used as coordinates along the vertical axes (see Fig. 15.8). In case of linear regression, the data points should align along the diagonal line that is included as a visual aid. An alternative would be to plot residuals $T_{a1}(A_{1ij}) - \hat{A}_{1i}$ [4] instead of observed measurements $T_{a1}(A_{1ij})$ along the vertical axis. In order to assess the goodness of fit, two lines that run parallel to the diagonal at a distance of two times the estimated noise standard deviation σ_{a1} are also included. In case of an adequate model fit, approximately 95% percent of the data points should fall in between these oblique lines. In case of our data set, a reasonable model fit was observed, but with some systematic deviations. In order to complement the visual impression, the user can request more detailed information about the regression. The result is presented in both graphical and textual form. In the graphical output, the 95% ACI for the linear regression coefficient f_1 is plotted. Since zero was outside this confidence interval, it could be concluded that there was evidence for a linear relationship. The complementary textual output contains a complete Analysis of Variance (ANOVA). Since there were repeated measures, ANOVA could also perform an F-test for the lack-of-fit [4]. This test, which is very often omitted, establishes whether or not there are variations within the dependent data that are not explained by the linear regression. The result $F(16,26) = 5.201$ ($p = 0.00011$) > 2.052($p = 0.05$) indeed indicates that there is a lack of fit. We discuss two options for how to (interactively) obtain more insight into this deviation from a linear regression.

The first option is to perform non-linear instead of linear regression. Within the model of Fig. 15.2, this corresponds to including a nonlinear response function R_{a1}. Increasingly complex response functions can be created, up to the point where increasing the number of parameters no longer contributes significantly to improving the regression. The LLD $\Delta\Lambda$ of equation (15.16) can be used to judge significance, since the XGms program can be requested to compare the current model with a previously stored model at any time during the interactive session. Two kinds of nonlinear transformations are supported by XGms, power-like transformations with up to 3 parameters, and monotonic spline transformations with up to 5 internal knot points, which corresponds to 6 parameters [10]. In both cases, only the first two parameters add significantly to improving the (nonlinear) regression. The optimal power-law and spline transformations are both presented in Fig. 15.5a. The optimal nonlinear transformation is also displayed during the interactive visualization (see Fig. 15.8), so that the observer gets a visual impression of it (for instance useful in judging the deviation from linearity).

The second option for analyzing the non-linearity is to compare the independent data with the optimal linear predictor. Within the model of Fig. 15.2, this corresponds to MDS optimization of the configuration $\boldsymbol{x}_i$ based on the observed

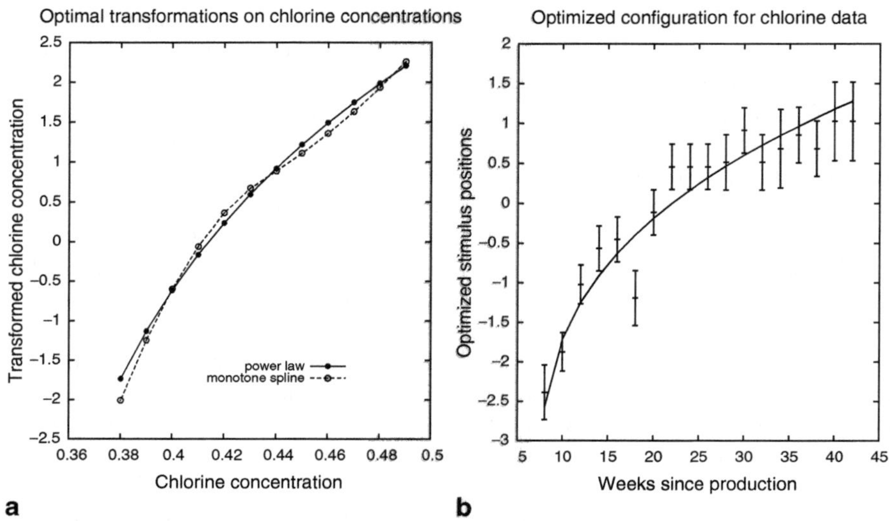

Fig. 15.5 Figure (**a**) shows optimized power-law and monotonically increasing spline transformations on chlorine concentrations. Figure (**b**) is an optimized (MDS) stimulus configuration with approximate linear relationship to the dependent variable (chlorine concentration), plotted as a function of the independent variable (weeks since production). The drawn line is an approximate power-law transformation with two parameters on the independent variable

data, and to plotting the optimized configuration as a function of the independent variable. The result of this MDS analysis is shown in Fig. 15.5b. As already observed in the previous section, the MDS stimulus configuration is geometrically (i.e., linearly) related to the dependent variable in case there is no output non-linearity. The observed relationship in Fig. 15.5b hence indicates which transformation needs to be applied to the independent variable (the weeks since production) to have an approximate linear effect on the dependent variable (the chlorine concentration). The difference with the first method, where the transformation was applied to the dependent variable, is that the second method determines the transformation that is required on the independent variable. The model in Fig. 15.2 does not allow for a transformation at this stage (i.e., on the scores x_{ki}, before they enter the linear regression). Nevertheless, the model can be used to find a suitable approximation. Indeed, by keeping the optimized MDS configuration fixed while changing the dependent data to what was originally the independent data (i.e., the weeks since production), one can apply the regression method of the previous section to find an optimum non-linear transformation on the independent variable. The optimum two-parameter power-law transformation derived in this way is also shown in Fig. 15.5b.

15.3.3 Example 3. Multiple Regression and Factor Analysis

The simple case treated in the previous example, where only one independent variable characterizes the objects under study, has its obvious limitations. In practice, the objects of interest will often vary in multiple aspects and the purpose of an experiment may be to establish a suitable compromise between conflicting attributes. This requires establishing how one or more dependent variables are (linearly or non-linearly) related to a number of independent parameters. With reference to the model in Fig. 15.2, this means that each object i under study, for $i = 1,\ldots,N$, is characterized by a vector $\boldsymbol{x}_i$, the elements of which are the independent variables. For these objects, one or more dependent variables may be measured. We will illustrate this case by an example where the perceived quality of images degraded by noise and blur is modeled [8, 10]. All combinations of four levels of blur with a binomial kernel and four levels of Gaussian additive white noise were applied to create 16 different processed images from an original image. Seven subjects rated the perceived quality of the images. All images were presented $R_a = 4$ times, in random order, to each of the subjects, resulting in $16 \times 4 = 64$ quality scores per subject. Integer scores between 0 and 10 were used by the subjects to express their judgments.

The multiple regression (MR) vectors ($f_k \cdot \boldsymbol{a}_k$ in the notation of Fig. 15.2) that describe the quality judgments of the individual subjects are plotted as dotted vectors in Fig. 15.6. The 4×4 stimulus configuration is square because the blur and the noise are assumed to be independent characteristics. For only one of the seven subjects was there evidence that nonlinear regression was significantly better than linear regression, so that linear regression was adopted for all judgments. Note that the 95%-confidence ellipses on the regression vectors (which are scaled by a factor of $1/\sqrt{2}$ in order to facilitate interpretation) indicate that some vectors have approximately the same orientation, while others have significantly different orientations. Establishing the number of independent factors underlying a set of attribute judgments is usually accomplished through mathematical procedures such as factor analysis. However, the interactive visualization within XGms also allows to gather evidence for which attributes share a common factor. More specifically, the number of parameters in the model of Fig. 15.2 can be reduced by letting some attribute vectors share the same orientation (i.e., by equating normalized attribute vectors, e.g., $\boldsymbol{a}_1 = \boldsymbol{a}_2$). Note that such vectors can still have unequal lengths (since f_1 need not be equal to f_2). If two attributes share the same orientation then the number of degrees of freedom in the model is reduced (by one in the case of a two-dimensional configuration), at the cost of a decrease in the log likelihood of the model.

The LLD of equation (15.16) can be used to decide whether or not this decrease is sufficiently large to prefer the more complex model, with unequally oriented attribute vectors, over the simpler model, with equally oriented attribute vectors. Within the interactive visualization program XGms, the user can select which attribute orientations to merge. For the specific data set considered in this example, an iterative procedure where the two most closely related orientations (i.e., with smallest mutual angle) are merged in each successive step, leads to the conclusion that there is statistical evidence for only two groups of quality vectors (i.e., two independent factors). The resulting dashed vectors are also shown in Fig. 15.6. The vectors in a group share the same orientation, but have different lengths. The obvious interpretation for these two groups is that one group (of four subjects) attributes more relative weight to blur than to noise in comparison to the other group (of three subjects). It is of course possible that we are not interested in individual or group quality judgments, but only in the average quality direction across subjects. This is easily accomplished by letting all vectors share the same orientation ($\boldsymbol{a}_1 = \ldots = \boldsymbol{a}_7$). The resulting average orientation for quality corresponds to the drawn vector in Fig. 15.6.

15.3.4 Example 4. Multidimensional Scaling

The original motivation for developing the XGms program was to create an interactive visualization for multidimensional scaling (MDS). Within the model of Fig. 15.2, MDS refers to cases where the stimulus positions $\boldsymbol{x}_i$ are estimated, together with the other parameters, from the observed data A_{kij}. We can for instance use the data from the previous example to perform MDS. The resulting optimum 2D configuration

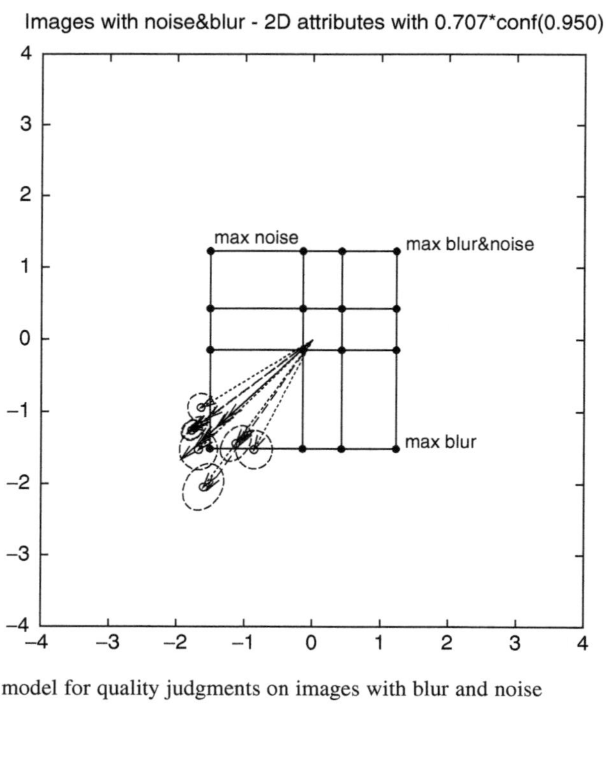

Fig. 15.6 MR model for quality judgments on images with blur and noise

is shown in Fig. 15.7, together with the regressed quality vectors (both the individual and group quality vectors, as well as the averaged quality orientation). This MDS solution has a significantly higher log likelihood than the multiple regression solution in the previous section ($\Delta\Lambda = 278.04 > \chi^2_{0.05}(28) = 41.35$), so that the MDS configuration of Fig. 15.7 is more accurate for predicting image quality than the MR configuration of Fig. 15.6. However, note the elongated confidence ellipses on the stimulus points, which indicate that the stimulus positions are ill determined in the direction orthogonal to the quality vectors. This is an instance where it would be interesting to compare the ellipsoidal ACIs with the "likelihood ratio" ACIs (something that is currently not implemented in XGms), since the elliptical approximation to the log likelihood may not be sufficiently accurate in this case. Comparison between a 2D and a 1D configuration using the log likelihood difference measure reveals that there is nevertheless statistical evidence ($\Delta\Lambda = 92.72 > \chi^2_{0.05}(16) = 26.31$) for a 2D configuration over a 1D configuration. Despite the fact that there is statistical evidence for a 2D solution, a 1D solution might be preferred because of the obvious difficulty of interpreting the configuration in Fig. 15.7. The problem is obviously due to the fact that the quality judgments only measure stimulus variations in one direction. It has been shown in [9, 10] that a much more stable 2D configuration arises when noise and blur judgments, which correspond to different directions in this space, are combined with the quality judgments.

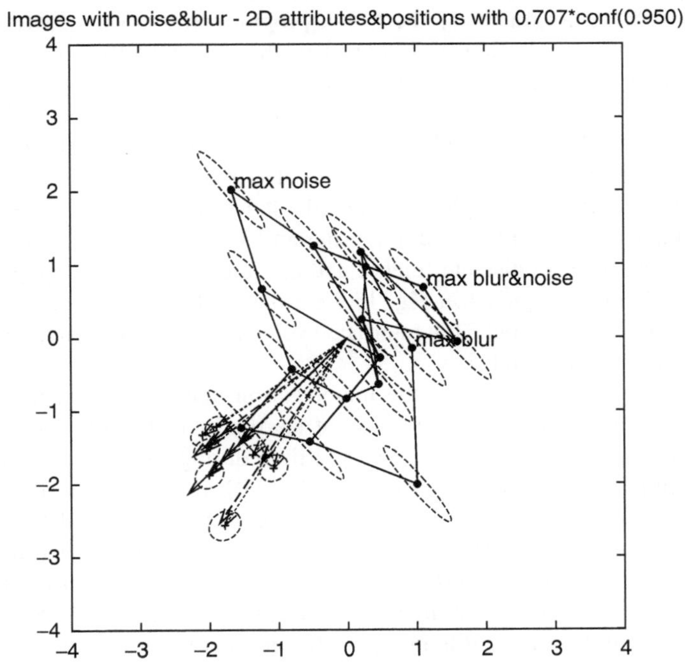

Fig. 15.7 MDS model for quality judgments on images with blur and noise

15.4 The XGms Interface to the Geometrical Model

In order to control model parameters and options, and in order to feedback the modeling results to the user, an appropriate interface to the geometrical model of Fig. 15.2 is required. Most existing statistical programs can be characterized as off-line programs (see for instance [1] for an overview of computer programs for MDS). This implies that the user must enter his/her choice of statistical method, and that the results are returned as text and graphs, to be examined after the analysis has finished. This makes it very difficult and cumbersome to appreciate the impact of alternative model choices, and hence to choose the model that most adequately describes the data. Also, since such programs are nonlinear optimization programs, the reported solution may correspond to a local optimum instead of a global one. The interactive program XGvis [2] is one of the few examples that has been developed to help remedy such problems. The program XGvis allows to interactively control the main parameters in an MDS model, and exchanges the calculated stimulus configuration with a second program, called XGobi [18].

This latter program is an interactive dynamic data visualization tool for the X Window environment. By combining the functionality of both programs, the user is not only able to dynamically alter the parameters of an MDS model within XGvis, but he can also view and manipulate the stimulus configuration in XGobi. This interactivity for instance allows the user to assist the optimization algorithm in avoiding sub-optimum solutions that correspond to local minima.

Like most MDS programs [1], the XGvis program only models continuous dissimilarity data of a single subject. In our view, this functionality is too limited for modeling more complex measurement situations, such as when relationships between multiple variables need to be established. In order to overcome these limitations, XGvis has been extended to include the joint analysis of data from single-stimulus scaling (such as in Fig. 15.2), double-stimulus difference scaling and dissimilarity scaling for multiple variables (the latter options are discussed in [10, 11]). Another extension of the resulting program XGms is that it not only supports continuous data but also discrete (metric and non-metric) data. The graphical user interface to XGms is depicted in Fig. 15.8 for the (Chlorine) data set in Example 15.2 of the previous section. This interface evolved from the graphical user interface of the XGvis program [2].

The panel at the top contains the major action buttons. The user can either specify an initial stimulus configuration at startup or can load a new stimulus configuration (using "Load CONF") at any time during the XGms session. The current stimulus configuration can be used for MR analysis against the experimental data. Alternatively, the current stimulus configuration can be used as the initial configuration in an MDS analysis. Either the original data (Ai), power-transformed data (At) or spline-transformed data (As) can be used in the MR or MDS analysis. In the example, power-transformed attribute data are used. The stimulus configuration is continuously exchanged between the statistical modeling program XGms and the visualization program XGobi [18], so that this latter program can be used to manipulate and render the configuration. In order to allow

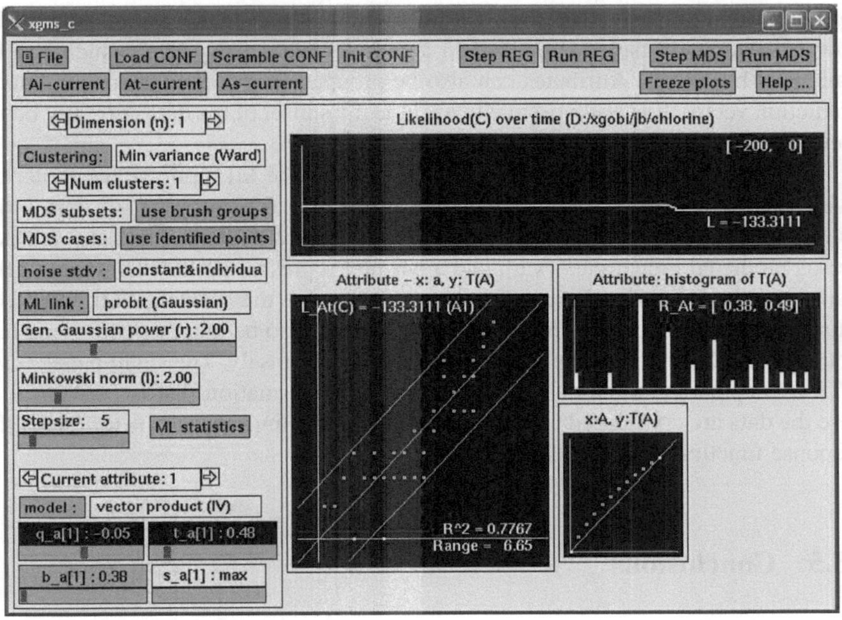

Fig. 15.8 XGms graphical user interface to the data set in Example 2 (*See Color Plates*)

processing by other data analysis or visualization programs, most intermediate data in the XGms program can also be output to ASCII files using the options in the "file" menu. File menu options can also be used to request more detailed graphical representations that include the ACIs needed for statistical inference.

The left panel in the interface allows the user to control the most important parameters of the geometrical model, such as

1. the dimension n of the stimulus space,
2. the noise model used,
3. the prediction model used (individual or shared attribute vector),
4. the parameters q, t and b that control the nonlinear power-like transformations on the variable data, and
5. the number s of internal knot points in a monotonically increasing spline transformation.

Xgms can also perform clustering on the stimulus configuration; and the left panel contains two action buttons that allow to interactively control this clustering. The user can obtain ML statistics, including the current number of DOF in the model and the likelihood value of the model, at any time in the XGms session by hitting the "ML statistics" button. XGms compares the outcomes on two successive calls to "ML statistics." In this way, χ^2-tests between alternative models can be made in order to infer which model is most appropriate. If data for several attributes are available, then the "current" selection allows to view the settings and model fits for the current attribute. The user can for instance select which parameters of the power-like transformation are fixed to a user-specified value, and which can be optimized by XGms. Attributes can also be grouped so that they share a common prediction vector. It is also possible to exclude the subset of the data currently being viewed from the model optimization.

The graph in the upper-right corner displays how the ML optimization criterion (which is the negated log likelihood) has varied as a function of time during the XGms session. In addition, a scatter plot of transformed experimental data (y:T(A)) versus predicted model data (x:a), and a bar plot representing the histogram of the transformed experimental data (T(A)) are shown for the `current' attribute. The data in the scatter plot "Attribute - x:a, y:T(A)" can also be output to the visualization program XGobi in order to examine them more closely. The small panel "x:A, y:T(A)" depicts the monotonically increasing transformation that is performed in case the data are considered to be non-metric. It is the inverse $T_{ak}(a) = R_{ak}^{-1}(A)$ of the response function in Fig. 15.2.

15.5 Conclusions

We have argued how statistical modeling can profit from interactive visualization. Moreover, we have introduced a specific class of geometrical models that we consider to be intuitive, but nevertheless general enough to capture a large number of interesting data analysis situations. We have developed the interactive visualization program XGms for interaction with this class of models. Although the mathematical basis for this work was already presented in earlier publications [10, 11], experience with other users than the author has revealed that some aspects of the model are fairly easy to understand and apply, but that exploiting the full potential requires an introduction to the less straightforward aspects. This was an important motivation for the introduction to ML statistics and the discussion of example applications provided in this chapter.

We propose that an interactive visualization system for statistical modeling should contain three main components. First, it should incorporate a statistical modeling engine (or expert system) that can perform ML estimations of statistical model parameters, and that can construct the CIs required for statistical inference. Second, it should provide an interface through which users can intuitively formulate their statistical questions. Third, it should render the results of the analysis in a way that can be easily and quickly assessed by the users. Further developments in each of these components within XGms are foreseen. Concerning component one, we should note that the model shown in Fig. 15.2 covers only part of the modeling capabilities of the interactive visualization program XGms. More precisely, next to individual scaling data, the model can also handle pairwise comparisons, such as dissimilarity data or difference data [10]. Another important aspect is that currently only ellipsoidal ACIs (using the "Wald" approximation) are available, while there is an obvious interest to also implement ACIs based on the "likelihood ratio" approximation. Concerning component two, it is clear that extensive usage scenarios, such as the ones described in the examples, are instrumental to establishing the kind of user actions that are potentially most useful. Additional support, such as for factor analysis of attribute vectors, could make the interaction at this stage less elaborate at times (currently, the reported factor analysis in Example 3 involved some text editing of input files and restarting of the program). A more intuitive interface than the current buttons and menus, i.e., one providing a more explicit relationship to the statistical model (such as in Fig. 15.2), would also be a great improvement, especially for first-time users. Inspiration might be drawn from related recent programs for Partial Least Squares modeling, i.e., Smart PLS (http://www.smartpls.de) and PLS-Graph (http://disc-nt.cba.uh.edu/plsgraph/), on how models can be graphically represented in an easy-to-understand way. The interface that is currently implemented within XGms (and XGobi) is heavily influenced by the options available within the low-level X Windows toolkit being used, and is clearly outdated. More advanced rendering techniques could obviously help to make the interface more appealing and revealing (for instance, better 3D rendering could lower the threshold for moving from 2D to 3D models).

15.6 Summary

This chapter explains how statistical models can be used in the interactive analysis of experimental data. It is discussed how maximum likelihood estimation can map experimental data into model parameters, and how confidence intervals on these parameters play a key role in drawing inferences. One frequent inference is whether or not similar data collected in two different experimental conditions require a significant change in model parameters, hence indicating that the conditions are not equivalent. Another frequent inference is whether a simple or a more complex model needs to be adopted for describing observed data. It is argued that the user, who has insight into the problem underlying the data, should be allowed to play an active part in selecting models and specifying the inferences of interest. Hence, the need for interactive visualization is identified and the program XGms that has been developed for this purpose is discussed. The fact that the statistical models implemented within XGms are geometrical in nature simplifies their visualization and interpretation. The flexibility of modeling diverse data in XGms is demonstrated by means of several examples.

It is proposed that an interactive visualization system for statistical modeling should contain three main components. First, it should incorporate a statistical modeling engine (or expert system) that can perform maximum likelihood estimations of statistical model parameters, and that can construct the confidence intervals required for statistical inference. Second, it should provide an interface through which users can intuitively formulate their statistical questions, such as which models to compare. Third, it should render the results of the analysis in a way that can be easily and quickly assessed by the users. The paper discusses how the program XGms meets with these demands and how it can possibly be extended in the future to overcome current limitations.

References

1. Borg I 0020, Groenen P (2005) Modern Multidimensional Scaling. Springer, New York
2. Buja A, SwayneD, LittmanM, Dean N, Hoffman H (2002) Visualization methodology for multidimensional scaling. Journal of Classification19, 7–44
3. Cox T, Cox M (1994) Multidimensional Scaling. Chapman & Hall, London
4. Draper N, Smith H (1998) Applied Regression Analysis. John Wiley and Sons Inc., New York
5. Fisher R (1992) On the interpretation of $\chi 2$ from contingency tables, and the calculation of p^2. Journal of the Royal Statistical Society 85, 87–94
6. Fleiss J, Levin B, Cho Paik M (2003) Statistical methods for rates and proportions. John Wiley and Sons Inc.,Hoboken, New Jersey
7. GreenP, Carmone Jr. F, Smith S(1998)Multidimensional Scaling, Concepts and Applications. Allyn & Bacon, Boston, Massachusetts
8. Kayargadde V, Martens JB (1996)Perceptual characterization of images degraded by blurand noise: Experiments. Journal of the Optical Society of America A13, 1166–1177
9. Kayargadde V, Martens JB (1996) Perceptual characterization of images degraded by blur and noise: Model. Journal of the Optical Society of America A13, 1178–1188
10. Martens J (2003) Image Technology Design – A Perceptual Approach.Kluwer Academic Publishers, Boston, Massachusetts
11. Martens JB (2002) Multidimensional modeling of image quality. Proceedings of the IEEE 90, 133–153
12. Masson M, Loftus G (2003) Using confidence intervals for graphically based data interpretation. Canadian Journal of Experimental Psychology 57, 203–220
13. Longman, an imprint of Addison Wesley Longman, Inc. New York – Reading, Massachusetts – Menlo Park, California – Harlow, England – Don Mills, Ontario – Sydney – Mexico City – Madrid – Amsterdam
14. Meeker W, Escobar L (1995)Teaching about approximate confidence regions based on maximum likelihood estimation.The American Statistician 49, 48–53
15. Ramsay J (1977) Maximum likelihood estimation in multidimensional scaling. Psychometrika 42,241–266
16. Ramsay J (1977) Monotonic weighted power transformations to additivity. Psychometrika 42,83–109
17. Stuart A, Ord J (1991) Kendall's Advanced Theory of Statistics: Volume 2 – Classical Inference and Relationship, 5th edn. Edward Arnold, London
18. Swayne D, Cook D, Buja A (1998) Xgobi: Interactive dynamic data visualization in the x window system. Journal of Computational and Graphical Statistics 7, 113–130
19. Tryon WW (2001) Evaluating statistical difference, equivalence, and indeterminacy using inferential confidence intervals: An integrated alternative method of conducting null hypothesis statistical tests. Psychological Methods 6(4), 371–386
20. Unwin A, Volinsky C, Winkler S (2003) Parallel coordinates for exploratory modeling analysis. Computational Statistics & Data Analysis 43(4), 553–564

Chapter 16
Interactive Mathematical Visualizations: Frameworks, Tools, and Studies

Kamran Sedig

Abstract This chapter discusses issues pertaining to the design of interactive mathematical visualizations in the context of performing epistemic activities. To this end, this chapter presents the following. It explains what mathematical visualizations are and their role in performing epistemic activities. It discusses the general benefits of making mathematical visualizations interactive. It emphasizes the need for having and using frameworks in order to describe, analyze, design, and evaluate the interactive features of mathematical visualization tools. It presents three such frameworks: micro-level interaction, micro-level interactivity, and macro-level interaction. It uses some of the elements of these frameworks to characterize and discuss five sample interactive mathematical visualization tools and to interpret the results of three usability studies. Finally, it offers some suggestions for future lines of research in this area.

Keywords: Mathematical visualizations, Interaction, Interactivity, Epistemic activities, Design, Micro- and macro-level frameworks, Descriptive frameworks, Interactive tools; Usability studies

16.1 Introduction

This chapter discusses issues pertaining to the design of interactive mathematical visualizations – specifically, the role of interaction in supporting users to perform epistemic activities using mathematical visualizations. Mathematics is a knowledge domain with potential for a vast number of entities to be visualized. Mathematical visualizations (MVs) represent concepts, objects, structures, and/or processes found in many areas of mathematics. In recent years, there has been an upsurge in the number of tools that not only visualize mathematical entities, but also allow users to interact with these visualizations. These tools are designed for many purposes, such as helping users understand mathematical ideas, solve mathematical problems, explore mathematical theories, and play mathematical games and puzzles. Most of these tools are not for productivity purposes; rather they are intended

E. Zudilova-Seinstra et al. (eds.) *Trends in Interactive Visualization*,
doi:10.1007/978-1-84800-269-2_16

for performing epistemic activities. The common factor in majority of these tools is: to interact with the visualizations in order to perform activities such as reasoning, sense-making, meaning-making, problem-solving, learning, and decision-making – in other words, epistemic activities.

This chapter focuses on the interactive component of mathematical visualization tools. It presents, defines, and examines a number of concepts and ideas dealing with the design and evaluation of interaction in the context of mathematical visualization tools. The chapter is organized as follows. Section 16.2 provides some terminological and conceptual background with regard to MVs and interaction. Section 16.3 discusses the importance of having interaction frameworks in order to describe, analyze, design, and evaluate interactive mathematical visualization tools. Section 16.4 briefly describes a few sample interactive tools. Section 16.5 presents three studies that have looked at the role of interaction in performing epistemic activities with MVs. Finally, Sect. 16.6 provides a summary of the chapter and suggests future lines of research in this area.

16.2 Mathematical Visualizations and Interaction

Mathematical visualizations refer to representations that encode causal, functional, logical, and semantic properties and relationships of mathematical structures, objects, concepts, problems, patterns, and ideas in a visual form [8, 22]. Some examples of such visualizations include visual representations of geometric structures, tiling patterns, graphs, and diagrams. Mathematical visualizations differ from information and scientific visualizations in what they visualize and what their concerns are [24]: information visualizations are more concerned with visualizing abstract data and concepts such as basketball scores, market prices, and relationships among people; scientific visualizations are more concerned with visualizing physical entities such as patterns of cloud formations, concepts in physics, and metamorphosis of stones; and mathematical visualizations are concerned with depicting and modeling mathematical entities. Although there are differences among these visualizations and their concerns, they are all visual representations of represented worlds and provide users with externalizations with which they can perform epistemic and cognitive activities.

Oftentimes MVs have deep, hidden, latent, and layered interiority of meaning and structure. This makes the job of decoding and making sense of the semantics and structure of such visualizations difficult and challenging, hence reducing their epistemic utility. When needing to utilize a visualization for epistemic purposes, users have three possibilities: exert a great deal of mental effort to adapt their thinking and reasoning to the visualization, use a different visualization, or adjust the visualization to fit their epistemic and cognitive needs. The third possibility is generally the desirable and user-centred option. One way of adjusting the visualization to the needs of the users is by designing it to be malleable – i.e., interactive.

Static, non-interactive information (or any kind of static visualization) is not malleable. But, when users think, reason, and problem-solve with static information, they often need to process it: deconstruct, decode, and understand its layers of meaning, make sense of it, and/or apply it [12, 14, 20]. In other words, to utilize information for epistemic activities, users of static information make it malleable by performing low-level epistemic actions and/or cognitive tasks on it. Examples of some of the epistemic actions that users perform on information are: they rearrange and reorganize it, add to it, look at it from different perspectives, focus on and look for specific elements within it, modify it, magnify it, hide or eliminate parts of it, decompose it, identify and locate parts of it, create links within it, and probe its parts. Interaction can allow users to perform such actions on the MVs to adjust the visual information to the epistemic needs of the users. Interaction can be viewed as a mediator between these visualizations and the users, supporting the mental tasks that can be performed on or with the static, displayed representations.

Many researchers from different disciplines have suggested that making information interactive can enhance its communicative power by allowing different features, elements, and layers of the static information to be made explicit and available when needed [2, 3, 6, 9, 16, 20, 22, 23, 27–30]. A few of the general benefits of making visualizations interactive include: interaction makes visualizations dynamic and malleable, hence increasing their syntactic and semantic expressibility; by adding a temporal dimension to visualizations, interaction makes their latent properties visible, hence amplifying their epistemic utility and extending their communicative power; by providing opportunities for experimentation and exploration of hypothetical "what if" situations (e.g., by redoing, reformatting, rearranging, and adapting the visualization), interaction can mediate dialectic, evolutionary, formative, emergent, qualitative, and intuitive reasoning and understanding of ideas before they are formally grasped; interaction can guide and transform the path of reasoning and understanding; and, finally, interaction coordinates users' internal mental models with external visual models of objects and processes. Therefore, the design of interaction can be viewed as creating support, enhancement, and scaffolds for the various epistemic and cognitive activities that users perform on or with visualizations.

Although there is agreement on the general benefits of interactive visualizations, nonetheless, as yet, there are no commonly-accepted definitions for interaction and interactivity; nor is there a sufficient body of research to guide designers to know what the various types of interactive features are, and how they facilitate, singly or in combination, the performance of specific cognitive and epistemic tasks.

16.3 Interaction Design and Frameworks

Interaction design is a relatively young discipline. Most of the early research and development in interaction design has been devoted to building and evaluating domain-specific tools, ranging from productivity and entertainment tools to educational and knowledge-centered tools. This research and development has resulted in many new interaction ideas and techniques. However, these ideas and techniques are fragmented, incoherent, and scattered across several disciplines, such as human-computer interaction, visualization technologies, and cognitive technologies. Many of these ideas and techniques do not seem to be directly applicable to the analysis and design of interactive mathematical visualization tools. This problem is compounded by the fact that in describing interactive tools, the term "interactive" usually carries a positive connotation. Designers are usually not clear, nor specific, about what types of interactions are available in these tools, how these interactions support the epistemic activities of the users, how their design can influence the cognitive processes of the users, and how to analyze the interactivity of the tools. As a result, a tool can be "interactive," yet its interactive features may not fit the cognitive and epistemic needs of users. This non-specificity of interactive features of visualization tools is partly due to the fact that there is lack of a coherent language when describing and characterizing the interactive features and properties of these visualizations. For instance, though not the same, terms such as "interactive" and "interactivity" are used interchangeably, loosely, and vaguely, with different people meaning different things. Frameworks can help address this problem.

In the analysis, design, and evaluation of all computational tools frameworks play an important role [5, 7, 10]. Frameworks can organize and give structure to a space of ideas by categorizing its constituent landmarks. These landmarks are usually abstractions of a set of elements within the space that have certain common characteristics. Frameworks can explicate and characterize these landmarks. They can provide a common language for referring to elements within the space. As such, frameworks bring order and coherence to a set of fragmented elements within the space and provide opportunities for the systematic analysis and comparison of different elements – be they techniques, concepts, objects, or design features. In addition, frameworks stimulate creativity and innovation in design. Without superimposition of frameworks upon a landscape of design, designers tend to develop tools in an ad hoc fashion, relying mostly on personal intuition and anecdotes, without being able to situate the tools in the landscape. This ad hoc development of tools not only may result in tools that do not address the needs of a situation, but also may have a negative effect on any posterior analysis and evaluation of the effectiveness of the tools.

Analysis and design of interactive visualization tools involves two levels of frameworks: macro and micro. Macro-level frameworks deal with macroscopic operations, structures, features, and components related to the design of these tools, and micro-level frameworks deal with their microscopic elements and issues. In addition to the levels of frameworks, there are two broad categories of frameworks: descriptive and prescriptive. Descriptive frameworks provide an organized way of thinking about design and a common language to express and substantiate design choices and decisions. Prescriptive frameworks can provide rules and guidelines for how to design interactive visualization tools. Generally, development of prescriptive frameworks requires descriptive frameworks to have been created first.

To help with the analysis, design, and evaluation of interactive mathematical visualization tools, three descriptive frameworks are described next: two micro-level frameworks which not only clearly distinguish between interaction and interactivity, but also systematically organize and characterize the elements which inhabit and define these spaces; and, a macro-level framework which classifies and characterizes the overall interaction operations performed in visualization tools.

16.3.1 Micro-Level Interaction Framework

Sedig and Sumner (2006) [22] have developed a taxonomic framework which characterizes interaction with MVs in the context of performing low-level epistemic actions and/or cognitive tasks. So far, in this chapter, interaction has been discussed in a general sense. But, more specifically, how should interaction be viewed in the context of interactive mathematical visualization tools? Interaction can be viewed as the action a user performs on an MV coupled with the subsequent response from the MV. In this sense, interaction involves the user acting upon the MV and its response happening in the space between the user's mind and the MV. The term "coupled" here does not refer to the temporal sequence of action-reaction so much as the logical, epistemic connection of the two. In other words, interaction here is like the glue that binds the visualization to the mind of the user and mediates between the two. The interaction framework categorizes and characterizes micro-level user-MV interactions according to their common features and properties, epistemic goals, and intended cognitive benefits. The framework organizes the space of interactions into two main categories: basic and task-based. Basic interactions are conversing, manipulating, and navigating, which are based on the root metaphors derived from how people use different parts of their body to interact with the physical world – i.e., mouth/talking, hands/handling, and feet/walking. Task-based interactions are built using the basic interactions and refer to the epistemic actions and/or cognitive tasks in which users engage when thinking and reasoning about or with visualizations. These micro-level operations include animating, annotating, chunking, composing, cutting, filtering, fragmenting, probing, rearranging, repicturing, scoping, and searching (for definitions, see Table 16.1). A distinction is made between interactions and interaction techniques. Interactions are abstract, conceptual units. Interaction techniques, on the other hand, are concrete implementations of these abstractions. For instance, fragmenting is an interaction that seeks to break an entity into its elemental parts. Fragmenting a checkered piece of paper can be implemented using various techniques. In the physical world, the paper could be fragmented by using scissors or torn with the hands. Each of these is a distinct technique, yet the interaction in all cases is fragmenting and is the same. This distinction between interaction and interaction technique not only makes the number of interactions in the framework manageable, but also allows the interactions to remain independent of the techniques by which they are implemented. Additionally, as the list of interactions in the framework is not exhaustive, it allows the list to be expanded if the need arises.

16.3.2 Micro-Level Interactivity Framework

Sedig and Liang [23] have developed a framework which characterizes the interactivity of mathematical visualizations. In the literature, oftentimes, the two terms interaction and interactivity are used interchangeably. However, they are different. Though interaction and interactivity are closely related; yet, they are distinct concepts. They can be thought of as the two sides of the same coin. Whereas interaction focuses on the epistemic actions upon visualizations, interactivity refers to the feel, properties, and quality of interaction [1, 31]. For instance, interaction with a visualization can be through manipulation. However, this interaction can be through direct manipulation of the visualization or through indirect manipulation of it – i.e., via an intermediary visual. Whereas in both cases, interaction is manipulation, the feel and properties (i.e., interactivity) of direct and indirect manipulation are different. Interactivity of visualizations can affect the amount of cognitive effort users put into thinking about the inherent features and meanings of the visualization, how their different thought and reasoning processes are supported, how engaged they become with the tool, and the interchange between them and the tool.

This framework organizes the space of interactivity into twelve factors and discusses each factor's effect on users' cognitive processes and epistemic actions on MVs. Each factor can be viewed as an aspect, or facet, of the interactivity of MVs. The twelve factors are: affordance, cognitive offloading, constraints, distance, epistemic appropriateness, feedback, flexibility, flow, focus, involvement, scaffolding, and transition (for definitions, see Table 16.1). As in the case of the interaction framework, not only are these factors abstractions and can have many different instantiations, but also the list of the interactivity factors is not exhaustive and can be expanded.

Table 16.1 The three interaction design frameworks

	Interactions		Descriptions
Interaction Framework	Basic	Conversing	Talking to a visualization using symbolic, lexical expressions or commands
		Manipulating	Handling a visualization using a pointing cursor
		Navigating	Moving on, over, or through a visualization
		Animating	Generating movement within a visualization
	Task-based	Annotating	Augmenting a visualization by placing marks on it
		Chunking	Grouping a number of similar or related, but disjoined, visual elements
		Composing	Putting together separate visual elements to form a new visualization
		Cutting	Removing unwanted or unnecessary portions of a visualization
		Filtering	Showing, hiding, or transforming a selected subset of visual elements of a visualization based on certain criteria
		Fragmenting	Breaking a visualization into its elemental parts
		Probing	Focusing on or drilling into some aspect, property, or component of a visualization for further analysis
		Rearranging	Changing the spatial position and/or direction of elements of a visualization
		Repicturing	Displaying a visualization in an alternative manner
		Scoping	Changing the degree to which a visualization is visually constructed/deconstructed by adjusting its field of view
		Searching	Seeking out the existence of or position of specific features, elements or structures within a visualization

(continued)

Table 16.1 (continued)

	Factors	Descriptions
Interactivity Framework	Affordance	Provision of interface cues to advertise possible interactions with a visualization
	Cognitive offloading	Provision of interactions that can shoulder the load of some cognitive processes for the user, such as how a visualization changes from one form to another
	Constraints	Restriction of possible interactions with a visualization to canalize and guide the user's cognitive processes
	Distance	Degree of difficulty in understanding how to act upon a visualization and to interpret its subsequent response (types: semantic, articulatory, conceptual, presentation)
	Epistemic appropriateness	Suitability and harmony of interactions in supporting exploration of a visualization
	Feedback	Exchange of information and the direction of communication between the user and a visualization
	Flexibility	Range and availability of interactive choices and options available to the user
	Flow	Duration of interaction with a visualization in time and its effects on the user's perception of the relationship between cause and effect (types: continuous, discrete)
	Focus	Locus of the user's attention during interaction with the visualization (types: direct, indirect)
	Involvement	Degree of users' engagement with and contribution to the information content of a visualization allowed by the available interactions
	Scaffolding	Provision of interactions to cognitively support and augment the user's reasoning and understanding of the encoded information in a visualization
	Transition	Communication of visual changes of a visualization (types: stacked, distributed)
Macro Interaction Framework	Macro Interactions	Descriptions
	Access-based	Accessing stored, available visualizations
	Annotation-based	Adding meta-information to existing visualizations
	Construction-based	Constructing new visualizations
	Combination-based	Combining two or more of access, annotation, or construction operations together

16.3.3 Macro-Level Interaction Framework

Sedig and Liang [24] have developed a framework which abstracts and characterizes all interactive visualization tools according to their macroscopic user-information interaction operations. The framework divides the analysis and design space of interactive visualization tools into four landmark categories: access-based, annotation-based, construction-based, and combination-based (see Table 16.1). Each category represents an overall structure within which users operate upon visual information. The framework discusses what knowledge and cognitive activities each category serves. In access-based interactive mathematical visualization tools, the overall operation by which users interact with information is access; that is, users access the stored, available, existent MVs or MV-templates which are already contained in the tools. In this type of tool, users do not add any new MVs to the tool through interaction with it; rather, they retrieve, access, browse, and interpret the existing MVs which have already been incorporated in the tool by its designers. In annotation-based tools, the overall operation by which users interact with visual information is addition; that is, users add further information to the MVs which are already contained in the tools. In this type of tool, not only users have access to the existing MVs, but also they can annotate these visualizations with meta-information – that is, information that highlights and describes elements of the MVs. In construction-based tools, the overall operation by which users interact with information is construction; that is, users construct new MVs. In this type of tool, the MVs are not necessarily provided in the tool; rather, users create, synthesize, and compose their own MVs. In a combination-based tool, the overall operation by which users interact with information is two or more of the previous macroscopic operations.

To highlight the utility of the above frameworks, some of their elements are used to characterize and discuss the tools and studies in the next two sections.

16.4 Tools

Over the past number of years, much effort has been devoted to the development of mathematical visualizations (for some examples, see: [8, 11] and tools that allow users to visualize and interact with mathematical objects and processes (for some examples, see: [15, 33–34]. These tools range from simple access-based applets with basic interactive operations to complex combination-based applications that allow users to perform many epistemic interactions. This section briefly reviews five sample interactive mathematical visualization tools with different degrees of complexity.

16.4.1 KaleidoTile

Figure 16.1 shows a screen capture of KaleidoTile [36]. According to the macro interaction framework, KaleidoTile is an access-based tool. It allows users to explore tessellations of different planes (i.e., spherical, Euclidian, and hyperbolic). It provides users with micro-level task-based interactions such as repicturing and animating. Using different patterns, users can repicture the tiles of a tessellation to create beautiful visualizations. They can directly interact with an existing visualization by rotating it in a continuous manner, or they can indirectly interact with it through a control point to animate (or morph) a tessellation to explore how symmetry groups are related – e.g., morph a cube to an cuboctahedron to discover that they share the same symmetries.

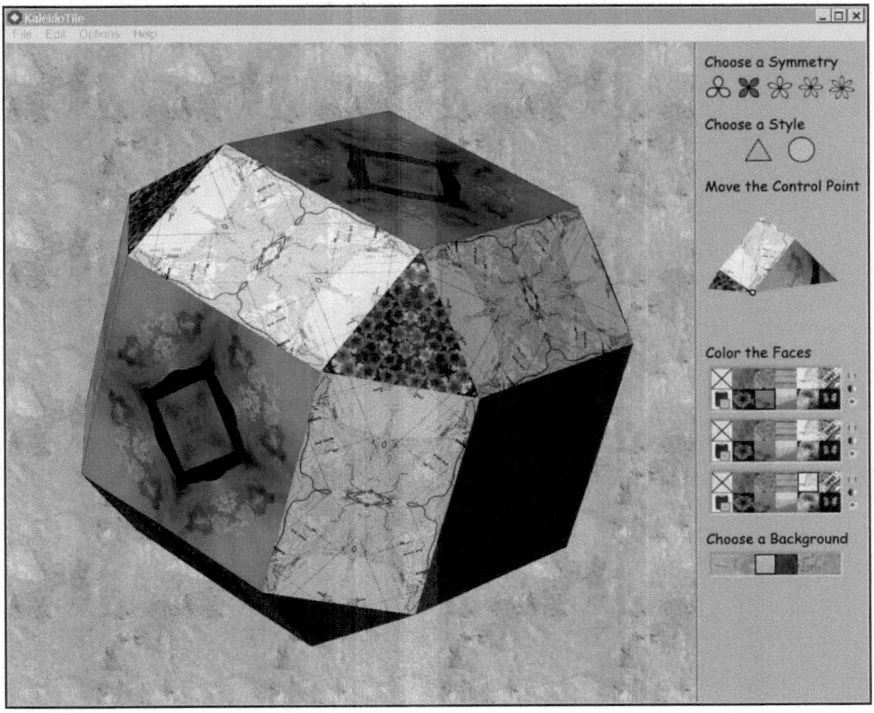

Fig. 16.1 KaleidoTile used to visualize and interact with 3D polyhedra (*See Color Plates*)

16.4.2 Tess

Figure 16.2 shows a screen capture of Tess [17]. Tess is a construction-based visualization tool. It provides users with a few basic geometric shapes and a palette of colors which they can use to compose a drawing. Users can directly manipulate control points on the created drawing to adjust its shape and size. They can then visualize quite sophisticated and intricate symmetric planar tesselations by selecting a group symmetry operation from a given set. The tool allows users to construct virtually an infinite number of visualizations. Users can further explore these visualizations by performing micro-level interactions on them, such as repicturing.

16.4.3 Archim

Figure 16.3 shows a screen capture of Archim [28]. Archim is a combination-based visualization tool. It provides both access- as well as construction-based interactions, though the main purpose of the tool is to allow users to construct and model

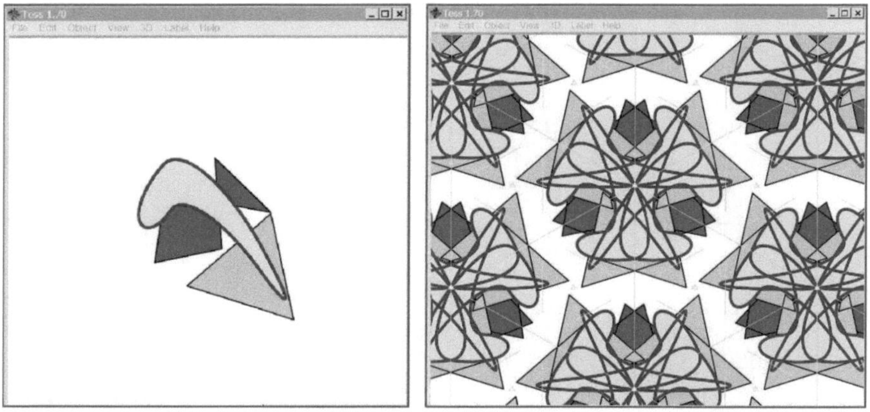

a b

Fig. 16.2 Tess used for visualizing tessellations

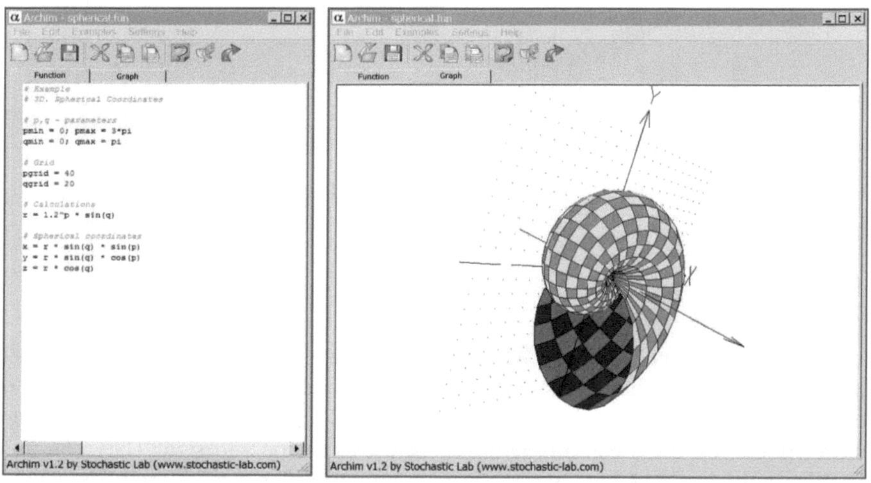

a b

Fig. 16.3 Archim used to visualize and interact with mathematical graphs

2D and 3D graphs of different kinds of mathematical functions. In Archim, users can access sample mathematical functions and observe and explore their corresponding 2D or 3D MVs. Additionally, they can create and visualize their own functions. The construction-based aspect of the tool offers a kit-set comprised of predefined functions (e.g., sine, cosine, and addition) which users can combine to create a variety of expressions. Using these expressions, users can construct virtually an infinite number of MVs. Through conversational interaction, users can change the parameters of these expressions and observe how these changes affect the visualization. Users can also manipulate, rotate, and repicture the constructed MVs.

16.4.4 KnotPlot

Figure 16.4 shows a screen capture of KnotPlot [18, 19] (Scharein, 2006). KnotPlot is a combination-based visualization tool. It allows users to visualize as well as interact with 3D and 4D mathematical knots. KnotPlot provides both access- as well as construction-based interactions. Users can access and explore a large variety of existing knots. They can also compose their own knots. Both accessed as well as constructed knots can be explored by users through micro-level interactions, mostly in the form of direct manipulation and repicturing.

16.4.5 Polyvise

Figure 16.5 shows a screen capture of Polyvise [13]. Polyvise is a complex access-based tool that allows users to visualize thousands of 4D polytopes and dynamically explore them. Four-dimensional polytopes are not easy to make sense of. A simple hypercube, for instance, is comprised of 16 vertices, 32 edges, 24 square faces, and

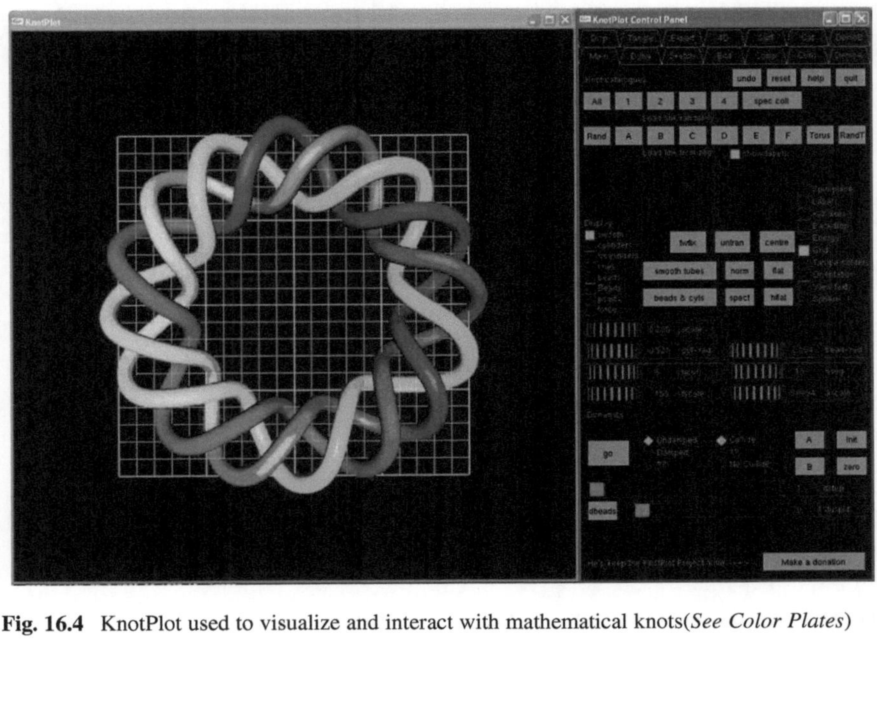

Fig. 16.4 KnotPlot used to visualize and interact with mathematical knots(*See Color Plates*)

8 cubic cells. As the number of components of a polytope increases, its 2D visualization grows in complexity and becomes prohibitively difficult to explore. For instance, an omnitruncated hypercube, which is not the most visually complex polytope, has 384 vertices, 768 edges, 464 faces, and 80 cells. In order to deal with the complexity of these visualizations, Polyvise provides users with a number of micro-level interactions to facilitate the exploration of the accessed visualizations. Three of these interactions are explained here. Users can apply discrete filtering to a visualization to filter out some of its visual elements (e.g., 3D cells) to make it less complex to explore. They can repicture a visualization by stacking its vertices, edges, and faces, by resizing it, by stretching it, and so on. Users can also use scoping to explore how the polytope grows and is constructed around a focal point.

16.5 Studies

This section reports three studies whose findings have implications for the design of interactive mathematical visualization tools, and beyond. As can be observed from the description of these studies, the frameworks not only are useful in having

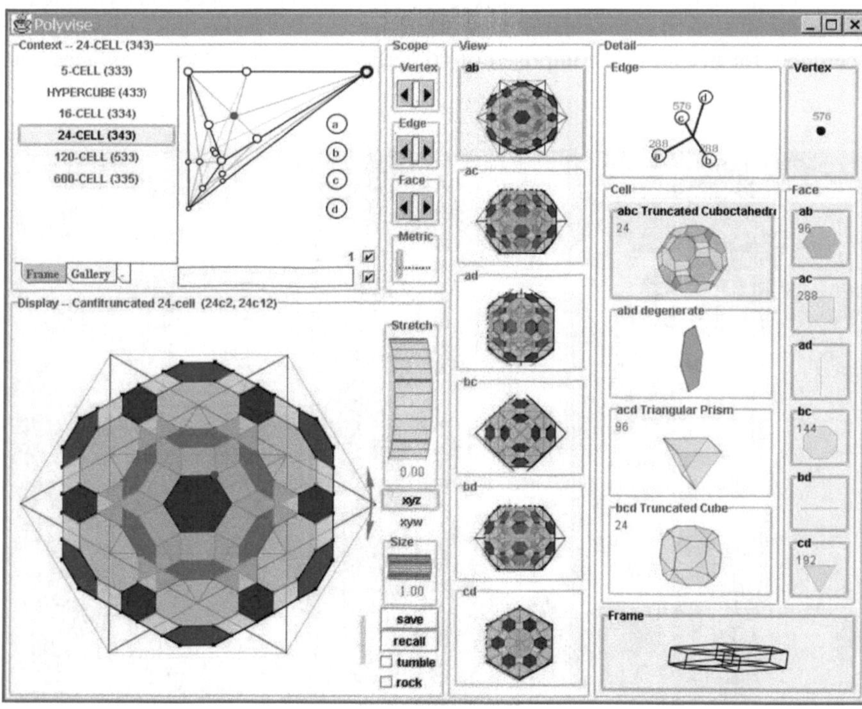

Fig . 16.5 Polyvise used to visualize and interact with 4D polytopes

a common language to more accurately characterize the experimental tools and techniques, but also assist in the interpretation of the results.

16.5.1 Focus and Scaffolding

Some researchers have suggested that there are indications that manipulating visual, graphical objects directly, as opposed to indirectly, can have a negative effect on users' thought processes. Though direct manipulation makes interaction easier, it is not necessarily conducive to reflective processing of information, an important aspect of conscious reasoning and problem solving. For instance, [32] found that, compared to direct manipulation, subjects who used a command-based interface (i.e., indirect interaction with objects) engaged in more reflective thought which was conducive to better learning – they made fewer errors, required fewer trials, and spent more time per trial. Golightly [4] argues that "less direct interfaces cause the user to build a more verbalisable and transferable body of knowledge about the domain" (p. 37). In solving the 8-puzzle game, moving the visual puzzle pieces using adjacent buttons rather than pointing at the pieces and moving them directly resulted in users paying more attention to each move and using a "look-ahead" strategy, as opposed to the ones who used the direct manipulation version of the activity. The direct manipulation strategy involved less planning on the part of the users and was based mainly on "trial-and-error" since recovering from errors was easy. It has, therefore, been concluded that "directness" of interaction is the main reason why this type of interaction does not promote reflective thought. As can be noticed from these two studies, in the first study, not only does the interaction vary, but also the interactivity factor of focus. Therefore, it is not clear whether it is variation in the interaction (manipulating vs. conversing) or the different focus (direct vs. indirect) which is conducive to better learning. The second study suggests that it is the focus of interaction that affects performance of epistemic activities.

To investigate the role of interaction on reflective cognition and concept learning and whether direct manipulation has a negative effect on learning and cognition, [21] designed and conducted a study. Their study focused on the two interactivity factors, focus and scaffolding (see Table 16.1 for their definitions). The tool that was used for the study was Super Tangrams, an interactive mathematical visualization tool intended to support children's understanding of and reasoning about transformation geometry concepts. According to the macro-level interaction framework, Super Tangrams is an access-based tool in which users need to understand the semantics of the MVs and make sense of the causal relationships among the visual elements. Super Tangrams embeds the MV figures in the context of a tangrams activity. Given a set of visual geometric figures scattered on the screen, the object of the activity is for users to move each figure from where it is to a given target area (see Fig. 16.6). For the purposes of this study, three different versions of the tool were created.

In one version, subjects directly manipulated the visual representations of the geometric figures in order to move them from one location to another. This is the

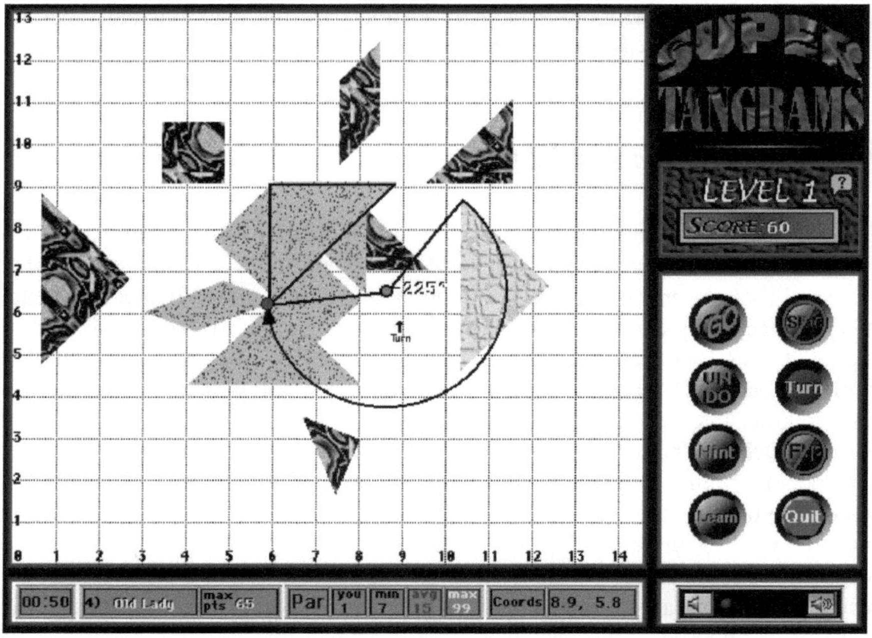

Fig. 16.6 Super Tangrams

manner in which users in other typical applications would move a visual figure: by selecting an operation, and then pointing at and clicking on the figure to translate, rotate, or reflect it. In the next version, subjects did not interact with the geometric figures directly; rather, they manipulated the geometric figures indirectly via directly manipulating the visualizations of the transformation operations (e.g., a translation vector) that acted upon the figures. And, in the third version, indirect manipulation was scaffolded; that is, the visual structure of the transformation visualizations would gradually fade and change, making interaction with the visualizations a more mindful and conscious activity. Hence, variation from the first version to the second was in terms of the interactivity factor "focus" (i.e., direct versus indirect), and variation between the second and third version was in terms of the interactivity factor "scaffolding" (i.e., non-scaffolded versus scaffolded). Empirical results of the study showed that subjects using the third version did significantly better on the administered transformation geometry test than those using the second version, who in turn did significantly better than those using the first version. Subjects using the third version had to process information consciously and think harder than those using the second and first versions. In the context of the interactivity framework, this study suggests that indirect manipulation of the visual figures – that is, direct manipulation of the visualized transformation operations – is more effective than direct manipulation of the geometric figures; and, scaffolded interaction is conducive to more reflective thought than non-scaffolded interaction. Hence, the deficiencies of interfaces that employ direct manipulation are not necessarily caused by their "directness," but by that with which users interact directly – in this study, directness toward geometric figures rather than directness toward visualizations of transformation geometry concepts (i.e., visualizations that are to be consciously processed and understood). The study also suggests that direct manipulation with the figures does not necessarily have to be replaced with command-based interaction (i.e., conversing) for the subjects to learn more. Rather, improved learning can result from using the same interaction (i.e., manipulating the figures), but by changing the interactivity factors of the interaction. Finally, this study also indicates that the degree of mental effort needed to figure out how to interact with visualizations to arrive at a goal is an important factor in the effectiveness of a micro-level interaction. In this study, scaffolding modified interaction, hence affecting the degree of mental effort exerted to process the MVs.

16.5.2 Multiplicity of Interactions

Sedig et al. [26] conducted a study to investigate the effect of incorporating a multiplicity of information visualization techniques into a mathematical visualization tool. The tool that was used for the study was PARSE, an interactive mathematical visualization tool intended to support users' understanding and reasoning about 3D geometric shapes, namely Platonic and Archimedean solids (see Fig. 16.7). According to the macro-level interaction framework, PARSE is an access-based tool in which users need to understand the structure of a set of geometric shapes and make sense of the relationships among them. PARSE uses many techniques, both visual and interactive, to support user reasoning. Here, only a few of the interactive features pertinent to the goals of this chapter are reported, namely interactive morphing, semantic magnification, and dynamic queries. Interactive morphing is an interaction technique in which, by directly manipulating a control point on a geometric shape, users re-arrange its structure and morph it from one state to another. Since visual re-arrangement of the shapes is generated dynamically and the flow of action is continuous, users can experiment with different formations of these geometric shapes through a manipulation-observation-modification feedback loop. Semantic magnification is an implementation of a probing interaction. Since Archimedean solids can be derived from the 5 Platonic solids, the space of relationships among the derived shapes can be visualized using 5 maps. A point on any of these maps semantically refers to a latent geometric shape. PARSE operationalizes this concept by allowing users to manipulate a dot on any of these maps and observe its magnified visualization. Finally, dynamic queries in PARSE allow users to interact with sliders to indirectly filter the space of possible shapes and explore objects that satisfy the specified criteria.

A usability study of PARSE was conducted, investigating how each feature influenced exploration of the visualized shapes. The study showed that, when multiple

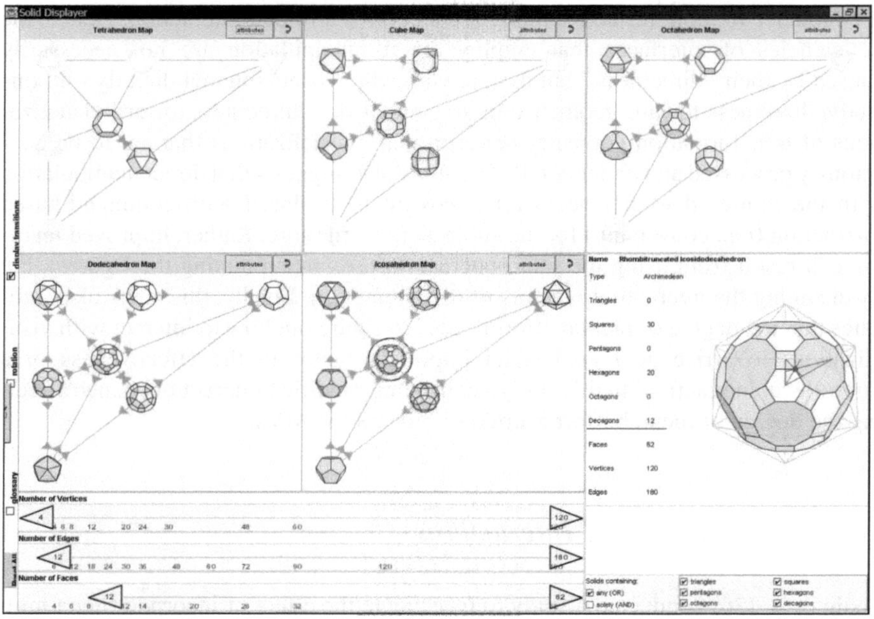

Fig. 16.7 PARSE

interactive features and techniques are provided in a tool, users use them to engage in different forms of mental activities: to vary their reasoning style, to switch from structural to process-based thinking and vice versa, to solve dissimilar tasks, and so on. For instance, interactive morphing was used extensively and helped subjects to have close control over how one shape transforms into another while observing all the intermediary stages of transition in a continuous manner; semantic magnification helped subjects to discover relationships among the shapes and reason about how one shape could be carved out from another; and, dynamic queries were used to identify and locate shapes, and to help formulate hypotheses about the shapes, their properties, and their relationships. The most important conclusion from this study is that different micro-level epistemic interactions in a tool can support and enhance different mental activities, each to different degrees of efficacy.

16.5.3 Transition

In many tools, interaction with a visualization results in a change in the visual image – i.e., a transition happening in the structure and form of the visualization. According to the interactivity framework, transitions in visualizations can be communicated using two distinct models: temporally-stacked or spatially-distributed. In the temporally-stacked model, transitional changes are unveiled in one location, where sequential visual images are stacked on top of one another, a new image replacing the previous one in time. Movies are prime examples of this model of narrating visual change. In the distributed model, communication of the transitional changes to the visualization is not limited to one location only, but it spans within a region in space. Storyboards are a good example of this model of narrating visual change.

In order to investigate how to communicate transitional changes that happen to visualizations to users, Sedig et al. [25] designed and conducted a study. Three different interactive mathematical visualization tools were designed, each having a different user interface: temporally-stacked, spatially-distributed, and spatio-temporal. These tools used a subset of the mathematical visualization objects and concepts as in PARSE – that is, Platonic and Archimedean solids. Each interface provided a different form of visualization of and interaction with the geometric shapes. The temporally-stacked interface (Fig. 16.8, right) employed a temporal model, providing users with a geometric shape at a time and allowing them to directly manipulate it to morph it from one form to another. The transitional changes to the visualizations were communicated in one location. The spatially-distributed interface (Fig. 16.8, left) employed a spatial model, providing users with a relational map of a set of geometric shapes and allowing them to navigate the map by clicking on links that would animate how one shape morphs and becomes

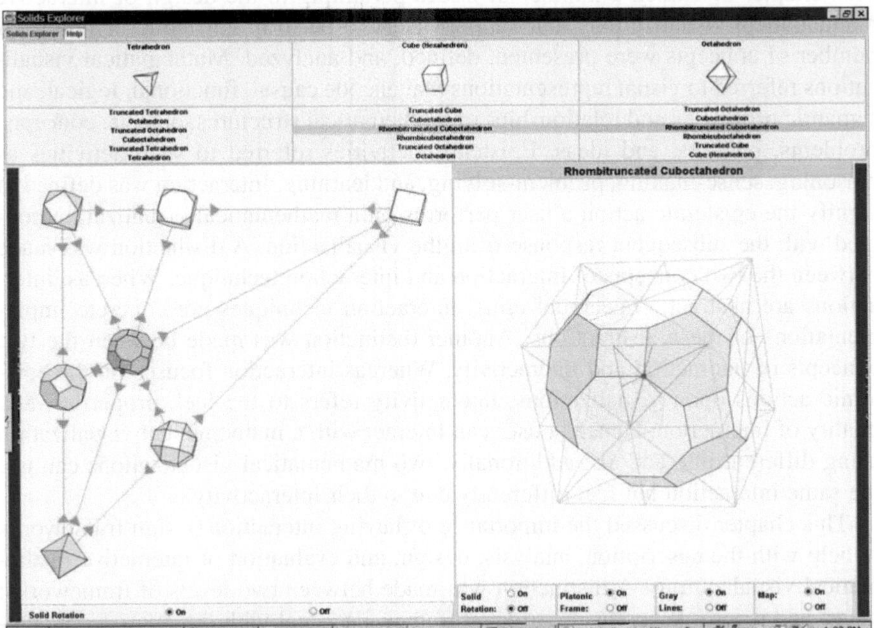

Fig. 16.8 Spatio-temporal interface: spatially-distributed (L) and temporally-stacked (R)

another. The transitional changes to the visualizations were communicated in a region in space. The spatio-temporal interface (Fig. 16.8) integrated the temporally-stacked and spatially-distributed interfaces into one interface, tightly coupling the two models. In this interface, direct manipulation of a shape in the temporally-stacked side of the interface would result in communication of changes in a stacked form as well as in a distributed form, and navigation of the map in the spatially-distributed side of the interface would result in communication of changes in both sides as well.

A usability study of the three interfaces indicated that the spatio-temporal interface was the most effective of the three interfaces in supporting the formation of cognitive maps of transitional changes in the mathematical visualizations. Although all three interfaces supported the formation of cognitive maps of these transitions to some degree, the spatio-temporal interface facilitated construction of a more complete understanding of the transitions from one shape to another. The study showed that simply offering users either a temporally-stacked or spatially-distributed interface does not seem to be sufficient to support proper understanding of transitional changes in visualizations.

16.6 Summary and Future Work

This chapter discussed a number of issues pertaining to the design of interactive mathematical visualizations that support users to perform epistemic activities. A number of concepts were presented, defined, and analyzed. Mathematical visualizations referred to visual representations that encode causal, functional, logical, and semantic properties and relationships of mathematical structures, objects, concepts, problems, patterns, and ideas. Epistemic activities referred to such activities as reasoning, sense-making, problem-solving, and learning. Interaction was defined to signify the epistemic action a user performs on a mathematical visualization coupled with the subsequent response from the visualization. A distinction was made between the two concepts of interaction and interaction technique. Whereas, interactions are abstract, conceptual units, interaction techniques are concrete implementations of these abstractions. Another distinction was made between the two concepts of interaction and interactivity. Whereas interaction focuses on the epistemic actions upon visualizations, interactivity refers to the feel, properties, and quality of interaction. Hence, a user can interact with a mathematical visualization using different interactions; additionally, two mathematical visualizations can use the same interaction but feel differently due to their interactivity.

This chapter discussed the importance of having interaction design frameworks to help with the description, analysis, design, and evaluation of interactive mathematical visualizations. A distinction was made between two levels of frameworks: micro and macro. Whereas micro-level frameworks deal with the microscopic elements and issues related to the design of interactive mathematical visualization tools, macro-level frameworks deal with the macroscopic operations, structures, features, and components related to the design of these tools. Another distinction was made between two categories of frameworks: descriptive and prescriptive. Whereas descriptive frameworks provide an organized way of thinking about design and a common language to express and substantiate design choices and decisions, prescriptive frameworks provide rules and guidelines for how to design such tools. Three descriptive frameworks were presented: micro-level interaction, micro-level interactivity, and macro-level interaction. Each framework classified and characterized the elements which inhabit these spaces. To highlight the utility of these frameworks, some of their elements were used to characterize and discuss five interactive mathematical visualization tools and to interpret the results of three usability studies.

Many ideas were presented briefly in this chapter. But because they were presented together, it can be seen that the different concepts that were discussed are related and what needs to be done is to unify and harmonize these concepts using conceptual frameworks. As in many other developing areas of design, it has gradually become clear that we cannot simply continue developing new interactive visualization tools without frameworks that help the research community to describe, analyze, and situate these tools and their embedded interactive visualizations. Although not demonstrated explicitly, many of the concepts and ideas that were discussed in this chapter can easily be applied to describe, analyze, design and evaluate all kinds of other interactive visualizations in other domains.

Most of the ideas presented in this chapter have been of a descriptive nature, though the studies are steps in developing prescriptions for how to interact with visualizations in more effective ways. One of the future areas of research should be to expand this type of investigation and develop a wider and more concrete set of prescriptive guidelines. Conceptualizing and developing these guidelines is not easy. As a long, organic process, some notable, inter-related lines of action that are needed include: creating a large repertoire of visualization tools that can be used as test-beds for experimenting with different design requirements; designing and conducting usability studies to investigate and compare different tools and interaction ideas to find out how they support users in performing different epistemic tasks using different visualizations; developing general rules and guidelines for interaction design as a result of usability studies performed with a large set of test-bed tools; developing prescriptive frameworks that taxonomize these design rules; and, evaluating and modifying these frameworks in light of new findings to enhance their validity.

References

1. Burgoon, J.K., Bonito, J.A., Bengtsson, B., Cederberg, C., Lundeberg, M., & Allspach, L. (2000) Interactivity in human-computer interaction: A study of credibility, understanding, and influence. Computers in Human Behavio r, 16,553–574.
2. Card, S.K., Mackinlay, J.D., & Shneiderman, B. (Eds.)(1999) Readings in information visualization: Using vision to think.Morgan Kaufmann Publishers.

3. Dix, A.J. & Ellis, G.(1998) Starting simple – adding value to static visualization through simple interaction.Proceedings of the 4th International Working Conference on Advanced Visual Interfaces (AVI '98)(pp.124–134).L'Aquilla, Italy. New York: ACM Press.
4. Golightly, D. (1996) Harnessing the interface for domain learning. In M.J. Tauber (Ed.),Proceedings of the CHI '96 Conference Companion on Human Factors in Computing Systems: Common Ground. April 13–18. Vancouver, British Columbia, Canada. (pp. 37–38).
5. Hannington, A. & Reed, K. (2001) Towards a taxonomy for guiding multimedia application development.Proceedings of the Ninth IEEE Asia-Pacific Software Engineering Conference, Dec. 4–6. (pp.97–106).
6. Hanson, A., Munzner, T., & Francis, G. (1994) Interactive methods for visualizable geometry. IEEE Computer, 27(7),73–83.
7. Heller, R.S., Martin, D., Haneef, N., & Gievska-Krliu, S.(2001) Using a theoretical multimedia taxonomy framework. ACM Journal of Educational Resources in Computing,1,1.
8. Hitt, F. (Ed.) (2002) Representations and mathematics visualization. Proceedings of the Twenty-Fourth North American Chapter of the International Group for the Psychology of Mathematics Education. Georgia, USA.
9. Holzl, R. (1996) How does dragging affect the learning of geometry? International Journal of Computers for Mathematical Learning, 1,169–187.
10. Hult, L., Irestig, M., & Lundberg, J. (2006) Design Perspectives. Human-Computer Interaction, 21(1), 5–48.
11. JVM (2007) Journal of Visual Mathematics. Available: http://www.mi.sanu.ac.yu/vismath/pap.htm
12. Kirsh, D., & Maglio, P. (1994) On distinguishing epistemic from pragmatic action. Cognitive Science, 18,513–549.
13. Morey, J., & Sedig, K. (2004) Adjusting degree of visual complexity: An interactive approach for exploring four-dimensional polytopes. The Visual Computer: International Journal of Computer Graphics, 20,1–21. Berlin: Springer-Verlag.
14. Neth, H., & Payne, S.J. (2002) Thinking by doing? Epistemic actions in the Tower of Hanoi. In W.D. Gray, & C.D. Schunn (Eds.), Proceedings of the Twenty-Fourth Annual Conference of the Cognitive Science Society. (pp. 691–696). Mahwah, NJ: Lawrence Erlbaum.
15. NLVM (2007) National Library of Virtual Manipulatives. Available: http://nlvm.usu.edu/en/nav/vlibrary.html
16. Otero, N., Rogers, Y., & du Boulay, B.(2001) Is interactivity a good thing? Assessing its benefits for learning. Proceedings of the 9th International Conference on HCI (pp. 790–794). New Orleans, USA. New Jersey: Lawrence Erlbaum Associates.
17. Pedagoguery Software (2006) Tess (Version 1.70) [Computer software]. Terrace, B.C., Canada: Pedagoguery Software Inc. Available: http://www.peda.com/
18. Scharein, R.G. (1998). Interactive topological drawing. Unpublished PhD thesis, Department of Computer Science, The University of British Columbia, Canada.
19. Scharein, R.G. (2006). KnotPlot [Computer software]. Vancouver, Canada: Hypnagogic Software. Available: http://knotplot.com/download/
20. Schwan, S. (2002) Do it yourself? Interactive visualizations as cognitive tools.International Workshop on Dynamic Visualizations and Learning. July, 18–19. (pp.1501–1506). Tübingen, Germany.
21. Sedig, K., Klawe, M., & Westrom, M.(2001) Role of interface manipulation style and scaffolding on cognition and concept learning in learnware. ACM Transactions on Computer-Human Interaction, 1(8), 34–59.
22. Sedig, K. & Sumner, M. (2006). Characterizing interaction with visual mathematical representations. International Journal of Computers for Mathematical Learning, 11(1), 1-55. Berlin: Springer-Verlag
23. Sedig, K.& Liang, H. (2006) Interactivity of visual mathematical representations: Factors affecting learning and cognitive processes. Journal of Interactive Learning Research, 17(2), 179–212.

24. Sedig, K. & Liang, H. (2008) Learner-information interaction: A macro-level framework characterizing visual cognitive tools. Journal of Interactive Learning Research, 19(1),147–173.
25. Sedig, K., Rowhani, S., & Liang, H. (2005) Designing interfaces that support formation of cognitive maps of transitional processes: An empirical study. Interacting with Computers: The Interdisciplinary Journal of Human-Computer Interaction, 17(4),419–452.
26. Sedig, K., Rowhani, S., Morey, J., & Liang, H. (2003) Application of information visualization techniques to the design of a mathematical mindtool: A usability study. Information Visualization, 2(3),142–160.
27. Spence, R. (2007) (2nd ed.) Information visualization: Design for interaction. Pearson/ Prentice Hall.
28. Stochastic-Lab (2006). Archim (Version 1.1). Available: http://www.stochastic-lab.com/ archim.html
29. Strothotte, T.(1998) Computational Visualization: Graphics, Abstraction, and Interactivity. Berlin: Springer-Verlag.
30. Stylianou, D. (2002) On the interaction of visualization and analysis: The negotiation of a visual representation in expert problem solving. Journal of Mathematical Behavior, 21,303–317.
31. Svanæs, D. (1999) Understanding interactivity: Steps to a phenomenology of Human-Computer Interaction. Unpublished doctoral Dissertation, Department of Computer and Information Science, Norwegian University of Science and Technology, Trondheim, Norway.
32. Svendsen, G.B. (1991) The influence of interface style on problem solving. International Journal of Man-Machine Studies, 35(3),379–397.
33. TMF (2007) The Math Forum Library. Available:http://mathforum.org/library/
34. VMM (2007)Virtual Math Museum. Available: http://virtualmathmuseum.org/index.html
35. Webb, R. (2003) Stella: Polyhedron navigator. Symmetry: Culture and Science, 11(1–4),231–268.
36. Weeks, J. (2005) KaleidoTile (Version 3.0) [Computer Software]. Available:http:// geometrygames.org/

Index

A

Ad hoc queries, 205, 206
Advanced Visualization in Solar System Exploration and Research (ADVISER), 232–233, 237–239, 241–242
Affordances, 166–168
Analysis of variance, 322, 333
Annotation, vii, 9, 217, 227, 273, 275, 277, 349, 350
ANOVA. *See* Analysis of variance
AR. *See* Augmented Reality
ARCHAVE, 229–230, 235
Archim, 351–353
Asynchronous collaborative visualization systems, 271, 275, 276
Attribute prediction, 329
Augmented reality (AR), 9, 112, 262, 271

B

Balancing, 205, 213, 214
Binocular cue, 145
Bookmark, 272, 274, 277, 278
Brushing, 110, 273, 274, 290

C

CA. *See* Cellular Automata model
Cave, 7, 226, 232–237, 239–244
Cellular automata model
    spatial, 312
Cellular shape
    dynamics simulation rules, 317–318
    models, 313–316
Classification
    pre-, vi, 104
    post-, vi, 104, 105
Client-server models, 134, 135
Closure, 158, 160
Cluster rendering environment, 134
Cognitive
    offloading, 348
    walkthrough, 178, 190
Coherent hierarchical culling (CHC), 82–84, 86, 87
Collaborative virtual environment (CVE)
    data logging, 202, 207, 217
    development life cycle, 202, 205
    event model, 208
Collaboration
    asynchronous, 270, 271
    collocated, 271
    remote, 271–273
Collaborative console views, 211
Color
    mapping, 81, 82, 84, 109
    maps, 100
Communication, 4, 7, 10, 120, 130, 132, 166, 186–188, 258, 270–272, 274, 275, 280, 304, 359, 360
Computational steering latency (CSL), 130, 131
Computed tomography (CT), 80, 100, 101, 104–106, 112, 113
Computer-supported cooperative work (CSCW), 169, 270
Conceptual learning, 355
Confidence intervals, 43, 322–325, 333
Consistency, 166, 168
Constraints, 23, 24, 32, 66, 122, 134, 166, 167, 185, 191, 226, 239, 305, 317, 348
Continuity, 157, 161
Closed contours, 158, 160
Coordination, 12, 274, 280
Correlation filter, 307
Correlation theorem, 307

CSCW. *See* computer-supported cooperative work
CT. *See* computed tomography
CVE. *See* Collaborative virtual environment

D
Data
  binary, 330, 331
  CVE, 203, 207
  discrete, 330
  exploration, 82, 84, 175
  interval, 322, 330
  multidimensional, 102, 166
  oceanographic, 317
  ordinal, 322, 330
  sharing, 276, 278
  structuring, 12, 42
  tomography, 106, 301
Data mining
  high dimensional, 76
  virtual environment, 202
Degree of certainty, 38, 39
Depth
  cues, 305
  perception, 226
Design, vi, vii, 8–10, 23, 45, 46, 52, 57
Design gallery, 107
Dialogue styles, 166
Diffusion MRI visualization, 231, 235
Discussion
  doubly-linked, 274, 277, 280
  embedded, 274, 277
  forum, 274, 276
  independent, 274
Display
  graphical, 160, 164, 165
  informative, 52
  haptic, vii, 259
  technologies, 7, 144, 145
Distance, 31, 55, 67, 70, 89, 90, 108, 243, 253, 255, 256, 289, 290, 294, 298, 328, 331, 333, 348
Dual uncertainty model (DUM), 38
DUM. *See* Dual uncertainty model

E
Economic visualisation, 216
EDA. *See* Data, exploration
Emergent events, 206, 207
Emission and absorption coefficient, 114
Environment traversal visualisation, 215
Epistemic appropriateness, 348
Error bars, 29, 30
Exploratory data analysis. *See* EDA
Evaluations
  controlled laboratory, 192
  formal, 234, 237, 239
  of IVR-based visualization systems, 9, 190, 192, 227

F
Factor analysis, 323, 335, 341
Fast fourier transform
  discrete, 307
  inverse, 307
Feedback
  auditory, 168, 258
  force, 258–260
  loop, 126, 127, 137, 357
  sensory, 258
  tactile, 168
  visual, 13, 40, 112, 127, 168, 258
  visual force, 258
Field of regard (FOR), 244–246
Field studies, 191–194
Field of view (FOV), 137, 235, 240, 244–246
Filtering, 125, 126, 131, 132, 168, 273, 280, 347, 354
Flexibility, 101, 170, 189, 261, 299, 341, 348
Focus
  groups, 178, 183, 190, 201, 206, 207, 212–214, 216, 218
  testing, 205, 214
Formal evaluation, 234, 237, 239
Frustum culling, 82, 90, 94
Fuzzy sets, 27, 28, 31, 32, 34, 36, 43

G
Geometric primitives, 109, 110, 125
Geometrical models
  for statistical data analysis, 328
  XGms Interface to, 338
Gestalt principles, 157, 159–164
GPU. *See* Programmable graphics processing unit
GROPE III, 259, 260
Graphical user interface (GUI), 6, 44, 53, 108, 112, 156, 226, 296, 297, 338, 339
Graphics hardware, vi, 81, 82, 93, 297, 298
Graphs
  bar, 42
  2D, 12, 31, 122, 160, 161, 352
  3D, 34, 352

line, 38–40, 122, 142
multidimensional, 75

H

Haptic
display, vii, 259
renderer, 259
Head mounted display (HMD), 226, 245–246
Heuristic evaluation, 178, 190
Hierarchical stop-and-wait occlusion culling (HSW), 83
High-resolution display walls, 244–245
Hypersurface, 62, 63, 65–67, 71–74, 253
Hue, 30, 33, 99, 168
Human
factors, 139–151, 169
perception, vi, 10, 120–122, 124, 144, 309
vision system, 304

I

Image
quality, 122, 139–140, 337
recognition, 50
Immersive environments, 9, 226, 242, 243, 248, 257, 289–291
Immersion experience, 206, 213
Immersive Virtual Reality (IVR), *See* also Virtual Reality
for scientific visualization, 9, 226, 227
IMVS, *See* Interactive molecular visualization
Information
foraging, 279–280
patches, 279
qualitative, 294
quantitative, 287, 292–294, 299
scent, 279
static, 124, 344, 345
Information uncertainty
invariance, 37
modeling, 37
models
possibility, 21
probability, 21
provability, 21
membership, 21
propagation, 22, 23, 36–40
sources, 21–22, 43
visualization
data-driven, 24
task-driven, 24
user-objective-driven, 24
InfoScope, 13, 14
IMD, *See* Interactive molecular dynamics
Input
devices, 8, 10, 147, 227, 244, 246–248
quantitative, 288, 290, 292, 295
Interaction
devices, *See* input devices
dual domain, 110
events, 206, 207, 212, 216, 219, 220
face-to-face, 272
loop, 130, 131
multimodal, 10
of uncertainty, 44–45
user, 3–6, 10, 124–126, 128–131, 134, 137, 139, 143–150, 186, 202, 204, 206
of variables, 23
Interaction/interactivity design
frameworks
basic, 347, 348
descriptive, 346, 361
macro-level, 346, 349–350, 355, 357, 360
micro-level, 346–349, 360,
prescriptive, 346, 361
task-based, 347, 348
Interactive
evolution, 107, 114
molecular dynamics (IMD), 257, 260, 261
molecular visualization (IMV), 251–257, 259–262, 264
ray tracing, 81, 82, 87–94
spatiotemporal reasoning, 303–316
statistical modeling, 321–340
Interactive visualization
applications, 244, 246, 247
challenges, 71
design principles for, 155–171
frameworks, 11–13
model, 4, 12
of particle-based simulation, 81, 93
pipeline, 7, 123, 126, 130, 133, 135
system architectures, 125–126, 129, 130, 133–134, 141, 144
Interactivity
recursive, 73
recursive multidimensional, 77
Interview, 178, 181–185, 190, 191, 214, 275
Inverse design, 107, 114
Involvement, 348
Iso-surfacing, 124, 131, 133
IV. *See* Interactive visualization
IVR. *See* Immersive virtual reality and Virtual Reality
IVR-based visualization systems, 227–242

J
Jalview, 180

K
Kinesthetic sensory systems, 261
KnotPlot, 353

L
Likelihood function, 323, 325
Lightweight visualization system, 141
Live console, 205, 207, 211, 212
Log specification
  in situ, 209–210
  aggregate, 210–211
  programmer, 212
Low-high-histogram, 111

M
3D mice, 247
MAF. *See* Multimod application framework
Many-Eyes.com, 278
Manipulation
  direct, 7, 131, 166, 168–170, 172, 227, 228, 259, 348, 353, 355–357, 360
  indirect, 168, 348, 356
  object, 149–150
  physical, 264
Mapping, 7, 23, 30, 39, 45, 51, 59, 81, 82, 84, 99, 101–106, 109, 112, 121, 125, 156, 166, 168, 172, 203, 328–330
Massively Multiplayer Online Roleplaying Game (MMORPG), 202–204, 217, 218
Maximum likelihood, 323
Measurement
  angular, 291
  cylindrical, 291
  ellipsoidal, 290
  interactive, 288, 292, 301
  linear, 290, 291
  quantitative, 237, 288, 290, 299
  tools, 288–291, 298, 299
Medical imagery, 124
Medical Imaging Interaction Toolkit (MITK), 12
Metrology, 287
MITK, *See* Medical Imaging Interaction Toolkit
Möbius strip, 74, 75
MolDRIVE, 257, 258
Molecular
  builders/editors, 255
  docking, 255, 256
  mechanics, 252, 253, 255, 256
  modeling, 252, 253, 255, 256
  models
    computer molecular, 252
    material, 252, 262
  searching/steering systems, 257, 261
  viewers, 253–255, 260
Monocular cue, 145
Motion cue, 146
Motion trackers, 246–247
Monitors, 61, 140, 211, 243–245, 257, 272, 304
Multi-display visualization environments, 194
Multidimensional
  contouring, 61
  scaling, 31, 323, 328, 336–338
Multimod Application Framework, 13, 14
Multiplicity of interactions, 357–358

N
Navigation
  controls, 227
  social, 203, 279
  through 3D dataset, 132
Navigational cues, 168
Nested Cavities (NC), 63–65
Nonlinear models, 49
Nonlinear multivariate relations, *See* Hypersurfaces
Numerical simulations, 229, 288

O
Observation
  ethnographic, 183
Opacity, 28, 30, 33, 38, 39, 101, 109, 231, 297
Output
  computational, 292
  quantitative, 288, 290, 292, 300, 301
  visual, 244, 299

P
PARSE, 357–359
Parallel coordinates
  3D extension of, 34
  foundations, 51, 67
Parameter range culling, 81, 84, 89
Particle visualization methods, 79, 93

Particles, 30, 79–95, 123, 125, 229, 231, 258, 292, 294, 301, 305
Pattern recognition, 50, 51, 62, 76, 304
Perception
  homogeneity of, 328
Perceptual illusions, 122
Planes
  clipping, 6, 12, 110
  proximate, 70–71
  tangent, 71, 72, 75
Plural value, 38, 39
PHANToM, 260, 261
Pointing, 11, 53, 128, 166, 227, 232, 247, 253, 256, 257, 270, 272, 273, 275–281, 355, 356
Position function, 108
Prefuse Information Visualization Toolkit, 12
Pre-attentive processing, 156, 162–164
Principle of requisite generalisation, 38
Polyvise, 353–354
Probability
  distribution, 27, 28, 39
Problem solving
  environment, 95, 304
Programmable graphics processing unit, 81
Projectors, 243–245, 317
Prototypes
  low Fidelity (Lo-Fi), 177, 186
  high Fidelity (Hi-Fi), 178, 186
Proximity, 30, 70, 156–158, 160, 161, 163, 164, 300
Publishing, 270, 275, 278–279, 281
Python Molecular Viewer (PMV), 254

Q
QA, *See* quality assurance
Quality assurance, 201, 205, 214, 218
Quantum mechanics, 252, 255
Questionnaire, 178, 181–184, 190, 191, 206, 214, 240, 241

R
Ray tracing, 81, 82, 87–94
RealityGrid project, 140
Reflective cognition, 355
Resource discovery, 131, 142
Response time, 129, 131–132
Responsive Workbench, 245, 258
Regression
  linear, 323, 330, 332–335
  multiple, 328, 335–338
Rendering
  adaptive, 134, 139–140
  non-photorealistic, 294, 295
  of spatial periodicities, 310
  volume, 5, 12, 26, 79, 94, 100, 102, 106

S
Scaling, 5, 31, 70, 323, 328, 336, 338, 340
Selective, Dynamic, Manipulation (SDM), 167, 168
Sense.us, 276–278, 281
Sensory data, 306
Sensory modalities, 10, 120
Simulation steering, 255–257
Shading
  soft, 90–91
Shading-based visualization environment, 297–298
Shape
  correlation, 306–309
Social network visualisation, 215–216
Space
  spatial, 306
  temporal, 306
Spatial-based frequency analysis, 310
Spatial proximity, 156, 163, 164, 300
Spatial periodicity, 309–312
Spatiotemporal patterns, 305
Statistical data analysis
  geometrical models for, 328–337
Statistical models, 321–341 (Chapter 15 deals with this topic)
Stereo imagery, 124, 137
Stereoscopic
  display, 243, 244, 246
  vision, 261, 305
Spotfire, 275, 276, 281
Surround-screen displays, 244
Symmetry, 158, 159, 237, 305, 350, 351
Swivel, 276, 278, 281

T
Talking, 270, 272, 274–281, 347
Task model, 184, 185, 214, 220
Tess, 351
Texture, 5, 11, 30, 34, 39, 84, 100, 168, 261, 297, 298, 309
Time events, 206, 207, 215
Time-varying data, 84, 86, 304
Tissue engineering, 289–291, 301
Touch, 45, 259–261, 264

Tracking
head-, 226, 233, 236, 243, 244, 246
interactive, 307, 309
system, 243, 246
target, 307
vision-based, 306
Transfer function
design, 102, 106–109, 111, 113, 114
multidimensional, 105–106, 110, 114
Transition
spatially-distributed, 358–360
temporally-stacked, 358–360

U
Unified uncertainty model, 38
Uncertainty visualisation techniques, 44
Usability
testing, 178, 191
of visualization systems, 114
User and task analysis, 179
User experience, 10, 169–172, 205
User interaction/control
direct, 3, 6, 10, 147–149
human factors guidelines for, 144–150
real-time, 6, 125, 128–129
User interfaces
for transfer function design, 109
UUM, *See* Unified uncertainty model

V
Vector glyph, 5, 41, 100
View-frustum culling (VFC), 82–84, 87
View sharing, 272–273, 275, 277, 281
Virtual Cardiovascular Laboratory, 227–230
Virtual
laboratory, 290
menus, 150
objects, 244, 247, 259, 301
scene, 291, 292
Virtual Reality (VR). *See also* Immersive virtual reality
FishTank, 226, 235, 239–241, 243, 244
Vis5D, 12, 14
Visual cues, 52, 54, 81, 90, 91, 121, 125, 133
Visual parameters
techniques for assignment of, 108
Visualization
client-server, 136
collaborative, 9, 141, 176, 192–194, 202, 270–272, 274–279, 281
communication-minded, 271
of CVE data, 203, 207–208
design, 156, 175–194, 202
distributed, 129–133, 137
of financial data, 58–62
of fuzzy rules, 31–36
GPU-based, 81
immersive, 231, 288, 290, 291, 296
information, 12, 14, 38, 110, 111, 121, 122, 184, 189, 192, 226, 270, 294, 344, 357
mathematical, 343–361
medical, 8, 11, 120
multidimensional, 75
multimodal, 7, 13
pipeline, 7, 123, 125, 126, 130, 135
scientific, 9, 11, 99, 100, 102, 120, 122–125, 133, 140, 142, 151, 156, 175, 225–248, 269, 271, 289, 304–306, 344
sparse, 296
of stress in flows, 292–294
web-based, 12, 271, 278–279, 281
Visible Human Explorer, 169
Visualization Toolkit, 11–14
VizServer, 135–137
VOlume eXplorer (VOX), 233, 236, 239
VR. *See* Virtual reality
VTK. *See* Visualization Toolkit

W
Wikimapia, 276, 277, 281
WIMP (Window, Icons, Menus, and Pointing), 253
Wizard of Oz, 188

X
XGms, 321–341
XGvis, 338

Z
Zipdecode, 12
Zoomable interfaces, 168
Zooming windows, 311

Color Plates

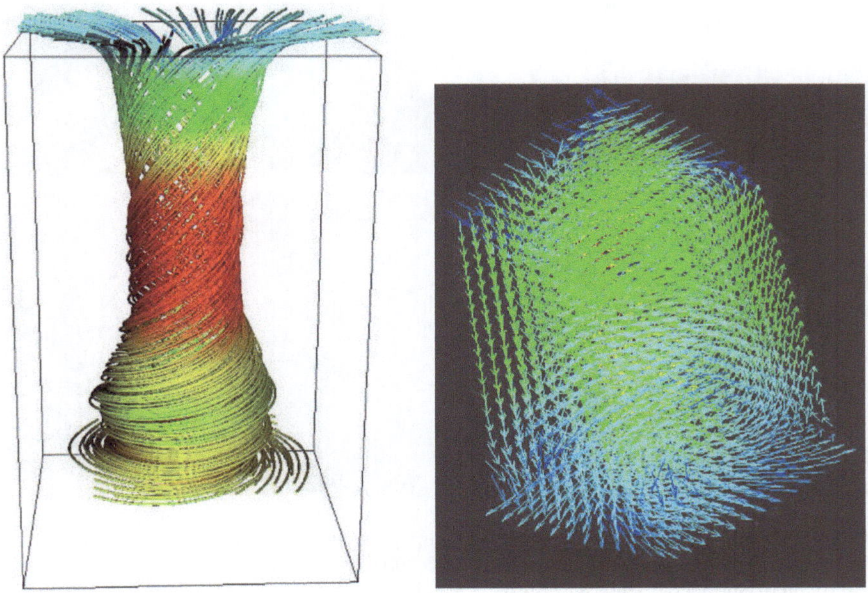

a b

Fig 1.2 Streamline (a) and glyph (b) based visualization techniques applied to validate the tornado CFD (Computational Fluid Dynamics) model

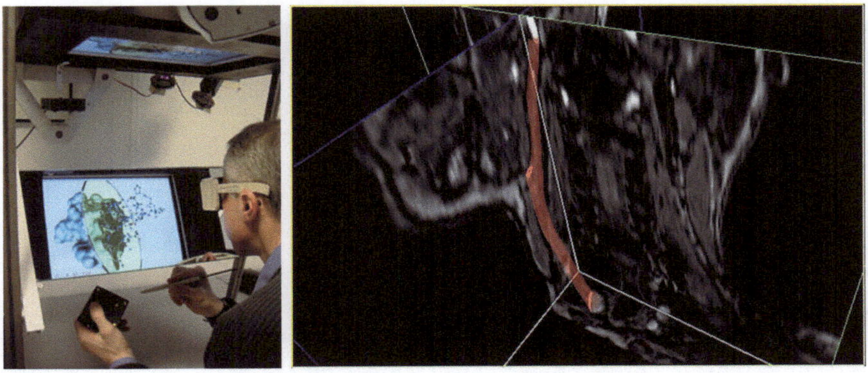

a b

Fig 1.3 Direct user interaction with the 3D visualization of a molecular structure (a); three orthogonal clipping planes within a 3D volumetric medical dataset (b) (Images courtesy of the Center for Mathematics and Computer Science (CWI) and the Division of Image Processing (LKEB), Leiden University Medical Center, the Netherlands)

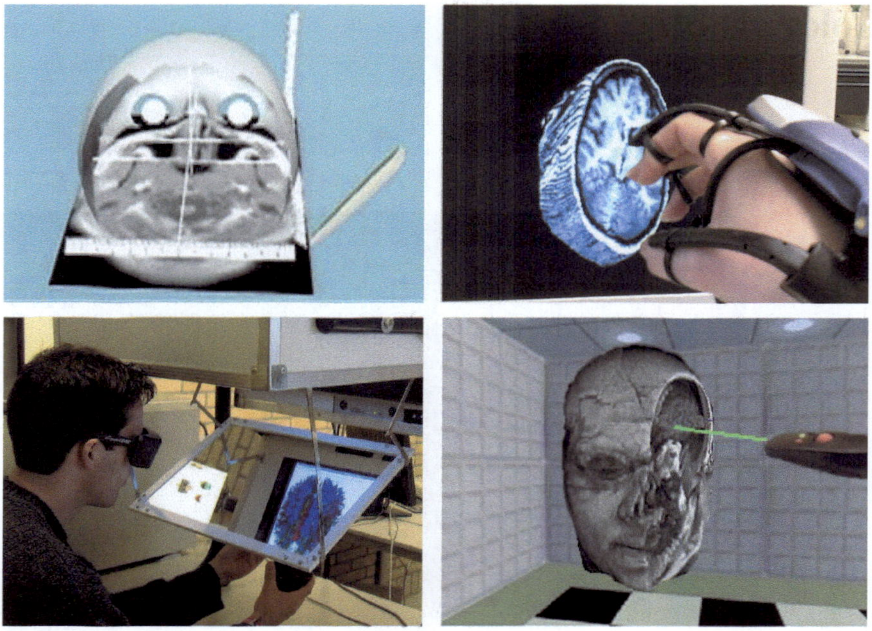

Fig 1.5 Interactive medical visualization in VR (Images courtesy of the CSIRO, Australia and the University of Amsterdam, the Netherlands [36], © 2004 Springer Verlag, included here with kind permission of Springer Science and Business Media)

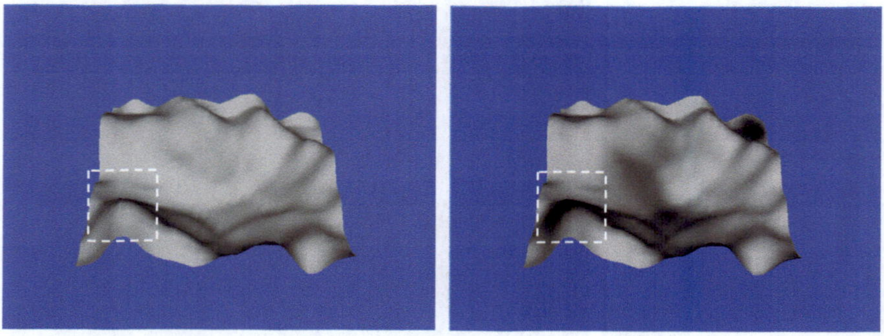

Fig. 2.1 Frames from a movie of the luminance oscillation technique, with the changes in values highlighted with the dashed rectangle

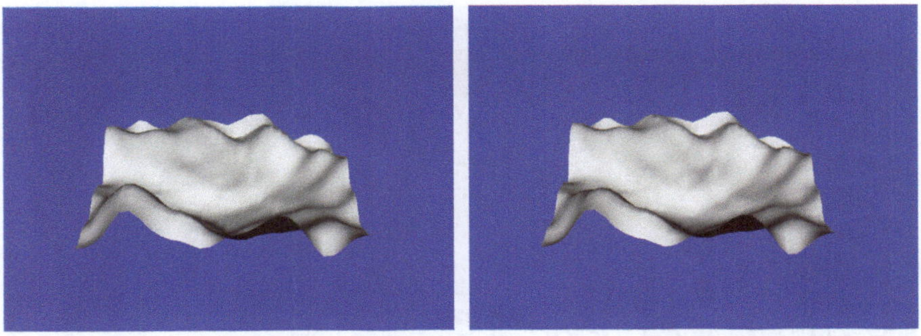

Fig. 2.2 Stereo pair with uncertainty at the peaks and in the centre rendered with vertex vibrations. This appears as a blurred uncertainty region due to an absence of binocular fusion

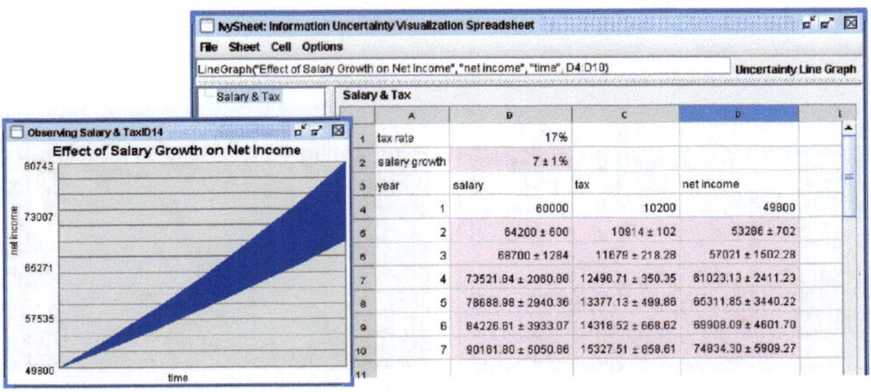

Fig. 2.8 Prototype information uncertainty spreadsheet system. The salary growth field (cell B2) is subject to uncertainty, which is propagated to other cells and from there to the visualisation

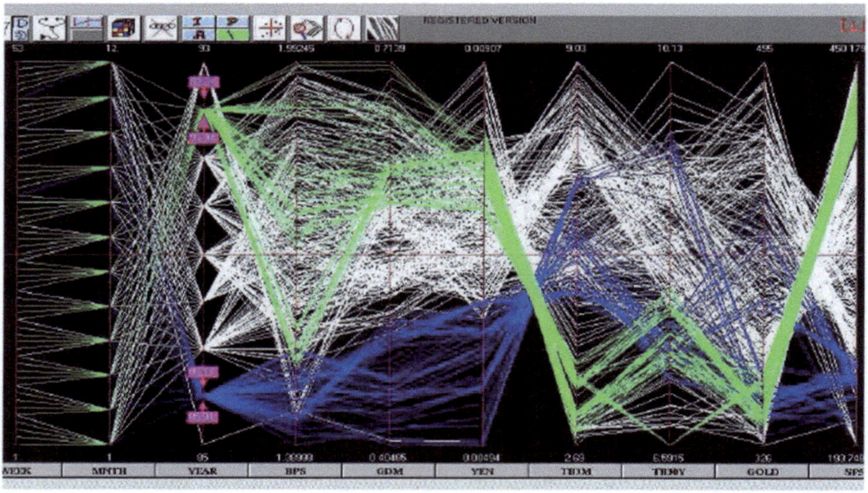

Fig. 3.9 Financial data. Quotes by Week-on Mondays, Month, Year – the first 3 axes fix the date; **S**terling, **D**mark, **Yen** rates per $ 4th, 5th, 6th axes; **3M**TB, **30Y**TB interest rates in %,7th, 8th axes; Gold in $/ounce, 9th, **SP**500 index values on 10th axes

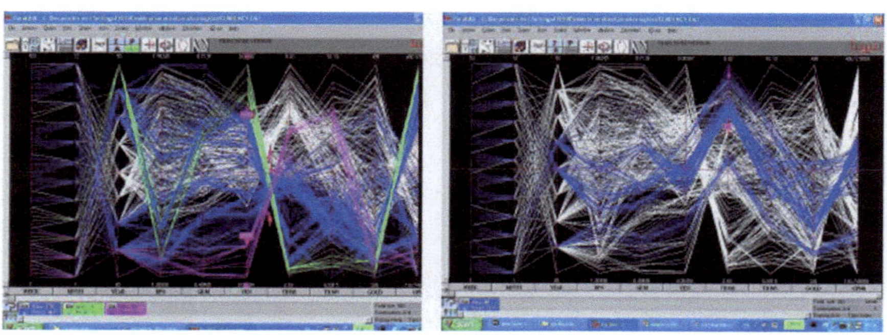

Fig. 3.11 (Left) Negative correlation. (Right) Positive correlation (Left) The crossing lines between the 6th and 7th axes in Fig. 3.9 show strong negative correlation between Yen and **3M**TB rates. One cluster is selected with the **P**inch query and combined with the high and low ranges on the **Yen** axis.(Right) A positively correlated cluster where the Yen and **3M**TB rates move *together when **Gold** prices are low to mid-range*

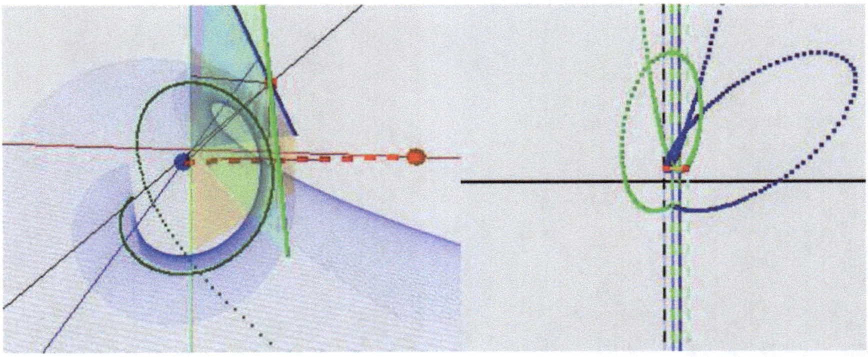

Fig. 3.27 A 3-D helicoid in Cartesian and ||-coords. The tangent plane determined by the two intersecting lines (left) is represented by a pair of points one on each of the curves at the same y (right). A helicoid in N-D is represented by $N-1$ such curves

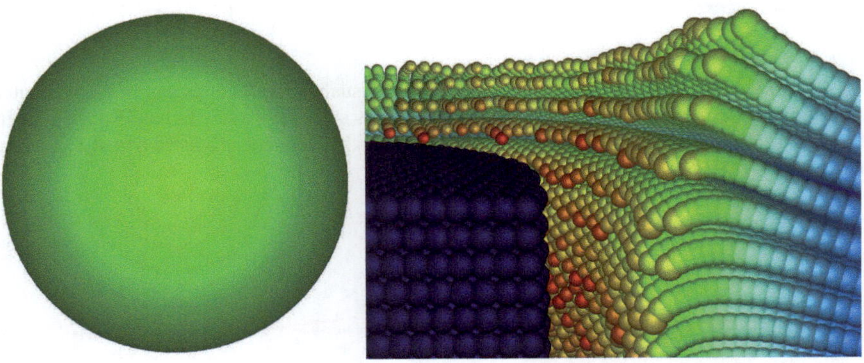

Fig. 4.2 *High quality particle rendering with point sprites*. View-aligned billboards serve as the base primitive. An individual particle is specified by a vertex position and other per-vertex attributes that control its representation (left). Efficiently rendering high quality particle glyphs enables simultaneous visualization of both large and small scale features within the data (right)

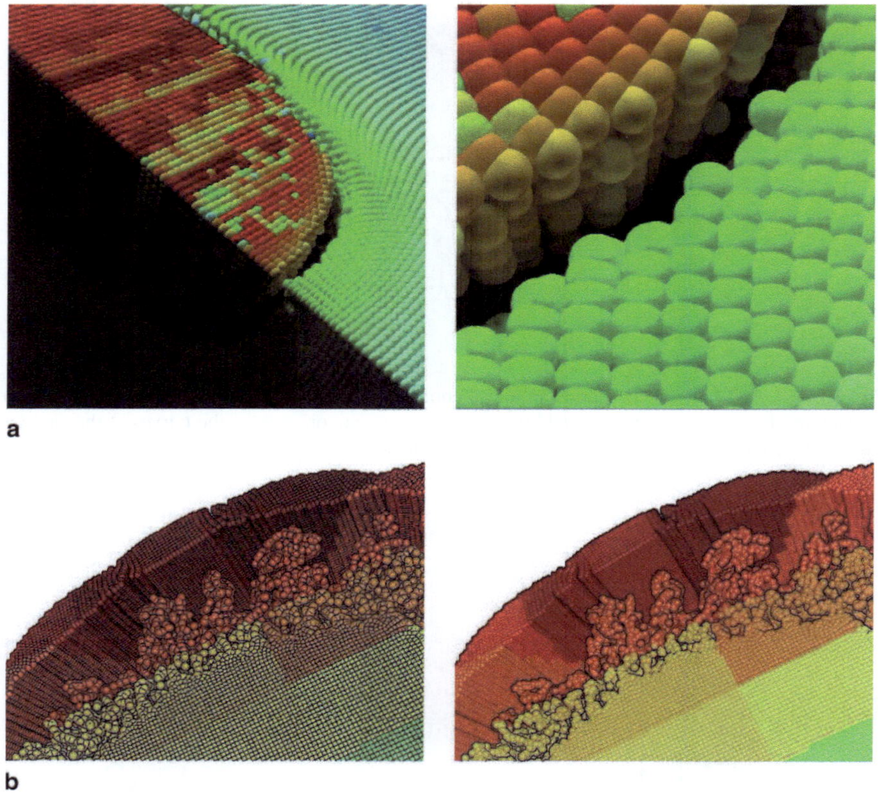

Fig. 4.3 *Enhancing particle visualization*. Advanced visualization features can be implemented using multipass fragment processing. **a** Shading models such as physically based diffuse interreflection lead to enhanced perception of particle datasets.**b** Silhouetteedges can be used to accentuate a set of view-dependent boundaries

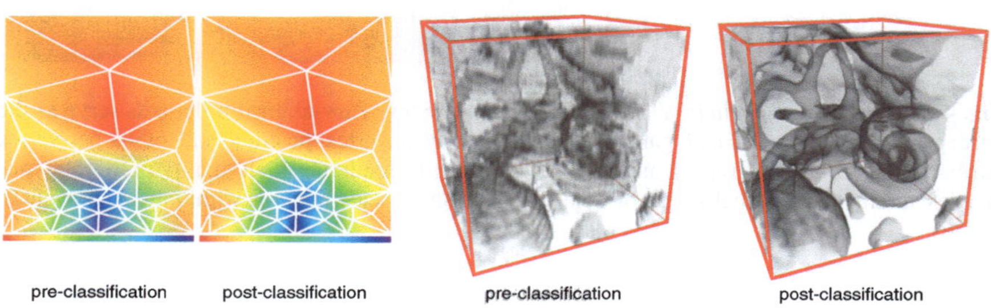

Fig. 5.4 Comparison of pre- and post-classification for the 2D heat distribution (left) and for a high-resolution CT of the inner ear (right)

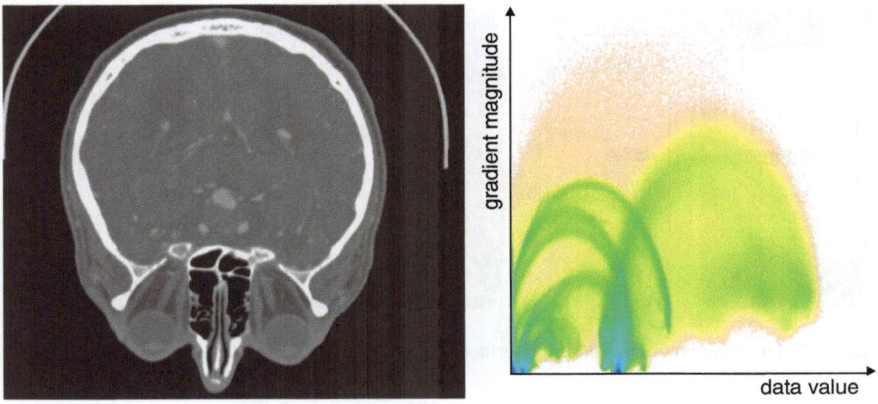

Fig. 5.5 Left: Slice image of a CT angiography of the human brain. Right: 2D histogram of data value and gradient magnitude for the same data set

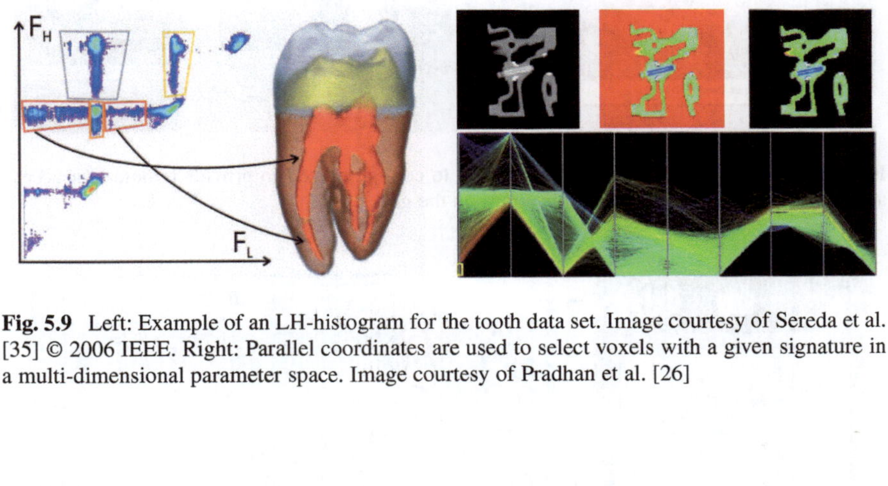

Fig. 5.9 Left: Example of an LH-histogram for the tooth data set. Image courtesy of Sereda et al. [35] © 2006 IEEE. Right: Parallel coordinates are used to select voxels with a given signature in a multi-dimensional parameter space. Image courtesy of Pradhan et al. [26]

Fig. 5.10 Examples of a semantic model for CT angiography, with the anatomical structures, brain, soft tissue bone and vasculature

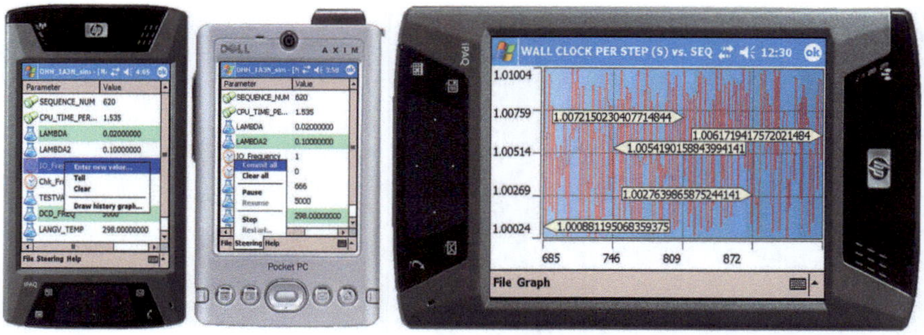

Fig. 6.12 The computational steering interface of the RealityGrid PDA Client

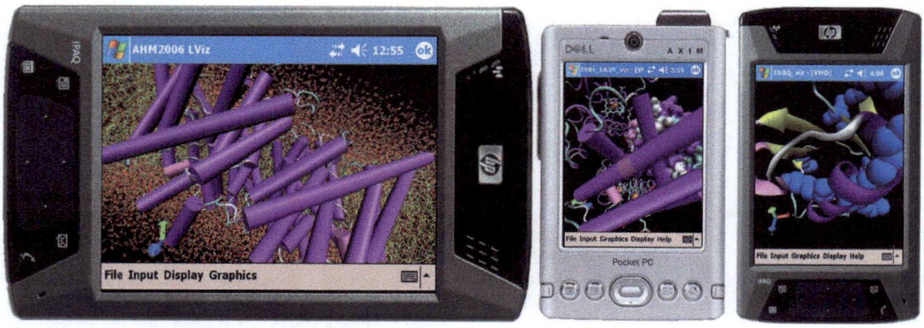

Fig. 6.13 The RealityGrid PDA Client is able to configure itself to provide remote user access and interaction for visualization applications on the grid

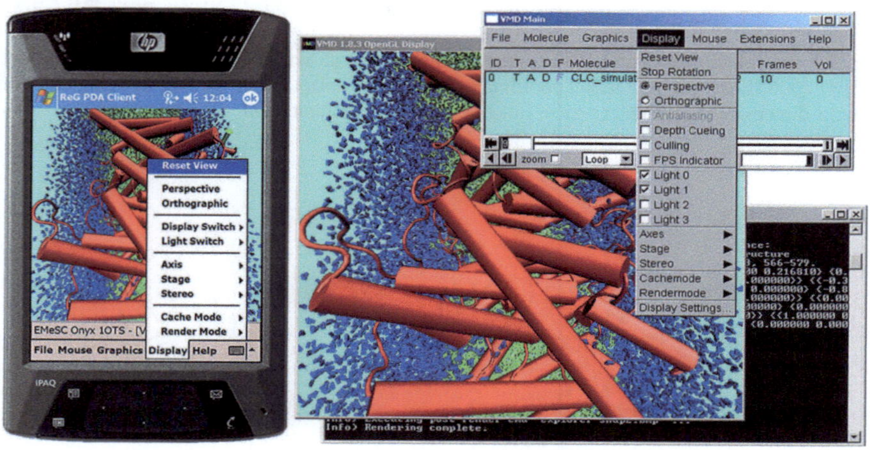

Fig. 6.14 The RealityGrid PDA Client visualization interface has been specifically designed to provide the same user services as the integrated VMD front-end

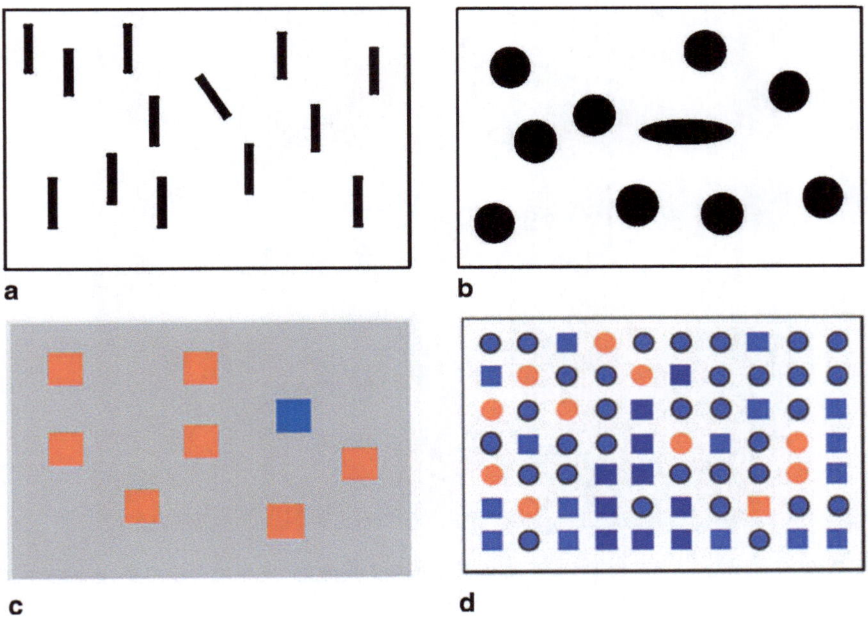

Fig. 7.8 (**a**) Orientation – the 'odd one out' can be quickly identified, (**b**) Different shapes can often pop out, (**c**) A different colour can be identified pre-attentively, (**d**) Pre-attentive processing does not occur – careful scrutiny is required to locate the orange square (Spence [34])

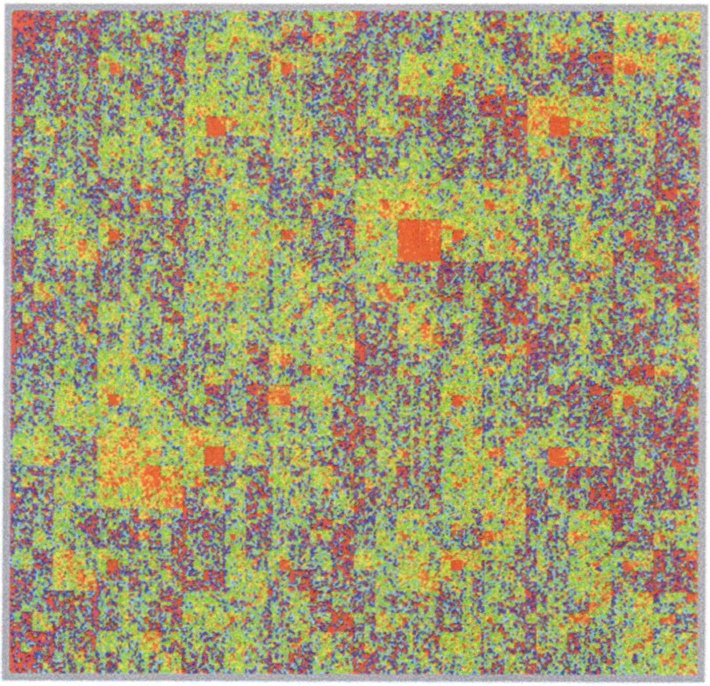

Fig. 7.10 Gene map of an E-coli visualisation. Colour and shape and used to support the pre-attentive recognition of related items (orange squares) and patterns in the data

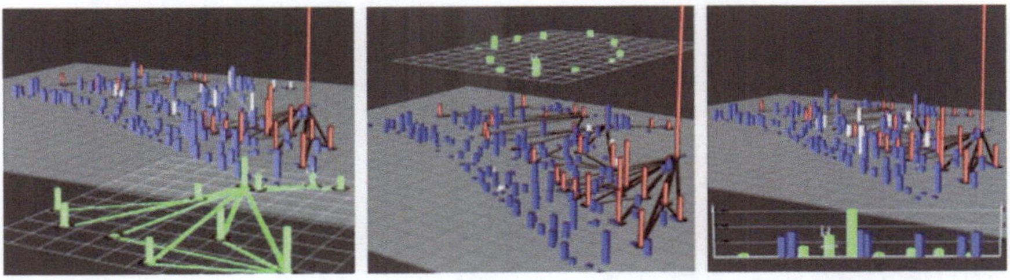

Fig. 7.12 SDM operations: pulling focus objects (green) to the front (left), selected object set (green) is raised to solve occlusion problems (centre), two sets of objects created for height comparisons (right)

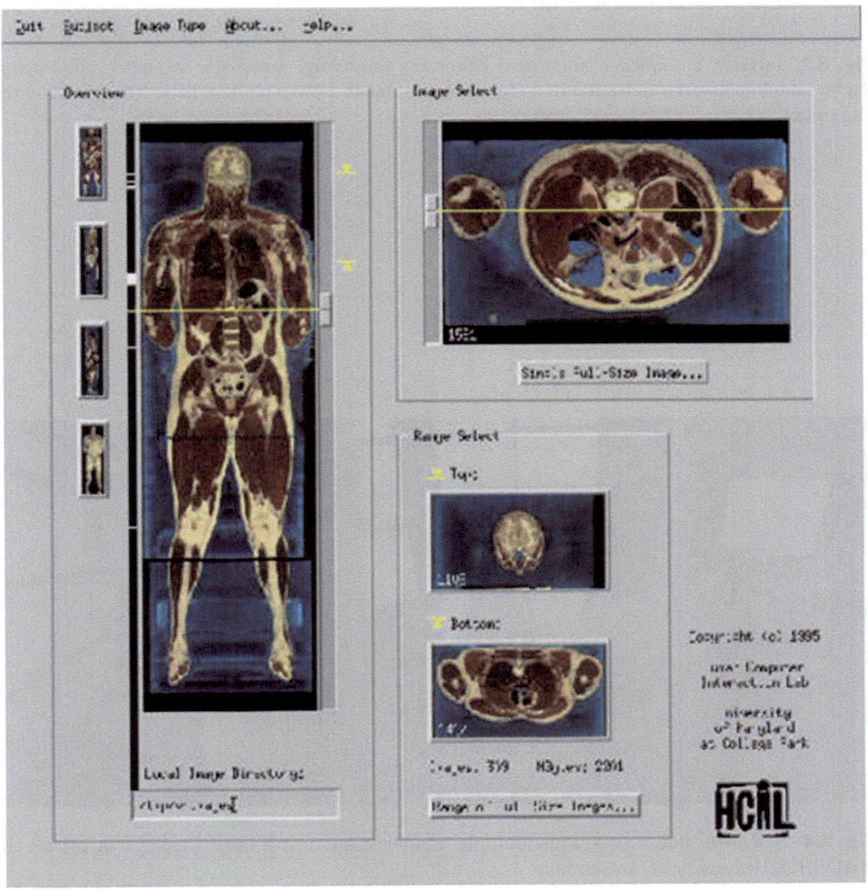

Fig. 7.13 The Visible Human Explorer [23] – dragging sliders animates the cross-sections through the body

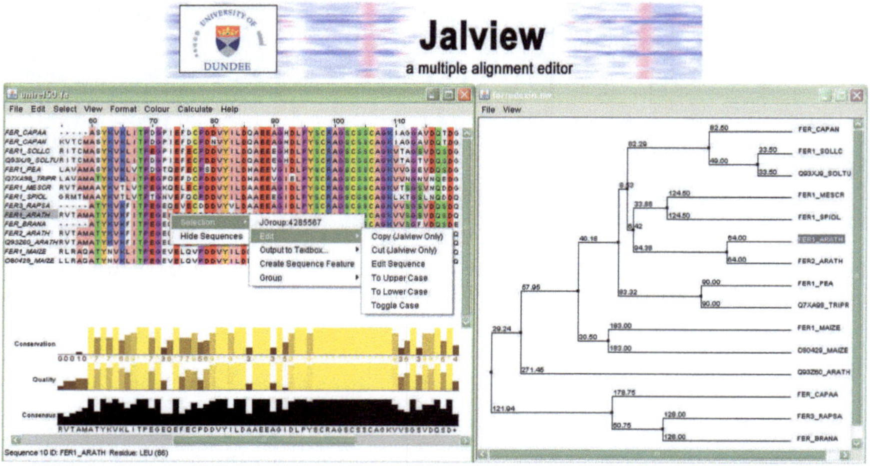

Fig. 8.2 Jalview, a sequence alignment editor for improving automatic sequence alignments. Right: an interactive visualisation of a sequence alignment. Left: a phylogenetic tree, based on the alignment

Fig. 8.4 Scientists interacting with multiple visualisations using large displays in e-BioLab, MAD/IBU, University of Amsterdam

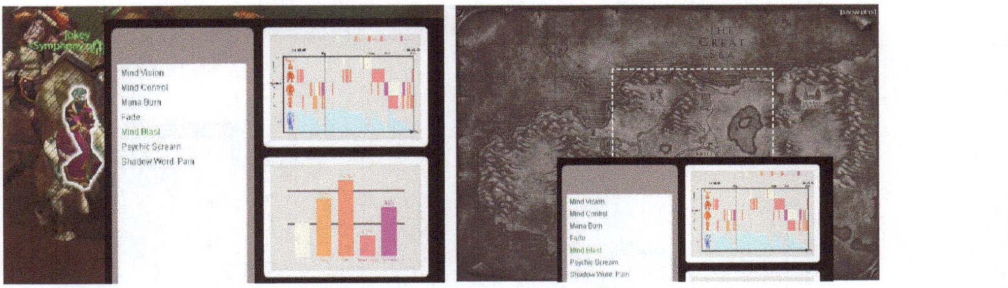

Fig. 9.3 Illustration of the in situ interfaces, with the designer highlighting a priest game character in the left image (white halo to left of menu), and requesting a data log and visualisation of the "Mind Blast" weapon. On the right a map region (white dotted rectangle) is being selected for the same weapon monitoring within the game

Fig. 9.10 Map indicating locations of a player chatting, trading, and using environmental content, for both World of Warcraft (left) and Second Life (right). The difference in transaction price to the average world price is shown. Both visualisations give designers insight into the usage of the environment from an economic perspective

Fig. 9.11 On the left is a spatial map of the deaths in the level, and their correlation with locations of negative comments by players (shown by black dots), with an overlay of content interactions for that region (deaths and kills). On the right is a spatial map showing traversal in the area around the wolf deaths, including overlays of interaction with content by players

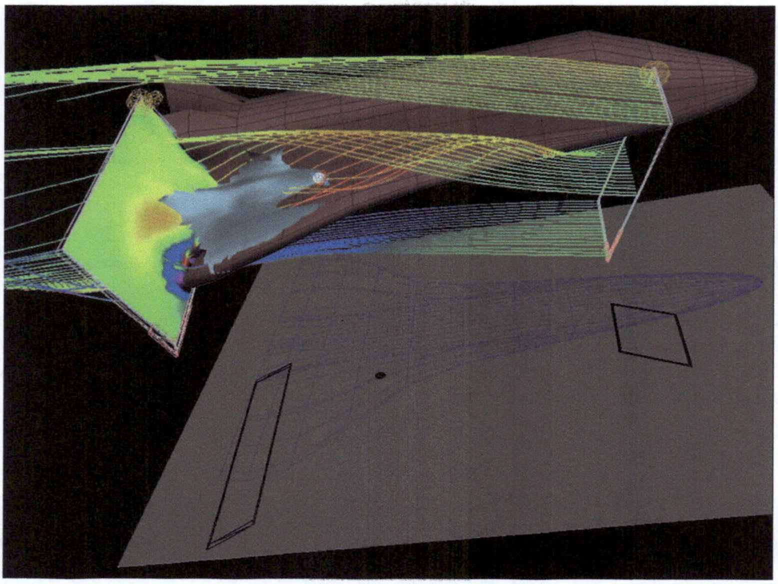

Fig. 10.1 Three example widgets developed as part of the Brown Widget Library developed in the mid-90s under NASA sponsorship to help scientists interactively visualize flow data past a space shuttle model. A color plane of flow speed (far left), an isosurface of flow speed widget (around the bluish-gray surface geometry), and a streamline source widget are shown. Each may have visualization parameters adjusted via direct manipulation of geometry "handles" making up the widget, as well as be transformed (resized, translated, or dragged via interactive shadows)

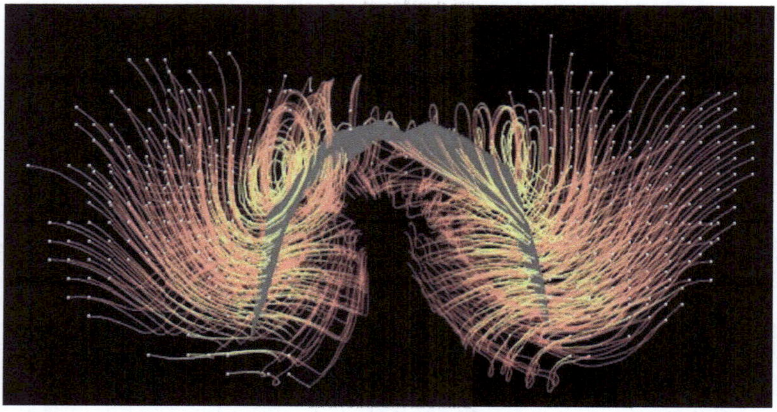

Fig. 10.5 Snapshot from an immersive visualization of bat flight highlighting vortical structure, a signature of lift, near the bat wing surface

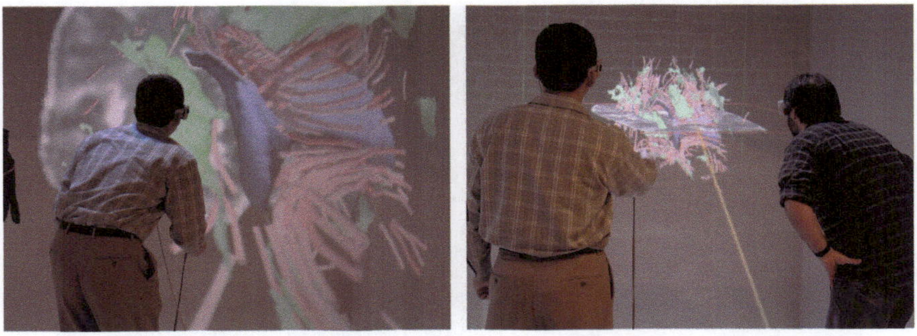

Fig. 10.6 Users interacting with the brain dataset in the Brown University Cave

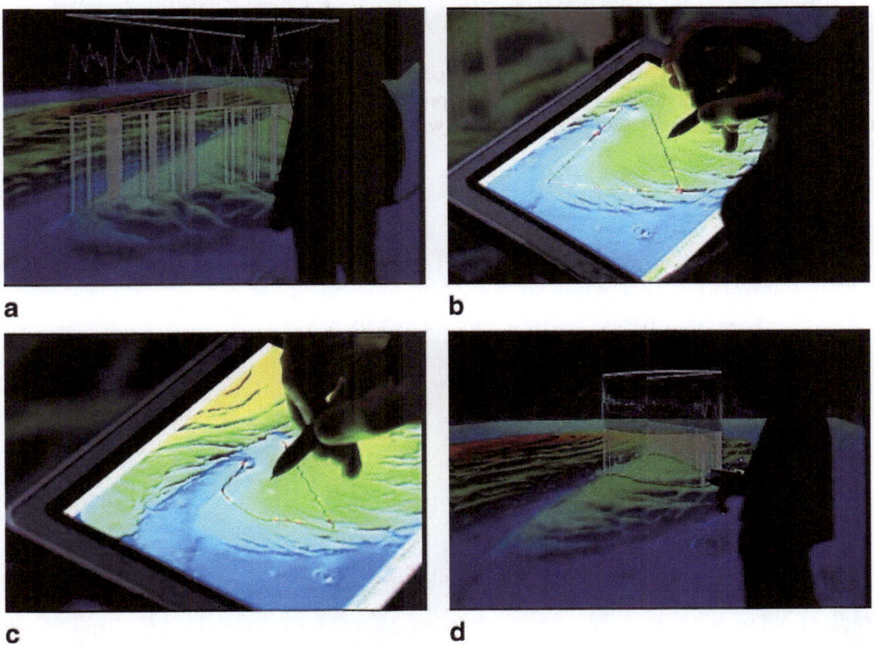

Fig. 10.7 A traverse planning operation in ADVISER. **a** Initial traversal is visualized in the IVR by a line that snaps to the terrain and vertical bars that connect it to a graph of slope (opaque bars indicate slopes too steep for rovers traversal, transparent bars indicate safe slopes), **b** The TabletPC's view of the initial traverse. **c** The user sketches out a new traverse and **d** the system updates the traverse and slope visualization

Fig. 11.3 MolDRIVE system running on a Responsive Workbench. A virtual spring manipulator (bent cone-shaped polyhedron) is employed to produce visual feedback of user-applied forces to atoms in a real-time simulation [29]. Reprinted with permission of M. Koutek

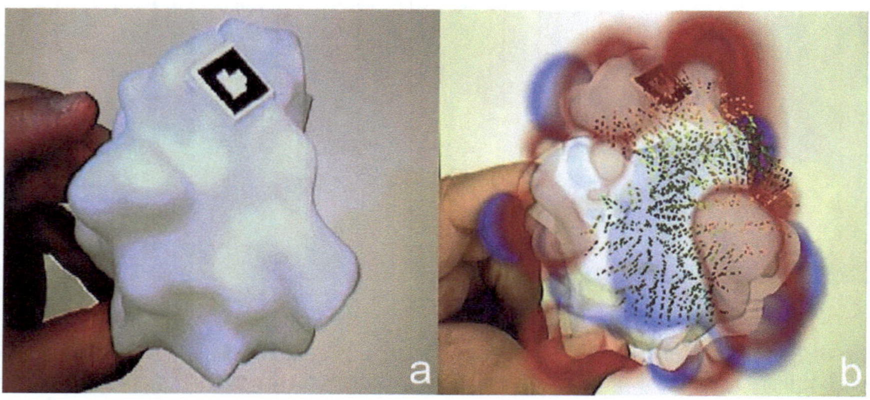

Fig. 11.5 Auto-fabricated molecular model of a protein with attached registration marker (**a**), and with superimposed computed properties (**b**) [17]. © 2004 IEEE. Included here by permission

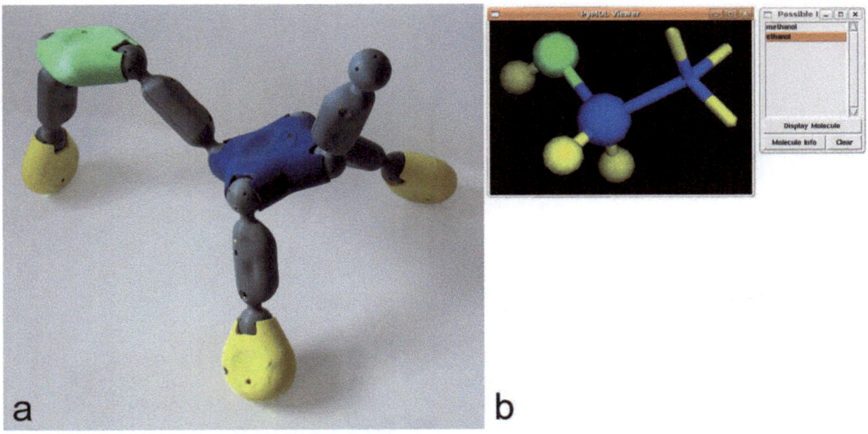

Fig. 11.6 Posey model of ethanol fragment (**a**) and computer image constructed in Molecular Explorer (**b**) [61]. Printed with permission of M. Gross

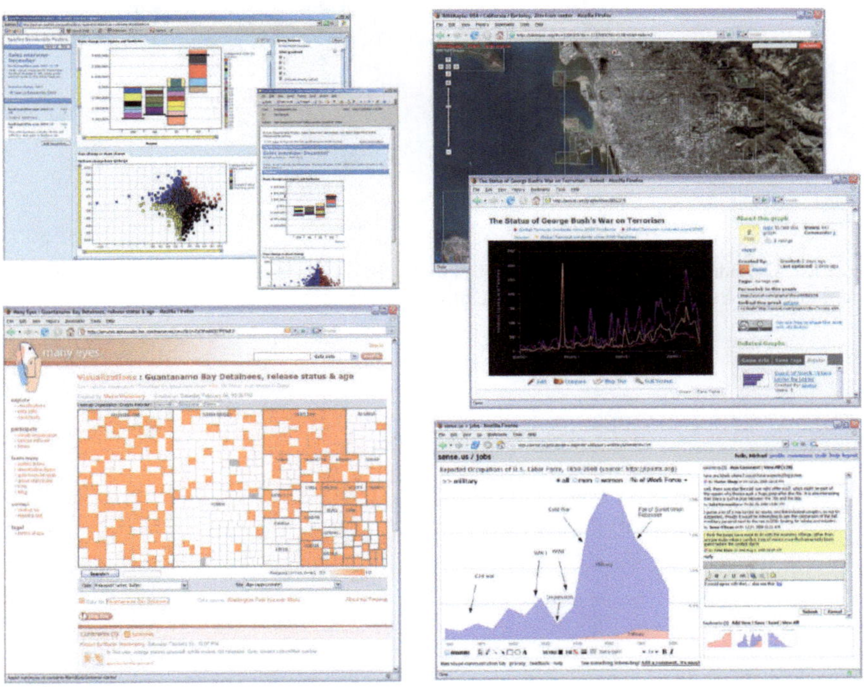

Fig. 12.2 Asynchronous collaborative visualization systems. Clockwise from top-left: Spotfire decisionSite posters, Wikimapia, Swivel, sense.us, and Many Eyes

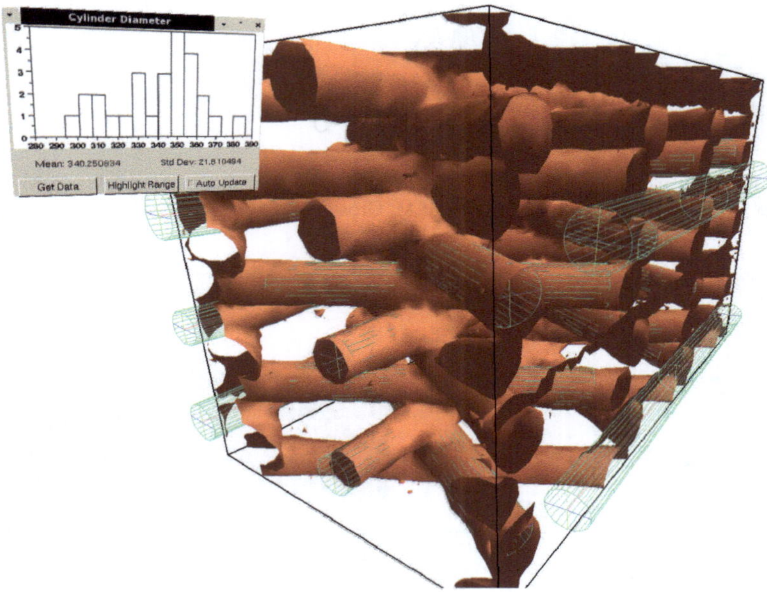

Fig. 13.1 Cylinder measurement and analysis tool used on rendered objects derived from measured data taken from a tissue engineering scaffold

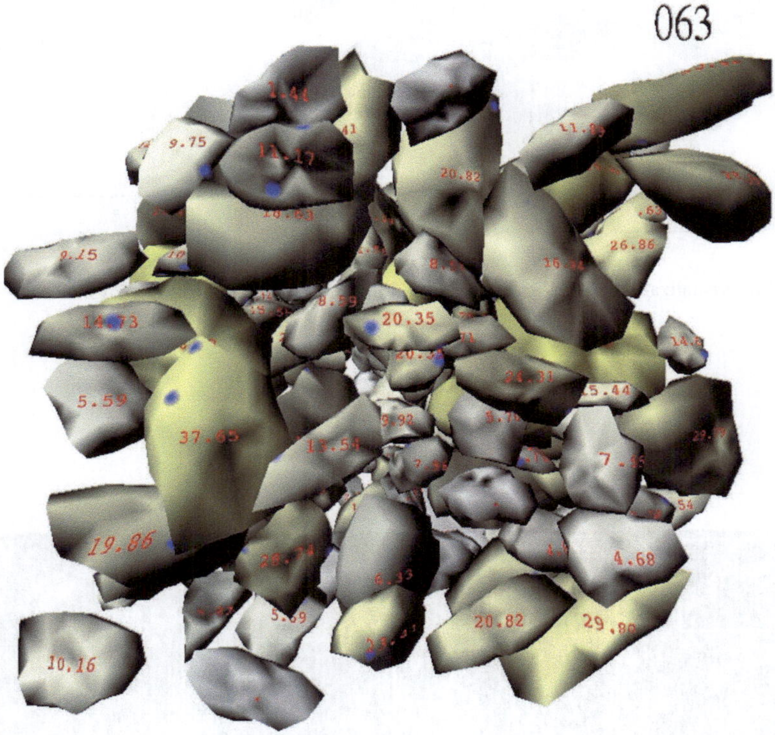

Fig. 13.3 Frame 63 in a simulation of the flow of rocks in a suspension. The per-rock stress is shown with a gray-yellow color scale, and also with a numeric value printed on the face for each rock

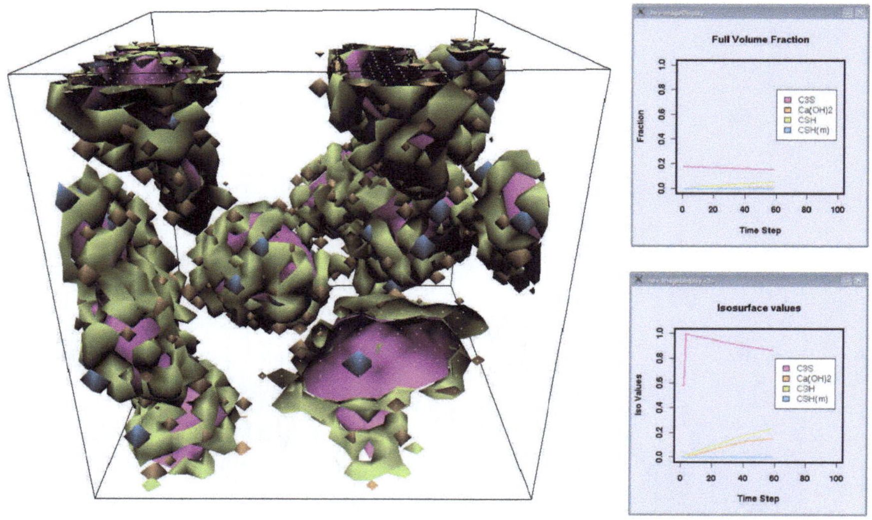

Fig. 13.6 Visualization of the cement hydration model with quantitative displays

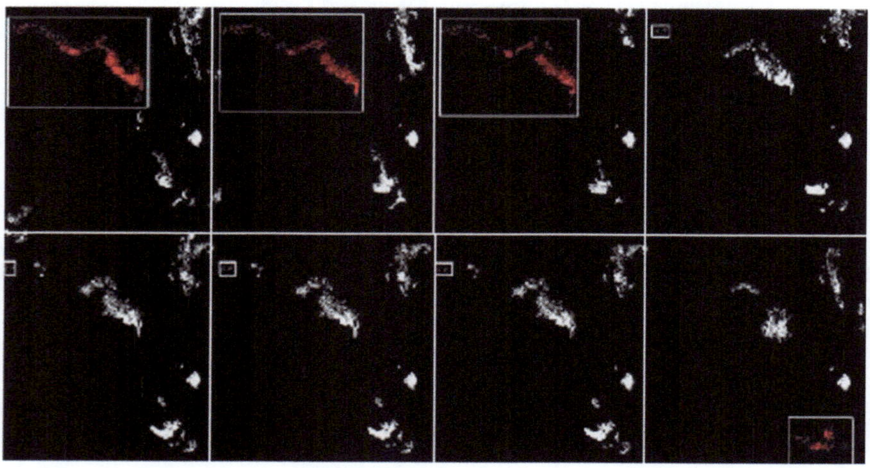

Fig. 14.3 Automatic tracking of a target which has split into two pieces

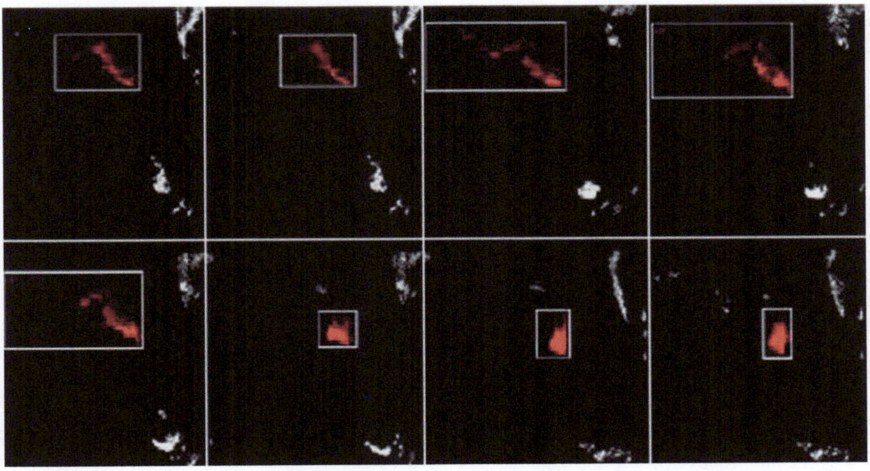

Fig. 14.5 Interactive tracking results: the computer tracks the object and the user makes decision at the "breaking point," notified by the computer

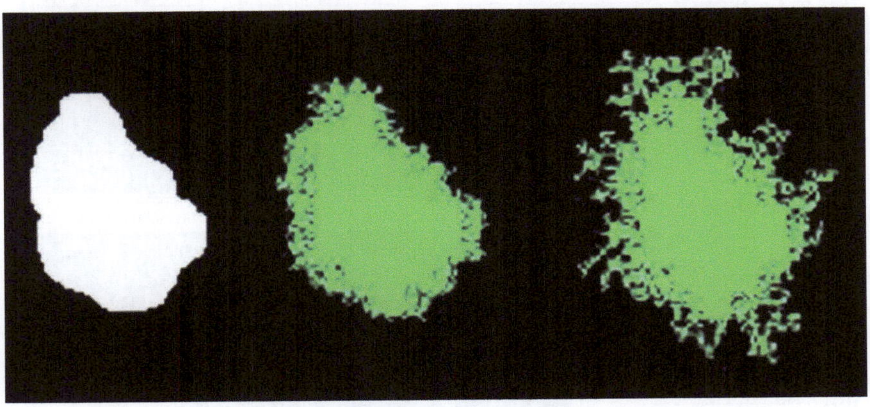

Fig. 14.9 Diffusion with resistance

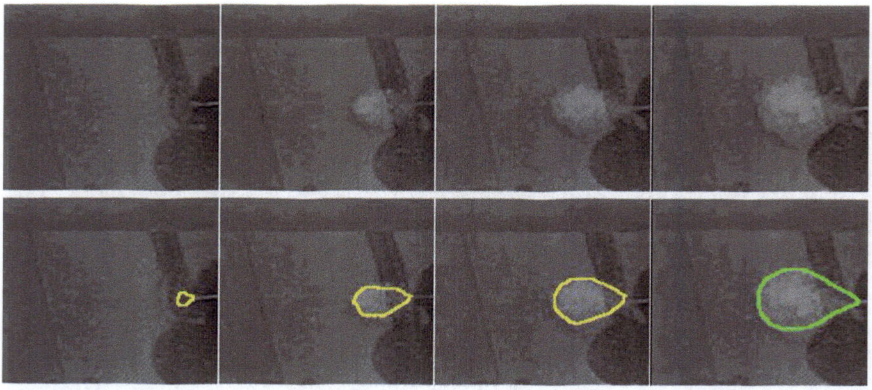

Fig. 14.11 Example of the output and interaction: the first row video is the physical river plume simulation with ink. The second row video is the superimposed results, where the yellow color in the first three images outlines tracked plumes and the green color in the last image indicates the envelop of the predicted shape

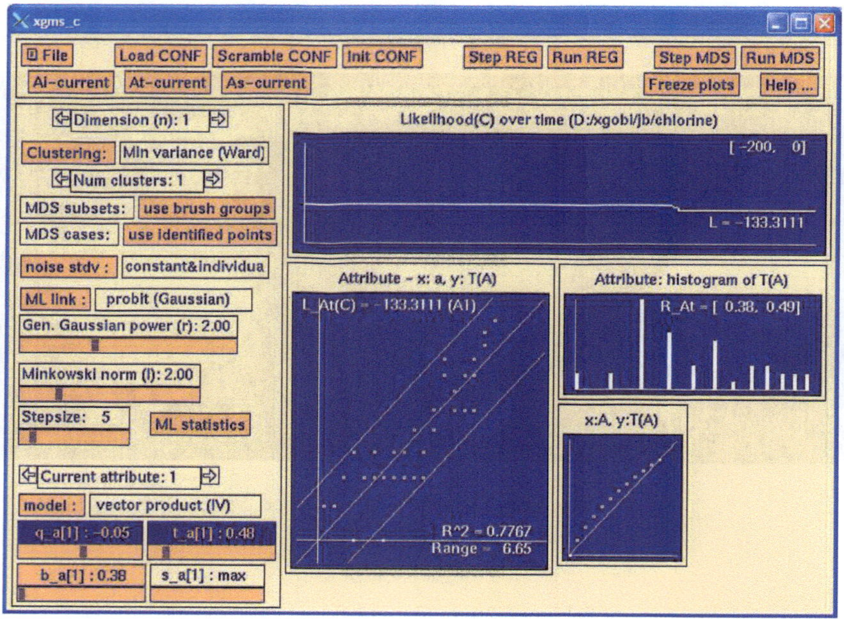

Fig. 15.8 XGms graphical user interface to the data set in Example 2

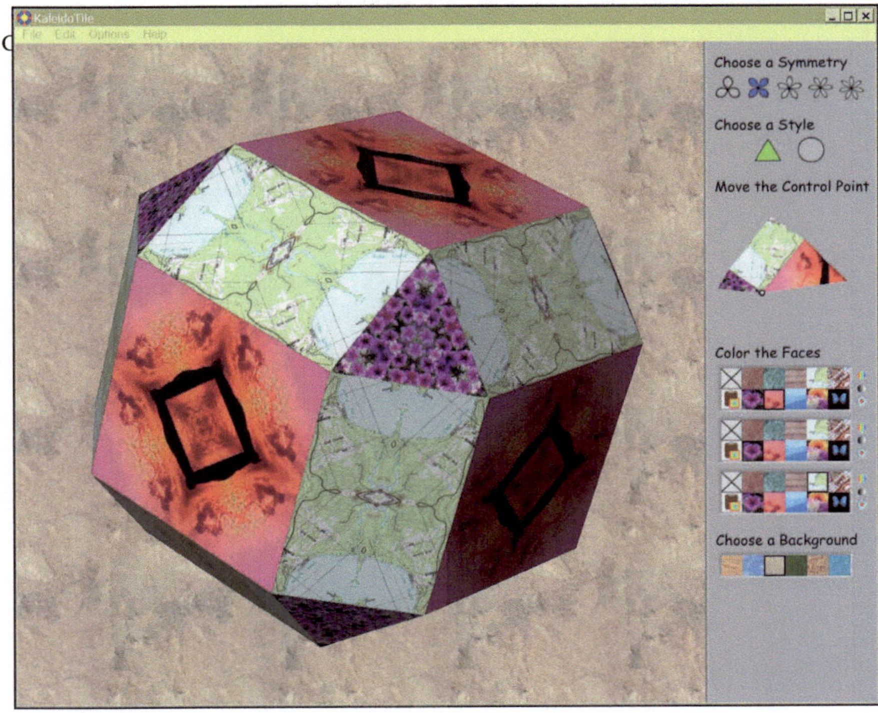

Fig. 16.1 KaleidoTile used to visualize and interact with 3D polyhedra

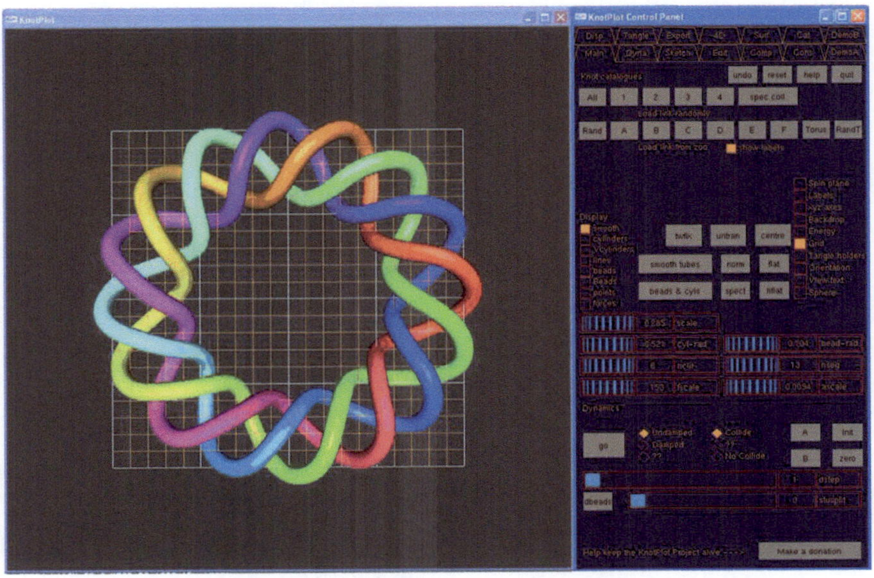

Fig. 16.4 KnotPlot used to visualize and interact with mathematical knots

MIX
Papier aus verantwortungsvollen Quellen
Paper from responsible sources
FSC® C105338

If you have any concerns about our products,
you can contact us on
ProductSafety@springernature.com

In case Publisher is established outside the EU,
the EU authorized representative is:
Springer Nature Customer Service Center GmbH
Europaplatz 3, 69115 Heidelberg, Germany

Printed by Libri Plureos GmbH
in Hamburg, Germany